John Laing, Samuel Halkett

A Dictionary of the Anonymous and Pseudonymous Literature of Great Britain

Including the works of foreigners written in, or translated into the English language

John Laing, Samuel Halkett

A Dictionary of the Anonymous and Pseudonymous Literature of Great Britain
Including the works of foreigners written in, or translated into the English language

ISBN/EAN: 9783337298036

Printed in Europe, USA, Canada, Australia, Japan

Cover: Foto ©Thomas Meinert / pixelio.de

More available books at **www.hansebooks.com**

A DICTIONARY

OF THE

ANONYMOUS AND PSEUDONYMOUS LITERATURE OF GREAT BRITAIN.

INCLUDING THE WORKS OF FOREIGNERS WRITTEN IN,
OR TRANSLATED INTO THE ENGLISH LANGUAGE.

BY THE LATE SAMUEL HALKETT,
KEEPER OF THE ADVOCATES' LIBRARY, EDINBURGH;

AND

THE LATE REV. JOHN LAING, M.A.,
LIBRARIAN OF THE NEW COLLEGE LIBRARY, EDINBURGH.

VOLUME FOURTH.

EDINBURGH: WILLIAM PATERSON.
1888.

EDITOR'S NOTE.

IN bringing this work to a close, I feel that some explanation of the
unexpected delay which has taken place in the issue of the several
volumes, is due to the subscribers. At the time of my father's death,
eight years ago, there came into my hands an enormous mass of
materials, comprising, in addition to his own collections, those of Mr
Halkett and Mr H. B. Wheatley. No attempt had been made to
arrange these materials. In the process of reducing the slips to some
rough alphabetical order, I discovered that a large number consisted of
merely a word or two of the title, with a reference to one or more
authorities. Consequently, those titles had to be completed, references
verified, and not infrequently, in the case of duplicate slips drawn from
different sources, rival claims of authorship examined.

Moreover, the strict rule laid down by the original projectors of
the Dictionary, that no book should be considered anonymous or
pseudonymous, if the author's real name was made known anywhere
throughout the work, imposed upon me the duty of carefully examining
the books themselves in all such cases where the memoranda in my
hands were defective, or where it was not clear that the books had
already been so examined. I have thus fortunately been able to add
an asterisk to many entries which had previously been taken at second
hand. It need hardly be said that all this involved much expenditure
of time. The Edinburgh libraries which were accessible to me did not
contain all the volumes I had to examine, or the bibliographical
works it was necessary to consult; nor did my references always
tell me where they were to be found. I was therefore obliged
to seek information from various libraries throughout the kingdom;
and a single incomplete or illegible slip has sometimes caused
much correspondence. A few titles, nevertheless, will be found
entered in the Dictionary on the authority of sale and booksellers'
catalogues, such as Leslie's Cat. and Bliss' Cat. Some of these may not

be strictly anonymous; but I have entered them, knowing that it was my father's intention to give them a place in the Dictionary, with this explanation.

Although I have taken every pains to complete this work in a manner worthy of those who originated and carried it on, I am deeply conscious how far I fall short of my aim; and I have to crave the indulgence of those whose superior knowledge will enable them to detect errors or omissions.

There remains for me now only the pleasant duty of acknowledging my obligations to the many librarians and bibliographers to whom I am indebted for assistance. My special thanks are due to Mr J. T. Clark, Keeper of the Advocates' Library, who, besides placing the large stores under his charge at my disposal, has, with great courtesy and kindness, been ready in every difficulty to help me with his valuable information and advice; to Mr T. G. Law of the Signet Library, Edinburgh, whose well-known acquaintance with Roman Catholic literature has been of great service; to Mr H. R. Tedder of the Athenæum Library, London, who has kindly compared with the books all the slips which refer to the Athenæum Catalogue; and to Dr Garnett of the British Museum, and Mr F. Madan of the Bodleian Library, with whom I have had much correspondence, and who, in the midst of their arduous duties, have, with unwearying patience, never failed to afford me the help which their wide knowledge and abundant stores of information enabled them to give.

CATHERINE LAING.

EDINBURGH, *June* 1888.

N.B.—The numerals in brackets which follow the authors' names are the dates on which the books indiced were published. The figures in brackets following, in several instances, the column references, indicate the number of books by the author in that column.

A DICTIONARY

ANONYMOUS AND PSEUDONYMOUS LITERATURE OF GREAT BRITAIN.

TIT — T—L

TIT for tat. Original poems for juvenile minds. By Q. in the corner. [John HARRIS.]

London : 1830. Octavo. 2¼sh. [*Smith's Cat. of Friends' books*, i. 99.]

TIT for tat, a comedy in three acts. Performed at the Theatres Royall Hay-market, Drury-Lane, and Covent-Garden. Printed under the inspection of James Wrighton, prompter. Exactly agreeable to the representation. [By George COLMAN, the elder.]

London : 1788. Octavo. Pp. 49. b. l.* [*Biog. Dram.*]

TITAN'S Letter to Milo. [By Albert WILLIAMS.]

London : N. D. Octavo. [*W.*]

TITCOMB'S letters to young people single and married. Timothy Titcombe, Esq. [By J. G. HOLLAND.] Low's cheap series of American authors. Fiftieth edition.

London : 1873. Octavo. Pp. x. 246.*

TITHES indefensible : or, observations on the origin and effects of tithes. Addressed to country gentlemen. [By Thomas THOMPSON.]

York : 1792. Octavo. Pp. 118.* [*Bodl.*]

TITHING (a) table, or a table of tithes and oblations, according to the ecclesiastical laws and ordinances established in the Church of England. By W. C. [Bp. CARLETON.]

London : 1662. Quarto. [*Lowndes, Bibliog. Man.*, p. 2687.]

TITLE (the) of a thorough settlement examined ; in answer to Dr Sherlock's Case of the allegiance due to sovereign powers, &c. With an appendix in answer to Dr. Sherlock's Vindication.

[By Dr JENKINS, Master of St. John's College, Cambridge.]

London : MDCXCI. Quarto. Pp. 6. b. l. 80 ; append. 12.*

TITLE (the) of kings proved to be jure divino ; and also that our royall Soveraign King Charles the Second is the right and lawfull heir to the crown of England, and that the life of his father, Charles the First, was taken away unjustly, contrary to the common-law, statute-law, and all other lawes of England. Wherein are laid down several proofs, both of Scripture and law, clearly and plainly discovering that there can be no full and free parliament without a King and House of Lords. By W. P. [William PRYNNE] Esq.

London : 1660. Sm. Quarto. [*Cat. Lond. Inst.*, ii. 325.]

TITUS Vespasian : a tragedy. [By John CLELAND.]

London : printed for the author MDCCLV. Octavo.* [*Lowndes, Bibliog. Man.*]

Though not mentioned on the title-page, this tragedy is followed, with continuous pagination, by " The Ladies subscription : a dramatic performance. Designed for an introduction to a dance."

TIVERTON (the) woolcomber's defence. By one unconcerned, but a friend to liberty. [Rev. William DADDO, A.M.]

London : 1750. Quarto. [*Boase and Courtney, Bib. Corn.*, i. 102.]

T—L—ND'S invitation to Dismal to dine with the Calves-head Club. Imitated from Horace, Epist. 5. Lib. 1. [By Jonathan SWIFT.]

N. P. N. D. Folio. S. Sh.*

Dismal is Daniel Finch, Earl of Nottingham, who was nicknamed the Dismal Orator.

TO ——: I said to you a few months ago : *See* " LETTER on Irish affairs."

TO all kings, princes, rulers, governours, bishops and clergy, that profess Christianity in Christendom being a distinction between the laws, commandments and ordinances of the higher powers, for the punishment of evil doers, and for the praise of them that do well : and the ordinances, doctrines and commands of men concerning religion and worship, which are not to be touched, tasted nor handled : and the hand-writing of ordinances among the Jews, which Christ hath blotted out. By G. F. [George Fox.]

London : 1685. Quarto. Pp. 27.*

TO all magistrates, teachers, schoolmasters, and people in Christendome, who teach your children the way of the heathen, out of their books, in naming the dayes, and months, and times, and observing your feasts, as followeth. To that intent is this given forth, that you may come off them, and teach your children according to the Scriptures, in which you may see your teaching is different from the Jews, and Christians in old time : but according to the heathen since the apostles dayes in the apostacy. Something concerning the naming of times, dayes, and moneths, &c. And their derivations or etymologies as they call them, which children have been taught, and are taught out of heathenish authors, and from heathenish customs. That parents may see, what their children are taught, and whether they can consent that they be so taught ; and consider what benefit they reap by being taught those things, and such authors as treats of those things. [By George Fox.]

London : 1660. Quarto. Pp. 8.* Signed G. F.

TO all people in all Christendom concerning perfect love, pure wisdome and the holy faith, and who they are that banisheth them, and who they are that entertains them: and how Christendome hath not received this love and this faith to edifie and build them, but hath received envy, and wrath, which sets them on heaps one against another, so not receiving love, they cannot edifie, nor receiving faith they cannot build. Also concerning Christs flesh which was offered, and Adams flesh which was defiled, and concerning the out-

ward offerings and sacrifices, and in what they were held, and concerning the belief in the outward offerings, and concerning the belief in Christ the offering, and concerning Adam in the fall, and concerning Adam before he fell, and concerning Christ that doth never fall, and concerning the eating of Christs flesh, and drinking his blood, and who hath life, and who hath not. [By George Fox.]

N. P. N. D. Quarto. Pp. 8.* Signed G. F.

TO all that professe Christianity, are these following particulars. Concerning their name of Christians. Loving enemies. The worship in spirit. Gospel-fellow-ship. Their many heads and baptismes. Their many Churches. Their disagreeing about Scriptures interpretation. By G. F. [George Fox.]

London, 1661. Quarto. Pp. 8.*

TO all the faithful brethren born of the immortal seed of the father of life, and sent forth in the great commission, and power of the king of eternal glory, to gather his elect from the winds of the earth, forth of all nations and kindreds where they are scattered ; this to you is the word of God. [By William Dewsbury.]

London, 1661. Quarto. Pp. 8.* Signed W. D., and dated from York Castle.

TO all the nations under the whole heavens : and to all those who have ministred the letter, and yet are ignorant, and haue kept others in the ignorance both of the letter and spirit also. From those people who are despitefully called Quakers, who tremble at the word of God in their hearts : to which word all the holy men of God haue brought forth their testimony after the same manner (and who are appeared in that which cannot be shaken) as the Scriptures of the Old and New Testament do eminently declare and set forth. G. F. [George Fox.]

London. 1660. Quarto. 1 sh. [*Smith's Cat. of Friends' books*, i. 660.]

TO all who smoke ! A few words in defence of tobacco : or, a plea for the pipe. By " Cavendish." [Samuel Bevan.]

London : 1857. Octavo. 6 sh. [*Smith's Cat. of Friends' books*, i. 262.]

TO farmers. A short account of the cause of the disease in corn, called by

farmers, the blight, the mildew, and the rust. By the Right Hon. Sir Joseph Banks, Bart. K.B. Re-edited with marginal annotations pointing out a remedy where this cause appears to arise from bad husbandry, insufficient tillage, improper manure, or from small inclosures, which prevent a free circulation of air : to which is added a receipt for preparing wheat for sowing. By an agriculturist, F.R.S. and F.S.A. [Sir Thomas HANMER, Bart.]

London : 1807. Octavo. [*IV.*]

TO Her Royal Highness the Princess of Wales, with the tragedy of Cato. Nov. 1714. To Sir Godfrey Kneller, on his picture of the King. [By Joseph ADDISON.]

London : 1716. Folio. Pp. 9. b. t.*

ΤΩ ΚΑΘΟΛΙΚΩ Stillingfleeton. Or, an account given to a Catholick friend, of Dr. Stillingfleets late book against the Roman Church. Together with a short postil upon his text, in three letters. By I. V C. [John Vincent CANE.]

Bruges, 1672. Octavo.*

TO Mr. E. L. on his Majesties dissolving the late parliament at Oxford, March 28, 1681. [By White KENNETT, D.D.]

Printed in the year, 1681. A broadside.* [*Bodl.*]

TO my Lady Morton on New-years-day, 1650. At the Louver in Paris. [By Edmund WALLER.]

London, 1661. Folio. S. L.* [*Bodl.*]

TO the author [Mr. Shepherd of Bath chapel] of Infant Baptism. Dated 1773. [By Mary GILLAM.]

Printed in the year 1777. Octavo. Pp. 4.* [*Bodl.*]

TO the beloved and chosen of God in the seed elected, particularly in London and elsewhere, who have seen the the day of Christ, and received the message of peace and reconciliation in these last dayes of his glorious appearance. [By Edward BURROUGH.]

London, 1660. Quarto. Pp. 8.* Signed E. B.

TO the bitter end A novel By the author of 'Lady Audley's secret' etc. etc. etc. [Mary Elizabeth BRADDON.]

London 1872. Octavo.*

TO the honourable Parliament of England now assembled at Westminster,

the humble petitions, serious suggestions, and dutifull expostulations of some moderate and loyall gentlemen, yeomen, and freeholders of the Eastern Association, &c. [By Rev. Nathaniel WARD.]

1648. [*N. and Q.*, 23 *March* 1867, p. 237.]

TO the electors of Great Britain. Serious reflexions on a dissolution of Parliament. By an elector. [T. PRESTON.]

London: 1784. Octavo. [*IV., Brit. Mus.*]

TO the Hundred of Blything. [An address on the subject of the Poor-Law assessment.] [By J. JERMYN ?]

[Southwold? 1821?] Octavo. [*IV., Brit. Mus.*]

TO the inhabitants of Berry Pomeroy. [By Rev. W. B. COSENS, vicar of Berry Pomeroy.]

1852. [*IV., Davidson, Bib. Devon.*, p. 108.]

TO the magistrates, the military, and the yeomanry of Ireland. [By Sir Richard MUSGRAVE, Bart., M.P. for Lismore.]

Dublin: 1798. Octavo. [*IV.*] Signed Camillus.

TO the majesty of the people, the Christian-political mouse-trap ! or the world reformed by order, truth and good humour, &c. [By P. LABELLIÈRE.]

London: 1789. Octavo. [*IV., Brit. Mus.*]

TO the memory of a lady lately deceased. [Mrs. Lyttelton, wife to George Lyttelton, Esq., one of the Lords of the Treasury.] A monody. [By George, Lord LYTTELTON.]

London: MDCCXLVII. Folio. Pp. 15. b. t.*

TO the most illustrious, John, Earle of Lauderdale, &c. His Majesties High Commissioner for the kingdom of Scotland, His Grace, A congratulatory welcome of an heart-well-wishing quill : Hecatombe. [By Mungo MURRAY.]

N. P. N. D. Folio. S. sh.* [*Adv. Lib.*] Signed M. M.

TO the no less vertuous than engeniou Mrs Mary More ; upon her sending Sir Thomas More's picture (of her own drawing) to the Long Gallery at the public schools in Oxon. R. W. [R. WHITHALL, of Merton College.]

N. P. 1674. Fol S.L.* Author's name in the handwriting of Wood.

TO the parliament of the Comonwealth of England. Fifty nine particulars laid down for the regulating things, and the taking away of oppressing laws, and oppressors, and to ease the oppressed. By G. F. [George FOX.] London, 1659. Quarto. Pp. 23.* [*Smith's Cat. of Friends' books*, i. 658.]

TO the patrons of ecclesiastical livings. [By Browne WILLIS, LL.D.]
N. P. N. D. Quarto. Pp. 8.*

TO the Right Honourable James Earl of Perth, Lord Drummond, and Stob-Hall, &c. Lord High Chancellour of his Majesties most ancient kingdom of Scotland. The congratulatory welcome of an obliged quill. [By Mungo MURRAY.]
N. P. N. D. S. Sh. Folio.* Signed M. M.

TO the Right Reverend the Ld. Bishop of Carlisle. Containing a third vindication of Edward the Third. Letter III. [By Thomas RYMER.]
London: 1706. Octavo.*

TO the Right Reverend the Ld. Bishop of Carlisle. Containing an historical deduction of the alliances between France and Scotland. Whereby the pretended old league with Charlemagne is disprov'd : and the true old league is produced and asserted. To which is added, a notable piece of church-history from her Majesty's archives ; never before publish'd. Letter II. [By Thomas RYMER.]
London : N. D. Octavo.*

TO the saints in Sion, a song of praise. Together with some short hints, especially in the 2nd part, by way of prophecy, concerning the judgments of God upon the world for their sins, by famine, by the sword, by pestilence, and by fire from heaven. Written at Carlisle in Cumberland, about 50 years ago, and now published by consent of the writer. T. S. [Thomas STORY.]
London: 1740. Octavo. 1¼ sh. [*Smith's Cat. of Friends' books*, i. 61 ; ii. 637.]

TO the Society of the people called Quakers. [By John PAYNE.] Signed Pacificus.
N. P. 1793. Folio. 1 sh. [*Smith, Bib. Anti-Quaker.*, p. 353.]

TO the Wh[ig]s Nineteen queries, a fair and full answer, by an honest Torie ; purely for the publick good of his country. [By Francis ATTERBURY.]
London : 1710. Duodecimo. Pp. 16.

TO thee Charls Stuart King of England, am I moved of the Lord to write ; and to thee it is the visitation of his love, through him whose travel hath been for thee, that thy soul may be saved in the day of the Lord, therefore hear that thy soul may live, and thy dayes be prolonged in the house of thy pilgrimage. [By George BISHOP.]
N. P. N. D. [1660.] Quarto. Pp. 8.* The second half of the above, to C. S. K. is signed J. P.

TO ὕψος ἅγιον : or, an exercise upon the creation. Written in the express words of the sacred text, as an attempt to shew the beauty and sublimity of Holy Scripture. [By Francis PECK.]
London: 1717. Octavo.*

TOAST (the). An heroick poem in four books, written originally in Latin, by Frederick Scheffer : now done into English, and illustrated with notes and observations, by Peregrine Odonald, Esq. [By William KING, LL.D., Principal of St. Mary Hall, Oxford.]
Dublin : printed. London : reprinted in the year MDCCXLVII. Quarto.*

TOBACCONIST (the), a comedy of two acts altered from Ben Johnson. Acted at the Theatres Royal in the Haymarket and Edinburgh. (With great applause.) [By Francis GENTLEMAN.]
London : M.DCC.LXXI. Octavo. Pp. 4. b. t. 50.* [*Biog. Dram.*]

TOCSIN (the), with several minor poems. By a member of the Honourable Society of Lincoln's Inn. [Daniel CABANEL.]
1811. Quarto. [*Gent. Mag.*, lxxxv. 1. 144. *Brit. Crit.*, xxxix. 191.]

TO-day and yesterday : a satire. [By Sir Henry Lytton BULWER.]
Chiswick, 1824. Octavo. Pp. 29. [*IV., Martin's Cat.*]

TO-day in Ireland. In three volumes. [By Eyre Evans CROW.]
London : 1825. Duodecimo.*

TOILE (a) for two-legged foxes. Wherein their noisome properties ; their hunting and vnkenelling, with the duties of the principall hunters and guardians of the spirituall vineyard is liuely discouered, for the comfort of all her Highnesse trustie and true-hearted subiects, and their encouragement against all Popish practises. By

J. B. [J. BAXTER] Preacher of the word of God.

London, 1600. Octavo.*

TOLERATION Act explained. An answer to a legal argument on the Toleration Act, shewing that the court of quarter sessions have a judicial function as to the administration of oaths to persons offering themselves for qualification as Protestant dissenting ministers. By a barrister of the Temple. [George Wharton MARRIOTT, B.C.L.]

London: 1812. Octavo. Pp. 39.* [Bodl.]

TOLERATION defended: or, the letter from a gentleman [James Ramsay] to a member of parliament concerning toleration considered; with some observes on Mr. Meldrum's sermon. [By George BROWN.]

Printed in the year, 1703. Quarto. Pp. 24. b. t.* [Adv. Lib.]

TOLERATION disapprov'd and condemn'd by the authority and convincing reasons of I. That wise and learned King James and his Privy-Councill. Anno Reg. 2do. II. The Honourable Commons assembled in this present parliament in their votes &c. Feb. 25. 1662. III. The Presbyterian ministers in the City of London met at Sion-Colledge Decemb. 18. 1645. IV. Twenty eminent divines most (if not all) of them members of the late assembly) in their sermons before the two Houses of Parliament on solemn occasions. Faithfully collected by a very moderate hand, and humbly presented to the serious consideration of all dissenting parties. [By William ASSHETON, D.D., of Brasen-Nose College.]

Oxford, 1670. Quarto. Pp. 78. b. t.* [Bodl.]

TOLERATION discuss'd; in two dialogues. I. Betwixt a conformist, and a non-conformist; laying open the impiety, and danger of a general liberty. II. Betwixt a presbyterian, and an independent; concluding, upon an impartial examination of their respective practises, and opinions, in favour of the independent. [By Sir Roger L'ESTRANGE.]

London, 1670. Octavo.* [Darling, Cyclop. Bibl.]

TOLERATION (a) in Scotland no breach of the Union. [By William STRAHAN, LL.D.]

London: MDCCXII. Quarto. Pp. 8.*

TOLERATION not to be abused. Or, a serious question soberly debated, and resolved upon presbyterian principles. Viz. Whether it be adviseable, especially for the presbyterians, either in conscience or prudence, to take advantage from his Majesties late declaration, to deny or rebate their communion with our parochial congregations, and to gather themselves into distinct and separate churches? By one that loves truth and peace. [Francis FULLWOOD, D.D.]

London, 1672. Quarto. Pp. 35.* [Orme's Life of Baxter, ii. 263.]

TOLERATION'S fence removed, the Thoughts [by Sir A. Sinclair] concerning the present state of affairs in so far as they respect a toleration considered, and exposed; Plain dealing with the presbyterians as it is not found, so not to be expected from prelatical pamphleteers. Or a vindication of a Letter from a gentleman to a member of parliament concerning toleration from all the cavils that have been advanced against it, and the wilfull mistakes about it. [By James RAMSAY.]

Edinburgh, 1703. Quarto. Pp. 36.* [Adv. Lib.]

TOLLERATION sent down from heaven to preach. Or godly religious meetings, and true gospell preachers, praying and preaching, in other places then parish churches and chappels, justified by the highest powers; and signally owned by testimonies from heaven, ought not to be condemned or forbiden, but rather allowed and tollerated by men upon earth. And likewise what it is to preach according to the laws and statutes of the kingdome, as to the matter of preaching, not punishable by the act against nonconformists. Also concerning the manner of Christian religious meetings, and the true ordination of ministers sent forth to preach, according to the Scriptures, since Christ's assention. And likewise what the gospel is, who have a true right to preach it; and what it is for preachers to live of the gospel, according to the Scriptures, or ordination of God in that case provided. Written in Glocestershire the begining of the 10th month, 1665. By R. F. [Richard FARNWORTH.]

Printed in the year, 1665. Quarto. Pp. 37. b. t.*

TOLONDRON. Speeches to John

Bowle, about his edition of Don Quixote ; together with some account of Spanish literature. [By Joseph BARETTI.]

London : 1786. Octavo. [*Gent. Mag.*, lviii. ii. 1029.]

TOM Brown at Oxford. By the author of "Tom Brown's school days." [Thomas HUGHES, Q.C.] In three volumes.

Cambridge : 1861. Octavo.*

TOM Brown's school days. By an old boy. [Thomas HUGHES.] Third edition.

Cambridge : 1857. Octavo. Pp. viii. 420.*

T O M Cladpoles journey to Lunnun, shewing the many difficulties he met with, and how he got safe home at last, told by himself, and written in pure Sussex doggerel by his Uncle Tim. Second edition, to which is added, Tom Cladpole's return, and a portrait of Tom in his travelling costume. [By Richard TOWER.]

Hailsham: N. D. Duodecimo. Pp. 38. [*W.*]

T O M Crib's Memorial to Congress. With a preface, notes, and appendix. By one of the Fancy. [Thomas MOORE.] Second edition.

London : 1819. Octavo. Pp. xxxi. 88.*

TOM Double return'd out of the country : or, the true picture of a modern Whig, set forth in a second dialogue between Mr. Whiglove and Mr. Double, at the Rummer tavern in Queen-Street. [By Charles DAVENANT, LL.D.]

London: 1702. Octavo. Pp. 64.* *Bodl.*]

TOM Essence : or, the modish wife. A comedy. As it is acted at the Dukes Theatre. [By Thomas RAWLINS.]

London, 1677. Quarto. Pp. 2. b. t. 67. 1.* [*Biog. Dram.*]

TOM Pippin's wedding. A novel. By the author of "The fight at Dame Europa's school.' [Henry William PULLEN.]

London : N. D. Octavo. Pp. 392.*

TOM Raw, the Griffin ; a burlesque poem, in twelve cantos : illustrated by twenty-five engravings descriptive of the adventures of a cadet in the East India Company's service, from the period of his quitting England to his obtaining a staff situation in India. By a civilian and an officer on the

Bengal establishment. [Sir Charles D'OYLY.]

London : M.DCCC.XXVIII. Octavo. [*Gent. Mag., Nov.* 1845, p. 531.]

T O M Thumb. A tragedy. As it is acted at the theatre in the Hay-market. [By Henry FIELDING.]

London, 1730. Octavo. Pp. 1. b. t. 16.* [*Biog. Dram.*]

TOM Treddlehoyle's peep at t'Manchester Art Treasures Exhebishon e 1857. [By J. ROGERS.]

Leeds : 1857. [*N. and Q., Feb.* 1869, p. 169.]

T O M B E S (the), monuments, and sepulchral inscriptions lately visible in St Paul's Cathedral and St Faith's under it, completely rendred in Latin and English, with several historical discourses on sundry persons intombed therein : a work never yet performed by any author old or new. By P. F. [Payne FISHER], student in antiquities, batchelor of arts, and heretofore one of his late Majesties Majors of foot, to the late Honorable Sir Patricius Curwen, Co. Cumberland, Baronet.

London: N. D. Quarto. [*W., Upcott.*]
In another edition it is said to be compiled by Major P. Fisher, student in antiquities, &c.

TOMBO-Chiqui : or, the American savage. A dramatic entertainment. In three acts. [By John CLELAND.]

London: 1758. Octavo.* [*Biog. Dram.*]

TONGVE-combat (a) ; lately happening betweene two English souldiers in the Tilt-boat of Grauesend, the one going to serve the king of Spaine ; the other to serue the States Generall of the Vnited Provinces. Wherein the cause, course, and continuance of those warres, is debated, and declared. [By Thomas SCOT.]

Printed at London. 1623. Quarto. Pp. 6. b. t. 104.*

TOO clever by half ; or the Harroways. By the Mofussilite. [John LANG.]

1853. [*N. and Q., Oct.* 1869, p. 373.]

TOO soon : a study of a girl's heart. By the author of "Patty," etc. [Katherine S. MACQUOID.] In three volumes.

London : 1873. Octavo.*

TOPICKS in the laws of England. Containing media, apt for argument, and resolution of law cases : also an

exposition of severall words, not touched by former glossaries. [By John CLAYTON, of the Inner Temple.]

London: 1646. Octavo. Pp. 16. b. l. 13S.* Dedication signed J. C.

TOPOGRAPHER (the). Numb. 1. for March 1821. [Edited by Sir T. PHILLIPS.]

[Middle Hill;] 1821. Octavo. [*W.* Privately printed.

TOPOGRAPHICAL (a) account of Tattershall, in the county of Lincoln. Collected from the best authorities. [By G. WEIR.] [The second edition.]

Horncastle, 1813. Octavo. Pp. 23.*

TOPOGRAPHICAL (a) and historical account of Linlithgowshire. By the late John Penny. [Really by George CHALMERS.]

Edinburgh: MDCCCXXXI. Duodecimo. Pp. xi. 223.*

The above work was copied, almost verbatim, from Chalmers' Caledonia, and was published as the work of Penney by Mr. Maidment, who added a preface and appendix.

TOPOGRAPHY (the) of all the known vineyards, containing a description of the kind and quality of their products and a classification. Translated from the French and abridged so as to form a manual and guide to all importers and purchasers in the choice of wines. [An abridged translation of "Topographie de tous les vignolles connus," by A. JULLIEN.]

London: 1824. Duodecimo. Pp. xvi. 248. [*W.*]

TOPSAIL-sheet blocks; or, the naval foundling. By "The old sailor:" author of "Tough yarns;" "Nights at sea;" "Greenwich Hospital;" &c. &c. [M. H. BARKER.] In three volumes.

London: 1838. Duodecimo.*

TOPSY turvy: with anecdotes and observations illustrative of leading characters in the present government of France. By the editor of Salmagundi. [George HUDDESFORD, M.A.]

London: M.DCC.XCIII. Octavo. Pp. 56. b. t.*

TOR (the) hill. By the author of "Brambletye House," "Gaieties and gravities," &c. &c. [Horace SMITH.] In three volumes.

London: 1826. Duodecimo.*

TORMENTS (of the) of hell. The

foundation and pillars thereof discovered, searched, shaken and removed. With many infallible proofs, that there is not to be a punishment after this life for any to endure that shall never end. To the glory of God, and comfort of those in fear of the torments of hell, and for the furtherance of a holy life. [By Samuel RICHARDSON.]

London: N. D. Octavo. Pp. 56.* [*Bodl.*]

TORRINGTON Hall: being an account of two days, in the autumn of the year 1844, passed at that magnificent and philosophically conducted establishment for the insane. By Arthur Wallbridge, author of "Jest and earnest," &c. [A. W. LUNN.]

London, MDCCCXLV. Octavo. Pp. x. 135.* [*Bodl.*]

TORY (the) Quaker: or, Aminadab's new vision in the fields, after a cup of the creature. [By Edward WARD.]

London: 1717. Octavo. 1½ sh. [*Smith, Bib. Anti-Quaker.*, p. 442.]

TOTALL (the) and finall demands already made by, and to be expected from, the agitators and army : vpon the concession whereof they will rest fully satisfied ; and disband when they shall think seasonable, but not before in all probability. Worthy all wise and honest mens serious consideration. [By William PRYNNE.]

London, 1647. Quarto. Pp. 8.*

TOTALL (the) svmme. Or no danger of damnation vnto Roman Catholiques for any errour in faith : nor any hope of saluation for any sectary vvhatsoeuer that doth knovvingly oppose the doctrine of the Roman Church. This is proued by the confessions, and sayings of M. William Chillingvvorth his booke. [By John FLOYD, Jesuit.]

Permissu superiorum. 1639. Quarto. Pp. 104.*

TOUCHING the subject of supremacy in causes ecclesiastical. Diatriba quædam Oxoniensis cujusdam. Tending to peace and setling, by shewing how the powers civil and ecclesiastical may act in their own sphæres without incroachment on one another. [By John GEREE, M.A.]

Printed by J. F. for Philemon Stephens. 1647. Quarto. Pp. 8.* [*Bodl.*]

TOUCH-STONE (a) for physick, directing by evident marks and characters to such medicines, as without purgers,

vomiters. bleedings, issues, minerals, or any other disturbers of nature, may be securely trusted for cure in all extreamities, and be easily distinguished from such as are hazardous or dangerous, exemplyfied by various instances of remarkable cures performed solely by such medicines. [By William WALWYN.]

London: 1667. Duodecimo. Pp. 110; [*W.*] "To the Reader" signed "W. W."

TOUCH-STONE (the) of the new religion : or sixty assertions of Protestants try'd by their own rule of Scripture alone, and condemn'd by clear and express texts of their own Bible. [By Richard CHALLONER, Bishop of Debra.]

London: 1748. Duodecimo. [*W.*]

TOUCHSTONE (a) or a perfect tryal by the scriptures, of all priests, bishops and ministers who have called themselves the ministers of the gospel, whose time and day hath been in the last ages past, or rather in the night of apostacy ; unto which is annexed, Women's speaking justified. [By Margaret FELL, afterwards Fox.]

London : 1667. Quarto. [*Brit. Mus.* Signed M. F.

TOUCH-STONE (the) : or, historical, critical, political, philosophical, and theological essays on the reigning diversions of the town. Designed for the improvement of all authors, spectators, and actors of operas, plays, and masquerades. In which every thing antique, or modern, relating to musick, poetry, dancing, pantomimes, chorusses, cat-calls, audiences, judges, criticks, balls, ridottos, assemblies, new oratory, circus, bear-garden, gladiators, prize-fighters, Italian strolers, mountebank stages, cock-pits, puppet-shews, fairs, and publick auctions, is occasionally handled. By a person of some taste and quality. [James RALPH.] With a preface, giving some account of the author and the work.

London : 1728. Duodecimo.*

TOUCH-stone (a) : whereby the Protestant religion, as it stands at this day in England may be tryed. That in the light of Christ, people of all sorts may see the degeneration, and great apostacy, which these last dayes and perillous times have produced. And by comparing the present apostatized state of the Protestant Church, with the Scriptures of truth, and its

state in the primitive purity thereof, every capacity may comprehend, how miserably it is corrupted in all its ordinances, order and discipline, and how it differs from the Christian Church, and religion ; and is become one with the Church of Rome in very many particulars : also it may appear thereby that the people called Quakers, are the true Protestants in practice, and principle. And this is written, to the intent, that the good people of this nation, may not be deceived with reprobate silver, instead of gold tryed in the fire. By a friend to all that love pure religion, and follow after righteousness. [John COLLINS.]

London, 1660. Quarto. Pp. 9. b. t. 18.* [*Bodl.*] Signed J. C.

TOUGH yarns ; a series of naval tales and sketches to please all hands, from the swabs in the shoulders down to the swabs in the head. By the old sailor, author of "Greenwich Hospital," &c. [Matthew Henry BARKER.] Illustrated by George Cruikshank.

London : 1835. Octavo. Pp. 3. b. t. 351.*

TOUR (a) in Connaught : comprising sketches of Clonmacnoise, Joyce country, and Achill. By the author of " Sketches in Ireland." [Caesar OTWAY.]

Dublin, 1839. Duodecimo.*

TOUR (a) in England and Scotland, in 1785. By an English gentleman. [Thomas NEWTE.]

London : 1788. Octavo. Pp. x. 367.*

TOUR in England, Ireland, and France, in the years 1828 & 1829 ; with remarks on the manners and customs of the inhabitants, and anecdotes of distinguished public characters. In a series of letters. By a German prince. [Hermann Ludwig Heinrich, Prinz von PÜCKLER-MUSKAU.] In four volumes.

London : 1832. Octavo.*

Vols. III. and IV. have the following title :—Tour in Germany, Holland and England, in the years 1826, 1827, & 1828, &c. This work is perhaps, strictly speaking, not anonymous, inasmuch as the translator in his preface states that rumour has generally ascribed it to Prince Pückler-Muskau. It is a translation of a part only of the original Briefe eines Verstorbenen.

TOUR (a) in Germany, and some of the Southern provinces of the Austrian empire, in the years 1820, 1821, 1822. [By John RUSSELL.] In two volumes.

Edinburgh : 1824. Duodecimo.*
A new edition, published at Edinburgh in
1828, has the author's name.

TOUR in Germany, Holland, and England. *See* TOUR in England, Ireland,
and France, &c.

TOUR (a) in Ireland in 1775. With a
map, and a view of the salmon-leap at
Ballyshannon. [By Richard TWISS.]

London, MDCCLXXVI. Octavo. Pp. 204.
b. t.* [*Bodl.*]

TOUR (a) in quest of genealogy, through
several parts of Wales, Somersetshire,
and Wiltshire, in a series of letters to
a friend in Dublin ; interspersed with
a description of Stourhead and Stonehenge; together with various anecdotes, and curious fragments from a
manuscript collection ascribed to
Shakespeare. By a barrister. [Rich-
ard FENTON.]

London : 1811. Octavo. Pp. iv. 338.*
[*Gent. Mag.*, xci. ii. 644.]

TOUR (a) in 1787, from London, to the
Western Highlands of Scotland. Including excursions to the lakes of
Westmoreland and Cumberland, with
minute descriptions of the principal
seats, castles, ruins &c. throughout the
tour. [By Stebbing SHAW.]

London : N. D. Duodecimo. Pp. ix. 303.*
[*Gent. Mag.*, lxxiii. i. 10 ; lviii. ii. 805.
Mon. Rev., lxxix. 537.]

TOUR (a) in Tartan-Land. By Cuthbert Bede, author of 'Glencreggan ;
or, a Highland home in Cantire,' etc.
[Edward BRADLEY.]

London: 1863. Octavo. Pp. xv. 430.*

TOUR (a) in Teesdale ; including
Rokeby and its environs. [By Richard
GARLAND.] Second edition.

York : 1813. Duodecimo. Pp. 96.
[*Boyne's Yorkshire Lib.*, p. 188-9.]

TOUR (a) in the Isle of Wight, in the
autumn of 1820. [By the Countess of
BLESSINGTON.]

London: 1822. Duodecimo. Pp. 84.
[*W., Martin's Cat.*]

TOUR in the prairies. By the author
of "The sketch book." [Washington
IRVING.]

London : 1835. Duodecimo.

TOUR (the) of Doctor Syntax, in search
of the picturesque. A poem. [By
William COMBE.]

[London: 1812.] Octavo. Pp. iii. b. t. 275.*

TOUR (the) of the Don. A series of
extempore sketches made during a
pedestrian ramble along the bank of
that river, and its principal tributaries.
Originally published in the 'Sheffield
Mercury,' during the year 1836. [By
John HOLLAND, of Sheffield.] In two
volumes.

London : 1837. Duodecimo. [*Boyne's
Yorkshire Lib.*, p. 108.]

TOUR (the) of Valentine. [By Joseph
Holden POTT.]

London : 1786. Octavo. [*Nichols, Lit.
Anec.*, ix. 73. *Mon. Rev.*, lxxv. 315.]

TOUR through Ireland in 1779. [By
Philip LUCKOMBE.]

1780. Duodecimo. [*N. and Q.*, 10 *April*
1858, p. 308.]

TOUR through Ireland ; particularly
the interior & least known parts :
containing an accurate view of the
parties, politics, and improvements, in
the different provinces ; with reflections and observations on the union of
Britain and Ireland ; the practicability
and advantages of a telegraphic com-
munication between the two countries,
and other matters of importance. By
the Rev. James Hall, A.M. [William
THOMSON, LL.D.] In two volumes.

London : 1813. Octavo.*

TOUR (a) through Normandy, described
in a letter to a friend. [By Andrew
Coltee DUCAREL, LL.D.]

London : MDCCLIV. Quarto.*

TOUR (a) through part of Belgium and
the Rhenish provinces. [By John
Henry MANNERS, Duke of Rutland.]

London : 1822. Quarto. Pp. i. b. t. 131.*
[*Bodl.*]

TOUR (a) through part of France, con-
taing a description of Paris, Cher-
bourg, and Ermenonville ; with a
rhapsody, composed at the tomb of
Rousseau. In a series of letters. [By
Right Hon. John Charles VILLIERS.]

London : MDCCLXXXIX. Octavo. Pp.
viii. 323.* [*Biog. Dict.*, 1816.]

TOUR (a) through part of Virginia in
the summer of 1808 ; also some
account of the Azores. [By J.
CALDWELL.]

Belfast : 1810. Octavo. Pp. 63. [*Rich,
Bib. Amer.*, ii. 51.]

TOUR through parts of England, Scotland and Wales in 1778. In a series

of letters. [By Richard Joseph SULI-
VAN.]

London: 1780. [*Watt, Bib. Brit.*]
The second edition is not anonymous.

TOUR through parts of the United
States and Canada. By a British
subject. [—— BEAUFOY.]

London: 1828. Octavo.* [*Rich, Bib.
Amer.*]

TOUR (a) through the Isle of Thanet,
and some other parts of East Kent,
including a particular description of
the churches in that extensive district,
and copies of monumental inscriptions
&c. [By Zachariah COZENS.]

London MDCCXCIII. Quarto. Pp. 507.*
[*Smith, Bib. Cant.*, p. 315. *Upcott*, i. 437.]

TOUR (a) through the South of England, Wales, and part of Ireland,
made during the summer of 1791. [By
Edward Daniel CLARKE, LL.D.]

London: M.DCC.XCIII. Octavo. Pp. xxx.
403.*

TOUR (a) through the upper provinces
of Hindostan; comprising a period
between the years 1804 and 1814:
with remarks and authentic anecdotes.
To which is annexed, a guide up the
river Ganges, with a map from the
source to the mouth. By A. D. [Mrs
A. DEANE.]

London: 1823. Octavo.*

TOUR (a) thro' the whole island of
Great Britain, divided into circuits or
journies. Giving a particular and
diverting account of whatever is
curious and worth observation, viz. I.
A description of the principle cities
and towns, their situation, magnitude, government, and commerce.
II. The customs, manners, speech,
as also the exercises, diversions,
and employment of the people. III.
The produce and improvement of
the lands, the trade, and manufactures.
IV. The sea ports and fortifications,
the course of rivers, and the inland
navigation. V. The publick edifices,
seats, and palaces of the nobility and
gentry. With useful observations
upon the whole. Particularly fitted
for the reading of such as desire to
travel over the island. [By a gentleman. [Daniel DEFOE.]

London: M DCC XXIV. Octavo.*
Vol. II. 1724. Vol. III. 1727. [*Wilson,
Life of Defoe*, 185, 186, and 195.]

TOUR (a) to the caves in the environs
of Ingleborough and Settle, in the
West Riding of Yorkshire. With
some philosophical conjectures on the
deluge, remarks on the origin of fountains, and observations on the ascent
and descent of vapours, occasioned by
facts peculiar to the places visited.
Also a glossary of old and original
words made use of in common conversation in the North of England.
In a letter to a friend. [By Rev. John
HUTTON, vicar of Burton in Kendal.]
The second edition, with large
additions.

London: 1781. Octavo. Pp. 100. [*Boyne's
Yorkshire Lib.*, p. 125.]

TOUR (a) to the Rhine, with anti-
quarian and other notices. [By G. W.
MEREDITH.]

London: 1825. Octavo. Pp. 106. [*W.,
Martin's Cat.*]

TOURIST'S (the) assistant: a popular
guide to watering places in England
and Wales, with a railway key to the
Paris exhibition. By Frank Foster,
author of "Number one; or, the way
of the world;" "A journey of life,"
etc., etc., etc. [D. PUSELEY.] First
annual issue. (Third thousand.)

London: 1867. Octavo. Pp. 234.*

TOURIST'S (the) guide; being a con-
cise history and description of Ripon,
Studley Royal, Fountains Abbey,
Markenfield, Brimham Rocks, Hack-
fall, and Newby Hall. [By John
Richard WALBRAN.]

Ripon: 1837. Duodecimo. Pp. 106.
[*Boyne's Yorkshire Lib.*, p. 138.]
A third edition appeared in 1841, under
the title of 'The Harrogate visitor's pictorial pocket guide to Ripon, Studley, &c.'
In 1844, a similar pictorial guide was
published, with the author's name.

TOURNAY; or Alaster of Kempen-
cairn. By the author of the Fire-
eater. [James WILSON.]

London. MDCCCXXIV. Duodecimo. Pp.
471.*

TOWER (the) of Percemont and Marianne. By George Sand. [Madame
DUDEVANT.]

London: 1881. Octavo. Pp. 240.*

TOWN and country. [By Lord Francis
EGERTON, afterwards Earl of Ellesmere.]

London: MDCCCXXXVI. Octavo. Pp. 16.*
Privately printed.

TOWN and forest. By the author of
"Mary Powell." [Anne MANNING.]

London: 1860. Duodecimo. Pp. iv. 286.*

T O W N (a) eclogue. [By George William Auriol Hay DRUMMOND.]

Edinburgh : 1804. Octavo. Pp. 33.*

TOWN fashions, or modern manners delineated, a satirical dialogue; with James and Mary, a rural tale. [By Hector MACNEILL.]

Edinburgh: 1810. Duodecimo.* [*Rogers, Mod. Scot. Minst.*, i. 79.]

TOXOPHILUS : the schole of shootinge conteyned in two bookes ; to all gentlemen and yomen of Englande, pleasaunte for theyr pastyme to rede and profitable for theyr use to folow, both in war and peace. [By Roger ASCHAM.]

Londini, E Whytchurch. 1545. Quarto. B. L. [*W.*]

TRACT (a) against the high rate of usurie. Presented to the High Court of Parliament, A.D. 1623. [By Sir Thomas CULPEPER, Kt.]

London : 1623. Quarto. [*M'Cull. Lit. Pol. Econ.*, p. 249.]

TRACT (a) concerning schisme and schismatiques. Wherein, is briefly discovered the originall causes of all schisme. Written by a learned and judicious divine. Together, with certain animadversions upon some passages thereof. [By John HALES.]

Oxford, 1642. Quarto. Pp. 33.*

TRACT entitled True and faithful relation of a worthy discourse, between Colonel John Hampden and Colonel Oliver Cromwell. Preceded by an explanatory preface. [By George Nugent Temple GRENVILLE, Lord Nugent.]

London ; 1847. Quarto. Pp. viii. 61.* [A ficticious work, purporting to be written by Dr. William Spurstowe, but really written by Lord Nugent.]

TRACT (a) for all time. The Christian or true constitution of man, versus the pernicious fallacies of Mr. Combe and other materialistic writers. By Stephen Seedair. [Phineas DESERET.]

Edinburgh : 1856. Octavo.

TRACT (a) for soldiers. By the author of "The faithful promiser," "Morning and night watches," &c. [John Ross MACDUFF, D.D.]

Edinburgh : MDCCCLIII. Duodecimo.*

TRACT (a) for the times. [Attributed to William PENNEY, Lord Kinloch.]

Edinburgh 1866. Octavo. Pp. 31.*

TRACT (a) for the times Is endless punishment true or false ? Dialogues between a Calvinist, Arminian, Baxterian and Berean. [By J. OAKESHOTT.]

Brighton : [1848.] Octavo. [*Brit. Mus.*]

TRACT (a) on the novel county-rates. Exeter, &c. [By William HOLMES.]

Exeter, 1800. Octavo. [*Davidson, Bib. Devon.*, p. 28.]

TRACT (a) upon the dispensing power. [By Daniel DEFOE.]

London : 1687. Quarto. [*Wilson, Life of Defoe*, 5.]

TRACT (a) upon tomb-stones ; or suggestions for the consideration of persons intending to set up that kind of monument to the memory of deceased friends. By a member of the Lichfield Society for the encouragement of ecclesiastical architecture. [By —— PAGET.] Third edition.

London : MDCCCLIII. Octavo. Pp. 23.* [With 7 plates.]

TRACTS by Warburton, and a Warburtonian [Richard Hurd] ; not admitted into the collections of their respective works. [Edited by Samuel PARR, LL.D.]

London : M,DCC,LXXXIX. Octavo. Pp. ii. 281.*

TRACTS [ix.] for the Church in 1856. [By Henry DRUMMOND and Nicholas ARMSTRONG.]

London : 1856-57-58. Octavo. Pp. 121.*

TRACTS for the last days. [By Henry DRUMMOND, M.P.] Vol. I.

London : 1844. Octavo. Pp. 400.* No more published. The volume consists of 24 tracts, each having a separate title.

TRACTS on practical agriculture and gardening ; in which the advantage of imitating the garden culture in the field is fully proved by a seven years course of experiments ; particularly addressed to the gentlemen farmers in Great Britain. With observations made in a late tour through part of France, Flanders and Holland ; also several useful improvements in stoves and green-houses. To which is added, a complete chronological catalogue of English authors on agriculture, gardening, &c. By a country gentleman. [Richard WESTON.]

London : 1769. Octavo. [*Mon. Rev.*, xliv. 298 ; xlix. 319.]

TRACTS on the relative duties of

married persons, parents, and servants. By a country clergyman. [Edward BERENS, M.A., Archdeacon of Berks.]

Oxford, 1820. Duodecimo.* Each of the tracts has a separate title and pagination.

TRACTS, written in the years 1823 & 1828. By C. L. Esq. [Chandos LEIGH.]

Warwick. 1832. Octavo. Pp. vi. 247.* [*Bodl.*] Privately printed.

TRADE (the) with France, Italy, Spain, and Portugal, considered : with some observations on the treaty of commerce between Great Britain and France. [By Daniel DEFOE.]

London, M.DCC.XIII. Octavo.*

TRADESMAN'S (the) jewel ; or, a safe, easie, speedy, and effectual means for the incredible advancement of trade, and multiplication of riches. [By W. POTTER.]

London : 1659. Quarto. [*M'Cull. Lit. Pol. Econ.*, p. 159.]

TRADIDI vobis : or the traditionary conveyance of faith cleer'd, in the rational way, against the exceptions of a learned opponent. [T. White]. By J. B. [John BELSON, Esquire.]

London: 1662. Duodecimo. [*IV.*] Published by S. W. without the author's consent, who (the Publisher) states in his Epistle to the Reader, that it is an answer to Rushworth's Dialogues [by T. White.]

TRADING : finishing the story of "The house in town," &c. By the author of "The wide wide world," "The old helmet," "Walks from Eden," etc. etc. [Susan WARNER.]

London : 1872. Octavo. Pp. 203—414.*

TRADITIONS etc. respecting Sir William Wallace, collected chiefly from publications of a recent date [by Major-General YUILLE].

Edinburgh : 1856. Octavo. Pp. 32. [*IV., Bibliotheca Wallasiana*, p. 19.]

TRADITIONS of London, historical and legendary. By "Waters." [William RUSSELL.]

London : 1859. Octavo.

TRADITIONS (the) of the Jews, or the doctrines and expositions contained in the Talmud and other Rabbinical writings : with a preliminary preface, or an inquiry into the origin, progress, authority, and usefulness of those traditions ; wherein the mystical

sense of the allegories in the Talmud, &c. is explained. [By Rev. John Peter STEHELIN, F.R.S.] In two volumes.

London : 1742. Octavo. [*Horne's Introduction*, v. 455.] Translated from the High Dutch of Dr. John Andrew Eisenmenger, professor of Oriental languages in the University of Heidelberg : the *preface* by Rev. J. P. Stehelin. [*IV.*]

TRAFALGAR, or the sailors play. [By William PERRY, M.D., of Hillingdon.]

Uxbridge : 1807. [*N. and Q.*, 20 *Dec.* 1856, p. 499.]

TRAGE-comedy, acted by the late ministry: or an answer to a scandalous pamphlet, entitul'd, A defence of the king. [By John ASGILL.]

London : N. D. Octavo. Pp. 22. b. t.* [*Bodl.*]

TRAGEDIE (the) of Alceste and Eliza. As it is found in Italian, in La croce racquistata. Collected, and translated into English, in the same verse, and number, by Fr. Br. Gent. [Francesco BRACCIOLINI.] At the request of the right vertuous lady, the Lady Anne Wingfield, wife unto that noble knight, Sir Anthony Wingfield Baronet, his Majesties High Shiriffe for the county of Suffolke.

London, 1638. Octavo. No pagination.* [*Bodl.*]

TRAGEDIE (the) of Antonie. [By Robert GARNIER.] Doone into English by the Countess of Pembroke.

Imprinted at London for William Ponsonby 1595. Octavo. No pagination.*

TRAGEDIE (the) of Mariam, the fair queene of Jewry. Written by that learned, vertuous, and truly noble ladie, E. C. [Lady Elizabeth CAREW.]

London, 1613. Quarto. No pagination.* [*Biog. Dram.*]

TRAGEDIE (the) of Solimon and Perseda. Wherein is laide open, loues constancie, fortunes inconstancie, and deaths triumphs. [By Thomas KYD.]

Imprinted at London, 1599. Quarto. No pagination.* [*Biog. Dram.*]

TRAGEDY (the) of Christopher Loue at Tower-hill. By the ingenious author of Iter boreale. [Robert WILD, D.D.]

London, 1660. Quarto. Pp. 8.* [*Bodl.*]

TRAGEDY (the) of Chrononhotontho-

logos : being the most tragical tragedy that ever was tragediz'd by any company of tragedians. Written by Benjamin Bounce, Esq ; [Henry CAREY.]

Dublin : MDCCLXXIII. Duodecimo. Pp. 22.*

TRAGEDY (the) of Count Alarcos. By the author of "Vivian Grey." [Benjamin DISRAELI.]

London : 1839. Octavo. Pp. vi. i. 108.* [*Brit. Mus.*] Dedication signed Δ.

T R A G E D Y (the) of Hoffman or a reuenge for a father. As it hath bin diuers times acted with great applause, at the Phenix in Druery-lane. [By Henry CHETTLE.]

London, 1631. Quarto. No pagination. The only edition.

"This tragedy was written by Henry Chettle a very voluminous dramaticke author having written at least as many plays as Shakspeare, either solely or with the assistance of other men. See the titles of 38 of his pieces in my Shakspeare, vol. I. P. 11. p. 308 & seq. The tragedy of Hoffman was first acted in Jany 1602-3. Of all his dramas this only, and *Patient Grissel* and *The blind beggar of Bethnal Green* remain. In the former he was assisted by Thos. Dekker and Wm. Haughton, in the latter by John Day. Chettle was a stationer. Since this was written I have observed that he likewise wrote the Second Part of Robert Earl of Huntingdon, in conjunction with Anthony Mundy, and the Valiant Welchman in conjunction with Drayton and Haughton : both which are extant."—MS. note by Malone.

TRAGEDY (the) of Julia Agrippina ; Empresse of Rome. By T. M. Esq. [Thomas MAY.]

London, 1639. Duodecimo. No pagination.* [*Biog. Dram.*]

TRAGEDY (the) of King Lear, as lately published, vindicated. [By Charles JENNINS or JENNENS.]

No separate title. N. P. [1772.] Octavo. Pp. 42.* [*Wilson's Shaksperiana*, 62.]

TRAGEDY (the) of King Saul. Written by a deceas'd person of honour, and now made publick at the request of several men of quality who have highly approv' of it. [By Joseph TRAPP.]

London, 1703. Quarto. Pp. 67.* The author's name appears in the duodecimo edition published in 1739.

TRAGEDY (the) of Mustapha. [By Fulke GREVILLE, Lord Brooke.]

London, 1609. Quarto.* [*Bodl.*]

"This is the first edition. It was printed without the author's knowledge. There is a second in folio, printed in 1633." M[alone].

TRAGEDY (the) of Nero newly written. [By Matthew GWINNE.]

London : 1633. Quarto. [*N. and Q.*, 22 Dec. 1849, p. 120.] Earlier edition in 1603.

TRAGEDY (the) of that famous Roman oratour Marcus Tullius Cicero. [By Fulke GREVILLE, Lord Brooke.]

London, 1651. Quarto. No pagination.* [*Bodl.*]

TRAGEDY (the) of Thierry King of France, and his brother Theodoret. As it was diuerse times acted at the Blacke-Friers by the Kings Majesties seruants. [By Francis BEAUMONT and John FLETCHER.]

London, 1621. Quarto.* [*Biog. Dram.*]

TRAGEDY (the) of tragedies ; or the life and death of Tom Thumb the great. As it is acted at the theatre in the Hay-Market. With the annotations of H. Scriblerus Secundus. [By Henry FIELDING.] The third edition.

London : MDCCXXXVII. Octavo. Pp. 6. b. t. 54.*

TRAGI-comicall (a) history of ovr times, vnder the borrowed names of Lisander, and Calista. [By G. de COSTA.]

London, 1627. Quarto. Pp. 2. b. t. 247.*

TRAGIC dramas from Scottish history. Heselrig. Wallace. (Second edition.) James the First of Scotland. [By Robert BUCHANAN, M.A., professor of logic in the University of Glasgow.]

Edinburgh : MDCCCLIX. Octavo. Pp. vi. 233.*

The above (with additional dramas) appeared in 1868, in two volumes, under the title, "Tragic dramas from history with legendary and other poems," and with the author's name.

TRAGICAL (the) history of two English louers, 1563. written by Ber. Gar. [Bernard GARTER.]

Printed by R. Tottell, 1565. Octavo. [*Lowndes, Bibliog. Man.*]

TRAGICALL (the) historie of the life and death of Doctor Faustus. With new additions. Written by Ch. Mar. [Christopher MARLOW.]

London. 1631. Quarto. No pagination. B. L.* [*Biog. Dram.*]

TRAGIDIE (the) of Ferrex and Porrex.

set forth without addition or alteration but altogether as the same was shewed on stage before the Queenes Maiestie, about nine yeares past, viz. the xviij. day of Ianuarie, 1561. By the gentlemen of the Inner Temple. [By Thomas NORTON.]

Imprinted at London N. D. Octavo. B. L. No pagination.*

The two last acts by Thomas Sackville, Lord Buckhurst.

TRAITOR (the) to him=self, or mans heart his greatest enemy. A moral interlude in heroic verse. Representing, the carless, hardned, returning, despairing, renewed heart. With intermaskes of interpretation at the close of each several act. As it was acted by the boys of a publick school at a breaking up, and published as it may be useful, on like occasion. [By William JOHNS.]

Oxford, 1678. Quarto. Pp. 6. b. t. 43.* [*Bodl.*]

TRAITS and stories of the Irish peasantry; second series. [By William CARLETON.] In three volumes.

Dublin, 1833. Octavo.

TRAITS and trials of early life. By L. E. L. author of " The improvisatrice," &c. [L. E. LANDON.]

London : 1836. Octavo.*

TRAITS of American humour, by native authors. Edited and adapted by the author of "Sam Slick," "The old judge," "The English in America," &c. &c. [Thomas Chandler HALIBURTON.] In three volumes.

London : 1852. Octavo.*

TRAITS of private life. By L. A. [Louisa ANTHONY.]

London : 1844. Octavo. Pp. vii. 364. [*N. and Q., Feb.* 1869, p. 169.]

TRAITS of travel ; or, tales of men and cities. By the author of " High-ways and by-ways." [Thomas C. GRATTAN.] In three volumes.

London: 1829. Duodecimo.*

TRANCE (a) : or, newes from hell, brought fresh to towne. By Mercurius Acheronticus. [James HOWELL.]

London, 1649. Quarto. Pp. 19.* [*Bodl.*]

TRANSACTIONEER (the) ; with some of his philosophical fancies, in two dialogues. [By William KING, LL.D.]

1700. [*Gent. Mag.,* xlvi. 465.]

TRANSACTIONS in India, from the commencement of the French war in seventeen hundred and fifty-six, to the conclusion of the late peace, in seventeen hundred and eighty-three. Containing a history of the British interests in Indostan, during a period of near thirty years ; distinguished by two wars with France, several revolutions and treaties of alliance, the acquisition of an extensive territory, and the administration of Governor Hastings. [Said to be by John MOIR.]

London. MDCCLXXXVI. Octavo. Pp. 505. [*Catalogue of Authors,* 1788.]

TRANSACTIONS of the Loggerville Literary Society. [By William SANDYS, F.S.A.]

London : 1867. Octavo. [*Adv. Lib.*]

TRANSALPINE memoirs ; or, anecdotes and observations, shewing the actual state of Italy and the Italians. By an English Catholic. [John Richard BEST.] In two volumes.

Bath : 1826. Duodecimo.*

TRANSITION (the) between the Christian and Millennial dispensations. A.D. 1848 proved to be A.M. 6000 ! [By Louis Albert du PUGET.]

London ; 1852. Octavo. Pp. 46.* [*Bodl.*] Signed L. A. du P.

TRANSLATION from the Italian of Fortiguerri of the first canto of Ricciardetto ; with an introduction concerning the principal romantic, burlesque and mock heroic poets. [Translated by Sylvester DOUGLAS, Lord Glenbervie.]

London: 1821. Duodecimo. [*W.*] Privately printed.

Reprinted with the translator's name in 1822.

TRANSLATION (a) of a charter granted to the city of Exeter by K. Charles I. By a citizen of Exeter. [W. HOLMES.]

[Exeter :] 1785. Sm. Quarto. Pp. xii. 78. [*Lowndes, Bibliog. Man.*]

TRANSLATION (the) of bishops. [By Samuel Roffey MAITLAND, D.D.]

London: 1834. Octavo. Pp. 24.*

TRANSLATION of divers parts of the Holy Scriptures, chiefly from Dr. Mill's printed Greek copy, with notes and maps. [By —— MORTIMER.]

London: 1761. Octavo. [*Leslie's Cat.,* 1843.]

TRANSLATION (a) of the Latin epistle in the Dreamer. [By William KING, D.D.]

London: 1754. Octavo. Pp. 28. b. t.*
[*Bodl.*]

TRANSLATION (a) of the passages from Greek, Latin, Italian, and French writers, quoted in the prefaces and notes to the Pursuits of literature; a poem, in four dialogues. To which is prefixed, a prefatory epistle, intended as a general vindication of the Pursuits of literature, from various remarks which have been made upon that work. By the translator. [Thomas James MATHIAS.]

London: 1798. Octavo. Pp. lxxv. b. t. 104.*

TRANSLATION (a) of the several charters &c granted by Edward IV, Henry VII, James I and Charles II to the citizens of Canterbury; also a list of the bailiffs and mayors, from the year 780 to the present period. By a citizen. [Alderman C. R. BUNCE.]

Canterbury: 1791. Octavo. [*W.*]

TRANSLATIONS and poems. [By E. H. ALDERSON.] Not published.

London: 1846. Duodecimo. Pp. 42. [*W.*]

TRANSLATIONS chiefly from the Italian of Petrarch and Metastasio. By * * * * * * *, M.A. Fellow of New College. [Thomas LE MESURIER, B.D.]

Oxford: MDCCXCV. Octavo. Pp. iv. 127.*
[*Bodl.*]

TRANSLATIONS from Camoens, and other poets, with original poetry, by the author of "Modern Greece," and the "Restoration of the works of art to Italy." [Felicia HEMANS.]

Oxford: 1818. Octavo. Pp. 95.*

TRANSLATIONS from the German, in prose and verse. [By Ellis Cornelia KNIGHT.]

Windsor: 1812. Duodecimo. Pp. 112.
[*W., Martin's Cat.*]

TRANSLATIONS, imitations, etc., etc. By the author of Ireland, a satire. [Rose Lambart PRICE.]

London: 1824. Duodecimo. Pp. 8. 179.
[*Boase and Courtney, Bib. Corn.,* ii. 527.]

TRANSLATIONS in verse. Mr. Pope's Messiah, Mr. Philips's Splendid shilling in Latin; the eighth Isthmian of Pindar in English. [By Thomas TYRWHITT.]

Oxford, MDCCLII. Quarto. Pp. 21. b. t.*
[*Dyce Cat.*, ii. 379.]

TRANSPROSER (the) rehears'd: or the fifth act of [Dryden] Mr Bayes's play. Being a postscript to the Animadversions on the preface to Bishop Bramhall's Vindication, &c. Shewing what grounds there are of fears and jealousies of Popery. [By Richard LEIGH, of Queen's College, Oxford.]

Oxford, Printed for the assignes of Hugo Grotius, and Jacob Van Harmine, on the North-side of the Lake-Lemane. 1673. Octavo. Pp. 149. b. t.*

TRANSUBSTANTIATION a peculiar article of the Roman Catholick faith, which was never own'd by the ancient Church or any of the Reform'd Churches, in answer to a late discourse call'd, Reasons for abrogating the test. [By —— GOODWIN.]

London, 1688. Quarto. Pp. 2. b. t. 48.*
[*Queen's Coll. Cat.*, p. 241.]

TRANSUBSTANTIATION contrary to Scripture: or, the Protestant's answer to the Seeker's request. [By Robert NELSON.]

London: 1688. Quarto. Pp. 24.* [*Jones' Peck*, ii. 364.]

TRANSUBSTANTIATION defended and prov'd from Scripture, in answer to the first part of a treatise [by Tillotson], intitled, A discourse against transubstantiation. [By John GOTHER.]

London: 1687. Quarto. Pp. xxii. 64.*
[*Jones' Peck*, ii. 389.]

TRANSUBSTANTIATION no doctrine of the primitive Fathers: being a defence of the Dublin letter herein, against the Papist misrepresented and represented, part 2. cap. 3. [By John PATRICK, D.D.]

London: 1687. Quarto. Pp. 72. b. t.*
[*Jones' Peck*, i. 108.]

TRAP (a) to catch a sunbeam. By the author of "Old Jolliffe." "A merry Christmas," etc. etc. [Mrs MACKARNESS.]

London: 1859. Duodecimo.

TRASH, dedicated without respect to James HALSE, Esq., M.P. [By Winthrop Mackworth PRAED.]

Penzance, 1833. Duodecimo. Pp. iv. 31.
[*Boase and Courtney, Bib. Corn.*, i. 204.]

TRAVAILES (the) of the three English brothers, Sir Thomas Sir Anthony Mr. Robert Shirley. An historical play.

As it is now play'd by her maiesties seruants. [By John DAY.]

London, 1607. Quarto. No pagination.*
"The authors, John Day, William Rowley, and George Wilkins, according to Kirkman." —MS. note by Malone in the Bodleian copy.

TRAVELLERS (the) ; a tale, designed for young people. By the author of Redwood. [Miss C. M. SEDGWICK.]

London: MDCCCXXV. Duodecimo. Pp. 202. b. t.* [*Bodl.*]

TRAVELLER'S (the) dream, and other poems. By Henrietta, authoress of "Poetical pieces on religion and nature." [Henrietta NETHERCOTT.]

Dublin: 1858. Duodecimo. Pp. 192.*

TRAVELLER'S (the) guide in Switzerland ; being a complete picture of that interesting country, describing every object of curiosity, and containing sketches of the manners, society and customs of its respective cantons ; with a detailed account of the cities of Geneva, Lausanne, Berne and Zurich and their environs, the Alpine passes of the Simplon, St Gothard, and St Bernard, the glaciers of Chamouny and Grindelwald, and a narrative of the various attempts to ascend Mont Blanc. By Henry Coxe, Esq. author of the Picture of Italy. [John MILLARD.]

London : 1816. Duodecimo. [*IV.*]

TRAVELLERS in search of truth. By the author of "The antidote to the miseries of human life," &c. &c. [Harriet CORP.]

London : 1849. Duodecimo.* [*Watt, Bib. Brit.*]

TRAVELLING anecdotes through various parts of Europe. [By James DOUGLAS.] In two volumes.

Rochester: M,DCC,LXXXII. Octavo. [*Gent. Mag., Dec.* 1819, p. 564.]

TRAVELLING notes in France, Italy and Switzerland of an invalid in search of health. [By John STRANG, LL.D.]

Glasgow : MDCCCLXIII. Octavo. Pp. xix. 266.*

Appeared originally in the Glasgow Herald.

TRAVELS (the) and observations of Hareach, the wandering Jew. Comprehending a view of the most distinguished events in the history of mankind since the destruction of Jerusalem by Titus. With a description of the manners, customs, &

remarkable monuments, of the most celebrated nations. Interspersed with anecdotes of eminent men of different periods. Second edition, revised and improved, with many valuable additions. By the Rev. T. Clark, author of "A tour of Europe," and "A tour of Asia," abridged from the most esteemed modern voyages and travels, for the use of schools. [John GALT.]

London : N. D. Duodecimo. Pp. xviii. 424.* [*Adv. Lib.*]

Preface dated Chelsea ; September, 1820.

TRAVELS at home, and voyages by the fire-side ; for the instruction and entertainment of young persons. [By Charles LLOYD, LL.D.] In two volumes.

London : 1814. Duodecimo. [*Mon. Rev.,* lxxiii. 437.]

TRAVELS By 'Umbra' [Charles Cavendish CLIFFORD.]

Edinburgh : MDCCCLXV. Octavo. Pp. vi. 278.*

TRAVELS in Europe, Asia, and Africa ; describing characters, customs, manners, laws, and productions of nature and art ; containing various remarks on the political and commercial interests of Great Britain ; and delineating, in particular, a new system for the government and improvement of the British settlements in the East Indies ; begun in the year 1777 and finished in 1781. In two volumes. [By William MACINTOSH.]

London : MDCCLXXXII. Octavo.* [*Adv. Lib.*]

TRAVELS in France, during the years 1814-15. Comprising a residence at Paris during the stay of the allied armies, and at Aix, at the period of the landing of Bonaparte. [By Sir Archibald ALISON, Bart., and Patrick Fraser TYTLER.] In two volumes. Second edition, corrected and enlarged.

Edinburgh : 1816. Octavo.

The first edition was published in 1815.

TRAVELS in Phrenologasto. By Don Jose Balscopo. Translated from the Italian. [Written by John TROTTER, jun.]

Calcutta : 1825. Octavo.* [*Adv. Lib.*]
Ascribed to Alexander Trotter. [*IV.*]

TRAVELS in Portugal. By John Latouche. [Oswald John Frederick CRAWFURD, H.B.M. Consul at Oporto, who writes also in the New Quarterly

Magazine under the name of John Dangerfield.] With illustrations by the Right Hon. T. Sotheron Estcourt.

London: [1875.] Octavo. Pp. xii. 354.* [*Lib. Jour.*, iii. 76.] *See* Athenæum, May 26, 1877, p. 672.

TRAVELS in Scotland, by an unusual route : with a trip to the Hebrides. Containing hints for improvements in agriculture and commerce. With characters and anecdotes. Embellished with views of striking objects, and a map, including the Caledonian Canal. By the Rev. James Hall, A.M. [William Thomson, LL.D.] In two volumes.

London : 1807. Octavo.*

TRAVELS in the Western Hebrides, from 1782 to 1790. By the Rev. George Lane Buchanan, A.M. Missionary minister to the Isles from the Church of Scotland. [By William Thomson, LL.D.]

London : 1793. Octavo. Pp. 251. [*Watt, Bib. Brit. Mon. Rev.*, xii. 154.]

TRAVELS in town. By the author of "Random recollections of the Lords and Commons," "The great metropolis," &c. &c. [James Grant.] In two volumes.

London : 1839. Duodecimo.*

TRAVELS into several remote nations of the world. In four parts. By Lemuel Gulliver, first a surgeon, and then a captain of several ships. [By Jonathan Swift, D.D.] [In three volumes.] The second edition. To which are prefixed, several copies of verses explanatory and commendatory; never before printed.

London : MDCCXXVII. Octavo.*

TRAVELS of Ali Bey [Domingo Badia y Leblich] in Morocco, Tripoli, Cyprus, Egypt, Arabia, Syria, and Turkey, between the years 1803 and 1807. Written by himself, and illustrated by maps and numerous plates. In two volumes.

London : 1816. Quarto.*

TRAVELS of an Irish gentleman in search of a religion. With notes and illustrations by the editor of "Captain Rock's memoirs." [Thomas Moore.] In two volumes.

London : 1833. Octavo.*

TRAVELS (the) of Edward Brown, Esq. ; formerly a merchant in London. Containing his observations on France

and Italy ; his voyage to the Levant ; his account of the Island of Malta ; his remarks in his journies through the Lower and Upper Egypt ; together with a brief description of the Abyssinian empire. Interspersed throughout with several curious historical passages relating to our own as well as foreign nations ; as also with critical disquisitions as to the present state of the sciences in Egypt, particularly physick and chemistry. [By John Campbell, LL.D.] In two volumes.

London : MDCCLIII. Duodecimo.* First edition appeared in 1739.

TRAVELS (the) of Persiles and Sigismunda: a Northern history : wherein, amongst the variable fortunes of the Prince of Thule, and this Princesse of Frisland, are interlaced many witty discourses, morall, politicall, and delightfull ; the first copie, beeing written in Spanish [by Miguel de Cervantes Saavedra], translated afterward into French ; and now last into English.

London, 1619. Quarto. Pp. 399. "Epistle dedicatory" signed 'M. L.'

TRAVELS (the) of the imagination ; a true journey from Newcastle to London, in a stage-coach. With observations upon the metropolis. By J. M. [James Murray.]

London: MDCCLXXIII. Duodecimo.* [*Adv. Lib.*]

TRAVELS of the late Duke du Chatelet in Portugal, with notes by J. F. Bourdoing. [By —— Cormartin, one of the Vendean Chiefs.] In two volumes.

London : 1809. Octavo. [*W., Lowndes, Bibliog. Man.*]

TRAVELS over the most interesting parts of the globe, to discover the source of moral motion ; communicated to lead mankind through the conviction of the senses to intellectual existence, and an enlightened state of nature. [By John Stewart.]

London : N. D. Duodecimo.* [*Watt, Bib. Brit.*]

The second volume of the above work bears the title of "The apocalypse of nature, &c."

TRAVELS through Denmark and some parts of Germany [by M. De La Combe De Vrigny] by way of Journal in the retinue of the English envoy [J. Vernon] in 1702. Done into English from the French original.

London: 1707. Octavo. [*W., Brit. Mus.*]

TRAVELS through parts of the United States and Canada. By a British subject. [—— BEAUFOY, brother of Henry.]

London: 1828. Octavo. Pp. 141. [*Rich, Bib. Amer.*, p. 203.]

TRAVELS through Sicily and the Lipari Islands, in the month of December, 1824. By a naval officer. [Capt. BOID.] Illustrated with views and costumes from drawings made on the spot, and on stone by L. Haghe.

London: 1827. Octavo. Pp. xvi. 367.*

TRAVELS through Spain and part of Portugal, with commercial, statistical, and geographical details. [By the Rev. —— WHITTINGTON.] In two volumes.

London: 1808. Duodecimo. [*W.*]

TRAYTOR (the) : a tragedy, as it is acted at the New Theatre in Little Lincolns-Inn-Fields. Reviv'd, with several alterations. [By Christopher BULLOCK.]

London: 1718. Octavo.*
This tragedy was originally written by Rivers, a Jesuit, and was published by James Shirley, with alterations and improvements, in 1635.

TRAYTORS (the) unvailed, or a brief and true account of that horrrid (*sic*) and bloody designe intended by those rebellious people, known by the names of anabaptists and Fifth monarchy [men] being upon Sunday the 14th of April 1661 in Newgate on purpose to oppose his Majesties person and laws. [By Thomas ELLIS.]

[London:] 1661. Quarto. Pp. 7. [*W.*]

TRÈ (the) Giuli. Translated from the Italian of G. B. Casti. With a memoir of the author, and some account of his other works. [By Captain MONTAGU MONTAGU, R.N.]

London : 1826. Octavo.*

TREACHERY. [By Mrs. Martin LUCAS.] In three volumes.

London: 1848. Duodecimo.*

TREASURIE of auncient and moderne times. [By Thomas MILLES.] In two volumes.

1613-19. Folio. *W., Bliss' Cat.*]

TREASURY (a) of pleasure books for young people. [Edited by Joseph CUNDALL.]

London: 1856. Octavo. [*W., Brit. Mus.*]
Signed J. C.

TREASURY (a) of theological knowledge; wherein Christianity and the divine authority of the Scriptures are proved, and the most plausible objections considered. [By Morgan WILLIAMS.] In two volumes.

Garm. 1791. Duodecimo. [*Darling, Cyclop. Bibl.*]

TREASURY (the) of wit, being a methodical selection of about twelve hundred, the best, apophthegms and jests from books in several languages. In two volumes ... By H. Bennet, M.A. [John PINKERTON.]

London : M,DCC,LXXXVI. Duodecimo.*
[*Gent. Mag.*, xcvi. i. 471.]
The contents of each volume, which are given on the title-pages, are omitted in the above.

TREATISE (a) cōcerning divers of the Constitucyons Provynciall and Legantines. [Probably written by S. GERMAIN, author of the Doctor and Student.]

London, by Thomas Godfray. Octavo. [*W., Lowndes, Bibliog. Man.*]

TREATISE (a) concerning the causes of the present corruptions of Christians, and the remedies thereof. In two parts. [Translated from the French of Jean Frederic OSTERVALD, by Charles MUTEL.] The second edition corrected.

London, 1702. Octavo. Pp. 10. b. 1. 468.* Part II. has a separate title; but the pagination is continuous.

TREATISE (a) concerning the dignities, titles, offices, pre-eminencies, and yearly revenues, which have been granted to the several kings of England, after the Conquest, for the honour and maintenance of the princes, their eldest sons ; with sundry particulars relating thereto. [By Duncan FORBES, Lord President of the Court of Session.]

London : MDCCXXXVII. Quarto. Pp. viii. 58. 6.*

TREATISE (a) concerning the division between the spiritualitie and temporalitie. [By Christopher ST GERMAIN.]

London, by Robert Redman. N. D. Octavo. [*W., Lowndes, Brit. Lib.*]
This book chiefly incited Sir Thomas More to write his Apology, printed by W. Rastell, 1533.

TREATISE (a) concerning the manner of fallowing of ground, raising of grass-seeds, and training of lint and hemp,

for the increase and improvement of the linnen-manufactories in Scotland. Publish'd for the benefit of the farmers in that kingdom, by the honourable Society for improving in the knowledge of agriculture. [By William MACINTOSH, of Borlum.]

Edinburgh: 1724. Octavo. Pp. 173.*

TREATISE (a) concerning the militia, in four sections. 1. Of the militia in general. 2. Of the Roman militia. 3. The proper plan of a militia for this country. 4. Observations upon this plan. By C. S. [Charles SACKVILLE, 2nd Duke of Dorset.]

1752. Octavo. [*Park's Walpole*, iv. 281. *Mon. Rev.*, vi. 90.]

TREATISE (a) concerning the origin and progress of fees ; or, the constitution and transmission of heritable rights ; being a supplement to Spotiswood's Introduction to the knowledge of the stile of writs. [By James MACKENZIE.]

Edinburgh, MDCCXXXIV. Octavo. Pp. xii. 276.* [*D. Laing.*]

TREATISE (a) concerning the payment of tythes and oblations in London. By B. W. [Brian WALTON] D.D.

1641. Octavo. [*Richard Thomson's Chronicles of London Bridge*, p. 297.]

TREATISE (a) concerning the regulation of the coyn of England, and how the East India trade may be preserved and encreased. By R. C. [Roger COOK.]

London : 1696. Quarto. Pp. 44. [*W.*]

TREATISE (a) concerning the sanctifying of the Lord's day. And particularly the right improvement of a Communion-Sabbath. Wherein the morality of the Sabbath, and its strict observation uuder the New Testament dispensation, is maintained against the adversaries thereof. And also many special advices and directions given for promoting the great and comprehensive duties of Sabbath-sanctification, and worthy - communicating. Necessary for families. By a minister of the Church of Scotland. [The Rev. John WILLISON, Dundee.]

Edinburgh, M DCC XVI. Octavo. Pp. 53. S. 456. 3.*

TREATISE (a) concerning the use and abuse of the marriage bed : shewing 1. The nature of matrimony, its sacred original, and the true meaning of its

institution. II. The gross abuse of matrimonial chastity, from the wrong notions which have possessed the world, degenerating even to whoredom. III. The diabolical practice of attempting to prevent childbearing by physical preparations. IV. The fatal consequences of clandestine or forced marriages, thro' the persuasion, interest, or influence of parents and relations, to wed the person they have no love for, but oftentimes an aversion to. V. Of unequal matches, as to the disproportion of age ; and how such, many ways, occasion a matrimonial whoredom. VI. How married persons may be guilty of conjugal lewdness, and that a man may, in effect, make a whore of his own wife. Also, many other particulars of family concern. [By Daniel DEFOE.]

London ; M.DCC.XXVII. Octavo. Pp. 406.* [*Wilson, Life of Defoe,* 200.]

TREATISE (a) concerning trespasses vi & armis. Wherein the nature of trespass is clearly explicated, and the gist of the action stated, and by whom such actions may be brought, and against whom and how to be laid. Together with the forms and learning of writs, declarations and pleadings, in reference to all sorts of torts or wrongs done to a man's person, estate or interest. And also wherein is contained all the learning of our law concerning pleadings and bars by way of excuse, justification, concord, amends, &c. With the general rules of pleading in this action, and particular rules applied to every case. Together also with a clear and methodical discourse of the curious learning of traverses, of replications in this action ; and of evidence, verdict, damages, costs and judgments therein. To which are added references to presidents and entries proper to each title. A work very useful for students and practisers of the common law. By the author of Lex customaria. [Samuel CARTER.]

London, 1704. Octavo.*

TREATISE (a) containing the acqvity of an hvmble svpplication which is to be exhibited vnto hir gracious Maiestie and this high court of parliament in the behalfe of the countrey of Wales, that some order may be taken for the preaching of the Gospell among those people. Wherein also is set downe as much of the estate of our people as without offence could be made known,

to the end that our case (if it please God) may be pitied by them who are not of this assembly, and as they also may bee driuen to labour on our behalfe. [By John PENRY.]

At Oxford, 1587. Octavo. Pp. 62. i.* [*Bodl.*]

TREATISE (a), containing the description and use of a new and curious quadrant, made by J. Rowley for taking altitudes and for solving various mathematical problems. By T. W. [T. WOODFORD.]

London: 1756. Quarto. [*W.*]

TREATISE (a) how by the Word of God, Christian mens almose ought to be distributed. [By Martin BUCER, translated by Bp. Ponet.]

N. P. N. D. Probably printed about 1566. Sm. Octavo. Pp. 29.
Herbert (p. 1753) quotes it from Maunsell's Catalogue.

TREATISE (a) in confutation of the Latin service practised, and, by the order of the Trent Council, continued in the Church of Rome. [By Daniel WHITBY.]

London, 1687. Quarto. Pp. 118.* [*Jones' Peck*, ii. 329.]

TREATISE (a) of agriculture. [By Adam DICKSON.]

Edinburgh: MDCCLXII. Octavo.*

TREATISE (a) of blazing starres in generall. As well supernaturall as naturall: To what countries or people soeuer they appeare in the spacious world. [Translated by Abraham Fleming from the Latin of Frederick NAUSE, Bishop of Vienna.]

London, 1618. Quarto. No pagination. B. L.* [*Herbert's ed. of Ames' Typogr. Antiq.*, vol. ii. p. 1196.]

TREATISE (a) of communion under both kinds. Faithfully rendered from the French and dedicated to Thomas Lord Petre. [By Jacques Bénigne BOSSUET; translated by John DAVIS.]

London: 1687. Quarto. Pp. vi. 116. [*Jones Peck*, p. 350.]

TREATISE (a) of divine worship; tending to prove, that the ceremonies imposed upon the ministers of the Gospel in England, in present controversie, are in their use unlawful. [By William BRADSHAW.] With a preface, containing an account of the antiquity, occasion, and grounds of non conformity: a vindication of the

dissenters from the charge of schism, and of occasional conformity from the charge of novelty and hypocrisie, and inconsistency with the principles of dissenters. And also, a postscript in defence of a book entituled, Thomas against Bennet, being a reply to Mr. Bennet's answer thereto.

London: 1703. Octavo. Pp. xxii. b. t. 40.*
The "Treatise," the only part by Bradshaw, was first printed in 1604. The "Preface" and "Postscript" were written probably by D. M., who signs the latter.

TREATISE (a) of ecclesiasticall and politike power. Shewing, the Church is a monarchicall gouernment, ordained to a supernaturall and spiritual end, tempered with an aristocraticall order, (which is the best of all and most comfortable to nature) by the great Pastor of soules Iesus Christ. Faithfully translated out of the Latin originall [of Edmundus RICHERIUS], of late publikely printed and allowed in Paris. Now set foorth for a further warrant and encouragement to the Romish Catholikes of England, for theyr taking of the oath of allegiance; seeing so many others of their owne profession in other countries doe deny the Popes infalibility in iudgement and temporall power ouer Princes, directly against the doctrine of Iesuits. To the Prince.

[London.] 1612. Quarto. No pagination.* Address to the Prince signed Δ.

TREATISE (a) of election and reprobation; in vindication of the universal grace and love of God to mankind. By B. L. [Benjamin LINDLEY.]

London: 1700. Quarto. 8 sh. [*Smith's Cat. of Friends' books*, ii. 124.]

TREATISE of equity. [By Thomas BALLOW.]

London: 1737. Folio. [*Lincoln's Inn Cat.*]

TREATISE (a) of fornication: shewing what the sin is. How to flee it: Motives and directions to shun it. Upon 1 Cor. vi. xviii. Also, a penitentiary sermon upon John viii. 11. By W. B. [William BARLOW, rector of Chalgrove, Oxford] M.A.

London, 1690. Octavo. Pp. 6. b. t. 110.* [*Darling, Cyclop. Bibl.*]

TREATISE (the) of heavenly philoso-

phie. By T. P. [Thomas PALFREY-MAN.]

London: 1578. Quarto. [*Lowndes, Bibliog. Man.*, p. 1765.]

TREATISE (a) of human nature; being an attempt to introduce the experimental method of reasoning into moral subjects. [By David HUME.] In two volumes.

London: 1739. Octavo.*

—— Vol. III. With an appendix, wherein some passages of the foregoing volumes are illustrated and explain'd. [By David HUME.]

London: 1740. Octavo.*

TREATISE (a) of humane reason. [By Martin CLIFFORD, Master of the Charter House, London.]

London, 1675. Duodecimo. Pp. 91.* [*Darling, Cyclop. Bibl.*]

TREATISE (a) of infallibility, shewing that the Church of Rome's claim to that high privilege is without foundation in Scripture, antiquity, or reason. In answer to a paper on that subject sent by a Popish missionary. With some animadversions on a book, entituled, The shortest way to end disputes about religion, and upon that author's way of reasoning. By a presbyter of the suffering Church of Scotland. [W. HARPER.]

Edinburgh: M.DCC.LII. Octavo.*

TREATISE (a) of magistracy, shewing the magistrate hath beene, and for ever is to be the cheife officer in the Church, out of the Church, and over the Church; and that the two Testaments hold forth. [By Mary POPE.]

Printed in the year 1647. Quarto. Pp. 23. b. t. 131.* [*Bodl.*] The Epistle dedicatory signed M. P.

TREATISE (a) of marriage, with a defence of the 32 Article of religion of the Church of England, viz. Bishops, priests and deacons are not commanded by God's law, either to vow the state of single life, or to abstain from marriage; therefore it is lawful for them, as for all other men, to marry at their own discretion, as they shall judge the same to serve better to godliness. [By Thomas HODGES.]

London, 1673. Octavo.* The epistles dedicatory to the Worshipful Robert Raworth Esq. and to the Reader, are both signed T. H.

TREATISE (a) of monarchie, contain-

ing two parts: 1. Concerning monarchy in generall. 2. Concerning this particular monarchy. Wherein all the maine questions occurrent in both, are stated, disputed, and determined: and in the close, the contention now in being is moderately debated, and the readiest meanes of reconcilement proposed. Done by an earnest desirer of his countries peace. [Philip HUNTON.]

London, Anno Dom. 1643. Quarto.* [*Jones' Peck*, i. 9.]

TREATISE (a) of paradise. [By John SALKELD.]

London: 1617. Octavo. [*Watt, Bib. Brit. Queen's Coll. Cat.*, p. 433.]

TREATISE (a) of power essential and mechanical. By J. H. [J. HUTCHINSON.]

1734. [*Watt, Bib. Brit. Gent Mag.*, ii. 684.]

TREATISE (a) of repentance and of fasting, especially of the Lent fast. [By Symon PATRICK, D.D., Bishop of Ely.]

London: 1686. Duodecimo. [*Darling. Cyclop. Bibl.*]

TREATISE (a) of taxes & contributions. Shewing the nature and measures of Crown-lands. Assessements. Customs. Poll-moneys. Lotteries. Benevolence. Penalties. Monopolies. Offices. Tythes. Raising of coins. Harth-money. Excize, &c. With several intersperst discourses and digressions concerning warres. The Church. Universities. Rents & purchases. Usury & exchange. Banks & Lombards. Registries for conveyances. Beggars. Ensurance. Exportation of money, wool. Free-ports. Coins. Housing. Liberty of conscience, &c. The same being frequently applied to the present state and affairs of Ireland. [By Sir William PETTY.]

London, 1662. Quarto. Pp. 75.* [*M'Cull., Lit. Pol. Econ.*, p. 318.]

TREATISE (a) of the celibacy of the clergy, wherein its rise and progress are historically considered. [By Rev. Henry WHARTON.]

London, 1688. Quarto. Pp. iv. 168.* [*Jones' Peck*, ii. 334.]

TREATISE (a) of the Chvrch. In which is proued M. Iohn White his Way to the true Church, to be indeed no way at all to any Church, true or false: by demonstrating, that his

visible company of protestants, is but a chymæra of his owne braine. For that there was neuer yet any one, eyther man, woman, or child a member of it, in all antiquity, by the confession of the most famous protestants themselues, that euer were. Written by W. G. [William WRIGHT] Professor in Diuinity : in manner of dialogue.

Permissu Superiorum. M.DC.XVI. Quarto.* [*Dodd, Ch. Hist.*, ii. 136.]

TREATISE (a) of the first principles of laws in general : of their nature and design, and of the interpretation of them. Translated out of French. Being a proper introduction to the New institute of the imperial or civil law, with notes, &c. lately published. [By Thomas WOOD, LL.D.]

London: 1705. Octavo. Pp. 1. b. t. 144.* [*Bodl.*]

TREATISE (a) of the grovndes of the old and newe religion. Devided into two parts, Whereunto is added an appendix, containing a briefe confutation of William Crashaw his first Tome of Romish forgeries and falsifications. [By Edward MAYHEW.]

Anno Domini M.D.C.VIII. Quarto.* [*Dodd, Ch. Hist.*, ii. 401.] The address from the printer to the reader is signed :—Your poore Catholike countriman, Thom R.

TREATISE (a) of the holy Communion. [By Dr Henry COMPTON.]

1677. Duodecimo. [*Leslie's Cat.*, 1843.]

TREATISE (a) of the Ivdge of controversies Written in Latin by the R. Father Martinus Becanus of the Society of Jesus, professour in diuinity. And englished by W. W. Gent. [William WRIGHT.]

Permissu superiorum. M.DC.XIX. Octavo.* [*Dodd, Ch. Hist.*, iii. 114.]

TREATISE (a) of the just interest of the kings of England, in their bill disposing power, and the validity of grants made to their subjects. Written at the request of a person of honour in the year 1657, by a person learned in the laws. [Sir Matthew HALE? Published by Blackerby Fairfax.]

London : 1703. Duodecimo. [*IV.*]

TREATISE (a) of the Lords Supper, in two sermons. [By Henry SMITH.]

Imprinted at London by Thomas Orwin for Thomas Man, dwelling in Paternoster row, at the signe of the Talbot. 1591. Octavo.* [*Bodl.*]

Each sermon has a separate pagination.

TREATISE (a) of the ministery of the Church of England. Wherein is handled this question, whether it be [better ?] to be separated from or joyned vnto. Which is discussed in two letters, the one written for it [by Arthur HILDERSAM], the other against it [by Francis JOHNSON]. Whervnto is annexed, after the preface, a brief declaration of the ordinary officers of the Church of Christ. And, a few positions. Also in the end of the treatise, some notes touching the Lordes prayer. Seven questions. A table of some principal thinges conteyned in this treatise.

N. P. N. D. Quarto. Pp. 6. b. t. 141. 2. B. L.*

TREATISE (a) of the natvre and vse of things indifferent. Tendinge to prove that the ceremonies in present controversie amongst the ministers of the gospell in the realme of England, are neither in nature or vse indifferent. [By William BRADSHAW.]

Printed 1605. Octavo. Pp. 30. b. t.*

TREATISE (a) of the nature of God. [By Thomas MORTON.]

London. 1599. Octavo. Pp. 12. b. t. 239.* [*Bodl.*]

TREATISE (a) of the perpetuall visibilitie, and succession of the true Chvrch in all ages. [By George ABBOT, Archbishop of Canterbury.]

[London.] 1624. Quarto. Pp. 5. b. t. 116.*

TREATISE (a) of the plague. Being an instruction how one ought to act, in relation, I. To apparel and lodging. II. To diet. III. To antidotes or preservatives. IV. To such medicines, as are necessary to be made use of, when any one shall be so unhappy, as to be visited with the distemper. Wherein is inserted a rare collection of a great many recipe's of very valuable medicines, made use of in the plague, by the greatest physicians in the world, and published for the general good of mankind, especially the meaner sort. By Eugenius Philalethes, Jun. [Robert SAMBER.]

London : MDCCXXI. Octavo.*

TREATISE (a) of the principall grounds and maximes of the lawes of this kingdome. Very usefull and commodious for all students, and such others as desire the knowledge, and understanding of the lawes. Written by that most excellent, and learned ex-

positor of the law, W. N. [William Noy] of Lincolns-Inn, Esquire.

London: 1641. Quarto. Pp. 4. b. t. 130.*

TREATISE (a) of the svfferings and victory of Christ, in the work of our redemption : declaring by the Scriptures these two questions : that Christ suffered for vs the wrath of God, which we may well terme the paynes of hell, or hellish sorrowes. That Christ after his death on the crosse, went not into hell in his soule. Contrarie to certaine errours in these points publiklie preached in London : anno 1597. [By Henry Jacob.]

N. P. 1598. Octavo. Pp. 174.* Signed II. I.

TREATISE (a) of the three-fold state of man, wherein is handled : 1. His created holiness ; 2. His sinfulness since the fall ; 3. His renewed holiness in his regeneration. [By Rev. Thomas Morton.]

London : 1596. Sm. Octavo. [*Darling, Cyclop. Bibl.*]

TREATISE (a) of the two sacraments of the Gospell : Baptisme and the Svpper of the Lord. Divided into two parts. The first treating of the doctrine and nature of the sacraments in generall, and of these two in speciall ; together with the circumstances attending them. The second containing the manner of our due preparation to the receiving of the Supper of the Lord ; as also, of our behaviour in and after the same. Whereunto is annexed an appendix, shewing ; first, how a Christian may finde his preparation to the Supper sweete and easie : secondly, the causes why the sacrament is so unworthily received by the worst ; and so fruitlesly by the better sort : with the remedies to avoyd them both. The third edition. By D. R. B. of divin. minister of the Gospel. [Daniel Rogers.]

London : 1636. Quarto. Pp. 14. b. t. 360. 15.*

TREATISE (a) of three conversions of England from Paganisme to Christian religion. The first under the Apostles, in the first age after Christ : the second under Pope Eleutherius and K. Lucius, in the second age. The third, under Pope Gregory the Great, and K. Ethelbert in the sixth age ; with divers other matters thereunto apperteyning. Divided into three partes, as appeareth in the next page. The former two where-

of are handled in this booke, and dedicated to the Catholikes of England. With a new addition to the said Catholikes, upon the news of the late Q. death, and succession of his Maiestie of Scotland, to the crowne of England. By N. D. author of the Ward-word. [Robert Parsons.]

Imprinted with licence, anno. 1603. Octavo.* [*Jones' Peck*, i. 150.]

TREATISE (a) of traditions. Part I. Where it is proved, that we have evidence sufficient from tradition ; 1. That the Scriptures are the Word of God. II. That the Church of England owns the true canon of the books of the Old Testament. III. That the copies of the Scripture have not been corrupted. IV. That the Romanists have no such evidence for their traditions. V. That the testimony of the present Church of Rome can be no sure evidence of Apostolical tradition. VI. What traditions may securely be relyed upon, and what not. [By Daniel Whitby.]

London, M DC LXXXVIII. Quarto.*

——. Part II. Shewing the novelty of the pretended traditions of the Church of Rome ; as being, I. Not mentioned by the ancients of their discourses of traditions apostolical, truly so called, or so esteemed by them. Nor, II. In their avowed rule, or symbol of faith. Nor, III. In the instructions given to the clergy, concerning all those things they were to teach the people. Nor, IV. In the examination of a bishop at his ordination. Nor, V. In the ancient treatises designed to instruct Christians in all the articles of their faith. VI. From the confessions of Romish doctors. With an answer to the arguments of Mr. Mumford for traditions. And a demonstration, that the heathens made the same plea from tradition as the Romanists do ; and that the answer of the Fathers to it doth fully justifie the Protestants. [By Daniel Whitby.]

London, M DC LXXXIX. Quarto.* [*Jones' Peck*, ii. 323.]

TREATISE (a) of vnion of the two realmes of England and Scotland. By I. H. [Sir John Haywarde, D.C.L.]

At London. 1604. Quarto. Pp. 4. 58.*

TREATISE (a) of vse and custome. [By Meric Casaubon.]

London M.D.C.XXXVIII. Quarto. Pp. 186. 6.*

TREATISE (a) of weights and measures. In which the antient and modern weights and measures of several nations are accurately compared, especially those of Scotland and England. [By William YOUNG.]

Aberdeen : 1762. Duodecimo.*

TREATISE (a) of wool, and the manufacture of it : in a letter to a friend. Occasion'd upon a discourse concerning the great abatements of rents, and low value of lands. Wherein is shewed how their worth and value may be advanced by the improvement of the manufacture and price of our English wool. Together with the presentment of the grand jury of the county of Somerset, at the general Quarter Session begun at Brewton the thirteenth day of January 1684. [By George CLARKE.]

London, 1685. Quarto. Pp. 31.* [*Bodl.*]

TREATISE (a) on air ; containing new experiments and thoughts on combustion ; being a full investigation of M. Lavoisier's system ; and proving, by some striking experiments, its erroneous principles ; with strictures upon the chemical opinions of some eminent men. By Richard Bewley, M.D. [Robert HARRINGTON, M.D.]

London : 1791. Octavo. Pp. 215. [*Mon. Rev.*, vi. 435 ; xiv. 462.]

TREATISE (a) on captures in war. By Richard Lee, Esq. Second edition ; corrected : with additional notes. [By Thomas Hartwell HORNE.]

London : 1803. Octavo. From a list of his works in the handwriting of the author.

TREATISE (a) on harmony ; dedicated to all lovers of musick by an admirer of this agreeable science. [By James, Lord PAISLEY of Abercorn.]

London : 1731. Oblong Quarto. [*IV.*]

TREATISE (a) on heresy, as cognizable by the spiritual courts ; and an examination of the statute 9th and 10th William III. C. 32. entitled, "An Act for the more effectual suppressing of blasphemy and profaneness, in denying by writing, printing, teaching, or advised speaking, the divine original of the Scriptures, or the doctrine of the Holy Trinity." By a barrister at law. [Sir Benjamin HOBHOUSE, Bart.]

London : 1792. Octavo. Pp. 146. [*Biog. Dict.*, 1816. *Mon. Rev.*, xi. 206.]

TREATISE (a) on mercury, shewing the danger of taking it crude for all manner of disorders, after the present fashion, from its nature, its manner of operating in the human body and facts, with some remarks on the Antient physician's legacy [of Thomas Dover]. [By Henry BRADLEY.]

London : 1733. Octavo. Pp. viii. 52. [*IV.*]

TREATISE (a) on military finance ; containing the pay, subsistence, deductions, and arrears of the forces on the British and Irish establishments ; and all the allowances in camp, garrison and quarters, &c. With an enquiry into the method of cloathing and recruiting the army ; and an extract from the report of the Commissioners of public accounts, relating to the office of the Paymaster General. [By John WILLIAMSON.]

London : 1782. Duodecimo. [*Gent. Mag.*, lxxi. ii. 957. *Mon. Rev.*, lxviii. 362.]

TREATISE (a) on naval discipline ; with an explanation of the important advantages which naval and military discipline might derive from the science of phrenology. To which are added, phrenological deductions from the cerebral developement of J——h H——e [Joseph Hume] Esq. [By Capt., afterwards Sir John ROSS.]

London, 1825. Octavo.*

TREATISE (a) on soap-making : containing, an account of the alkaline materials ; tests for discovering the presence of an alkali, &c. ; with full directions for manufacturing yellow, pure, white, and perfumed hard soap : also, complete instructions for the making of green or soft soap : with other requisites necessary to finish the soap-boiler. To which is added abstract of the excise laws relative to hard and soft soap-makers. By a manufacturer. [John CARMICHAEL.]

Edinburgh : 1807. Duodecimo. Pp. xxii. 132.*

TREATISE (a) on tennis. By a member of the Tennis Club. [Robert LUKIN.]

London : 1822. Octavo. Pp. viii. 120.*

TREATISE (a) on the application of certain terms and epithets to Jesus Christ. [By Paul CARDALE.]

London : 1774. Octavo. Pp. 74. [*Darling, Cyclop. Bibl.*]

TREATISE (a) on the arts, manufactures, manners and institutions of the Greek and Romans. [By Thomas Dudley FOSBROOKE, M.A., Rev. Dionysius LARDNER, LL.D., and Samuel Astley DUNHAM, LL.D.] In two volumes.

London: 1833. Duodecimo. Lardner's Cab. Cyclopædia.

TREATISE (a) on the beneficial effects of cold and warm bathing : with an appendix ; containing a description of the baths erected at Portobello, near Edinburgh. [By John MILLAR, M.D.]

Edinburgh: 1807. Octavo. Pp. 62. b. t.*

TREATISE (a) on the breeding, training, and management of horses, with practical remarks & observations on farriery, etc. ; to which is prefixed the natural history of horses in general, and the antiquity of horse-racing in England ; together with an appendix containing the whole law relating to horses. By an old sportsman, etc. [William FLINT.]

Hull : 1815. Duodecimo. [W., Brit. Mus.] Signed 'W. F.'

TREATISE (a) on the Coco-nut tree... By a Fellow of the Linnæan and Horticultural Societies. [J. W. BENNETT.]

London: 1831. Octavo. [N. and Q., Feb. 1869, p. 168.]

TREATISE (a) on the Court of Exchequer : in which the revenues of the crown ; the manner of receiving and accounting for the several branches of them ; the duty of the several officers employed in the collection and receipt ; the nature of the processes for the recovery of debts due to the crown ; are clearly explained : as also occasionally, the nature of the feudal and other antient tenures, the origin of parliaments, convocations, the several courts of justice ; and many other curious and useful particulars, are shewn. By a late Lord Chief Baron of that court. [Sir Jeffrey GILBERT.]

In the Savoy : MDCCLVIII. Octavo. Pp. xvi. 343.*

TREATISE (a) on the game of cribbage ; shewing the laws and rules of the game, as now played at St. James's, Bath, and Newmarket ; with the best methods of laying out your cards, and exposing all the unfair arts practised by sharpers. By Anthony Pasquin, Esq. [John WILLIAMS.]

London: 1792. Octavo. Pp. 96. [Biog. Dict., 1816. Mon. Rev., viii. 468.]

TREATISE (a) on the improvements made in the art of criticism. Collected out of the writings of a celebrated hypercritic. By Philocriticus Cantabrigiensis. [John JACKSON.]

London, MDCCXLVIII. Octavo. Pp. 58.* [Sutton's Life of Jackson, p. 184.]

TREATISE (a) on the indefinite and infinite powers of credit, circulation of money, and industry. [By —— GARBETT.]

London : 1784. Octavo. [Brit. Mus.]

TREATISE (a) on the manner of raising forest trees, &c. In a letter from the Right Honourable, the Earl of —— to his grandson. [Thomas HAMILTON, Earl of Haddington.] To which are added, two memoirs ; the one on preserving and repairing forests ; the other on the culture of forests. Both translated from the French of M. de Buffon of the Royal Academy at Paris.

Edinburgh: M.DCC.LXI. Duodecimo: Pp. 129. b. t.*

TREATISE (a) on the nature and causes of doubt, in religious questions: (with a particular reference to Christianity). With an appendix, on some common difficulties ; lists of books &c. &c. [By David Bristow BAKER, M.A., of St. John's College, Cambridge.]

London : 1831. Duodecimo.*

TREATISE (a) on the nature and constitution of the Christian Church ; wherein are set forth the forms of its government, the extent of its powers, and the limits of our obedience. By a layman. [William STEVENS.]

London: 1773. Octavo. [Watt, Bib Brit. Mon. Rev., xlviii. 419.]

TREATISE (a) on the nature and virtues of the Buxton waters. With a preliminary account of the external and internal use of natural and artificial warm waters among the ancients. By a physician. [Alexander HUNTER, M.D.]

London : M.DCC.LXI. Octavo. Pp. 68.* The third edition, published in 1773, has the author's name.

TREATISE (a) on the nature, uses, and effects of the Harrogate mineral waters. by a member of the Royal College of Surgeons. [John THOMSON, formerly Mayor of Ripon.]

[Ripon : 1841.] Duodecimo. Pp. 93. [*Boyne's Yorkshire Lib.*, p. 138.]
The above is appended to the third edition of "The Tourist's guide," by John Richard Walbran, published at Ripon in 1841, under the title of 'The Harrogate visitor's pictorial pocket guide to Ripon, Studley, &c.'

TREATISE (a) on the origin, progressive improvement, and present state, of the silk manufacture. [By George Richardson PORTER.]

London : 1831. Octavo. Pp. xv. 339.* Lardner's Cab. Cyclop.

TREATISE (a) on the parallactic angle, extracted from a letter to the late Earl of Macclesfield on that subject. To which is added an appendix : containing a compleat set of solar and lunar tables, entitled Tabulae Dunelmenses, for computing the places of those luminaries, both in and out of Syzigies. [By the Hon. Spencer COWPER, Dean of Durham.]

London : M.DCC.LXVI. Quarto. Pp. viii. 31.* The appendix has a separate pagination [viii. 33]. Dedication signed S. C.

TREATISE (a) on the passions, so far as they regard the stage ; with a critical enquiry into the theatrical merit of Mr G——k, Mr Q——n, and Mr B——y. [Garrick, Quin, and Barry.] The first considered in the part of Lear, the two last opposed in Othello. [By Samuel FOOTE.]

London, N. D. Octavo.*

TREATISE (a) on the pleadings in suits in the Court of Chancery by English bill. In two books. [By John MITFORD, 1st Lord Redesdale.]

London, 1780. Octavo. Pp. 12. b. t. 128.*

TREATISE (a) on the police of the metropolis, explaining the various crimes and misdemeanors which at present are felt as a pressure upon the community ; and suggesting remedies for their prevention. By a magistrate. [Patrick COLQUHOUN, LL.D.]

London : M DCC XCVI. Octavo.*
The edition of 1800 has the author's name.

TREATISE on the progress of literature, and its effects on society : including a sketch of the progress of English and Scottish literature. [By Robert THOMSON.]

Edinburgh : MDCCCXXXIV. Octavo.*

TREATISE (a) on the progressive improvement & present state of the

manufactures in metal. [By John HOLLAND.] [In three volumes.]

London : 1831-1834. Octavo.*

TREATISE (a) on the proper condition for all horses. By Harry Hieover. [Charles BINDLEY.]

London. 1852. Octavo.*

TREATISE (a) on the religious observation of the Lord's-day, according to the express words of the fourth commandment. [By Dr Samuel WRIGHT.] The second edition. With a new preface, and a table of contents, and other additions.

London : 1724. Octavo.*

TREATISE (a) on the safety and maintenance of states by the means of fortresses. Written originally in French, by M. Maigret, Ingineer in Chief, and Knight of the Royal and Military Order of St. Louis. [Translated by John HEATH.]

London ; MDCCXLVII. Octavo.*

TREATISE (a) on the second sight, dreams and apparitions : with several instances sufficiently attested ; and an appendix of others equally authentic : the whole illustrated with letters to and from the author on the subject of his treatise ; and a short dissertation on the mischievous effects of loose principles. By Theophilus Insulanus. [—— M'LEOD.]

Edinburgh : M,DCC,LXIII. Duodecimo. Pp. vi. xx. 4. 192.*
Reprinted in Miscellanea Scotica, vol. iii.

TREATISE (a) on the theory and practice of seamanship : containing general rules for manœuvring vessels, with a moveable figure of a ship, so planned that the sails, rudder, and hull may be made to perform the manœuvres according to the rule laid down. To the above is added a miscellaneous chapter on the various contrivances against accidents, and a copper plate of the diagrams and figures explained in the work : the whole forming a useful compendium to the officer, to instruct him when young, and to remind him when old. By an officer in the service of the India Company. [Richard Hall GOWER.]

London : 1793. Octavo.*

TREATISE (a) on trade, or the antiquity and honour of commerce, shewing how

trade was esteemed by the Egyptians, Jews, Greeks, and Romans, and on what footing of worship it stands with us. Addressed to the country-gentlemen of England. [By —— PERRY of Penshurst, Kent.]

London: 1750. Octavo. Pp. viii. 64. [*H.*]

TREATISE on wheel carriages, showing their present defects ; with a plan and description of a new constructed waggon, which will effectually preserve and improve the public roads, and be more useful, cheap, and handy to the proprietor. [By Samuel BOURN.] In three parts.

London: 1768. Octavo. [*Watt, Bib. Brit.*]

TREATISE (a) partly theological, and partly political, containing some few discourses, to prove that the liberty of philosophizing (that is making use of natural reason) may be allow'd without any prejudice to piety, or to the peace of any common-wealth ; and that the loss of public peace and religion it self must necessarily follow, where such a liberty of reasoning is taken away. Translated out of Latin [of Benedict de SPINOZA].

London, 1689. Octavo. Pp. 27. b. t· 452.* [*N. and Q.*, 28 Feb. 1863, p. 168.]

TREATISE (a) shewing how useful, safe, reasonable and beneficial the inrolling and registring of all conveyances of lands may be to the inhabitants of this kingdom. By a person of great learning and judgment. [Sir Matthew HALE.]

London: 1694. Quarto. [*Wood, Athen. Oxon.*, iii. 1096.]

TREATISE (a) tending to mitigation tovvardes Catholicke - subiectes in England. Wherein is declared, that it is not impossible for subiects of different religion, (especially Catholickes and Protestantes) to liue togeather in dutifull obedience and subiection, under the gouernment of his Maiesty of Great Britany. Against the seditious wrytings of Thomas Morton minister, & some others to the contrary. Whose two false and slaunderous groundes, pretended to be dravvne from Catholicke doctrine & practice, concerning rebellion and equivocation, are ouerthrowne, and cast vpon himselfe. Dedicated to the learned schoole-deuines, cyvill and canon lavvyers of the tvvo Vniuersities

of England. By P. R. [Robert PARSONS.]

Permissu Superiorum. 1607. Octavo.*

TREATISE (a) touching the East-Indian trade: or, a discourse (turned out of French into English) concerning the establishment of a French company for the commerce of the East-Indies. To which are annexed the articles, and conditions, whereupon the said company for the commerce of the East-Indies is established. [By François CHARPENTIER.]

London ; 1664. Quarto. Pp. 4. b. t. 62.* [*Bodl.*]

TREATISE (a) upon coal-mines: or, an attempt to explain their general marks of indication, acknowledg'd and probable. Together with particular instances of their public utility ; objections to the mode of their discovery, and to their manufacture, obviated, &c. [By William SHARP, vicar of Long Burton.]

London : MDCCLXIX. Octavo. Pp. 105.*

TREATISE (a) upon gout, in which the primitive cause of that disease and likewise of gravel is clearly ascertained ; and an easy method recommended, by which both may be with certainty prevented, or radically cured. [By Murray FORBES.]

London: M.DCC.LXXXVI. Octavo.* [*Mon. Rev.*, lxxvi. 220 ; xiii. 233.]

TREATISE (a) upon the culture of peach trees. Translated from the French [of DE COMBES].

London, 1768. Octavo.*

TREATISE (a) upon the modes : or, a farewell to French kicks. [By John HARRIS, D.D., Bishop of Llandaff.]

London: 1715. Octavo. Pp. viii. b. t. 64.* [*Bodl.*]

TREATISE (a) wherein is declared the sufficiencie of English medicines for cure of all diseases, cured with medicines. Whereunto is added a collection of medicines growing (for the most part) within our English climat, approoved and experimented against the jaundice, dropsie, stone, falling sicknesse, pestilence. [By Timothy BRIGHT?]

At London, printed by H. L. for Tho. Man, 1615. Duodecimo. Title, 5 leaves, pp. 127. [*W.*] The dedication to Lord Zouch is subscribed "T. B."

TREATISE (a) wherein is demonstra-

ted, I. That the East-India trade is the most national of all foreign trades. II. That the clamors, aspersions, and objections made against the present East-India Company, are sinister, selfish, or groundless. III. That since the discovery of the East-Indies, the dominion of the sea depends much upon the wane or increase of that trade, and consequently the security of the liberty, property, and protestant religion of this kingdom. IV. That the trade of the East-Indies cannot be carried on to national advantage in any other way than by a general joynt-stock. V. That the East-India trade is more profitable and necessary to the kingdom of England, than to any other kingdom or nation in Europe. By Φιλοπάτρις. [Sir Josiah CHILD.]

London, 1681. Quarto. Pp. 43.* [*M'Cull. Lit. Pol. Econ.*, p. 99.]

TREATISE (a) wherein is manifestlie proved, that Reformation and those that sincerely favor the same are unjustly charged to be enemies unto his Majestie, & the state. [By John PENRY.]

1590. Quarto. Running title, "Reformation no enemy to her majestie and the state."

TREATISE (a) written by an author of the communion of the Church of Rome touching transubstantiation. Wherein is made appear, that according to the principles of that Church, this doctrine cannot be an article of faith. [From the French of Louis DUFOUR, abbé de Longuerne. Published by Abp. TENISON.]

London, MDCLXXXVII. Quarto. Pp. 73.*

TREATISES concerning reg'.eration. 1. Of repentance; 2. Of ..ie diet of the soule. Shewing, the one, how it ought to be sought ?°_r, and may be attained vnto. T .e other, how it being gotten, is to be preserued and continued. [By Thomas MORTON.]

London. 1613. Octavo. Pp. 11. b. t. 119.* [*Bodl.*]

TREATMENT (the) of our domestic dogs. [By Captain MAHON.]

Edinburgh: 1868. Octavo.

TREATYSE (a) shewing and declaring the pryde and abuse of women now a dayes. By Charles Bansley. [Edited by John Payne COLLIER.]

Reprinted from an unique copy. [London: 1841.] Octavo. Pp. 15. [*IV.*]

TREMAINE; or, the man of refinement. [By Robert Plumer WARD.] Second edition. In three volumes.

London: 1825. Duodecimo.*

TREPAN (the); or virtue rewarded. An opera. [Probably by John MAXWELL, a blind man.]

York: 1739. Octavo. [*Biog. Dram.*]

TREVELYAN. By the author of "A marriage in high life." [Lady SCOTT.] Second edition. In three volumes.

London: 1834. Duodecimo.*

TREVLYN Hold; or, Squire Trevlyn's heir. By the author of "East Lynne," "Danesbury House," &c. [Mrs Henry WOOD.] In three volumes.

London: 1864. Octavo.*

TREW (the) report of the dysputacyon had & begonne in the convocaycyon hows at london among the clargye there assembled the xviii daye of October in the yeare of our lord M.D.LIIII. [By John PHILPOT, Archdeacon of Winchester.]

Imprinted at Basil by Alexander Edmonds. Duodecimo.* [*See Maskell's Selected centuries of books*, p. 98.]

TREWE (a) and feythfull hystorie of the redoubtable Prynce Radapanthus. [A pretended reprint from a unique copy by Wynken de Worde; but the reputed author is John Adey REPTON.]

London: 1820. Sq. Duodecimo. [*Gent. Mag., Jan.* 1861, p. 109. *Lowndes, Bibliog. Man., s.v. Radapanthus. Martin's Cat.*]

TRIAL (the) and life of Eugene Aram; several of his letters and poems; and his plan and specimens of an Anglo-Celtic lexicon; with copious notes and illustrations, and an engraved facsimile of the handwriting of this very ingenious but ill-fated scholar. [By Michael FRYER, of Reeth.]

Richmond: 1842. Octavo. Pp. 126.

TRIAL (the): more links of the Daisy chain. By the author of "The heir of Redclyffe." [Charlotte Mary YONGE.]

London and Cambridge: 1864. Octavo.*

TRIAL (the) of a student at the college of Clutha. In the kingdom of Oceana. [By William THOM, minister of Govan.]

Glasgow: MDCCLXVIII. Octavo. Pp. 76.* Re-printed among "The works of the Rev.

William Thom . . . ." Glasgow : 1799, 12mo.

TRIAL (the) of Abraham ; a dramatic poem. [By —— FARRER.]

Stamford, 1790. Octavo. [*W., Brit. Mus.*]

TRIAL (the) of Elizabeth Fenning for murder. With an investigation of the mysterious case, and full particulars by Dr J. Watkins. [William HONE.]

1815. [*Nattali and Bond's Cat., Feb.* 1858.]

T R I A L (the) of Farmer Carter's dog Porter, for murder. Taken down verbatim et literatim in short-hand, and now published by authority, from the corrected manuscript of Counsellor Clear-point, barrister at law. N.B. This is the only true and authentic copy ; and all others are spurious. [By Edward LONG.]

London, MDCCLXXI. Octavo.* [*Gent. Mag., May* 1813, p. 490.]

TRIAL (the) of Mr. Whitefield's spirit. In some remarks upon his fourth journal, publish'd when he staid in England on account of the embargo. [By Rev. Samuel WELLER, minister of Maidstone.]

London : MDCCXL. Octavo. Pp. 55. b. t.* [*Smith, Bib. Cant. Gent. Mag., Nov.* 1740, p. 576.]

TRIAL (the) of republicanism : or, a series of political papers, proving the injurious and debasing consequences of republican government, and written constitutions. With an introductory address to the Hon. Thomas Erskine, Esq. By Peter Porcupine. [William COBBETT.]

London : 1801. Octavo. Pp. 63.*

TRIAL (the) of Selim the Persian [Lord Lyttelton], for divers high crimes and misdemeanours. [By Edward MOORE, the dramatist.]

London : MDCCXLVIII. Quarto. Pp. 20. b. t.*

TRIAL (the) of the Unitarians, for a libel on the Christian religion. [By George WILKINS.]

London : 1830. Octavo. Pp. i. b. t. 313.* [*Aberdeen Lib.*]

TRIAL (the) of tractarianism by the divine rule "Beware of false prophets... Ye shall know them by their fruits." By Cornelius. [Charles Henry CORBETT.]

London : 1851. Duodecimo. [*W.*]

TRIALL (a) of svbscription, by way of a preface vnto certaine svbscribers ; and, reasons for lesse rigour against non-subscribers. Both modestly written ; that neither should offend. [By William BRADSHAW.]

N. P. 1599. Octavo. Pp. 10. b.t. 28.*

TRIALOGUS. A conference betwixt Mr. Con, Mr. Pro, and Mr. Indifferent concerning the Union. To be continued weekly. [By George MACKENZIE, Earl of Cromarty.]

Printed in the year 1706. Quarto.*

TRIALS : a tale. By the author of "The favourite of nature," &c. &c. [M. A. KELTY.] [In three volumes.]

London, 1824. Duodecimo.*

TRIALS (the) of a village priest. By Ruth Buck. [Mrs Joseph LAMB.]

London : [1862.] Octavo. [*Adv. Lib.*]

TRIALS (the) of life. By the author of "De Lisle." [Mrs Elizabeth C. GREY.] Second edition. In three volumes.

London : 1829. Duodecimo.*

TRIALS (the) of Margaret Lyndsay. By the author of Lights and shadows of Scottish life. [Professor John WILSON.]

Edinburgh and London. MDCCCXXIII. Octavo.*

TRIANGULAR (a) canon logarithmicall ; or, a table of artificiall sines, tangents, and the complements arithmeticall of sines supplying the use of secants, to radius 100,000,000 and to every degree and minute of the quadrant. [By Richard NORWOOD, teacher of mathematics.] In two parts.

[1665 ?] Quarto. [*W., Brit. Mus.*]

TRIBE (the) of Levi. A poem. [By John TUTCHIN.]

London, M DC XCI. Quarto.* [*Bodl.*]

TRIBUNE (the). [By Patrick DELANY, D.D.]

Printed at Dublin : London reprinted, MDCCXXIX. Octavo. Pp. 84. b. t.* Consists of xii. numbers.

TRIBUTE (the) ; a panegyrical poem dedicated to the Honorable the Lady Ann Coke, of Holkham Hall. By Philo. [—— MAITLAND.]

Norwich : N. D. Octavo. Pp. viii. 28.* [*Bodl.*] Address to the reader dated 1832.

TRIBUTE (the) of a humble muse to an

unfortunate captive Queen, the widow of a murdered King. By W. T. F*** G****, Esq. [W. T. FITZGERALD.]

London: 1793. Quarto. [*Mon. Rev.*, x. 457.; xiii. 238.]

TRIBUTE to O'Connell. By a Catholic priest of the house of Leinster. [By the Hon. Arthur Philip PERCEVAL, B.C.L.]

Dublin. 1844. Octavo. Pp. 11.* [*Bodl.*]

TRIBUTE (a) to the memory of Dr. Chalmers. By a former pupil. [James M'Cosh, D.D., Principal of Princeton College.]

Brechin: MDCCCXLVII. Octavo. Pp. 8.* [*D. Laing.*] Signed J. M.

TRIBUTE (a) to the memory of William Cowper, author of the Task and other poems, occasioned by the perusal of his works, and the memoirs of his life, by Hayley. [By John Talwyn SHEWELL.]

Ipswich: 1808. Quarto. 4 sh. [*Smith's Cat. of Friends' books*, i. 82 ; ii. 567.]
Another edition in octavo, was published in the same year, with the author's initials, I. T. S.

TRIBUTE (a) to the memory of William Grover, of Stanstead, in Essex, who died the 11th of 10th month, 1825. By A. F. G. [Atkinson F. GIBSON.]

Warwick, 1826. Octavo. ½ sh. [*Smith's Cat. of Friends' books*, i. 95.]

TRIBUTES of affection; with the Slave; and other poems. By a lady, and her brother. [Elizabeth Sophia TOMLINS; published by her brother, Sir Thomas Edlyne Tomlins.]

London: 1797. Duodecimo. [*Gent. Mag.*, xcviii. ii. 471. *Mon. Rev.*, xxiv. 214.]

TRICK (a) to catch the old-one. As it hath beene lately acted, by the children of Paules. [By Thomas MIDDLETON.]

At London Printed by George Eld, and are to be sold at his house in Fleete-lane at the signe of the Printers-Presse. 1608. Quarto. No pagination.* [*Biog. Dram.*]
There is another copy of the same play with the following title :—A tricke to catch the old-one. As it hath beene often in action, both at Paules, and the Black-Fryers. Presented before his Maiestie on New-yeares night last. Composde by T. M. [Thomas MIDDLETON.]
At London Printed by G. E. and are to be sold by Henry Rockytt, at the long shop in the Poultrie vnder the Dyall. 1608.

TRICOTRIN The story of a waif and stray. By Ouida, author of 'Strathmore,' 'Chandos,' 'Idalia,' 'Under two flags,' &c. [Louise de LA RAMÉ.] In three volumes.

London : 1869. Octavo.*

TRIDENT (the): or, the national policy of naval celebration : describing a hieronauticon, or naval temple, with its appendages ; proposing a periodical celebration of naval games, and, on occasion of victories of the first magnitude, the granting of triumphs : these works and institutions being intended to foster the rising arts of Britain into a full maturity, and a successful rivalship with those of Rome and Greece ; and to keep alive, and in full lustre, to the latest generations, the present heroic spirit of the British navy. By a private gentleman. [Major John CARTWRIGHT.]

London, 1802. Quarto. Pp. xvi. 208.*

TRIFLER (the), a new periodical miscellany by Timothy Touchstone of Saint Peter's College, Westminster. [By —— OLIPHANT and —— ALLEN, of Trinity College Cambridge ; Hon. W. ASTON and —— TAUNTON, Students of Christ Church, Oxford, all of whom were under the age of 20.]

London : 1788. Octavo. [*Lowndes, Bibliog. Man.*]

TRIFLER (the); or a ramble among the wilds of fancy, the works of nature, and the manners of men. [By Henry MAN.]

London : 1776. Duodecimo.

—— Vols III and IV.

London : 1777. Duodecimo.

TRIFLES from my portfolio. [By Walter HENRY, surgeon of the forces.] In two volumes.

Quebec : 1838? [*W.*]
This book was republished with the author's name in two volumes post 8vo, London, 1843, under the title of "Events of a military life : being recollections after service in the Peninsular war, invasion of France, the East Indies, St Helena, Canada and elsewhere."

TRIFLES in verse. [By Henry, Lord LYTTELTON.]

London : 1803. Octavo. Pp. 52. [*W., Martin's Cat.*]

TRIFLING (a) mistake in Lord Erskine's recent preface, corrected in a letter to his Lordship by the author of the "Defence of the people." [J. C. HOBHOUSE.]

London : 1819. Octavo. [*W., Brit. Mus.*]

T R I M E S T E R (a) in France and Swisserland; or a three months' journey in the months of July, August, September, and October, 1820, from Calais to Basle, through Lyons; and from Basle to Paris, through Strasburg and Reims. By an Oxonian. [Stephen WESTON.]

London: MDCCCXXI. Octavo. Pp. 88.* [*Lowndes, Bibliog. Man.*, p. 2882.]

TRIMMER (the): or, some necessary cautions, concerning the union of the kingdoms of Scotland and England; with an answer to some of the chief objections against an incorporating union. [By Sir John SPOTSWOOD.]

Edinburgh, 1706. Quarto.*

TRIMMING (the) of Thomas Nashe Gentleman, by the high-tituled patron Don Richardo de Medico Campo, Barber Chirurgion to Trinitie Colledge in Cambridge. [Gabriel HARVEY.]

London, 1597. Quarto. Pp. 53.*

TRINCULO'S trip to the jubilee. [By Edward THOMPSON.]

Moran: 1769. Quarto. [*Newsam's Poets of Yorkshire. Mon. Rev.*, xli. 393.]

TRINITARIAN (the) controversy reviewed: or, a defence of the Appeal to the common sense of all Christian people, &c. Wherein every particular advanced by the Reverend Dr M'Donnell in his Sincere Christian's answer to the Appeal, is distinctly considered; several other subjects relative to the question, are discussed; and an humble attempt is made to put a final period, if possible, to this controversy, by a solemn address to the most judicious defenders of the Athanasian Trinity. By the author of the Appeal. [William HOPKINS.]

London: M DCC LX. Octavo.*

TRINITARIAN (the) investigator: or an examination into the origin, amongst Christians, and Scripture proofs, of the doctrine of the Trinity, &c. A dispassionate inquiry, whether certain opinions held by the Society of Friends, are the peculiar doctrines of Christianity, or whether they are not heathenish, absurd, unscriptural, antichristian, and derogatory of God, addressed to John Wilkinson, Josiah Forster, Joseph John Gurney, & William Allen, acknowledged by that Society to be "true ministers of Christ, and inwardly moved to the work by the Holy Ghost." [By Joseph SHIPTON.]

Birmingham. [1830.] Octavo. 4 sh. [*Smith's Cat. of Friends' books*, i. 99; ii. 573.] Signed "An unlearned layman."

TRIP (a) to Holland, containing sketches of characters; together with cursory observations on the manners and customs of the Dutch. [By Andrew BECKET.] In two volumes.

London: 1786. Sm. Octavo. [*Biog. Dict.*, 1816. *Mon. Rev.*, lxxiv. 67; lxxv. 138.]

TRIP (a) to London; or, the humours of a Berwick smack. Interspersed with topographical notices. [By —— JAMESON.]

Edinburgh: 1815. Duodecimo. Pp. x. 241.*

TRIP (a) to New-England. With a character of the country and people, both English and Indians. [By Edward WARD.]

London, 1699. Folio. Pp. 16.*

TRIP (a) to Paris in July and August 1792. [By Richard TWISS.]

London: 1792 or 3. Octavo. Pp 131. [*Mon. Rev.*, x. 65.]

TRIP (the) to Portsmouth; a comic sketch of one act, with songs. [By George Alexander STEVENS.]

London: [1773.] Octavo. Pp. 51.*

TRIP (a) to Scotland. As it is acted at the Theatre Royal in Drury-Lane. [By William WHITEHEAD.]

London: M.DCC.LXX. Octavo. Pp. 40.* [*Biog. Dram. Mon. Rev.*, xlii. 145.]

TRIP (a) to Shetland. By a Scotsman. [David Dakers BLACK.]

Edinburgh: 1872. Octavo. Pp. 49.* Signed T. G.

TRIPLE (the) cord or a treatise proving the truth of the Roman religion, by Sacred Scriptures. Taken in the literall sense. Expounded by ancient Fathers. Interpreted by Protestant writers. With a discouery of sundry subtile sleights vsed by Protestants, for euading the force of strongest arguments, taken from cleerest texts of the foresaid Scriptures. [By Laurence ANDERTON.]

Permissu Superiorum, M.DC.XXXIIII. Quarto. Pp. 70. b. t. 801. 11.* Epistle dedicatory signed N. N.

TRISTIA; or, the sorrows of Peter. Elegies to the king, Lords Grenville, Petty, Erskine, the Bishop of London,

Messrs. Fox, Sheridan, &c. &c. By P. Pindar, Esq. [John WOLCOTT, M.D.]

London: 1806. Octavo. Pp. 2. b. t. 169.*

TRITHEISM charged upon Dr. Sherlock's new notion of the Trinity, and the charge made good, in an answer to the Defense of the said notion against the Animadversions upon Dr. Sherlock's book, entituled, A vindication of the doctrine of the holy and ever blessed Trinity, &c. By a divine of the Church of England. [Robert SOUTH.]

London, M DC XCV. Quarto.*

TRIUMPH (the) of acquaintance over friendship. An essay for the times. By a lady. [Mrs HAYLEY.]

London : 1796. Duodecimo. Pp. 87. [European Mag., xxix. 183 ; xxxii. 359.]

TRIUMPH (the) of benevolence ; a poem. Occasioned by the national design of erecting a monument to John Howard, Esq. A new edition, corrected and enlarged ; to which are added, stanzas on the death of Jonas Hanway, Esq. [By Samuel Jackson PRATT.]

London: MDCCLXXXVI. Quarto. Pp. 30.* [Nichols, Lit. Anec., ix. 7. Mon. Rev., lxxv. 392.]

TRIUMPH (the) of Christianity : or, the life of Cl. Fl. Julian. the apostate : with remarks, contain'd in the resolution of several queries. To which is added, reflections upon a pamphlet, call'd, Seasonable remarks on the fall of the Emperor Julian. And on part of a late pernicious book, entituled, A short account of the life of Julian, &c. [By John DOWELL, M.A., of Christ's College, Cambridge.]

London: 1683. Octavo. Pp. 14. b. t. 237.*

TRIUMPH (the) of fashion ; a vision. [By Henry James PYE.]

London : 1771. Quarto. [Wall, Bib. Brit. Crit. Rev., xxxi. 314.]

TRIUMPH (the) of friendship, an historical poem. [By William GOLDEN.]

London 1791. Quarto.*

TRIUMPH (the) of Isis, a poem. Occasioned by [William Mason's] Isis, an elegy. [By Thomas WARTON.] The third edition.

London, MDCCL. Quarto. Pp. 16.* [Coleridge's Worthies of Yorkshire, p. 403.]

TRIUMPH (the) of the Orwell, with a

dedicatory sonnet, and prefatory stanzas. [By Bernard BARTON.]

Woodbridge : [1817.] Octavo. 1 sh. [Smith's Cat. of Friends' books, i. 196.]

TRIUMPH (the) of truth ; being an account of the trial of Mr E. Elwall [written by himself] for heresy and blasphemy, at Stafford Assizes, before Judge Denton. To which are added extracts from William Penn's Sandy foundation shaken, and a few additional illustrations. By the author of An appeal to the serious and candid professors of Christianity &c. [Joseph PRIESTLEY.]

London: 1776. Duodecimo. [Mon. Rev., liv. 79, 80.]

TRIUMPH (the) over Midian. By A. L. O. E., author of " The Shepherd of Bethlehem," " Exiles in Babylon," " Rescued from Egypt," &c. &c. [Charlotte TUCKER.]

London: 1867. Octavo. Pp. 280.*

TRIUMPHS (the) of Europe in the campaigns of 1812, 1813, 1814, commemorated by a series of twelve views from original drawings in the collection of the Emperor of Russia, to which is prefixed a concise history of those important events. [By T. H. HORNE.]

London : 1814. Folio. [W., Brit. Mus.]

TRIUMPHS (the) of perseverance and enterprise: recorded as examples for the young. [By Thomas COOPER.]

London : [1856.] Octavo. Pp. viii. 280.*

TRIUMPHS (the) of religion: a sacred poem, in four parts. [By Harriett COPE.]

London: 1811. Duodecimo. Pp. 121. [Lond. Cat. Mon. Rev., lxvi. 320. Brit. Crit., xxxviii. 519.]

TRIUMPHS (the) of Rome over despised, Protestancie: [By George HALL, Bishop of Chester.]

London; 1655. Quarto. Pp. 2. b. t. 148.* The address "to the victorious Roman Catholique knight, that foyld the vicar, and won the lady" is signed Your truly Catholique wel-willer, faithfull will-bee vicar of Non-such.

TRIUMPHS (the) of the Prince d'Amour. A masque presented by his Highnesse at his pallace in the Middle Temple, the 24th of Februarie 1635. [By Sir William D'AVENANT.]

London, 1635. Quarto. Pp. 2. b. t. 16. 1.* [Bodl.] Address to every reader

signed W. D. "Will. D'Avenant the author."—Wood.

TRIUMPHS (the) of time. The previsions of Lady Evelyn ; with the conclusion. By the author of " Two old men's tales," " Emilia Wyndham," &c. [Mrs Anne MARSH.]

London : 1849. Octavo. Pp. 348.*

TRIUMPHS (the) ouer death : or, a consolatorie epistle, for afflicted minds, in the affects of dying friends. First written for the consolation of one : but nowe published for the generall good of all, by R. S. the authour of S. Peters complaint, and Mœoniæ his other hymnes. [Robert SOUTHWELL.]

London printed by Valentine Simmes for Iohn Busbie, and are to be solde at Nicholas Lings shop at the West end of Paules Church. 1596. Quarto. No pagination.* Original edition.

TRIUMVIRATE (the) ; or the authentic memoirs of A. B. and C. [By Richard GRIFFITH.] In two volumes.

London : 1765. Duodecimo. [Watt, Bib. Brit. Mon. Rev., xxxii. 316.]

TRIVIAL poems, and triolets. Written in obedience to Mrs. Tomkin's commands, by Patrick Carey, 20th Aug. 1651. [Edited by Sir Walter SCOTT.]

London : 1820. Quarto. [IV.]

TROADES Englished. By S. P. [Samuel PORDAGE.]

London, 1660. Octavo. Pp. 6. b. t. 67.*

TROJAN (the) horse of the Presbyteriall government unbowelled. Wherein is contained, I. The power of the Presbyterian government. II. The persons in whom this power is placed. III. The exercise of the Presbyterian power in Scotland, and the lawes there imposed on the peoples necks. [By Henry PARKER, of Lincoln's Inn.]

Printed in the yeere 1646. Quarto. Pp. 22. b. t.*

TROUBADOUR (the) ; catalogue of pictures, and historical sketches. By L. E. L. author of The improvisatrice. [Letitia Elizabeth LANDON, afterwards Mrs. M'Lean.] Third edition.

London : 1825. Octavo. Pp. 326. b. t.*

TROUBLESOME (the) and hard adventures in love, lively setting forth the feavers, the dangers and the jealousies of lovers ; and the labyrinths and wildernesses of fears and hopes

through which they dayly passe, illustrated by many admirable patterns of heroical resolutions in some persons of chivalry and honour, and by the examples of incomparable perfections in some ladies, a work very delightfull and acceptable to all, written in Spanish, by that excellent and famous gentleman, Michael Cervantes, and exactly translated into English by R. C. [Robert CODRINGTON] Gent.

London, printed by B. Alsop, dwelling in Grubstreet near the Upper Pump. 1652. Quarto. 139 leaves, unpaged. [IV.] The Epistle dedicatory signed R.C.

TROUBLESOME (the) life and raigne of King Henry the Third. Wherein five distempers and maladies are set forth. Viz. 1. By the Pope and churchmens extortions. 2. By the places of best trust bestowed upon unworthy members. 3. By patents and monopolies for private favourites. 4. By needlesse expences and pawning of jewels. 5. By factious Lords and ambitious peeres. Sutable to these unhappie times of ours ; and continued with them till the king tied his actions to the rules of his great and good Councell, and not to passionate and single advice. [By Sir Robert COTTON.]

Imprinted at London for George Lindsey. 1642. (Quarto.*

A reprint of A short view of the long life and raigne, &c.

TRUCKLEBOROUGH Hall ; a novel. In three volumes. [By William Pitt SCARGILL.]

London : 1827. Duodecimo.*

TRUE (a) account and declaration of the horrid conspiracy against the late king, his present Majesty, and the government : as it was order'd to be published by his late Majesty. [By Thomas SPRAT, D.D., Bishop of Rochester.] The second edition.

In the Savoy : 1685. Folio. Pp. 2. b. t. 167.* [Brit. Mus.]

TRUE (a) account of the behaviour and conduct of Archibald Stewart, Esq. ; late Lord Provost of Edinburgh. In a letter to a friend. [By David HUME.]

London : MDCCXLVIII. Octavo. Pp. 51.*

TRUE (a) account of the life and writings of Thomas Burnett, Esq. [By George SEWELL.]

London : 1715. Octavo. [W.]

A satirical account of Sir Thomas Burnet,

one of the Justices of the Court of Common Pleas, and youngest son of Bishop Burnet.

TRUE (a) account of the present state of Trinity College in Cambridge, under the oppressive government of their master Richard Bentley, late D.D. [By Conyers MIDDLETON, D.D.]

London: 1719. Octavo. Pp. 43.* [*Rawlinson's English Topographer*, p. 20.]

TRUE (a) account of the proceedings at Perth; the debates in the secret council there; with the reasons and causes of the suddain finishing and breaking up of the rebellion. Written by a rebel. [John, Master of SINCLAIR.]

London: 1716. Octavo. Pp. 76. b. t.* [*See Preface* (p. viii.) to *Memoirs of the insurrection in Scotland in* 1715. *By John, Master of Sinclair. . . With notes by Sir Walter Scott, Bart. Printed at Edinburgh:* M.DCCC.LVIII, 4to.]

T R U E (a) account of the sensible, thankful and holy state of God's people. And of his speaking to them both in the Old and New Covenant. By the servant of Christ, G. F. [George FOX.]

Printed in the year 1686. Quarto. 1½ sh. [*Smith's Cat. of Friends' books*, i. 686.]

TRUE (a) account of this present blasing-star. Presenting it self to the view of the world. This August. 1682. with sundry considerable remarks and observations thereupon. [By Christopher NESSE.]

London 1682. Folio. S.L.* [*Bodl.*]

TRUE (the) and briefe relation of the great victory obtained by Sir Ralph Hopton, neare Bodmin, in the county of Cornwall, Ianuary 19. Ann. Dom. 1642. [By Peter HEYLIN, D.D.]

Printed by H. Hall for W. Webb. M.DC.XLII. Quarto. Pp. 37-42. [*Bodl.*] The above is complete in itself; but the pagination shows it to be only a part of a larger work.

TRUE (a) and exact history of the succession of the Crown of England: collected out of records, and the best historians. Written for the information of such as have been deluded and seduced by the pamphlet [by Lord Somers], called The brief history of the succession, &c. pretended to have been written for the satisfaction of the Earl of H. [By Robert BRADY, M.D.]

London, MDCLXXXI. Folio. Pp. 46. b. t.*

TRUE (a) and exact relation of the strange finding out of Moses his tombe,

in a valley neere unto Mount Nebo in Palestina. With divers remarkable occurrences that happened thereupon, and the severall judgements of many learned men concerning the same. Communicated by a person of quality residing at Constantinople, to a person of honour in England, and by him permitted to be published, for the satisfaction of the ingenious. [By Thomas CHALONER.]

London, 1657. Octavo. Pp. 2. b. t. 39.* [*Wood, Athen. Oxon.*, iii. 531.]

"This book, at its first appearance, made a great noise, and pusled the presbyterian Rabbies for a time: at length the author thereof being known, and his story found to be a meer sham, the book became ridiculous, and was put to posterior uses." —Ant. à Wood, Athen.Oxon., ed Bliss, iii. 533.

Ascribed also to Joseph Georgirenes, Archbishop of Samos. [*Douce Cat.*]

TRUE (a) and faithful narrative of the unjust and illegal sufferings and oppressions of many Christians (injuriously and injudiciously called fanaticks, holding all the fundamentals of the Christian religion, believing all the articles of the Christian faith; and whose lives and conversations are as consonant and agreeable to the laws of God as theirs that persecute them) under, and by several of his Majesties Justices of peace, and others, who are no officers, but informers, in the county of Devon, since the 10th of May, 1670, from a pretended zeal, to put the laws against conventicles in execution. As also of the most malicious prosecution of nine innocent persons, to take away their lives under a false pretence of murdering an informer: and of the tryals that were betwixt Matthew Hale, of Halwell, in the parish of Pool, William Bastard, of Garston, in the parish of West-Alvington, Esquires, and Mr. Edmund Reynel, and John Bear, (called by a nick-name Cocky Bear) two informers for pretended neglects, of putting the Act against conventicles in execution, and the hard measure they met with from the judge, with the horrid perjuries of the witnesses brought against them at the assizes held at Exon, in the county of Devon, April 1671. [By John HICKS, minister at Kingsbridge.]

Printed in the year 1671. Quarto.* [*Davidson, Bib. Devon.*, p. 96.]

Somers' Collection of Tracts, 2d. ed. vol. vii. pp. 586-615.

TRUE (a) and ful relation of the officers and armies forcible seising of divers eminent members of the Commons House, Decemb. 6. & 7. 1648. As also, a true copy of a letter lately written by an agent for the army in Paris, dated 28 of Novemb. 1648. to a member of the said House, a great creature and patriot of the army; clearly discovering, that their late remonstrance and proceedings do drive on and promote the Jesuits and Papists designes, to the subversion of religion, parliament, monarchy, and the fundamental laws and government of the kingdom. [By William PRYNNE.]
London, 1648. Quarto. Pp. 15.*

TRUE (a) and impartial account of the life of the Most Reverend Father in God, Dr. James Sharp, Arch-bishop of St. Andrews, Primate of all Scotland, and Privy-Counsellor to his Most Sacred Majesty King Charles II. With a short, but faithful narrative of his execrable murder, taken from publick records, original letters, and other manuscripts. With a preface, wherein a clear discovery is made of the malicious falshoods contained in some late scandalous books and pamphlets, concerning that affair. To both which is subjoined an appendix, containing copies of such papers as are therein referred to. [By David SIMSON.]
Printed in the Year M.DCC.XXIII. Octavo.*
[Adv. Lib.]

TRUE (a) and impartial account of the parliamentary conduct of Sir T. D. Acland, Bart. By a freeholder of the county of Devon. [Rev. J. JONES, of North Bovey.]
Exeter: 1819. Octavo. [Davidson, Bib. Devon., p. 135.]

TRUE (a) and impartial history of the most material occurrences in the kingdom of Ireland during the two last years. With the present state of both armies. Published to prevent mistakes, and to give the world a prospect of the future success of their Majesties arms in that nation. Written by an eye-witness of their Majesties arms in that nation. Written by an eye-witness to the most remarkable passages. [George STORY.]
London: 1691. Quarto. [IV.]

TRUE (a) and impartiall relation of the battaile betwixt, his Majesties army and that of the rebells, neare Newbury in Berk-shire, Sept. 20. 1643. With the severall actions of the kings army since his Majesties removing it from before Gloucester. Sent in a letter from the army to a noble Lord. [By Lord George DIGBY.]
Printed, 1643. Quarto. Pp. 9. b. t.*
[Bodl.]
"This was writt by my Lord George Digby."—MS. note by Bishop Barlow.

TRUE (a) and lively representation of Popery, shewing that Popery is only new modelled Paganism, and perfectly destructive of the great ends and purposes of God in the Gospel. [By Henry HALLYWELL.]
London: 1679. Quarto. Pp. 82. [Jones' Pick, i. 251.]

TRUE (a) and perfect narrative of the strange and unexpected finding the crucifix & gold = chain of that pious prince, St. Edward the King and Confessor, which was found after 620 years interment : and presented to his most sacred Majesty, King James the Second. By Charles Taylour, Gent. [Henry KEEPE.]
London, 1688. Quarto. Pp. 2. b. t. 34.*
[Bodl.]

TRUE (the) and real violations of property; offered to consideration in some expostulatory queries, concerning the criminal and mischievous nature of those unjust practices, whereby just possessions, rights, or dues, are injuriously invaded, detained, or diminished. [By John GRAILE, A.M.]
London; 1683. Octavo. Pp. 28. b. t. 160.* [Bodl.]

TRUE (a) answer to Dr. Sacheverell's sermon before the Lord Mayor, Nov. 5. 1709. In a letter to one of the Aldermen. [By White KENNETT, D.D.]
London; 1709. Octavo.*

TRUE-bleu Presbyterian loyalty; or, the Christian loyalty of Presbyterians, in Britain and Ireland, in all changes of government, since the Reformation, asserted. More particularly, of the Presbyterians in Ulster, since their first plantation there : when King James the First came to possess the crown of England. And a true discovery of the real authors and causes of the civil wars, insurrections, and rebellions in these nations since. To which is added an apology for the Declaration of the Presbytery of Bangor, July, 7th, 1649. [By William TISDAL, D.D., vicar of Belfast.]
Dublin, 1709. Quarto. Pp. 31.*

The title of the above is taken from the
Reply by John M'Bride, and must be re-
garded as ironical, since Dr Tisdall was a
violent opponent of the Presbyterians. The
work has been ascribed (see Wodrow's Correspondence, i. 412), to Mr Campbell,
probably Dr William Campbell, minister
of Armagh, who wrote a Vindication of
the character and principles of the Presbyterians of Ireland. Dr Reid, however, in
his History of the Presbyterian Church of
Ireland (iii. 127, 128, 166, 167), ascribes
it unhesitatingly to Dr Tisdall.

TRUE-born (the) Englishman. A satyr.
[By Daniel DEFOE.]

Printed in the year MDCCI. Quarto.*

TRUE (the) Briton. [By Philip, Duke
of WHARTON.] In two volumes.

London: 1723-4. Octavo. [*W.*]
This Paper consists of seventy-four numbers.

TRUE (the) character of a churchman,
shewing the false pretences to that
name. [By Richard WEST, D.D.]

No separate title-page. Quarto. Pp. 7.*
[*Bodl.*]

TRUE (the) character of a rigid Presbyter: with a narrative of the dangerous
designes of the English and Scotch
Covenanters, as they have tended to
the rouine of our Church and kingdom. Also, the articles of their dog-
matical faith, and the inconsistency
thereof with monarchy. [By Marchamont NEDHAM.] To which is added,
a Short history of the English rebellion : compiled in verse, by Marchamont Nedham ; and formerly extant,
in his Mercurius Pragmaticus.

London: 1661. Quarto. Pp. 4. b. t. 94.*
The "Short history" has a separate title ;
but the pagination is continuous. The
address to the reader is signed Mercurius
Pragmaticus. A MS. note by Wood states
that Nedham "published this merely to
curry favour at the king's restauration, wn
he had lost his credit so much, yt he was
many times in danger of his life."

TRUE (the) character of an honest
man : particularly with relation to the
publick affairs. Dedicated to his
Grace the Duke of Marlborough. [By
Thomas BURNET.]

London, 1712. Octavo. Pp. 6. b. t. 32.*
[*Bodl.*] Dedication signed Timon.

TRUE (a) character of Mr Pope, and
his writings. In a letter to a friend.
[By Charles GILDON.]

London: 1716. Octavo. Pp. 18.* [*Lowndes,*

Bibliog. Man., p. 1920. *Dyce Cat.*, ii. 189.]
Ascribed also to John Dennis.

TRUE (the) Christian religion againe
discovered ; after the long and darke
night of apostacy ; which hath over-
shadowed the whole world ; and the
profession and practice thereof for
many ages ; witnessed unto by the
Scriptures, &c. [By Edward BUR-
ROUGH.]

London: 1658. Quarto. 3⅞ sh. [*Smith's
Cat. of Friends' books*, i. 35.]

TRUE (the) Christians distinguished
from such as go under the name of
Christians. With a short epistle concerning the Holy Scriptures of truth.
As also concerning Christ the offering ;
and such as are chosen in Christ, and
haue their names written in the book
of life before the foundation of the
world. By G. F. [George FOX.]

London, 1689. Quarto. 2½ sh. [*Smith's
Cat. of Friends' books*, i. 688.]

TRUE Church of Christ, shewed by
concurrent testimonies of Scripture
and primitive tradition ; in answer to
"Leslie's Case stated." Three parts.
[By J. HAWARDINE.]

1715-38. Octavo. [*Leslie's Cat.*, 1841.]

TRUE (a) collection of the writings of the
author of the True born English-man.
[Daniel DEFOE.] Corrected by himself.

London: M DCC III. Octavo.* [*Wilson,
Life of Defoe*, 39.]

TRUE (the) copies of some letters occasioned by the demand for dilapidations
in the archiepiscopal see of Canterbury.
[By Archdeacon TENISON.]

1716. Quarto. [*W., Upcott.*]

TRUE (a) declaration of our innocency,
who in scorn are called Quakers, and
how we are clear (if we have justice)
from the penalties of the late Act made
against seditious meetings, and conventicles, as exprest in the preamble
and reason of the said Act, &c. Also
several reasons, and proofs by the
Common-Prayer-Book, and the Holy
Scriptures directed to in it, that our
meetings, and the manner of them, are
according to the Scriptures of truth,
and therefore allowed by the liturgy of
the Church of England, &c. By J. S.
[John STUBBS.]

Printed in the year 1670. Quarto. 1 sh.
[*Smith's Cat. of Friends' books*, ii. 641.]

TRUE (the) defēce of peace, wherin is
declaredde the cause of all warres now

a dayes, and how they maye be pacified, called before the Pollecye of warre devysed & lately recognised by Theodore Basille. [Thomas BECON.]

London: 1543. Duodecimo. B. L. [*IV.*] Reprinted in his works under the title of The policy of war.

TRVE (a) discovrse historicall, of the svcceeding governovrs in the Netherlands, and the ciuill warres there begun in the yeere 1565. With the memorable seruices of our honourable English generals, captaines and souldiers, especially vnder Sir Iohn Norice knight, there performed from the yeere 1577. vntill the yeere 1589. and afterwards in Portugale, France, Britaine and Ireland vntill the yeere 1598. Translated and collected by T. C. [Thomas CHURCHYARD] Esquire, and Ric. Ro. [Richard ROBINSON] ovt of the reuerend E. M. [Emanuel METERANUS] of Antwerp, his fifteene bookes Historiæ Belgicæ; and other collections added: altogether manifesting all martiall actions meete for euery good subiect to reade, for defence of prince and countrey.

London 1602. Quarto. Pp. 9. b. t. 154. B. L.* Epistle dedicatorie signed T. C.

TRUE (a) discourse of the two infamous upstart prophets, Richard Farn'ham weaver of White-chappell, and John Bull weaver of Saint Butolphs Algate, now prisoners, the one in Newgate, and the other in Bridewell: with their examinations and opinions taken from their owne mouthes April 16. Anno. 1636. As also of Margaret Tennis now prisoner in Old Bridewell, with the hereticall opinions held by her, at the same time examined. Written by T. H. [Thomas HEYWOOD.]

London, 1636. Quarto. Pp. 2. b. t. 19.* Reprinted by J. Caulfield, 1795.

RUE (the) dissenter, or, the cause of those that are for gathered Churches. Being a right state thereof, proposed and settled upon its proper foundations: in opposition to all compliance that is sinful, but in order to that obedience which is lawful, and conducive to the healing of the nation. Occasion'd by some late writings, and especially by a book entituled, The cause of their mix'd Churches against (or The axe laid to the root of) separation. [By Stephen LOBB.]

Printed in the year MDCLXXXV. Octavo. Pp. 11. b. t. 142.* [*Darling, Cyclop. Bibl.*]

TRUE (the) doctrine of the New Testament concerning Jesus Christ, considered; wherein the misrepresentations that have been made of it, upon the Arian hypothesis, and upon all Trinitarian and Athanasian principles, are exposed; and the honour of our Saviour's divine character and mission is maintained. Drawn up originally at the request of a friend. To which are added, an appendix, containing some strictures upon the first chapter of St. John's Gospel. And a prefatory discourse upon the right of private judgment in matters of religion; proving, that there cannot be a visible infallible judge of controversy in the Church of Christ. [By Paul CARDALE, Unitarian minister at Evesham.] The second edition, corrected and enlarged.

London: MDCCLXXI. Octavo. Pp. iii. 428.*

TRUE (the) effigies of the most eminent painters and other famous artists, that have flourished in Europe, curiously engraven on copper plates; together with an account of the time when they lived, the most remarkable passages of their lives, and most considerable works. [By —— RESTA.]

Antwerp: 1694. Folio. [*IV., Brit. Mus.* The plates only of Belgians.]

TRUE (the) English government, and mis-government of the four last kings, with the ill consequences thereof, briefly noted in two little tracts. [By Edward STEPHENS.]

London, 1689. Quarto. Pp. 8.* [*Bodl.*]

TRUE (the) Englishman's miscellany, in two parts. Part. I. The false guardians outwitted: a ballad opera, containing twenty one airs. With a prologue and preface, giving some account of the author, and his reasons for this publication. Part. II. Containing a collection of dismal songs, pleasant satires, bitter encomiums, terrible poems, epigrams, epitaphs, &c. Never before published. By W. G. [William GOODALL.]

[London:] 1740. Octavo.*

TRUE (a) estimate of the light of inspiration and the light of human learning, before and since the apostolic age: submitted to the candidates for Holy Orders, &c. [By C. E. de COETLOGON.]

1788. Quarto. [*Watt, Bib. Brit. Mon. Rev., lxxix. 560.*]

TRUE (a) exemplary and remarkable history of the Earl of Tirone. By an eye witnesse. [Thomas GAINSFORD.]

London: 1619. Quarto. [*Lowndes, Bibliog. Man.*, p. 854.]

TRUE (the) faith, by Herman Heinfetter, author of "Rules for ascertaining the sense conveyed in ancient Greek manuscripts," &c. &c. [Frederick PARKER.]

London: 1862. Duodecimo. Pp. 20.*

TRUE (the) foundations of natural and reveal'd religion asserted. Being a reply to the Supplement to the Treatise [by Waterland] entitul'd, The nature, obligation, &c. of the Christian sacraments. [By Arthur Ashley SYKES.]

London: M DCC XXX. Octavo. Pp. 96.* [*Brit. Mus.*]

TRUE (the), genuine, Tory-address. To which is added, an explanation of some hard terms now in use : for the information of all such as read, or subscribe, addresses. [By Benjamin HOADLY.]

[London:] 1710. Folio. Pp. 2.*

TRUE genuine Tory-address, and the true genuine Whig-address, set one against another. To which is added a farther explanation of some hard terms now in use, for the information of all such as read, or subscribe addresses. Being an answer to a late scandalous paper, falsly call'd The true genuine Tory-address, &c. [By Joseph TRAPP, D.D.]

London: 1710. Folio. Pp. 12.*

TRUE (the) good old cause rightly stated, and the false uncaved. [By William PRYNNE.]

[London: 1659.] Quarto. [*IV., Brit. Mus.*]

TRUE (the) grounds of ecclesiasticall regiment set forth in a breife dissertation. Maintaining the kings spirituall supremacie against the pretended independencie of the prelates &c. Together with some passages touching the ecclesiasticall power of parliaments, the use of synods, and the power of excommunication. [By Henry PARKER.]

London, 1641. Quarto.*

TRUE (a) history of a late short administration.] [By Charles LLOYD.]

London: 1766. Octavo. Pp. 22.* [*Almon's Biog. Anec.*, ii. 110.

TRUE (the) history of a little ragamuffin. By the author of "A night in a work house." [James GREENWOOD.]

London: [1866.] Octavo. [*Adv. Lib.*]

TRUE (the) history of Joshua Davidson. [By Mrs E. Lynn LINTON.]

London 1872. Octavo. Pp. viii. 279.*

TRUE (the) history of the Jacobites, of Ægypt, Lybia, Nubia, &c. their origine, religion, ceremonies, laws, and customs. Whereby you may see how they differ from the Jacobites of Great Britain. Translated by a person of quality [Sir Edward SADLEIR] from the Latin of Josephus Abudernus, a man of integrity, and born in Cairo in Ægypt.

London: MDCXCII. Quarto. Pp. 10. b. t. 32.*

TRUE (the) idea of Jansenisme, both historick and dogmatick. By T. G. [Theophilus GALE.]

London, 1669. Octavo. Pp. 30. b. t. 166.*

TRUE (the) institution of sisterhood : or, a message and its messengers. By L. N. R. [Mrs RANYARD.]

London: N. D. Octavo. Pp. 32.*

TRUE (the) interest of families : or, directions how parents may be happy in their children, and children in their parents. To which is annexed a discourse about the right way of improving our time. By a divine of the Church of England. [James KIRKWOOD.] With a preface by A. Horneck, D.D.

London: 1692. Octavo. Pp. 18. b. t. 224.*

TRUE (the) interests of the European powers and the Emperor of Brazil, in reference to the existing affairs of Portugal. By a friend of truth and peace. [W. WALTON.]

London: 1829. Octavo. [*IV., Brit. Mus.*] With autograph letter from the author.

TRUE jvdgement, or, the spiritual man judging all things, but he himself judged of no man. To them who are growing up into discerning and judgement : and to them, who cannot endure sound judgement. [By George FOX.]

London, 1654. Quarto. 1 sh. [*Smith's Cat. of Friends' books*, i. 33.]

TRVE (the) lawe of free monarchies. Or the reciprock and mutuall dutie betwixt a free king, and his naturall subjects. [By James VI. of Scotland.]

At London Printed by T. C. according to the copie printed at Edinburgh. 1603. Duodecimo. No pagination.*

The advertisement to the reader is signed Φιλοπατρις. The first edition was published at Edinburgh in 1598.

TRUE (the) liberty and dominion of conscience vindicated, from the usurpations & abuses of opinion, and persuasion. [By John Nalson, LL.D. prebendary of Ely.]

In the Savoy, 1677. Octavo. Pp. 4. b. t. 142.* [Bodl.]

TRUE (the) meaning of Rom. 13. 7, stated, in a sermon preached in the city of Chester. By a now persecuted clergyman. [Thomas Parry.]

N. P. 1751. Quarto. [Darling, Cyclop. Bibl.]

TRUE (a) method, 1. For raising of souldiers. 2. For bringing those seamen that are in the land into the navy, &c. &c. [By Peter Rowe.]

London : 1703. Quarto. [Brit. Mus.]

TRUE (the) mother Church, or, a short practical discourse upon Acts ii. [41. 42] concerning the first Church at Jerusalem. [By Rev. Samuel Johnson.]

London, 1688. Octavo. Pp. 20. b. t.* [Bodl.]

TRUE (a) narrative of the sufferings and relief of a young girle ; strangely molested, by evil spirits and their instruments, in the West : collected from authentic testimonies there-anent. With a preface and postscript containing reflections on what is most material or curious ; either in the history, or trial of the seven witches who were condemn'd to be execute in that country. [By Francis Grant, of Cullen, one of the Lords of Session.]

Edinburgh : M.DC.XCVIII. Octavo. Pp. xlvi. 21. 1.*

TRUE (a) narrative of what pass'd at the examination of the Marquis De Guiscard, at the cock-pit, the 8th of March, 17½?. His stabbing Mr. Harley, and other precedent and subsequent facts, relating to the life of the said Guiscard. [By Jonathan Swift, D.D.]

London : 1711. Octavo. Pp. 43.*

TRUE (the) non-conformist in answere to the Modest and free conference [by Gilbert Burnet] betwixt a conformist and a non-conformist, about the present distempers of Scotland. By a lover of truth, and published by its order. [Robert M'Ward.]

Printed in the year 1671. Octavo.* [Wodrow.]

TRUE (the) notion of imputed righteousness, and our justification thereby ; being a supply of what is lacking in the late book of that most learned person Bishop Stillingfleet, which is a discourse for reconciling the dissenting parties in London ; but dying before he had finished the two last and most desired chapters thereof, he has left this main point therein intended, without determination. By the Reverend M. S. a country minister. [Matthew Smith.]

London : 1700. Octavo. Pp. 14. b. t. 222.*

A presentation copy to Ralph Thoresby who has given the author's name.

TRUE (the), pathetic history of poor Match. By Holme Lee, author of "Legends from fairy land," "Adventures of Tuflongbo and his companions," etc. [Harriet Parr.] With four illustrations.

London : M.DCCC.LXIII. Octavo. Pp. viii. 219.*

TRUE patriotism. [By T. Robinson, Lincolnshire bard.]

[Gent. Mag., Sept. 1799, p. 748.]

TRUE (the) penitent instructed. [By Jeremy Taylor.]

1697. Duodecimo. [Leslie's Cat., 1843 (415).]

TRUE (the) picture of a modern Whig, set forth in a dialogue between Mr Whiglove & Mr. Double, two under-spur-leathers to the late ministry. [By Charles Davenant, LL.D.] The seventh edition.

London : 1705. Octavo. Pp. 96.* r

TRUE (the) picture of Quake ·
summary view of the ⌐
heresies and treasonal⸜
the Quakers of old
most noted and ᵃ·
a lover of truth. ·

1736. [Watt
vi. 295.]

TRUE (the
man co·

to the ordinary occupations and pursuits of life. By the author of The morning and evening sacrifice,—The last supper,—and Farewell to time. [Thomas WRIGHT.] In three volumes. Edinburgh and London. MDCCCXXX. Duodecimo.*

TRUE (the) portraiture of the kings of England ; drawn from their titles, successions, raigns and ends. Or, a short and exact historical description of every king with the right they have had to the crown, and the manner of their wearing of it especially from William the Conqueror. Wherein is demonstrated, that there hath been no direct succession in the line to create an hereditary right, for six or seven hundred years ; faithfully collected out of our best histories, and humbly presented to the parliament of England. To which is added the Political Catechism. [By Henry PARKER, of Lincoln's Inn.]
London, 1688. Quarto. Pp. 2. b. t. 63.* Address " to the reader " signed H. P.

TRUE (the) principles of the English Reformation, being the substance of a lecture (occasioned by a discussion between the Catholick Church and the Church of England) delivered in Canon-Street chapel, Louth. By the author of " Notitiæ ludæ ;" " Evidence for Infant baptism "; and " The new Hebrew concordance " (now in the course of publication.) &c. [R. S. BAYLEY.]
London : MDCCCXXXV. Octavo. Pp. 46.*

TRUE (a) protestant bridle : or some cursory remarks upon a sermon [by William Stephens, rector of Sutton in Surrey] preached before the Right Honourable the Lord Mayor and Aldermen of the city of London at S. Mary le Bow, 30 Jan. 1693. in a letter to Sir P. D. [By Thomas ROGERS.]
London : 1694. Quarto. [*Wood, Athen. Oxon.*, iv. 401.]

TRUE (a) reformer. [By Lieut.-Col. Francis Rawdon CHESNEY, R.A.] In volumes. Originally published [in Blackwood's] Magazine.
London MDCCCLXXIII. Oc-

and journall of the and magnificent Prince Charles the VILLIERS,

Bliss' Cat.]

TRUE (a) relation of that memorable parliament, which wrought wonders, begun at Westminster, 1386, in the tenth yeare of the reign of King Richard the Second. Whereunto is added an abstract of those memorable matters, before and since the said king's reign, done by parliaments. Together with the character of the said amiable, but unhappy king, and a briefe story of his life and lamentable death. [By Thomas FANNANT.]
Printed in the yeare 1641. Quarto.* [*Brit. Mus.*] Scott's ed. of Somers' Tracts, iv. 174-190.

TRUE (a) relation of the apparition of one Mrs. Veal, the next day after her death, to one Mrs. Bargrave at Canterbury, the 8th of September. 1705, which apparition recommends the perusal of Drelincourt's Book of consolations against the fear of death. [By Daniel DEFOE.]
London : 1705. Quarto. [*Wilson, Life of Defoe*, 78.]

TRUE (a) relation of the faction begun at Wisbich, by Fa. Edmonds, alias Weston, a Iesuite, 1595. and continued since by Fa. Walley, alias Garnet, the Prouinciall of the Iesuits in England, and by Fa. Parsons in Rome, with their adherents : against vs the secular priests their brethren and fellow prisoners, that disliked of nouelties, and thought it dishonourable to the auncient ecclesiasticall discipline of the Catholicke Church, that secular priests should be gouerned by Iesuits. [By Christopher BAGSHAW.]
Newly imprinted. 1601. Quarto. Pp. 6. b. t. 90.*

TRUE (a) relation of the last sicknes and death of Cardinal Bellarmine, who died in Rome the seaventeenth day of September, 1621 : by C. E. [Edward COFFIN] of the Society of Jesus.
1622. Duodecimo. [*Oliver's Jesuits.*]

TRUE (a) relation of the several facts and circumstances of the intended riot and tumult on Queen Elizabeth's birthday. Gathered from authentick accounts : and published for the information of all true lovers of our constitution in Church and State. [By Jonathan SWIFT.]
London, 1711. Octavo. Pp. 16.*

TRUE relation of what hath been transacted in behalf of those of the reformed religion, during the treaty of peace at

Reswick; with an account of the present persecution in France. By P. G. D. [Peter GALLY de Gaujac.]

London: 1698. Quarto. [*Mendham Collection Cat.*, p. 118.]

TRUE (a) relation of what past betweene the fleet of his Highnes the Prince of Wales [Charles II.] and that under the command of the Earle of Warwick. [By Sir William BATTEN.]

1648. Quarto. [*IV., Brit. Mus.*]

TRUE (of) religion, haeresie, schism, toleration, and what best means may be us'd against the growth of Popery. The author J. M. [John MILTON.]

London, 1673. Quarto. Pp. 16.*

TRUE (a) reporte of the death and martyrdome of M. [Edmund] Campion, Jesuite and Prieste, and M. [Rodulph] Sherwin and M. [Alexander] Bryan, Priestes, at Tiborne, the first of December 1581. Observed and written by a Catholike priest [Robert PARSONS] which was present thereat. Whereunto is annexid certayne verses made by sundrie persons.

[Doway: 1582.] Octavo. [*IV., Lowndes, Bibliog. Man.*]

This tract was written in answer to one by Ant. Munday, entitled, "A discoverie of Edmund Campion, and his confederates."

TRUE (a) reporte of the late discoveries, and possession, taken in the right of the Crowne of Englande of the New-found Landes, by that valiaunt and worthye gentleman, Sir Humfrey Gilbert, Knight. Wherein is also breefly sette downe her Highnesse lawfull tytle thereunto, &c. [By Sir George PECKHAM.]

London: J[ohn] C[harlewood] for John Hinde, 1583. Quarto. [*IV., Lowndes, Bibliog. Man.*] Dedication signed G. P.

TRUE (a) representation of Presbyterian government wherein a short and clear account is given of the principles of them that owne it. The common objections against it answered, and some other things opened that concern it in the present circumstances. The second edition corrected and much enlarged. By a friend to that interest. [Gilbert RULE, D.D.]

Edinburgh, 1690. Quarto. Pp. 2. b. t. 19.* Address to the reader signed G. R.

TRUE (a) representation of the absurd and mischievous principles of the sect, commonly known by the name of

Muggletonians. [By John WILLIAMS, D.D.]

London, MDCXCIV. Quarto. Pp. 2. b. t. 30.* [*Bodl.*]

TRUE (the) Scripture doctrine of the most holy and undivided Trinity, continued and vindicated from the misrepresentations of Dr. Clarke. In answer to his Reply. By the author of the Scripture-Doctrine published and recommended by Robert Nelson, Esq. [By James KNIGHT, D.D.]

London: MDCCXV. Octavo. Pp. 2. 304.* [*Darling, Cyclop. Bibl.*]

TRUE (the) sentiments of America: contained in a collection of letters sent from the House of Representatives of the province of Massachusetts Bay, to several persons of high rank in this kingdom: together with certain papers relating to a supposed libel on the governor of that province, and a dissertation on the canon and feudal law. [By Thomas HOLLIS.]

London: 1768. Octavo. Pp. 158. [*Rich, Bib. Amer.*, i. 164.]

TRUE (the) settlement of a Christians faith, after shaking assaults, by its own evidence; and by the internal sealing work of the Spirit; pointed at, in some special enquiries thereon, in a letter to a friend. With some serious reflections on the present times we are in, and these great vicissitudes of Providence, which have been in the publick state of Britain in this last age, in a II. letter. By a minister of the Gospel. [Robert FLEMING.]

Printed in the year 1692. Octavo. Pp. 2. b. t. 208.*

TRUE, sincere, and modest defence of English Catholiques that suffer for their faith both at home and abroad, against a false, seditious and slaunderous libel [by Lord Burghley] intituled, "The execution of justice in England." [By William ALLEN, Cardinal.]

N. P. N. D. Octavo.

TRUE (the) Sonship of Christ investigated. And his person, dignity and offices explained and confirmed from the Sacred Scriptures. By a clergyman. [William DALGLEISH, D.D., of Peebles.]

London: MDCCLXXVI. Duodecimo. Pp. 4. b. t. 198.*

TRUE (the) speeches of Thomas Whitebread, Provincial of the Jesuits in England, William Harcourt, pretended

Rector of London, John Fenwick, Procurator for the Jesuits in England, John Gavan, and Anthony Turner, all Jesuits and priests; before their execution at Tyburn, June the 20th. MDCLXXIX. With animadversions thereupon : plainly discovering the fallacy of all their asseverations of their innocency. [By David CLARKSON.] Published by authority.

London, 1679. Folio. Pp. 24. b. t.*

TRUE (the) spirit of the Methodists, and their allies, (whether other enthusiasts, Papists, deists, Quakers, or atheists) fully laid open ; in an answer to six, of the seven pamphlets, (Mr Law's being reserv'd to be consider'd by itself;) lately publish'd against Dr. Trapp's sermons upon being righteous over-much. By which it appears that the said pamphlets united make up one of the greatest curiosities that even this curious age has produced. [By Joseph TRAPP, D.D.]

London : 1740. Octavo. Pp. 98. b. t.*

TRUE (a) state of the case concerning the election of a Provost of Queens-College in Oxford. [By Francis THOMPSON, B.D.]

Oxford : 1704. Quarto. Pp. 32. b. t.* [*Bodl.*]

Most of the materials for this pamphlet were collected by Dr. Thomas Crosthwait.

TRUE (the) state of the process against Mr. Ebenezer Erskine minister of the Gospel at Stirling ; setting forth the proceedings of the Synod of Perth and Stirling against him, and the Act of the late Assembly concerning him, and some other ministers adhering to his protest. Together with a preface and appendix, containing some remarks on the preface to the two Acts of Assembly lately publish'd. [By Ebenezer ERSKINE.]

Edinburgh, M,DCC,XXXIII. Octavo. Pp. 80.* [*M'Kerrow's History of the Secession Church* (ed. 1841), p. 818.]

TRUE stories of cottagers. The drunkard's boy. The cottage in the lane. Robert Lee. Annie's grave. Mary Cooper. The railroad boy. [By Edward MONRO, M.A.]

London : MDCCCXLIX. Duodecimo.* [*Bodl.*]

Each story has a separate title and pagination.

TRUE (the) subject to the rebell : or the hurt of sedition, how greivous it is to a commonwealth. Written by Sir John Cheeke, Knight (Tutor and Privy-Councellour to King Edward the Sixt) 1549. Whereunto is newly added by way of preface a briefe discourse of those times, as they may relate to the present, with the author's life [by G. LANGBAINE].

Oxford : 1641. Quarto. [*IV.*]

TRUE (a) subjects wish. For the happy successe of our royall army preparing to resist the factious rebellion of those insolent Covenanters (against the sacred Maiesty, of our gracious and loving King Charles) in Scotland. [By Martin PARKER.] [In two parts.]

London. N. D. S. Sh. Folio. B.L.* Signed M.P.

TRUE (a) testimony from the people of God : (who by the world are called Quakers) of the doctrines of the prophets, Christ, and the apostles, which is witnessed unto, by them who are now raised up by the same power, and quickened by the same Spirit and blood of the everlasting Covenant, which brought again our Lord Jesus from the dead. Published for this end (viz.) that all sober minded people may see the unity and agreement of our doctrine and testimony, with the testimony of Jesus, and all the holy men of God. With the difference between us, and them that have the form of words, but not the power thereof. By M. F. [Margaret FELL.]

London, 1660. Quarto. Pp. 3. b. t. 28.*

TRUE (the) text of the Holy Scriptures. By Herman Heinfetter, author of " Rules for ascertaining the sense conveyed in ancient Greek manuscripts," &c. &c. [Frederick PARKER.] Second edition.

London : 1861. Duodecimo. Pp. 30.*

TRUE (the) theory of the earth, and philosophy of the predicted end ; a solution of some of the great problems of science, and sacred prophecy, on the testimony of the two witnesses, the book of nature and the Word of God ; specially considered as elucidating the origin and distribution of auriferous deposits in Australasia and elsewhere, now offering the attraction of gold in inexhaustible quantities, to "allure to the wilderness " "the nations of them that are saved," in the calamities now impending over Europe. By Research. [J. Wood BEILBY, Frankston, Victoria.]

Edinburgh : MDCCCLXIX. Octavo. Pp. vii. 229.*

TRUE (the) time of keeping St. Matthias's-day in leap years, shewn in a familiar conference between a church-man and a dissenter ; wherein is inserted Dr. Wallis's letter to Bp. Fell written on that subject. [By Robert WATTS, LL.B.]

Oxford: 1711. Octavo. [*Bodl.*]

TRUE to her trust ; or, "womanly past question." [By Miss Dora HAVERS.] With illustrative initial devices by F. W. Waddy. [In three volumes.]

London: 1874. Octavo.* [*Title page of* "*Pretty Miss Bellew.*"]

TRUE to life, a simple story. By a sketcher from nature. [Mary STANLEY.]

London: 1873. Octavo.

TRUE (the) translation of the Holy Scriptures, by Herman Heinfetter, author of "Rules for ascertaining the sense conveyed in ancient Greek manuscripts," &c. &c. [Frederick PARKER.]

London: 1861. Duodecimo. Pp. 55.*

TRUMPET (the) of fame, or Sir F. Drakes and Sir J. Hawkins Farewell. By H. B. [Henry ROBERTS.]

London, by T. Creede, 1595. Quarto. Pp. 12. [*W., Lowndes, Bibliog. Man.*]

TRUMPET (the) of the Lord sounded, and his sword drawn, and the separation made between the precious and the vile ; and the vineyard of the Lord dressed by his own husbandmen, and the dead trees cut down, and all the mystery of witchcraft discovered in all professions : by them who have come thorow great tribulation, whose garments have been washed in the blood of the Lamb, who are accounted as the off-scowring of all things for Christs sake, scornfully called by the world Quakers. [By George FOX.]

London, 1654. Quarto. Pp. 17. b. t.*

One of what may be called the blasts of the trumpet is signed G. F.

TRUST in God ; or, Jenny's trials. By Cousin Kate. [Catherine Douglas BELL.]

London: 1871. Duodecimo.

TRUSTEE (the). By the author of the tragedy of "The Provost of Bruges," &c. [G. W. LOVELL.] In three volumes.

London: 1841. Duodecimo.*

TRUSTWORTHINESS (the) of the Earl Street committee examined. [By James M. M'CULLOCH, D.D., Greenock.]

Edinburgh: 1828. Octavo.

TRUTH and error : a calm examination of the doctrines of the Church of Rome for all who are sincere in the search after truth. By an octogenarian. [Mrs. TYNDALL, of Oxford.]

Oxford: MDCCCLXX. Octavo. Pp. 211. xxxii.*

TRUTH and innocence vindicated : in a survey of a discourse [by Samuel Parker] concerning ecclesiastical polity ; and the authority of the civil magistrate over the consciences of subjects in matters of religion. [By John OWEN.]

London, 1669. Octavo.* [*Bodl.*]

TRUTH, if you can find it : or, a character of the present M -----y and P ------t. In a letter to a member of the March Club. [By Sir Thomas BURNET.]

London: 1712. Octavo. Pp. 37.*

TRUTH its manifest, or a short and true relation of divers main passages of things (in some whereof the Scots are particularly concerned) from the very first beginning of these unhappy troubles to this day. [By David BUCHANAN.] Published by authority.

London. Printed in the yeer, 1645. Pp. 16. b. t. 142.*

"The author of the present vol. was, I believe, David Buchanan, who in 1644, republished Knox's History of the Reformation in Scotland—and was the author of various other works."—MS. note by Dr. David Laing.

TRUTH (the) of revelation demonstrated by an appeal to existing monuments, sculptures, gems, coins, and medals. By a Fellow of several learned Societies. [John MURRAY.]

London: MDCCCXXXI. Duodecimo. Pp. xviii. 276.*

The author's name appears on the title-page of the second edition published in 1840.

TRUTH (the) of the Christian religion vindicated from the objections of unbelievers ; particularly of John James Rousseau. In a series of dissertations. By the editors of the Christian's Magazine. [By William DODD, LL.D.]

1766. Octavo. [*Gent. Mag.*, xlvii. 421.]

TRUTH triumphant. By T. B. [Timothy BROWN, P.P. of Castle Lyon, Co. Cork.]

Cork: 1745. Quarto.

TRVTH-triumphant: in a dialogue between a Papist and a Quaker: wherein (I suppose) is made manifest, that Qvaking is the off-spring of Popery. At the least, the Papist and the Quaker, are [patres vterini] both of one venter. [By Charles STANLEY, Earl of Derby.]

London, MDCLXXI. Quarto. Pp. 45-58.*

TRUTH unlocked; in gleanings and illustrations from the Scripture originals. By a pioneer witness. [William BENNET.]

Edinburgh: 1875. Octavo. Pp. 454. b. t.

TRUTH (the) unvailed, &c. in behalf of the Church of England, and at the importunity of one that calls loudly on Mr. Standish for particular instances of such (amongst her profess'd sons) as have ventured upon innovations in her doctrine; taking occasion from his sermon preach'd before his Majesty, and ordered to be published by royal authority. By a person of quality. [Arthur ANNESLEY, Earl of Anglesey.]

Printed in the year, 1667. Quarto. Pp. 20-39. b. t.*

TRUTH vindicated: being an appeal to the light of Christ within, and to the testimony of Holy Scripture; by way of answer to a pamphlet, entitled, "Extracts from periodical works on the controversy amongst the Society of Friends." [By Henry MARTIN.]

London: 1835. Duodecimo. 9½ sh. [Smith's Cat. of Friends' books, i. 221.]

TRUTH vindicated: or a detection of the aspersions and scandals cast upon Sir Rob. Clayton and Sir Geo. Treby, justices; and Slingsby Bethel and Henry Cornish sheriffs of the city of London, in a paper published in the name of Dr. Francis Hawkins minister of the Tower entit. The confession of Edw. Fitzharris, Esq; &c. [By Sir George TREBY.]

London: 1681. Quarto. 4 sh. [Wood, Athen. Oxon., iv. 500.]

TRUTH will out: or, a discovery of some untruths smoothly told by Dr. Ieremy Taylor in his Disswasive from Popery: with an answer to such arguments as deserve answer. By his friendly adversary E. W. [Edward WORSELEY.]

Printed, in the year, 1665. Quarto. Pp. 6. b. t. 217. 4.* [Jones' Peck, ii. 465.]

TRUTH without prejudice. [By Miss WYNDHAM, afterwards Mrs Alfred Montgomery.]

London: 1842. Octavo.* [N. and Q., 5 Nov. 1864, p. 376.]

TRUTHS and fancies from fairy land, or fairy stories with a purpose. [By W. H. Davenport ADAMS.]

London, Edinburgh, and New York. N. D. Octavo. Pp. 128.* Preface signed W. H. D. A.

TRUTHS and their reception, considered in their relation to homœopathy. To which are added various essays on the principles and statistics of homœopathic practice. [By Marmaduke B. SAMPSON.] Second edition.

London: 1849. Octavo. Pp. 251. [Manchester Free Lib. Cat., p. 620.]

TRUTHS defence: or, the pretended examination by John Alexander of Leith, of the principles of those (called Quakers) falsly termed by him Jesuitico-Quakerism, re-examined and confuted, together with some animadversions on the dedication of his book to Sir Robert Clayton, then Mayor of London. By G. K. [George KEITH.]

London, 1682. Octavo. Pp. 254. b. t.* [Smith's Cat. of Friends' books, ii. 22.]

TRUTHS for the day of life and the hour of death. By the author of "God is love." [James GRANT.]

London: 1864. Octavo.

TRUTHS illustrated by great authors. A dictionary of nearly four thousand aids to reflection, quotations of maxims, metaphors, counsels, cautions, aphorisms, proverbs &c. &c. in prose and verse. Compiled from Shakespeare, and other great writers, from the earliest ages to the present. [By William WHITE, publisher.]

London: 1852. Duodecimo.*

TRUTH'S triumphs in the eternal power over the darke inventions of fallen man. G. F. [George FOX.]

London, 1661. Quarto. 4 sh. [Smith's Cat. of Friends' books, i. 666.]

TRUTH'S triumph over Trent: or, the great gvlfe betweene Sion and Babylon. That is, the vnreconcileable opposition betweene the apostolicke Church of Christ, and the apostate synagogue of Antichrist, in the maine and fundamentall doctrine of ivstification, for which the Church of England Christs spouse, hath iustly, through

Gods mercie, for these manie yeares, according to Christs voyce, separated her selfe from Babylon, with whom from henceforth she must hold no communion. By H. B. [Henry BURTON] rector of S. Mathews Friday-Street.

London, 1629. Quarto. Pp. 13. b. t. 373.*

TRUTH'S victory over error. Or, an abridgement of the chief controversies in religion, which since the apostles days to this time, have been, and are in agitation, between those of the orthodox faith, and all adversaries whatsoever ; a list of whose names are set down after the epistle to the reader. Wherein, by going through all the chapters of the Confession of faith, one by one, and propounding out of them, by way of question, all the controverted assertions; and answering by Yes, or No, there is a clear confirmation of the truth ; and an evident confutation of what tenets and opinions, are maintain'd by the adversaries. A treatise most useful for all persons, who desire to be instructed in the true Protestant religion, who would shun in these last days, and perillous times, the infection of errors and heresies, and all dangerous tenets and opinions, contrary to the Word of God. [A translation of Professor David DICKSON'S Prælectiones in Confessionem fidei by Geo. Sinclar, who signs the dedication to the Lord Provost, Magistrates and Town Council of the City of Edinburgh.]

Edinburgh, 1684. Octavo.*

T R Y. A book for boys. By "Old Jonathan." [David Alfred DOUDNEY, D.D.]

London : 1857. Duodecimo. [Adv. Lib.]

TRY and try again : being an outline of the lives of two youths who became clergymen of the Church of England. By "Old Jonathan." [David Alfred DOUDNEY, D.D.]

London : 1864. Octavo.

TRYAL (the) and examination of a late libel, intituled, A new test of the Church of Englands loyalty. With some reflections upon the additional libel, intituled, An instance of the Church of Englands loyalty. [By Samuel JOHNSON.]

No title page. Quarto.* [Jones' Peck, i. 66.]

T R Y A L (the) of dramatic genius : a

poem. To which are added, a collection of miscellaneous pieces. By the same author. [William HEARD.]

London : [1770.] Octavo.* [J. Maidment.] Heard's father kept the Philobiblian Library in Piccadilly, and was prompter of the theatre at China Hall.

TRYAL (the) of the time-killers. A comedy of five acts. [By Phanuel BACON.]

London : MDCCLVII. Octavo.* [Biog. Dram.]

T R Y A L (the) of the witnesses of the resurrection of Jesus. [By Thomas SHERLOCK.]

London : M DCC XXIX. Octavo. Pp. 110.*

TRYAL (the) of William Whiston, clerk. For defaming and denying the Holy Trinity, before the Lord Chief Justice Reason. To which is subjoined, a new catechism for the fine ladies : also a specimen of a new version of the Psalms. By Mr. Pope, &c. [By Thomas GORDON.] The third edition.

London : MDCCXL. Octavo. Pp. 67. From 19 to 26 a double pagination.* [Nichols, Lit. Anec., i. 710.]

TRYAL (the) of witchcraft ; or, witchcraft arraign'd and condemned. In some answers to a few questions anent witches and witchcraft. Wherein is shewed, how to know if one be a witch, as also when one is bewitched ; with some observations upon the witches mark, their compact with the devil, the white witches &c. [By John BELL.]

N. P. N. D. Duodecimo.* [Adv. Lib.]

TRYALS per pais ; or, the law concerning juries by nisi-prius, &c. methodically composed for the publick good, in the 16th year of the reign of our Soveraigne Lord Charls the Second, King of England, Scotland, France and Ireland, &c. By S. E. [Giles DUNCOMBE] of the Inner-Temple Esquire.

London, 1665. Duodecimo. Pp. 22. b. t. 238.*

This work has been erroneously ascribed to Sampson Ever. The letters S. E. are the finals of Duncombe's names.

TUDORS & Stuarts. By a descendant of the Plantagenet. [Frances Mary ENGLISH.] In two volumes. Vol. I.—Tudors.

London : 1853. Duodecimo.*

TUFLONGBO'S journey in search of

ogres ; with some account of his early life, and how his shoes got worn out. By Holme Lee, author of "Legends from fairy land," "Adventures of Tuflongbo and his companions," etc. [Harriet PARR.] With six illustrations by H. Sanderson.

London : M.DCCC.LXII. Octavo. Pp. vii. 240.*

TUILERIES (the). A tale. By the author of "Hungarian tales," "Romances of real life," &c. &c. [Mrs Catherine Frances GORE.] In three volumes.

London : MDCCCXXXI. Duodecimo.*

TULLIUS de Amicicia, in English. Here after ensueth a goodly treatyse of amyte or frendshyp, composed in latyn by the most eloquente Romayne, Marcus Tullius Cicero, and lately translatyd in to Englyshe [by J. TIPCROFT, Earl of Worcester].

[London : 1530?] Folio. [*IV.*]
A Reprint from the edition, published with Cicero De Senectute by Caxton in 1481.

TUNBRIDGE (the) miscellany. [By Sir Charles Hanbury WILLIAMS.] In two parts.

London, 1713. Octavo. [*Smith, Bib. Cant.*, p. 320.]

TUNBRIDGE-walks : or, the Yeoman of Kent ; a comedy. As it is acted at the Theatre Royal by her Majesty's servants. By the authour of the Humour o' the age. [Thomas BAKER.]

London : MDCCIII. Quarto. Pp. 12. b. t. 64.* [*Biog. Dram.*]

TUNBRIDGE - WELLS ; or, a day's courtship : a comedy, as it is acted at the Dukes-Theatre. Written by a person of quality. [Attributed to Thomas RAWLINS, and by Wood, doubtfully, to Sir Charles SEDLEY.]

London, 1678. Quarto. Pp. 2. 42. 1.*

TUNBRIDGIALIA, a poem, being a description of Tunbridge, in a letter to a friend at London, by the author of "My time, O ye muses." [Dr BYROM.]

London, 1726. Quarto. [*Smith, Bib. Cant.*, p. 320.]

TUNER (the). [By Paul HIFFERNAN.]

London: MDCCLIV. 1755. Octavo.* [*Watt, Bib. Brit. Mon. Rev.*, Feb. 1754.]
The work consists of five letters, each with a separate title and pagination. It is supposed that no more was published.

TURF characters : the officials, and the

subalterns. By Martingale, author of "Sporting scenes," "English country life," &c. [—— WHITE.]

London : 1851. Octavo. Pp. xvi. 128.* [*Adv. Lib.*]

TURKISH (a) tale. In five cantos. [By George GREY, of Southwick, father-in-law of the first Earl Grey.]

London, M DCC LXX. Duodecimo.* [*Autograph on J. Maidment's copy.*]

TURNING out ; or, St. S—'s in an uproar ; containing particulars of the death and resurrection of the heaven-born ministers ; or, the pilots that weathered the storm. A poem. By Peter Pindar, Jun. author of the Royal Bloods, and Royal Lover. [John AGG.]

London : 1812. Octavo. Pp. 24.*

TURNUS and Drances : being an attempt to shew, who the two real persons were, that Virgil intended to represent under those two characters. [By William BEARE.]

Oxford, MDCCL. Octavo. Pp. 30.*
"Given by the author, William Beare, M.A. of C.C.C."—MS. note in the Bodleian copy.

TUTAMEN evangelicum : or, a defence of Scripture-Ordination, against the exceptions of T. G. [Thomas Gipps] in a book intituled, Tentamen novum, proving, that ordination by Presbyters is valid ; Timothy and Titus were no diocesan rulers ; the Presbyters of Ephesus were the apostles successors in the government of that Church, and not Timothy ; the First Epistle to Timothy was written before the meeting at Miletus ; the ancient Waldenses had no diocesan Bishops, &c. By the author of the Plea for Scripture-Ordination. [James OWEN.]

London : 1697. Octavo. Pp. 30. b. t. 190.* Preface signed J. O.

TUTOR (the) of truth. By the author of the Pupil of pleasure &c. [S. J. PRATT.] In two volumes.

London : 1779. Duodecimo. [*Watt, Bib. Brit. Mon. Rev.*, lxii. 324.]

TUTOR'S (the) assistant ; or, comic figures of arithmetic, slightly altered and elucidated from a Walking-game, by Alfred Crowquill. [Alfred Henry FORRESTER.]

London : 1843. Duodecimo.

TUTOR'S (the) ward. A novel. By the author of "Wayfaring sketches,"

"Use and abuse," etc. [Felicia M. F. SKENE.] In two volumes.

London : 1851. Octavo.* [*Adv. Lib.*]

TWA (the) cuckolds [by A. STEEL]; and the Pint quey, or thrawart Maggy [by R. GALL]. Two tales in the Scottish dialect.

Edinburgh : 1796. Duodecimo. [*W., Brit. Mus.*]

TWEEDS teares of joy, to Charles Great Brittains King. [By George LAUDER.]

N. P. N. D. [1641.] Quarto. Pp. 8.* No separate title-page.

TWELFTH (the) note of the Church examined, viz The light of prophecy. [By William CLAGETT, D.D., Preacher to the Society of Gray's Inn.]

London, 1687. Quarto. Pp. 23.* [*Jones' Peck*, p. 439.]

TWELVE generall arguments, proving that the ceremonies imposed upon the ministers of the gospell in England, by our prelates, are unlawfull ; and therefore that the ministers of the gospell, for the bare and sole omission of them in church service, are most unjustlie charged of disloyaltie to his Majestie. [By William BRADSHAW.]

N. P. 1605. Duodecimo.* [*Adv. Lib.*]

TWELVE letters on the evidences of the Christian religion. By an enquirer. [W. CUNNINGHAME.] First printed in the Oriental Star.

Scrampore ; 1802. Sm. Octavo. [*W., Brit. Mus.*]

TWELVE months in the British legion. By an officer of the Ninth regiment. [C. W. THOMPSON, Capt.]

London : MDCCCXXXV. Duodecimo. Pp. viii. 273 ; appendix xxx.*

TWELVE (the) nights. [By Baron Karl von MILTIE.]

London : 1831. Duodecimo. Pp. xv. 404.*

TWELVE (the) Pagan principles, or opinions, for which Thomas Hicks hath published the Quaker to be no Christian, seriously considered, and presented to Mr. N. L., citizen of London. By W. L., a lover of every man whose conversation is honest. [William LODDINGTON.]

N. P. 1764. Octavo. 2½ sh. [*Smith's Cat. of Friends' books*, ii. 127. *Wilson, Hist. of Diss. Ch.*, iii. 392.]

T W E L V E sermons, preached to a country congregation. [By Alexander DALLAS, M.A.]

Oxford, 1827. Duodecimo. Pp. vii. 231.*

TWELVE tales for the young. [By Gertrude PARSONS, née HEXT.]

London : N. D. [1860.] Duodecimo. [*Boase and Courtney, Bib. Corn.*, ii. 426.] Of the above tales, "The old dripping pan" was written by Daniel Parsons ; and "Too late for school," by Miss A. M. Bridges.

TWELVE years' military adventure in three quarters of the globe : or, memoirs of an officer who served in the armies of his Majesty and of the East India Company, between the years 1802 and 1814, in which are contained the campaigns of the Duke of Wellington in India, and his last in Spain and the south of France. [By Lieutenant BLAKISTON, Engineers.] In two volumes.

London : 1829. Octavo.* [*See his "Twenty years in retirement."*]

TWENTY cases of conscience propounded to the bishops, or others, who are called fathers in God. For them to answer ; that the blind may not be turned out of the way, nor the people perish for lack of knowledge. And that the way of truth may be known from the way of errour. The which also may serve as a glass, to shew to the ignorant the spots and deformities in the way of their worship, as also some of the reasons why many godly people refuse to worship with the multitude. By J. C. [John CROOK.]

London, N. D. [1667.] Quarto. Pp. 8.*

XXIV (the) cases concerning things indifferent in religious worship considered. Or the resolver better resolved by his own principles ; and non-conformists more confirmed. Also the grand case touching ministers conformity, with the double supplement thereunto annexed, briefly discussed. [By Edward BAGSHAW.]

London, 1663. Quarto. Pp. 64. b. l.* The above is the second part of the "The great question concerning things indifferent in religious worship, briefly stated, &c." The third part has the author's name.

TWENTY-ninth (the) of May : rare doings at the Restoration. By Ephraim Hardcastle, author of "Wine and walnuts." [William Henry PYNE.] In two volumes. Second edition.

London : MDCCCXXV. Duodecimo.* [*Bodl.*]

TWENTY years ago. From the journal of a girl in her teens. [Beatrice Walford.] Edited by the author of ' John Halifax, Gentleman.' [Dinah Maria MULOCK.]

London : 1871. Octavo. Pp. v. 1. 277.*

TWICE lost. A novel. By the author of "Queen Isabel," "Nina," "The story of a family," etc. etc. [Miss Menella Bute SMEDLEY.]

London : 1863. Octavo. Pp. 1. b. 1. 323.*

TWICKENHAM (the) hotch-potch, for the use of the Rev. Dr. Swift, Alexander Pope, Esq ; and company. Being a sequel to the Beggar's opera, &c. Containing, I. The state of poetry, and fate of poets, in the reign of King Charles the IId. II. Seriosities and comicalities, by Peter Henning, a Dutchman. III. Two dozen of infallible maxims, for court and city. IV. The present war among authors, viz. Swift, Pope, Theobald, Rolli, Voltaire, Parson B——dy, and Mr. Ozell. V. The rival actresses, viz. Mrs. O - - - d, Mrs. P - - - r, Mrs. B - - - h, Miss Y——ger, and Miss Polly Peachum. VI. A poetical catalogue of Polly Peachum's gallants. VII. An epistle from Signora F - - - na to a lady. VIII. A true copy of Polly Peachum's opera. Also, her panegyrick. Written by Caleb D'Anvers. [Nicholas AMHURST.]

London : 1728. Octavo. Pp. vii. b. t. 54.*

"This work will be continued. The end of the first part."

TWIN (the) sisters ; or, the advantages of religion. [By Mrs Elizabeth SANDHAM.]

1809. Duodecimo. [Biog. Dict., 1816, Mon. Rev., lix. 321.]

TWO apologetical odes, and an elegy. [By —— COURTNEY.]

1808. Octavo. [IV.] Not published.

TWO (the) babies. A sketch of every-day life. By a mother. [Mrs Henry DAVIDSON.]

London : 1859. Duodecimo. Pp. 17. b. t.* Signed H. D.

TWO (the) banners and the old battle, or the Established & Free Churches as they are. By a Highlandman. [Hugh M'Intosh, M.A.] Third edition (25th thousand).

Edinburgh : N. D. Octavo. Pp. 72.*

TWO (the) books of Francis Bacon : Of the proficience and advancement of learning, divine and human. [Edited by Thomas MARKBY.]

London : 1852. Duodecimo. [IV.] Preface signed T. M., King's College.

TWO (the) brothers. By the author of "The discipline of life," "Clare Abbey," "The young Lord," &c., &c. [Lady Emily PONSONBY.] In three volumes.

London : 1858. Octavo.*

TWO (the) brothers ; or the family that lived in the first society. [Translated from the German of Mathilde RAVEN.] In two volumes.

London : 1850. Octavo. [IV., Brit. Mus.]

TWO centuries of St. Pauls Church Yard ; una cum Indice expurgatorio in Bibliotheca Parliamenti, sive qui librorum prostant venales in vico vulgo vocato Little Brittain. Done into English for the benefit of the Assembly of Divines and the two Universities. [By Sir John BERKENHEAD.]

About 1650. Octavo. [Cat. Lond. Inst., ii. 195.

TWO charges as they were delivered by T. E. [Thomas EDGAR] Justice of the peace for the county of Suffolke ... wherein appears the necessity of government, and of steps and degrees in it, and the duty .. not to desert the present government.

London : 1650. Quarto. [IV., Brit. Mus.]

TWO Christmas stories Sam Franklin's saving-bank A miserable Christmas and a happy new year By Hesba Stretton author of ' Lost Gip ' Cassy' ' Jessica's just prayer ' etc. [Sarah SMITH.] With two illustrations. Ninth thousand.

London 1876. Octavo. Pp. 68.*

TWO conferences, one betwixt a papist and a Jew, the other betwixt a protestant and a Jew ; in two letters from a merchant in London to his correspondent in Amsterdam. [By Richard MAYO.]

London 1699. Duodecimo.* [Wilson, Hist. of Diss. Ch. Mon. Rev., xi. 314.] Ascribed to John Jacob. [Mendham Collection Cat., p. 162.]

TWO copies of verses on the meeting of King Charles the First and his Queen Henrietta Maria, in the Valley

of Kineton, below Edge-Hill, in Warwickshire, July 13, 1643. [Edited by William HAMPER.]

Birmingham : 1822. Quarto. [*IV., Martin's Cat.*]

TWO (the) cousins ; a moral story, for the use of young persons. By the author of "The blind child." [Mrs PINCHARD.]

London : 1794. Octavo. [*IV., Brit. Mus.*]

TWO dialogues ; containing a comparative view of the lives, characters, and writings, of Philip, the late Earl of Chesterfield, and Dr. Samuel Johnson. [By William HAYLEY.]

London : M.DCC.LXXXVII. Octavo. Pp. xxiv. 240.* [*Gent. Mag.*, lxxxi. ii. 448. *Mon. Rev.*, lxxvii. 457.]

TWO dialogues in English, between a doctour of divinity, and a student in the laws of England, of the grounds of the said laws and of conscience. [By C. SAINT GERMAIN.] Newly revised and reprinted.

London: 1668. Octavo. B. L. [*IV., Brit. Mus.*]

TWO discourses. The first concerning the spirit of Martin Luther, and the original of the Reformation. The second, concerning the celibacy of the clergy. [By Abraham WOODHEAD.]

Printed at Oxford, An. 1687. Quarto.* [*Jones' Peck*, i. 196.
The two discourses are separately paged, and have also separate titles, besides the general title given above.

T W O discourses concerning the adoration of our B. Saviour in the H. Eucharist. The first : Animadversions upon the alterations of the rubrick in the communion-service, in the Common-prayer-book of the Church of England. The second : The Catholicks defence for their adoration of our Lord, as believed really and substantially present in the holy sacrament of the Eucharist. [By Abraham WOODHEAD.]

At Oxford printed, Anno 1687. Quarto.* *Jones' Peck*, ii. 355.]

TWO discourses concerning the affairs of Scotland ; written in the year 1698. [By Andrew FLETCHER, of Salton.]

Edinburgh, 1698. Octavo. Pp. 50. 54.* [*M'Cull. Lit. Pol. Econ.*, p. 296.]

TWO discourses delivered at the public meetings of the Royal Academy of

Sciences and Belles Lettres at Berlin, in the years 1785 and 1786 ; I. On the population of states in general, and that of the Prussian dominions in particular. II. On the true riches of states and nations, the balance of commerce and that of power. By the Baron de Hertzberg, minister of State and member of the Academy. Translated from the French [by Joseph TOWERS, LL.D.].

London : 1786. Octavo. [*Gent. Mag.*, lxxiii. i. 355. *Mon. Rev.*, lxxvi. 42.]

TWO discourses for the furtherance of Christian piety and devotion. The former asserting the necessity and reasonableness of a positive worship, and particularly of the Christian. The later considering the common hinderances of devotion, and the divine worship, with their respective remedies. By the author of the Method of private devotion. [Edward WETENHALL, D.D.]

London, 1671. Duodecimo. Pp. 18. b. t. 379.* [*Bodl.*]
Each discourse has a separate title-page ; but the pagination is continuous.

TWO discourses : of purgatory, and prayers for the dead. [By William WAKE, D.D.]

London, MDCLXXXVII. Quarto. Pp. 71.* [*Brit. Mus.*

TWO discourses wherein it is prov'd that the Church of England blesseth and offereth the Eucharistick elements. With a preface, shewing in what sense she allows praying for the saints departed : and that mixt wine is not contrary to any of her rubricks. [By George SMITH.]

Printed in the year M,DCC,XXXII. Octavo.*

T W O disputations concerning the Messiah, one between a papist and a Jew, the other between a protestant and a Jew ; contained in two letters from a merchant in Amsterdam. [By Richard MAYO.]

1754. Octavo. [*Mon. Rev.*, xi. 314.]
Same as "Two conferences."

TWO dissertations concerning sense, and the imagination. With an essay on consciousness. [By Zachary MAYNE.]

London: MDCCXXVIII. Octavo. Pp. 231.*

T W O dissertations on the subject of Carausius, Emperour of Britain, together with that of his supposed wife and son A 3d. Also of him and his

successor Allectus. Illustrated with three copper plates, of hitherto unpublished coins. To which is added A letter to the Reverend Dr. S - - k - - y [Stukeley] on the first volume of his extraordinary medallick History of Carausius, observing the many mistakes, unwarrantable assertions, and amazing productions therein. [By John KENNEDY.]

London, N. D. Quarto.*

A general title to "A dissertation," "Further observations," and "A letter to the Reverend Dr S—k—y."

TWO elegies, consecrated to the never dying memorie of the most worthily admyred &c Prince, Henry Prince of Wales. [By Christopher BROOKE and William BROWNE.]

London: 1613. Quarto. [W., Bliss' Cat.]

TWO enquiries into the meaning of demoniacks in the New Testament. By T. P. A. P. O. A. B. I. T. C. O. S. [Arthur Ashley SYKES, D.D.]

London: 1737. Octavo.

The initials on the title stand for "The Precentor and Prebendary of Alton Borealis in the Church of Salisbury."

TWO epistles to Mr. Pope, concerning the authors of the age. [By Edward YOUNG, LL.D.]

London: MDCCXXX. Octavo. Pp. 44.* [Dyce Cat., ii. 191.]

TWO (the) families : an episode in the history of Chapelton. By the author of "Rose Douglas." [Mrs S. R. WHITEHEAD.] [In two volumes.]

London: 1852. Octavo.*

TWO (the) fathers. An unpublished original Spanish work; by Adadus Calpe [anagram of A[ntonio] D. de PASCUAL]; translated into the English language by the author, and Henry Edgar. In three volumes.

New York: 1852. Duodecimo. [W.]
The title is headed "He who taketh the sword shall perish by the sword."

TWO first books of Lucretius, De rerum natura, translated into blank verse. [By Sir J. S. TRELAWNY and [Sir] Robert Porrett COLLIER.]

Devonport: 1842. Octavo. [Boase and Courtney, Bib. Corn., i. 80.]

TWO general epistles to the flock of God, where-ever they are dispersed on the face of the earth, who are separated from the world to bear testimony for the Lord God [by Mrs Margaret

Fox, née Fell]; also Pure consolation proclaimed from the spirit of life to the faithful followers of the Lamb etc. [by J. PARK].

London: 1664. Quarto. [W., Brit. Mus.] Signed M. F.

TWO grammatical essays. First on a barbarism in the English language, in a letter to Dr. S——. Second on the usefulness and necessity of grammatical knowledge in order to a right interpretation of the Scriptures. [By William SALISBURY, B.D.]

London: 1768. Octavo.* [Mon. Rev., xl. 84, and Index.]

TWO great questions considered, I. What is the obligation of parliaments to the addresses or petitions of the people, and what the duty of the addressers? II. Whether the obligation of the covenant or other national engagements, is concern'd in the treaty of union? Being a sixth essay at removing national prejudices against the union. [By Daniel DEFOE.]

[Edinburgh.] Printed in the year M.DCC.VII. Quarto. Pp. 31.* [Wilson, Life of Defoe, 100.]

TWO (the) great questions consider'd. I. What the French king will do with respect to the Spanish monarchy. II. What measures the English ought to take. [By Daniel DEFOE.]

London, printed in the year, 1700. Quarto.* [Wilson, Life of Defoe, 13.]

TWO (the) great questions further considered. With some reply to the Remarks. By the author. [Daniel DEFOE.]

London: MDCC. Quarto. Pp. 2. b. t. 20.* [Wilson, Life of Defoe, 14.]

TWO (the) guardians; or, home in this world. By the author of "Henrietta's wish," "Kenneth," etc., etc. [Charlotte M. YONGE.]

London: MDCCCLII. Octavo. Pp. vii. 430.*

TWO (the) homes A tale by the author of Amy Grant. [Miss —— HOPTON.]

Oxford: MDCCCLVI. Octavo. Pp. i. b. t. 146.* [Bodl.]

TWO introductory lectures on the study of the early Fathers, delivered in the University of Cambridge by the Rev. J. J. Blunt B.D. Margaret Professor of Divinity. Second edition, with a brief memoir of the author, and table of

lectures delivered during his professorship [by William SELWYN].

Cambridge: 1856. Octavo. [*W.*] Memoir is signed W. S.

TWO journeys to Jerusalem, containing first, a strange and true account of the travels of two English pilgrims some years since, and what admirable accidents befel them in their journey to Jerusalem, Grand Cairo, Alexandria, &c. By H. T. Secondly, the travels of fourteen Englishmen in 1669. from Scanderoon to Tripoly, Joppa, Ramah, Jerusalem, Bethlehem, Jericho, the river Jordan, the lake of Sodom and Gomorrah, and back again to Aleppo. By T. B. With the rare antiquities, monuments, and memorable places and things mentioned in holy Scripture: and an exact description of the old and new Jerusalem, &c. To which is added, a relation of the Great Council of the Jews assembled in the plains of Agayday in Hungaria in 1650. to examine the Scriptures concerning Christ. By S. B. an Englishman there present. With an account of the wonderful delusion of the Jews, by a counterfeit Messiah, or false Christ at Smyrna, in 1666. and the event thereof. Lastly, the fatal and final extirpation and destruction of the Jews throughout Persia, in 1666 and the remarkable occasion thereof. Beautified with pictures. [By Richard BURTON.]

London, 1683. Duodecimo. Pp. 2. b. t. 232.*

TWO Lancashire lovers: or the excellent history of Philocles and Doriclea. By Musæus Palatinus. [Richard BRATHWAIT.]

London: 1640. Octavo. Pp. 268. [*W.*, *Lowndes, Bibliog. Man.*]

TWO lectures read before the Essay Society of Exeter College, Oxford. [By R. J. KING.]

1840. Octavo. [*W.*, *Bliss' Cat.*]

TWO letters, addressed to a noble Lord, on the manufactures, agriculture, and apparent prosperity of Scotland. With a few strictures on the speculations, morals, and manners, of the nineteenth century. [By —— M'NEIL.]

Edinburgh: 1804. Octavo. Pp. 55. The letters are signed, Anti-speculator.

TWO letters, addressed to the Right Rev. prelates, who a second time rejected the Dissenters' bill. [By E. RADCLIFF.]

London, MDCCLXXIII. Octavo. Pp. 108. b. t.* [*Bodl.*]

TWO letters containing a further justification of the Church of England, against dissenters. The first, by one of the reverend commissioners for the review of the Liturgy, at the Savoy, 1661. [Thomas PIERCE, D.D.] The second by Dr Laurence Womock Archdeacon of Suffolk, author of the Verdict upon Melius inquirendum.

London: 1682. Octavo. Pp. 1. b. t. 89.*

TWO letters from a deist [Nicholas STEVENS, A.M.] to his friend, concerning the truth and propagation of deism, in opposition to Christianity. With remarks. [By Samuel WESLEY, M.A.]

London: MDCCXXX. Quarto. Pp. vi. 37.* [*Bodl.*]

II. letters in defence of the British and Foreign Bible Society, addressed to a friend in the country. [By David BROWN, bookseller.]

Edinburgh: 1826. Octavo.*

Each letter has a separate title and pagination, and is signed Amicus.

TWO letters of advice. I. For the susception of holy orders. II. For studies theological. [By Henry DODWELL.]

London: 1662. Octavo. [*Lincoln's Inn Cat.*]

TWO letters on Scottish affairs, from Edward Bradwardine Waverley Esq. [John Wilson CROKER] to Malachi Malagrowther, Esq. [Sir Walter Scott, Bart.]

London and Edinburgh. MDCCCXXVI. Octavo. Pp. 63. b. t.*

TWO letters on the subject of the Catholics, to my brother Abraham, who lives in the country. By Peter Plymley. [Sydney SMITH.]

London: 1807. Octavo.

TWO letters on the subject of the present vacancy in the Professorship of the Oriental languages. [By Thomas BROWN.]

Edinburgh: 1813. Octavo. Pp. 31. 7.* [*New Coll. Cat.*, p. 116.] The Letters are signed E. P.

TWO letters, one from John Audland a Quaker, to William Prynne. The other, William Prynnes answer. By the author of Hudibras. [Samuel BUTLER.]

London, 1672. Folio. Pp. 22.*

TWO letters, to a British merchant, a short time before the expected meeting of the new parliament in 1796 ; and suggesting the necessity and facility of providing for the public exigencies, without any augmentation of debt, or accumulation of burdens. [By John BOWLES.]　The second edition.

London : M.DCC.XCVI.　Octavo.　Pp. 1. b. t. 84.*　[*Bodl.*]

TWO letters to a clergyman in the country, concerning the choice of members, and the execution of the parliament writ, for the ensuing Convocation. [By Francis ATTERBURY, D.D.]

London : 1701.　Quarto.　[*Bodl.*]

TWO letters to the Rev. Dr. Chalmers, on his proposal for increasing the number of churches in Glasgow.　By an observer. [James HALDANE.]

Glasgow : 1818.　Octavo.　Pp. 38.*　[*New Coll. Cat.*, p. 163.]

T W O letters to the Reverend Dr. Kennicott, vindicating the Jews from the charge of corrupting Deut. xxvii. 4. The first of which was published in the Library for July, 1761.　The second is now first published, being an answer to Dr. Kennicott's remarks, in the Library for August, 1761 ; and a farther illustration of the argument. [By Robert FINDLAY, D.D.]

London : 1762.　Octavo.　Pp. 34.*　Letters signed Philalethes.

TWO letters to the Rev. Dr. Thomas M'Crie, and the Rev. Mr. Andrew Thomson, on the parody of Scripture, lately published in Blackwood's Edinburgh Magazine. By Calvinus. [James GRAHAME, advocate.]

Edinburgh : 1817.　Octavo.　Pp. 30.*

Of these letters of Calvinus, there were, in all, five, besides a postscript.　Their titles are "Another letter"; "Two more letters"; and "Postscript to the letters of Calvinus."

TWO letters to the Right Honourable Lord Viscount Townshend : shewing the seditious tendency of several late pamphlets ; more particularly of, A review of the Lutheran principles, by Tho. Brett, L.L.D. Rector of Betteshanger in Kent, and of A letter to the author of the Lutheran Church, from a country school-boy.　By a presbyter of the Church of England. [Robert WATTS, LL.B., St. John's Coll., Oxford.]

London, 1714.　Octavo.　Pp. 40.*　Signed R. W.

TWO letters, written by a minister of the gospel to a gentleman, concerning Professor Campbell's divinity.　Letter I. Wherein his scheme concerning the origine, or primary source of moral virtue, contained in his answer to the author of the Fable of the bees, is shewed to be irrational, and antiscriptural.　Letter II. Wherein his discourse, proving that the Apostles were no enthusiasts, is considered ; and the poisonous nature of enthusiasm, together with his mistakes of it, are detected. [By James HOG.]

Edinburgh, M.DCC.XXXI.　Octavo.　Pp. 63.*

TWO letters written to [Samuel Hill] the author of a pamphlet entituled, Solomon and Abiathar ; or, the case of the deprived bishops and clergy discussed. [By Samuel GRASCOME.]

London, MDCXCII.　Quarto.　Pp. 43.*

TWO little wooden shoes.　A sketch. By Ouida, author of "Chandos," "Tricotrin," "Under two flags," etc. [Louise de LA RAMÉ.]

London ; 1874.　Octavo.　Pp. 322.*

TWO love stories ; an Anglo-Spanish romance.　By "Waters." [William RUSSELL.]

London : 1861.　Octavo.

TWO lyric epistles : one to my cousin Shandy, on his coming to town ; and the other to the grown gentlewomen, the Misses of * * * * [By John HALL-STEVENSON.]

London : MDCCLX.　Quarto.*

TWO marriages.　By the author of "John Halifax, Gentleman," "Christian's mistake," "A noble life," &c. &c. [Dinah Maria MULOCK.]　In two volumes.

London : 1867.　Octavo.*

TWO (the) mentors : a modern story. By the author of The old English baron. [Clara REEVE.]　The third edition.

London : 1803.　Duodecimo.　Pp. 1. b. t. 386.*　[*Nichols, Lit. Anec.*, viii. 138.]

TWO (the) misers : a musical farce.　As it is performed at the Theatre Royal in Covent-Garden.　By the author of Midas, and the Golden Pippin. [Kane O'HARA.]

London, 1775.　Octavo.　Pp. 32.*　Taken from "Les deux avares" of Fenouillot de Falbaire.

TWO more letters (being the fourth and the last), to the Rev. Dr. Thomas M'Crie, and the Rev. Mr. Andrew Thomson, on the parody of Scripture, lately published in Blackwood's Edinburgh Magazine. Including a brief view of ministerial character and duty. By Calvinus. [James GRAHAME, advocate.]

Edinburgh : 1817. Octavo. Pp. 29.*

TWO (the) Mr. Clarks. (From the "Witness" of 12th April 1843.) [By Hugh MILLER.]

Edinburgh, 1843. Duodecimo. Pp. 18. Reprinted in 1870 in a volume entitled "Leading articles on various subjects. By Hugh Miller."

TWO novels. In letters. By the authors of Henry and Frances. [Richard and Elizabeth GRIFFITH.] In four volumes.

London : M DCC LXIX. Duodecimo.*

TWO odes of Horace, relating to the civil wars of Rome, and against covetous rich men. Translated into English [by Richard FANSHAW.]

London : 1664. Octavo. [Lowndes, Bibliog. Man.]

TWO old men's tales. The deformed, and the Admiral's daughter. [By Mrs Anne MARSH.] In two volumes. Second edition.

London : 1834. Duodecimo.*

TWO papers : a theatrical critique, and an essay (being No. 999 of the Pretender) on sonnet writing, and sonnet-writers in general, including a sonnet on myself, attributed to the editor of the Ex-m-n-r, preceded by proofs of their authenticity, founded upon the authority of internal evidence. [By John POOLE.]

London : 1819. Octavo. Pp. xi. 24.* [Athen. Cat., p. 486.]

TWO (the) parties in the Church brought to the test ; or, moderatism and evangelism contrasted. [By Rev. David CARMENT.]

Edinburgh : 1843. Octavo. Pp. 8. [New Coll. Cat., p. 152.]

TWO penny-worth of truth for a penny, or a true state of facts; with an apology for Tom Bull [William Jones of Nayland] in a letter to Brother John. [By Ann JEBB.] Second edition.

London : 1793. Octavo. Pp. 16. [IV.] Signed W. Bull.

TWO petitions presented to the supreame authority of the nation, from thousands of the Lords, owners, and commoners of Lincolneshire ; against the old court-levellers, or propriety-destroyers, the prerogative undertakers. [By John LILBURNE.]

London, 1650. Quarto. Pp. 10. b. t.* [Bodl.]

TWO questions, previous to Dr. Middleton's Free enquiry, impartially considered : viz. What are the grounds upon which the credibility of miracles, in general, is founded ? and Upon what grounds the miracles of the Gospel, in particular, are credible ? To which is added, A dissertation upon Mark xvi. 17. 18. These signs shall follow them that believe, &c. [By Arthur Ashley SYKES.]

London : M DCC L. Octavo. Pp. 129.*

—— Part II. In which the evidence for the miracles of the primitive Church is fully examined into ; and the miracles of the Gospel are shewn to have sure marks of credibility. [By Arthur Ashley SYKES, D.D.]

London : MDCCLII. Octavo. Pp. ix. 5. 209.*

TWO (the) rectors. [By George WILKINS, D.D.]

London : 1824. Duodecimo. Pp. xvi. 458.*

TWO seasonable discourses concerning the present parliament. [By Anthony Ashley COOPER, 1st Earl of Shaftesbury.]

Oxford, 1675. Quarto. Pp. 10. b. t.* [Bodl.]

TWO sermons, etc. I. on the national jubilee ; II. On the thanksgiving and poems on the majesty of the Godhead.] [By Rev. S. BARKER, A.M.] Not published.

[Yarmouth :] 1815. Quarto. Pp. 63. [IV., Martin's Cat.]

TWO sermons formerly preach'd in the cathedral-church of Worcester. P... late prebendary of the said ...ur ...y a [Miles STAPYLTON, D.D., p... church. of Worcester.] ...rebendary

London : M.DCCXXXVI. C... ...ctavo. Pp. 73.*

TWO sermons preach... during the late wa... ...ed on a fast day Francis BLACKI... ...with France. [By ...URNE, M.A.]

London : MD... ...CCLXXVIII. Octavo. Pp. 11. b. t. 28... [Bodl.]

TWO sermons, preached to a congregation of black slaves, at the parish

church of S. P. in the province of Maryland. By an American pastor. [Thomas BACON.]

London : [date cut off.] Duodecimo. Pp. 79.* [*Bodl.*]

TWO sermons : the first addressed to seamen ; the second to British West-India slaves. [By James Mackittrick ADAIR, M.D.] To which are subjoined Remarks on female infidelity, and a plan of Platonic matrimony, by F. G.

1791. Octavo. [*Cat. Lond. Inst.*, ii. 8.]

TWO sketches of France, Belgium, and Spa, in two tours, during the summers of 1771 and 1816 ; with a portrait of Napoleon's guide at Waterloo. By the author of " Letters from Paris, in 1802-3." [Stephen WESTON, F.R.S.]

London. 1817. Octavo. Pp. vii. 176.*

TWO speeches made in the House of Peers. The one November 20. 1675. The other in November 1678. By a Protestant peer of the realm of England. [Anthony Ashley COOPER, 1st Earl of Shaftesbury.]

Hague, 1680. Quarto. Pp. 15.*

TWO speeches of a late Lord Chancellor. [Charles YORKE, Earl of Hardwicke.] Printed from an authentic copy.

London : 1770. Octavo. Pp. 64.*

TWO summers in Norway. By the author of " The angler in Ireland." [—— BELTON.] In two volumes.

London : 1840. Duodecimo.*

TWO stories of the seen and the unseen The open door Old Lady Mary [By Mrs Margaret O. W. OLIPHANT.]

Edinburgh and London MDCCCLXXXV. Octavo. Pp. 212.*

TWO tales translated out of Ariosto : the one in dispraise of men, the other in disgrace of women, with certaine other [illegible] Italian stanzas and proverbes. By R. [illegible] [Robert TOFTE] gentleman.

Printed at L[ondon] by Valentine Sims, 1597. Quarto. [*W.*[illegible]]

TWO tellings to [illegible] Pet. [By Thomas S. MUIR.]

[Edinburgh : 1877.] Quarto. Pp. 33. b. t.* Privately printed.

TWO tracts shewing that Americans, born before the independence, are by the laws of England, not aliens. First, a

discussion, &c. ; second, a reply, &c. By a barrister. [—— REEVES.]

1814. Octavo. Pp. 100. [*Rich, Bib. Amer.*, ii. 72.]

TWO treatises of government : in the former, the false principles and foundation of Sir Robert Filmer, and his followers, are detected and overthrown. The latter is an essay concerning the true original, extent, and end of civil-government. [By John LOCKE.]

London, 1694. Octavo. Pp. 6. b. t. 358.*

TWO treatises : the first, proving both by history & record that the bishops are a fundamental & essential part of our English parliament : the second, that they may be judges in capital cases. [By Laurence WOMOCK, D.D.] London : 1680. Folio.*

TWO useful cases resolved. I. Whether a certainty of being in a state of salvation be attainable ? II. What is the rule by which this certainty is to be attained ? [By Richard BLECHYNDER, prebendary of Peterborough.] London : 1685. Quarto. Pp. 32.* [*Bodl.*]

TWO wise men and all the rest fooles : or a comicall morall, censuring the follies of the age, as it hath beene diverse times acted. [By George CHAPMAN.]

Anno. 1619. Quarto. Pp. 104. b. t.* [*Biog. Dram.*]

TWO words of counsel and one of comfort. [By William COMBE.]

1795. [*Gent. Mag.*, *May* 1852, p. 467.]

TWO years after and onwards or the approaching war amongst the powers of Europe and other future events described as foretold in Scripture prophecy. By the author of " The coming struggle." [David PAE.]

London MDCCCLXIV. Octavo. Pp. viii. 192.*

TWO years before the mast. A personal narrative of life at sea. [By Richard Henry DANA, Junr.]

London : MDCCCXLI. Octavo. Pp. 124. b. t.*

Reprint of the original American edition. Preface signed R. H. D. Jr.

TWO years in Ava. From May 1824, to May 1826. By an officer on the Staff of the Quarter-Master-General's department. [Capt. Thomas Abercrombie TRANT.]

London : MDCCCXXVII. Octavo.* [*Gent. Mag.*, *April* 1832, p. 371.]

TWOFOLD vindication of the Archbishop of Canterbury [Tillotson], and of the author of the History of religion. [By Sir Robert HOWARD.]

1696. Octavo. [*Leslie's Cat.*, 1843.]

TYPES (the), and a selection from the writings in verse and prose of a lady recently and suddenly deceased. [By Lucy CROGGAN.]

London: MDCCCXXXVI. Duodecimo. Pp. viii. 195.*

TYPES and antitypes of our Lord Jesus Christ. [By Miss GIMINGHAM, Weston-Super-Mare.]

London. [1884.] Oblong Quarto. Pp. 29, with 29 plates.*

TYRANNICALL-government anatomized: or, a discourse concerning evil-councellors. Being the life and death of John the Baptist. And presented to the Kings most excellent Majesty by the author. [A translation of George Buchanan's Baptistes by John MILTON.]

London, 1642. Quarto. Pp. 34.* [*See Peck's Memoirs of Milton*, p. 265.]

TYRANNICIDE proved lawful, from the practice and writings of Jews, heathens, and Christians; a discourse, delivered in the mines at Symsbury, in the colony of Connecticut, to the loyalists confined there by order of the Congress, on September 19, 1781. By Simeon Baxter, a licentiate in divinity, and voluntary chaplain to those prisoners in the apartment called Orcus. [Rev. Samuel PETERS.]

Printed in America: London: reprinted, MDCCLXXXII. Octavo. Pp. vi. 31.*
"I believe this squib is by the Rev. Samuel Peters."—MS. note in the Bodleian copy.

TYRANNUS or the mode: in a discourse of sumptuary lawes. [By John EVELYN.]

London, 1661. Octavo. Pp. 30. b. t.*
The address "To him that reades" signed I. E.
"This, which is corrected throughout, by the author (Mr. Evelyn) with his own hand, for a second edition . . ."—MS note on the Mason copy in the Bodleian.

TYRANNY and popery lording it over the consciences, lives, liberties, and estates both of king and people. [By Roger L'ESTRANGE.]

London, 1678. Quarto. Pp. 94.*
The second edition, 1681, has the author's name.

TYTLER'S History of Scotland examined. A review. [By Patrick Fraser, LL.D.]

Edinburgh: MDCCCXLVIII. Octavo. Pp. 246. b. t.* Appeared first in the North British Review.

U.

UGBROOKE park, a poem. [By Rev. Joseph REEVE.]

London: 1776. Quarto. [*Davidson, Bib. Devon.*, p. 128.]
A second edition, Exeter, 1794, has the author's name.

ULGHAM: its story. Printed in aid of the funds for rebuilding Ulgham church. [By William WOODMAN, of Morpeth.]

Newcastle: 1861. Quarto. Pp. 40.

ULLSMERE, a poem. [By John Charles BRISTOW.]

London: MDCCCXXXV. Octavo.*

ULTIMATE (the) remedy for Ireland. [By Rowley LASCELLES.]

London: 1831. Octavo. [*Gent. Mag.*, April 1831, p. 345.]

ULTRA-Protestant developements at Liverpool. An old warning to evangelicals repeated. By a Liverpool layman. [Dan. RADFORD.]

Liverpool: MDCCCLVI. Octavo. Pp. 36.* [*Bodl.*]

ULYSSES Homer; or a discovery of the true author of the Iliad and Odyssey. By Constantine Koliades, Professor in the Ionian University. [Jean Baptiste LE CHEVALIER; translated by the Rev. P. FRASER.]

London: 1829. Octavo. Pp. xxiv. 67. [*W.*]
This tract is abridged from J. B. Le Chevalier's "Voyage dans la Troade," 3 vols. 8vo, Paris, 1802.

VLYSSES upon Aiax. Written by

Misodiaboles to his friend Philaretes. [By Sir John HARINGTON.]

London, Thomas Gubbins 1596. Duodecimo. [*IV., Lowndes, Bibliog. Man.*]

UNANIMITY. A poem. Most respectfully inscribed to that truly patriotic nobleman the Duke of Leinster. [By John MACAULAY.]

London: 1780. Quarto. [*Watt, Bib. Brit. Mon. Rev.*, lxii. 319.]

UNANSWERABLE (an) conviction of the impostures of Popery, and deceits of the Papal agents. With a necessary caution to all sincere and conscientious Christians to beware of them. Recommended to all the clergy of England; especially of such parishes, as have any of these deceivers or deceived in them. [By Edward STEPHENS, of Cherington.]

London, 1706. Quarto. Pp. 4.* [*Bodl.*]

UNAUTHORISED (an) appeal to Irish Catholics. [By Rev. Robert R. SUFFIELD.]

New York: 1864. [*Author.*]

UNAWARES: a story of an old French town. By the author of "One year.' [Frances Mary PEARD.]

London: 1870. Octavo. Pp. 295. b. t.*

UNBELEEVERS (the) preparing for Christ. By T. H. [Thomas HOOKER.]

London, 1638. Quarto.* [*Bodl.*]

VNBISHOPING (the) of Timothy and Titus. Or a briefe elaborate discourse, prooving Timothy to be no bishop (much lesse any sole, or diocæsan bishop) of Ephesus, nor Titus of Crete; and that the power of ordination, or imposition of hands, belongs Iure divino to presbyters, as well as to bishops, and not to bishops onely. Wherein all objections and pretences to the contrary are fully answered; and the pretended superiority of bishops over other ministers and presbyters Iure divino, (now much contended for) utterly subverted in a most perspicuous maner. By a well-wisher to God's truth and people. [William PRYNNE.]

N. P. In the yeare M.DC.XXXVI. Quarto. Pp. 173. 5.*

UNCERTAINTY (the) of the signs of death, and the danger of precipitate interments and dissections, demonstrated, I. From the known laws of the animal oeconomy. II. From the structure of the parts of the human body. And, III. From a great variety of amusing and well-attested instances of persons who have return'd to life in their coffins, in their graves, under the hands of the surgeons, and after they had remain'd apparently dead for a considerable time in the water. With proper directions, both for preventing such accidents, and repairing the misfortunes brought upon the constitution by them. To the whole is added, a curious and entertaining account of the funeral solemnities of many ancient and modern nations, exhibiting the precautions they made use of to ascertain the certainty of death. Illustrated with copper plates. [By Jean Jacques BRUHIER-D'ABLAINCOURT.]

London: MDCCXLVI. Octavo. Pp. 6. b. t. 219.* [*N. and Q.*, Oct. 1868, p. 287. *Douce Cat.*]

UNCLAIMED (the) daughter; a mystery of our own day. Edited by C. J. H. [C. J. HAMILTON], author of "The curate of Linwood," "Amy Harrington," etc. Second edition.

Bath: N. D. Octavo. Pp. xv. 175.*

UNCLE Armstrong. A narrative. In three volumes. By Lord B * * * * * * m, author of "Masters and workmen," "The fate of folly," "Naples," &c. [Probably by Lord BELFAST.]

London: 1866. Duodecimo.*

UNCLE Horace, a novel. By the author of "Sketches of Irish character," "The Buccaneer," &c. &c. [Anna Maria HALL.] In three volumes.

London: MDCCCXXXVII. Octavo.*

UNCLE Peregrine's heiress. A novel. By Ann of Swansea, author of Guilty or not guilty; Woman's a riddle; Deeds of the olden time; Gonzalo de Baldivia; Conviction, &c. [Frances Ann KEMBLE.] In five volumes.

London: 1828. Duodecimo.* [*Bodl.*]

UNDECEIVING (the) of the people in the point of tithes. Wherein is shewed, I. That never any clergy in the Church of God hath been, or is maintained with lesse charge to the subject, then the established clergy of the Church of England. II. That there is no subject, in the realme of England, who giveth any thing of his own, towards the maintenance of his parish-minister, but his Easter-offering. III. That the change of tithes into stipends, will bring greater trouble to the clergy, then is yet considered; and far lesse

profit to the country, then is now pretended. By Ph. Treleinie Gent. [Peter HEYLIN.]

London, 1651. Octavo. Pp. 28.*

UNDER a charm. A novel. From the German of E. Werner [E. BUERSTENBINDER], by Christina Tyrrell. In three volumes.

London: 1877. Octavo.*

UNDER a cloud. By one who knows what shadows are. [Mrs Sawers MITCHELL.]

Edinburgh 1867. Octavo. Pp. x. 434.* Printed for private circulation.

UNDER seal of confession. By Averil Beaumont, author of "Thornicroft's model." [Mrs A. W. HUNT.] In three volumes.

London: 1874. Octavo.* [Adv. Lib.]

UNDER temptation. By the author of "Ursula's love story," "Beautiful Edith," &c., &c. [Gertrude PARSONS, née Hext.] In three volumes.

London: 1878. Octavo.*

UNDER the greenwood tree A rural painting of the Dutch school. By the author of 'Desperate remedies.' [Thomas HARDY.] In two volumes.

London: 1872. Octavo.*

UNDER the spell. By the author of "Grandmother's money," "Wild-flower," "One-and-twenty," &c. [Frederick William ROBINSON.] In three volumes.

London: 1861. Octavo.*

UNDER two flags A story of the household and the desert. By Ouida, author of "Strathmore," "Chandos," "Idalia," &c. [Louise de LA RAMÉ.] In three volumes.

London: 1867. Octavo.*
Originally written for a military periodical.

UNDERCURRENTS overlooked. By the author of "Flemish interiors," "Realities of Paris life." [Mrs William Pitt BYRNE.] In two volumes.

London: 1860. Duodecimo.*

UNDERGRADUATE subscription. Extracts from a collection of papers published in Oxford in 1772 on the subject of subscription to the xxxix Articles, required from young persons at their matriculation. With a preface by the Editor. [Vaughan THOMAS, B.D.] To which is added, the debate in the House of Commons upon Sir William Meredith's motion on the same subject, Feb. 1773.

Oxford. 1835. Octavo. Pp. xix. 44.* [Bodl.] Editor's name in the handwriting of Dr Bliss.

UNDISCOVERED crimes. "By Waters." [William RUSSELL.]

London: 1862. Octavo.

UNERRABLE (an) Church or none, being a rejoynder to the uncrring unerrable Church against Dr. Andrew Salls repley entituled The Catholic Apostolic Church of England. Written by J. S. [Ignatius BROWN] and dedicated to the most illustrious Prince James Duke of Ormond, &c.

Anno 1678. Octavo. Title, an adv. to the Reader, 1 leaf; To the most illustrious Prince James, &c., 3 leaves; the preface, 7 leaves; pp. 342, the last leaf of errata not numbered. [W.]

VNFOULDYNG (the) of sundry vntruths and absurde propositions, latelye propounded by one I. B. a greate fauourer of the horrible heresie of the Libertines. [By Thomas WILCOCKS.]

Imprinted at London for Thomas Man. 1581. Octavo. No pagination. B. L.* [Bodl.]

UNFULFILLED prophecy respecting Eastern nations, especially the Turks, the Russians, and the Jews. [By A. MACLEOD.]

London: 1841. Duodecimo.*

VNHAPPY (an) game at Scotch and English. Or, a full answer from England to the papers of Scotland. Wherein their Scotch mists and their fogs; their sayings and gain-sayings; their juglings, their windings and turnings; hither and thither backwards and forwards, and forwards and backwards again; their breach of Covenant, articles and treaty, their king-craft present design against the two Houses of Parliament, and people of England. their plots and intents for usurpation and government over us and our children detected, discovered, and presented to the view of the world and predreadfull omen, and warning to the kingdome of England. [By John LILBURNE.]

Edinburgh, 1646. Quarto. Pp. 26.*

UNHAPPY (the) princesses. In two parts. Containing, first, the secret history of Queen Anne Bullen. Mother to Queen Elizabeth of renowned

memory. With an impartial account of the first loves of Henry VIII. to that lady; the reasons of his withdrawing his affections from her, and the real cause of her wilful and calamitous fall. Secondly, the history of the Lady Jane Grey. Who was proclaimed Queen of England; with a full relation of her admirable life, short reign, and most deplorable death. Adorn'd with pictures. By R. B. [Richard, or Robert, BURTON, *i.e.* Nathaniel CROUCH.]

London: 1710. Duodecimo. Pp. 159.*

U N I O politico - poetico - joco - seria. Written in the latter end of the year 1703: and afterwards, as occasion offered, very much enlarged, in severall paragraphs. By the author of Tripatriarchicon. [Andrew SYMSON.]

Edinburgh. Printed by the author, 1706. Quarto. Pp. 32.*
The two concluding lines give the author's initials:—"And if you ask the author's name, here 'tis, A. S. Philophilus, Philopatris."

UNIOMACHIA, or the battle at the Union, an Homeric fragment, lately given to the world by Habbakukius Dunderheadius [Thomas JACKSON], and now rendered into the English tongue by Jedediah Puzzlepate [John Douglas GILES].

Oxford: 1833. Octavo. Pp.8.* [*F. Madan.*]

U N I O N and no union. Being an enquiry into the grievances of the Scots and how far they are right or wrong, who alledge that the Union is dissolved. [By Daniel DEFOE.]

London: 1713. Octavo. Pp. 24.* [*Lee's Defoe*, 150.]

UNION (the) of Christ and the Church; in a shadow. By R. C. [Ralph CUDWORTH.]

London, 1642. Quarto. Pp. 35.*

U N I O N (the): or, select Scots and English poems. [Edited by Thomas BLACKLOCK.] The second edition.

WARRINGTON: M.DCC.LIX. Octavo. Pp. 6. London: ... b. t. 152.*
The first edition ... was published in 1753.

UNION-proverb (the): viz. If Skiddaw has a cap, Scruffell wots full well of that. Setting forth, I. The necessity of uniting. II. The good consequences of uniting. III. The happy union of England and Scotland, in

case of a foreign invasion. [By Daniel DEFOE.]

London: N. D. Octavo. [*Wilson, Life of Defoe*, 105.]

UNION pursued; in a letter to Mr. Baxter, concerning his late book of National churches. Published for a fuller disquisition about this subject, by the sober and composed of all sides, in order to comprehension which hath been forming, and a larger constitution of the Church to be formed, when that day of concord comes, which the gentle aspect of heaven in God's appointment (and the king's) of so many choice moderate bishops together at this time does presage to the nation. That the Presbyterians and Independants, that have united within themselves, may both be united also with the Church of England. By a lover of him, and follower of peace. [John HUMFREY.]

London, 1691. Quarto. Pp. 38.* [*Bodl.*]

UNITE or fall. [By Frederick HOWARD, 5th Earl of Carlisle.] Fifth edition.

London: 1798. Duodecimo. Pp. 23.* [*Bodl.*]

UNITY (the) of God not inconsistent with the divinity of Christ. Being remarks on the passages in Dr. Waterland's Vindication, &c. relating to the unity of God and to the object of worship. [By Joseph HALLET.]

London: MDCCXX. Octavo.* [*Watt, Bib. Brit. Darling, Cyclop. Bibl.*]

UNITY of priesthood necessary to the unity of communion in a Church. With some reflections on the Oxford Manuscript, and the preface annexed. Also a collection of canons, part of the said Manuscript, faithfully translated into English from the original, but concealed by Mr. Hody, and his prefacer. [By Nathaniel BISBIE.]

London, MDCXCII. Quarto. Pp. 72.*
This work has been assigned to Mr. Webster: but it is ascribed to Bisbie by Rawlinson, in his MS. continuation of the Athenæ. *See* also Lathbury's Nonjurors, p. 137.

UNIVERSAL and saving grace, asserted and demonstrated, or, a Scriptural refutation of the doctrines of absolute and unconditional predestination, in letters to the proprietors of the Gospel Magazine. Letter the first, in which are noticed, chiefly, some of the argu-

ments, inconsistencies, and contradictions, contained in a treatise on the subject, by the late A. Toplady, A.B., vicar of Hembury, Devon. [By Thomas SCANTLEBURY.]

Sheffield: 1813. Duodecimo. 1¼ sh. [*Smith's Cat. of Friends' books*, i. 84 ; ii. 541.]

UNIVERSAL angler ; or, that art improved in all its parts, especially in fly-fishing ; the whole interspersed with many curious and uncommon observations. ["This book is copied from Bowlker's Art of Angling, printed at Worcester, with some few additions taken from Walton, Cotton and Hawkins."—Wm. White.]

London: 1766. Duodecimo. [*IV.*, *Smith, Bib. Ang.*]

UNIVERSAL beauty, a philosophical poem in six books. [By Henry BROOKE.]

London: 1735. Folio. [*Gent. Mag.*, v. 55.]

UNIVERSAL (the) Church : an essay on nature, as the universal basis of truth, perfection, and salvation, and their universality, &c. [By J. CROOK.]

London: 1807. Octavo. [*IV.*, *Brit. Mus.*]

UNIVERSAL (the) doom : or, the state of mortality. Humbly presented to the Right Reverend Father in God Thomas Tanner, D.D. Lord Bishop of St. Asaph. [By W. HOWARD.]

London : 1733. Quarto. Pp. 12. b. t.* [*Bodl.*]

UNIVERSAL (the) historical bibliotheque : or an account of the most considerable books, printed in all languages in the month[s] of January [February and March] 1686. Wherein a short description is given of the design and scope of almost every book : and of the quality of the author, if known. [By G. WELLS, and J. D. de LA CROSE.]

London : 1687. Quarto. [*IV.*]

UNIVERSAL (the) passion. *See* "The love of fame."

UNIVERSAL (the) passion. A comedy. As it is acted at the Theatre-Royal in Drury-Lane by His Majesty's servants. [By James MILLER.]

London: MDCCXXXVII. Octavo.* [*Biog. Dram.*]

UNIVERSAL (the) prayer. By the author of the Essay on man. [Alexander POPE.]

London : MDCCXXXVIII. Folio. Pp. 7.* First edition.

UNIVERSAL restitution, a scripture doctrine. This proved in several letters wrote on the nature and extent of Christ's kingdom. Wherein the scripture passages, falsely alledged in proof of the eternity of hell torments, are truly translated and explained. [By James STONEHOUSE.]

London : 1762. Octavo. [*Queen's Coll. Cat.*, i. 151. *Mon. Rev.*, xxvi. 181.]

UNIVERSAL (the) revival of religion. A few words to Christian ministers, and others. By M. Justitia. [John FREARSON.]

London : [1858.] Duodecimo.* Pp. 26.* Dated Dec. 1. 1858.

UNIVERSAL (the) Spectator. [By Daniel DEFOE.] No. 1.

1728. Quarto. 1 sh. [*Lee's Defoe*, 246.]

UNIVERSAL (the) Spectator, by Henry Stonecastle, of Northumberland, Esq. [The ostensible author of these papers was John KELLY, the dramatic writer.] In four volumes.

London : MDCCLVI. Duodecimo.* [*Athen. Cat.*]

UNIVERSE (the) : a poem. By the Rev. C. R. Maturin. [In reality by Rev. James WILLS.]

London : MDCCCXXI. Octavo. Pp. 108. b. t.* [*N. and Q.*, 5*th Ser.*, iii. p. 20, 172, 240, 280, 340.]

UNIVERSITIES of Scotland Bill.—Remarks on the condition, necessities, and claims of the Universities of Scotland ; with an appendix. By a graduate. [John Rose CORMACK, M.D.]

London : 1858. Octavo. Pp. xvi. 72. [*IV.*]

UNIVERSITY (the) commission, or Lord John Russell's post bag of April 27, 1850. The first instalment. [By William SEWELL, D.D.]

Oxford, 1850. Octavo. Pr. b. t.* Pp. vii. 35.*

—— The second instalment.

Oxford, 1850. Octavo. Pp. i. b. t. 41.*

—— The third instalment.

Oxford, 1850. Octavo. Pp. iv. 37.*

—— Containing Mister Anthony Pepys his diary, he being a member of the

said commission. The fourth instalment.

Oxford, 1850. Octavo. Pp. 1. b. t. 47.*

UNIVERSITY (the) of Cambridge vindicated from the imputation of disloyalty it lies under on the account of not addressing : as also from the malicious and foul aspersions of Dr. B - - - - ly, late Master of Trinity College ; and of a certain officer, and pretended reformer in the said University. Written by the author. [Styan THIRLBY.]

London : 1710. Octavo. Pp. 35.*

VNKINDE (the) desertor of loyall men and true frinds. [By Nicholas FRENCH, titular Bishop of Ferns.] Superiorum permissu, Año. 1676. Octavo. Pp. 246 [misprinted 446]. 8. b. t.*

Of the above work, seven copies only are known to exist. The Bodleian copy has the author's autograph, and memoranda of donation to Sir Christopher French, his brother.

UNKIND (the) word and other stories. By the author of " John Halifax, Gentleman," &c., &c. [Dinah Maria MULOCK.]

London : N. D. Octavo. Pp. 303. b. t.*

UNKNOWN (the) Eros. [By Coventry Kearsey Dighton PATMORE.]

London : 1877. Octavo. [Lib. Jour.]

VNLAVVFVLNES (the) and danger of limited Prelacie, or perpetvall presidensie in the Chvrch briefly discovered. [By Robert BAILLIE, A.M.]

Printed in the yeare, 1641. Quarto. Pp. 2. b. t. 19.* [Brit. Mus.]

UNLAWFULNESS (the) of bonds of resignation. First written in the year 1684. for the satisfaction of a private gentleman. And now made publick for the good of others. [By John WILLES.]

London : 1696. Octavo. Pp. 28. b. t.* [Bodl.]

VNLAWFVLNESSE (the) of subjects taking up armes against their soveraigne, in what case soever. Together an answer to all objections ... together with ... their severall bookes. And scattered in the ... notwithstanding such a proofe, that ... they plead for, were not ... resistance as they ... present warre made damnable, yet the pre... because those upon the king is so, ... men have cases, in which onely som... evidently not dared to excuse it, are evidently not now ; his Majesty fighting ... onely to

preserve himselfe, and the rights of the subjects. [By Dudley DIGGES.]

Printed in the yeare 1643. Quarto. Pp. 170. b. t.* [Bodl.]

UNLUCKY (the) citizen experimentally described in the various misfortunes of an unlucky Londoner, calculated for the meridian of this city but may serve by way of advice to all the cominalty of England, but more particularly to parents and children master and servants husbands and wives. Intermixed with severall choice novels. Stored with variety of examples and advice president and precept. Illustrated with pictures fitted to the severall stories. [By Francis KIRKMAN.]

London, 1673. Octavo. Pp. 17. b. t. 296.* The work has an engraved title The unlucky citizen by F. K.

UNMASKING (the) of the politique atheist. By J. H. Batcheler of Divinitie. [John HULL.]

At London, 1602. Octavo.* [W., Bliss. Cat.]

VNPARALLEL'D reasons for abollishing Episcopacy. 1. It will assure his Majesties authority royall. 2. Increase his revenue. 3. Settle a good union in his Majesties owne kingdomes, and between them and other reformed Churches. 4. Cause a good understanding betweene his Majesty and his people. By N. F. Esquire. [Nathaniel FIENNES.]

London. 1642. Quarto. Pp. 8.* [Bodl.]

UNPARALLEL'D varieties : or, the matchless actions and passions of mankind. Displayed in near four hundred notable instances and examples. Discovering the transcendent effects ; I. Of love, friendship, and gratitude. II. Of magnanimity, courage and fidelity. III. Of chastity, temperance, and humility. And, on the contrary, the tremendous consequences, IV. Of hatred, revenge, and ingratitude. V. Of cowardice, barbarity, and treachery. VI. Of unchastity, intemperance, and ambition. Imbelished with pictures. By R. B. [Richard BURTON]. The third edition.

London, 1699. Duodecimo. Pp. 1. b. t. 168.* [Bodl.]

"The contents of this volume were pillaged from Wanley's Wonders of the little world." —MS. note by Douce.

UNPROTECTED females in Norway ;

or, the pleasantest way of travelling there, passing through Denmark and Sweden. With Scandinavian sketches from nature. [By Miss Lowe.]

London : 1857. Octavo.* [*Adv. Lib.*]

UNPROTECTED (the) : or facts in dressmaking life. By a dressmaker. [Mary Guignard.] [Edited, with an introduction, by Rev. W. Landels.]

London : 1857. Octavo. [*W., Brit. Mus.*]

UNRAVELLED convictions. [By Lady Amabel Cowper, afterwards Kerr.]

Liverpool Printed at the Boys' Refuge, St. Anne Street. 1876. Octavo. Pp. 128.* Privately printed. Preface dated Nov. 16. 1868. Published shortly afterwards, still anonymously, by Burns & Oates, London.

UNREASONABLENESS (the) and impiety of Popery : in a second letter written upon the discovery of the late plot. [By Gilbert Burnet, D.D.]

London, 1678. Quarto. Pp. 36. b. t.*

UNREASONABLENESS (the) o atheism made manifest. [By Sir Charles Wolseley.]

London. 1669. Sm. Octavo. Pp. 197.*

UNREASONABLENESS (the) of separation : the second part. Or, a further impartial account of the history, nature, and pleas of the present separation from the communion of the Church of England. Begun by Edw. Stillingfleet D.D. Dean of St. Pauls. Continued from 1640 to 1681. With special remarks on the life and actions of Mr. Richard Baxter. [By Thomas Long, B.D.]

London : 1682. Octavo. Pp. 6. b. t. 167. 1.* [*Bodl.*]

UNREASONABLENESS (the) of the Romanists, requiring our communion with the present Romish Church : or, a discourse drawn from the perplexity and uncertainty of the principles, and from the contradictions betwixt the prayers and doctrine of the present Romish Church ; to prove that 'tis unreasonable to require us to joyn in communion with it. [By William Squire.]

London, 1670. Octavo. Pp. 34. b. t. 170.* [*Bodl.*]

UNSEEN (the) universe or physical speculations on a future state. [By Professors Peter Guthrie Tait, and Balfour Stewart.]

London 1875. Octavo. Pp. xvi. 212.* Published subsequently with the authors' names.

UNSEEN (the) world ; communications with it, real or imaginary, including apparitions, warnings, haunted places, prophecies, aerial visions, astrology, &c. &c. [By John Mason Neale.]

London : MDCCCXLVII. Octavo.*

UNSEX'D (the) females. A poem, addressed to the author of the Pursuits of literature. [By Richard Polwhele.]

London : 1798. Octavo. Pp. 37. [*Boase and Courtney, Bib. Corn.*, ii. 509.]

'UNTIL the shadows flee away ;' a tale. [By Miss M'Laren.]

Edinburgh : 1869. Octavo. [*Adv. Lib.*]

UNVEILING (the) of the everlasting gospel ; with the scripture philosophy of happiness, holiness and scriptural power, specially addressed to the ministers and Church of God at the present crisis. [By Ebenezer Cornwall.]

London : 1848. Duodecimo.*

UP and war them a' Willie. A letter of congratulation to the Burgher-hero William Smith ; upon the glory of his late atchievement in routing the whole body of Antiburghers. [By Adam Gib.]

Edinburgh : MDCCLXVI. Octavo. Pp. 15.*

UPHOLSTERER (the) or what news ? A farce, in two acts. As it is performed at the Theatre Royal, in Drury-Lane. By the author of the Apprentice. [Arthur Murphy.]

London. M DCC LIII. Octavo.* [*Biog. Dram.*]

UPLAND (the) tarn A village idyll [By John E. H. Thomson.]

Edinburgh : 1881. Octavo. Pp. 167. b. t.* *Adv. Lib.*]

UPON Mr. Bobards yew-men of the guards to the Physick Garden. To the tune of the counter-scuffle. [By Edm. Geyton.]

N. P. [1662.] Folio. S. L.* [*Bodl.*] "By G. E. [*i.e.*] Edm. Geyton Esq ; Bedle of Arts. Oxon."—MS. note by Wood.

UPON nothing. A poem. By a person of honour. [John Wilmot, 2d Earl Rochester.]

N. P. N. P. Folio. S. L.* See "Nothing (upon)."

UPON the most hopefull and ever-flourishing sprouts of valour, the indefatigable centrys of the Physick-Garden. [By John DROPE, M.A.]

Printed 1664. Folio. S.L.* [*Bodl.*]
"Joh. Drope M. of A. Fellow of Magd. Coll. the author."—MS. note by Wood.

UPWARDS and downwards, and other stories. By A. L. O. E., author of "The silver casket," "Crown of success," etc., etc. [Charlotte TUCKER.]

London: 1873. Octavo. Pp. 120.*

URAICECHT na Gaedhilge. A grammar of the Gaelic language. [By William HALLIDAY.]

Dublin, 1808. Duodecimo. Pp. xv. 201.*
Introduction signed E. O'C. *i.e.* Edmond O'Connell.

URIEL, and other poems. [By T. J. de POWIS.]

London: 1857. Octavo. Pp. 169.*

URIM and Thummim: or the apostolical doctrines of light and perfection maintained; against the opposite plea of Samuel Grevill (a pretended minister of the gospel) in his ungospellike discourse against a book, intituled, A testimony of the light within, anciently writ by Alexander Parker. By W. P. [William PENN.]

Printed in the year 1674. Quarto.*

URSULA. A tale of country life. By the author of "Amy Herbert," "Ivors," &c. &c. [E. M. SEWELL.] In two volumes.

London: 1858. Octavo.*

URSULA'S love story. [By Mrs. Gertrude PARSONS.] In three volumes.

London: 1869. Octavo.*

USAGE (the) of holding Parliaments and of preparing and passing bills of supply, in Ireland, stated from record. [By John LODGE.] Published by authority.

Dublin: M,DCC,LXX. Octavo.
To which is added, Annotations, together with an address to His Excellency George Lord Viscount Townshend, lord lieutenant general and general governor of Ireland. By C. Lucas, M.D. one of the representatives of the city of Dublin, in Parlement.
Dublin: Re-printed M,DCC,LXX. Octavo. Pp. 76.*

USE and abuse, a tale. By the author of "Wayfaring sketches amongst the Greeks and Turks, and on the shores of the Danube, by a seven years resi-

dent in Greece." [Felicia M. F. SKENE.]

London: 1849. Duodecimo.*

USE (the) and abuse of Parliaments, in two historical discourses. [Published and edited by James RALPH. The first discourse was written by Algernon SIDNEY, the remaining portion of the work by Lord POLWARTH, afterwards Earl of Macclesfield.] In two volumes.

London: 1744. Octavo. [*IV.*]

USE (on the) and abuse of satire. [By Charles ABBOT, afterwards Lord Tenterden.]

Oxford: 1786. Octavo. [*Gent. Mag. Aug.* 1839, p. 157. *Watt, Bib. Brit.*]

USE (the) of catechisms further considered. With a more full account of God's ambassadors; of saving faith; and of the faith of devils. In a letter to a friend. [By John GLAS.]

Edinburgh, 1737. Duodecimo. Pp. 45. 2.*

USE (the) of daily pvblick prayers, in three positions. [By Meric CASAUBON.]

London, 1641. Quarto. Pp. 28. b. t.* [*Bodl.*]

USE (the) of reason recovered, by the data in Christianity. Whereby we know, the state we are in; that there are Elahim; what they have done for us; the state they offer us; the terms upon which they offer it. So have evidence to reason upon, and may make a reasonable choice. By J. H. [John HUTCHINSON.]

London: MDCCXXXVI. Octavo.*

USE (the) of sunshine. A Christmas narrative. By S. M. [Menella Bute SMEDLEY] authoress of "The story of a family," "The maiden aunt," "Lays and ballads from English history," etc.

London: 1852. Octavo.* [*Adv. Lib.*]

USEFUL miscellanies: or serious reflections, respecting men's duty to God, and one towards another. With advices civil and religious, tending to regulate their conduct in the various occurrences of human life. Published for general service. By a well-wisher to all mankind. [William DOVER.]

London: 1739. Octavo. 6 sh. [*Smith's Cat. of Friends' books,* i. 59, 542.]

USEFUL transactions in philosophy, and other sorts of learning, for the months of January and February 170⅚.

To be continu'd monthly, as they sell. [By William KING, LL.D.]

London [1709.] Octavo. Pp. 4. b. t. 59.* [Bodl.]

There were six numbers in all.

USEFULNESS (the) of catechisms considered, in a letter to a friend. [By John GLAS.]

Edinburgh, 1736. Duodecimo. Pp. 34.*

USURER (the); or, the departed not defunct; a comedy, in five acts. [By John Radcliffe ROBINS.]

London : 1833. Octavo.*

USURER'S (the) daughter, by a contributer to "Blackwood's Magazine." [W. P. SCARGILL.] In three volumes.

London: 1832. Duodecimo.*

USURPATIONS (the) of France upon the trade of the woollen manufacture of England briefly hinted at ; being the effects of thirty years observations, by which that king hath been enabled to wage war with so great a part of

Europe. By W. C. [William CARTER, clothier.]

London: 1695. Quarto. [IV., Brit. Mus.]

USURY explain'd ; or, conscience quieted in the case of putting out mony at interest. By Philopenes. [Jo. DORMER, S.J.]

London: 169⅝. Octavo. Pp. 8. b. t. 116.* [Bodl.]

UTOPIA found ; being an apology for Irish absentees. Addressed to a friend in Connaught, by an absentee, residing in Bath. [Edward MANGIN.]

Bath: 1813. [N. and Q., Dec. 9, 1865, p. 475; 3 Feb. 1866, p. 107.]

UTOPIA: written in Latin by Sir Thomas More, Chancellor of England; translated in English [by Gilbert BURNET, Bishop of Salisbury]. First edition.

London : 1685. Octavo. Pp. xxii. 206. [IV.]

V.

VADE mecum : a manuall of essayes, morrall, theologicall. Inter-woven with moderne obseruations, historicall, politicall. [By Daniel TUVILL.]

London, 1629. Duodecimo. Pp. 6. b. t. 246.* [Bodl.]

To the reader, signed Thine Anonym. Musophil.

VAIN boastings of Frenchmen, the same in 1386 as in 1798. Being an account of the threatened invasion of England by the French the 10th year of King Richard II. Extracted from ancient chronicles. [By Craven ORD.]

London: 1798. Octavo. Pp. 15.* [Bodl.]

VALE (the) of Chamouni. [By John CHALONER, Capt. in H.M. 36th Regt.]

1822. [N. and Q., 5 March 1864, p. 204.]

VALENTINE Duval: an autobiography of the last century. . . [By Anne MANNING.]

London : 1860. Octavo.

VALENTINE'S day, a musical drama, in two acts. As it is performed at the

Theatre Royal in Drury-Lane. [By William HEARD.]

London : 1776. Octavo. [Biog. Dram., Mon. Rev., liv. 341.]

VALERIUS; a Roman story. [By John Gibson LOCKHART.] In three volumes.

Edinburgh: 1821. Octavo.*

VALETTA. A novel, by the author of "Denton Hall." [—— CROSS.] In three volumes.

London: 1851. Octavo.*

VALIANT (the) Welshman, or the trve chronicle history of the life and valyes; deedes of Caradoc the Great, King of Cambria, now called Wales. As it hath beene sundry times acted by the Prince of Wales his seruants. Written by R. A. Gent. [Robert ARMIN.]

London, 1615. Quarto. No pagination.* [Brit. Mus.]

VALIDITY (the) of baptism administred by dissenting ministers, and the unreasonableness of refusing burial to children so baptiz'd. First offer'd to

the consideration of a dissenting congregation, at two publick baptisms, on the occasion of that new notion, denying all such to be Christians, who have been baptiz'd by persons not episcopally ordain'd ; and the late agreement of some neighbouring clergy-men not to bury any such. Now publish'd (with some alterations) for the conviction of unprejudic'd Church-men, and the satisfaction of Protestant dissenters. By a Presbyter of the Church of Christ. [Ferdinando SHAW.]

Nottingham : 1713. Octavo. Pp. 22.* [*Cresswell's Printing in Nottinghamshire.*] Ascribed also to James Peirce.

VALIDITY (the) of the orders of the Church of England made out against the objections of the Papists, in several letters to a gentleman of Norwich, that desired satisfaction therein. [By Dr. Humphry PRIDEAUX.]

London : 1688. Quarto. [*Queen's Coll. Cat.*, i. 224.]

VALLEY (the) of a hundred fires. [By the author of "Margaret and her bridesmaids," "Mr. and Mrs. Asheton," &c. &c. [Mrs MARSH.] In three volumes.

London : 1860. Octavo.*

VALLEY (the) of the Rea. By V. author of "IX. poems." "The Queen's ball," etc. etc. [Mrs CLIVE.]

London 1851. Duodecimo.*

VALOUROUS (a) and perillous sea-fight. Fought with three Turkish ships, pirats or men of warre on the coast of Cornwall, (or westerne part of England) by the good ship named the Elizabeth of Plimmouth, she being of the burthen of 200 tuns, which fight was bravely fought, on Wednesday the 17 of June last past, 1640. [By John TAYLOR.]

London, 1640. Quarto. [*Davidson, Bib. Devon.*, p. 61.]

VALPERGA ; or, the life and adventures of Castruccio, prince of Lucca. By the author of "Frankenstein." [Mrs SHELLEY.] [In three volumes.]

London, 1823. Duodecimo.*

VALUE (the) of a child ; or, motives to the good education of children. In a letter to a daughter. [By John TAYLOR, dissenting teacher.]

1751. Duodecimo. [*Chalmers, Biog. Dict. Mon. Rev.*, v. 461.]

VAMPIRE (the). A tragedy [in five acts.] [By George STEPHENS.] Second edition.

London: 1821. Octavo. [*W., Brit. Mus.*]

VAMPYRE (the) : a tale. [By J. W. POLIDORI?]

London : 1819. Octavo.* [*Dyce Cat.*, ii. 385.]

VANDELEUR ; or, animal magnetism. A novel. [By Madame PISANI.] In three volumes.

London : 1836. Duodecimo.*

VANESA. [By Margaret Agnes PAUL.] The second edition. In two volumes.

London : 1878. Octavo. [*Lib. Jour.*, iii. 125.]

VANITIE (the) of self-boasters. Or, the prodigious madnesse of tyrannizing Sauls, mis-leading Doegs (or any others whatsoever) which peremptorily goe on, and atheistically glory in their shame and mischiefe. In a sermon [on Psalm 52. 1.] preached at the funerall of John Hamnet, Gent. late of the parish of Maldon in Surrey. By E. H. minister of the same, and late Fellow of Merton Colledge in Oxford. [Edward HINTON.]

London : 1643. Quarto. Pp. 1. b. t. 52.* [*Bodl.*]

VANITY Church. [By J. M. WHITE-LAW ?] In two volumes.
London : 1861. Octavo.*

VANITY (the) of scoffing : or a letter to a witty gentleman, evidently shewing the great weakness and unreasonableness of scoffing at the Christian's faith, on account of its supposed uncertainty. Together with the madness of the scoffers unchristian choice. [By Clement ELLIS, M.A., rector of Kirkby, Nottinghamshire.]

London, 1674. Quarto. Pp. 38. b. t.* [*Bodl. Wood, Athen. Oxon.*, iv. 517.] Ascribed to J. Fell, Bishop of Oxford. [*W., Brit. Mus.*]

VANITY (the) of the life of man. Represented in the seven several stages thereof, from his birth to his death. With pictures and poems exposing the follies of every age. To which is added, several other poems upon divers subjects and occasions. By R. B. [Richard BURTON.]

London, 1688. Duodecimo. Pp. 30. b. t.*

VARIETIE (the), a comoedy, lately presented by his Majesties servants at

the Black-Friers. [By William CA-
VENDISH, Duke of Newcastle.]

London, 1649. Duodecimo. Pp. 2. b. t.
87.* [*Bodl.*]

VARIETIES, by a wanderer. [Arthur
MOBERLEY, formerly of St. Peters-
burg.]

London : 1849. [*Brit. Mus. Copy.*]

VARIETIES of literature, from foreign
literary journals and original MSS.
now first published. [By William
TOOKE.] In two volumes.

London : M.DCC.XCV. Octavo.* [*Nichols, Lit. Anec.*, ix. 159. *Brit. Crit.*, vii.
41.]

VARIETY. A tale, for married people.
[By William WHITEHEAD.]

London: M.DCC.LXXVI. Quarto. Pp. 24.*
[*Watt, Bib. Brit. Mon. Rev.*, liv. 241.]

VARIETY : a collection of essays.
Written in the year 1787. [By Humphrey REPTON.]

London : M DCC LXXXVIII. Octavo. Pp.
viii. 297.* [*Watt, Bib. Brit. Mon. Rev.*,
lxxix. 440.]

VARIETY ; a comedy, in five acts : as
it is performed at the Theatre-Royal in
Drury-Lane. [By Richard GRIFFITH.]

London : MDCCLXXXII. Octavo. Pp. 71.*
[*Biog. Dram.*]

VARIOUS accounts of the great convul-
sion at Axmouth in Devonshire, &c.
[Edited by J. H. HALLETT.]

Exeter : 1840. Octavo. [*Davidson, Bib.
Devon.*, p. 118.

VARIOUS prospects of mankind, nature
and providence. [By Robert WAL-
LACE, D.D.]

London : MDCCLXI. Octavo.* [*M'Cull.
Lit. Pol. Econ.*, p. 257.]

VARNISHANDO : a serio-comic poem ;
addressed to collectors of paintings.
By an admirer of the arts. [Francis
Duckinfield ASTLEY.]

Manchester, 1809. Octavo. *Biog. Dict.*,
1816. *Brit. Crit.*, xxxiii. 632.]

VATICAN (the) Council. Eight months
at Rome during the Vatican Council.
Impressions of a contemporary. By
Pomponio Leto. [Cardinal VITELLES-
CHI.] Translated from the original.

London : 1876. Octavo. Pp. xx. 340.*
Although the above work was prepared for
the press, and edited by the Marchese
Vitelleschi, there is no doubt that the real
author was the Cardinal, who was present
at the Council, and kept a journal of the
proceedings. See The Church Quarterly
Review, July, 1876.

VAURIEN : or, sketches of the times ;
exhibiting views of the philosophies,
religions, politics, literature, and manners of the age. In two volumes. [By
I. DISRAELI.]

London : 1797. Duodecimo.*

VEGETABLE physiology. [By J.
LINDLEY.]

London: 1827. Octavo. [*IV., Brit. Mus.*]
Library of Useful Knowledge.

VEGETABLE substances used for the
food of man. [By Dr Edwin LAN-
KESTER.] In two volumes.

London : 1846. Duodecimo. [*IV.*]

VELINA ; a poetical fragment. [By
Andrew MACDONALD.]

London: 1782. Octavo. [*Chalmers' Notes.
Mon. Rev.*, lxvii. 470.]

VELITATIONES polemicae ; or,
polemicall short discussions of certain
particular and select questions. By I.
D. Phil-Iren-Alethius. [John DOUGH-
TIE, Fellow of Merton.]

London, 1651. Octavo. Pp. 4. b. t. 335.*
[*Wood, Athen. Oxon.*, iii. 977.]

VELVET (the) cushion. [By Rev. J.
W. CUNNINGHAM, of St. John's College, Cambridge.]

London : 1814. Octavo.

VENETIA. By the author of "Vivian
Grey" and "Henrietta Temple"
[Benjamin DISRAELI.] In three vol-
umes.

London : MDCCCXXXVII. Duodecimo.*
Dedication to Lord Lyndhurst signed Δ.

VENETIAN (the) bracelet, The lost
Pleiad, A history of the lyre, and other
poems. By L. E. L. author of the
Improvisatrice, the Troubadour, and
the Golden violet. [Letitia Elizabeth
LANDON.]

London: 1829. Octavo.*

VENETIA'S lovers An uneventful history
By Leslie Keith author of "Sur_ender,"
Alasnam's lady, etc. [Miss Ke_th JOHN-
STON.] In three volumes.

London 1884. Octavo.*

VENICE under the yoke of France and
of Austria : with memoirs of the courts,
governments, & people of Italy ; presenting a faithful picture of her present
condition, and including original anecdotes of the Buonaparte family. By a

lady of rank. [Catherine HYDE, Marchioness Broglio Solari.] Written during a twenty years residence in that interesting country; and now published for the information of Englishmen in general and of travellers in particular. In two volumes.

London: 1824. Octavo.* [*Adv. Lib.*]

V E N T A, and other poems. By the author of "Pericula urbis." [Rev. William MOORE, rector of Appleton.]

London: 1882. Octavo. Pp. 3. 133.* [*Crockford's Clerical Directory.*]

VÉRA. By the author of "The hôtel du Petit St. Jean." [Charlotte Louisa Hawkins DEMPSTER.]

London: 1871. Octavo. Pp. viii. 289.*

VERBAL (of) criticism: an epistle to Mr. Pope. Occasioned by Theobald's Shakespear, and Bentley's Milton. [By David MALLET.]

London: 1733. Folio. Pp. 14. b. t.* [*Dyce Cat.*, ii. 192.]

VERBEIA; or, Wharfdale. A poem, descriptive and didactic. With historical remarks. [By Thomas MAUDE.]

1783. Quarto. [*Mon. Rev.*, lxix. 167.] Edition of 1782 mentioned in Upcott, p. 1410, not anon.

VERDICT (the) upon the dissenters plea, occasioned by their Melius inquirendum [by Vincent Alsop]. To which is added, a letter from Geneva to the Assembly of Divines. Printed by his late Majesties special command; with some notes upon the margent, under his own royal and sacred hand. Also a postscript touching the union of Protestants. [By Lawrence WOMOCK, D.D., Bishop of St. David's.]

London, 1681. Octavo. Pp. 12. b. t. 281; letter and postscript, pp. 45.* [*Bodl.*]

V E R I T A S in semente; a moderate discourse concerning the principles and practices of the Quakers. [By —— HUMPHREYS.]

1707. Octavo. [*Leslie's Cat.*, 1843.]

VERNAL (the) walk: a poem. [By Ebenezer ELLIOTT.]

London: 1801. Octavo. [*Watkins' Life of Elliott. Mon. Rev.*, xxxv. 109.]

VERS de société: historical fragments, sonnets, etc. [By Joseph DENISON, M.P.] In two volumes.

London: 1849. Octavo. [*IV., Martin's Cat.*]

VERSES. [By J. R. FINLAY.]

Printed for private circulation 1874. Octavo. Pp. 2. b. t. 41.*
"Nearly all the following pieces were written more than twenty years ago.—J. R. F."

VERSES addressed to Lady Brydges, in memory of her son Edward William George Brydges. [By Sir Samuel Egerton BRYDGES.]

Lee Priory: 1816.] Quarto. Pp. 8. [*IV.*] Privately printed.

VERSES and translations. By C. S. C. [Charles Stuart CALVERLEY.]

Cambridge: 1862. Octavo. Pp. vi. 203.*

VERSES, edited by M[ilitia] M[ea] M[ultiplex]. [William TOOKE.]

London, for private distribution only, 1860. Octavo. Pp. 31. [*IV.*] Verses relating to Mr. Tooke's family, &c., by various persons.

V E R S E S for children. [By Jane BRAGG.]

Carlisle: 1862. Duodecimo. Pp. 31. [*Smith's Cat. of Friends' books*, i. 312.]

VERSES for holy seasons; with questions for examination. By C. F. H. [C. F. ALEXANDER.] Edited by Walter Farquhar Hook, D.D., vicar of Leeds.

London: 1846. Octavo. Pp. xi. 232.*

VERSES in memory of Dunbar Collegiate Church. [By George MILLER.]

Edinburgh: 1819. Octavo. Pp. 40.* [*J. Maidment.*]

VERSES occasioned by reading some strictures on Barclay's Apology. [By Joseph BECK.]

Printed in the year 1785. Octavo. 2⅜ sh. [*Smith's Cat. of Friends' books*, i. 73.]

VERSES occasioned by seeing the Palace and Park of Dalkeith anno MDCCXXXII. [By S. BOYSE.] Humbly inscribed to his Grace the Duke of Buccleugh.

Edinburgh: 1732. Octavo. Pp. 14.

VERSES on Sir Joshua Reynolds's painted window at New College, Oxford. [By Thomas WARTON.]

1782. Quarto. [*Gent. Mag.*, lii. 342.]

VERSES on the death of Dr. Samuel Johnson. [By Thomas PERCY, LL.D., Fellow of St. John's College, Oxford, nephew of the Bishop of Dromore.]

London: 1785. Quarto. Pp. 16. [*Gent. Mag., May* 1808, p. 470.]

VERSES, sacred and miscellaneous.

By Harriet. [Miss WHITE, of Cashel.]

1853. [*Olphar Hamst*, p. 5.]

VERSES spoken to the King, Queen, and Dutchesse of Yorke in St. John's library in Oxford. [By Thomas LAURENCE.]

N. P. N. D. Quarto. Pp. 2.* [*Bodl.*] "These verses were spoken by Thom. Laurence a gent. com. of St. John Coll—Afterwards Fellow of Univ. coll."—MS. note by Wood.

VERSES to Sir Thomas Hanmer on his edition of Shakspeares works. By a gentleman of Oxford. [W. COLLINS.]

London: 1743. Folio. [*Lowndes, Bibliog. Man.*, p. 2314.]

VERSES to the memory of a brother. [By William Laurence BROWN, D.D. Principal of Marischal College, Aberdeen.]

N. P. [1784.] Octavo. Pp. 15.* [*D. Laing.*]

VERSES to the Right Rev. Father in God, Edward, Lord Bishop of Durham. With an essay towards restoring the original texts of Scripture and reconciling the Hebrew and Septuagint, by the Oriental languages, Fathers, &c. [By John MAWER, M.A.]

London, 1731. Octavo. Pp. 27. [*Davies' Mem. of the York press*, p. 182.]

VERSES written on several occasions, between the years 1712 and 1721. [By Sir Thomas BURNET.]

London: MDCCLXXVII. Quarto.*

VERSION (a) of the Psalms of David, attempted to be closely accommodated to the text of Scripture; and adapted, by variety of measure, to all the music used in the versions of Sternhold and Hopkins, and of Brady and Tate: by a lay-member of the Church of England. [John STOW, of Greenwich.]

London: 1809. Duodecimo. Pp. xix. 7. 704.*

VERTUMNUS: an epistle [in verse] to Mr. Jacob Bobart. By the author of the Apparition. [Abel EVANS.]

Oxford: 1713. Octavo. [*Watt, Bib. Brit.*]

VERTUOUS (the), holy, christian life and death of the late Lady Lettice, Vicountess Falkland, with some additionals. [By John DUNCON.]

London: 1653. Duodecimo. [*IV., Brit. Mus.*]

VERULAMIANA; or opinions on men, manners, literature, politics, and theology, by Francis Bacon, Baron of Verulam, &c. &c. To which is prefixed a life of the author, by the editor. [P. L. COURTIER.]

London: 1803. Duodecimo. [*Lowndes, Bibliog. Man.*, p. 97.]

VERY (a) godly and learned exposition, vpon the whole Booke of Psalmes. Wherein is contained the diuision and sense of euery Psalme: as also manifold, necessary and sound doctrines, gathered out of the same, all seruing for the great furtherance and instruction of euery Christian reader. Heretofore penned and written, and now diligētly and faithfully reuiued by the author (who hath added many worthy things thereto) and newly published at the no smal cost of the printer, for the glory of God, and the good of the Church. [By Thomas WILCOCKS.]

London printed by Thomas Orwin for Thomas Man. 1591. Quarto. Pp. 6. b. t. 600.* [*Bodl.*]
Epistle dedicatory signed T. W.

VERY (a) simple story... [By Florence MONTGOMERY.]

Sleaford, 1867. Quarto. [*Adv. Lib.*]

VESPERTINA, by A. H. B., commoner of St. John's College, Oxford. [A. H. BALDWIN.]
Oxford: 1853. Octavo. Pp. viii. 118.* [*F. Madan.*]

VESTIGES of the natural history of creation. [By Robert CHAMBERS, LL.D.] Eleventh edition. Illustrated by numerous engravings on wood.

London: MDCCCXL. Octavo. Pp. iv. 286. lxiv.*

VETERANS (the) of Chelsea Hospital. By the author of "The subaltern," "Traditions of Chelsea College," "Country curate," etc. [George Robert GLEIG.] In three volumes.
London: 1842. Duodecimo.*

VETERES vindicati, in an expostulatory letter to Mr Sclater of Putney, upon his Consensus Veterum &c. Wherein the absurdity of his method, the weakness of his reasons are shewn, his false aspersions upon the Church of England are wiped off, and her faith concerning the Eucharist proved to be that of the primitive Church. To-

gether with animadversions on Dean Boileau's French translation of, and remarks upon Bertram. [By Edward GEE.]

London, 1687. Quarto.*

VIA dolorosa: being the Catholic devotion of the stations ; prepared as a special office for the use of English people, with reference to the sins, the responsibilities, and the portents of these times. Translated and arranged by the author of "From Oxford to Rome," "Rest in the Church," etc. [E. F. S. HARRIS.]

London : 1848. Octavo.* The preface is signed E. F. S. H.

VIA (the) media; or, Anglican orthodoxy, by a member of the Oxford Convocation. [J. HIPPISLEY.]

London : MDCCCXXXVIII. Octavo. Pp. 53.*

VIA, veritas, vita : discursive notes on preaching and on some types of the Christian life. By a presbyter. [Rev. Peter BARCLAY, M.A.]

London, 1881. Octavo. Pp. 94. [Author.] Published in 1882, with the Author's name, with the title—"The Way, the Truth, and the Life."

VIÆ per Angliam stratæ : editio altera. [By T. L. CLAUGHTON.]

Oxford : 1841. Octavo. Pp. 15.* [F. Madan.]

VIAGGIANA : or, detached remarks on the buildings, pictures, statues, inscriptions, &c. of ancient and modern Rome. [By Stephen WESTON.]

London : [1776.] Duodecimo. Pp. iv. b. t. 4. 176.* [Dyce Cat., ii. 417.

VIATOR, a poem : or a journey from London to Scarborough, by the way of York. With notes historical and topographical. [By Thomas MAUDE.]

London. MDCCLXXXII. Quarto. Pp. 40. xix.* [Boyne's Yorkshire Lib., p. 128.]

VICE versâ or a lesson to fathers. By F. Anstey. [F. Anstey GUTHRIE.] New and revised edition.

London 1883. Octavo. Pp. vi. 1. 370.*

VICEROY (the) : a poem. Addressed to the Earl of Halifax. [By John LANGHORNE, D.D.]

London : M DCC LXII. Quarto. Pp. xi. 11.* [Watt, Bib. Brit., Mon. Rev. xxvii. 75.]

VICEROY (the) of Catalonia; or, the

double cuckhold. [By Gabarel de BREMOND.] Made English by James Morgan, Gent.

London, 1678. Duodecimo. Pp. 5. b. t. 155. 2.*

VICES (on the) of horses. By B. C. [Bracy CLARK.]

London : 1839. Quarto. [W., Brit. Mus.]

VICISSITUDES (the) of Bessie Fairfax, By Holme Lee, author of "Basil Godfrey's caprice," "The beautiful Miss Barrington," "Katherine's trial," etc. etc. [Harriet PARR.] [In three volumes.]

London : 1874. Octavo.*

VICISSITUDES (the) of commerce A tale of the cotton trade. [By Thomas GREENHALGH.] In two volumes.

London 1852. Duodecimo.*

VICISSITUDES of life; exemplified in the interesting memoirs of a young lady, in a series of letters. [By Jane WEST.] In two volumes.

London : 1815. Duodecimo.*

VICTIM (the) of fancy. By a lady; author of "The conquests of the heart." [Elizabeth Sophia TOMLINS.] In two volumes.

London : 1787. Duodecimo. [Mon. Rev., xxvii. 331 ; lxxvi. 446.]

VICTORIAISM ; or, a re-organization of the people: moral, social, economical, and political : suggested as a remedy for the present distress. Respectfully addressed to the Right Hon. Sir Robert Peel, Bart. [By William C. COWARD.]

London : 1843. Octavo.* Signed W. C.C.

VICTORIES (the) of the British armies ; with anecdotes illustrative of modern warfare. By the author of "Stories of Waterloo," "Captain Blake," "Wild sports of the West," "The bivouac," &c. [William Hamilton MAXWELL, rector of Ballagh, Connaught.] In two volumes.

London : 1839. Octavo.*

VICTORIOUS (the) stroke for old England all preachers make all hearers one man against her enemies and down Jericho, etc. [By J. HENLEY.] The third edition.

London : 1748. Octavo. [W., Brit. Mus.]

VICTORY (the). And other stories.

By A. L. O. E., author of " Fairy Frisket," " Fairy Know-a-bit," " The giant-killer," &c., &c. [Charlotte TUCKER.]

London : 1875. Octavo. Pp. 64.*

VICTORY (the) of the vanquished : a tale of the first century. By the author of " Chronicles of the Schönberg-Cotta family," &c. [Mrs CHARLES.]

London : 1871. Octavo. Pp. 458.*

" V I C T O R Y (the) won." A brief memorial of the last days of G. R. [By Miss Catherine MARSH.] Second edition.

London : 1855. Octavo. Pp. 84.* Preface signed W. M.

VIDA Study of a girl By Amy Dunsmuir. [Miss OLIPHANT.] In two volumes.

London : 1880. Octavo.*

VIENNA wherein is storied, ye valorous atchieuements, famous triumphs, constant loue, greate miseries, & finall happiness of the well-deseruing, truly noble and most valiant Kt, Sr Paris of Vienna, and ye most admired amiable Princess, the faire Vienna. [By Richard MYNSHULL.]

London N. D. Quarto. Pp. 6. b. t. 180.* Attributed also to Manwaring by Hazlewood.

VIEW (a) of a printed book [by Henry Parker] intituled Observations upon His Majesties late answers and expresses. [By Sir John SPELMAN.]

Oxford, 1642. Quarto. Pp. 45.* [Bodl.] Author's name in the handwriting of Barlow.

VIEW (a) of antient history ; including the progress of literature and the fine arts. By William Rutherford, D.D. master of the academy at Uxbridge. [In reality by John LOGAN, minister of Leith.] [In two volumes.]

London : MDCCLXXXVIII. MDCCXCIII. Octavo.*

The title of vol. ii. (2d. ed.) is different from that of vol. i.

VIEW (a) of antiquity. See "ΑΡΧΑΙΟΣ-ΚΟΠΙΑ."

Ascribed also to J. Howell, and to Jonathan Harmer.

VIEW of Christianity, containing a short account of religion from the creation to the end of the 4th cent. ; with the complete duty of a Christian : laid down in two catechisms. [By U. DEACON.

1747. Octavo. [Lathbury's Nonjurors.]

VIEW (a) of Fraunce. [By Sir Thomas DALLINGTON.]

London, 1604. Quarto. No pagination.*

VIEW (a) of Lord Bolingbroke's philosophy, compleat, in four letters to a friend. In which his whole system of infidelity and naturalism is exposed and confuted. With the apology prefixed. [By William WARBURTON, D.D.] The third edition.

London, MDCCLVI. Duodecimo. Pp. xlviii. 335.* [Bodl.]

VIEW (a) of many errors and some gross absurdities in the old translation of the Psalms in English metre ; as also in som other translations lately published : shewing how the Psalms ought to be translated, to be acceptable and edifying. Together with sundry epigramms and suffrages of many godly and learned men in behalf of the author's translation, and reasons for publishing the same. By W. B. M.A. and minister of the Gospel. [William BARTON.]

London, M.DC.LIV. Quarto. Pp. 6. b. t. 18.*

VIEW (a) of real grievances, with remedies proposed for redressing them ; humbly submitted to the consideration of the legislature. [By —— POWELL.]

London : 1772. Octavo. [Queen's Coll. Cat. Mon. Rev., xlviii. 19.]

VIEW (a) of society and manners in France, Switzerland, and Germany : with anecdotes relating to some eminent characters. By a gentleman who resided several years in those countries. [John MOORE, M.D.] In two volumes.

London : M DCC LXXIX. Octavo.*

VIEW (a) of some exceptions which have beene made by a Romanist to the Lord Viscount Falkland's Discourse of, the infallibilitie of the Church of Rome. Submitted to the censure of all sober Christians. Together with the Discourse it selfe of infallibilitie prefixt to it. [By Henry HAMMOND, D.D.]

Oxford, 1646. Quarto. Pp. 4. b. t. 204.*

VIEW (a) of Stourton Gardens with strictures on a late abusive Ode upon the same subject : somewhat, it is said, in imitation of Horace, Book II, Ode 13. [By Rev. John CHAPMAN.] Octavo. Pp. 11. [W. Upcott.]

VIEW of the agriculture of Oxfordshire, drawn up for the Board of Agriculture and internal improvement. By the secretary to the Board. [Rev. Arthur YOUNG.]

London : 1809. Octavo. [*W.*]

VIEW (a) of the British Empire, more especially Scotland ; with some proposals for the improvement of that country, the extension of its fisheries, and the relief of the people. [By John KNOX, bookseller.]

London: 1784. Octavo.*

The author's name appears in the third edition, 1785.

VIEW of the conduct of the English clergy, as relates to civil affairs. [By Sir E. THOMAS.]

1737. Octavo. [*Leslie's Cat.*, 1843 (414).]

VIEW (a) of the controversy between Great-Britain and her colonies : including a mode of determining their present disputes, finally and effectually ; and of preventing all future contentions. In a letter to the author of A full vindication of the measures of the Congress, from the calumnies of their enemies. By *A. W.* Farmer. Author of Free thoughts, &c. [Dr. Samuel SEABURY, Bishop of Connecticut.]

New-York, printed : London reprinted, 1775. Octavo. Pp. 90. b. t.* [*Bodl.*]

VIEW (a) of the Dissertation upon the Epistles of Phalaris, Themistocles, &c. Lately publish'd by the Reverend Dr. Bentley. Also of the examination of that Dissertation by the Honourable Mr. Boyle. In order to the manifesting of the incertitude of heathen chronology. [By Rev. John MILNER, B.D.]

London: 1698. Octavo. Pp. 5. b. t. 78.* [*Bodl.*]

VIEW (a) of the elections of bishops in the primitive Church: wherein is shewed, what were the several shares of the bishops, inferior clergy and people in these elections ; as also, of the Emperors, after they became Christians : and the nature of the Church, its unity and government are likewise explained. By a presbyter of the Church of Scotland. [James DUNDASS.]

Edinburgh: M.DCC.XXVIII. Octavo. Pp. 242.*

VIEW of the evidence for proving that the present Earl of Galloway is the

lineal heir male and lawful representative of Sir William Stuart of Jedworth, so frequently mentioned in history from the year 1385 to the year 1429. [Drawn up by Rev. E. WILLIAMS, his lordship's chaplain.]

1796. Quarto. [*W., Martin's Cat.*]

VIEW (a) of the gold coin and coinage of England from Henry the Third to the present time, with copper plates. [By Thomas SNELLING.]

London: 1763. Folio. [*W., Brit. Mus.*]

VIEW (a) of the internal evidence of the Christian religion. [By Soame JENYNS.]

London : M.DCC.LXXVI. Octavo.*

VIEW (a) of the Jewish religion containing the manner of life, rites, ceremonies and customes of the Jewish nation throughout the world at this present time ; together with the articles of their faith, as now received. Faithfully collected by A. R. [Alexander ROSS.]

London, 1656. Octavo. Pp. 5. b. t. 427.* [*Lowndes, Brit. Lib.*, p. 1253.]

VIEW (a) of the Lancashire dialect, by way of dialogue ; to which is added, a glossary of all the Lancashire words and phrases therein used. By T. Bobbin, Opp'n Speyker o' th' Dialect. [John COLLIER, of Milnrow.]

Manchester : [1746.] Duodecimo. [*W.*] First edition.

VIEW (a) of the naval force of Great Britain ; in which its present state, growth, and conversion of timber ; construction of ships, docks and harbours ; regulations of officers and men in each department, are considered and compared with other European powers. To which are added, observations and hints for the improvement of the naval service. By an officer of rank. [Sir John Borlase WARREN.]

London : 1791. Octavo. Pp. 203. 74. [*Watt, Bib. Brit. Mon. Rev.*, vi. 221.]

VIEW (a) of the new directorie, and a vindication of the ancient liturgie of the Church of England. In answer to the reasons pretended in the ordinance and preface, for the abolishing the one, and establishing the other. [By Henry HAMMOND, D.D.] The third edition.

Oxford, 1646. Quarto. Pp. 10. b. t. 106.* An edition, said to be the third, with some variations in the spelling, both on the title-page and throughout the work, was printed

at Oxford, by the same printer [Henry Hall], in the same year, with a different pagination.

VIEW (a) of the political state of Scotland at Michaelmas 1811 : comprehending the rolls of the freeholders, an abstract of the setts or constitutions of the royal burghs, and a state of the votes at the last elections throughout Scotland : to which is prefixed an account of the forms of procedure at elections to parliament from the counties and burghs of Scotland. [By James BRIDGES, W.S.]

Edinburgh : 1812. Octavo.* [*Watt, Bib. Brit.*]

VIEW (a) of the political state of Scotland at the late general election. Containing, an introductory treatise on the election laws ; lists of the peers, and the procedure at their late election, with the effect of their protests ; the rolls of the freeholders of Scotland ; an abstract of the sets of the Royal boroughs, and the names of their delegates, &c. &c. Exhibiting the manner in which every peer, freeholder, and borough in Scotland voted at the late general election ; with other interesting political information. [By Alexander MACKENZIE.]

Edinburgh : Anno 1790. Octavo.*

VIEW (a) of the present state and future prospects of the free trade and colonization of India. [By John CRAWFURD.]

London : 1829. Octavo. [*M'Cull. Lit. Pol. Econ.*, p. 110.]

VIEW of the real power of the Pope, and of the power of the priesthood over the laity ; with an account how they use it. [By T. HAWKINS.]

London : 1733. Octavo. [*Leslie's Cat.*, 1841.]

Ascribed also to T. Hart.

VIEW (a) of the relative situations of Mr Pitt and Mr Addington, previous to, and on the night of, Mr Patten's motion. By a member of parliament. [Robert Plumer WARD.] Second edition.

London : 1804. Octavo. [*Pellew's Life of Sidmouth*, ii. 146. *Mon. Rev.*, xliii. 328.]

VIEW of the Romish hydra and monster, traison against the Lord's Anointed ; condemned by David, 1 Sam. 26, and nowe confuted in seven sermons, to perswade obedience to princes, concord among ourselves, and a general refor-

mation and repentance in all states. [By Laurence HUMPHREY.]

Oxford : 1588. Duodecimo. B. L. [*Wood, Athen. Oxon.*]

VIEW (a) of the Scots rebellion. With some inquiry into what we have to fear, [from the rebels? and what is the properest method to take with them? [By Daniel DEFOE.]

London : 1715. Octavo. Pp. 40. [*Lee's Defoe*, 171.]

VIEW (a) of the Scripture revelations concerning a future state : laid before his parishioners by a country pastor. [Richard WHATELY.]

London : 1829. Duodecimo. Pp. 322.* [*Darling, Cyclop. Bibl.*]

VIEW (a) of the several schemes with respect to America, and their comparative merit in promoting the interest and dignity of Great Britain. [By Capel LOFFT.]

1776. Octavo. Pp. 55. [*Rich, Bib. Amer.*, i. 468.]

VIEW (a) of the silver coin and coinage of England, from the Norman Conquest to the present time ; considered with regard to type, legend, sorts, rarity, weight, fineness and value. [By Thomas SNELLING.]

London : 1762. Quarto. [*W., Brit. Mus.*]

VIEW (a) of the soul, in several tracts. The first, being a discourse of the nature and faculties, the effects and operations, the immortality and happiness of the soul of man. The second, a cordial against sorrow, or a treatise against immoderate care for a man's own posterity, and grief for the loss of children. The third consists of several epistles to the Reverend John Tillotson, D.D. and Dean of Canterbury, tending to the further illustration of the former arguments concerning the soul of man, and the proof of a particular providence over it. By a person of quality. [R. SAUNDERS.]

London, MDCLXXXII. Folio.* [*Lowndes, Brit. Lib.*, p. 804.]

VIEW (a) of the state of religion in the diocese of St David's about the beginning of the eighteenth century. With some account of the causes of its decay, together with considerations of the reasonableness of augmenting the revenues of impropriate Churches. By E. S. [Erasmus SAUNDERS] D.D.

London : 1721. Octavo. Pp. 128. [*Darling, Cyclop. Bibl.*]

VIEW (a) of the times, their principles and practices, in the Rehearsals by Philalethes. [Charles LESLIE.]

First edition, 1708-9. Folio. Second edition in six volumes, London, 1750. Duodecimo. [*Darling, Cyclop. Bibl.*]

VIEW (a) of the treaty &c. [By Denis O'BRIEN.]

London: 1787. Octavo. [*Chalmers' Notes. Mon. Rev.*, lxxvi. 169.]

VIEW (a) of the whole controversy between the Representer and the Answerer, with an answer to the Representer's last reply : in which are laid open some of the methods by which Protestants are misrepresented by Papists. [By William CLAGETT, D.D., preacher to Gray's Inn.]

London : MDCLXXXVII. Quarto. Pp. 123.* [*Bodl.*]

VIEWS and opinions. By Matthew Browne. [W. B. RANDS.]

London and New York 1866. Octavo. Pp. xviii. 294.* [*Athenæum, April*, 1882.]

VIEWS in London, by an amateur. [The Hon E. S. ABBOT, afterwards Baroness Colchester.] Sketched from a window in the Palais de la Vérité : and extracts from an album.

Chiswick, 1833. Octavo.

VIEWS in Orkney, and on the North-Eastern Coast of Scotland, taken in M.DCCC.V. and etched in M.DCCC.VII. [By the late Duchess of SUTHER-LAND.]

Folio. Pp. 27. [*W., Martin's Cat.*]

VIEWS of Canada and the colonists, embracing the experience of a residence ; views of the present state, progress and prospects of the colony; with detailed and practical information for intending emigrants. By a four year's resident. [James Bryce BROWN.]

Edinburgh : MDCCCXLIV. Octavo.*

VIEWS of ports and harbours, watering places, fishing villages, and other picturesque objects on the English coast. Engraved by W. and E. Finden. [With a descriptive letterpress by W. A. C. ; William Andrew CHATTO.]

London, 1838. Quarto. [*Universal Cat. of books on art*, i. 275.]

VIEWS of society and manners in America ; in a series of letters from that country to a friend in England, during the years 1818, 1819, and 1820.

By an Englishwoman. [Frances WRIGHT.]

London : 1821. Octavo. Pp. x. 523.* [*Rich, Bib Amer.*, ii. 130.]

VIEWS of the seats of noblemen and gentlemen in England, Wales, Scotland and Ireland. From drawings by J. P. Neale. [With letterpress descriptions by Thomas MOULE.]

In six volumes. London : 1818-23. Second series. In five volumes. London: 1824-9. [*IV.*]

VILLAGE belles. A tale of English country life. By the author of " Mary Powell." [Anne MANNING.] New edition, revised.

London : 1860. Octavo. Pp. iv. 348.*

VILLAGE (a) commune By Ouida [Louise de LA RAMÉ.] In two volumes.

London 1881. Octavo.*

VILLAGE conversations ; or, the vicar's fire-side. [By Sarah RENOU.] Dedicated to Mrs. Hannah More.

London: 1815. Duodecimo. Pp. xvii. 227.* Dedication signed S. R.

VILLAGE (the) curate. A poem. [By James HURDIS, D.D.]

Bishopstone : 1797. Octavo. [*IV.*]

VILLAGE (the) lesson book ; for the use of schools. By Martin Doyle, author of " Hints to small farmers, &c., &c." [Ross HICKEY.]

London : 1855. Duodecimo. Pp. 116.*

VILLAGE memoirs ; in a series of letters between a clergyman and his family in the country, and his son in town. [By Joseph CRADOCK.]

London: 1775. Duodecimo. [*Cradock's Mem.*, i. xix. *Mon. Rev.*, lii. 139.]

VILLAGE (the) on the cliff. By the author of " The story of Elizabeth." [Miss THACKERAY.] With six illustrations by Frederick Walker.

London : 1867. Octavo. Pp. 3. b. t. 318.*

VILLAGE (the) pastor. By one of the authors of Body and soul. [George WILKINS, D.D.]

London : 1825. Duodecimo.*

VILLAGE (the) pastor. By the author of The retrospect, Ocean, Morning meditations, Village observer, Village church yard, &c. formerly a Lieutenant in the Royal Navy, and now a minister

in the Established Church. [Richard MARKS.] In two volumes.

London : MDCCCXXVII. Duodecimo.*

VILLAGE reminiscences. By an old maid. [Mrs MONKLAND.] In three volumes.

London : 1834. Duodecimo.*

VILLAGE scenes : a poem. In two parts. [By James Cargill GUTHRIE.] Edinburgh and London. M.DCCC.L. Duodecimo.*

VILLAGE sermons. By a country clergyman. [Edward BERENS, Archdeacon of Berks.]

Oxford, 1820. Duodecimo. Pp. viii. 202.*

VILLAGE sermons. By a Northamptonshire rector. [Granville Hamilton FORBES.] With a preface on the inspiration of Holy Scripture.

London and Cambridge : 1863. Octavo. Pp. xliv. 321.*

VILLAGE sketches : or, hints to pedestrians. Reprinted from the 'Doncaste Gazette,' 1849-50. [By C. W. HATFIELD.]

Doncaster : N. D. Duodecimo. Pp. 350. [Boyne's Yorkshire Lib., p. 108.]

VILLAGE virtues : a dramatic satire. In two parts. [By Matthew Gregory LEWIS.]

London : 1796. Quarto. Pp. 45.* [N. and Q., 8 June 1861, p. 458.]

V I L L A G E (the) wedding : or the faithful country maid. A pastoral entertainment of music. As it is performed at the Theatre - Royal at Richmond. [By James LOVE or DANCE.]

1767. Octavo. [Biog. Dram. Mon. Rev., xxxvii. 152.]

VILLAINY (the) of stock-jobbers detected, and the causes of the late run upon the bank and bankers discovered and considered. [By Daniel DEFOE.]

London, MDCCI. Quarto.* [Wilson, Life of Defoe, 19.]

VILLANIES discouered by lanthorne and candle-light, and the helpe of a new cryer called O per se O. Being an addition to the belman's second nightwalke, and a laying open to the world of those abuses, which the bel-man (because he went i' the darke) could not see, with canting songs neuer before printed. [By Thomas DEKKER.]

London, 1616. Quarto. B.L. No pagination.*

VILLETTE. By Currer Bell, author of "Jane Eyre," "Shirley," etc. [Charlotte BRONTË.] In three volumes.

London : 1853. Octavo.*

VINDICATION (a) and defence of Mr. George Meldrum's Sermon, preached May 16. 1703. against the reflections and censure of [John Sage] the author of the Examination of some things in the sermon, and [George Brown] the author of Toleration defended. [By George MELDRUM, minister at Edinburgh.]

Edinburgh, 1703. Quarto. Pp. 30. b. t.*

VINDICATION (a) of a book, intituled, A brief account of many of the prosecutions of the people call'd Quakers, &c. Lately presented to the members of both Houses of Parliament; shewing the fallacy and injustice of the calculations and remarks in a late book call'd An examination, &c.; the evasions and disingenuity of the clergy of the diocese of London in their answers and reflections; and the falshood and inconsistency of the intelligences by them published. To which are added, remarks on the poor vicar's Plea. With Bishop Burnet's description of the ecclesiastical courts. [By Joseph BESSE.]

London : 1737. Octavo. Pp. 138. b. t.* [Smith's Cat. of Friends' books, i. 254.]

VINDICATION (a) of a book, intituled, A brief account of many of the prosecutions of the people called Quakers, &c. Presented to the members of both Houses of Parliament : in answer to a late Examination thereof in behalf of the church-men of the diocese of Hereford. [By Joseph BESSE.]

London : 1741. Octavo. 4 sh. [Smith's Cat. of Friends' books, i. 256.

VINDICATION (a) of a book, intituled, A brief account of many of the prosecutions of the people called Quakers, &c. Presented to the members of both Houses of Parliament : in answer to a late Examination thereof, in defence of the clergy of the diocese of York. [By Joseph BESSE.]

London : 1741. Octavo. Pp. 2. b. t. 228.* [Smith's Cat. of Friends' books, i. 256.]

VINDICATION (a) of a book intituled, A brief account of many of the prosecutions of the people called Quakers,

&c. Presented to the members of both Houses of Parliament : in answer to a late Examination thereof, so far as the clergy of the diocese of Canterbury are concerned in it. With an appendix, demonstrating, that tithes are an oppression to the husbandman, a burden too heavy for him to bear, and undoeth many. [By Joseph BESSE.]

London : 1742. Octavo. 14 sh. [*Smith's Cat. of Friends' books*, i. 256.]

VINDICATION (a) of a book, intituled, A brief account of many of the prosecutions of the people called Quakers, &c. Presented to the members of both Houses of Parliament : in answer to a late Examination thereof, so far as the clergy of the diocese of Carlisle are concerned in it. [By Joseph BESSE.]

London : 1741. Octavo. 3 sh. [*Smith's Cat. of Friends' books*, i. 256.]

VINDICATION (a) of a book intituled A brief account of many of the prosecutions of the people call'd Quakers, &c. Presented to the members of both Houses of Parliament, in answer to a late Examination thereof, so far as the clergy of the diocese of Lichfield and Coventry are concerned in it : with an appendix, in reply to the objections of two clergymen of the diocese call'd St. David's. [By Joseph BESSE.]

London : MDCCXXXIX. Octavo. Pp. 96.* [*Smith's Cat. of Friends' books*, i. 254.]

VINDICATION (a) of a book intituled, A brief account of many of the prosecutions of the people called Quakers, &c. Presented to the members of both Houses of Parliament ; in answer to a late Examination thereof, so far as the clergy of the dioceses of Oxford, Glocester, and Chester, are concerned in it. [By Joseph BESSE.]

London : 1740. Octavo. 2¾ sh. [*Smith's Cat.of Friends' books*, i. 255.]

VINDICATION (a) of a discourse concerning the unreasonableness of a new separation, on account of the oaths [by Edward Stillingfleet], from the exceptions made against it in a tract called, A brief answer to a late discourse, &c. [By John WILLIAMS, D.D.]

London : MDCXCI. Quarto. Pp.2.b.t.40.* Ascribed by some to Stillingfleet.

VINDICATION (a) of a discourse entituled the Principles of the Cyprianic age, with regard to episcopal power and jurisdiction : being a reply to Gilbert Rule's Cyprianic bishop examin'd and found not to be diocesan. Wherein besides a great many things more briefly considered, the usefulness of fixing the principles of the Cyprianic age is succinctly represented ; the main controversie between those of the Church and the Presbyterians is fully and distinctly stated ; Mr. Rule's main subterfuges are utterly overthrown ; large supplements are added to the Principles of the Cyprianic age ; the Cyprianic episcopacy is shewn to be inconsistent with a papacy ; and it is demonstrated that episcopal government was universally delivered to be of divine right in the days of St. Cyprian. [By Bishop John SAGE.]

London : MDCCI. Quarto.*

VINDICATION (the) of a late pamphlet, (entituled, Obedience and submission to the present government, demonstrated from Bp. Overal's Convocation-book) from the false glosses, and illusive interpretations of a pretended answer [by Thomas Wagstaffe]. By the author of the first pamphlet. [Zachary TAYLOR.]

London : MDCXCI. Quarto. Pp. 36.* [*Cat. Lond. Inst.*, ii. 34.]

VINDICATION (a) of a late pamphlet, intituled, The case of the Hanover troops considered : with some further observations upon those troops ; being a Sequel to the said pamphlet. [By Philip Dormer STANHOPE, Earl of Chesterfield.]

London : MDCCXLIII. Octavo. Pp. 56. b. t.*

VINDICATION (a) of an undertaking of certain gentlemen, in order to the suppressing of debauchery, and profaneness. [By Edward FOWLER, D.D., Bishop of Gloucester.]

London, 1692. Quarto. Pp. 16.* [*Bodl.*]

VINDICATION (a) of Bishop Taylor, from the injurious misrepresentation of him by the author of the Letter to the clergy of the Church of England in the county of Northumberland. With a few remarks upon some other passages in that letter. [By Thomas SHARP, D.D., Archdeacon of Northumberland.]

Printed in the year 1733. Octavo. 1 sh. [*Smith, Bib. Anti-Quaker.*, p. 39, 392.]

VINDICATION (a) of commerce and the arts ; proving that they are the source of the greatness, power, riches and populousness of a state. Being an examination of Mr. Bell's Dissertation

upon populousness, read in the schools, and honoured with the Lord Viscount Townshend's prize, by the University of Cambridge. Wherein Mr. Bell's calumnies on trade are answered, his arguments refuted, his system exploded, and the principal causes of populosity assigned. With a large appendix, containing remarks on that part of the estimate of the manners and principles of the times, which relates to trade and commerce. By I—— B——, M.D. [William TEMPLE.]

London: MDCCLVIII. Octavo. Pp. xvi. 137.*

VINDICATION (a) of Dr Sherlock, Dean of St. Paul's, in answer to Mr. Nathaniel Taylor's late treatise, entituled, Dr Sherlock's Case of Church communion, and his letter to Anonymous, consider'd, &c. Together with a reply to his vindication of the dissenters from the charge of schism. [By Benjamin HOADLEY, D.D.]

London: 1702. Quarto. Pp. 5. b. t. 72.*

VINDICATION (a) of Doctor Tail [Traill], from the charge of heresy: being a defence of a sermon entitled, The happiness of dead clergymen, &c. By the Reverend Doctor Tail. [William THOM, minister at Govan.]

Glasgow: M DCC LXX. Octavo.*

VINDICATION (a) of Exeter School, by its master. J. L. [John LEMPRIÈRE, D.D.]

Exeter, 1818. Octavo. [Davidson, Bib. Devon., p. 29.]

V I N D I C A T I O N (a) of God's sovereignty, the doctrines of election, reprobation, and original sin; from a late pamphlet intituled, Free and impartial thoughts on the sovereignty of God, &c. By W. B. [Richard FINCH.]

London: 1745. Octavo. 2½. sh. [Smith's Cat. of Friends' books, i. 610.]
Afterwards formed part of a volume entitled "Tracts,—By Richard Finch."

VINDICATION (a) of his Excellency the Lord C——t from the charge of favouring none but Tories, high-churchmen and Jacobites. By the Reverend Dr. S——t. [Jonathan SWIFT, D.D.]

London MDCCXXX. Octavo. Pp. 27. b. t.*

VINDICATION (a) of his Majesties government and judicatures, in Scotland; from some aspersions thrown on them by scandalous pamphlets, and

news-books: and especially, with relation to the late Earl of Argyle's process. [By Sir George MACKENZIE.]

Printed at Edinburgh: and re-printed at London, M.DC.LXXXIII. Quarto. Pp. 29. b. t.*

VINDICATION of informers of the breaches of the laws against prophaneness and immorality. Asserting and proving the lawfulness and necessity of informing. Shewing that all sober Christians, and good neighbours, are called in duty to joyn therein. And answering objections made by ill or ignorant men, against those pious and useful persons, who out of love to God and their neighbours, do reckon themselves obliged in conscience, to inform against the vicious. [By Francis GRANT, Lord Cullen.]

Printed at Edinburgh. Anno 1701. Quarto.*

VINDICATION (a) of Isaac Bickerstaff Esq; against what is objected to him by Mr. Partridge, in his Almanack for the present year 1709. By the said Isaac Bickerstaff Esq; [Jonathan SWIFT, D.D.]

London: MDCCIX. Octavo. Pp. 8.*

VINDICATION (a) of King Charles the Martyr, proving that His Majesty was the author of ΕΙΚΩΝ ΒΑΣΙΛΙΚΗ. Against a memorandum, said to be written by the Earl of Anglesey: and against the exceptions of Dr. Walker, and others. [By Thomas WAGSTAFFE, A.M.]

London, 1693. Octavo. Pp. 46.* [Wood.]
A second edition appeared in 1697, with a preface containing a refutation of a passage in Bayle's Dictionary relating to the controversy; and a third, in 1711, with large additions, and some original letters of Charles I.

VINDICATION (a) of lawful authority: against some principles lately advanc'd to undermine the same; or a confutation of Hobbism in politicks, as it is reviv'd by some modern doctors; wherein Dr Broughton's Grand apostacy is consider'd; and his notion concerning the divine right of power is set in its true light; according to the Holy Scriptures, and the testimony of the primitive Church. [By George SMITH.]

[London:] 1718. Octavo. Pp. 80. [W., Brit. Mus.]

VINDICATION (the) of liturgies, lately

published by Dr. Falkner, proved no vindication of the lawfulness, usefulness and antiquity of set-forms of publick ministerial prayer, to be generally used by, or imposed on all ministers; and consequently an answer to a book, intituled, A reasonable account why some pious nonconformists judge it sinful, for them to perform their ministered acts in by the prescribed forms of others. Wherein with an answer to what Dr. Falkner hath said on the book aforesaid, the original principles are discovered, from whence the different apprehensions of men in this point arise. By the author of the Reasonable account, and supplement to it. [John COLLINGES, D.D.]

London, 1681. Octavo. Pp. 30. b. t. iv. 258. 3.*

VINDICATION (a) of mankind, or freewill asserted in answer to a philosophical inquiry concerning human liberty [by Anthony Collins]; to which is added an Examination of Mr. Lock's scheme of freedom. [By S. LOWE?]

London: 1717. Octavo. [*IV., Brit Mus.*]

VINDICATION (a) of marriage, as solemnized by Presbyterians, in the North of Ireland. Wherein, 1. Their principles, practice, and reasons thereof, are candidly shown, with the causes of their non-conformity to the form prescribed in the liturgy. 2. The libels exhibited against ministers and people, in the official courts, examined and answered. 3. And such marriages proven to be agreeable to Scripture, light of nature, laws of nations, and customs of other reformed Churches, and not inconsistent with the civil laws of this land; and therefore lawfull tho not canonical. By a minister of the Gospel. [John MACBRIDE.]

Printed in the year 1702. Quarto. Pp. 71.*

VINDICATION (a) of Mr. George Buchanan, in two parts. Part I. Vindicating him from the vile aspersion cast on him by Camden, that he repented, when dying, of what he wrote against Mary Queen of Scots: which falshood has been since retailed and propagated by Messieurs Sage and Ruddiman. Part. II. Vindicating him from the horrible ingratitude he is charged with to Q. Mary, in extolling her so high in his dedication of his paraphrase of the Psalms, and there

after writing so bitterly against her in the Detection and History. With an appendix, containing a letter from the illustrious Mons. de Thou President of the Parliament of Paris, to Mr. William Camden, relating to Q. Mary's reign, and apologizing for his following Buchanan in his narration thereof: With a translation of that letter. [By John LOVE.]

Edinburgh: M.DCC.XLIX. Octavo. [*Chalmers' Life of Ruddiman*, p. 224.]

VINDICATION (a) of Mr. James Colmar Bachelor of physick and Fellow of Exeter College in Oxford. From the calumnies of three late pamphlets. 1. A paper publish'd by Dr. Bury, 1659. 2. The account examin'd. 3. The case of Exeter College related and vindicated. To which are annex'd the authentick copies of the affidavits relating to that affair. [By James HARRINGTON.]

London: 1691. Quarto. Pp. 4. b. t. 43.*

VINDICATION (a) of Mr. Pope's Essay on man, from the misrepresentations of Mr de Crousaz, professor of philosophy and mathematicks in the university of Lausanne. By the author of The divine legation of Moses demonstrated. In six letters. [By William WARBURTON, D.D.]

London: M.DCC.XL. Duodecimo. Pp. 118.*

There is added A seventh letter, which finishes the Vindication, with a separate title-page, and having the author's name. The pagination is continuous, and the date 1740.

VINDICATION (a) of Mr. Robert Keith, and of his young grand nephew Alexander Keith, from the unfriendly representations of Mr Alexander Keith junior of Ravelstone, one of the under-clerks in the Court of Session. [By William DOUGLAS.]

N. P. [1750.] Octavo. Pp. 22.*

"A few copies of this tract were printed for private circulation, in the year 1750, by Bishop Keith, author of the History of the affairs of Church and State in Scotland." —MS. note by Dr. David Laing.

VINDICATION (a) of my Lord Bishop of Worcester [George Morley]'s letter touching Mr. Baxter from the animadversions of D. E. [Edward Bagshaw.] [By Sir Henry YELVERTON.]

London, 1662. Quarto. Pp. 14. b. t.* [*Bodl.*]

VINDICATION (a) of my Lord Shaftesbury on the subject of ridicule, being remarks upon [John Brown's] "Essays on the characteristics." [By Charles BULKLEY.]

London: 1751. Octavo. [*Brit. Mus. Mon. Rev.*, v. 285 ; vii. 41.]

VINDICATION (a) of natural society : or a view of the miseries and evils arising to mankind from every species of artificial society. In a letter to Lord ****. By a late noble writer. [Edmund BURKE.]

London: 1756. Octavo. Pp. 1. b. t. 106.* [*Bodl.*]

VINDICATION (a) of Plain-dealing, from the base and malicious aspersions of two country curates, contained in a little scurrilous pamphlet, entitled, Plain-dealing proved to be plain-lying. [By Rev. Charles OWEN, D.D.]

London: 1716. Octavo. [*IV., Lowndes, Bibliog. Man.*]

VINDICATION (a) of Presbyterian ordination ; from Scripture and antiquity, the judgment of the Reformed Churches, and particularly of the Church of England. With a brief reflection upon the arguments offered by Mr. Cautrell of Derby against it. [By the Rev. John HARTLEY, of Ashby-de-la-Zouch.]

Nottingham: 1714. Octavo. Pp. 72. [*Darling, Cyclop. Bibl.*]

VINDICATION (a) of Protestant charity, in answer to some passages in Mr. E[dward] M[eredith]'s Remarks on a late conference. [By James HARRINGTON.]

Oxford, 1688. Quarto. [*Jones' Peck*, i. 140.]

The above is printed with "Some reflexions upon a treatise called Pietas Romana et Parisiensis, &c.," *q.v.*

VINDICATION (a) of Protestant principles, by Phileleutherus Anglicanus. [John William DONALDSON, D.D., head-master of King Edward's School, Bury St. Edmunds.]

London : M.DCCC.XLVII. Octavo.*

VINDICATION (a) of St. Gregorie his dialogues : in which the great St. Gregory is proved the author of that work. [By James MUMFORD, S.J.]

London, 1660. Quarto. Pp. 19. b. t.*

VINDICATION (a) of scriptural Unitarianism, and some other primitive Christian doctrines, in reply to Vindex's Examination of an appeal to the Society of Friends. By Verax. [Thomas FOSTER.]

London: 1810. Octavo. Pp. 324. [*Mon. Rev.*, lxiii. 442.]

VINDICATION (a) of some among our selves against the false principles of Dr. Sherlock. In a letter to the Doctor, occasioned by the sermon which he preached at the Temple-Church, on the 29th of May, 1692. In which letter are also contained reflexions on some other of the Doctor's sermons, published since he took the oath. [By George HICKES, D.D.]

London, MDCXCII. Quarto. Pp. 51.*

VINDICATION (a) of some passages in a Discourse concerning communion with God, from the exceptions of William Sherlock, rector of St. George Buttolph-Lane. By the author of the said Discourse. [John OWEN, D.D.]

London, 1674. Octavo. Pp. 237.* [*Bodl.*]

VINDICATION (a) of some truths contained in the Scriptures, by the exercise of reason only. [By Joseph LANCASTER.]

London: 1801. Duodecimo. 1 sh. [*Smith's Cat. of Friends' books*, i. 78.]

VINDICATION (a) of the account of the double doctrine of the ancients. In answer to a Critical enquiry into the practices of the antient philosophers. [By Arthur Ashley SYKES, D.D.]

London: MDCCXLVII. Octavo. Pp. 38.*

VINDICATION of the Address made by the Episcopal clergy to the General Assembly of the Presbyterians anno M.DC.XC.II. From the sinistruous and false constructions put upon it, by the enemies of that order : but more especially of that particular address, given in by Mr. Robert Irving minister of Towie, and Mr. John Forbes minister of Kincardine ; in name of, and by commission from, their brethren, the ministers of the synod of Aberdeen : they being expressly reflected upon, and named by [James Hadow] the author of the Remarks upon the case of the Episcopal clergy. [By Robert IRVING.]

Printed, in the year M.DCC.IV. Quarto. Pp. 40.* [*Adv. Lib.*]

VINDICATION (a) of the Answer to some late papers concerning the unity and authority of the Catholick Church, and the reformation of the Church of

England. [By Edward STILLING-FLEET, D.D.]

London, MDCLXXXVII. Quarto.* [*Jones' Peck*, i. 16.]

VINDICATION (a) of the Answer to the Humble remonstrance, from the uniust imputations of frivolousnesse and falsehood : wherein the cause of liturgy and episcopacy is further debated, by the same Smectymnuus. [Stephen MARSHALL, Edmund CALAMY, Thomas YOUNG, Matthew NEWCOMEN and William SPURSTOWE.]

Printed in the yeare. 1641. Quarto.*

VINDICATION (a) of the Answer to the Popish address presented to the ministers of the Church of England. In reply to a pamphlet abusively intituled, A clear proof of the certainty and usefulness of the Protestant rule of faith, &c. [By John WILLIAMS, D.D.]

London : MDCLXXXVIII. Quarto. Pp. 41.* [*Jones' Peck*, ii. 316.]

VINDICATION (a) of the Apamean medal : and of the inscription ΝΩΕ. Together with an illustration of another coin struck at the same place, in honour of the Emperor Severus. By the author of the Analysis of ancient mythology. [Jacob BRYANT.]

London : 1775. Quarto. [*W.*]

VINDICATION (a) of the authenticity of the narratives contained in the first two chapters of the Gospels of St. Matthew & St. Luke; being an investigation of objections urged by the Unitarian editors of the improved version of the New Testament : with an appendix, containing strictures on the variations between the first and fourth editions of that work. By a layman. [John BEVAN.]

London : 1822. Octavo.* [*Smith's Cat. of Friends' books*, i. 91. *Horne's Introduction.*]

VINDICATION (a) of the authority of Christian princes over ecclesiastical synods from the exceptions made against it by Mr Hill. [By —— TURNER.]

London : 1701. Octavo.

VINDICATION (a) of the Bishop of Condom's Exposition of the doctrine of the Catholic Church. In answer to a book [by W. Wake] entituled, An exposition of the doctrine of the Church of England, etc. With a letter from the said Bishop. [By Joseph JOHNSTON.] Permissu superiorum.

London, 1686. Quarto. Pp. 122.* [*Jones' Peck*, i. 113.

VINDICATION (a) of the Brief discourse concerning the Notes of the Church. In answer to a late pamphlet, entituled, The use and great moment of the Notes of the Church, as delivered by Cardinal Bellarmin, De Notis Ecclesiæ, justified. [By William SHERLOCK.]

London ; MDCLXXXVII. Quarto.*

VINDICATION (a) of the British colonies, against the aspersions of the Halifax gentleman, in his letter to a Rhode-Island friend. [By James OTIS.]

Boston : 1765. Octavo. Pp. 32.* Reprinted with author's name, 1769.

VINDICATION of the ca'endar tables and rules annexed to the Act for regulating the commencement of the year, and correcting the calendar, against the objections made to it, with respect to the time appointed for the celebration of Easter-day. To which is added a more full account of that Act ; written whilst it was depending in the House of Commons. [By Peter DAVAL.]

1761. Quarto. [*Nichols, Lit. Anec.*, ii. 372. *Mon. Rev.*, xxiv. 468.]

VINDICATION (a) of the Case of indifferent things, used in the worship of God: in answer to a book, intituled, The case of indifferent things used in the worship of God, examined, stated on the behalf of the dissenters, and calmly argued. [By John WILLIAMS, D.D.]

London, 1684. Quarto. Pp. 57.*

VINDICATION (a) of the Character of a Popish successor : in a reply to two pretended answers to it. By the author of the Character. [John PHILLIPS.]

London : 1681. Folio. Pp. 15.* [*Bodl.*]

VINDICATION of the character of the late Right Hon. William Pitt, from the calumnies against him contained in the fifth article of the Edinburgh Review for April, 1810. [By James WALKER.]

Edinburgh : 1810. Octavo. [*N. and Q.*, 28 *June* 1862.]

VINDICATION (a) of the Church and clergy of England, from some late reproaches rudely and unjustly cast upon them. [By White KENNETT, D.D.]

London: 1709. Octavo. Pp. vi. b. t. 120.* [*Bodl.*]

VINDICATION (a) of the Church and clergy of England from the misrepresentations of the Edinburgh Review. By a beneficed clergyman. [Henry SOAMES, M.A., Dean of St. Paul's.]

London: 1823. Octavo.* [*Crockford's Clerical Directory.*]

VINDICATION (a) of the Church of England from the aspersions of a late libel, intituled, Priestcraft in perfection, &c. Wherein the controverted clause of the Church's power in the xxth Article is shewn to be of equal authority with all the rest of the Articles; and the fraud and forgery, charged upon the clergy on the account of that clause, are retorted upon their accusers. With a preface containing some remarks upon the Reflections on that pamphlet. By a priest of the church of England. [Hilkiah BEDFORD.]

London: 1710. Octavo.*

VINDICATION (a) of the Church of England from the foul aspersions of schism and heresie unjustly cast upon her by the Church of Rome. [By Michael ALTHAM.] Part I. [and II.]

London, MDCLXXXVII. Quarto.* [*Jones' Peck*, i. 168.]

VINDICATION (a) of the Church of England, in answer to Mr. Peirce's Vindication of the dissenters. Wherein abundance of historical mistakes are rectified; several groundess calumnies thrown upon the most worthy and deserving prelates of our Church, refuted; and many Fathers of the most primitive ages of Christianity clear'd from misrepresentations. In two parts. By a presbyter of the Church of England. [Zachary GREY, LL.D., vicar of St. Peter's and Giles', Cambridge.]

London, 1720. Octavo.* [*Bodl.*] Each part has a separate title and pagination.

VINDICATION (a) of the Church of Scotland. Being an answer to a paper, intituled, Some questions concerning episcopal and presbyterial government in Scotland. Wherein the latter is vindicated from the arguments and calumnies of that author; and the former is made appear to be a stranger in that nation. By a minister of the Church of Scotland, as it is now established by law. [Gilbert RULE.]

London, 1691. Quarto.* [*Adv. Lib.*]

VINDICATION (a) of the "Clanronald of Glengary" against the attacks made upon them in the Inverness Journal and some recent printed performances. With remarks as to the descent of the family who style themselves "of Clanronald." [By John RIDDELL.]

Edinburgh 1821. Octavo. Pp. 97. xxx.*

VINDICATION (a) of the clergy, from the contempt imposed upon them by [John Eachard] the author of The grounds and occasions of the contempt of the clergy and religion. [By John BRAMHALL, Bishop of Derry.]

London: 1686. Octavo. Pp. 13. b. t. 135.* [*Bodl.*] "First edit. of this came out in 1672. Oct. at Lond."—MS. note by Wood.

VINDICATION (a) of the conforming clergy from the unjust aspersions of heresie, &c. In answer to some part of M. Jenkyn's funeral sermon upon Dr. Seaman. With short reflexions on some passages in a sermon preached by Mr. J. s. upon 2. Cor. 5. 20. In a letter to a friend. [By Robert GROVE, D.D.]

London, 1676. Quarto. Pp. 74. b. t.* [*Bodl.*]

VINDICATION (a) of the convention lately concluded between Great Britain and Russia, in six letters. Addressed to —— —— [By Charles JENKINSON, Earl of Liverpool.]

London: 1801. Octavo. Pp. 124. b. t.*

VINDICATION (a) of the deprived bishops, asserting their spiritual rights against a lay-deprivation, against the charge of schism, as managed by the late editors of an anonymous Baroccian MS. In two parts. I. Shewing, that though the instances collected in the said MS. had been pertinent to the editors design, yet that would not have been sufficient for obtaining their cause. II. Shewing, that the instances there collected are indeed not pertinent to the editors design, for vindicating the validity of the deprivation of spiritual power by a lay-authority. To which is subjoined the latter end of the said MS. omitted by the editors, making against them and the cause espoused by them. In Greek and English. [By Henry DODWELL.]

London, 1692. Quarto.*

VINDICATION (a) of the divine attributes. In some remarks on his Grace [W. King] the Archbishop of Dublin's

sermon, intituled, Divine predestination and foreknowledg consistent with the freedom of man's will. [By John EDWARDS, D.D.]

London, M.DCC.X. Octavo. Pp. 38.*

VINDICATION (a) of the Divine perfections, illustrating the glory of God in them, by reason and revelation: methodically digested into several meditations. By a person of honour. [James DALRYMPLE, 1st. Viscount of Stair.]

London, M DC XCV. Octavo.*
The preface is signed W. Bates, J. Howe, the editors.

VINDICATION (a) of the doctrine of grace, from the charge of antinomianism: contained in a letter to a minister of the gospel [Ralph Erskine]. [By James HOG.]

Edinburgh: M.DCC.XVIII. Octavo. Pp. 24.* Signed I. II.

VINDICATION (a) of the doctrine of the Trinity from the exceptions of a late pamphlet entituled An essay on spirit &c. By a divine of the Church of England. [Thomas RANDOLPH, D.D.] Part I.

Oxford, M DCC LIII. Octavo.* [Darling, Cyclop. Bibl.]
Part II. was also published in 1753, and part III. in 1754. The name of the author is given in the Appendix, which also appeared in 1754.

VINDICATION (a) of the ecclesiastical part of Sir James Dalrymple's Historical Collections: in answer to a late pamphlet [by John Gillane], intituled, The life of the Reverend Mr. John Sage, &c. Wherein some things are added towards the clearing the ancient government of the Church of Scotland from the mistakes of a late author. Together with a defence of what Sir James hath advanced concerning the opinion of the Scottish historians in relation to King Robert the Second's marriage with Elizabeth Muir, in answer to Mr. John Sage his criticism on that subject in his introduction to Hawthornden's works. [By Sir James DALRYMPLE, Bart., of Borthwick.]

Edinburgh, 1714. Octavo. Pp. 5. b. t. 73.* [D. Laing.]

VINDICATION (a) of the Enquiry into charitable abuses, with an exposure of the misrepresentations . . . in the Quarterly Review . . . [By Henry Bellenden KERR.]

London: 1819. Octavo. Pp. 129. [Manchester Free Lib. Cat.]

VINDICATION (a) of the Faithful rebuke to a false report against the rude cavils of the pretended Defence. [By Vincent ALSOP.]

London: 1698. Octavo. Pp. 152.*
The Report and Defence were written by Stephen Lobb.

VINDICATION (a) of the Faults on both sides, from the reflections of the Medley, the Specimen-maker, and a pamphlet, [by Joseph Trapp] entituled, Most faults on one side. With a dissertation on the nature and use of money and paper-credit in trade, and the true value of joint-stocks, maintaining the assertions of the author, in relation to those matters. By the author of the Faults on both sides. [Richard HARLEY.]

London: 1710. Octavo. Pp. 43.*
"Faults on both sides" has been ascribed to Defoe, and to Clements, secretary to the Earl of Peterborough, as well as to Harley. —Note in Adv. Lib. Cat.

VINDICATION (a) of the freedom &. lawfulness of the late General Assembly begun at St. Andrews, and continued at Dundee; in answer to the reasons alledged against the same in the Protestation and Declinatore given in at St. Andrews, and in another paper contrived since, and spread abroad amongst such as were conceived more inclinable to follow that way, but kept up from others. Now published by a lover of the Church of Scotland for preventing and removing prejudices and misrepresentations which some emissaries have endeavoured to possesse us with here, who are strangers to the true estate of the late differences there, by dispersing papers against the judicatories of that Church, and disseminating calumnies against their brethren and countrymen. [By James WOOD, Professor at St. Andrews.]

London, printed in the year 1652. Quarto. Pp. 49. b. t.* [D. Laing.]

VINDICATION (a) of the Friendly conference between a minister and a parishioner of his, inclining unto Quakerism, from the exceptions of Thomas Ellwood, in his pretended Answer to the said conference. By the same author. [Thomas FOWLER, D.D.]

London: 1678. Octavo. 21½ sh. [Smith, Bib. Anti-Quaker., p. 21.]

VINDICATION (a) of the Fundamental charter of presbytery [by Sage] from the exceptions of [John Anderson] the contry-man in his letter to [R. Calder] a curate. Wherein these queries are considered : I. Whether it was the constant and uniform practice of our reformers to join in the communion of the Church of England, when they had occasion? II. Whether our reformers, in their public deeds, openly and solemnly professed, that they were of one communion with the Church of England? III. Whether the English liturgy was used in Scotland, for several years, by our reformers? By a true son of the afflicted Church of Scotland. [John GILLAN.]

Edinburgh : 1713. Octavo.*

VINDICATION (a) of the government, doctrine, and worship, of the Church of England, established in the reign of Queen Elizabeth : against the injurious reflections of Mr. Neale, in his late History of the Puritans. Together with a detection of many false quotations and mistakes in that performance. [By Isaac MADOX, D.D.]

London: MDCCXXXIII. Octavo. Pp. 362. b. t.*

VINDICATION of the Hindoos from the aspersions of the Rev. Claudius Buchanan, M.A. ; with a refutation of the arguments exhibited in his Memoir on the expediency of an ecclesiastical establishment for British India, and the ultimate civilization of the natives by their conversion to Christianity. Also remarks on an address from the missionaries in Bengal to the natives of India, condemning their errors, and inviting them to become Christians. The whole tending to evince the excellence of the moral system of the Hindoos, and the danger of interfering with their customs and religion. By a Bengal officer. [Charles STUART.]

London: 1808. Octavo. Pp. 171. [*Gent. Mag.*, cii. ii. 194. *Mon. Rev.*, lvii. 109.]

VINDICATION (a) of the Historiographer of the University of Oxford, and his works, from the reproaches of the Lord Bishop of Salisbury [Gilbert Burnet] in his Letter to [Lloyd] the Lord Bishop of Coventry and Litchfield, concerning a book lately published, called, A specimen of some errors and defects in the History of the reformation of the Church of England, by Anthony Harmer [*i.e.* Henry Wharton]. Written by, E. D. To

which is added the Historiographer's Answer to certain animadversions made in the before-mentioned History of the reformation, to that part of Historia & antiquitates universitatis Oxon, which treats of the divorce of Queen Catherine from King Henry the Eighth. [By Dr. Thomas WOOD, of New College, Oxford.]

London, MDCXCIII. Quarto. Pp. 30.* [*Wood, Athen. Oxon.*, i. cxiv. note.]

Ascribed to James Harington. [*Upcott*, p. 1089.]

VINDICATION (a) of the history of the Gunpowder-treason, and of the proceedings and matters relating thereunto, from the exceptions which have been made against it, and more especially of late years by the author of the Catholic apology, and others. To which is added, a parallel betwixt that, and the present Popish plot. [By John WILLIAMS, D.D.]

London, 1681. Quarto. Pp. 2. b. t. 95. i.* [*Bodl.*]

Ascribed to Gilbert Burnet, D.D. [*Mendham Collection Cat.*, p. 51.]

VINDICATION (of the history of the Septuagint from the misrepresentations of the learned Scaliger, Dupin, Dr. Hody, Dr. Prideaux, and other modern criticks. [By Charles HAYES.]

London : M.DCC.XXXVI. Octavo. Pp. v. b. t. 174.* [*Orme, Bib. Bib. Nichols, Lit. Anec.*, ii. 323. *Lowndes, Brit. Lib.*]

This work has been attributed to Sir Richard Ellys, Bart.

VINDICATION (a) of the honour and justice of Parliament against a most scandalous libel entitled the Speech of John A—— Esq. [By Daniel DEFOE.]

London : N.D. [1721.] 2 leaves, pp. 36. [*Lee's Defoe*, 209.]

VINDICATION (a) of the honour of King Charles I. against the prodigious calumnies of the regicide, Ludlow, publisht in what he calls A letter from Major-General Ludlow, to Sir E. S. [By Edmund ELYS.]

Printed in the year, 1691. Octavo. Pp. 14. b. t.* [*Bodl.*]

Author's name in the handwriting of Wood.

VINDICATION (a) of the imprisoned and secluded members of the House of Commons, from the aspersions cast upon them, and the maiority of the House, in a paper lately printed and published : entituled, An humble answer to the generall councel of the officers of the army under his Excellency Thomas Lord Fairfax, to the

demands of the Honourable Commons of England in parliament assembled : concerning the late securing or secluding some members thereof. [By William PRYNNE.]

London, 1649. Quarto. Pp. 34.*
[Pagination erroneous; dupl. of 24, 25, 29, 30.]

VINDICATION (a) of the king's sovereign rights : together with a justification of his royal exercise thereof, in all causes, and over all persons ecclesiastical (as well as by consequence) over all ecclesiastical bodies corporate, and cathedrals: more particularly applyed to the King's Free Chappel and Church of Sarum. Upon occasion of the Dean of Sarum's Narrative and Collections, made by the order and command of the most noble and most honourable the Lords Commissioners, appointed by the King's Majesty for ecclesiastical promotions. By way of reply unto the answer of the Lord Bishop of Sarum, presented to the aforesaid most honourable Lords. The first part. Printed only to save the labour of transcribing several copies, and to prevent the mistakes thereby apt to be incurr'd, and meerly for the satisfaction of private friends, who either want or desire a most impartial information of that affair. [By Thomas PIERCE, Dean of Salisbury.]

London, 1683. Folio. Pp. 2. b. t. 44.*
[Bodl.]

VINDICATION (a) of the late Archbishop Sancroft, and of his brethren the rest of the depriv'd bishops, from the reflections of Mr. Marshal in his Defence of our constitution in Church and State : particularly with regard to their refusing to publish an abhorrence of the Prince of Orange's invasion ; their meeting at Guild-Hall, and their endeavours for a regency. In a letter to a friend. [By Hilkiah BEDFORD.]

London, 1717. Octavo.*

VINDICATION (a) of the late House of Commons, in rejecting the Bill for confirming the eighth and ninth articles of the treaty of navigation and commerce between England and France. By a citizen. [John EGLETON.]

London: 1714. Octavo. [W., Brit. Mus.]

VINDICATION (a) of [Lord King] the learned and honourable author of The history of the Apostles Creed, from the false sentiment, which Mr. Simson has injuriously imputed to him. [By James HADOW, D.D.]

Edinburgh, M.DCC.XXXI. Octavo.* [Adv. Lib.]

VINDICATION (a) of the Letter out of the North concerning Bp. Lake's declaration of his dying in the belief of passive obedience, &c. [By —— EYRE.]

London: 1690. Quarto.

VINDICATION (a) of the licensed chapels in Scotland : being an answer to the objections exhibited against them, in a Letter addressed to the Reverend Mr. Grant at Edinburgh. By Philanthropos. [James GRANT.]

Edinburgh, 1749. Octavo. Pp. 46.* [D. Laing.]

VINDICATION (a) of the literal sense of three miracles of Christ : I. His turning water into wine ; II. His whipping the buyers and sellers out of the Temple ; III. His exorcising the devils out of two men ; against the objections of Thos. Woolston. [By Benjamin Andrews ATKINSON.]

London: 1729. Octavo. [Cat. Lib. Trin. Coll. Dub., p. 145.]

VINDICATION (a) of the literary character of the late Professor Porson, from the animadversions of the Right Reverend Thomas Burgess, D.D. F.R.S. F.A.S. P.R.S.L. Lord Bishop of Salisbury, in various publications on 1 John v. 7. By Crito Cantabrigiensis. [Thomas TURTON, D.D.]

Cambridge: 1827. Octavo.* [N. and Q., 28 April 1860, p. 332.]

VINDICATION (a) of the Lord Bishop of Ely's visitatorial jurisdiction over Trinity-College in general, and over the Master thereof [Bentley] in particular. [By John COLBATCH, D.D.]

London : MDCCXXXII. Quarto. Pp. 44.* [Bodl.]

VINDICATION (a) of the ministers and ruling elders of the Church of Scotland who have taken the abjuration ; wherein it is made evident, that they are not thereby engaged in their stations to oblige the successor when he comes to the crown, to join in communion with the Church of England, as some ignorant people are made to believe. [By Alexander LAUDER, minister at Mordentoun.]

Edinburgh, 1712. Quarto.* [Adv. Lib.]

VINDICATION of the ministers of the Church of Scotland, who have

prayed for the Queen by name, notwithstanding the order in Council on that subject. By a presbyterian. [Thomas M'CRIE, D.D.] The second edition.

Edinburgh : 1820. Octavo.*

Ascribed also to Andrew Thomson, D.D.

VINDICATION (a) of the ministers of the Gospel in, and about London, from the unjust aspersions cast upon their former actings for the Parliament, as if they had promoted the bringing of the king to capitall punishment. With a short exhortation to their people to keep close to their covenant-ingagement. [By Cornelius BURGES.]

London, 1648. Quarto.*

VINDICATION (a) of the Miscellanea Analytica : in answer to a late pamphlet entitled Observations, &c. [By John WILSON, M.A., St. Peter's College, Cambridge.]

Cambridge, M.DCC.IX. Octavo. Pp. 22.*

VINDICATION (a) of the modern history of Hindostan, from the gross misrepresentations, and illiberal strictures of the Edinburgh reviewers, by the author. [Thomas MAURICE.]

London : 1805. Octavo. Pp. 88. b. t.*

VINDICATION (a) of the New theory of the earth from the exceptions of Mr. Keill and others. With an historical preface of the occasions of the discoveries therein contained : and some corrections and additions. [By William WHISTON.]

London : 1698. Octavo. Pp. 10. b. t. 52.*

VINDICATION (a) of the nine reasons of the House of Commons, against the votes of bishops in parliament : or, a reply to the Answers made [by John Williams, Abp. of York] to the said reasons, in defence of such votes. [By Cornelius BURGES.] Printed by order of a Committee, of the Honourable House of Commons, now assembled in Parliament.

London, 1641. Quarto.*

The above is the same as "An Humble examination of a printed abstract of the answers &c.," q.v.

VINDICATION (a) of the opposition to the late intended bill for the relief of Roman Catholics in Scotland ; in which an address to the people on that subject, by the Reverend Dr Campbell, Principal of Marischal College, Aberdeen, is

particularly considered. [By John ERSKINE, D.D.]

Edinburgh: MDCCLXXX. Octavo. Pp. 53.*

VINDICATION (a) of the ordinations of the Church of England. In which it is demonstrated that all the essentials of ordination, according to the practice of the primitive and Greek Churches, are still retained in our Church. In answer to a paper written by one of the Church of Rome to prove the nullity of our Orders ; and given to a person of quality. [By Gilbert BURNET, D.D.] The second edition.

London : MDCLXXXVIII. Quarto. Pp. xxviii. b. t. 94.* The first edition, 1677, has the author's name on the title-page.

VINDICATION (a) of the Oxford Reply to two discourses [by Abraham Woodhead] there printed 1687; concerning the adoration of our blessed Saviour in the Eucharist, from the exceptions made to it in the second appendix [by Obadiah Walker] to a compendious discourse on the Eucharist [by Abraham Woodhead], published from the same press. [By Henry ALDRICH, D.D.]

N. P. N. D. Quarto. Pp. 91. [Jones' Peck, p. 359.]

VINDICATION (a) of the people of God, called Quakers ; directed unto Roger Boyle, called Earl of Orrery. Charles Coote, called Earl of Mountrath. Theophilus Jones, called Sir Theophilus Jones. Being an ansvver to a book, dedicated to them, by one George Pressick of Dublin. In which book many lyes and calumnies are presented against the innocent people of God. And this is for the clearing of the truth, that no lye may rest upon it ; and for the satisfaction of all sober people in Ireland, and elsewhere. With a word of good advice to the chief governours there. By E. B. [Edward BURROUGH.]

London, N. D. Quarto. Pp. 24.*

VINDICATION (a) of the Presbyterian ministers in the North of Ireland ; subscribers and non-subscribers : from many gross and groundless aspersions cast upon them, in a late scandalous libel, entituled, An account of the mind of the Synod at Belfast 1721. in a short reply to Mr. Dugud's remarks upon their declaration. By a sincere lover of truth and peace. [James KIRKPATRICK.] Published and recommended by Victor Ferguson, M.D.

Belfast: MDCC.XXI. Octavo. Pp. 82.*

VINDICATION (a) of the primitive Church, and diocesan episcopacy: in answer to Mr. Baxter's Church history of bishops, and the councils abridged: as also to some part of his Treatise of episcopacy. [By Henry MAURICE, D.D.]

London, 1682. Octavo. Pp. 64. b. t. 567.* [*Watt, Bib. Brit.* [*Orme's Life of Baxter*, ii. 383.]

VINDICATION (a) of the principles of the author of the answer to the compiler of the Nubes Testium from the charge of popery. In answer to a late pretended letter from a dissenter to the divines of the Church of England. [By Rev. Edward GEE, rector of St. Benedict, Paul's Wharf, London.]

London, 1688. Quarto.* [*Darling, Cyclop. Bibl.*]

VINDICATION (a) of the proceedings against the six members of E[dmund] Hall, Oxford. By a gentleman of the University. [William BROWNE.]

London: MDCCLXVIII. Octavo. Pp. 16. b. t.* [*Bodl.*]

VINDICATION (a) of the proceedings of his Majesties ecclesiastical commissioners against [Hen. Compton] the Bishop of London, and the Fellows of Magdalen College. [By Henry CARE.]

London, MDCLXXXVIII. Quarto.*

VINDICATION (a) of the proceedings of some members of the Lower House of the last Convocation, with relation to the archbishop's prorogation of it upon the eighth of May. In a letter to the publisher of the Late narrative of the proceedings of that House about adjournments. [By Charles TRIMNELL.]

[London:] 1702. Quarto. Pp. 8.* [*Bodl.*]

VINDICATION (a) of the proceedings of the Edinburgh Bible Society, relative to the Apocrypha, against the aspersions of the "Eclectic Review;" in a letter to the members of the commitee of the parent institution. [By James HALDANE.]

London: M.DCCC.XXV. Octavo. Pp. 35. [*Brit. Mus.*]

VINDICATION (a) of the proceedings of the late Parliament of England, An. Dom. 1689. Being the first in the reign of their present Majesties King William and Queen Mary. [By John, Lord SOMERS.]

London, 1690. Quarto. Pp. 25. b. t.*

VINDICATION (a) of the proceedings of the University of Oxford, against the allegations of an act of the council of the city of Oxford, dated Sept. 6. 1703. By a private hand. [Thomas WOOD, D.C.L.]

No separate title-page. Quarto. Pp. 7.* [*Bodl.*]

VINDICATION (a) of the Protestant doctrine concerning Justification, and and of its preachers and professors, from the unjust charge of Antinomianism. In a letter from a minister in the city, to a minister in the countrey. [By Robert TRAILL, M.A.]

London: 1692. Quarto. Pp. 42. b. t.* [*Aberdeen Lib.*]

VINDICATION (a) of the real Reformation-principles of the Church of Scotland concerning separation, &c. In which the Essay on separation is vindicated; and the arguments of the Reverend Mr. Wilson, for separation from this Established Church, in his Defence, are considered, where sundry Anti-Reformation principles, historical errors, &c., in that Defence, are noticed; and many things, neither truth, nor matter of fact in the Testimony of the seceding brethren, are discovered and collected. To which, in an appendix, a further argument against separation, taken from the conduct of the famous martyr Mr. James Guthric, and other Protesters in his day, is largely insisted on. By the author of the Essay on separation. [John CURRIE.]

Edinburgh, MDCCXL. Octavo. Pp. xiv. 8. 360.* [*New Coll. Cat.*] Address to the reader signed J. C.

VINDICATION (a) of the realm, and Church of England, from the charge of perjury, rebellion, & schism, unjustly laid upon them by the non-jurors: and the rebellion and schism shewn to lie at their own doors. [By William WAKE.]

London: MDCCXVI. Octavo. Pp. 68.* *Darling, Cyclop. Bibl.*]

VINDICATION (a) of the Reasonableness of Christianity, &c. from Mr. Edwards's Reflections. [By John LOCKE.]

London: 1695. Octavo. Pp. 40.* [*Brit. Mus.*]

VINDICATION (a) of the Reasons and Defence, &c. Part I. Being a reply to the first part of No sufficient reason

[by Spinckes] for restoring some prayers and directions of King Edward VI's first liturgy. By the author of Reasons and Defence. [Jeremy COLLIER.]

London: MDCCXVIII. Octavo.*

———. Part II. Being a reply to the second part of No sufficient reason for restoring some prayers and directions of King Edward VI's first liturgy. By the author of the Reasons and Defence. [Jeremy COLLIER.]

London: 1719. Octavo.*

VINDICATION (a) of the religious and civil principles of the Irish Catholics, in a letter, addressed to his Excellency the Marquis Wellesley, K.G. Lord Lieutenant General, and General Governor of Ireland, &c. &c. Second edition. By J. K. L. [James Warren DOYLE, Roman Catholic Bishop of Kildare and Leighlin.] Author of "Letters to his Grace the Protestant Archbishop of Dublin," of "Essays on domestic nomination," &c. &c.

Dublin: 1823. Octavo.*

VINDICATION (a) of the Remarks upon Mr. Cha. Leslie's First Dialogue on the Socinian controversy. [By Thomas EMLYN.]

No separate title-page. Quarto. Pp. 8.*

VINDICATION (a) of the Reverend Dr. Henry Sacheverell, from the false, scandalous, and malicious aspersions cast upon him in a late infamous pamphlet, entitled, The modern fanatick [by William Bisset]. Intended chiefly to expose the iniquity of the faction in general, without taking any considerable notice of their poor mad tool B—t in particular. In a dialogue between a Tory and a Wh—g. [By William LAMBE.]

London: N. D. Octavo. Pp. 5. b. t. 99.* This tract is also attributed to William King, LL.D., who appears only to have had a share in it. Lambe owns it as being principally his own in his "Possibility of leaving the Tories."—Note in Bodl. Cat.

VINDICATION (a) of the Rev. Mr. Wesley's last minutes: occasioned by a circular, printed letter, inviting principal persons, both clergy and laity, as well of the dissenters as of the established Church, who disapprove of those minutes, to oppose them in a body, as a dreadful heresy; and designed to remove prejudice, check rashness, promote forbearance,

defend the character of an eminent minister of Christ, and prevent some important Scriptural truths from being hastily branded as heretical. In five letters, to the Hon. and Rev. author [Walter Shirley] of the Circular letter. By a lover of quietness and liberty of conscience. [John William FLETCHER.] Bristol: 1771. Duodecimo. Pp. 98.* [Gent. Mag., lvi. 29.] Letters signed J. F.

VINDICATION (a) of the Right Reverend the Lord Bishop of Exeter [Dr. Blackall], occasioned by Mr. Benjamin Hoadly's reflections on his Lordship's two sermons Of government, preached in St. Dunstan's church, March 8, 1704. And before her Majesty, March 8, 1708. [By William OLDISWORTH.] London: 1709. Octavo. Pp. 87.* [Bodl.]

VINDICATION (a) of the Right Reverend the Ld. Bishop of Norwich, from the undeserved reflections of the Reverend Mr. John Johnson, in his book entituled The unbloody sacrifice and altar unvailed and supported. Wherein is shewn how groundless and unreasonable this Reverend man's exceptions and complaints are, and how little service he has done himself by them. In a letter to the Reverend Mr. Johnson. By a Christian. [John LEWIS, D.D., Vicar of Margate.]

London: N. D. Octavo. Pp. 23.* [Bodl.]

VINDICATION (a) of the Right Reverend the Lord Bishop of Winchester, against the malicious aspersions of those who uncharitably ascribe the book, intituled, A plain account of the nature and end of the Sacrament of the Lord's Supper, to his Lordship. By the author of the Proposal for the revival of Christianity. [Philip SKELTON, rector of Fintona, Ireland.]

Dublin printed, London, reprinted, MDCCXXXVI. Octavo. Pp. 71.*

VINDICATION (a) of the rights of men, in a letter to the Right Honourable Edmund Burke; occasioned by his Reflections on the Revolution in France. [By Mary WOOLSTONECRAFT.]

London: 1790. Octavo. [W.]

VINDICATION (a) of the Roman Catholicks of the English nation, from some aspersions lately cast upon them. In a letter from a Protestant gentleman in the country, to a citizen of London. [By R. CARON.]

London, 1660. Quarto.* [Bibliotheca Grenvilliana, i. 117.]

VINDICATION (a) of the royal martyr King Charles I. from the Irish massacre in the year 1641, cast upon him in the "Life of Richard Baxter," wrote by himself, and since in the "Abridgement" by Edmund Calamy : being a case of present concern. In a letter to a member of the House of Commons. [By Rev. Thomas CARTE.] Second edition.

1704. [*Cat. Lond. Inst.*, ii. 320.]

VINDICATION (a) of the Scotish Presbyterians & Covenanters, against the aspersions of the author of " Tales of my landlord." By a member of the Scotish bar. [James GRAHAME.]

Glasgow, 1817. Octavo. Pp. 32.*

VINDICATION (a) of the Scottish Covenanters : consisting of a review of the first series of the " Tales of my landlord," extracted from the Christian Instructor for 1817. [By Thomas M'CRIE, D.D.] With an appendix, containing various extracts, illustrative of the principles and character of the Reformers.

Glasgow, 1824. Duodecimo.*

VINDICATION (a) of the scripture doctrine of original sin from Mr Taylor's Free and candid examination of it. [By Rev. David JENNINGS, D.D.]

London: 1740. Octavo. Pp. vi. 130. [*Darling, Cyclop. Bibl.*]

VINDICATION (a) of the Short history of the Corporation and Test Acts. [By Capel LOFFT.]

London: M.DCC.XC. Octavo. Pp. 35. b. t.* [*Bodl.*]

VINDICATION (a) of the Surey demoniack as no impostor: or, a reply to a certain pamphlet publish'd by Mr. Zach. Taylor, called The Surey impostor. With a further clearing and confirming of the truth as to Richard Dugdale's case and cure. By T. J. [Thomas JOLLY] one of the ministers who attended upon that affair from first to last : but replies only as to matter of fact, and as he therewithal is more especially concerned. To which is annexed a brief narrative of the Surey demoniack, drawn up by the same author, for the satisfaction of such who have not seen the former narrative.

London, 1698. Quarto. Pp. 32.* [*Bodl.*]

VINDICATION (a) of the Theory of Mahometanism unveiled, against the strictures of a writer in No. XIII. of the British Critic, and Quarterly Theological Review. In a letter to the Rev. Hugh James Rose, B.D., Christian Advocate in the University of Cambridge. [By the Rev. Charles FORSTER, author of the work.] Not published.

[London :] 1830. Octavo. [*IV., Martin's Cat.*]

VINDICATION (a) of the Treatise of monarchy, containing an answer to Dr. Fernes reply; also a more full discovery of three maine points; 1. The ordinance of God in supremacie. 2. The nature and kinds of limitation. 3. The causes and meanes of limitation in governments. Done by the authour of the former treatise. [Philip HUNTON.]

London, M.DC.XLIV. Quarto.*

VINDICATION (a) of the Twenty third Article of the Church of England, from a late exposition, ascribed to my Lord Bishop of Sarum. [By William THORNTON, of Hart-Hall.]

London: 1702. Quarto. Pp. 26. b. t.* [*Bodl.*]
Ascribed also to Bernard de Mandeville, and to Robert Burscough.

VINDICATION (a) of the worship of the Lord Jesus Christ, on the Unitarian principles : in answer to what is said on that head by Mr. Jos. Boyse, in his Vindication of the Deity of Jesus Christ. [By Thomas EMLYN.] Note the references are made to the 4to. edition of Mr. B's book.

N. P. M.DCC.V. Quarto.*

VINDICATION (a) of their Majesties authority to fill the sees of the deprived bishops ; in a letter out of the country. Occasioned by Dr. B—— [Beveridge]'s refusal of the bishoprick of Bath and Wells. [By Edward STILLINGFLEET, D.D.]

London : MDCXCI. Quarto. Pp. 27.*

VINDICATION (a) of those who take the oath of allegiance to his present Majestie from perjurie, injustice, and disloyaltie, charged upon them but such as are against it ; wherein is evidently shewed that the common good of a nation is what is primarily and principally respected in an oath, and therefore when the oath is inconsistent with that, the persons who have taken it, are absolved from it ; in proving of which the case of Maud and King Stephen is particularly consider'd. In

a letter to a non-juror. [By Thomas HEARNE.]

1731. Octavo. [*W.*] Preface to the Reader by —— Bilstone, M.A., of All Souls.

VINDICIÆ Academiarum containing, some briefe animadversions upon Mr. Webster's book, stiled, The examination of academies. Together with an appendix concerning what M. Hobbs, and M. Dell have published on this argument. [By Seth WARD.]

Oxford, 1654. Quarto. Pp. 65.* [*Wood, Athen. Oxon.*, iv. 249.]
The tract is signed H. D. being the final letters of the author's names. There is a wood-cut on the title-page. Prefatory epistle signed N. S. John Wilkins [finals] of Wadham College.
The prefatory epistle has been assigned to Nathaniel Stephens.

VINDICIÆ Biblicæ; a series of notices and elucidations of passages in the Old and New Testament, which have been the subject of attack and misrepresentation by deistical writers. [By David WALTHER.]
London: 1832. Octavo. [*Horne's Introduction*, v. 424. *Lowndes, Brit Lib.*, p. 314.]

VINDICIÆ Britannicæ: being strictures on a late pamphlet by Gilbert Wakefield, A.B. late Fellow of Jesus College, Cambridge, intitled, "The spirit of Christianity compared with the spirit of the times in Great Britain. By an undergraduate. [William PENN, descendant of the Quaker.]
1794. Octavo. Pp. 66. [*Gent. Mag.*, June 1863. p. 800. *Mon. Rev.*, xv. 225.]

VINDICIÆ Calvinisticæ: or some impartial reflections on the Dean of Londonderry's Considerations, and Mr. Chancellor King's Answer thereto, in which he no less unjustly than impertinently reflects on the Protestant dissenters. In a letter to a friend, by W. B., D.D. [Joseph BOYSE.]
Dublin: 1688. Quarto. [*Jones' Peck*, i. 155.]
Published among Boyse's Works, ii. 45.]

VINDICIÆ Carolinæ: or, a defence of Ἐικων Βασιλικὴ. the portraicture of his sacred Majesty in his solitudes and sufferings. In reply to a book intituled Ἐικονοκλαστής, written by Mr. Milton, and lately re-printed at Amsterdam. [By Richard HOLLINGWORTH, D.D.]

London, MDCXCII. Octavo. Pp. 12. b. t. 141.* [*Lowndes, Bibliog. Man.*, p. 723.]

Ascribed to John Wilson, author of a Treatise on necromancy. [*W., Brit. Mus.*]

VINDICIÆ contra tyrannos; a defence of liberty against tyrants; or of the awfull power of the prince over the people, and of the people over the prince; being a treatise written in Latin and French by Junius Brutus [Hubert LANGUET] and translated out of both into English [by William WALKER].
London: 1648, 1689. Quarto.
"The original of this work has been attributed to Theodore Beza. M'Crie in his Life of Andrew Melville, vol. 1. p. 424, says that this work resembles Hotman's Franco Gallia, and that Languet's work is properly only an enlargement of Beza's supprest work, De Jure Magistruum, and although more guarded yet is still far from evasive in the expression of liberal opinions. In the British Museum copy of the edition of 1689, is the following Manuscript note — "This translation of the Vindiciæ contra tyrannos was the work of Mr William Walker of Darnal near Sheffield, Yorkshire, the person who cut off King Charles's head. It was first printed in 1649 [1648] and reprinted at the Revolution as above."

VINDICIAE Flavianae: or, A vindication of the testimony given by Josephus concerning our Saviour Jesus Christ. [By Jacob BRYANT.]
London: M.DCC.LXXVII. Octavo. Pp. 83. b. t.* [*Dyce. Cat.*]

VINDICIÆ juris regii: or, remarques upon a paper [by Gilbert Burnet, D.D.], entituled, An enquiry into the the measures of submission to the supream authority. [By Jeremy COLLIER.]
London, MDCLXXXIX. Quarto. Pp. 48. b. t.*

VINDICIÆ Landavensis: or strictures on the Bishop of Landaff's late charge, in a letter to his Lordship. [By William MAVOR, LL.D.]
Oxford: MDCCXCII. Quarto. Pp. 19. b. t.*

VINDICIÆ pietatis: or, a vindication of godlinesse, in the greatest strictness and spirituality of it, from the imputations of folly and fansy. Together with several directions for the attaining and maintaining of a godly life. By R. A. [Richard ALLEINE.]
London: 1664. Octavo. Pp. 12. 331.* [*Brit. Mus.*]

VINETUM Britannicum: or, a treatise of cider, and such other wines and

drinks that are extracted from all manner of fruits growing in this kingdom. Together with the method of propagating all sorts of vinous fruit-trees. And a description of the new-invented ingenio or mill, for the more expeditious and better making of cider. And also the right method of making metheglin and birch-wine. With copper-plates. By J. W. Gent. [John WORLIDGE.]

London: 1676. Octavo. Pp. 19. b. t. 186. 6.* [*Bodl.*]

VINEYARD (the) of Naboth; a dramatic fragment. Translated from the original Hebrew. [By Dr. Edward ANDREWS, minister of Beresford Church, Walworth.] Printed for private circulation.

London: 1825. Octavo. Pp. 36.

VIOLA. By the author of "Caste," "My son's wife," "Pearl," &c. &c. [Emily JOLLY.]

London: 1869. Octavo.*

VIOLA; or 'tis an old tale. [By Isabel GOLDSMID.]

London: 1852. Octavo.
Another edition of "'Tis an old tale," *q.v.*

VIOLENZIA, a tragedy. [By W. C. ROSCOE.]

London: MDCCCLI. Octavo. Pp. xiii. 1. 140. 1.* [*Bodl.*]

VIOLET Bank and its inmates. [By Mrs C. JENKIN.] In three volumes.

London: 1858. Octavo.

VIOLET; or the danseuse: a portraiture of human passions and character. [By ——BEASLEY.] In two volumes.

London: 1836. Octavo.*
See discussion as to authorship in N. and Q., 4th Ser., p. 176, 324, 397, 492, 543. [The above name, Beasley, is in Mr. Laing's handwriting; but his reasons for thus assigning it are not given. —ED.]

VIOLET Stuart, a tale of Gibraltar. By H. E. P. [Harriet Eleanor PHILLIMORE.]

London: 1879. Octavo. [*Lib. Jour.*, iii. 310.]

VIRGIDEMIARUM. The three last bookes. Of byting satyres. [By Joseph HALL.]

London, 1598. Octavo. Pp. 2. b. t. 105.*

VIRGIDEMIARUM, sixe bookes. First three bookes, of tooth-less satyrs.

1. Poeticall. 2. Academicall. 3. Morall. [By Joseph HALL.]

London, 1597. Octavo. Pp. 14. b. t. 67. 1.*

VIRGIL in London; or, town eclogues. To which are added, imitations of Horace. [By George DANIEL.]

London, 1814. Octavo.*

VIRGILIUS. This Boke treateth of the lyfe of Virgilius, and of his deth, and many marvayles that he did, in hys lyfe-tyme, by whychcrafte and nygromancye thorough the helpe of the devyls of hell. [Reprinted and edited by E. Vernon UTTERSON.]

London: [1812.] Quarto. Pp. 22. [*W., Martin's Cat.*]

VIRGILS Eclogves translated into English. By W. L. Gent. [William LISLE.]

London, 1628. Octavo. Pp. 14. b. t. 193.*

VIRGIL'S husbandry, or an essay on the Georgics: being the first book. Translated into English verse. To which are added the Latin text, and Mr. Dryden's version. With notes critical, and rustick. [By William BENSON.]

London: MDCCXXV. Octavo. Pp. xv. 50, and 6 leaves of notes unpaged. [*Lowndes, Bibliog. Man.*, p. 2784.]
The second book, with title-page as above, was published in the previous year, 1724.

VIRGIN (the) Mary misrepresented by the Roman Church, in the traditions of that Church, concerning her life and glory; and in the devotions paid to her, as the mother of God. Both shewed out of the offices of that Church, the lessons on her festivals, and from their allowed authors. Part I. Wherein two of her feasts, her conception and nativity are considered. [By John PATRICK.]
London: MDCLXXXVIII. Quarto. Pp. 153.* [*Jones' Peck*, p. 417.]

VIRGIN (the) of Eden. [By Charles POVEY.]

[*Gent. Mag.*, liii. 941.]

VIRGINIA. A tragedy. As it is acted at the Theatre-Royal in Drury-Lane, by his Majesty's Servants. [By Henry CRISP.]

London, MDCCLIV. Octavo. Pp. 74.* [*Biog. Dram.*]
Ascribed to Frances Moore, afterwards Mrs Brooke. [*Dyce Cat.*]
Baker, Biog. Dram., gives the date of Mrs. Brooke's Virginia as 1756.

VIRTUE the source of pleasure. [By E. BARNARD.]

1757. Octavo. [*Biog. Dram.*, i. 21. *Mon. Rev.*, xvii. 603.]

VIRTUS post funera vivit ; or, honour tryumphing over death, being true epitomes of honourable, noble, learned and hospitable personages. By W. P. [William SAMPSON.]

London: 1636. Quarto. Thirty-six leaves. [*W.*, *Lowndes*, *Bibliog. Man.*]

VIRTUS rediviva. A panegyric on our late King Charles the First of ever blessed memory, attended with several ingenious pieces from the same pen. By T. F. [Thomas FORD.]

London: 1660. Octavo. [*Wood, Athen. Oxon.*, iii. 1097 ; iv. 245.]

VISIBLE (of the) sacrifice of the Church of God by Anonymus Eremita. [Simon STOCK, or, according to his professed name, Simon a. S. MARIA.] In two parts.

At Bruxelles 1637-8. Quarto.

VISION (the), a poem. [By Thomas HAMILTON, 6th Earl of Haddington.]

N. P. N. D. Quarto. Pp. 4.*

VISION (the) compylet in Latin be a most learnit clerk, in time of our hairship and oppression, anno 1300, and translatit in 1524. [By Allan RAMSAY.]

Printed in the year 1748. Octavo. Pp. 15.*

VISION (a) of hell. A poem. [By John Abraham HERAUD.]

Glasgow, MDCCCXXXI. Duodecimo. Pp. 1. b. t. 165.*

VISION (the) of judgment, by Quevedo Redivivus [George Gordon BYRON, Lord Byron], suggested by the composition so entitled by the author [Robert Southey] of "Wat Tyler."

London: N. D. Octavo. Pp. 24.*

VISION (the) of Mary ; or, a dream of joy. Poem in honour of the immaculate conception. By R. B. J. barrister-at-law : Temple. [R. B. JONES.]

London: MDCCCLVI. Octavo.* [*Olphar Hamst*, p. 108.]

VISION (the) of Pierce Plowman, now fyrste imprynted by Roberte Crowley, dwellyng in Ely rentes in Holburne. Anno Domini. 1505. Cum priuilegio ad imprimendū solum. [By Robert LANGLAND.]

Imprinted at London by Roberte Crowley, dwellyng in Elye rentes in Holburne. The yere of our Lord. M.D.L. Quarto. Fol. i. b. t. cxvii. B. L.*

VISION (the), or a dialog between the soul and the bodie fancied in a morning dream. [By James HOWELL.]

1651. Octavo. [*Bliss' Cat.*, 154.]

VISIONS in verse, for the entertainment and instruction of younger minds. [By E. COTTON.]

London: MDCCLI. Octavo. Pp. 104.* [*Bodl.*]

VISIONS (the) of Sir Heister Riley. [By Charles POVEY.]

1710. [*N. and Q.*, 24 *March* 1855, p. 234.]

VISIONS (the) of the soul, before it comes into the body. In several dialogues. Written by a member of the Athenian Society. [John DUNTON.]

London, 1692. Octavo. Pp. 4. b. t. 151.*

VISIT (the) for a week ; or, hints on the improvement of time. Containing original tales, anecdotes from natural and moral history, &c. Designed for the amusement of youth. By the author of The six princesses of Babylon, Juvenile Magazine, and Knight of the rose. [Lucy PEACOCK.]

London: 1794. Duodecimo. Pp. 330. b. t.*

VISIT (a) to Dublin. [By William KNOX.]

Edinburgh: 1824. [*N. and Q.*, 26 *Dec.* 1863, p. 529.]

VISIT (a) to Iona : by an American clergyman. [James C. RICHMOND.]

Glasgow: MDCCCXLIX. Sq. Octavo.* [*Presentation copy.*]

VISIT (a) to Saint Saviour's, Southwark, with advice to Dr Sacheverell's preachers there. By a divine of the Church of England. [White KENNETT, D.D.]

London: 1710. Octavo.

VISIT (a) to the Eastern necropolis of Dundee, on 30th August 1865, in seven chapters. By Norval. [James SCRYMGEOUR.]

Dundee: N. D. Duodecimo. Pp. 33. b. t.* [*A. Jervise.*]

Reprinted from the "Dundee Advertiser" for private circulation.

VISIT (a) to the New Forest A tale By Harriet Myrtle, author of "The Water-lily," "The ocean child," etc.

etc. [Mrs Lydia Falconer MILLER.] Illustrated with twenty-five engravings, from drawings by William Harvey, George Thomas, Birket Foster, and Harrison Weir.

London : 1859. Octavo. Pp. 158.*

VISIT (a) to the rectory of Passy, with sketches of character and scenery. [By J. W. PEERS.]

London : MDCCCXXVI. Octavo. Pp. 2. b. t. 228.*

VISIT (a) to the United Service Institution in 1849 by Bosquecillo. [Lieutenant SHAW.]

London : 1849. Duodecimo.

VISIT (a) to Vaucluse, Nismes, Orange, Pont-du-Gard, Avignon, Marseilles, &c. &c. in May, MDCCCXXI. By the author of the Trimester, in MDCCCXX. [Stephen WESTON.]

London : 1822. Octavo. Pp. 1. b. t. 111.*

Author's name in the hand-writing of Dyce.

VISITATION (a) of heavenly love unto the seed of Jacob yet in captivity; to whom the love of the Lord is, who is gathering, and will gather it, for it belongs unto him. By one who feeleth the springs of life opened from which this is given forth, D. W. [Dorothy WHITE, of Weymouth.]

London, 1660. Quarto. Pp. 9. b. t.*

VISITATION (a) speech at Colchester in Essex, 1692. [By John HANSLEY, Archdeacon of Colchester.]

London, 1662. Quarto. Pp. 14.*

VISITATION (a) to the Jewes from them whom the Lord hath visited from on high, among whom he hath performed his promise made with Abraham, Isaac, and Jacob, and to his seed, which Moses saw, &c. Given forth by G. F. [George FOX.]

London, 1656. Quarto. 5 sh. [Smith's Cat. of Friends' books, i. 651.]

VISITATIONS for Cornwall. [By Sir Nicholas Harris NICOLAS.]

N. P. N. D. Folio. Pp. 28.* The above is a made-up title. The work was never published.

VISITED on the children. A novel. By Theo. Gift [Dora HAVERS.] In three volumes.

London : 1881. Octavo.

VISITING my relations, and its results; a series of small episodes in the life of a recluse. [By Mary Ann KELTY.]

London. 1851. Octavo.*

VISITING societies and lay readers : a letter to the Lord Bishop of London. By Presbyter Catholicus. [Rev. William HARNESS, incumbent of All-Saints, Knightsbridge.]

London : 1844. Octavo.* [Darling, Cyclop. Bibl.]

VISITOR'S hand-book for Cheltenham; containing brief notices of the spas, pump rooms, and places of fashionable resort and amusement ; also of its churches, chapels, and public institutions ; with chronological notices of events connected with its history, &c. &c. [By H. DAVIES.]

London, 1840. Octavo. Pp. viii. 78.* [[Bodl.] Advertisement signed H. D.

VITIS degeneris : or, the degenerate-plant. Being a treatise of ancient ceremonies. Containing an historical account of their rise and growth, their first entrance into the Church, and their gradual advancement to superstition therein. Written originally in French, but now, for general information and benefit, faithfully translated into English [by Thomas Douglas]. [By John WILSON.]

London, 1668. Octavo. Pp. 45. b. t. 173.* [Bodl.]

"The author one Mr. Wilson a non-conformist who lived in, or about Chester."— MS. note in the hand-writing of Barlow.

VITTORIA Colonna: a tale of Rome in the nineteenth century. [By Charlotte A. EATON.] In three volumes.

Edinburgh : 1827. Duodecimo.

VIVE Jesus. The Rule of St Austin with the Constitutions and Directory for the religious sisters of the Visitation. Translated out of French [by Charles TOWNELY].

Paris, 1678. Pp. 312.

VIVIAN Grey. [By Benjamin DISRAELI.] A new edition. [In five volumes.]

London : 1826, 27. Duodecimo.*

VIXEN A novel By the author of "Lady Audley's secret," etc., etc., etc. [M. E. BRADDON.] In three volumes.

London : 1879. Octavo.*

VIZIER'S (the) son; or, the adventures of a Mogul. By the author of "Pandurang Hari." [William Brown HOCKLEY.] In three volumes.

London : 1831. Octavo.

VOCABULARY (a) of the English, Bugis, and Malay languages, contain-

ing about 2000 words. [By Th. THOM-
SEN.]

Singapore: 1833. Octavo. Pp. vi. 66.*

VOCABULARY (a) to Bland's Latin
Hexameters and Pentameters, by a
Harrow tutor. [Cecil Frederick
HOLMES.]

London: 1863. Duodecimo. Pp. vii. 45.*
Introduction signed C. F. H.

VOCAL parts of an entertainment [by
Mr. Rich], called Apollo and Daphne:
or, the Burgo-master trick'd. As perform'd in the Theatre Royal in Lincoln's-Inn-Fields. [By Lewis THEO-
BALD.] The fourth edition, with alterations and additions.

London: 1726. Octavo. Pp. 15. b. t.*

VOICE (a) from America to England.
By an American gentleman. [Calvin
COTTON.]

London: MDCCCXXXIX. Octavo.* [Alli-
bone.]

VOICE (a) from Palace Yard ! addressed
to Sir Robert Peel and members of
both houses of parliament by George
Canning. [By Serjeant MURPHY.]

London: [1844.] Octavo. Pp. 24.* [Athen.
Cat.]

VOICE (a) from the factories. In serious
verse. Dedicated to the Right Honourable Lord Ashley. [By the Hon.
Caroline Elizabeth Sarah NORTON.]

London: MDCCCXXXVI. Octavo.*

VOICE (a) from the font. [By George
WILKINS, D.D.]

London: 1838. Duodecimo.*

VOICE (a) from the North. An appeal
to the people of England on behalf of
their Church. By an English priest.
[Samuel Brown HARPER.] No. I.
State of the dogmatic teaching of the
English Church.

London: MDCCCL. Octavo. Pp. 32.*

——. No. II. The legal position of the
English Church.

London: MDCCCL. Octavo.*

——. No. III. Internal disorganization
of the Church.

London: MDCCCL. Octavo. Pp. 68. b. t.*

VOICE (a) from the place of S. Mor-
wenna, in the rocky land, uttered to
the sisters of mercy, at the Tamar
Mouth ; and to Lydia, their lady in the
faith, "whose heart the Lord opened."
By the vicar of Morwenstow, a priest

in the diocese of Exeter. [Robert
Stephen HAWKER.]

London: MDCCCXLIX. Duodecimo. Pp.
13.* Signed R. S. H.

VOICE (a) from the sea ; or the wreck
of the Eglantine. By Ruth Elliott.
[Lillie PECK.]

London: 1876. [Lib. Jour., iii. 379.]

VOICE (a) from the South : or, an
address from some Protestant dissenters in England to the Kirk of
Scotland. [By Daniel DEFOE.]

No separate title-page. [1707.] Quarto.
Pp. 8.* [Wilson, Life of Defoe, 99.]

VOICE (a) from the vintage, on the
force of example, addressed to those
who think and feel. By the author of
" The women of England. [Mrs William ELLIS, née Sarah Stickney.] Dedicated, by permission, to the Very Rev.
Theobald Mathew. [The second edition.]

London: 1843. Duodecimo. Pp. 5. b. t.
80.*

VOICE (the) of Christian life in song ;
or, hymns and hymn-writers of many
lands and ages. By the author of
" Tales and sketches of Christian life."
[Mrs CHARLES.]

London: M.DCCC.LVIII. Octavo. Pp.
v. i. 303.*

VOICE (the) of one crying in a wilderness. Or, the business of a Christian,
both antecedaneous to, concomitant of,
and consequent upon, a sore and
heavy visitation ; represented in several sermons. First preach'd to his
own family, lying under such visitation :
and now made publick as a thank-
offering to the Lord his Healer. By
S. S. a servant of God in the Gospel
of his Son. [Samuel SHAW.]

London, 1668. Duodecimo. Pp. 21. b. t.
248.*

VOICE (the) of the addressers : or, a
short comment upon the chief things
maintain'd, or condemn'd in our late
modest addresses. [By Benjamin
HOADLY, D.D.]

London: MDCCX. Octavo. Pp. 31.*
[Bodl.]

VOICE (the) of the people, in a memorial
to the Prince Regent of Great Britain
and Ireland. By an elector of Westminster. Author of "The universal
Church," and of " Religious and civil
union," &c. [John CROOK.]

Westminster: 1819. Octavo. Pp. 62.
b. t.* [Brit. Mus.]

VOICE (the) of the people, no voice of God : or, the mistaken arguments of a fiery zealot, in a late pamphlet entitl'd Vox populi, vox Dei, since published under the title of the Judgment of whole kingdoms and nations, &c. fully confuted, and his designs prov'd to be pernicious and destructive to the publick peace ; which he cannot answer, without blasphemy and perverting the Holy Scriptures. Publish'd for the rectifying men's judgment in their duty to the establish'd government. By F. A. [Francis ATTERBURY, D.D.]

Sold by the booksellers. 1710. Octavo.*

VOLPONE, or, the fox. By way of fable, very applicable to the present times. [By Joseph BROWNE, D.D.]

London, 1706. Quarto. Pp. 19. b. t.* [Bodl.]

VOLTAIRE in the shades ; or, dialogues on the deistical controversy. [By William Julius MICKLE.]

London : M D CC LXX. Octavo. Pp. xvi. 214.* [Watt, Bib. Brit.]

VOLUNTARY (the) principle tried by the Scriptures of the New Testament. [By the Hon. Arthur Philip PERCEVAL.]

London : 1836. Duodecimo. Pp. 24.*

VOLUNTARY (the) system. By a churchman. [Samuel Roffey MAITLAND.] 7 parts.

London, 1834-5. Octavo.*

VOLUNTEER (the) levee or the remarkable experiences of Ensign Sopht. Written and illustrated by himself. Edited by the author of " How not to do it." [Robert Michael BALLANTYNE.]

Edinburgh : MDCCCLX. Octavo. Pp. 56.*

VOLUNTEERS (the) ; or, taylors to arms ! a comedy in one act ; as performed at the Theatre Royal, Covent Garden. [By George DOWNING.] The music by Mr. Hook.

London : 1780. Octavo. [Biog. Dram. Mon. Rev., lxii. 411.]

VORTIGERN, an historical tragedy, in five acts ; represented at the Theatre-Royal, Drury Lane, and Henry the Second, an historical drama. Supposed to be written by the author of Vortigern. [By William Henry IRELAND.]

London : [1799.] Octavo.* Each play has a separate title and pagination.

VORTIGERN under consideration ; with general remarks on Mr. James Boaden's Letter to George Steevens, Esq. relative to the manuscripts, drawings, seals, &c. ascribed to Shakespeare, and in the possession of Samuel Ireland, Esq. [By W. C. OULTON.]

London : 1796. Octavo. Pp. 67.* Author's name in the handwriting of Samuel Ireland, to whom the pamphlet belonged.

VOTIVAE Angliae : or, the desires and wishes of England. Contained in a patheticall discourse, presented to the king on new-yeares day last. Wherein are vnfolded and represented, many strong reasons, and true and solide motiues, to perswade his Majestie to drawe his royall sword, for the restoring of the Pallatynat, and Electorat, to his sonne in law Prince Fredericke, to his onely daughter the Lady Elizabeth, and their princely issue. Against the treacherovs vsvrpation, and formidable ambition and power of the Emperour, the King of Spaine, and the Duke of Bavaria, who unjustlie possesse and detaine the same. Together with some aphorismes returned (with a large interest) to the Pope in answer of his. Written by S. R. N. I. [Thomas SCOT.]

Printed at Vtrecht. MDCXXIIII. Quarto. No pagination.* [Bodl.]

VOW (the) of the peacock, and other poems. By L. E. L. author of " The improvisatrice," " The golden violet," &c. [By L. E. LANDON.]

London : 1835. Octavo.*

VOX cleri : or, the sense of the clergy, concerning the making of alterations in the established liturgy : with remarks on the discourse concerning the Ecclesiastical Commission, and several letters for alterations. To which is added, an historical account of the whole proceedings of the present Convocation. [By Thomas LONG, B.D., Exeter.] The second edition.

London : 1690. Quarto.*

VOX coeli, or newes from heaven. Of a consultation there held by the high and mighty princes, King Hen. 8. King Edw. 6. Prince Henry, Queene Mary, Queene Elizabeth, and Queene Anne ; wherein Spaines ambition and treacheries to most kingdomes and free estates of Evrope, are vnmaskd and truly represented, but more particularly towards England, and now more

especially under the pretended match of Prince Charles, with the Infanta Dona Maria. Whereunto is annexed two letters written by Queene Mary from heaven, the one to Count Gondomar, the ambassadour of Spaine, the other to all the Romane Catholiques of England. Written by S. R. N. I. [Thomas SCOT.]
Printed in Elisium. 1624. Quarto.*

VOX Dei. [By Thomas SCOT.]
[1624.] Quarto. Pp. 9. b. t. 86. Engraved title.*

VOX militis: foreshewing what perils are procvred where the people of this, or any other kingdome liue without regard of marshall discipline, especially when they stand and behold their friends in apparent danger, and almost subuerted by there enemies vniust persecution, and yet with hold their helping hand and assistance. Diuided into two parts, the first manifesting for what causes princes may enter into warre, and how necessary and vsuall it is, drawne from the actions of the Prince of Orange. The second discourseth of warre, souldiers, and the time when it is conuenient : collected out of the heroicall examples of Count Mansfield. Where, as in a mirrour, meet to be perused by kings, princes, nobles, knights, gentlemen, and men of all degrees throughout the whole kingdome, to behold with what consideration they should first enter into the warre, with what courage they should prosecute them, and how to deale with a common enemy. Dedicated to Count Mansfield, and the honourable councell of warre. [By Gervase MARKHAM.]
London, 1625. Quarto. Pp. 8. b. t. 38.*
Epistle dedicatorie signed G. M.
"This is Barnaby Rich's Allarum to England originally printed 4° 1578. the matter abridged, the language modernized, and the whole newly adapted to the age in which it appeared, by Gervase Markham, who has added the two dedications & the lines entitled "Vox militis," but not improved, in the main, on the original."—MS. note by Dr. Bliss.

"VOX oculis subjecta;" a dissertation on the most curious and important art of imparting speech and the knowledge of language, to the naturally deaf, and (consequently) dumb; with a particular account of the academy of Messrs. Braidwood of Edinburgh, and a proposal to perpetuate, and extend the benefits thereof. By a parent. [Francis GREEN.]

London: MDCCLXXXIII. Octavo.* [Nichols, Lit. Anec., viii. 125.]

VOX piscis, or the book fish, containing three treatises, which were found in the belly of a cod-fish in Cambridge Market, on Midsummer Eve last, Ao. 1626. [By Richard TRACEY, or TRACY.]
1627. Octavo. [Lowndes, Bibliog. Man., p. 2704. Wood, Athen. Oxon., i. 245.]
Vox piscis is a reprint of "Preparation (of the) to the cross and to death, and of the comfort under the cross and death." In two books. London, 1540, 8°.

VOX populi. Or newes from Spayne, translated according to the Spanish coppie. Which may serve to forewarn both England and the United Provinces how far to trust to Spanish pretences. [By Thomas SCOT, Utrecht.]
Imprinted in the yeare 1620. Quarto. No pagination.*

V O X populi, expressed in XXXV. motions to this present Parliament. Being the generall voyce and the humble and earnest request of the people of God in England to that most honorable and religious assembly. For reforming the present corrupt state of the Church. Published by Irenæus Philadelphus. [Lewis DU MOULIN.]
Printed in the yeare, 1641. Quarto. Pp. 12. b. t.*

V O X populi, vox Dei. Being true maxims of government; proving, I. That all kings, governors and forms of government proceed from the people. II. The nature of our constitution is fairly stated, with the original contract between king and people, and a journal of the late revolution. III. That resisting of tyrannical power is allowed by Scripture and reason. IV. That the children of Israel did often resist and turn out their evil princes, and that God Almighty did approve of resistance. V. That the primitive Christians did often resist their tyrannical emperors, and that Bishop Athanasius, St. Chrysostom, Luther, and Melancthon &c. did approve of resistance. VI. That the Protestants in all ages did resist their evil and destructive princes. VII. Together with a historical account of the depriving of kings for their evil government, in Israel, France, Spain, Scotland &c., and in England before and since the Conquest. VIII. That absolute passive obedience is a damnable and treasonable doctrine; by contradicting the glorious attributes

of God, and encouraging of rebellion, usurpation, and tyranny. To which no answer will be made, or dare be made, or can be made, without treason ; not to be behind Mr. Lesley, or any Jacobite in assurance. [By Daniel DEFOE.]

London, 1709. [*Wilson, Life of Defoe*, 113.] Reprinted under the title of "The judgment of whole kingdoms and nations," &c.

VOX regis. [By Thomas SCOT.]

[1624.] Quarto. Pp. 5. b. t. 74.* Address to the reader signed T. S.

VOYAGE (a) into the Levant : a brief relation of a journey lately performed by Mr. Henry Blunt gentleman, from England by the way of Venice, into Dalmatia, Sclavonia, Bosnia, Hungary, Macedonia, Thessaly, Thrace, Rhodes and Egypt, unto Gran Cairo : with particular observations concerning the moderne condition of the Turks, and other people under that empire. [By Sir Henry BLUNT.] The fourth edition.

London, 1650. Duodecimo. Pp. 228.* [*Bodl.*]

VOYAGE (the) of Captain Popanilla. By the author of "Vivian Grey." [Benjamin DISRAELI.]

London : 1828. Duodecimo. Pp. viii. 243.*

VOYAGE (the) of Columbus. A poem. [By Samuel ROGERS.]

London : 1810. Quarto. Pp. viii. 48.*

VOYAGE (the) of France or a compleat journey through France with the character of the people, and the description of the chief towns, fortresses, churches, monasteries, universities, pallaces and antiquities, as also of the interest, government, riches, &c. By P. H. [Peter HEYLIN] D.D.

London, 1673. Octavo. Pp. 362. b. t.*

"This is the spurious edition alluded to in Wood's Athenæ ii. 283 : but there must have been a previous edition."—Douce.

"Reprint of the first of Heylin's Two journeys, published in 1656."—Note in Bodl. New Cat.

VOYAGE (a) round the world, in the years MDCCXL., I, II, III, IV. By George Anson, Esq ; commander in chief of a squadron of his Majesty's ships, sent upon an expedition to the South-Seas. Compiled from papers and other materials of the Right Honourable George Anson, and pub-

lished under his direction, by Richard Walter, M.A., chaplain of his Majesty's ship the Centurion, in that expedition. Illustrated with forty-two copper-plates. [In reality by Benjamin ROBINS, F.R.S.]

London : MDCCXLVIII. Quarto. Pp. 30. b. t. 417.*

The copper-plates occupy a separate volume.

VOYAGE (a) round the world : or, a pocket-library, divided into several volumes. The first of which contains the rare adventures of Don Kainophilus, from his cradle to his 15th. year. The like discoveries in such a method never made by any rambler before. The whole work intermixt with essays, historical, moral and divine ; and all other kinds of learning. Done into English by a lover of travels. Recommended by the wits of both universities. [By John DUNTON.]

London, N. D. Octavo. Pp. 24. b. t. 158.*

VOYAGE (a) to the East Indies in 1747 and 1748 ; containing an account of the islands of St Helena and Java, of the city of Batavia, of the government and political conduct of the Dutch ; of the empire of China, with a particular description of Canton, interspersed with many useful and curious observations and anecdotes, and illustrated with copper-plates. [By C. F. NOBLE ?]

London : 1762. Octavo. [*W., Brit. Mus.*]

VOYAGE (a) to the South-Seas, and to many other parts of the world, performed from the month of September in the year 1740, to June 1744, by Commodore Anson, in his Majesty's ship the Centurion, having under his command the Gloucester, Pearl, Severn, Wager, Trial, and two storeships. . . By an officer of the squadron. [Richard Walter, *i.e.* Benjamin ROBINS.] London, MDCCXLIV. Octavo. Pp. 408. [*Dyce Cat.*]

VOYAGE (a) to the world of Cartesius. Written originally in French [by Gabriel DANIEL], and now translated into English.

London : 1692. Octavo. Pp. 12. b. t. 298. 6.*

The translator was T. Taylor, who signs the dedication.

This has been attributed to Defoe, but in Wilson's list of Defoe's works, it is set down as doubtful.

VOYAGE (a) up the Thames 1738. [By —— WEDDELL.]

[*His "Incle and Yarico." Gent. Mag.*, viii. 224.]

VOYAGES (the) and adventures of Captain Robert Boyle, in several parts of the world. Intermixed with the story of Mrs. Villars, an English lady, with whom he made his surprising escape from Barbary. Likewise including the history of an Italian captive, and the life of Don Pedro Aquilo, &c. Full of various and amazing turns of fortune. [By W. R. CHETWOOD.]

Edinburgh: M.DCC.LXXVIII. Duodecimo. Pp. 266.* [*Lowndes, Bibliog. Man.*, p. 249.]

Ascribed to Benjamin Victor. [*Brit. Mus.*]

VOYAGES (the), dangerous adventures and imminent escapes of Captain Richard Falconer, containing the laws, customs and manners of the Indians of America, and intermixed with voyages and adventures of Thomas Randall, Cork pilot. [By William Rufus CHETWOOD.]

1734. [London, 1838, 5th ed. in 12mo.] [*N. and Q.*, 28 *Jan.* 1860, p. 66.]

VOYAGES to the Madeira, and Leeward Caribbean Isles: with sketches of the natural history of these islands. By Maria R ****** [Maria RIDDELL.]

Edinburgh: 1792. Duodecimo. Pp. ix. 105.*

VOYCE (the) of him that is escaped from Babylon. Reasons given forth to all sober minded people, why I departed from the ministery of those called ministers of parishes; and why I departed from the ministery of those called Anabaptists; and why I have, and what I have contended for, some years past. [By Robert WEST, of Devizes.]

London, 1658. Quarto. 2½ sh. [*Smith's Cat. of Friends' books*, i. 36.]

VULGAR errors in divinity removed. [By Ralph BATTELL.]

London: 1683. Octavo. [*Leslie's Cat.*, 1844, p. 21.]

VULGUS Britannicus: or, the British Hudibrass. [By Edward WARD.]

London: 1710. Octavo.*

W.

WACOUSTA; or, the prophecy: a tale of the Canadas. By the author of "Écarté." [Major John RICHARDSON.] In three volumes.

London: 1832. Duodecimo.*

WAES (the) o' war: or, the upshot o' the History o' Will and Jean. In four parts. [By Hector MACNEILL.]

Edinburgh: M.DCC.XCVI. Octavo. Pp. 32.*

W A L D E N B E R G; a poem, in six cantos, by M. E. M. J. [Margaret Elizabeth Mary JONES.]

London: 1837. Duodecimo. Pp. viii. ix. 108.* [*N. and Q.*, 25 *July* 1857, p. 71.]

WALK (a) from the town of Lanark to the Falls of Clyde, on a summer afternoon. [By C. BUCHANAN.]

Glasgow: 1816. Octavo. Pp. 88.*

A presentation copy with the author's signature.

WALK knaves, walk. A discourse intended to have been spoken at court, and now published for the satisfaction of all those that have participated of the sweetnesse of publique employments. By Hodg Turbervill, chaplain to the late Lord Hewson. [Edmund GAYTON.]

London: 1659. Quarto. Pp. 14.* [*Wood, Athen. Oxon.*, iii. 756.]

WALK (a) round the boundaries of Morayshire. With map specially prepared from Ordnance survey, by a pedestrian. [James PIRIE.]

Banff. 1877. Octavo. Pp. viii. 91.*

WALK (a) through Leeds, or stranger's guide to everything worth notice in that ancient and populous town; with an account of the woollen manufacture of the West Riding of Yorkshire. With plates. [Said to have been written by Francis T. BILLAM.]

Leeds: 1806. Duodecimo. Pp. 55. [*Boyne's Yorkshire Lib.*, pp. 84, 85.]

WALK (a) through Leicester ; being a guide to strangers, containing a description of the town and its environs ; with remarks upon its history and antiquities. [By Susanna WATTS.]
Leicester: 1804. Duodecimo.* [*Upcott*, i. 548.]

WALKS abroad and evenings at home. [By Robert Kemp PHILP.] With numerous illustrations.
London, 1861. Octavo. Pp. viii. 328. [*Boase and Courtney, Bib. Corn.*, ii. 494.]

WALKS and wanderings in the world of literature. By the author of "Random recollections," "The great metropolis," "Travels in town," &c. &c. [James GRANT.] In two volumes.
London : MDCCCXXXIX. Duodecimo.*

WALKS through Leeds ; or the stranger's companion to the public buildings, churches, chapels, charitable institutions, &c., in that ancient and populous town ; and various historical occurrences connected therewith. [Said to have been written by John Robert BLESARD.]
Leeds: 1835. Duodecimo. Pp. viii. 132. [*Boyne's Yorkshire Lib.*, p. 85.]

WALKS through London, including Westminster and the borough of Southwark, with the surrounding suburbs ; describing every thing worthy of observation in the public buildings, places of entertainment, exhibitions, commercial and literary institutions, &c. down to the present period : forming a complete guide to the British metropolis. By David Hughson, LL.D. [Dr. R. PUGH.] In two volumes.
London : 1817. Octavo.* [*Upcott*, iii. 1478.]
Ascribed also to William Hamilton Reid, and Mrs Reid.]

WALLACE : a tragedy. [By James GRAHAME.]
Edinburgh : 1799. Octavo. Pp. 94.*

WALLACE : a tragedy, in five acts. [By Robert BUCHANAN, professor of rhetoric in the University of Glasgow.]
Glasgow : MDCCCLVI. Octavo. Pp. 96.*

WALLACE ; or, the fight of Falkirk, a metrical romance. [By Miss Margaret HOLFORD, afterwards Mrs Hodson.]
London : 1809. Quarto.* [*Gent. Mag.*, *March* 1810, p. 251.] Second ed., 1810, has authoress' name.

WALLACE ; or, the vale of Ellerslie. With other poems. [By John FINLAY.]
Glasgow : 1802. Octavo.*

WALLADMOR : "freely translated into German from the English of Sir Walter Scott." And now freely translated from the German into English. [By Wilhelm HAERING.] In two volumes.
London : 1825. Octavo.*

WALLENSTEIN'S camp, from the German ; and original poems. [By Lord Francis LEVESON-GOWER.]
London: MDCCCXXX. Octavo. Pp. 167.*

WALLIS'S pocket itinerary: being a new and accurate guide to all the principal direct and cross-roads, throughout England, Wales, and Scotland. [By Thomas Hartwell HORNE.]
London : 1803. Octodecimo.
"The publisher inscribed his own name on the title-page." From a list of his works in the handwriting of the author.

WALLOGRAPHY ; or the Britton describ'd ; being a pleasant relation of a journey into Wales, wherein are set down several remarkable passages that occur'd in the way thither. And also many choice observables, and notable commemorations, concerning the state and condition, the nature and humor, actions, manners, customs, &c. of that countrey and people. By W. R. a mighty lover of Welch travels. [William RICHARDS.]
London, 1682. Octavo.* [*Wood.*]

WALPOLIANA. [Collected by John PINKERTON.] [In two volumes.]
London. N. D. Duodecimo.* [*N. and Q.*, 26 *Dec.* 1863, p. 516.]

WALPOLIANA ; or, a few anecdotes of Sir Robert Walpole. [By Philip, 2nd Earl of HARDWICKE.]
London : 1783. Quarto.

WALTER Clayton : a tale of the Gordon riots. [By —— M'GAURAN.] In three volumes.
London : 1844. Duodecimo.*

WALTER Colyton ; a tale of 1688. By the author of "Brambletye House," &c. &c. [Horace SMITH.] In three volumes.
London : 1830. Duodecimo.*

WALTER, the schoolmaster. [By Edward MONRO, M.A.]
London : MDCCCLIV. Octavo. Pp. 2. b. t. 252.*

WALTZ; an apostrophic hymn. By Horace Hornem, Esq. [Lord BYRON.] Paris: 1821. 12mo. [*IV.*]

WANDA By Ouida [Louise de LA RAMÉ.] In three volumes. London: 1883. Octavo.*

WANDERER (the). By Owen Meredith, author of "Clytemnestra, The Earl's return, The artist, and other poems." [Edward Robert BULWER-LYTTON.] Second edition. London: 1859. Octavo. Pp. xvi. 436.*

WANDERER (the). Fantasia and Vision. &c. By The Smith of Smitheden. [Daniel M'IVOR.] Edinburgh: MDCCCLVII. Octavo. Pp. vii. 381.*

WANDERER (the) in Africa: a tale illustrating the thirty-second Psalm. By A. L. O. E., authoress of "Clermont tales," "Ned Franks," "Glimpses of the unseen," &c. [Charlotte TUCKER.] Edinburgh: N. D. Octavo. Pp. 96.*

WANDERER (the); or, Edward to Eleonora. A poem. [By John BELL.] [London:] MDCCLXXXV. Quarto.* [*Adv. Lib.*]

WANDERING (the) bard: and other poems. [By John Walker ORD.] Edinburgh: MDCCCXXXIII. Octavo. Pp. 135.* [*Tweddell's Bards and Authors of Cleveland and South Durham*, p. 251.]

WANDERING (the) islander; or, the history of Mr Charles North. [By Charles Henry WILSON, Middle Temple.] In three volumes. London: 1792. Duodecimo. [*Gent. Mag., May* 1808 p. 469. *Mon. Rev.*, xii. 338.]

WANDERING (the) Jew: or the travels and observations of Hareach the Prolonged: comprehending a view of the most distinguished events in the history of mankind since the destruction of Jerusalem by Titus; with a description of the manners, customs, and remarkable monuments, of the most celebrated nations; interspersed with anecdotes of celebrated men of different periods. Compiled from a MS supposed to have been written by that mysterious character. By the Rev. T. Clark. [John GALT.] London: 1820. Duodecimo. [*IV.*] At p. 437, the letters of the author's name are found commencing the sentences in the last paragraph of the book. Thus the following are the first words of each sentence:—*It, Over, History, Nevertheless, Greatness, All, Literally, To.*

WANDERING (the) Jews chronicle: or, The old historian His brief declaration Made in a mad fashion Of each coronation That past in this nation Since William's invasion For no great occasion But meer recreation To put off vexation. [By Martin PARKER.] N. P. N. D. S. Sh. Folio. B. L.* [*Bodl.*] Signed M. P.

WANDERING Willie. The sponsor. [By Edward MONRO, M.A., perpetual curate of Harrow Weald.] London: 1845. Octavo. Pp. 29.* [*Bodl.*] Signed E. M.

WANDERINGS (the) of Persiles and Sigismunda; a northern story by Miguel de Cervantes Saavedra. [Translated by Louisa Dorothea STANLEY.] London: 1854. Duodecimo. Pp. xvii. 477. [*IV.*]

WANDERINGS over Bible lands and seas. By the author of "Chronicles of the Schönberg-Cotta family," &c. &c. [Mrs. CHARLES.] London: 1868. Octavo. Pp. 301.*

WANDRING (the) lover. A tragycomedie. Being acted severall times privately at sundry places by the author and his friends with great applause. Written by T. M. gent. [Thomas MERITON.] London, 1658. Quarto. Pp. 6. b. t. 31.* [*Biog. Dram.*]

WAR; an epic satire. [By Stephen BARRETT.] 1747. [*Gent. Mag.*, xvii. 156.]

WAR and peace. A tale of the retreat from Caubul. By A. L. O. E., authoress of "The young pilgrim," "Flora," "The giant killer," "Pride and his prisoners," &c. &c. [Charlotte TUCKER.] London: MDCCCLXII. Octavo. Pp. 256.*

WAR in disguise; or, the frauds of the neutral flags. [By James STEPHEN.] The second edition. London: 1805. Octavo.* [*Rich, Bib. Amer.*, p. 21.]

WAR (the): is it just or necessary? Signed R. W. S. [R. W. SMILES.] Quarto. Pp. 4. [*N. and Q., Feb.* 1869, p. 169.]

WAR lyrics. By A. and L. [SHORE.] London: 1855. Octavo. [*IV., Brit Mus.*]

WAR with France, the only security of Britain, at the present momentous

crisis, set forth in an earnest address
to his fellow subjects. By an old
Englishman. [James RENNELL.]
London : 1794. Octavo.

WAR with the devil : or the young mans
conflict with the powers of darkness :
in a dialogue. Discovering the corrup-
tion and vanity of youth, the horrible
nature of sin, and deplorable condition
of fallen man. Also, a definition, power,
and rule of conscience, and the nature
of true conversion. To which is added,
an appendix, containing a dialogue between an old apostate, and a young
professor. Worthy the perusal of all,
but chiefly intended for the instruction
of the younger sort. The fourth
impression. By B. K. [Benjamin
KEACH.]
London, 1676. Octavo. Pp. 208. b. t.*
[*Brit. Mus.*]

WAR with the saints. By Charlotte Elizabeth. [Charlotte Elizabeth
Browne, afterwards Mrs Phelan, afterwards Mrs TONNA.]
[London :] 1848. Duodecimo.

WAR with the senses ; or, free thoughts
on snuff-taking. By a friend to female
beauty. [Richard RUSSELL, wool-
stapler.]
London : 1782. Octavo. [*Gent. Mag.*,
liv. 821. *Mon. Rev.*, lxvii. 234.]

WARD (the) of the crown. A historical
novel. By the author of " Seymour of
Sudley," " The Pope and the actor,"
" The forester's daughter." [Hannah
D. WOLFENSBERGER.] In three vol-
umes.
London : 1845. Duodecimo.*

WARDS (the) of London ; comprising
a historical and topographical description of every object of importance
within the boundaries of the city.
With an account of all the companies,
institutions, buildings, ancient remains,
&c. &c. and biographical sketches of
all eminent persons connected therewith. By Henry Thomas. [Henry
RIDE.] [In two volumes.]
London : 1828. Octavo.*
" This book is said to have been written by
Henry Ride, formerly of S. John's Coll.
Oxford. Vide ' Memoirs of Shakspeare's
tavern the late Boar's Head, Eastcheap '—
note at bottom of page 3."—MS. note on
the Douce copy in the Bodleian.

WARFARE and work, or life's progress.
[By Helen CLACY.]
London : 1859. Duodecimo. [*W., Brit.
Mus.*] Signed Cycla.

WARLEY : a satire. Addressed to the
first artist in Europe. [By Thomas
MAURICE.] Part the first.
London : 1778. Quarto.*

WARLICK (a) captain attack'd by a
single soldier : or, a letter from A . . . . w
S . . . . . . n [Andrew STEVENSON]
writer in Edinburgh, to the Reverend
Mr T . . . . s N . . . n [Thomas Nairn]
minister of the Gospel at Abbotshall.
Wherein the said Mr N . . . n's reasons
of secession from the A . . . . e
P . . . . y [Associate Presbytery],
and the bad effects it hath already produced, are briefly consider'd. In which,
more particularly, the said Mr. N . . . n's
chief reason of separation from the said
Presbytery, viz. their not disowning the
present civil powers over these nations,
on account of the want of some of
these qualifications magistrates ought
to have by the word of God and our
covenants, is shewn to be contrary unto
the principles and practice of the
Church of Scotland, unto the practice
of the most eminent saints recorded in
Scripture, and unto many Scripture
precepts.
Edinburgh : MDCCXLIII. Duodecimo. Pp.
55.*
Letter signed A . . . . w S . . . . n.

WARLOCK (the). By the old sailor,
author of " Land and sea tales,"
" Tough yarns," &c. [Matthew Henry
BARKER.] A new edition.
London : 1860. Octavo. Pp. 272. b. t.*

W A R N - word (the) to Sir Francis
Hastinges Wast-word : conteyning the
issue of three former treateses, the
Watch-word, the Ward-word and the
Wast-word (intituled by Sir Francis,
an apologie or defence of his Watch-
word ;) togeather with certaine admonitions & warnings to the said Knight
and his followers. Whereunto is
adioyned a brief reiection of an insolent
and vaunting minister [Matthew Sut-
cliffe] masked with the letters O. E.
who hath taken vpon him to wryte of
the same argument in supply of the
Knight. There are also foure seuerall
tables, one of the chapters, another of
the controuersies, the third of the cheif
shiftes, and deceits, the fourth of the
particular matters conteyned in the
whole book. By N. D. author of the
Ward-word. [Robert PARSONS.]
Permissu Superiorum. Anno. 1602. Octavo.* Pp. 15. Fol. 131. 138 ; pp. 21.
[*Jones' Peck*, i. 54.]"

The initials N. D. represent Nicholas Doleman, a name frequently assumed by Parsons.

WARNING (the). Recommended to the serious attention of all Christians, and lovers of their country. [By Eliza COLTMAN.]

London: N. D. Duodecimo. [*Smith's Cat. of Friends' books*, i. 80.]

WARNING (a) agaynst the dangerous practices of Papistes, and specially the parteners of the late rebellion. [By Thomas NORTON.]

Imprinted by John Daye [1569.] Octavo. B. L. [*See Stryfe's Annals*, p. 554, 562.]

WARNING (a) from the Lord to the Pope and to all his train of idolatries: with a discovery of his false imitations, and likenesses, and traditional inventions, which is not the power of God. And a testimony against his foundation, to the overthrow of the whole building: and a witness by the Spirit of God against his dead-worship of dead idols; and the false imitation of false crosses, which is not the power of God unto salvation, but delusion and damnation. By a lover of souls, G. F. [George FOX.]

London, 1656. Quarto. 2¾ sh. [*Smith's Cat. of Friends' books*, i. 651.]

WARNING (a) to all teachers of children, which are called schoolmasters and school-mistresses, and to parents, which doth send their children to be taught by them, that all schoolmasters and school-mistresses may train up children in the fear of God, etc. By G. F. [George Fox.]

[London: 1657.] Quarto. [*W., Brit. Mus.*]

WARNING (a) to all the merchants in London, and such as buy and sell. With an advisement to them to lay aside their superfluity, and with it to nourish the poor. By G. F. [George Fox.]

London, 1658. Quarto. 1 sh. [*Smith's Cat. of Friends' books*, i. 656.]

WARNING (a) to the Church of England. [By J. BRAMHALL, Archbishop of Armagh.]

London: [1706.] Quarto. [*W., Brit. Mus.*] A reprint of the "Fair warning against the deception of the Scotch discipline," &c.

A work with title as above is in Adv. Lib. Cat. ascribed to Charles Leslie. London, [1706], 4°, pp. 4. b. l. 52.

WARNING (a) to the dragon and all his angels. [By Eleanor AUDELEY.]

N. P. 1625. Quarto. [*Cat. Lib. Trin. Coll. Dub.*, p. 152.]

WARNING to the eldership. [By John LONGMUIR, LL.D.]

N. P. [1869.] Duodecimo. Pp. 4.* [*A. Jervise.*] Reprinted from the "Aberdeen Free Press" of 19th March, 1869.

WARNING (a) to wives: or, the Platonic lover. A novel. In three volumes. By the author of "Cousin Geoffrey," "The marrying man," "The match-maker," "The jilt," "The breach of promise," and "The life of a beauty." [Mrs Yorick SMYTHIES, née Gordon.]

London: 1847. Duodecimo.*

WARNING (the) voice. [By P. L. COURTIER.]

1798. Quarto. [*Watt, Bib. Brit. Mon. Rev.*, xxv. 476.]

"WARNINGS (the) of the war." A letter to the Right Hon. Lord Palmerston, Prime Minister. By "A British Commoner." [Edward Rupert HUMPHREYS, LL.D., Head Master of the Cheltenham Grammar School.]

London: 1855. Octavo. Pp. 53. [*W.*]

WARP and woof: or, the reminiscences of Doris Fletcher. By Holme Lee, author of "Sylvan Holt's daughter," "Against wind and tide," etc. [Harriet PARR.] In three volumes.

London: MD.CCC.LXI Octavo.*

WARRANTABLENESS (the) of the Associate Synod's sentence, concerning the religious clause of some Burgess-Oaths, proved; and some notes of two sermons vindicated: upon occasion of a late pamphlet [by Ralph Erskine], intitled, The lawfulness of the religious clause of some Burgess Oaths asserted; in several remarks upon some notes of sermons delivered lately, at a certain occasion, by some brethren, who therein attempted publickly to shew the unlawfulness thereof. In two parts. [Part I. by Rev. Thomas MAIR, of Orwell; Part II. by Rev. Alexander MONCRIEFF, of Abernethy.]

Edinburgh, MDCCXLVII. Octavo. Pp. 55.*

WARRENIANA, with notes, critical and explanatory, by the Editor of a Quarterly Review. [By William Frederick DEACON.]

London: 1824. Duodecimo.* [*Talfourd's Memoir of Deacon prefixed to his "Annette."*]

WARRES (the) of Pompey and Cæsar. By G. C. [George CHAPMAN.]

London : 1631. Quarto. [*W., Bliss Cat.*]

WARRIOR and Pacificus; or, dialogues on war. By the author of " Remarks on the theatre, &c." [Ann ALEXANDER, *née* Tuke.]

York : 1819. Duodecimo. 2 sh. [*Smith's Cat of Friends' books,* i. 8.]

WARS (the) of Wapsburgh. By the author of " The heir of Redclyffe," etc. etc. [Charlotte Mary YONGE.]

London : 1864. Octavo.*

WAS it a dream? and, The new churchyard. By the author of " Stories on the Lord's Prayer," etc. [Miss E. M. SEWELL.]

London : 1849. Sm. Octavo. [*W., Brit. Mus.*]

WAT Tyler. A dramatic poem. [By Robert SOUTHEY, LL.D.]

London : 1817. Duodecimo. Pp. xi. 70.*

VVATCH-vvoord (a) to Englande to beware of traytours and tretcherous practises, which haue beene the ouerthrowe of many famous kingdomes and common weales. Written by a faithfull affected freend to his country : who desireth God long to blesse it from traytours, and their secret conspiracyes. Seene and allowed, according to the order appointed in the queenes iniunctions. [By Anthony MUNDAY.]

London 1584. Quarto.* B. L. Epistle dedicatory signed A. M.

WATER (the) lily By Harriet Myrtle. [Mrs. Lydia Falconer MILLER.] With illustrations by Hablot K. Browne ; engraved by Thomas Bolton.

London : MDCCCLIV. Octavo. Pp. 84.*

WATER-Lily (the) on the Danube : being a brief account of the perils of a pair-oar during a voyage from Lambeth to Pesth. By the author of the ' Log of the Water Lily ' [Robert Blackford MANSFIELD] and illustrated by one of the crew.

London : MDCCCLIII. Octavo.*

WATER-queen (the) or the mermaid of Loch Lene (translated from the Gaedhic) and other tales. [By H. COATES.] In three volumes.

London : 1832. Duodecimo. [*Adv. Lib.*]

WATER (the) witch ; or, the skimmer of the seas. A tale. By the author of

" The borderers," " The prairie," &c. &c. [James Fenimore COOPER.] In three volumes.

London : 1830. Duodecimo.*

WATERDALE (the) neighbours. By the author of " Paul Massie." [Justin M'CARTHY.] In three volumes.

London : 1867. Octavo.*

WATERLOO, a poem, in two parts : inscribed by permission, to his Grace the Duke of Wellington, &c. &c. by his respectful and obliged humble servant, the author of Triumphs of religion ; Suicide, a poem ; and other works. [Harriett COPE.]

London : N. D. Octavo.*

WATERLOO, a poetical epistle to Mr. Sergeant Frere, master of Downing College, and Vice Chancellor of Cambridge in 1820. [By Rev. J. WING.]

London : 1820. Octavo. Pp. viii. 28.* [*Bodl.*]

WATERMAN (the) ; or, the first of August : a ballad opera, in two acts. As it is performed at the Theatre-Royal, Hay - Market. [By Charles DIBDIN.]

London : 1774. Octavo.* [*Biog. Dram.*]

WATERS of comfort. A small volume of devotional poetry of a practical character, addressed to the thoughtful and the suffering. By the author of " Visiting my relations." [Mary Ann KELTY.]

Cambridge : 1856. Octavo.*

WATERS (the) of Marah sweetned. A thanks-giving sermon, [on Exod. 15. 23, 24, 25.] Preached at Taunton, in the county of Somerset, May 11. 1647. for the gracious deliverance of that poore towne from the strait and bloody siege. By T. B. Master of Arts, and a minister of the Gospel in that county. [Timothy BATT.]

London. 1648. Quarto. Pp. 2. b. t. 20.*

WATTY and Meg, or, the wife reform'd : a tale. [By Alexander WILSON.]

Paisley, 1826. Duodecimo. Pp. 8.* [*Paton's " Wilson the ornithologist,"* p. 6.]

WAVERLEY ; or 'tis sixty years since. [By Sir Walter SCOTT.] In three volumes.

Edinburgh : 1814. Duodecimo.*

WAY (the) home. [By Mrs. BARBOUR.] Edinburgh : 1856. Duodecimo.*

WAY (the) of the wilderness, and other poems. By E. C. C. B. author of " The protoplast." [E. C. C. BAILLIE.]
London : N. D. Octavo.*

WAY (a), propounded to make the poor in these and other nations happy, by bringing together a fit, suitable, and well qualified people unto one household government or little-commonwealth. Whereunto is also annexed an Invitation to this society or little commonwealth. By Peter Cornelius. [" I believe this pamphlet was made by Mr Hugh PEETERS, who hath a man named *Cornelius* Glover." MS. note by George Thomason in the British Museum copy.]
London: [1659.] Octavo. 2 pts. 4to, 1659. [*W.*]
The 'Invitation' has a separate title page, but the pagination is continuous.

WAY (the) to be happy ; or, the story of Willie the gardener's boy. By Cousin Kate. [C. D. BELL.]
London : 1871. Duodecimo.

WAY (the) to be wise and wealthy ; or, the excellency of industry and frugality. By Mr. J. S. [John SOWTER.]
Exon : 1716. Octavo. Pp. 95. [*Manchester Free Lib. Cat.*, p. 673.]

WAY (the) to health, long life and happiness, or, a discourse of temperance and the particular nature of all things requisit for the life of man, as all sorts of meats, drinks, air, exercise, &c. with special directions how to use each of them to the best advantage of the body and mind. Shewing from the true ground of nature whence most diseases proceed, and how to prevent them. To which is added, a treatise of most sorts of English herbs, with several other remarkable and most useful observations, very necessary for all families. The whole treatise displaying the most hidden secrets of philosophy, and made easie and familiar to the meanest capacities by various examples and demonstrances. The like never before published. Communicated to the world for a general good, by Philotheos Physiologus. [Thomas TRYON.]
London, 1683. Octavo. Pp. 12. b. t. 669.* [*Bodl.*]
Address to the reader signed Philotheos Physiologus.

WAY (the) to keep him, a comedy in three acts. [By Arthur MURPHY.]
London : 1760. Octavo.* [*Biog. Dram.*]

WAY (the) to make all people rich ; or, wisdoms call to temperance and frugality, in a dialogue between Sophronio and Guloso, one a lover of sobriety, the other addicted to gluttony, and excess. By Philotheos Physiologus, the author of The way to health, The countrymans companion. [Thomas TRYON.]
[London.] 1685. Octavo. Pp. 6. b. t. 130.* [*Douce Cat.*, 279.]

WAY (the) to peace amongst all Protestants : being a letter of reconciliation sent by Bp. Ridley to Bp. Hooper. With some observations upon it. [By Samuel JOHNSON, chaplain to William, Lord Russell.]
London : 1688. Quarto. Pp. 8. b. t.* [*Bodl.*]

WAY (the) to things by words, and to words by things ; being a sketch of an attempt at the retrieval of the antient Celtic, or, primitive language of Europe. To which is added, a succinct account of the Sanscort, or learned language of the Bramins. Also two essays, the one on the origin of the musical waits at Christmas. The other on the real secret of the Free Masons. [By John CLELAND.]
London, MDCCLXVI. Octavo.* [*Lowndes, Bibliog. Man. Mon. Rev.*, xxxv. 363.]

VVAY (the) tovvards the finding of a decision of the chiefe controversie now debated concerning Church government. [By John HALES, of Eaton.]
London, 1641. Quarto. Pp. 42. b. t.* [*Wood, Athen. Oxon.*, iii. 413.]
" Authore John Hales è Coll. Eatonensi, ut creditur."—MS. note by Barlow in the Bodleian copy.
By some ascribed to John Dury.

WAY (the) women love. A novel. By E. Owens Blackburne, author of " A woman scorned," etc. [Elizabeth CASEY.] In three volumes.
London : 1877. Octavo.*

WAYFARING sketches among the Greeks and Turks, and on the shores of the Danube. By a seven years' resident in Greece. [Felicia M. F. SKENE.]
London : MDCCCXLVII. Octavo. Pp. 343. b. t.*

WAYS and means whereby his Majesty may man his navy with ten thousand able sailors, etc. [By T. ROBE.]
London : 1726. Octavo.

—— Second edition, to which is added a method whereby criminals liable to

transportation, may be render'd not only useful but honest members of the publick.

London: [1726?] Octavo. [*W., Brit. Mus.*]

WAYS (the) of the line. A monograph on excavators. [By Anna R. TREGELLES.]

N. P. 1858. Octavo. [*Smith's Cat. of Friends' books*, ii. 821.]

WAYS to kill care. A collection of original songs, chiefly comic. Written by Young D'Urfey. [Frederick FORREST.]

London: MDCCLXI. Octavo. Pp. xii. b. t. 112.* [*Lowndes, Bibliog. Man.*]

WAYWARD Dosia, and the generous diplomatist. By Henry Gréville. [Madame DURAND.]

London: 1880. Octavo. Pp. 212.*

WE'RE all low people there, and other tales. By the author of "Caleb Stukely." [Samuel PHILLIPS.] Eighth thousand.

London: 1854. Octavo. Pp. 2. b. t. 255.* Reprinted from Blackwood's Magazine.

"WE can't afford it!" Being thoughts upon the aristocracy of England. Part the second. By Isaac Tomkins, Gent. [Lord BROUGHAM.]

London: MDCCCXXXV. Octavo. Pp. 30.*

WE know what we worship. [By Rev. John Henry BLUNT.]
London. 1858. Sm. Octavo. Pp. 16.

"WE pity the plumage, but forget the dying bird." An address to the people on the death of the Princess Charlotte. By the Hermit of Marlow. [Percy Bysshe SHELLEY.]

[London.] N. D. Octavo. Pp. 16.*

WEALTH and labour. A novel. By Lord B******* author of "Masters and workmen," "Farce of life," &c. [Probably Lord BELFAST.] In three volumes.

London: 1853. Duodecimo.

WEALTH discovered; or, an essay upon a late expedient for taking away all impositions .. By F. C. [Francis CRADOCK] a lover of his country. ..

London: 1661. Quarto. Pp. 43. [*Manchester Free Lib. Cat.*, p. 167.]

WEALTH the name and number of the

beast, 666, in the Book of Revelation. [By John TAYLOR.]

London: 1844. Octavo.* [*Adv. Lib.*]

WEARING the willow; or, Bride Fielding. A tale of Ireland and of Scotland sixty years ago. By the author of 'The nut-brown maids.' [Henrietta KEDDIE.]

London: 1860. Octavo. Pp. 1. b. t. 343.*

WEATHERCOCK (the), a musical entertainment of two acts; as performed at the Theatre-Royal, Covent-Garden. [By Theodosius FORREST.]

London: M.DCC.LXXV. Octavo. Pp. 3. b. t. 37.* [*Biog. Dram.*]

WEATHER-COCKE (the) of Romes religion: with her severall changes. Or: the world turn'd topsie-turvie by Papists. [By Alexander COOKE.]

London: 1625. Quarto. Pp. 16. b. t.* [*Bodl.*]

WEAVER'S (the) family. By the author of "Dives and Lazarus," "A tale for the Pharisees," &c., &c. [William GILBERT.]

London: N. D. Octavo. Pp. 347.*

WEAVERS (the) pocket-book: or, weaving spiritualized. In a discourse, wherein men employed in that occupation are instructed how to raise heavenly meditations, from the several parts of their work. To which also are added, some few moral and spiritual observations, relating both to that and other trades. By J. C. [John COLLINGES, or COLLINGS] D.D.

Edinburgh: M.DCC.XXIII. Octavo. Pp. 8. b. t. 145. 4.*

WEDDING! and bedding! The R—l nuptials!! or, epithalamium extraordinary!! A poem, by Peter Pindar, Esq. author of the R—l courtship. &c. &c. &c. [John WOLCOTT, M.D.] Third edition.

London: N. D. Octavo. Pp. 27.*

WEDLOCK; or, yesterday and to-day. By the author of "The maid's husband." [Mrs. JENKINS.] In three volumes.

London, 1841. Duodecimo.

WEDNESDAY Club Law; or the injustice, dishonour, and ill policy of breaking into parliamentary contracts for public debts. [By —— BROOME.]

London: 1717. Octavo. Pp. 38. [*N. and Q., June* 1853, p. 576.]

WEE wifie. A tale. By the author of

'Nellie's memories.' [Rosa Nouchette CAREY.] In two volumes.
London : 1869. Octavo.*

WEEDS and wild flowers. By E. G. L. B. [Sir Edward George BULWER-LYTTON.]
Paris : 1826. Privately printed. [*W.*, *Martin's Cat.*]

WEEK (a) at a cottage. A pastoral tale. [By William HUTCHINSON.]
1776. Duodecimo. [*Nichols, Lit. Illust.*, i. 421. *Mon. Rev.*, lv. 77.]

WEEK (the) of darkness; a short manual for the use and comfort of mourners in a house wherein one lies dead. By the author of "Ye maiden and married life of Mary Powell, afterwards Mistress Milton. [Anne MANNING.]
London : 1856. Duodecimo. Pp. viii. 195.*

WEEKLY (the) Journal ; or Saturday's Post (Mist's.) [Daniel DEFOE first found in it at No. 37, and continued to No. 101, 15 Nov. 1718. Defoe again connected with Mist's Journal, 31. January, 1719, and continued its management, writing letters introductory until the beginning of July, 1720 ; after which he only watched the paper, and translated the articles on foreign affairs and occasionally contributed articles.]
Each number 1½ sheets. Small folio. 24 August, 1717, to 15 Nov. 1718. 3 Jan. 1719 to July, 1720 ; and occasionally afterward, until Oct. 24. 1724. [*Lee's Defoe*, 183.]

WEEKLY memorials for the ingenious : or, an account of books lately set forth in several languages. With other accounts relating to arts and sciences. [By —— BEAUMONT.]
London, M.DC.LXXXIII. Quarto. Pp. 6. b. t. 390. 8.* [*Bodl.*]
The work consists of 50 numbers.

WEEKLY (the) Miscellany. Giving an account of the religion, morality and learning of the present times. By Richard Hooker, of the Temple, Esq. [William WEBSTER, D.D.] In two volumes.
London 1736. Octavo. [*W.*]
The first number of this paper was published on Dec. 16, 1732, and was continued until June 27, 1741. It met with but little success, and from the number of religious essays that it contained, it acquired the appellation of "Old Mother Hooker's Journal." See Nichols, Lit. Anec., ii. 36 ; v. 161, 169, 175, &c.

WEEKLY (the) pacquet of advice from Rome : or the history of Popery. A deduction of the usurpations of the Bishops of Rome, and the errors and superstitions by them from time to time, brought into the Church. In the process of which the Papists arguments are answered, their fallacies detected, their cruelties registred, their treasons and seditious principles observed, and the whole body of papistry anatomized. Perform'd by a single sheet, coming out every Friday, but with a continued connexion. To each being added, The Popish Courant : on some occasional joco-serious reflections on Romish fopperies. [By Henry CARE.] In four volumes.
London : 1679-83. Quarto. [*W.*]
The first number was published on the 3 of Dec. 1678 and the last of vol. 5 on July 13, 1683.

WEESILS (the), a satyrical fable, giving an account of some argumental passages happening in the Lion's Court about Weesilion's taking the oaths. [By Thomas BROWNE, B.D.]
London, 1691. Quarto. [*Lathbury's History of the Convocation . . . . 2d. ed. pp. 338-9.*]

WEIGHT (the) of a crown, a tragedy, by Feragus. [C. H. WILLIAMS.]
1852. [*N. and Q., March* 26, 1870, p. 332.]

WELCH (the) freeholder's farewell epistles to the Right Rev. Samuel, Lord Bishop (lately of St David's), now of Rochester ; in which the Unitarian dissenters, and the dissenters in general, are vindicated from the charges advanced against them in his Lordship's circular letter on the case of the emigrant French clergy ; with a copy of that letter. [By David JONES.]
London : 1794. Octavo. Pp. 68.

WELCH (the) freeholder's vindication of his letter to the Right Rev. Samuel [Horsley] Lord Bishop of St David's ; in reply to a letter from a clergyman of that diocese ; together with strictures on the said letter. [By David JONES.]
London : 1791. Octavo. Pp. 61. [*March's Dissenters*, p. 518. *Mon. Rev.*, v. 354.]

WELCH peasant boy. By the author of the Maid of Avon. [Mrs PECK.] In three volumes.
1808. [*Biog. Dict.*, 1816. *Brit. Crit.*, xxxii. 95.]

WELCOME & farewell, a tragedy. [By Rev. William HARNESS.]

London: N. D. [1837.] Octavo. Pp. 2. b. t. 119.* [*Gent. Mag.*, *Jan.* 1838, p. 49. *Martin's Cat.*]

WELCOME (the) of Isis. A poem, occasioned by an unexpected visit of the Duke of Wellington to the University of Oxford. By the author of "The Oxford Spy." [James Shergold BOONE, M.A.]

Oxford. 1834. Octavo. Pp. 31.*

WELL met gossip : or, tis merrie when gossips meete Newly enlarged with diuers merrie songs [By Samuel ROWLANDS.]

London, 1619. Quarto. No pagination.*

WELLS of Baca ; or, solaces of the Christian mourner, and other thoughts on bereavement. By the author of "The faithful promiser," "Morning and night watches," &c. &c. [John Ross MACDUFF.] Fourth edition.

London : MDCCCXLV. Duodecimo. Pp. 70.*

WELLS (the) of Scripture, illustrated in verse. By the author of The pastor's legacy. [Henrietta Joan FRY.]

London: 1847. Octavo. 3½ sh. [*Smith's Cat. of Friends' books*, i. 816.]

WELSH sketches, chiefly ecclesiastical, to the close of the twelfth century. By the author of " Proposals for Christian union." [Ernest Silvanus APPLEYARD.] Second edition.

London : MDCCCLII. Duodecimo. Pp. viii. 160.*
Advertisement signed E. S. A. The first edition appeared in 1851.

—— Second series.

London : MDCCCLII. Duodecimo. Pp. viii. 153.*

—— Third series.

London : MDCCCLIII. Duodecimo. Pp. viii. 192.*

WENSLEYDALE ; or rural contemplation : a poem. [By Thomas MAUDE.] The third edition.

London : MDCCLXXX. Quarto. Pp. xii. 13-54. [*Gent. Mag.*, lxix. 163. *Mon. Rev.*, xlvii. 114.]
The fourth edition, published at Richmond in 1816, 8vo, has the author's name.

WERNERIA, or short characters of earths : with notes according to the improvements of Klaproth, Vauquelin and Hauy. By Terræ Filius. [Stephen WESTON.]

London : 1805. Duodecimo. Pp. 113. [*Lowndes, Bibliog. Man., s.v. Werner. Mon. Rev.*, xlix. 99 ; liii. 92.]

WESLEYAN Methodism in Scotland. [By H. W. HOLLAND.]

Leeds : 1864. Octavo. Pp. 12.* [*Bodl.*]

WEST-country (the) farmer, or, a fair representation of the decay of trade, and badness of the times : in a letter of complaint from a tenant in the country, to his landlord in London. [By Francis SQUIRE.]

Taunton : N. D. Duodecimo. Pp. 50.* [*Bodl.*] The preface is signed Ofellus.

WEST (the) country farmer, (Number 2,) consisting of three parts : I. The landlord's answer to his tenant's complaint, wherein he objects to the farmer's arguments, blames the conduct of the country in several particulars, but yet promises for the future to be their friend and advocate. II. The farmer's reply, in which the errors of his brethren are excused, their honesty and loyalty defended, their interest farther asserted and maintained, with some hints of expedients that would be serviceable to them, and to the whole kingdom. III. A postscript to the farmers themselves, exhorting them to put a due value on their persons and professions, to judge for themselves, and assert their true liberty, and not to be seduced, and beguiled by crafty and designing men. [By Francis SQUIRE.]

Taunton, N. D. Octavo.* [*Bodl.*]
The Farmer signs himself Ofellus ; the Landlord, X. Y. Z.

WEST India eclogues. [By Edward RUSHTON.]

London : 1787. Quarto. [*Sketches of obscure poets*, p. 58. *Mon. Rev.*, lxxvii. p. 283.]

WEST (the) Indian : a comedy. As it is performed at the Theatre Royal in Drury-Lane. By the author of the Brothers. [Richard CUMBERLAND.]

London : MDCCLXXI. Octavo. Pp. 102.* [*Biog. Dram.*]

WESTERN (the) mail. Being a series of letters, &c. [By Annabella PLUMPTRE.]

1801. Duodecimo. [*Watt, Bib. Brit. Mon. Rev.*, xxxv. 219.]

WESTERN (the) martyrology: or, bloody assizes. Containing the lives, trials, and dying-speeches of all those eminent Protestants that suffer'd in the West of England, and elsewhere, from the year 1678, to this time. Together with the life and death of George L. Jeffreys. The fifth edition. To which is now added, to make it compleat, an account of the barbarous whippings of several persons in the West. Also the trial and case of Mr John Tutchin (the author of the Observator) with the cruel sentence pass'd upon him ; and his petition to K. James to be hang'd : never before printed. With an alphabetical table to the whole. [By Thomas PITTS.]

London : MDCCV. Octavo. Pp. 14. 279.* [*Mendham Collection Cat.*, p. 240.]

WESTMINSTER Abbey : a poem. [By John DART.]

London : 1721. Octavo. Pp. 3. b. t. 64.* [*Dyce Cat.*]

WESTMINSTER Abbey ; or, the days of the Reformation. By the author of "Whitefriars," "Caesar Borgia," &c. [Miss Jane ROBINSON.] In three volumes.

London : MDCCCLIV. Duodecimo.*

WESTMINSTER Abbey; with other occasional poems, and a free translation of the Oedipus Tyrannus of Sophocles. By the author of Indian antiquities. [Thomas MAURICE.]

London : 1813. Octavo. [*IV.*]

WESTMINSTER Hall; or anecdotes and reminiscences of the bar, the bench, and the woolsack. [Compiled by Henry and Thomas ROSCOE.] In three volumes.

London : 1825. Sm. Octavo. [*Lowndes, Bibliog. Man.*, p. 2880.]

WESTMORLAND (the) dialect, in three familiar dialogues : in which an attempt is made to illustrate the provincial idiom. By A. W. [A. WALKER.]

Kendal : MDCCXC. Duodecimo. Pp. 95. 12.* [*Bodl.*]
Ascribed also to H. Wheeler.

WHARNCLIFFE : a play, in three acts. Time occupied, one day. [By J. H. AVELING, M.D.]

London : MDCCCLIV. Duodecimo. Pp. 36.*

WHAT am I? Where am I? What ought I to do? How am I to become qualified and disposed to do what I ought? By the author of "Outlines of social economy," &c. &c. &c. [William ELLIS.]

London : 1852. Octavo. Pp. 66 b. t.* [*Bodl.*]

WHAT an old myth may teach By Leslie Keith [Miss Keith JOHNSTON] author of "A simple maiden." Illustrated by O. A. Von Glehn, B.A.

London : 1878. Octavo. Pp. 139.* [*Adv. Lib.*]

WHAT are the English Roman Catholics to do? The question considered in a letter to Lord Edward Howard. By Anglo-Catholicus. [Lord John MANNERS.]

London : 1841. Octavo.* [*Bodl.*] Letter signed Anglo-Catholicus.

WHAT election and reprobation is, clearly discovered, and the ignorance of such who hold election and reprobation of persons, manifested. By G. F. [George FOX.]

Printed in the year 1679. Quarto. 9½ sh. [*Smith's Cat. of Friends' books*, i. 679.]

WHAT have thirty years of Church revival done? [By Rev. John Henry BLUNT.]

London. 1861. Octavo. Pp. 24.

WHAT if the Swedes should come? With some thoughts about keeping the army on foot, whether they come or not. [By Daniel DEFOE.]

London : MDCCXVII. Octavo. Pp. 38.* [*Wilson, Life of Defoe*, 160.]

WHAT is a Christian? By A. L. O. E., authoress of "The Claremont tales," "Christian conquests," "Glimpses of the unseen," "Sheer off," etc. [Charlotte TUCKER.] Six woodcuts.

Edinburgh : N. D. Octavo. Pp. 208.*

WHAT is baptism? Is it a fiction? Considered by a no-party man. [Henry HAYES.]

Holloway : 1859. Octavo. [*IV., Brit. Mus.*]

"WHAT is he." By the author of "Vivian Grey." [The Rt. Hon. Benjamin D'ISRAELI.]

London : 1833. Octavo. Pp. 16. [*IV.*]

WHAT next? or the peers and the third time of asking. [By —— RICH.]

London : 1837. Octavo. Pp. iv. 82. Fifth edition. [*IV.*]

WHAT ought the Church and people of

Scotland to do now? By a Seceder. [Rev. William WHITE, minister of Knox's Free Church, Haddington.] Second edition.

Edinburgh, 1840. Octavo. Pp. 28. [*New Coll. Cat.*]

WHAT ought the General Assembly to do at the present crisis? [By Thomas M'CRIE, D.D.]

Edinburgh; M.DCCC.XXXIII. Octavo. Pp. 58. b. t.*

WHAT peace to the wicked? Or, an expostulatorie answer to a derisorie question, lately made concerning peace. By a free-man, though a prisoner. [George WITHER.] The author spares his name ; not, that he dares not to let you know it ; but, that he cares not.

N. P. Printed in the year 1646. Quarto. Pp. 6. b. t.*

WHAT shall be the end of these things? An inquiry regarding the probable issues of the Scottish Free Church controversy. By the author of "Considerations for the conscientious." [Rev. James W. TAYLOR, of Flisk.]

Perth. MDCCCXLIV. Duodecimo. Pp. 117.*

WHAT she came through By Sarah Tytler author of "Citoyenne Jacqueline," "Lady Bell," "The Huguenot family," etc. [Henrietta KEDDIE.] In three volumes.

London 1877. Octavo.*

"WHAT she could." By the author of "The wide wide world." [Susan WARNER.]

London : MDCCCLXX. Octavo. Pp. 259. b. t.*

WHAT we must all come to. A comedy in two acts, as it was intended to be acted at the Theatre-Royal in Covent-Garden. [By Arthur MURPHY.]

London, MDCCLXIV. Octavo. Pp. 52.* [*Biog. Dram.*]

Afterwards produced as "Three weeks after marriage."

WHAT will he do with it? By Pisistratus Caxton, author of "My novel," etc. [Sir Edward BULWER-LYTTON.] In four volumes.

Edinburgh : 1859. Octavo. [*W.*]

WHEAT and tares A tale [By H. S. CUNNINGHAM.]

London 1861. Duodecimo. Pp. 411.*

WHEN I was a little girl. Stories for children by the author of 'St Olaves.' [Miss TABOR.] Illustrated by L. Frolich.

London 1871. Octavo. Pp. vi. 2. 249.*

WHERE ought the new cemetery to be placed? In the Meadows? or in the King's Park? [By Pat. NEILL, printer.]

Edinburgh; 1832. Octavo. Pp. 7. [*W.*] Signed A Citizen.

WHERE was Protestantism before Luther? With an appendix. By a layman. [James Creighton M'CLELLAN.]

York : 1852. Duodecimo. Pp. 52.

VVHETHER Christian faith maye be kepte secret in the heart, without confession therof openly to the worlde as occasion shal serue. Also what hurt cōmeth by thē that hath receiued the gospell, to be presēt at masse vnto the simple and vnlearned. [By John HOOPER, Bishop of Gloucester.]

From Roane. Anno, M.D.LIII. the. iii. of October. Octavo. No pagination.*

WHETHER the parliament be not in law dissolved by the death of the Princess of Orange? And how the subjects ought, and are to behave themselves in relation to those papers emitted since by the stile and title of Acts? With a brief account of the government of England. In a letter to a country gentleman, as an answer to his second question. [By Robert FERGUSON.]

No separate title-page. Quarto. Pp. 59.* Letter dated April 24, 1695.

WHICH party breaks the law and resists God's ordinance? [By Alexander Murray DUNLOP.]

Edinburgh, N. D. Octavo. Pp. 4.* [*New Coll. Cat.*]

WHICH party still breaks the law? [By Alexander Murray DUNLOP.]

Edinburgh, N. D. Octavo. Pp. 8. [*New Coll. Cat.*]

WHICH wins, love or money? By the author of "Whitefriars," etc. etc. etc. [Jane ROBINSON.]

London : M DCCC LXII. Octavo. Pp. 262. b. t.*

WHIG'S (a) apology for his consistency; in a letter from a member of parliament to his friend in the borough of * * * *. [By Robert ADAIR.]

London : 1795. Octavo. Pp. 198. [*Watt, Bib. Brit. Mon. Rev.*, xix. 368.]

WHIGS turn'd Tories, and Hanoverian-

Tories, from their avow'd principles, prov'd Whigs : or, each side in the other mistaken. Being a plain proof, that each party deny that charge which the other bring against them : and that neither side will disown those principles, which the other profess. With an earnest exhortation to all Whigs, as well as Hanoverian-Tories, to lay aside those uncharitable heats among such Protestants, and seriously to consider, and effectually provide against those Jacobite, Popish, and conforming Tories ; whose principal ground of hope to ruine all sincere Protestants, is from those unchristian and violent feuds amongst our selves. [By Daniel DEFOE.]

London : 1713. Octavo. Pp. 4. b. t. 40.* [*Wilson, Life of Defoe*, 145.]

WHIGS (the) unmask'd : being the secret history of the Calf's-Head-Club. Shewing the rise and progress of that infamous society since the grand rebellion. Containing all the treasonable songs and ballads, sung as anthems by those saints, at their king-killing anniversaries. Much enlarg'd and improv'd by a genuine account of all the plots and conspiracies of the Whiggish faction against the Queen and ministry, since the persecution of the Church under the disguise of moderation. With animadversions in prose and verse. Adorn'd with cuts suitable to every particular design. To which are added, Several characters by Sir John Denham and other valuable authors. Also a vindication of the royal martyr, King Charles the First ; wherein are expos'd the hellish mysteries of the old republican rebellion. By Mr. Butler, author of Hudibras. [By Edward WARD.] The eighth edition, with large additions.

London : MDCCXIII. Octavo. Pp. 14. vi. 224.*

WHIGS (the) unmask'd : or, the history of the Calf's-Head-Club farther expos'd ; in a full account of the rise and progress of that impious society, since their horrid rebellion in forty-one. With all the treasonable ballads, sung by the villanous Whigs, as anthems, on the xxxth of January. Much enlarg'd, by an impartial account of all the plots and conspiracies form'd by the Low-Church faction, against the Queen and present ministry. With animadversions in prose and verse. Adorn'd with curious cuts, by the best hands.

To which is added, several characters by that most ingenious poet, Sir John Denham. And the hellish mysteries of the old republicans, set forth in vindication of King Charles the First, by Mr. Samuel Butler, author of Hudibras. [By Edward WARD.] The ninth edition.

London : MDCCXIV. Octavo. Pp. 14. b. t. vi. 224.*

WHIMZIES : or, a new cast of characters. [By Richard BRATHWAYT.]

London, 1631. Duodecimo. Pp. 17. b. t. 211.* [*Bodl.*]
Epistle dedicatorie, signed Clytus-Alexandrinus.

WHIPPER (the) whipt. Being a reply upon a scandalous pamphlet, called the Whip : abusing that excellent work of Cornelius Burges, Dr in divinity, one of the Assembly of divines, entituled, The fire of the sanctuary newly discovered. [By Francis QUARLES.]

Imprinted M.DC.XLIV. Quarto. Pp. 2. b. t. 44.*

WHIRL-WIND (the) of the Lord gone forth as a fiery flying roule, with an alarm sounded against the inhabitants of the North-countrey. Being a forewarning to all the rulers in England, of the mighty and terrible day of the Lord which shall overtake the wicked ; but especially and in particular, to the persecuting rulers, priests, and people, in the county of Westmorland. Who by their priests are made manifest to all, to be open enemies to Sion's converts, and a generation of evil doers, with whom the Lord Jehovah is coming to plead the cause of the oppressed, and to redeem Zion with judgement, and her converts with righteousness. C. T. [Christopher TAYLOR.]

London, 1656. Quarto. Pp. 17. b. t.* [*Bodl.*] First printed in 1655.

WHISKERS (the) whisk'd : or, a farewel sermon prepared to be preach'd in Turners-Hall in Phillpot-Lane. By the Irreverend J—— J—— [Joseph Jacob], doctor of enthusiasm. [By John TUTCHIN, author of the Observator.]

London 1703. Quarto. Pp. 26.* [*Bodl.*]

WHISPERER (the) ; or tales and speculations. By Gabriel Silvertongue. [James MONTGOMERY.]

London : 1798. Duodecimo. [*W.*]
Containing 24 Nos., the first dated May 28, 1795 ; the last, Nov. 5, 1795.

The copy in the British Museum contains the following note by Archdeacon Wrangham : " There is only one other copy, it is believed, of this work in existence, and that is in the author's hands. He has sedulously destroyed the remaining few which ever got into circulation."

WHIST : a poem, in twelve cantos. [By Alexander THOMSON.]

London : M DCC XCI. Octavo. Pp. 194.* [_Title-page of his "Paradise of taste."_]

WHITE (the) charger that cost me two hundred pounds ; lost me seventy thousand pounds ; drove me from society ; eventually deprived me of my friends ; and finally compelled me to quit the service. By the author of " The horse guards," " The days when we had tails on us " &c. [Lieut. Col. HORT.

London : 1850. Octavo.*

WHITE (the) chateau. A tragedy. [By Thomas M'NICOLL, for some years editor of the British Quarterly Review.]

London : 1852. Octavo. Pp. 68.* [_K. Inglis._]

WHITE (the) cottage, a tale. [By Arthur MOWER.]

Edinburgh : 1817. Duodecimo. Pp. 344.* [_Noctes Ambrosianae, iv. 306._]

WHITE (the) slave ; and the Russian prince. By the author of " Revelations of Russia." [C. F. HENNINGSEN.] In three volumes. Second edition.

London : 1846. Duodecimo.*

WHITE (the) wife ; with other stories, supernatural, romantic and legendary ; collected and illustrated by Cuthbert Bede [Edward BRADLEY], author of " Verdant Green," " Glencreggan," " A tour in Tartan Land," etc.

London : 1865. Octavo. Pp. vii. 252.*

WHITEFRIARS ; or, the days of Charles the Second. An historical romance. In three volumes. [By Miss Jane ROBINSON.]

London : 1844. Octavo.*
Ascribed also to Joseph Robinson.

WHITEHALL (the) Evening Post. [Commenced and edited by Daniel DEFOE. Published every Tuesday, Thursday, and Saturday. He continued to write in it occasionally until June, 1720.]

18 Sep. 1718. to June, 1720. 2 leaves. Sm. Quarto. [_Lee's Defoe, 189._]

WHITEHALL ; or, the days of Charles I., an historical romance. By the author of Whitefriars. [Jane ROBINSON.] [In three volumes.]

London : 1845. Duodecimo.*
Ascribed also to Joseph Robinson.

WHITEHALL ; or, the days of George IV. [By William MAGINN, LL.D.]

London : [1827.] Octavo.* [_Dub. Univ. Mag._, xxiii. 86.]

WHITTINGTON and his cat. The " Royal " grand Christmas pantomime for 1881-82. Written by R. L. Westland. [Robert W. LOWE.] Produced Saturday, 17th December 1881.

Edinburgh : 1881. Octavo. Pp. 38.* [_Adv. Lib._]

WHITTLINGS from the West. With some account of Butternut Castle. By Abel Log. [Charles Butler GREATREX, rector of Stanton-upon Hine.]

Edinburgh and London, MDCCCLIV. Octavo. Pp. vi. 442.* [_Adv. Lib._]

"WHO breaks—pays." (Italian proverb.) By the author of " Cousin Stella." [Mrs. C. JENKIN.]

London : 1861. Octavo.

WHO fares best, the Christian, or the man of the world? Or, the advantage of a life of real piety to a life of fashionable dissipation. By a marine officer. [Andrew BURN.]

London : 1789. Octavo. [_Watt, Bib. Brit._]

WHO'S afraid? A farce of one act : with songs. [By Sir Richard Paul JODRELL, M.D.]

London : 1787. Octavo. [_W., Biog. Dram._]

WHO is to have it? A novel. By the author of " The Netherwoods of Otterpool." [J. C. BATEMAN.]

London : 1859. Octavo. Pp. 433. b. t.*

WHO'D be an author? With the answer. By Frank Foster. [D. PUSELEY.]

London : N. D. Octavo. Pp. vi. 264.*

WHO wrote Cavendish's Life of Wolsey? [By Joseph HUNTER, of Bath.]

London : M.DCCC.XIV. Quarto. Pp. 56. b. t.* [_Bodl. Gent. Mag., Jan._ 1825, p. 23.]

WHO wrote the Waverley novels? Being an investigation into certain mysterious circumstances attending their production, and an inquiry into the literary

aid which Sir Walter Scott may have received from other persons. [By William John FITZPATRICK.]

London: 1856. Octavo. Pp. 88.* [*Brit. Mus.*] The Introduction is signed W. J. F.

WHOLE Book of Psalms, as they are now sung in churches, with the singing notes of time and tune set to every syllable, made plain and easie to the understanding of all that can read, etc. "Never before done in England." By T. M. [Thomas MAY.]

1688. Octavo. [*W.*]

WHOLE (a) crew of kind gossips, all met to be merry. [By Samuel ROW-LANDS.]

London, 1609. Quarto. No pagination.* Address "To the maids of London," signed S. R.

WHOLE (the) duty of a Christian, by way of question and answer; exactly pursuant to the method of the Whole duty of man, and designed for the use of the charity schools, lately erected in and about London. [By Robert NELSON.]

London: 1705. Duodecimo. Pp. 93. 3.* [*Bodl.*]

WHOLE (the) duty of man consider'd, under its three principal and general divisions, namely, the duties we owe to God, ourselves, and neighbours. Faithfully extracted from that excellent book so entitled, and published for the benefit of the poorer sort. By a gentleman. [Browne WILLIS, LL.D.]

London, 1717. Duodecimo. Pp. x. 52.*

WHOLE (the) duty of woman. By a lady. Written at the desire of a noble lord. [By William KENRICK.]

London: M.DCC.LIII. Octavo.* [*Watt, Bib. Brit. Mon. Rev., viii. 143.*]

WHOLE (the) Psalter, translated into English metre [by Matthew PARKER, Archbishop of Canterbury], which contayneth an hundreth and fifty Psalmes. The first Quinquagene.

London by John Daye. [1557.] Quarto. [*W., Lowndes, Bibliog. Man.*]

WHOLE (the) question of ecclesiastical establishments stated and considered. [By —— LOWRIE, Lauder.]

Edinburgh: 1833. Duodecimo. [*New Coll. Cat., p. 273.*]

WHOLSOME advices from the Blessed Virgin, to her indiscreet worshippers. Written by one of the Roman com-munion [Adam WIDENFELT] and done out of the French into English, by a gentleman of the Church of England (James Taylor). With a preface shewing the motives to the translation.

London: 1687. Quarto. Pp. xvi. 20.* [*Jones' Peck*, i. 102; ii. 421.]

WHOLSOME severity reconciled with Christian liberty. Or, the true resolution of a present controversie concerning liberty of conscience. Here you have the question stated, the middle way betwixt popish tyrannie and schismatizing liberty approved, and also confirmed from Scripture, and the testimonies of divines, yea of whole Churches. The chiefe arguments and exceptions used in The bloudy tenent, The compassionate Samaritane, M. S. to A. S. &c. examined. Eight distinctions added for qualifying and clearing the whole matter. And in conclusion a parænetick to the five apologists for choosing accomodation rather than toleration. [By George GILLESPIE.]

London, 1645. Quarto.*

WHOM shall we hang? The Sebastopol enquiry. [By Peter Benson MAX-WELL.]

London: 1855. Octavo.* [*Scotsman, Jan. 14, 1856.*]

WHOSE poems? [By E. D. GIRDLE-STONE.]

London: 1850. Octavo.*

WHY are you a churchman? A plain question answered in a dialogue between Mr Fitz Adam and John Oakley. [By Thomas DREWITT, of Chedder.]

London: 1800. Duodecimo. [*Mon. Rev., xxxii. 314.*]

"WHY Johnny didn't interfere." An answer to "The fight at Dame Europa's school." [By Fr. CHANCELLOR.]

London: 1871. Duodecimo. Pp. 11.* [*F. Madan.*] Signed Johnny.

WHY Paul Ferroll killed his wife. By the author of "Paul Ferroll." [Mrs Archer CLIVE.]

London: 1860. Duodecimo.*

WHY should you secede? Containing observations on spiritual independence and non-intrusion in reference to secession. [By —— MUNRO, advocate.]

Edinburgh: MDCCCXLIII. Octavo. Pp. 31.*

WHYCHCOTTE of St. John's; or, the court, the camp, the quarter-deck, and

the cloister. [In two volumes.] [By Erskine NEALE.]

London : 1833. Duodecimo.* [*N. and Q.*, 3 *Feb.* 1855, p. 91.]

WHY'S? (the) and the How's? or, a good enquiry : a sermon [on Matt. ii. ver. 3.] preach'd before their Majesties in their chappel at St. James's the 2d. Sunday of Advent, December 6th. 1685. By J. D. of the Society of Jesus. [John DORMER.] Published by his Majesties command.]

London, MDCLXXXVII. Quarto. Pp. 34. b. t.*

WHYTE dyed black. Or a discouery of many most foule blemishes, impostures, and decciptes, which D. Whyte haith practysed in his book entituled The way to the true Church. Deuyded into 3 sortes Corruptions, or deprauations. Lyes. Impertinencies, or absurd reasoninges. Writen by T. W. P. [Thomas WORTHINGTON, Priest.] And dedicated to the Vniuersity of Cambridge.

N. P. 1615. Quarto. Pp. 18. b. t. 183.* [*Bodl.*]

WICKED (the) plots, and perfidious practises of the Spaniards, against the 17. provinces of the Netherlands, before they took up armes. Being gathered out of severall Dutch writers, by a lover of truth, and an unfained hater of oppression and tyrannie, the bane of commonwealths. [By Thomas SCOT.]

N. P. N. D. Quarto. No pagination.*

Printed at the end of Scot's Second part of Spanish practises, under the title of "An adioynder of sundry other particular wicked plots and cruell, inhumane, perfidious ; yea, unnatural practises of the Spaniards." Signed S. O.

WICKHAM wakened, or, The Quaker's madrigall in rime dogrell. [By Martin LLEWELLYN.]

Printed in the yeare, 1672. Quarto. 1 sh. [*Smith, Bib. Anti-Quaker.*, p. 275.]

WIDDOWES (the) teares, a comedie. Written by Geor. Chap. [George CHAPMAN.]

London : 1612. Quarto. [*W., Brit. Mus.*]

WIDE of the mark. . . [By Mrs HOUSTOUN.] In three volumes.

London : 1871. Octavo.

WIDE (the), wide world. By Elizabeth

Wetherell. [Susan WARNER.] Complete edition.

London : N. D. [1877.] Octavo. Pp. 446.*

WIDOW (the) bewitch'd. A comedy. As it is acted at the Theatre in Goodmans-Fields. [By John MOTTLEY.]

London : MDCCXXX. Octavo. Pp. 64.* [*Biog. Dram.*]

WIDOW (the) of the city of Nain ; and other poems : by an under-graduate of the University of Cambridge. [Thomas DALE.]

London : MDCCCXIX. Octavo.*

WIDOW (the) of the wood. [By Benjamin VICTOR.]

London : MDCCLV. Duodecimo. Pp. iii. b. t. 208.* [*Lowndes, Bibliog. Man. Mon. Rev.*, xii. 392.]

WIDOW'S (the) lodgings. A novel. [By John BALLANTYNE.] In two volumes.

Edinburgh : 1813. Duodecimo. [*Cat. Philos. Inst. Edin.*, p. 336.]

WIDOW'S (the) mite. Or, questions of the greatest moment. Humbly offered for reviving true piety and religion in the life and power thereof. [By John WARDEN.]

Edinburgh : 1721. Duodecimo.* [*Adv. Lib.*]

WIDOW'S (the) tale : and other poems. By the author of Ellen Fitzarthur. [Caroline BOWLES, afterwards Mrs Southey.]

London : 1822. Duodecimo. Pp. 1. b. t. 222.*

WIDOW'S (the) vow. A farce, in two acts, as it is acted at the Theatre Royal, Hay-Market. [By Elizabeth INCHBALD, née Simpson.]

London : 1786. Octavo. Pp. 35.* [*Biog. Dram.*]

WIFE (the). By Mira, one of the authors of The female spectator, and Epistles for ladies. [Eliza HAYWOOD.]

London : M.DCC.LVI. Duodecimo. Pp. v. b. t. 282.*

WIFE (the) and Woman's reward. [By Mrs NORTON.] In three volumes.

London 1835. Duodecimo.*

WIFE (the) hunter, and Flora Hunter : tales by the Moriarty family. Edited by Denis Ignatius Moriarty, Esq. [By

John O'Brien GRANT.] In three volumes.

London : 1838. Duodecimo.* [*Bodl.*]

WIFE (a), not ready made, but bespoken by Dicus the batchelor, and made up for him by his fellow shepheard Tityrus : in four pastorall eclogues. [By Robert AYLETT.] The second edition; wherein are some things added but nothing amended.

London. 1653. Octavo. [*W., Brit. Mus.*] Signed R. A.

WIFE (a), now a widdowe. [By Sir Thomas OVERBURY.]

London, Imprinted for Laurence L'isle dwelling at the Tygres head in Paul's Church-yard. 1614. Octavo. No pagination.* [*Bodl.*]

WIFE'S (a) story, and other tales. By the author of "Caste," "Safely married," &c., &c. [Miss Emily JOLLY.] In three volumes.

London : 1875. Octavo.*
Reprinted from "Household words," "All the year round," "Blackwood's Magazine," "The Cornhill Magazine," and "Chambers's Magazine."

WIFE'S (the) temptation, a tale of Belgravia. By the authoress of "The sister of charity," "The laurel and the palm," "The village school fête," &c. [Mrs A. E. CHALLICE.] In two volumes.

London : 1859. Duodecimo.*

WIFE'S (the) trials. A novel. [By Emma Jane WORBOISE.] In three volumes.

London : 1855. Octavo.*

WILD (the) flower of Ravensworth. By the author of "John and I," "Doctor Jacob," &c. &c. [Matilda Betham EDWARDS.] In three volumes.

London : 1866. Octavo.*

WILD (the) garland ; or, prose and poetry connected with English wild flowers. Intended as an embellishment to the study of botany. By the author of "The life of Linnæus, in a series of letters. [S. WARING.]

London : 1827. Duodecimo. 31⁷⁄₂ sh. [*Smith's Cat of Friends' books*, ii. 859.]

WILD Mike and his victim. By the author of 'Misunderstood.' [Florence MONTGOMERY.]

London 1875. Octavo. Pp. 146.*

WILD sports of the West. With legendary tales, and local sketches. By the author of "Stories of Waterloo." [By W. H. MAXWELL.] In two volumes.

London : 1832. Octavo.*

WILDFLOWER. By the author of "The house of Elmore." [F. W. ROBINSON.] In three volumes.

London : 1857. Octavo.*

WILFUL (the) ward. A novel. By the author of the "Young doctor," "Sir Arthur Bouverie," &c. [Miss PINKNEY.] In three volumes.

London : 1853. Duodecimo.*

WILHELM Meister's apprenticeship, A novel. From the German of Goethe. [By Thomas CARLYLE.] In three volumes.

Edinburgh and London. 1824. Octavo.*

WILL (the) of a certain Northern vicar. [By Rev. W. COOPER, rector of Kirkby Wiske near Thirsk, N. R., Yorkshire.] Second edition to which is annex'd a codicil.

London : 1765. Quarto. [*N. and Q.*, 18 *March* 1882, p. 209.]

WILL (the) ; or, the half-brothers. A romance. [By —— M'GAURAN.] In three volumes.

London : 1846. Octavo.*

WILL-worship (of). [By Henry HAMMOND, D.D.]

Oxford, 1644. Quarto. Pp. 26. b. t.*

WILLIAM and Ellen. A tale. [By Eaglesfield SMITH.]

London : 1796. Duodecimo. Pp. 22. [*Mon. Rev.*, xxi. 467 ; xxiii. 108.]

WILLIAM and Lucy. An opera of two acts. An attempt to suit the style of the Scotch music. [By —— PATON.]

Edinburgh MDCCLXXX. Octavo.* [*Biog. Dram.*]

WILLIAM and Nanny ; a ballad farce, in two acts. As performed at the theatre in Covent Garden. [By Richard Josceline GOODENOUGH.]

London : 1779. Octavo. [*Biog. Dram. Mon. Rev.*, lxii. 171.]

WILLIAM Douglas ; or, The Scottish exiles. A historical novel. In three volumes. [By Henry DUNCAN, D.D.]

Edinburgh : 1826. Duodecimo.*

WILLIAM Penn and the Quakers either impostors, or apostates, which they please : proved from their avowed principles, and contrary practices. By Trepidantium Malleus. [Samuel YOUNG.]

London : 1696. Duodecimo. Pp. 4. b. t. 134.* [*Smith, Bib. Anti-Quaker.*, p. 459.]

WILLIAM Shakespeare not an impostor. By an English critic. [G. H. TOWNSEND.]

London : 1857. Octavo.* [*Olphar Hamst*, p. 180.]

WILLIAM Tell, a tragedy. Translated from the German of Schiller by "Tarkari." [Peter REID, Aberdeen.]

Aberdeen : 1879. [*R. Inglis.*]

WILLIAM Wyrcestre redivivus. Notices of ancient church architecture, in the fifteenth century, particularly in Bristol. With hints for practicable restorations. [By Rev. T. DALLAWAY.]

Bristol : N. D. Quarto. Pp. 32.*

WILLIE Armstrong : a Scottish drama, in three acts, by a man wise enough to know that amusement, even though somewhat coarse, is at times as salutary as any article in the pharmacopœia. [By Dr. Richard POOLE.]

Edinburgh : 1843. Octavo. Pp. 60.*

WILLIE Wabster's wooing and wedding on the braes of Angus. [By Dorothea OGILVY, of Clova.]

Montrose : MDCCCLXVIII. Octavo. Pp. 62.* [*A. Jervise.*]

WILLOW brook. A sequel to "The little camp on Eagle hill." By the author of "The wide wide world," "Queechy," "Melbourne house," etc. [Susan WARNER.]

London : 1874. Octavo.

WILMINGTONS (the). A novel. By the author of "Two old men's tales," "Emilia Wyndham," "Mordaunt Hall," &c. [Mrs Anne MARSH.] In three volumes.

London : 1850. Octavo.*

WIN her and take her, or, old fools will be medling ; a comedy, as it is acted at the Theatre-Royall, by their Majesties servants. [By John SMYTH, M.A.]

London, 1691. Quarto.* [*Biog. Dram.*]

WINCHESTER, and a few other compositions, in prose and verse. [By Rev. Charles TOWNSEND, rector of Kingston-on-the-sea, near Brighton.]

Winchester, 1835. Quarto. Pp. 82. [*W., Martin's Cat.*]

WINCHESTER (the) converts : or, a full and true discovery of the real usefulness and design of a late right seasonable and religious treatise, entitled, A plain account of the nature and end of the sacrament of the Lords Supper. In three dialogues. [By Thomas TOVEY, D.D., Principal of New Inn Hall, Oxford.]

Oxford : 1735. Octavo. Pp. 78.* [*Bodl.*]

WINCHESTER (the) guide ; or, a description of the antiquities and curiosities of that ancient city. [By Thomas WARTON, B.D.] A new edition. Illustrated with copper plates.

Winton : 1780. Duodecimo. Pp. 115. b. t. 1.*

WINDING-sheet (a) for England's ministry, which hath a name to live, but is dead. Sent to John Owen, called Dr. in that ministry, and late Vice-Chancellor of Oxford. And is in answer to his printed paper concerning tythes, or an examination of those Scriptures by which he seems to prove "that the publike maintenance for preachers of the Gospel by way of tythes, is a Gospel-maintenance." But upon examination thereof by the Scriptures, he is found to be a subverter of them, and, that tythes is no lawful maintenance for Gospel ministers. [By T. FOSTER, of Norfolk ?]

N. P. N. D. Quarto. 1 sh. [*Smith's Cat. of Friends' books*, i. 626. Signed "By a member of the true Church and of that Society, which the world calls Quakers."

WINDSOR Castle ; or, the fair maid of Kent, an opera, as performed at the Theatre-Royal, Covent-Garden, in honour of the marriage of their Royal Highnesses the Prince and Princess of Wales. By the author of Hartford-Bridge, Netley Abbey, etc. [William PEARCE.]

London : 1795. Octavo. Pp. 40.*

WINE and walnuts ; or, after dinner chit-chat. By Ephraim Hardcastle, citizen and dry-salter. [W. H. PYNE.] In two volumes.

London : 1823. Octavo.*

WINE and wisdom : or, the tippling philosophers. A lyric poem. To which

are subjoin'd, the most remarkable memoirs of the following ancients. Thales. Solon. Pherecydes. Anaxagoras. Archelaus. Socrates. Xenophon. Aristippus. Hegesias. Theodorus. Bion. Euclides. Eubulides. Menedemus. Plato. Speusippus. Polemo. Arcesilaus. Aristotle. Theophrastus. Strato. Lycon. Diogenes. Menippus. Zeno. Antipater. Pythagoras. Heraclitus. Xenophanes. Parmenides. Leucippus. Democritus. Anaxarchus. Pyrrho. Epicurus. Longinus. Porphyrius. Iamblicus. Ædesius. Eustathius. Maximus. Priscus. Julianus. Proceresius. Xantus. Demosthenes. Zalucus. Seneca. Piso. Cato. Copernicus. [By Edward WARD.]

London : 1719. Octavo. Pp. 5. b. t. 40.*

WINGS and stings. A tale for the young. By A. L. O. E. authoress of the "Claremont tales," "Glimpses of the unseen," "True heroism," &c. [Charlotte TUCKER.]

London: MDCCCLXIII. Octavo. Pp. 160.*

WINIFRED Bertram, and the world she lived in. By the author of "Chronicles of the Schönberg-Cotta family," &c. &c. [Mrs CHARLES.]

London : 1866. Octavo. Pp. 476.*

WINTER (a) dreame. [By James HOWELL.]

Printed Anno Domini, 1649. Quarto. Pp. 20. b. t.* [Bodl.]

WINTER evenings at college : a familiar description of the manners, customs, sports, and religious observances of the Ancient Greeks : with a short account of the state of Modern Greece ; and reflections on the revolutions of empires. By a clergyman. [Benjamin Thomas Holcott COLE.] In two volumes.

London : M.DCCC.XXIX. Octavo.*

WINTER evenings ; or, lucubrations on life and letters. [By Vicesimus KNOX, D.D.] In three volumes.

London: M.DCC.LXXXVIII. Duodecimo.*

WINTER (a) in Edinburgh ; or, the Russian brothers. A novel. By Honoria Scott. [Mrs FRAZER.] In three volumes.

London : 1822. Duodecimo.*

"Mrs Frazer, who some years ago published several popular works under the name of Honoria Scott, has a work nearly ready for the press," &c.—Newspaper cutting (July 1824) in Mr. Maidment's copy.

WINTER leaves. [Poems by John FAIRBAIRN and Charles M'DOWAL.]

Edinburgh. 1835. Octavo.*

WINTER-piece (the). A poem. [By Joseph PHIPPS.] Written in 1740.

London ; 1763. Folio. 5 sh. [Smith's Cat. of Friends' books, i. 66.]

WINTER (a) story By the author of 'The rose garden' 'Thorpe Regis' etc. [Frances Mary PEARD.]

London 1875. Octavo. Pp. i. b. t. 292.*

WISDOM, a poem. [By Edward WILKINSON, M.D.] The fourth edition.

London : M.DCC.XCVIII. Octavo. Pp. 21.* [Gent. Mag., Dec. 1809, p. 1176. Mon. Rev., lviii. 305. Smith's Cat. of Friends' books, ii. 933.]

WISDOM from above: or, considerations tending to explain, establish, and promote the Christian life, or that holiness, without which no man shall see the Lord. By a lover of truth, and of the souls of men. [John MAPLETOFT, D.D.]

London ; 1714. Duodecimo. Pp. 155.* There is a second part, published in 1717, with the same title and separate pagination.

WISDOM (the) of looking backward, to judge the better of one side and t'other by the speeches, writings, actions, and other matters of fact on both sides, for the four years last past. [By White KENNETT, D.D.]

London: M DCC XV. Octavo.*

WISDOM the first spring of action in the Deity. A discourse, in which, among other things, the absurdity of God's being actuated by natural inclinations, and of an unbounded liberty, is shewn, the moral attributes of God are explain'd, the origin of evil is consider'd. The fundamental duties of natural religion are shewn to be reasonable ; and several things, advanc'd by some late authors, and others, relating to these subjects, are freely examin'd. [By Henry GROVE, of Taunton.]

London, MDCCXXXIV. Octavo. Pp. iv. b. t. 110.*

WISDOM'S conquest, being an explanation and grammatical translation of the 13th Book of Ovid's Metamorphoses [by Thomas HALL].

London : 1651. Octavo. [*W., Lowndes, Bibliog. Man.*]

WISE (a) and moderate discourse, concerning Church-affaires. As it was written, long since, by the famous authour [Francis, Lord BACON] of those Considerations, which seem to have some reference to this. Now published for the common good.

Imprinted in the yeere 1641. Quarto.*

Reprinted in 1663, title, "True peace: or, a moderate discourse to compose the unsettled consciences and greatest differences in ecclesiastical affaires."

WISE (the) judgment : being a chapter on the competing models for the Manchester Wellington testimonial. By Gabriel Tinto, Esq. [G. W. ANTHONY.]

Manchester : 1853. Octavo. Pp. 11. [*Manchester Free Lib. Cat.*, p. 18.]

WISE (the) or foolish choice : or the wisdom of choosing Christ, and the folly of choosing the world for our portion. Discovered and asserted by Solomon the Wise. In a paraphrase on the Song of Solomon, and an abstract of the book of Solomon called Ecclesiastes. Wherein the sweetness of union and communion with Christ, and the bitterness and vanity of all worldly things is held forth. Both done in metre by one of the ministers of the Gospel in Glasgow. I. C. [Rev. James CLARK, minister at Innerwick, afterwards at Glasgow.]

Edinburgh, M.D.CC.III. Octavo. Pp. 62. b. l.*

WISEMAN versus Pascal the younger. The Church of Rome's defence against "Cases of conscience," with a reply. By Pascal the younger. [Pierce CONNELLY.]

London : 1851. Octavo. [*New Coll. Cat.*, p. 591.]

WISHES (the) of a free people : a dramatic poem. [By Paul HIFFERNAN.]

London : 1761. Octavo. [*Biog. Dram. Mon. Rev.*, xxv. 396.]

WIT a sporting in a pleasant grove of new fancies. By H. B. [Henry BOLD.]

London : 1657. Sm. Octavo. [*Lowndes, Bibliog. Man.*]

WIT against reason, or the Protestant champion, the great, the incomparable Chillingworth, not invulnerable. By E. W. [Edward HAWARDEN.]

Brussels : 1735. Octavo. [*W.*]

WIT (the) of a woman. As it now acted at the New Theatre in Little Lincoln's-Inn-Fields. By Her Majesty's sworn servants, [By Thomas WALKER.]

London, 1705. Quarto. Pp. 8. b. t. 34.* [*Biog. Dram.*]

WIT revived : or, a new excellent way of divertisement, digested into most ingenious questions and answers. Published under the name of Asdryasdust Tossoffacan. [Edmund GAYTON.]

London : 1660. Duodecimo. [*Wood, Athen. Oxon.*, iii. 756.]

WITCH-FINDER (the); or, the wisdom of our ancestors. A romance. By the author of "The Lollards," "Other times," "Calthorpe," &c. [Thomas GASPEY.] In three volumes.

London : 1824. Duodecimo.*

WITCH (the) of the woodlands : or, the cobler's new translation : written by L. P. [Lawrence PRICE.]

London, 1655. Octavo. Pp. 22. B. L.* [*Bodl.*]

WITCHCRAFT cast out from the religious seed and Israel of God : and the black art, or, necromancy, inchantments, and witchcraft discovered, with the ground, fruits and effects thereof… Also some things to clear the truth from reproaches, and false accusations, occasioned by D. Bott, and his slander-carriers, etc. By Richard FARNWORTH.]

London : 1655. Quarto. [*W., Brit. Mus.*] Signed R. F.

WITCHCRAFT farther display'd. Containing I. An account of the witchcraft practis'd by Jane Wenham of Walkerne, in Hertfordshire, since her condemnation, upon the bodies of Anne Thorn and Anne Street, and the deplorable condition in which they still remain. II. An answer to the most general objections against the being and power of witches : with some remarks upon the case of Jane Wenham in particular, and on Mr. Justice Powel's procedure therein. To which are added, the tryals of Florence Newton, a famous Irish witch, at the assizes held at Cork, anno 1661 ; as also of two witches at the assizes held at Bury St. Edmonds in Suffolk, anno 1664, before Sir Matthew Hale, (then Lord Chief Baron of the Exchequer) who were found guilty and executed. [By Francis BRAGGE, A.B., late of Peterhouse in Cambridge.]

London, 1712. Octavo. Pp. 3. b. t. 39.* Introduction signed F. B.

WITENHAM-Hill, a descriptive poem. By T. P — — A.M. [Thomas Pye, A.M.]

London: 1777. Quarto. Pp. 26. b. t.* [Bodl.]

Ascribed to Thomas Pentycross. [Watt, Bib. Brit.]

WITH brains, Sir. [By John Brown, M.D.]

N. P. N. D. Octavo. Pp. 12.* From the Monthly Journal of Medical Science, for February 1851. Signed J. B.

WITH harp and crown. A novel. By the authors of "Ready-money Mortiboy," "My little girl," "This son of Vulcan," etc. [Walter Besant and James Rice.] In three volumes.

London: 1875. Octavo.*

WITHIN, without and over; or memorials of the earnest life of Henry C. Hall. [By Amanda H. Hall.]

Northampton : 1878. [Lit. Jour., iv. 24.]

WITS (the) and beaux of society. By Grace and Philip Wharton, authors of "The Queens of society." [Katherine and J. C. Thomson.] With illustrations from drawings by H. K. Browne and James Godwin. Engraved by the brothers Dalziel. In two volumes.

London : [1860. Octavo.*

WIT'S bedlam, where is had, whipping cheer to cure the mad. [By John Davies, of Hereford.]

London: 1617. Octavo. [W., Lowndes, Bibliog. Man.

WITS common-wealth : or a treasury of divine, moral, historical, and poetical admonitions, similies and sentences for the use of schools. [Compiled by John Bodenham.] Newly corrected and enlarged.

London : 1722. Sm. Octavo. Pp. 270. [W.]

—— ; the second part, a treasury of divine, morall, and phylosophicall similies, and sentences generally usefull, but more particularly published for the use of schooles, by F. M. [Francis Meres], Master of Arts of both Universities.

London, printed by William Stansby, 1634. Duodecimo. [W.]

Engraved title, 'Witts Academy, a treasurie of Goulden Sentences, Similies, and Examples, by Fr. M.' 7 leaves, pp. 741, and 4 leaves.

WITS extraction, conveyed to the ingenious in riddles, observations and morals. By W. B. [William Bagwell], Truth's servant.

London: 1664. Duodecimo. [W., Lowndes, Bibliog. Man.]

WITS interpreter : the English Parnassus. Or, a sure guide to those admirable accomplishments that compleat our English gentry, in the most acceptable qualifications of discourse or writing. In which briefly the whole mystery of those pleasing witchcrafts of eloquence and love, are made easie in the following subjects : viz. 1. Theatre of courtship, accurate complements. 2. The labyrinth of fancies, new experiments and inventions. 3. Apollo and Orpheus, several love-songs, epigrams, drollerys, and other verses. 4. Cyprian goddess, description of beauty. 5. The muses Elizium, severall poetical fictions. 6. The perfect inditer, letters a la mode. 7. Games and sports now us'd at this day among the gentry of England, &c. 8. Cardinal Richeleiu's Key to his manner of writing of letters by cyphers. As also an alphabetical table of the first devisers of sciences and other curiosities; all of which are collected with industry and care, for the benefit and delight of those that love ingenious enterprises. The 3d edition with many new additions, by J. C. [John Cotgrave.]

London, MDCLXXI. Octavo. Pp. 11. b. t. 520.*

WITS private wealth, stored with choyse commodities to content the minde. [By Nicholas Breton.]

London : 1625. Sm. Quarto. [W.] Sheets A to D inclusive, not paged.

WITS (the), or, sport upon sport. In select pieces of drollery, digested into scenes by way of dialogue. Together with variety of humors of several nations, fitted for the pleasure and content of all persons, either in court, city, countrey, or camp. The like never before published. [By Francis Kirkman.] Part I.

London, 1662. Octavo. Pp. 186. b. t.*

WITS theater of the little world. [By John Bodenham.]

Printed by I. R. for N. L. & are to be sold at the west doore of Paules. 1599. Octavo. Fol. 3. b. t. 269. 6.* [Bodl.]

WITTY apophthegms delivered at several times, and upon several occa-

sions, by King James, King Charles, the Marquess of Worcester, Francis, Lord Bacon, and Sir Thomas Moor. Collected and revised [by Dr. Thomas BAILY].

[London] 1671. Octavo. Pp. 2. b. t. 186.*

WITTY (a) combat: or, the female victor. A tragi-comedy. As it was acted by persons of quality in Whitsun-week with great applause. Written by F. P. Gent. [Thomas PORTER.]

London, 1663. Quarto. No pagination.* [*Bodl.*]

WIZARD (the) Peter. A song of the Solway. [By Charles Kirkpatrick SHARPE.]

Edinburgh: M.D.CCC.XXXIV. Octavo. Pp. 32.*

WOLF (the) stript of his shepherd's cloathing: in answer to a late celebrated book [by James Owen] intituled Moderation a vertue; wherein the designs of the dissenters against the Church; and their behaviour towards her Majesty both in England and Scotland are laid open. With the case of occasional conformity considered. Humbly offer'd to the consideration of her Majesty and her three estates of parliament. By one call'd an High-churchman. [Charles LESLIE.] With my service to Dr. D'Avenant.

Sold by the booksellers of London and Westminster. 1704. Quarto.*

WOLSEY, the cardinal, and his times; courtly, political, and ecclesiastical. By George Howard, Esq. author of Lady Jane Grey, and her times. [Lieut. F. C. LAIRD, R.N.]

London: 1824. Octavo.*

WOMAN. Sketches of the history, genius, disposition, accomplishments, employments, customs, and importance of the fair sex, in all parts of the world. Interspersed with many singular and entertaining anecdotes. By a friend to the sex. [—— ADAMS.]

London: 1790. Duodecimo. Pp. 400. [*Watt, Bib. Brit. Mon. Rev.*, iii. 227.]

WOMAN (the) hater. As it hath beene lately acted by the children of Paules. [By F. BEAUMONT and John FLET-CHER.]

London. 1607. Quarto. No pagination.*
The above is the first edition. The edition published in 1648 has the name of John Fletcher, and the edition of 1849 has the names of both Beaumont and Fletcher.

WOMAN (the) I loved, and the woman who loved me. By the author of "Agnes Tremarne," "The cost of a secret," "A story of two lives," &c., &c. [Isabella BLAGDEN.]

London: 1865. Octavo. Pp. 292. b. t.*

WOMAN (the) of Samaria. [By Ann ALEXANDER, *née* Tuke.]

London: 1846. Duodecimo. [*Smith's Cat. of Friends' books*, i. 8.]

WOMAN (the) of the world. A novel. By the authoress of the Diary of a désennuyée. [Mrs. Catherine Frances GORE.] Three volumes.

London: 1838. Duodecimo.*

WOMAN (a) scorned. A novel. By E. Owens Blackburne, author of "The quest of the heir," "Philosopher Push," "Dean Swift's ghost," etc. [Elizabeth CASEY.] In three volumes.

London: 1876. Octavo.*

WOMAN'S devotion. A novel. In three volumes. [By Mrs. MARSH.]

London: 1855. Octavo.*

WOMAN'S (the) kingdom. A love story. By the author of 'John Halifax, Gentleman,' &c. &c. [Dinah Maria MULOCK.] In three volumes.

London: 1869. Octavo.*

WOMAN'S (a) riddle. A romantic tale. In four volumes. By Ann of Swansea, author of Conviction, Cesario Rosalba, Secrets in every mansion, Chronicles of an illustrious house, Lovers and friends, Gonzalo di Baldivia, Guilty or not guilty, &c. &c. [Miss Frances Ann KEMBLE.]

London: 1824. Duodecimo.*

WOMAN'S (a) thoughts about women. By the author of "John Halifax, Gentleman," &c. &c. [Dinah Maria MULOCK.] In one volume.

London: 1858. Octavo. Pp. v. 348.*

WOMAN'S (a) vengeance. A novel. By the author of "Cecil's tryst," "Lost Sir Massingberd," etc., etc. [James PAYN.] In three volumes.

London: 1872. Octavo.*

WOMAN'S (a) victory. A novel. By the author of "Elsie: a lowland sketch." [Agnes C. MAITLAND.] In three volumes.

London: 1876. Octavo.*

WOMEN as they are; or, the manners of the day. [By Mrs Catherine Frances

GORE.] Second edition. In three volumes.

London: 1830. Duodecimo.*

WOMEN in the East. (Les femmes en Orient, par Mme. la Comtesse Dora d' Istria.) [The Princess KOLTZOFF-MASSALSKY, *née* Helena Ghika, daughter of the Prince Alexander Ghika, Ex-hospodar of Wallachia.] In two volumes.

Zurich & London: 1861. [*Athenæum, Aug.* 3, 1861, p. 148.]

WOMEN of the last days of old France. By the author of "On the edge of the storm," "Mademoiselle Mori," "Sydonie's dowry," etc. [Margaret ROBERTS.] With original illustrations by J. W. Petherick.

London: 1872. Octavo. Pp. vi. 1. 403.*

WOMEN (the) of the Gospels, The three wakings, and other verses. By the author of "Chronicles of the Schönberg-Cotta family." [Mrs CHARLES.] New edition, with additions.

London: 1868. Octavo. Pp. 276.*

WOMEN; or, pour et contre. A tale. By the author of "Bertram," &c. [Charles Robert MATURIN.] In three volumes.

Edinburgh: 1818. Duodecimo.*

WOMENS (the) conquest: a tragi-comedy. As it was acted by his Highness the Duke of York's servants. Written by the Honourable E. H. [Edward HOWARD.]

London, 1671. Quarto.*

WOMENS speaking justified, proved and allowed by the Scriptures, all such as speak by the spirit and power of the Lord Jesus, and how women were the first that preached the tidings of the resurrection of Jesus, etc. [By Margaret FOX, *née* Fell.]

London: 1667. Quarto. [*IV., Brit. Mus.*] Signed 'M. F.'

WONDER (the) of the Bishop of Meaux [Bossuet], upon perusal of Dr. Bull's books, consider'd and answer'd. [By Edward STEPHENS.]

London; 1704. Quarto. Pp. 12.*

WONDER (a); or, an honest Yorkshire-man. A ballad opera, as it is perform'd at the theatres with universal applause. [By Henry CAREY.]

London, 1736. Octavo.* [*N. and Q.,* 18 *Feb.* 1860, p. 126.]

WONDERFUL (the) adventures of Tuflongbo and his elfin company, in their journey with Little Content through the enchanted forest. By Holme Lee, author of "Legends from fairy land," etc. [Harriet PARR.] With eight illustrations by W. Sharpe.

London: M.DCCC.LXI. Octavo. Pp. vi. 245.*

WONDERFUL (the) confirmation of the succession of the Kingdom of Christ at 1697, derived from the 42 moons then ending; given by prophecy, &c. [By T. BEVERLEY.]

[London: 1690?] Quarto. [*IV., Brit. Mus.*]

WONDERFUL (a) cure. *See* "HOME plays for ladies."

WONDERFUL (the) life. By Hesba Stretton, author of "Lost Gip," "The king's servants," etc., etc. [Miss Sarah SMITH.]

London. 1875. Octavo. Pp. viii. 251.*

WONDERFUL prodigies of judgment and mercy: discovered in above three hundred memorable histories, containing I. Dreadful judgments upon atheists, perjured persons, blasphemers, swearers, cursers and scoffers. II. The miserable ends of divers magicians, witches, conjurers, &c. with several strange apparitions. III. Remarkable presages of approaching death, and of appeals to divine justice. IV. The wicked lives, and woful deaths of wretched popes, apostates, and desperate persecutors. V. Fearful judgments upon cruel tyrants, murderers, &c. with the wonderful discoveries of murders. VI. Admirable deliverances from imminent dangers and deplorable distresses at sea and land. VII. Divine goodness to penitents, with the dying thoughts of several famous men concerning a future state after this life. Faithfully collected from antient and modern authors, of undoubted authority and credit, and imbellished with divers curious pictures, of several remarkable passages therein. By R. B. author of the History of the wars of England, and the Remarks of London, &c. [Richard BURTON.]

London, 1682. Duodecimo. Pp. 2. b. t. 235.* [*Bodl.*]

WONDERFULL (a), strange and miraculous, astrologicall prognostication for this yeer of our Lord God,

1591. Discouering such wonders to happen this yeere, as neuer chaunced since Noes floud. Wherein if there be found one lye, the author will loose his credit for euer. By Adam Fouleweather, student in asse-tronomy. [Thomas NASH.]

London [1591.] Quarto. B. L. No pagination.*

WONDERFULL (the) yeare, 1603. Wherein is shewed the picture of London, lying sicke of the plague. At the ende of all (like a mery epilogue to a dull play) certain tales are cut out in sundry fashions, of purpose to shorten the liues of long winter nights, that lye watching in the darke for us. [By Thomas DEKKER.]

London, N. D. Quarto. Pp. 48. B. L.* [*Corser's Collectanea Anglo-Poetica*, Part v. p. 129.]

W O N D E R S no miracles; or, Mr Valentine Greatrates gift of healing examined, upon occasion of a sad effect of his stroaking, March the 7. 1665. at one Mr. Cressets house in Charter-House-Yard. In a letter to a reverend divine living near that place. [By David LLOYD, M.A., Canon of St. Asaph.]

London, 1666. Quarto.* [*Bodl.*]

WONDERS (the) of the vegetable kingdom display'd. In a series of [xiv.] letters. By the author of "Select female biography." [Mary ROBERTS.]

London: 1822. Octavo. Pp. 5. b. t. 243.* [*Smith's Cat. of Friends' books*, ii. 500.]

WONDERS of the vegetable world. [By W. H. Davenport ADAMS.]

London: 1867. Duodecimo. Pp. 127.* Preface signed W. H. D. A.

WONDROUS strange. A novel. By the author of "Mabel," "Sunshine and shadow," "Margaret Hamilton," "Right and left," etc. [Mrs C. J. NEWBY.] Second edition. [In three volumes.]

London: 1864. Duodecimo.*

WONDROUS (the) tale of Alroy. The rise of Iskander. By the author of "Vivian Grey," "Contarini Fleming," &c. [Benjamin DISRAELI.] In three volumes.

London: 1833. Duodecimo.*

WONSTON Confirmation tracts. [By Alexander Robert Charles DALLAS, rector of Wonston, Hants.]

London: 1840. Duodecimo.*

These tracts are twelve in number, having all the general title as given above. Each tract has, however, an addition, explanatory of the particular aspect in which Confirmation is viewed by the author.

WOO-CREEL (the), or the Bill o' Bashan; a tale. [By Sir Alexander BOSWELL.]

Auchinleck: 1816. Quarto. Pp. 11. b. t.* Dedication signed A. B.

WOOD-SPIRIT (the). A novel. In two volumes. [By Ernest JONES.]

London: 1841. Duodecimo.*

WOODEN (the) world dissected: in the character of a ship of war: as also, the the characters of all the officers, from the captain to the common sailor; viz. I. A sea-captain. II. A sea lieutenant. III. A sea-chaplain. IV. The master of a ship of war. V. The purser. VI. The surgeon. VII. The gunner. VIII. The carpenter. IX. The boatswain. X. A sea-cook. XI. A midshipman. XII. The captain's steward. XIII. A sailor. By the author of the London spy. [Edward WARD.] The seventh edition.

London: MDCCLVI. Duodecimo. Pp. 4. b. t. 86.*

WOODLAND (the) companion: or a brief description of British trees, with some account of their uses. By the author of Evenings at home. [John AIKIN, M.D.]

London: 1815. Duodecimo. [*IV., Brit. Mus.*] Signed J. A.

WOODLEIGH. By the author of "One and twenty," "Wildflower," "The house of Elmore," &c. [F. W. ROBINSON.] In three volumes.

London: 1859. Octavo.*

WOODSTOCK; an elegy. [By Hugh DALRYMPLE.]

1761. Quarto. [*N. and Q.*, 1. Ser. ix. 589. *Mon. Rev.*, xxv. 62.]

WOODSTOCK; or, the Cavalier. A tale of the year Sixteen hundred and fifty-one. By the author of "Waverley," "Tales of the Crusaders," &c. [Sir Walter SCOTT.] In three volumes.

Edinburgh: 1826. Octavo.*

WOOING!! and cooing!! The R—— courtship; or, C——tle and Co——gh. A poem, by Peter Pindar, Esq. [John WOLCOTT, M.D.] Fifth edition.

London: N. D. Octavo. Pp. 27.*

WOOING (the) o't. A novel. By Mrs Alexander. [Annie HECTOR, _née_ French.] In three volumes.

London : 1873. Octavo.*

WOOLLEN draper's (a) letter on the French treaty to his friends and fellow tradesmen all over England. [By Lieut. J. MACKENZIE.]

London : 1786. Octavo. Pp. 48. [_W., Author's MS. Dedication._]

Signed ' R. J. Woollen Draper.

WORCESTER dumb-bells ; a ballad. To the tune of All in the land of Essex. [By Thomas WARTON.]

N. P. N. D. S. L.* [_Bodl._]

WORCESTER gaudy, 1858. By A late fellow. [J. T. B. LANDON, M.A.]

N. P. N. D. Quarto. Pp. 3.*

WORCESTER-SHIRE (the) petition to the parliament for the ministry of England defended, by a minister of Christ in that county ; in answer to xvi. queries, printed in a book, called, A brief discovery of the threefold estate of Antichrist : whereunto is added, xvii. counter-queries, and an humble monition to parliament, people and ministers. [By Richard BAXTER.]

London, 1653. Quarto. Pp. 4. b. t. 40.* [_Smith, Bib. Anti-Quaker._, p. 59.]

WORCESTERS elegie, and evlogie. By J. T. [John TOY] Mr. of Arts.

London : 1638. Quarto. No pagination. [_Lowndes, Bibliog. Man._]

WORD (the). Walks from Eden. By the author of " The wide, wide world." [Susan WARNER.]

London : MDCCCLXVI. Octavo. Pp. vi. 1. 284.*

WORD (a) about a new election, that the people of England may see the happy difference between English liberty and French slavery ; and may consider well, before they make the exchange. [By Daniel DEFOE.]

Printed in the year 1710. Octavo.* [_Wilson, Life of Defoe_, 122.]

WORD (a) for that section in the Church, who, in the recent struggle, took up what may be called a medium position. [By David LOGAN, minister of Stenton.]

Edinburgh : N. D. [1844.] Octavo. Pp. 4.* [_D. Laing._]

WORD (a) in behalf of the king, that he may see who they are that honour all men, and love the brother-hood, that

fear God, and honour the king, according as it is written in the Scriptures of truth, see 1 Pet. 2. 17. Which is a beesom to sweep away all sin and wickednesse which dishonours the king and the nation. For who live in all manner of sin and wickednesse, drunkennesse, oaths, and uncleannesse, and ungodlinesse, these live out of Gods fear, so cannot honour the king. But they that depart from all manner of sin, ungodliness, unrighteousness, uncleanness, filthiness, swearing, are them that fear God, and honour the king ; and also how that Christ ends the Jews law, by which they were to kill about religion such as were contrary-minded, and he never gave out any since to do so, but to love enemies ; but all laws by which the Christians do now persecute, are gotten up in the apostacy since the dayes of the apostles ; and though the Jews and Gentiles were to hate enemies, and to kill them ; yet you may see that Christ's command and doctrine was to love enemies and they that do so are the true Christians. [By George FOX.]

London, 1660. Quarto. Pp. 15.* [_Smith's Cat. of Friends' books_, i. 659.] Signed G. F.

WORD (a) in season : being a parallel between the intended bloody massacre of the people of the Jews, in the reign of King Ahasuerus ; and the hellish powder-plot against the Protestants, in the reign of King James. Together with an account of some of the wicked principles and practices of the Church of Rome, demonstrated in their barbarous and cruel murders and massacres of the Protestants in the Netherlands, France, Ireland, Piedmont, the Albigenses, &c. Also shewing that the present Church of Rome is an apostate Church and so discovered to be that mystery Babylon, mother of harlots, and abominations of the earth, mentioned in the Revelations. By H. C. a lover of true Protestants. [Henry CARE.]

London, 1679. Quarto. Pp. 2. b. t. 47.*

WORD (a) in season ; or, how the corn-grower may yet grow rich, and his labourer happy. Addressed to the Stout British Farmer. [By Samuel SMITH, M.A., vicar of Lois-Weedon-by-Weston, Towcester.]

London : 1849. Octavo.* [_Adv. Lib._]

WORD (a) in season to all in authority.

With weighty considerations what persons, practices and things, doth chiefly cause division and contention, rending of kingdoms, and distresse of nations. As also, a plain discovery of those things and that ministery, that will bring blessings and unity, with deliverance from bondage, into liberty ; and instead of strife, wars and fightings, righteousnesse, reconciliation and peace in the land of our nativity. Published by a lover of truth and the kingdom of peace, J. C. [John COLLENS.]

London, 1660. Quarto. Pp. 26. b. t.*
The Postscript was written by J. Anderson.

WORD (a) in season to all sorts of well-minded people in this miserably distracted and distempered nation, plainly manifesting, that the safety and well-being of the commonwealth under God dependeth on the fidelity and steadfast adherence of the people to those whom they have chosen, and on their ready compliance with them &c. [By J. SADLER.]

London: 1646. Quarto. [*IV., Brit. Mus.*]

WORD (a) in season to the traders and manufacturers of Great Britain. [By William COMBE.] Sixth edition.

London, printed: Edinburgh, reprinted. M,DCC,XCII. Octavo. Pp. 22.*
Signed A true-born Englishman.

WORD (the) made flesh; or the true humanity of God in Christ demonstrated from the Scriptures. [By Thomas CARLYLE, advocate.]

Edinburgh: 1829. Octavo. Pp. 234.*
[*G. C. Boase.*]

WORD (a) more on the Moderatorship; in a letter to the Rev. William Cunningham, of Trinity College Church, Edinburgh. By a bystander. [James MONCRIEFF.]

Edinburgh: 1837. Octavo. Pp. 54.

WORD (a) of caution and of comfort to the middle and lower classes of society being a pastor's advice to his flock in time of trouble. [By Rev. T. F. DIBDIN.]

London: 1831. [*Olphar Hamst*, p. 182.]

WORD (the) of God the best guide to all persons, at all times, and in all places : or, a collection of Scripture-texts, plainly shewing such things as are necessary for every Christians knowledg and practice. By the author of the Best companion. . [William HOWELL.]

Oxford, M.DC.LXXXIX. Octavo. Pp. 10. b. t. 213. 3.* [*Bodl.*]

WORD (a) of information to them that need it ; briefly opening some most weighty passages of God's dispensations among the sons of men, from the beginning ; and insisting a little upon the state and condition of the nations, wherein they now stand, and particularly of England : for this end, that men may remember themselves, and turn unto the Lord ; and seek to be delivered from the mysteries of iniquity, to walk with God in fellowship and communion. To which (as pertinent hereunto) is annexed, an addition concerning Lord-Bishops, and Common-Prayer-Book. With a tender admonition to those called priests, or ministers : and also, a loving exhortation to those that have separated from their superstitions. By W. T. [William TOMLINSON.]

London, 1660. Quarto. Pp. 47.* [*Bodl.*]

WORD (a) of reproof, and advice to my late fellow-souldiers and officers of the English, Irish and Scotish army ; with some inrhoad made upon the hireling and his mass-house, university, orders, degrees, vestments, poperies, heathenism, &c. With a short catalogue of some of the fighting priests, and for just cause given, have given them a blow in one of their eyes, (pickt out of the whores head) which they call, a fountain of religion, but is a sink of iniquity. Also a word to those old creatures who are old in iniquity, and in the fallen estate, yet deny falling away. Likewise a word to those magistrates and rulers who whip, or suffer to be whipt or imprisoned the saints of the Most High as vagabonds, amongst whom there is no begger. As also a word to that bad generation of people, who in their reprobate minds, and with their unwholsome tongues blaspheme and belye the dreadful and just God, in saying that he hath created some men intentionally to be damned, and a particular number to be saved and damn'd. Wherefore then doth the hireling preach, and for what hath he his hire? Mark, the decrees of God are yea, amen, and unalterable. A word to these who are called dukes, marquesses, earls, viscounts, lords, barrons, bannerets, baronets, knights of all sorts, esquires and gentlemen (so called.) Also let that generation that desire a signe, read some of the examples that have befallen the per-

secutors of the innocent. By a lover of good men, good laws, good governments and governours, good judges and ministers, as at the beginning : who hates nor fears no man, and is a lover and honourer of all men in the Lord, but cannot give flattering title, or respect the person of any man. E. B. [Edward BILLING.]

London, 1659. Quarto. Pp. 96.* [*Bodl.*]

WORD (the) of the Lord, To his beloved Citty New-Ierusalem, come from God, cloathed with the excellency of the glory of his love; and is the bride the Lambs wife, with the flowings of the tender compassionate bowels of the Lord Jesus, to all the mourners in Sion, and the afflicted desolate people, who waite for his comming as for the morning, and hath not satisfaction in any thing but in the enjoyment of his sweet and comfortable presence. [By William DEWSBURY.] (Given forth in York Castle, the 19. of the first moneth, 1663.)

N. P. N. D. [1663.] Quarto. Pp. 7.*

WORD (the) of the Lord to Sion the new Jerusalem, the bride the Lambs wife, the excellency of all the glory that is amongst the people; though she be now in deep sufferings, in fulness of time God will clear the innocency of her children ; and all the nations of the earth shall call her the blessed of the Lord, yea, the holy city, in whom the Lord dwells, to manifest his glory upon the earth amongst the children of men for ever. [By William DEWSBURY.]

London, 1664. Quarto. Pp. 8.* Signed W. D.

WORD (a) of wisdom for the witty, addressed to Isaac Tomkins, author of "Thoughts upon the aristocracy of England." [By John RICHARDS, M.P.]

London : 1835. Octavo. Pp. 24. [*Manchester Free Lib. Cat.*, p. 596.]

WORD (a) or two of advice to William Warburton ; a dealer in many words. By a friend. With an appendix containing a taste of William's spirit of railing. [By Zachary GREY, LL.D.]

London: MDCCXLVI. Octavo. Pp. 26. b. t.* [*Bodl.*]

The Advice is signed Thy friend in the truth, A. E. See "FREE and familiar letter."

WORD (a) or two in vindication of the University of Oxford and of Magdalen College in particular from the posthumous aspersions of Mr. Gibbon. [By James HURDIS, D.D.]

[London : 1797.] Quarto. Pp. 44.*

WORD (a) or two; or, architectural hints : in lines, in two parts, addressed to those Royal Academicians who are painters : written prior, as well as subsequent to the day of annual election for their president, 10th December 1805. To which a few notes are added : a dedication, a preface, and postscript to reviewers. By Fabricia Nunnez, Spinster. [Peter COXE.]

London : 1806. Quart. Pp. 49.* [*Gent. Mag.*, Dec. 1844, p. 653; *Feb.* 1808, p. 143.] See "ANOTHER word or two."

WORD (a) to a drunkard. [By John WESLEY, M.A.]

N. P. N. D. Duodecimo. Pp. 4.*

WORD (a) to Mr Madan ; or, free thoughts on his late celebrated defence of polygamy ; in a letter to a friend. [By Henry MOORE.]

1781. Octavo. [*March's Dissenters*, p. 512. *Mon. Rev.*, lxv. 158.]

WORD (a) to Mr Peters, and two words for the parliament and kingdom, &c. [By Rev. Nathaniel WARD.]

1647. [*N. and Q.*, *March* 1867, p. 237.]

WORD (a) to Mr. Wil. Prynn, Esq; and two for the parliament and army. Reproving the one, and justifying the other in their late proceedings. Presented to the consideration of the readers of Mr. William Prynn's last books. [By Henry MARTEN.]

London: 1649. Quarto. Pp. 16.* [*Bodl.*]

WORD (a) to the Hutchinsonians ; or, remarks on three extraordinary sermons lately preached before the University of Oxford, by the Rev. Dr. Patten, the Rev. Mr. Wetherall, and the Rev. Mr. Horne. By a member of the University. [Benjamin KENNICOTT, D.D.]

London : 1756. Octavo. Pp. 44. [*Darling, Cyclop. Bibl.*]

WORD (a) to the public; by the author of "Lucretia," "Rienzi," &c. [Sir Edward Lytton BULWER-LYTTON.]

London : 1847. Duodecimo. [*W.*]

WORD (a) to the sons of Africa. [By Luke HOWARD.]

London : 1822. Octavo. 1 sh. [*Smith's Cat. of Friends' book*, i. 92.]

WORD (a) to the wavering : or an answer to the Enquiry into the present state of affairs : whether we owe allegiance to the King in these circumstances ? &c. With a postcript of subjection to the higher powers ; by Dr. G. B——. [Gilbert BURNET.]

London, printed in the year MDCLXXXIX. Quarto. Pp. 10.*

WORD (a) to the wise. In a letter to a city clergyman, recommended to the consideration of his brethren of the clergy especially those of the younger sort. [Said to be by Dr. RAWSON.]

London : 1711. Octavo. [*Kennett's Wisdom*, p. 110.]

WORD (a) to the wise ; or, an exhortation to the Roman Catholic clergy of Ireland. By a member of the Established Church. [George BERKELEY, Bishop of Cloyne.]

Dublin : 1749. Octavo. [*Cat. Lib. Trin. Coll. Dub.*, p. 273.]

WORD (a) upon Deuteronomy. [By Rev. Daniel EDWARD.]

Edinburgh : MDCCCLXXVII. Octavo. Pp. 58.*

WORDS (the) and works of our Blessed Lord and their lessons for daily life. By the author of " Brampton rectory." [Miss Mary M. HOWARD.] In two volumes.

London : 1860. Octavo.*

WORDS made visible : or grammar and rhetorick accommodated to the lives and manners of men. Represented in a country school for the entertainment and edification of the spectators. [By Samuel SHAW.]

London, 1679. Octavo. Pp. 6. b. t. 187.* [*Dyce Cat.*, ii. 295.]

WORDS (the) of Jesus. By the author of " The morning and night watches," " The faithful promiser," &c. &c. [John Ross MACDUFF, D.D.] Fourth edition of 5000.

London : MDCCCLIV. Octavo. Pp. 127.*

WORDS of life's last years : containing Christian emblems ; metrical prayers and sacred poems, translated from foreign writers. By the author of " Thoughts on devotion," etc. etc. [John SHEPPARD.]

London : 1862. Octavo.* [*Olphar Hamst.*]

WORDS (the) of the hymnal noted complete : with scriptural references. [By Thomas HELMORE, M.A.]

London : N. D. Duodecimo. Pp. 132. 8. b. t.*

WORDS (the) of the wise, designed for the entertainment and instruction of younger minds. [By John POTTER.]

London : 1768. Duodecimo. [*European Mag.*, v. 283. *Mon. Rev.*, xxxviii. 410.]

WORK about the Five Dials. [Attributed to the Hon. Alethea Maude STANLEY.]

London : 1878. [*Lib. Jour.*, iv. 25.] Ascribed to George Barnett Smith. [*International Review, Nov. Dec.*, 1878.] See Lib. Jour., iii. 348.

WORK among the lost. By the author of " Home thoughts for mothers and mothers' meetings." [Miss Ellice HOPKINS.]

London : 1870. Sm. Octavo. Pp. 95.

WORK for a cooper. Being an answer to a libel, written by Thomas Wynne the cooper, the aleman, the quack, and the speaking-Quaker. With a brief account how that dissembling people differ at this day from what at first they were. By one who abundantly pities their ignorance and folly. [William JONES, of North Wales.]

London : 1679. Quarto. 4½ sh. [*Smith, Bib. Anti-Quaker.*, p. 257.]

WORK (a) for none but angels & men. That is, to be able to look into, and to know our selves. Or a book shewing what the soule is, subsisting and having its operations without the body ; its more then a perfection or reflection of the sense, or temperature of humours : how she exercises her powers of vegetative or quickning power of the senses. Of the imaginations or common sense, the phantasie, sensative memory, passions, motion of life, the local motion, and intellectual powers of the soul. Of the wit, understanding, reason, opinion, judgement, power of will, and the relations betwixt wit & wil. Of the intellectuall memory, that the soule is immortall, and cannot dye, cannot be destroyed, her cause ceaseth not, violence nor time cannot destroy her ; and all objections answered to the contrary. [By Sir John DAVIES.]

London, 1653. Quarto. Pp. 54. b. t.* [*Bodl.*]

The second elegy of the " Nosce te ipsum.'

WORKE for a masse-priest. [By Alexander COOKE.]

London, 1617. Quarto. Pp. 14. b. t.* [*Bodl.*]

WORKE, more worke, and a little more worke for a masse-priest. [By Alexander COOKE.]

London. 1630. Quarto. [*Mendham Collection Cat.*, p. 83.]

WORKING-man's (the) companion. The results of machinery, namely, cheap production and increased employment, exhibited : being an address to the working men of the United Kingdom. [By Henry BROUGHAM, Lord Brougham.] Third edition.

London, 1831. Duodecimo. Pp. 216.*

——. The rights of industry : addressed to the working-men of the United Kingdom. By the author of " The results of machinery." [Henry BROUGHAM, Lord Brougham.] I. Capital and labour.

London : 1831. Duodecimo. Pp. 213.*

WORKING-man's (the) way in the world : being the autobiography of a journeyman printer. [By Charles Manby SMITH.]

London : N. D. Duodecimo.* [*N. and Q.*, *Feb.* 1869, p. 168.]

WORKING of the Tithe Commutation Act. [By the Hon. Arthur Philip PERCEVAL.]

London : 1838. Octavo.* [*Bodl.*]

WORKS (the) of Anacreon and Sappho, with pieces from ancient authors [Bion, Moschus, Virgil, and Horace], and occasional essays ; illustrated by observations on their lives and writings, explanatory notes from established commentators, and additional remarks by the editor ; with the Classic and introductory poem. [By Edward Burnaby GREENE.]

London : 1768. Duodecimo.

Classic signed E. B. G.

WORKS (the) of Ben Jonson ; with a memoir of his life and writings, by Barry Cornwall. [Bryan Waller PROCTER.]

London : 1838. Octavo. Pp. lvi. 819. [*IV.*]

WORKS (the) of Geoffrey Chaucer, compared with the former editions and many valuable MSS., out of which, three Tales are added which were never before printed ; by John Urry, Student

of Christ Church, Oxon, deceased : together with a glossary, by a Student of the same College [Timothy THOMAS]. To the whole is prefixed the author's life, newly written [by —— DART, corrected and enlarged by William THOMAS], and a preface, giving an account of this edition [by Timothy THOMAS].

London : 1721. Folio. [*IV.*]

WORKS (the) of Mr Hogarth moralized. [By Rev. John TRUSLER, LL.D.]

London : [1768.] Octavo. [*IV.*]

WORKS (the) of Mr John Cleveland, containing his poems, orations, epistles, collected into one volume, with the life of the author. [Edited by J. LAKE and S. DRAKE.]

London : 1687. Octavo. [*IV.*]

" The Epistle Dedicatory " is signed J. L., S. D.

WORKS (the) of Peter Pindar, Esq. [John WOLCOTT, M.D.] In four volumes.

London : 1794-6. Octavo. [*IV.*]

WORKS (the) of the Caledonian bards. Translated from the Galic. [by John CLARK.] Volume I.

Edinburgh : M,DCC,LXXVIII. Octavo. Pp. 200.* [*Lowndes, Bibliog. Man.*, p. 347. *Brydges, Cens. Lit.*, vi. 110.]

WORKS (the) of the ever-memorable John Hales of Eton, collected [by Sir David DALRYMPLE, Lord Hailes]. In three volumes.

Glasgow : 1765. Sm. Octavo. [*IV.*, *Lowndes, Brit. Lib.*]

WORKS (the) of the very learned and Reverend Father in God, John Jewell, not long since Bishop of Salisburie, newly set forthe with some amendment of divers quotations ; and a brief discourse of his life. [Edited by —— FULLER.]

London : 1611. Folio. [*IV.*]

The Dedication was written by Overal ; the life by Featley ; and the appendix by Bishop Morton. ¦ The book was published under the direction of Archbishop Bancroft.

WORKS (the) of William Browne ; containing Britannia's Pastorals : with notes and observations by the Rev. W. Thompson, late of Queen's-College, Oxford. The Shepherd's Pipe : consisting of Pastorals, the Inner Temple Masque, never published before ; and other poems ; with the life of the author [by Thomas DAVIES].

London : 1772. Duodecimo. [*IV.*]

WORKS (the) of William Hogarth (including the Analysis of beauty), elucidated by descriptions, critical, moral, and historical: to which is prefixed some account of his life. By Thomas Clerk. [Thomas Hartwell HORNE.] Two volumes.

London: 1821. Octavo.
The engravings were executed by Thomas Clerk. From a list of his works in the handwriting of the author.

WORLD (the). By Adam Fitz-Adam. [By Philip Dormer STANHOPE, Earl of Chesterfield, and others.] A new edition. [In four volumes.]

London: MDCCLXXXII. Duodecimo.*

WORLD (the) as it goes, a poem. By the author of the Diaboliad. Dedicated to one of the best men in his Majesty's dominions, &c. [By William COMBE.] The second edition.
London, MDCCLXXIX. Quarto. Pp. 37. b. t.*

WORLD (the) at Westminster, a periodical publication. By Thomas Brown, the younger. [Thomas MOORE.]
London; 1816. Duodecimo.*
The work consists of thirty numbers.

WORLD (the) conquered, or a believer's victory over the world. Laid open in several sermons on 1 John 5, 4. By R. A. [Richard ALLEINE.]
London, 1668. Octavo. Pp. 6. 314.*

WORLD (the): how to square it. By Harry Hieover. [Charles BINDLEY.]
London: 1854. Octavo.

WORLD (the) in the Church. By F. G. Trafford, author of "The moors and the fens," "Too much alone," and "City and suburb." [Mrs J. R. RIDDELL.] In three volumes. Second edition.
London: 1863. Octavo.*

WORLD (the) to come; the glories of heaven and the terrors of hell lively described under the similitude of a vision. By G. L. [G. LARKIN.]
1711. Octavo. [IV.]

WORLD (the) unmask'd: or, the philosopher the greatest cheat; in twenty-four dialogues between Crito a philosopher, Philo a lawyer, and Erastus a merchant. In which true virtue is distinguished from what usually bears the name or resemblance of it: the many prejudices and mistakes in judgment and practice, in

regard to conscience and religion, are examined and rectified: and the value of truth is shewn; with the reasons why it is not more generally known. To which is added, the state of souls separated from their bodies: being an epistolary treatise, wherein is proved, by a variety of arguments deduced from Holy Scripture, that the punishments of the wicked will not be eternal; and all objections against it solved. In answer to a treatise, entitled, An enquiry into Origenism. Together with a large introduction, evincing the same truth from the principles of natural religion. Translated from the French [of Mary HUBER].

London: MDCCXXXVI. Octavo.* [N. & Q., 13 Dec. 1856, p. 476; 28 March 1857, p. 256; 25 April 1857, p. 334.]

WORLD (a) without souls. [By the Rev. J. W. CUNNINGHAM, A.M., vicar of Harrow.]
London: 1805. Duodecimo. [Darling, Cyclop. Bibl.]

WORLD'S (the) great restavration. Or, the calling of the Ievves, and (with them) of all the nations and kingdomes of the earth, to the faith of Christ. Published by William Gouge, B. of D., and preacher of God's Word in Blackfryers, London. [Written by Henry FINCH.]
London. 1621. Quarto. Pp. 8, b. t. 234.* [Bodl.]

WORLD'S (the) honour detected, and, for the unprofitableness thereof, rejected; and the honour which comes from God alone, asserted, and reduced to practice; or, some reasons why the people of God called Quakers do deny the accustomary honour and salutations of the world, consisting in putting off the hat, bowing, titling, bidding good-morrow, good-night, &c., upheld by them in a respect of persons, contrary to the royal law of liberty, Jam. 2. Their several pleas for the same impleaded, and divers objections answered, by a friend to truth, who is no respecter or regarder of persons, called a Quaker, B. F. [Benjamin FURLY.]
London, 1663. Quarto. 8½ sh. [Smith's Cat. of Friends' books, i. 827.]

WORLD'S (the) idol. Plutus; a comedy written in Greek by Aristophanes. Translated by H. H. B. [Henry BURNELL.]
London: 1659. Sm. Quarto. [IV.]

WORLD'S (the) mistake in Oliver Cromwell; or, a short political discourse, shewing that Cromwell's maladministration, (during his four years and nine moneths pretended Protectorship), layed the foundation of our present condition in the decay of trade. [By Slingsby BETHEL.]

London, 1668. Quarto.* [*Lowndes, Bibliog. Man.*]

WORLD'S (the) verdict. By the author of "The morals of May Fair," "Creeds," etc. etc. [Mrs Annie EDWARDES.] In three volumes.

London: 1861. Octavo.*

WORME (the) of Lambton. [Edited by Sir Cuthbert SHARP.]

Durham: 1830. Quarto. Pp. 15. [*W., Martin's Cat.*]

WORTH (the) of a baby and How Apple-Tree Court was won. By Hesba Stretton, author of 'Lost Gip' 'Cassy' 'Jessica's first prayer' etc. [Sarah SMITH.]

London: 1876. Octavo. Pp. 58.*

WORTLEBANK (the) diary, and some old stories from Kathie Brande's portfolio. By Holme Lee, author of "Sylvan Holt's daughter," etc. [Harriet PARR.] In three volumes.

London: M.DCCC.LX. Octavo.*

WREATH (a) from the wilderness: being a selection from the metrical arrangements of Accola Montis-Amœni. [By Robert BARNARD.]

Ironbridge: 1816. Octavo. 10½ sh. [*Smith's Cat. of Friends' books*, i. 87, 193.] Reprinted in 1817, with the author's name, and with a change in the latter part of the title.

WREATH (the) of fashion, or, the art of sentimental poetry. [By Richard TICKELL.]

London: MDCCLXXVIII. Quarto. Pp. iv. 14.*

WREATH (a) of Indian stories. By A.L.O.E., honorary missionary at Amritsar, author of "The young pilgrim," "Rescued from Egypt," &c., &c. [Charlotte TUCKER.]

London: N.D. Octavo. Pp. 211.*

WREATH (a) of ivy, and Christmas wild flowers: gathered and twined by "Amicitiæ." [By Charles Augustus HULBERT.]

Shrewsbury. Christmas, 1823. Octavo. Pp. 34, 1.* [*Bodl.*]
A few copies only, printed for presentation.

WREATH (a) of smoke. By A.L.O.E., authoress of "The wanderer in Africa," "What is a Christian?" "Sheer off," &c. [Charlotte TUCKER.]

London: N.D. Octavo. Pp. 191.*

WRECK (the) of the "Grosvenor." [By W. Clarke RUSSELL.]

London: N.Y. 1878. [*Lib. Jour.*, iii., 271.]

WRINKLES; or, hints to sportsmen and travellers on dress, equipment, and camp life. By the Old Shekarry, author of "The forest and the field," etc. [H. A. LEVERSON.] A new edition, fully illustrated.

London: 1874. Octavo. Pp. 2. b. t. 294.*

WRONGS (the) of Africa. [By William ROSCOE.] In two parts.

London: 1787-8. Quarto. [*W.*]

WRONGS (the) of Poland, a poem in three cantos: comprising the siege of Vienna, with historical notes. By the author of "Parental wisdom." [J. ANTROBUS.]

London: 1849. Octavo.*

WRONGS (the) of woman. By Charlotte Elizabeth. [Mrs Charlotte Elizabeth TONNA, née Browne, afterwards Mrs Phelan.] [In four parts.]

London: 1843-44. Duodecimo.

WUTHERING Heights and Agnes Grey. By Ellis and Acton Bell. [Emily Jane, and Anne BRONTÉ.] A new edition, revised, with a biographical notice of the authors, a selection from their literary remains, and a preface, by Currer Bell [Charlotte BRONTÉ].

London: 1850. Pp. xxiv. Duodecimo.*

WYCH Hazel. By the author of 'The wide, wide world,' 'The golden ladder,' 'Queechy,' &c., &c. [Susan WARNER.]

London: MDCCCLXXVI. Octavo. Pp. iv. 422.*

WYCLIFFE to Wesley; heroes and martyrs of the Church in Britain. [By Gregory J. ROBINSON.]

London: 1879. Octavo. Pp. 8. 248.*

WYLLARD'S weird A novel By the author of "Lady Audley's secret," "Vixen," "Ishmael," &c. [Miss M. E. BRADDON.] In three volumes.

London: [1885.] Octavo.*

X.

X. Y. Z. A farce, in two acts, by George Colman, Esq. author of Inkle and Yarico, Who wants a guinea, &c. Printed from the acting copy, with remarks, biographical and critical, by D — G. [George DANIEL.] To which are added, a description of the costume, — cast of the characters, entrances, and exits, —relative positions of the performers on the stage,—and the whole of the stage business. As performed at the theatres royal, London. Embellished with a fine engraving, by Mr. Bonner, from a drawing taken in the theatre by Mr. R. Cruikshank.

London : N. D. Duodecimo. Pp. 41.*

XANTIPPE, or the scolding wife, done from the Conjugium of Erasmus. By W. F. of D. [W. FORBES of Disblair.]

Edinburgh, MDCCXXIV. Quarto. Pp. 27.*

XENOPHON'S defence of the Athenian democracy ; translated from the Greek. With notes, and an appendix, containing observations on the democratic part of the British government, and the existing constitution of the House of Commons. [By Henry James PYE.]

London : 1794. Octavo. Pp. iv. 106.*

Y.

YACHTMAN'S (a) holidays or cruising in the West Highlands By the "Governor." [John INGLIS.]

London 1879. Octavo. Pp. viii. 151.*

YARICO to Inkle, an epistle. By the author of an Elegy written among the ruins of an abbey. [Edward JERNINGHAM.]

London : 1766. Quarto. Pp. 19.

YARICO to Inkle, and other poems. [By Paul METHUEN, Baron Methuen of Corsham House, Wilts.]

London : 1810. Duodecimo. [W., Martin's Cat.]

YARNS by a Manchester spinner. [John CAMERON.]

Manchester : N. D. Octavo. [N. and Q., Feb. 1869, p. 168.]

YEA or nay? or, the union question tried and tested. By "a country minister" of the Free Church. [—— PHILIP.]

Edinburgh : 1870. Octavo. Pp. 16.*

YEAR (a) abroad : stories and sights in France and Italy. By Grace Greenwood. [Sarah Jane CLARKE.]

Edinburgh : N. D. Octavo. Pp. 221.*

YEAR after year A tale. By the author of " Paul Ferroll," and " IX

poems by V." [Lady CLIVE.] Third edition.

London : 1858. Duodecimo. Pp. vii. 365.*

YEAR (a) in Spain. By a young American. [Captain Alexander Slidell MACKENZIE.] In two volumes.

London : 1831. Octavo.*

YEAR (the) nine. A tale of the Tyrol. By the author of " Mary Powell." [Anne MANNING.]

London : 1858. Octavo.*

YEAR (the) of liberation : a journal of the defence of Hamburgh against the French army under Marshal Davoust, in 1813, with sketches of the battles of Lutzen, Bautzen, &c., &c. [By George CROLY, LL.D., rector of St. Stephen's, Walbrook.] In two volumes.

London : MDCCCXXXII. Duodecimo.*

YEAST : a problem. [By Charles KINGSLEY.] Reprinted, with corrections and additions, from Fraser's Magazine.

London : MDCCCLI. Duodecimo. Pp. vi. 1. 379.*

YEOMAN'S (the) [Sir William Cusack SMITH'S] second letter to the Right Honourable William Wickham, one of his Majesty's most honourable privy

council, &c. &c. &c. Occasioned by the second edition of an Irish Catholic [Mr. Scully]'s advice to his brethren. Second edition.

Dublin: 1804. Octavo. Pp. 98.*

YES and no : a tale of the day. By the author of "Matilda." [Constantine Henry PHIPPS, Marquis of Normanby.] In two volumes.

London: 1828. Duodecimo.*

YESTERDAY in Ireland. By the author of "To-day in Ireland." [Eyre Evans CROWE.] In three vols.

London: 1829. Duodecimo.*

YET a course at the Romyshe foxe. A disclosynge or openynge of the Manne of Sinne, cōtayned in the late declaratyon of the Popes olde faythe, made by Edmunde Boner, Bysshopp of London ; wherby Wyllyam Tolwyn was then newelye professed at Paules Crosse openlye into Antichristes Romyshe relygyon agayne, by a new solempne othe of obedyence, notwythstādinge the othe made to hys prynce afore to the contrarye, &c. Compyled by Johan Harrison. [John BALE, Bishop of Ossory.]

Zurich, 1543. 16mo. [Watt, Bib. Brit.]

YORK-shire (a) dialogue in its pure natural dialect, as it is now commonly spoken in the north parts of Yorkshire : being a miscellaneous discourse or hotchpotch of several country affaires. [By George MERITON.]

York: 1683. Quarto. Pp. 18. [W.] Reprinted with "The Praise of York-shire ale," York, 1697, 12mo.

YORKSHIREMAN (the), a religious and literary journal. By a Friend. [Luke HOWARD.] [In five volumes.]

Pontefract: 1833-1837. Octavo.* [Bodl.]

YOUNG (a) artist's life. [By Alexander Baillie COCHRANE, of Lamington, M.P.] In one volume.

London: 1864. Octavo. [Adv. Lib.]

YOUNG (the) baronet A novel. By the author of "The Scottish heiress," "The young widow," &c. &c. &c. [Robert Mackenzie DANIEL.] In three volumes.

London: 1846. Duodecimo.*

YOUNG Brown or the law of inheritance By the author of 'The member for Paris' 'Men of the second empire' &c.

[Eustace Clare Grenville MURRAY.] In three volumes.

London, 1874. Octavo.*

YOUNG (the) churchman's manual ; containing reasons for, and explanations of, the services of morning and evening prayer. By a member of the Church of England. [J. A. THORNTHWAITE.]

London : 1837. Duodecimo. [W., Brit. Mus.]

YOUNG (the) clergyman's companion, in visiting the sick. [By Rev. Richard BATTY.]

1756. [Watt, Bib. Brit.]

YOUNG (the) commander. A novel. By the author of "The two midshipmen," "The Warhawk," &c. [F. Claudius ARMSTRONG.] In three volumes.

London : 1856. Duodecimo.*

YOUNG (the) communicants, written for the use of the poor school, Bermondsey, and respectfully dedicated to the Reverend Peter Butler, by the author of "Geraldine, a tale of Conscience." [E. C. AGNEW]. With the approbation of the Right Reverend Dr. Griffiths, V.A.L.

London : MDCCCXL. Duodecimo. Pp. 116. b. t.* [Bodl.]

YOUNG (the) cottager ; a true story. By the author of "The dairyman's daughter. [Legh RICHMOND, M.A., rector of Turvey, Bedfordshire.]

London : N.D. Duodecimo. Pp. 40.*

YOUNG (the) doctor: a novel. By the author of "Lady Granard's nieces," "Sir Arthur Bouverie." [Miss PINKNEY.] [In three volumes.]

London : 1851. Octavo.*

YOUNG (the) duke. By the author of "Vivian Grey." [Benjamin DISRAELI.] In three volumes.

London : 1831. Duodecimo.*

YOUNG Emily. By [Mrs] Ann Jane [MORGAN].

London: 48mo. Pp. 16. [W.] Groom's Publications.

YOUNG heads on old shoulders. By Ascott R. Hope, author of "A peck of troubles," "The young rebels," "Stories of Whitminster," etc., etc. [Robert Hope MONCRIEFF.]

London: [1879.] Octavo. Pp. 3. b. t. 179.*

YOUNG (the) housekeeper as daughter, wife, and mother Forming a perfect "young woman's companion" in all her social relations, including practical instructions in plain and ornamental needlework, letter-writing, sick-room management, dress and clothing, house-furnishing, gardening, etiquette, and every other variety of household economy in the nursery, kitchen, and parlour With copious notes of the months, complete history of domestic manufactures, moral and religious readings in prose and poetry, and four hundred golden rules of life Compiled by the editor of "The family friend." [Robert Kemp PHILP.]

London N. D. Octavo. Pp. viii. b. t. 376.*

YOUNG (the) Lord. By the author of "The discipline of life," "Clare Abbey," "Edward Willoughby," &c. [Lady Emily PONSONBY.] In two volumes.

London : 1856. Octavo.*

YOUNG (the) man's guide in the choice of a benefit society ; or, the danger of choosing a bad club, and the advantage of entering a well-regulated friendly society, illustrated. In three dialogues. By a Suffolk clergyman. [Samuel HOBSON.]

London : M.DCCC.XLVI. Duodecimo.*

YOUNG (the) mechanic. A book for boys. Containing directions for the use of all kinds of tools, and for the construction of steam engines and mechanical models, including the art of turning in wood and metal. By the author of "The lathe and its uses," "The amateur mechanic's workshop," &c. [Rev. James LUKIN.]

London : 1871. Octavo. Pp. iv. 346.*

YOUNG (the) mountaineer, or Frank Miller's lot in life : the story of a Swiss boy. [From the French of Gouraud.] By Daryl Holme. [David HERBERT.]

Edinburgh : 1870. Octavo. [Adv. Lib.]

YOUNG Mrs. Jardine. By the author of "John Halifax, gentleman," &c., &c. [Dinah Maria MULOCK.] In three volumes.

London : 1879. Octavo.*

YOUNG (the) pilgrim : a tale illustrative of "The Pilgrim's progress." By A. L. O. E., author of "The Shepherd of Bethlehem," "The silver casket," "The robbers' cave," &c. [Charlotte TUCKER.]

London : 1871. Octavo. Pp. 286.*

YOUNG (the) Quaker ; a comedy : as it is performed at the Theatre Royal in Smock-Alley, with great applause. [By John O'KEEFE.]

Dublin: 1784. Duodecimo. 2½ sh. [Smith, Bib. Anti-Quaker., pp. 45, 345.]

YOUNG Scarron. [By Thomas MOZEEN.]

London : 1751. Duodecimo. [Lowndes, Bibliog. Man., s. v. Scarron.]

YOUNG (the) sportsman's instructor in angling, fowling, hawking, hunting, ordering singing birds, hawks, poultry, coneys, hares and dogs, and how to cure them. By G. M. [Gervase MARKHAM.]

[London:] N. D. Octavo. Pp. I. b. t. 140.*

YOUNG (the) step-mother ; or, a chronicle of mistakes. By the author of 'The heir of Redclyffe,' 'Heartsease,' etc. [Charlotte Mary YONGE.]

London : 1861. Octavo. Pp. 482.*

YOUNG (the) widow. A novel in three volumes. By the author of the "Scottish heiress," &c. &c. [Robert Mackenzie DANIEL.]

London : 1844. Duodecimo.*

YOUNG (the) widow ; or, the history of Cornelia Sedley, in a series of letters. [By William HAYLEY.] In four volumes.

London : 1789. Duodecimo. [Nichols, Lit. Anec., ix. 50. Mon. Rev., i. 332.]

YOVNGER (the) brother his apologie, or a fathers free power disputed, for the disposition of his lands, or other his fortunes to his sonne, sonnes, or any one of them : as right reason, the lawes of God and nature, the civil, canon, and municipall laws of this kingdome doe command. [By J. ALLEN.]

Oxford, 1624. Quarto. Pp. 8. b. t. 56.* [Lowndes, Bibliog. Man., p. 31.] Epistle to the reader signed J. A.

YOUNGER (the) sister. [By Anne DAWE.] In two volumes.

London : 1770. Duodecimo. [Gent. Mag., xciv. 1. 136. Mon. Rev., xlii. 487.]

YOUTH (the) and manhood of Cyril Thornton. [By Capt. Thomas HAMILTON.] In three volumes.

Edinburgh and London. M.DCCC.XXVII. Octavo.* [Adv. Lib.]

YOUTH (the) and womanhood of Helen Tyrrel. By the author of 'Brampton

Rectory,' 'Compton Merivale,' etc. [Mary Matilda HOWARD.]

London: MDCCCLIV. Duodecimo. *

YOUTH (the) of Shakspeare. By the author of "Shakspeare and his friends." [R. Folkestone WILLIAMS.] In three volumes.

London: 1839. Duodecimo. *

YOUTH'S comedy, by the author of Youth's tragedy. [T. SHERMAN.]

London: 1680. Octavo. [Lowndes, Bibliog. Man.]

YOUTH'S tragedy, a poem, drawn up by way of dialogue between youth, the devil, wisdom, time, death, the soul and the Nuncius. By T. S. [T. SHERMAN.]

London: 1671. Quarto. [Lowndes, Bibliog Man.]

YULE-tide: faces in the fire. By a clergyman's wife. [Mrs HART, née Fanny Wheeler.]

Manchester: N. D. Duodecimo. Pp. 15. *

Z

ZADOC, the outcast of Israel; a tale. By Charlotte Elizabeth. [Mrs TONNA, formerly Mrs Phelan, née Browne.]

London: 1825. Duodecimo. '

ZAIDA'S nursery note-book. For the use of mothers. By A. L. O. E., author of "Shepherd of Bethlehem," "Rescued from Egypt," "The young pilgrim," &c. &c. [Charlotte TUCKER.]

London: 1867. Octavo. Pp. 135. *

ZANA; or the heiress of Clair Hall. By the author of "Fashion and famine." [Mrs Ann S. STEPHENS.]

London: 1854. Duodecimo. *

ZARA, at the Court of Annamaboe, to the African Prince now in England. [By William DODD, LL.D.]

London: M,DCC,XLIX. Quarto. Pp. 15. *

ZARA: or, the black death. A poem of the sea. By the author of "Naufragus." [—— HORNE.]

London: 1833. Octavo. Pp. xii. 220. *

ZAREEFA a tale and other poems By the author of "Cephalus and Procris," "The prophecy" etc. [Miss Helen LOWE.]

London 1844. Octavo. Pp. vii. 171. *

ZASTROZZI, a romance. By P. B. S. [Percy Bysshe SHELLEY.]

London: 1810. Octavo. Pp. 252. b. t. *

ZAYDA, a Spanish tale, in three cantos; and other poems, stanzas, and canzonets. By Oscar. [Mrs Leman GRIMSTONE.]

London: 1820. Duodecimo. Pp. ix. 163. * [Adv. Lib.]

ZEAL without innovation: or the present state of religion and morals considered; with a view to the dispositions and measures required for its improvement. To which is subjoined, an address to young clergymen; intended to guard them against some prevalent errors [By Rev. James BEAN, vicar of Olney.]

London: 1808. Octavo. *

ZELIA in the desert. From the French. By a lady. [Mad. Marguérite DAUBENTON.] In three volumes.

London: 1789. Duodecimo. [Barbier. Mon. Rev., lxxxi. 363.]

ZELMANE; or, the Corinthian Queen, a tragedy. As it is acted at the New-Theatre in Lincoln's-Inn-Fields by Her Majesties servants. [By William MOUNTFORT.]

London: 1705. Quarto. * [Biog. Dram.]

ZELOTES and Honestus reconciled: or, an equal check to Pharasaism and Antinomianism continued: being the first part of the Scripture-scales to weigh the gold of Gospel-truth:—to balance a multitude of opposite Scriptures;—to prove the Gospel-marriage of free-grace and free-will: and restore primitive harmony to the Gospel of the day. With a preface, containing some strictures upon the Three letters of Richard Hill, Esq.; which have been lately published. By a lover of the whole truth as it is in Jesus. [John FLETCHER.]

London: 1705. Duodecimo. Pp. xxvi. 204. *

There is a second part, with a half title, occupying from p. 205 to p. 443.

ZELUCO. Various views of human nature, taken from life and manners, foreign and domestic. [By John MOORE, M.D.] In two volumes.

London: M DCC LXXXIX. Octavo.*

ZENITH distances, observed with the mural circle at the Royal Observatory, Cape of Good Hope, and the calculation of the geocentric south polar distances for 1836-7. [By Thomas MACLEAR, F.R.A.S., Her Majesty's astronomer at the Cape of Good Hope.]

1837. Quarto. [*W.*]

ZENOBIA : a tragedy. As it is performed at the Theatre Royal in Drury-Lane. By the author of the Orphan of China. [Arthur MURPHY.]

London : MDCCLXVIII. Octavo. Pp. 82.* [*Biog. Dram.*]

ZENOBIA ; or the fall of Palmyra. A historical romance. In letters of Lucius M. Piso from Palmyra, to his friend Marcus Curtius at Rome. [By Rev. William WARE.] [In two volumes.

London: 1844. Octavo.*

ZETETIC astronomy. A description of several experiments which prove that the surface of the sea is a perfect plane, and that the earth is not a globe ! Being the substance of a paper read before the Royal Astronomical Society on the evening of Dec. 8, 1848. By Parallax. [Dr. Samuel ROWBOTHAM.]

Birmingham : 1849. Duodecimo. Pp. 16.* [*Bookseller, Jan. 7. 1885.*]

ZILLAH ; a tale of the Holy City. By the author of " Brambletye House, "The Tor Hill," " Reuben Apsley," &c. [Horace SMITH.] Second edition. In three volumes.

London: 1828. Duodecimo.*

ZOË : an Athenian tale. [By John Campbell COLQUHOUN, of Killermont.]

Edinburgh : 1824. Duodecimo. Pp. ix. 115.*

Printed for private circulation.

ZOE'S 'brand'. . . [By Mrs HOUSTOUN.] In three volumes.

London : 1864. Octavo.

ZOFLOYA ; or, the Moor : a romance of the fifteenth century. In three volumes. By Charlotte Dacre. [Mrs BYRNE, better known as Rosa Matilda, author of the Nun of St. Omers, Hours of solitude, &c.]

London : 1806. Duodecimo.*

ZOHRAB the hostage. By the author of "Hajji Baba." [James MORIER.] In three volumes.

London: 1832. Duodecimo.*

ZOPHIEL ; or, the bride of seven. By Maria del Occidente. [Maria BROOKS.]

London : 1833. Octavo.*

ZORAIDA : a tragedy. As it is acted at the Theatre-Royal in Drury-Lane. To which is added a postscript, containing observations on tragedy. [By William HODSON.]

London : M DCC LXXX. Octavo. Pp. 104.* [*Biog. Dram.*]

ZULNEIDA : a tale of Sicily. By the author of the White cottage. [A. MOWER.] In three volumes.

London : 1837. Octavo.* [*Adv. Lib.*]

FINIS

The figures within brackets denote the number of times the name appears in the preceding column.

INDEX TO AUTHORS' PSEUDONYMS.

A. Bp. Zachary Pearce
        1625, 1626, 1627, 1628
A. Matthew Arnold   744, 2503
A. A. Adam Anderson, M.R.I.A.   1267
A. A. John Arnway, D.D.   1744, 2537
A. A. A. Baroness B. de Bury,
   M. P. Rose   67 (2), 1520
A. and L. A. and L. Shore   2788
AARON PHILOMIRTH. John H.
   Parr   1684
A * * * * *, MAJOR. C. B. Coles 2379
A. B. A. Bayne   1245
A. B. Abraham Cowley   1955
A. B. A. Brasher   2078
A. B. Alexander Brome   529
A. B. Andrew Borde   1605
A. B. Ann Beaty   2452
A. B. Aphra Behn   77, 1519
A. B. Edmund Hickeringill   2107
A. B. Henry Stebbing, D.D.   1842
A. B. Humphrey Prideaux, D.D.   1295
A. B. Jonathan Swift, D.D.   111, 1376
A. B. Joseph Skidmore   821
A. B. Richard Kidder   1369
A. B. Robert Ferguson   1385
A. B. Sir Alexander Boswell   2830
A. B. William de Britaine   1187
ABBOT GUALDI. Gregorio Leti 1473
ABBOT JACOB. T. S. Henderson 288
A. (B.) C. Archibald Campbell   2564
A. B. C. John Cockburn   2369
A. B. C. D. E. F. Major Edward
   Moor   1447
A. B. C. D. E. F. G. Walter Moyle 173
ABDIELS. Joshua W. Brooks   3
A. B. DON. Captain A. Bruce   649
ABEDA, FRANCISCO LOPEZ
   DE. Andreas Perez   2462
ABEL DRUGGER. John Hardman 945
ABEL KNOCKDUNDER. Lieut.
   H. P. Andrew Shortrede   1355
ABEL LOG. Charles B. Greatrix 2810
ABERDONENSIS PATRICIUS.
   Patrick Forbes   833
ABNER PARK. Rev. Alexander
   Stevenson Twombly   1605
A. B. R. Arthur B. Rowan   1314

ABRABANEL   SOLOMON.
   William Arnall   451
ABRAHAM ELDON, Dr. Thomas
   Wyse   499
ABRAHAM JOHNSON. Sir John
   Hill, M.D.   1523
ABRAHAM PHILOTHEUS. A.
   Wright   83
ABRICHT, JOHANN, A.M. Jon-
   athan Birch   683
A. B. Z. W. Arthur Brett, M.A.   601
A. C.   2062
A. C. A. Cameron   1408
A. C. Alexander Chalmers   1570
A. C. Alexander Chapman   380
A. C. Alexander Cumming   2338
A. C. Andrew Cant   2333, 2334
A. C. Anne Cooke   951
A. C. A. C. Copley   104
A. C. Ant. Conanus   2415
A. C. Anthony Collins   674
A. C. Anthony Copley   128, 922
A. C. John Fisher or Piercy   110
A. C. Robert Chambers   49
ACADEMICUS. Charles Seager,
   M.A.   200
ACADEMICUS. John Green, D.D.,
   Bp. of Lincoln   2015 (2)
A. C. C. Arthur C. Coxe   2260
A. C. C. PHILIPPUS PHILA-
   RETES. Thomas Comber   46
ACHERONTICUS MERCU-
   RIUS. James Howell   2621
ACHETA. L. M. Budgen   1546, 1561
ACHETA DOMESTICA, M.E.S.
   L. M. Budgen   779
A. C. M. Agnes C. Maitland   742
A. C. M. A. Alexander Cunningham 791
A. C. S. Anthony Champney   1544
ACTON BELL. Anne Brontë
        58, 1946, 2552, 2844
A. D. A. Deane   2613
A. D. A. Dutton   1693
ADADUS CALPE. Antonio D. de
   Pascual   2693
ADAM FITZ-ADAM. P. D. Stan-
   hope, Earl of Chesterfield   2841

ADAM FOULEWEATHER.
 Thomas Nash 2829
ADAM, UNCLE. C. A. Wetterburgh
 2325
ADAM, UNCLE. George Mogridge
 371
A——D B——R. Archibald Bower 252
ADDINGTON, Mr. Hugh Kelly 2269
ADELER, MAX. Charles H. Clark
 1810, 1836
ADELINE. R. A. Sergeant
 789, 2263, 2503
ADELPHUS PHILUS. John Ley 642
A. D. T. W. Adelina D. Train
 Whitney 880, 994
A. E. Andrew Edward 560
A. E. Arthur Ellis 1254
ÆMELIA JULIA. Emily Blacke 294
ÆSCHINES. Francis William Blag-
 don 914
A. E. P. Ann Eaton Polglase 2352
A. F. Abraham Fleming 290
A. F. G. A. F. Gaston 1834
A. F. G. Atkinson F. Gibson 2653
A. F. G. John Lister 777
A. F. T. Anne Fraser Tytler 1553
A. G. 224
A. G. A. Gardner 1663
A. G. Agnes Giberne
 77, 220, 1488, 1529, 1614
A. G. Alfred Gatty 222
A. G. Anthony Gilby 121
A. G. Archibald Gardner 581
A. G. Peter Walsh 2424
A. G. O. T. U. O. C. Owen Manning
 1229
A. H. Abraham Hartwell 2277
A. H. Abraham Hayward, Q.C. 906
A. H. Anthony Hammond 1006
AHAB SALEM. Rev. James Murray
 1724
A. H. B. A. H. Baldwin 2728
A. T. C. Morton Eudes 341
AILO THORNY. John Taylor 978
AIN. William Stevens 2202
AINSLIE HERBERT, B.A. Ed-
 ward Maitland 1913
A. J. Alexander Justice 1002
A. J. Anne Jenkinson 1565
AJAX. —— Ainley 2413
A. K. Anne Kemp 497
A. K. H. B. Andrew Kennedy Hutchi-
 son Boyd, D.D. 538
A. KINGSMAN. R. W. Essington 1838

A. L. Alexander Leighton 2467
A. L. Anthonie Linton 1738
ALASTOR. James Orton 853
ALAZON. Richard William Barnes 1342
ALAZONOMASTIX PHILA-
 LETHES. Henry More 1788
ALBERT. John Armstrong 2454
ALCIPHRON. Samuel Dickson,
 M.D. 1906
ALETHES, CLEROPHILUS. John
 Constable 2160, 2464
ALETHIUS. PHIL-IREN — I.D.
 John Doughtie 2724
ALETHOPHILUS GOTTINGEN-
 SIS. G. W. Alberti 2444
ALEXANDER DRAWCAUSIR,
 Sir, Knt. Henry Fielding 529
ALEXANDER, Mrs. Annie Hector
 née French 2831
ALEXANDER SMITH. Sydney
 Dobell 2454
ALEXANDER THE COPPER-
 SMITH. W. Boles 1616
ALEXANDRINUS CLITUS.
 Richard Brathwayt 336
ALEXANDRINUS CLYTUS.
 Richard Brathwayt 2808
ALFRED ALLENDALE. Theo-
 dore E. Hook 1539
ALFRED BURTON. John Mitford,
 R.N. 50
ALFRED CROWQUILL. Alfred
 Henry Forrester 9, 65, 291, 757, 984,
 1024, 1256, 1302, 1497, 1895, 1908, 1909,
 2386, 2541, 2686
ALFRED LEE. John Clark Fer-
 guson 744
ALI BEY. Domingo B y Leblich 2627
ALICE COUSIN. Alice Neal 67
ALIQUIS. James Barr, D.D. 1407
ALIQUIS. Richard Marks 2189
ALISTER, R. Alexander Robert-
 son 213, 222, 866
ALLENDALE, ALFRED. Theo-
 dore E. Hook 1539
ALLEN, William. Silas Titus 1301
A. L. M. Thomas Scantlebury 1510
A. L. O. E. Charlotte Tucker 1, 253,
 327, 371, 386, 406, 410, 411, 544, 556,
 724, 726, 838, 857, 879, 936, 969, 989,
 1013, 1018, 1025, 1028, 1074, 1080, 1169,
 1181, 1196, 1203, 1313, 1314, 1477, 1486,
 1503, 1515. 1606, 1617, 1620, 1685, 1708,
 1736, 1737, 1810, 1835, 1861, 1992, 2008,

2076, 2183, 2220, 2350, 2351, 2385 (2), 2461, 2496, 2498, 2500, 2519, 2658, 2717, 2731, 2787, 2788, 2804, 2819, 2843, 2844, 2849, 2851
ALPHA. G. Walker, M.D.   571
ALUMNUS CANTABRIGENSIS. T. Forster   1070
A. M. Alexander Monro, D.D.   770
A. M. Alexander Mudie   2273
A. M. A. Mannington   939
A. M. A. Money   2341
A. M. A. Murray   413
A. M. Anne Mackenzie   2315
A. M. Anthony Monday   255, 579, 663, 891, 1611, 2527, 2793
A ***** MAJOR. C. B. Coles   2379
AMBULATORIA VOLUNTAS. Henry Walker   2547
A. MACARONI. —— Taylor   2559
AMELIA, ANNIE. Annie Amelia Garrett   2341
AMELIA, ELLEN. Ellen Amelia Garrett   2341
AMERICAN. —— Woodmas   1966
AMERICAN, AN. Aurthr Lee   795
AMICITIÆ. Charles Augustus Hulbert   2843
AMICUS. David Brown   586, 2696
AMICUS. William Alexander   2060
AMICUS CURIÆ. John Payne Collier   541
AMICUS SECUNDUS. Rev. William Aird Thomson, D.D. 272, 2090
A—— M——L. Andrew Marvel   425, 1922
A. M. OXONIENSIS. Nathaniel Tillson Marsh   1832
A. M. Y. Marion Pritchard   2013
AMY DUNSMUIR. Miss Oliphant   2731
AMY LOTHROP. A. B. Warner   697, 1017, 1684, 2466
A. N. Alexander Nowell   336
A. N. Anthony Nixon   632
A. N. Arthur Newman.   227
ANASTASIUS. H. Drummond   624
A. N. C. Archibald N. Carmichael   996
ANDREW BORDE   1606
ANDREW HALLIDAY. Andrew Halliday Duff 50, 2261 (2), 2348, 2519
ANDREW, JAMES. Andrew Mackay   190
ANDREW MORETON. Daniel Defoe   838, 1863, 2042, 2309, 2314

ANDREW RIVETUS. Jun. Andrew Marvell   1675
ANSTEY, F. F. Anstey Guthrie   2729
ANGLICANUS PHILELEUTHERUS. John William Donaldson, D.D.   2747
ANGLICANUS PRESBYTER. Joseph Hemington Harris   200, 2390
ANGLICUS BECCARIA. Richard Wright   1444
ANGLICUS MERCURIOPHILUS. Elias Ashmole   900
ANGLO - CATHOLICUS. Lord James Manners   2804
ANG., PHIL. John Pennyman   279
ANGLUS, PHIL. Joseph Pennyman   1511
ANGLUS, PHIL. William Penn   751, 1835, 2045
ANNA MATILDA. Hannah Cowley   1959, 1960
ANNE FRANCIS RANDALL. Mary Robinson   1419
ANNE, SISTER   1518
ANNE-SON, IAMES. James Maxwell   310
ANNIE AMELIA. Annie Garret   2341
ANN JANE. Ann Jane Morgan   65, 1271, 2848
ANN OF SWANSEA. Frances Ann Kemble 303, 354, 391, 509, 577, 1011, 1059, 1520, 2311, 2314, 2706, 2826.
ANONIMUS. John Lilburn   1186
ANONYMOUS. Benjamin Dawson 99
ANONYMUS. John Disney, D.D. 2371
ANONYMUS LONDINESIS. Thomas Lewis   1378
AN. SC. Anthony Scoloker   625
ANSTEY, F. F. Anstey Guthrie   2729
ANTHONY GRIFFINHOOF. George Colman, Yr.   1555
ANTHONY HARMER. Henry Wharton   2465
ANTHONY PASQUIN. John Williams 201, 546, 549, 721, 1481, 1715, 1914, 1946, 1954, 1980, 2643
ANTI-DRACO. John Disney   932
ANTI-HUDIBRASTON. William Rhinde   2079
ANTI-SCRIBLERUS HISTRIONICUS. John Roberts   117
ANTI-THEATRICUS. Thady Fitzpatrick   772
ANTI-TINDALIAN. Robert Lyon 1409

A. O. Abraham Oakes, LL.D. 2498
A. P. A. Parkinson 422
A. P. F. Alexander Penrose Forbes, D.C.L. 439, 1170, 1574, 1622
A. P., M.D. Alexander Pennecuik, M.D. 1009
A. PRIMCOCK. James Ralph 2547
AQUILA. Samuel Alexander 2332
A. R. Alexander Read 1666
A. R. Alexander Ross 2734
A. R. Alexander Rowley 2268
A. R. Athelstan Riley 2049
ARACHNOPHILUS. Adam Whyte 504
ARCHÆOPHILUS CONSTANTIUS. Father Hatton 1590
ARCHIBALD JOBBRY. John Galt 1568
ARCHIBALD MAC SARCASM, Rev. Sir. William Shaw, D.D. 1474
ARCHIMAGIRUS METAPHORICUS. William Kenrick, LL.D. 1297
ARCHY MACSARCONICA, F.R.S. Thomas Hastings 248
ARISTO. Rev. E. Irving 624
ARISTOBULUS. Thomas Woolston 1403, 2300
ARISTOGEITON. P. Fraser 35
ARLEY. M. P. Andrews 1960
ARMAR GREYE. Mrs. Maria Greer 1301
ARMIG, S. P. Samuel Pordage 1678
ARMYTAGE, DUDLEY. William E. Axon 2347
ARNETT, JOHN ANDREWS. John Hannett 230, 1230
A——R O——W. Arthur Onslow 2470
ARTEMUS WARD. Charles F. Browne 185
ARTH., HEN. Henry Arthur 2048
ARTHUR BROOKE. John Chalk Claris 710, 2189
ARTHUR LOCKER. J. H. Forbes 2389, 2493, 2529
ARTHUR PENDENNIS. William Makepeace Thackeray 1737
ARTHUR SKETCHLEY. George Rose 1634, 1675 (5), 1676 (11), 1677 (3), 1835
ARTHUR WALLBRIDGE. Arthur W. Lunn 239, 517, 2608
A. S. 1236
A. S. Abednego Seller 2164
A. S. Abraham Shackleton 527

A. S. Abraham Sharp 1010
A. S. Adam Stewart 2427
A. S. J. Digby 1620
A. S. A——. Alfred S. Atcheson 254
ASCOTT, R. HOPE. Robert Hope Moncrieff 244, 245, 1091, 1557, 1598, 1686, 1847, 1879, 2230, 2342, 2472, 2496 (3), 2497 (2), 2709, 2848
ASDRYASDUST TOSSOFFACAN. Edmund Gayton 2822
ATTICUS SECUNDUS. John M'Diarmid 1432
AUGUSTINUS ELEUTHERIUS. Sebastianus Francker 940
AUGUSTUS STAWEL. Alfred O. Legge 1543
AUNT FANNY. Fanny Barrows 879, 1029, 1497, 1726, 1812
AURA. Mary Catharine Irvine 188, 972
AUSTRALIE. Mrs Heron, née E. Manning 209
A. V. Arthur Ashley Sykes 1406
A. V. A. Vickaris 794
AVERIL BEAUMONT. A. W. Hunt 1532, 2573, 2707
A. V. G. M. Mrs Molesworth 2549
A. W. H. D. Adams 609
A. W. Anna Weamys 500
A. W. A. Walker 2803
A. W. Mrs Webb 528
A. W. FARMER. Dr Sam. Seabury 477, 965
A. W., M.D. Andrew Wilson 215
AWL., SIL. Ralph Wallis 1662
A. W., Sir Sir Anthony Weldon 526
A----W S-------N. Andrew Stevenson 1409, 2790
A. X. Caleb Fleming 847
A. Y. Arthur Young 1700

B.

B. George B. Bubier 1197
B. John B. Bishop 1819
B. Nathaniel Ward 638
B——. William Thorn 2158
B. A. Benjamin Antrobus 290
BABINGTON WHITE. Mary E. Braddon 404
BAGWEEL. Rev. Joshua Barnes and six others 428
BALDWIN, EDWARD. William Godwin 872, 1135, 1138, 1146, 1687, 1713, 1838, 1849
BALLINASLOE. Frederick Taylor 472

BALWHIDDER, REV. MICAH. John Galt   101

BARBICAN, GEOFFREY. Richard Thomson   391

BARD, SAMUEL A. Ephraim G. Squier   51

BAREBONES, CAUSTIC. Thomas Bridges   930, 1732

BARNIVELT ESDRAS. Alexander Pope   1299

BARONESS DESPENCER. R. F. A. Lee   2139

BARRISTER AT LAW. Sir J E. Eardley   5

BARRY CORNWALL. Bryan Waller Proctor   704, 728, 763, 935, 1546, 1569, 1573, 1621, 1958, 2099, 2381, 2839

BASILEUS, PHILO-, PHILO-CLERUS. William Carpender   1288

BASILICUS. Edmund Lenthal Swift   724

BASILIUS PHILOMUSUS. Robert Waring, M.A.   16

BASILIUS PHILOMUSUS. Thomas Barlow, D.D.   1880

BASILIUS PHILOMUSUS. Thomas Pierce   2566

BASILLE THEODORE. Thomas Becon 387, 565, 1024, 1738, 1871, 1939, 1980, 2211, 2667

BATAVUS, BRITTO. John Toland 606

BATHONIENSIS. Jonas Dennis, B.C.L.   355

BAVIUS. Dr John Martyn   1590

BAXTER, SIMEON. Rev. Samuel Peters   2704

BAYLE, Mr. Rev. Henry Penneck, M.A.   156

B. C. Benjamin Camfield   2330

B. C. Benjamin Chandler   155

B. C. Benjamin Clark   389

B. C. Benjamin Coole   2061

B. C. Bracy Clark, F.L.S.   865, 1721, 1828, 2417, 2730

B. C. Clement Barksdale   1420

B. C. Robert Parsons   223, 696

B. C. B. Sir Benjamin Collins Brodie 2053

B. D. Benjamin Dorr   1131

B——, EARL OF. Earl of Balcarres, C. Lindsay   17

BEATRICE, Anne Manning   756

BEAUFORT, JOHN, LL.D. —— Thelwall   564

BEAUMONT, AVERIL. A. W. Hunt   1532, 2573, 2707

BEAUMONT, SIR HARRY. Rev. Joseph Spence   542, 1659, 1865

BECCARIA ANGLICUS. Richard Wright   1444

BEDE CUTHBERT, B.A. Rev. Edward Bradley, B.A. 50, 549, 878, 1017, 1068, 1521, 1560, 1670, 1675, 1834, 1905, 2226, 2351, 2540, 2611, 2809

BEE, HOOKANIT. S. R. Wigram, 936

BEE, JON. John Badcock   629, 1504, 2406

BEELZEBUB. H. Newton Goodrich   1201

BELL, ACTON. Anne Brontë   58, 1946, 2552, 2844

BELL, CURRER. Charlotte Brontë   1261, 1946, 2026, 2352, 2740, 2844

BELL, ELLIS. Emily Jane Brontë   1946, 2844

BELLAMY, THOMAS. Sir Henry Janson   1896

BEN DAVID. John Jones, LL.D.   2178, 2587

BENEDICK WHIPEM. Richard Harris   1726

BENEVOLUS HILARIUS. John Britton   1940

BENJAMIN BOUNCE. Henry Carew   2619

BENJAMIN GOOSEQUILL. J. M. Adair, M.D.   91

BENJAMIN PLACE. Edward Thring   2577

BENNET, H., M.A. Morgan Williams   2630

BEN TROVATO. Samuel Lover 2217

BER. GAR. Bernard Garter 2063, 2620

BERNARD BLACKMANTLE. Charles Molloy Westmacott   763, 930

BERWICK, E.L.A. James Reynolds   713, 837, 2064

BETA. E. B. Bassett   1637

BETTY MONTGOMERY. William Cullen   985

BEWLEY, RICHARD, M.D. R. Harrington, M.D.   2641

BEY, ALI. Domingo B y Leblich 2627

B. F. Benjamin Furly   2842

B. F. H. B. F. Hartshorne   560

B. F. J. Francis Beaumont   241

B. F. J. John Fletcher   241

B. G. Barnaby Gooch   1839

B. G. Benjamin Grosvenor   2418
B. G. Bernard Garter   1281
B. G. Dr Robinson   1627
B. H. Brian Hunt   1863
BIBLICUS. Alexander Tulloch, D.D.   680
BIBLIOPHILOS. John M'Hale, D.D.   2439
BICKERSTAFF, ISAAC. Jonathan Swift, D.D.   233, 1993, 2744
BICKERSTAFF, ISAAC. Sir Richard Steele   1028, 1254, 1524, 1993
BIGLOW, HOSEA. James Russell Lowell   1567
BILLY, SILLY. Eustace C. G. Murray   2501
BIRD AT BROOMSGROVE. John Crane   35, 286, 2207
B—— I. C—— M & C. C. C. Maclaurin and J. Boswell   2452
B. J. HARCOURT. J. Harcourt Bland   155
B. JON. Benjamin Johnson   207
B. K. Benjamin Keach   163, 1018, 1040, 2789
B·······KE, L--D. Henry St John, Lord Viscount Bolingbroke   1358, 1512
B. L. Benjamin Lindley   2634
BLACKBURNE, E. OWENS. Elizabeth Casey   1207, 1649, 2796, 2826
BLACKMANTLE, BERNARD. Charles Molloy Westmacott   763, 930
BLANCH. John Blanch   2530
B. LE BOVIER DE FONTENELLE. W. Gardiner   508
BLINKINSOP, VICESIMUS, LL.D. Theodore Hook   2552
B., LORD. Lord Belfast   1557, 1692, 2706, 2797
B ...., LORD. Lord Brougham   894
B——. Abel Boyer   1899
B. M. Barclay de Mounteney   1383
B. M. Bernard de Mandeville   964
B. M. A. D. Elie Benoist   1154
B. N. Nicholas Breton   753, 1201
B——N, CH——. Charles Bateman   765
B'NEY FIZLE. Robert Hunter   90
BOBBIN, TIM. John Collier   1316, 1630, 1940, 2593, 2734
BON GUALTIER. Theodore Martin   245
BON GUALTIER. William E. Aytoun, D.C.L.   245
BOOMERANG, OLD. John Richard Houlding   201

BORDE, ANDREW   1606
BOSQUECILLO. Lieutenant Shaw   2773
BOUNCE, BENJAMIN. Henry Carew   2619
BOWCHIER, JOSHUA, M.A. George Trosse   289
BOYD, WALTER, M.P. William Combe   1416
BOZ. Charles Dickens   1582, 1816, 2401, 2500
B. R. Barnaby Rich   892
B. R. Robert Hegge   1339
B. R. Sir Benjamin Rudyerd   2013
BRANCASSINE, R. F. Hughes R. P. Fraser Halle   540
BRAZEN, ROBERT, F.N.S. C. Maclaurin   1947
BRERELY, IOHN. James Anderton   2044
BRERELY, JOHN. James Anderton   1526, 1530, 2044, 2249
BR., FR. Franceso Bracciolini   2618
BRIGHTWELL, RICHARDE. John Frith   1917
BRITAIN'S REMEMBRANCER. George Wither   2513
BRITANNICO SCOTO. Miss Webster   1476
BRITANICUS PROBUS. Samuel Johnson, LL.D.   1549
BRITANNICUS. Allan Ramsay, Jun.   1448
BRITANNICUS. John S. Hardy   2326
BRITANNICUS. Thomas Gordon   956
BRITANNICUS MELA. Charles Kelsall   1178, 2157
BRITANNICUS PHILELEUTHERUS. John Hildrop, D.D.   2113
BRITANNO SED DUNENSI. James Hodges   594
BRITANNUS, PHILO-. C. Davenport, LL.D.   2114
BRITANNUS, SCOTO-. Thomas M'Crie, D.D.   964
BRITISH COMMONER. Edward R. Humphreys, LL.D.   1424
BRITON, A. Lord Rokeby   795
BRITTO-BATAVUS. John Toland   606
BROOKE, ARTHUR. John Chalk Claris   710, 2189
BROOMSGROVE, BIRD AT. John Crane   35, 286, 2207
BROWN, JAMES. Joseph Robertson   1717

BROWN, POLEMOPHILUS.
Alexander Geddes, LL.D.   1737
BROWN, THOMAS YOUNGER.
Thomas Moore   872. 976 (2), 1239,
     2169, 2207 (2), 2536, 2841
BROWNE, H. K.   Mrs Hawkshaw   200
BROWNE, MATTHEW.   W. B.
Rands   2737
BRUTUS, JUNIUS.   Charles Blount 156
BRUTUS, JUNIUS.   Johannes .
Crellius   1334
BRUTUS, JUNIUS.   Robert Fer-
guson   156
B. SERGEANT.   Robert Butler   1697
B——T WILLIAM.   William
Bisset   1672
BUCK, RUTH.   Mrs Joseph Lamb
     1183, 1262, 1939, 2652
BULL, THOMAS.   William Jones'
     1818 (2)
BULL, W.   Ann Jebb   2699
BULLCALF, PETER.   Joseph S.
Fry   1140
BUNYAN JOHN, Jun.   Rev. Wil-
liam Arnot   706
BURGHLEY FELTHAM.   C. A.
Ward   748, 1991, 2389, 2454
BURTON, ALFRED.   John Mit-
ford, R.N.   50
BURTON, RICHARD.   Nathaniel
Crouch   2709
BURTON, ROBERT.   Nathaniel
Crouch   2709
BUSHMAN, OLD.   H. W. Wheel-
wright   293
B. W.   Browne Willis   2535
B. W., D.D.   Bryan Walton, D.D.   2631
BYEFIELD, J.   John Freind, M.D.
     1399
BYFIELD, Dr.   John Freind, M.D.
     1399

C.

C.   Arthur Cleaveland Cope   192
C.   Arthur Cleaveland Coxe   375
C.   Ed. Capper   1626
C. A.   Charlotte Anley   1621
C. A.   Christopher Anstey   279
C. A.   David Stansfield   306
CADWALLADER, GEORGE.   G.
B. Doddington   2166
C. A. J.   C. A. Jones
     1833, 2082, 2251, 2518

CALEB D'ANVERS.   Nicholas
Amhurst   118, 171, 425, 529, 1414 (2),
     2149, 2303, 2589, 2689
CALEB D'ANVERS.   William Pul-
teney, Earl of Bath   2032
CALEDONIUS CINCINNATUS.
John Gordon Barbour   1487 (2), 2066
CALEDONNICUS.   Whitelaw
Ainslie, M.D.   931
CALPE ADADUS.   Antonio D. de
Pascual   2693
CALVINIANUS PRESBYTER.
Archibald Bruce   103, 2065
CALVIN, PHILANAX.   Samuel
Young   972
CALVINUS.   James Grahame
     104, 1980, 2697, 2699
CALVINUS MINOR SCOTO-
BRITANNUS.   Archibald Bruce 965
CAMBRIDGE GENTLEMAN.
—— Rawson   1404
CAMLAN GORONVA.   Rowland
Williams   1332, 1825
CANADIAN.   De Salles Later-
rière   1962
CANDIDUS.   Dr Smith   1927
CANDIDUS.   Thady Fitzpatrick   772
CANTABRIGENSIS ALUMNUS.
T. Forster   1070
CANTABRIGIENSIS.   Dr Taylor
     1626 (2)
CANTABRIGIENSIS CRITO.
Thomas Turton, D.D.   2758
CANTABRIGIENSIS DICAIO-
PHILUS.   Roger Long, D.D.   2213
CANTABRIGIENSIS PHILA-
LETHES.   Bishop Kaye   2141, 2178
CANTABRIGIENSIS PHILA-
LETHES.   James Jurin, M.D.
     165, 1010, 1619
CANTABRIGIENSIS PHILA-
LETHES.   John Jackson   900, 2141
CANTABRIGIENSIS PHILA-
LETHES.   Zachary Grey   2267
CANTABRIGIENSIS PHILE-
LEUTHERUS.   Thomas Herne
     798, 886, 1405, 2586
CANTABRIGIENSIS PHILO-
BIBLICUS.   J. Chapman, D.D. 2137
CANTABRIGIENSIS PHILO-
CRITICUS.   John Jackson   2644
CANTABRIGIENSIS THEO-
PHANES.   Samuel Squire, D.D.,
Bishop of St David's   88

CAPTAIN CRAWLEY. George Frederick Pardon
208, 234 (3), 1060, 1066 (2)
CAPTAIN ROBERTS. Augustus Charles Hobart, R.N.　1710
CAPTAIN ROCK. Roger O'Connor　1451
CARELESS, FRANCK. Richard Head　935
CARNABY CURRYCOMB. John Wolcott　1893
CARRE, THOMAS. Miles Pinckney　2530
CARRIBBER. Sir George Duncan Gibb, Bart.　1800
CARTHUSIAN. W. J. D. Ryder　391
CASSANDER, J. John Bruckner　541
CASPIPINA, TAMOC. Jacob Duché　326
CATHOLICUS. Henry Cotton, D.C.L.　1755
CATHOLICUS. Henry Portsmouth　812
CATHOLICUS. William Matthews　1713
CATHOLICUS. Rev. Joseph Mendham　778
CATHOLICUS-ANGLO. Lord John Manners　2804
CATHOLICUS JOHANNES. John Rutty　815
CATHOLICUS PRESBYTER. Rev. W. Harness　2774
CATO PARVUS. Thomas Frognall Dibdin　231
CAUSIDICUS. Samuel Whitcombe　2122
CAUSTIC BAREBONES. Thomas Bridges　930, 1732
CAUSTIC CHRISTOPHER. Thomas Green Fessenden　1957
CAVEAT EMPTOR. Sir George Stephen　48
CAVENDISH. Henry Jones
1327, 1328, 1942
CAVENDISH. Samuel Bevan　2598
CAXTON PISISTRATUS. G. E. Bulwer-Lytton　243
C. B. Charles Bathurst　1337
C. B. Charles Bucke　1256
C. B. Christopher Brooke　1013
C. B. Clement Barksdale
204, 1335, 1810, 2166
C. B. Jonathan Swift　1540

C. C. Charles Clark　234
C. C. Charles Coghlan　1517
C. C. Chr. Cartwright　352
C. C. C. Caleb C. Colton, M.A.　2134
C. D. Charles Dunster　1961, 2532
C. D. Mrs Charles Dyson　1595
C—— DE LA B——. Calderon de la Barca　1470
C. D'OLLINCAN. Charles Ancillon　834
C. E. Charlotte Elliot　1181
C. E. Edward Coffin　2121, 2674
CECIL. Cornelius Tongue
1179, 1194, 2101, 2481, 2508
C. E. H. Charlotte E. Hawker　938
CELATUS. Robert Owen　1643, 2054
CELTOPHILE, A. Rev. Francis Crawford, LL.D.　788
CELER LYSIPONIUS, M.D.L. Johann Groenevelt, M.D.　1321
C. E. M. Charles E. Mudie　2502
CENSOR. W. C. Taylor　2063
CERVANTES HOGG, F.S.M. Eaton Stannard Barrett　2217
CERVANTES HOGG, F.S.M. T. P. Lathy　2217
C. E. S., Sir, Bart. Sir Claude Edward Scott, Bart　434
C. F. A. Cecil Frances Alexander　1197
C. F. and E. C. Catherine Foster and Elizabeth Colling　1726
C. F. G. Charles Fitz Geoffrey　1022
C. F. G. Mrs Gore　1639
C. F. H. Cecil Frances Alexander　2726
C. F. H. Cecil Frederick Holmes　2775
C. F——N. C. Ferguson　1343
C. G. Charles Gataker　931
C. G. Charles Gibbon　1344
C. G. Charles Gildon　1978
C. G. H. C. G. Hamilton
494, 549, 857, 1547, 1749
C. H. Chambers Hall　1909
C. H. Charles Hope, Lord President　1752
C. H. Christ Hunt　1021
CHAP., GEOR. George Chapman　2813
CHARFY GUINIAD. George Smeeton　930
CHARLES CLIFFORD. William Henry Ireland　92
CHARLES DELORME. Charles Rumball　1553, 1879
CHARLES DODD. Hugh Tootle　352
CHARLES MARTELL. Thomas Delf　1519, 1558, 2016, 2017 (2)

CHARLES RANGER. Arthur Murphy   1044
CHARLES ROCKINGHAM, Sir Count de Jarnac   346
CHARLES TAYLOUR. Henry Keepe   2664
CHARLEY, CHILLY. Charles Clark   234
CHARLEY, SNARLY. Charles Clark   901
CHARLIE, MUSSEL MOU'D. G. R. Kinloch   209
CHARLOTTE DACRE. Mrs Byrne, Rosa Matilda   1181, 2854
CHARLOTTE DACRE. Rosa Matilda, Mrs Byrne   1181, 2854
CHARLOTTE ELIZABETH. Charlotte Elizabeth Tonna, Mrs Phelan *née* Browne   66, 227, 357, 379, 402, 475, 493, 562, 603, 609, 759, 886, 918, 1018, 1082, 1258, 1281, 1282, 1302, 1428, 1570, 1618, 1831, 1868, 1880, 1890, 1978, 2014, 2073, 2221, 2292, 3375, 2403, 2533, 2539, 2789, 2844, 2851
CHAS. DIRRILL. Richard Sill   2146
CH—— B——N. Charles Bateman   765
C. H. ED. Christian H. Erndtel   2125
CHESHIRE WEAVER. J. D. Latouche   93, 853
CHEVALIER, THE. A. M. Ramsay, LL.D.   1930
CHILLY CHARLEY. Charles Clark   234
CHIRURGUS. John Dix   1047
CHIUSO GIORGIONE DI CASTEL. Peter Bailey   2401
CH. MAR. Christopher Marlowe   2620
C. H. P. Charles Henry Parry, M.D.   1571
CHRISTIAN EMANUEL. George Ensor   1262
CHRISTIAN SEARCH, LL.D. Sir W. C. Smith, Bart.   1607
CHRISTIAN, THEOPHILUS. John Owen, M.A.   901
CHRISTIAN UVEDALE, M.D. Sir John Hill   496
CHRISTIANUS PHILELEUTHERES. Rev. T. Broughton   385
CHRISTIANUS, PHILO-. William Brough, D.D.   2247
CHRISTIANUS SOCRATES. Edward Stephens OR Stevens   158, 1261

CHRISTODULUS ECCLESTON. John Danks   573
CHRISTOPHER CAUSTIC. Thomas Green Fessenden   1957
CHRISTOPHER MERRET. Henry Stubbe   1564
CHRISTOPHER NORTH. Prof. John Wilson   2102, 2425
CHRISTOPHILUS, WILLIAM PIKE. Wm. Lucy, Bp. of St David's   1768
CHRYSAL. Sir William Scott, Lord Stowell   1447
C. H. T. C. H. Timperley   2453
CHURCHMAN, THEOPHILUS. Henry Hickman   2198
CHURCHMAN, THEOPHILUS. Peter Heylin, D.D.   1124, 2198
CHURNE, WILLIAM. Francis E. Paget   1177
C. I. Cosmo Innes.   463
CICERO, MARCUS TULLIUS. William Melmoth   341
CICESTRENSIS, PRESBYTER. Henry Latham   130
CINCINNATUS. Joseph Cawthorne   885
CINCINNATUS CALEDONIUS. John Gordon Barbour   1487 (2), 2066
CIRUJANO, M. M. C. George Borlase Childs   64, 212, 699
CIVIS. Alexander Dunlop   743
CIVIS. Baron Stowell   2432
CIVIS. George Thomson   2489
C. J. Charles Jenner   1539
C. J. H. C. J. Hamilton   2706
C. K. P., Rev. Charles Kegan Paul   2554
C. L. Chandos Leigh   2617
C. L. Charles Lumisden   864
C. L. Christopher Love   572
CLARA, FRANCIS A SANCTA. Francis Davenport   862, 2187
CLARIBEL. Mrs Barnard   925
CLARK, Rev. T. John Galt   2626, 2787
CLAUDERO. James Wilson   180, 551, 1951, 1952
CLAYTON, THOMAS. Peter Motteux   180
CLEESHBOTHAM, JEDEDIAH. Sir Walter Scott   2541 (4)
CLERICUS. Charles Page Eden   2320
CLERICUS. George Smith   875
CLERICUS. Rev. Augustus Clissold   1411

CLERICUS. Rev. David Murray　229
CLERICUS. Rev. W. Cartwright　395, 874, 2076
CLERICUS DORCESTREINSIS. Rev. J. L. Jackson, M.A.　389
CLERICUS LYVECANUS. C. Otway　106
CLERICUS, NON. —— Cottle　2224
CLERICUS SEPTENTRIONALIS. J. Richardson　2137
CLERK, THOMAS. Thomas Hartwell Horne　2841
CLEROPHILUS ALETHES. John Constable　2160, 2464
CLERUS-PHILO, PHILO-BASILEUS. William Carpender　1288
CLIFFORD, CHARLES. William Henry Ireland　92
CLINTON, WALTER. W. H. Davenport Adams　2530
CLITUS-ALEXANDRINUS. Richard Brathwayt　336
C. LL - - -, Rev. Charles Lloyd, LL.D.　1775
CLYTUS-ALEXANDRINUS. R. Brathwayt　2808
CLUTTERBUCK, CUTHBERT. A. Hamilton, W.S.　726
C. M. Charles Mackinnon　2059
C. M. Charles Maclaren　2075
C. M. Charles Marriott, M.A.　2361
C. M. Charles Northland　20
C. M. Charles Moss, D.D.　840
C. M. Christopher Marlowe　68, 777
C—— M. and B—— I, C. C. C. Maclaurin and James Boswell　2452
C. M. and I. D. Christopher Marlowe and John Davies　777
C. M., D.D. Cotton Mather　1813
C. MELMONTH. Samuel Jackson Pratt　1717, Errata, Vol. iv.
C. M. E. M. Mrs M‘Fie　2495
C. N. C. F. P. D. Cornelius Nary　1731
C. O. Cæsar Otway　2402 (2)
COBHAM, HARRY. Edward Long　136
CŒLEBS. Edward Augustus Carlyon　1327
COLLET, STEPHEN, A.M. John S. Byerley　2128
COLLIER, JOEL. J. L. Bicknell　1683
COLQUHOUN, P. R. Shaw　1770
COMMENT, CUTHBERT. Abraham Tucker　1538

COMMONER, BRITISH. E. R. Humphreys, LL.D.　1424
COMMONER OF OXFORD, GENTLEMAN. Samuel Croxall, D.D.　876
COMUS. Robert Michael Ballantyne　1635, 1685, 2219
CON CREGAN. Charles James Lever　473
CONNY - CATCHER, CUTHBERT. Robert Greene　579
CONSTABLE, HIGH. William Lee　494
CONSTANS. G. Berkeley, E. of Berkeley　1113
CONSTANTINE KOLIADES. J. P. Le Chevalier　2704
CONSTANTIUS ARCHÆOPHILUS. Father Hatton　1590
CONSTITUTIO. John Cartwright　1380
CONTRASTS. William Gilbert　873
CONWAY, DERWENT. Henry David Inglis　1890, 2415, 2530, 2540
COOPER, REV. WM. U., B.A. James G. Bertram　933
COPPER-FARTHING, THE, DEAN. Jonathan Swift　1669
COPYWELL, J. William Woty　2381
CORIAT, JUNIOR. Samuel Paterson　104, 159
CORNELIUS. Charles Henry Corbett　2651
CORNELIUS O'DOWD. Charles James Lever　514
CORNELIUS PAETS. Arthur A. Sykes, D.D.　1188
CORNELIUS, PETER. Hugh Peeters　2795
CORNUBIAN. Henry John Daniel　137
CORVINUS. Travers Twiss, D.C.L.　1193
CORVINUS VALERIUS. Thomas Blacklock　2151
CORNWALL, BARRY. Bryan Waller Procter　704, 728, 763, 935, 1546, 1569, 1573, 1621, 1958, 2099, 2381, 2839
CORY. William Johnson　Errata, Vol. iv.
CORYMBÆUS. Richard Brathwait　213
COSMO. John Hall Stevenson　1537
COTTON, ROBERT TURNER. Mortimer Collins　1672
COUNCILLOR DREENAN. J. B. Endean　1963

COUNT REGINALD DE ST LEON. Edward du Bois   2250

COURTNEY MELMOTH. Samuel Jackson Pratt   1781, 2057, 2346, 2510, 2548

COUSIN ALICE. Alice Neal   67

COUSIN KATE. Catherine D. Bell   178, 1177, 1518, 1520, 1547, 1554, 1710, 2341, 2679, 2795

COXE, HENRY. John Millard   1006, 1909, 2625 (2)

C—— P——. Constantia Phillips   1067

C. P. C. Charles Purton Cooper   312

C. R. Clara Reeve   1828, 2028

C. R. Richard Smith, Bishop of Chalcedon   682

CRAFT, ZACHARY. Charles Kelsall   929

CRAIG, J. H. James Hogg   1193

CRANMER. John Disney, D.D.   2393

CRAVEN. Captain John W. Carleton   1195, 2102

CRAWLEY, CAPTAIN RAWDON. George Frederick Pardon   208, 234 (3), 1060, 1066

CRAYON GEOFFREY. Washington Irving   66, 252, 2397, 2540

CREGAN, CON. Charles James Lever   473

CREWDSON, ISAAC. Benjamin Dockray   1684

CRI IN HOPE. John Price   418

CRINE, GEORGE, M.D. Sir John Hill   1540

CRISPIN. William Wagstaffe, M.D.   535

CRITHANNAH, JOB. Jonathan Birch   922

CRITICUS. Rev. William Orme   1572

CRITICUS. Thomas Barnes   1861

CRITICUS, PHILANAGNOSTES. Thomas Herne   13

CRITICUS, PHILO-. Francis Hare, D.D.   414

CRITO. J. H. Frere   624

CRITO CANTABRIGIENSIS. Thomas Turton, D.D.   2758

C. R. M. Charles Robert Manning, M.A.   307

C. R. MATURIN, Rev. Rev. James Wills   2712

CROUCH, NATH. Richard Burton   757

CROWQUILL, ALFRED. Alfred Henry Forrester   9, 65, 291, 757, 984, 1024, 1256, 1302, 1497, 1895, 1908, 1909, 2386, 2541, 2686

CRUSCA DELLA. Robert Merry   682, 1960

C. S. Charles Sackville, Duke of Dorset   2631

C. S. Charles Shadwell   877

C. S. Charles Snart   1985

C. S. Christopher Shutte   2555

C. S. S. Charles Stuart Calverley   937, 2726

C. S., SIR. Sir Charles Sedley   1711

C. S. W. Charles Stuart Wortley   1277

C. SYLVESTER. Lady Wood   2229

C. T. Christopher Taylor   2808

C. T. Dr Christopher Terne   2433

C. U. Charles Usher   1372

CUMBRIENSIS. John Rooke   2157

CURATE, JACOB. Robert Calder   2273

CURIAE, AMICUS. John Payne Collier   541

CURIO. Richard Howell   2401

CURRER BELL. Charlotte Brontë   1261, 1946, 2026, 2352, 2740, 2844

CURRYCOMB CARNABY. John Wolcott   1893

CUTHBERT BEDE, B.A. Rev. Edward Bradley, B.A.   50, 549, 878, 1017, 1068, 1521, 1560, 1670, 1675, 1834, 1905, 2226, 2351, 2540, 2611, 2809

CUTHBERT CLUTTERBUCK. A. Hamilton, W.S.   726

CUTHERT COMMENT. Abraham Tucker   1538

CUTHBERT CONNY-CATCHER. Robert Greene   579

C. V. Charles Vallancey   817

C. V. G. C. V. Grinfield   1913

C. V. S. Sir Richard Davis Hanson   1451

C. W. Charles Wase   733

C. W. Charles Wright   328

C. W. William Collins   1634

C. W. H. Charles Wren Hoskyns   2545

C. W., M.D., ... Clifton Wintringham   1772

CYCLA. Helen Clacy   200, 1867, 1875, 2789

CYCLOS. George Anderson   184

C——Y, J——N. John Courteney   2137

D.

Δ. Benjamin Disraeli   2619, 2724

Δ. Edmundus Richerius   2634

Δ. Francis Barham   1522

D. Rev. Joseph Wasse
     1626 (6), 1627 (6), 1628 (6)

DACRE, CHARLOTTE. Rosa Matilda, Mrs Byrne   1181. 2854

DALMOCAND. George Macdonald   1945

DALRYMPLE, GILBERT, D.D. Gerrard Legh   1356

DANGERFIELD, JOHN. Oswald John Frederick Crawfurd, H.B.M. 2627

DANIEL HARDCASTLE. Richard Page   31, 211, 1452

DANMONIENSIS. William Burt 611

D'ANVERS, CALEB. Nicholas Amhurst   118, 171, 425, 529, 1414 (2), 2032, 2149, 2303, 2589, 2686

D'ANVERS, CALEB. Wm. Pulteney, Earl of Bath   2032

DARYL, HOLME. David Herbert   1515, 2849

DARYL, SIDNEY. Douglas Straight   1072, 2231

DAVID BEN. John Jones, LL.D.   2178, 2587

DAVID HILTON. David Hilton Wheeler   279

DAVID HUGHSON, LL.D. Dr Edward Pugh   787, 1506, 2785

DAWPLUCKER, JONATHAN. John Barclay, M.D.   2144

D. B. P. Dr William Bishop   2118

D. C. Daniel Cawdrey   12, 2520

D. D. B. David Dakers Black   1337

D. E. Edward Bagshaw   1420, 2302

DEAN COPPER-FARTHING. Jonathan Swift   1669

DEAN, JONATHAN. Jonathan Swift, D.D.   568

DEAN SWIFT. Benson Earle Hill 1915

DECANUS. Edward N. Hoare, Dean of Achonry   763

DECANVER, H. C. C H. Cavender   333

DECLAN. William Phelan, D.D. 2300

DEENE KENNER. Charlotte Smith   101, 387, 708, 1497, 2221, 2242, 2271

DELLA CRUSCA. Robert Merry   682, 1960

DELORME, CHARLES. Charles Rumball   1553, 1879

DELTA. David Macbeth Moir   698, 1338, 1958

D'EMILLIANNE, GABRIEL. Antoine Gavin   958, 1770, 2368

DEMETRIUS WYSEMAN. Duke Willis   2062

DEMOCRITUS JUNIOR. Robert Burton   86

DENARIUS. Henry Cole   2349

DENIS IGNATIUS MORIARTY. John O'Brien Grant   2814

DERWENT CONWAY. Henry David Inglis   1890, 2415, 2530, 2540

DESPENCER, BARONESS. R. F. A. Lee   2139

DETECTOR. Rev. H. Gauntlett 1453

D. F. Daniel Defoe   770, 1385, 1970, 2002, 2196, 2310, 2437

D. F. Dr Frances Atterbury   557

D. G. David Garrick   1803

D——, G. George Daniel   1534, 1961, 2407, 2845,

D. HARDCASTLE. R. Page   31

D. H. K. Dr Henry King, Bishop of Chichester   578

D—— I——. Duncan Innes 1350, 1979

DICAIOPHILUS CANTABRIGIENSIS. Roger Long, D.D.   2213

DIEDRICH KNICKERBOCKER. W. Irving   1144

DIRRILL, CHAS. Richard Sill   2146

DISSENTER, ——. —— Hudson 1781

D'ISTRIA, MME. LA COMTESSE DORA, Princess Koltzoff Massalsky née Helena Ghika   2827

D. J. David Jones   1161, 2014

D. J. P. B. D. R. VV. Dr J. Ponet, Bishop of Rochester and Winchester   2380

D. K. Daniel King   337

D. L. David Laing   1757, 2464

D--MM--D, Mrs. Mrs Drummond   911

D****N. J**N, D.D. John Duncan, D.D.   1934

D——N S——T, Rev. Jonathan Swift, D.D.   1141, 1222, 1934

D. O. —— Owen   1891

DOBLADO, DON LEUCADIO. John Blanco White, M.A.   1429

DOCTOR. Dr Kingsley   2458

DODD, CHARLES. Hugh Tootle 352

DOD, PIERCE, M.S. Dr Barrowby   1403

DOD, PIERCE, M.S. Dr Schomberg, Jun.   1403

DODS, MARGARET. Christina J. Johnstone 510
DOGGREL, ILIAD, SIR. Sir Thomas Burnet 1173
DOLEMAN, NICHOLAS. Robert Parsons 2791
DOLEMAN, R. Robert Parsons 470
D'OLLINCAN, C. Charles Ancillon 834
DOLOS MISO-. Charles Leslie 1029
DOMESTICA ACHETA, M.E.S. L. M. Budgen 779
DOM CLAUDE LAUNCELOT. Mary Anne Schimmelpenninck 1693
DON, A. B. Captain A. Bruce 649
DON DIEGO PUEDE-SER. James Mabbe 855, 2460
DON LEUCADIO DOBLADO. Joseph Blanco White, M.A. 1429
DON RICHARDO DE MEDICO CAMPO. Gabriel Harvey 2655
DON, T. B. LEEVITT. James Mudie Spence, F.R.G.S. 1484
D---- OF A-----E. Duke of Argyle 557
DORA D'ISTRIA, MME. LA COMTESSE. Princess Koltzoff-Massalsky née Helena Ghika 2827
DORCESTRIENSIS CLERICUS. Rev. J. L. Jackson, M.A. 389
DOUGLAS. Andrew Reed 2584
DOULEY, GEORGE. William Warford 275, 276
DOYLE, MARTIN. Ross Hickey 60, 442 (2), 517, 555, 895, 897, 936, 1100 (2), 1251, 1310, 1552, 1984, 2240, 2408, 2738
D. P. Dig. Polwheele 2547
D. P. D. Paseley 563, 2216
D. P. C. Drummond Percy Chase, M.A. 2091
DRACO, ANTI-. John Disney 932
DRALLOC, N. John Collard 787, 1467
DRAPER, M. B. Jonathan Swift, D.D. 1402
DRAPIER, M. B. Jonathan Swift, D.D. 1402, 1415
DRAWCAUSIR, KNT., SIR ALEXANDER. H. Fielding 529
DRAWDE REKATIHW. Edward Whitaker 1204
D. R. B. Daniel Rogers, B.D. 1983
D. R., B. OF D. Daniel Rogers, B.D. 2639

DREENAN, COUNCILLOR. J. R. Endean 1963
DRUGGER, ABEL. John Hardman 945
DRUID. Henry Hall Dixon 1978, 2276, 2385
D. S. Edward Stephens 1479
D. T. Daniel Tuvill 791
D—T—, R—V—D. William Thom, M.A. 1067
DUBLINIENSIS, PHILELEUTHERUS. Patrick Delany, D.D. 2113
DUDLEY, ARMYTAGE. William E. A. Axon 2347
DUFFLE, THOMAS. John Galt 2492
DUNCAN MACCARTE. Samuel Squire, D.D. 1383
DUNDERHEADIUS HABBAKUKIUS. Thomas Jackson 2709
DUNENSI, BRITANNO SED. James Hodges 594
DUNSMUIR, AMY. Mrs Oliphant 2731
D'URFEY, YOUNG. Frederick Forrest 2080, 2797
DVCTOR OPTATVS. James Mumford 2069
D. W. Daniel Wilson, LL.D. 2064
D. W. Dorothy White 273
D. W. William Denton, M.D. 1178
DWALPHINTRAMIS. John Barnard 84, 87
ΔΥΝΑ'ΜΙΚΟΣ. Lynall Thomas 2209

E.

E. Henry John Temple, Viscount Palmerston 1735
E. Thomas Erskine 897
E. A. Edward Aggas 579, 636, 1823
E. A. Edward Archer 2407
E. A., M.A. Edmund Arwaker, M.A. 734
E. A. P. 958
EARL. G. R. C. Herbert, Earl of Pembroke 2458
EARL OF B. Earl of Balcarres, C. Lindsay 17
EARL OF HAD ----TON, Right Honbl. Thomas Baillie Hamilton, Earl of Haddington 195
EARLE OF ESSEX. Francis Lord Bacon 145
E. B. Edmund Bolton 737

E. B.   Edmund Borlase   270
E. B.   Edward Benlowes   570
E. B.   Edward Bentham   349
E. B.   Edward Billing   884, 2835
E. B.   Edward Bohun   145
E. B.   Edward Brotherton   2003
E. B.   Edward Budge   406
E. B.   Edward Burrough   321, 547, 576,
   1185, 1291, 2190, 2259, 2447, 2599, 2760
E. B.   Edward Bush   2335
EBENEZER LAZARUS.   Robert
   Mason   1866
EBENEZER PENTWEAZLE.   C.
   Smart   1179
EBENEZER TOM-TIT.   Charles
   Smith   1343
E. B. G.   Edward Burnaby Green
   538, 1090, 2839
E. B. L.   E. G. E. L. Bulwer Lytton   1072
EBN SHEMAYA.   David Parkes   2483
E. B. P.   Edward Bouverie Pusey,
   D.D.   687, 2476
E. C.   Edward Capel   1752
E. C.   George Mackenzie, Earl of
   Cromarty   9, 1356
E. C.   James Canceller   1
E. C.   Lady Elizabeth Carew   2618
E. C. A.   E. C. Agnew   1011
E. C. C. B.   E. C. C. Baillie   2795
ECCLESTON CHRISTODULUS.
   John Danks   573
E. C., C. F. and.   Catherine Foster
   and Elizabeth Colling   1726
ECCLETUS.   Luke Howard   915
ECLEA-NOBJ-MONI.   Benjamin
   Coole   1349
E. C. P.   E. C. Price   1818
E. C. S.   Sir Edward Cecil   1036
E. D.   Edward Dennant   2513
E. D.   Sir Edward Dyer   1990
EDEN WARWICK.   George Jabet
   1699, 1960
EDGAR, SIR JOHN.   Sir Richard
   Steele   2558
EDMUND FALCONER.   Edmund
   O'Rourke   870, 1597, 1680
EDMUND KIRKE.   J. R. Gilmore
   1470, 1686
ED. SP.   Edmund Spenser
   452, 1678, 2039, 2548
E. D., SR.   Sir Edward Dering   479
EDWARD BALDWIN.   William
   Godwin   872, 1135, 1138, 1146, 1687,
   1713, 1838, 1849

EDWARD BRADWARDINE
   WAVERLEY.   John Wilson
   Croker   2696
EDWARD GARRETT.   Isabella
   Fyvie   294, 307, 545, 1799, 1994
EDWARD KNOTT.   Matthew
   Wilson   365, 1603
EDWARD SEARCH.   Abraham
   Tucker   966, 1486
EDWARD TREVOR.   E. R. Bul-
   wer-Lytton   2546
E. E.   Edmund Ellis or Elys   71, 616 (2),
   685, 2279
E. F.   Ebenezer Forsyth   32
E. F.   Edward Fielde   558
E. F.   Edward Fisher   376, 1551, 2306
E. F.   Edward Fannant   1160
E. F.   E. Field   1545
E. F.   E. Fletcher   739
E. F.   Lord Vis. Falkland, H. Cary   1160
E. F. D.   E. F. Dagley   879
E. F. S. H.   E. F. S. Harris   2729
E. G.   Rev. Edmond Hogan, S.J.   1167
EGLANTIN, J.   J. Nightingale   1636
E. G. L. B.   Sir Edward George
   Bulwer-Lytton   2799
E. GLORIA NON NUMIS.   John
   Longmuir, D.D.   431
E. H.   Ebenezer Henderson, D.D.   1013
E. H.   Edmund Hickeringill   1682
E. H.   Edward Hinton   2722
E. H.   Ellis Hookes   179, 1236
E. H.   Hon. Edward Howard   2827
E. H. K. H.   Edward H. K. Hugessen
   2040
E. H. M.   E. H. Mair   2100
E. H. S.   Rt. Hon. Lord Stanley   2396
E. H. T.   E. Healy Thomson   1308
E. I.   Roger Widdrington   1736
E. I.   Thomas Preston   1736
E—— J——.   E. Jeffrys   2590
EKAL GAOLG.   J. A. Lake Gloag   1264
E. L.   Edward Leigh   1899
E. L.   Edward Llewellin   684
E. L.   E. Lamb   2262
E. L.   E. Lord   665
E. L.   E. Lydecott   2025
E. L. A. BERWICK.   James
   Reynolds   713, 837, 2064
E. L. B.   Edward G. E. L. Bulwer-
   Lytton   707, 1313, 1875
ELDER, AN.   James Mathieson   2212
ELDON, Dr ABRAHAM.   Thomas
   Wyse   499

ELEUTHERIUS, AUGUSTINUS. Sebastianus Francken   940

ELEUTHERUS PHILONO-MOUS. J. Arbuthnot, M.D.   1270

E. L. H. Edward Law Hussey   868

ELIOT, GEORGE. Marian Evans   32, 562, 908, 1217, 1338, 1613, 1616, 2226, 2263, 2385, 2461

ELIZA. Elizabeth Draper   1427

ELIZABETH CHARLOTTE. Charlotte Elizabeth Tonna, Mrs Phelan née Browne   66, 227, 357, 379, 402, 475, 493, 562, 603, 609, 759, 886, 918, 1018, 1082, 1258, 1281, 1282, 1302, 1428, 1570, 1618, 1831, 1868, 1880, 1890, 1978, 2014, 2073, 2221, 2292, 2375, 2403, 2533, 2539, 2789, 2844, 2851

ELIZABETH WETHERELL. Susan Warner   741, 2063, 2814

ELLEN AMELIA. Ellen Amelia Garrett   2341

ELLIOTT, RUTH. Lillie Peck   2776

ELLIS BELL. Emily Jane Brontë   1946, 2844

ELMLICHT TWINROCK. Thomas Peter Mitchell   2562

E. M. Edward Maitland   1267

E. M. Edward Marbury   437

E. M. Edward Mice   1278

E. M. Edward Monro, M.A.   2788

E. M. E. Mangin   1800

E. M. Emanuel Meteranus   2647

E. M. Everard Maynwaring, M.D.   1204

EMANCIPATUS. Rev. Joseph Mendham   2478, 2547

EMANUEL, CHRISTIAN. George Ensor   1262

E-M-D L-TT-N. Edmund Litton   1900

EMERITUS. —— Prower   1616

E. M. H——. Emily Marion Harris   78

EMILLIANE, GABRIEL D'. Antoine Gavin   958, 1770, 2368

EMPTOR CAVEAT. Sir George Stephen   48

E. M. S. Elizabeth M. Stewart   2221

E. N. Erskine Nicol, A.R.A.   1267

ENGLISH CONNAUGHT RAN-GER. Edward Cooper   550

ENNIS GRAHAM. Elizabeth Molesworth   404, 547, 1520, 1751, 2549

ENOS. Cecil Percival Stone   188, 1903

E. O'C. Edmond O'Connell   2717

E. O'C. E. O'Conor   1038

E. OWENS BLACKBURNE. Elizabeth Casey   1207, 1649, 2796, 2826

E. P. Edward Pearson   1372

E. P. Edward Phillips   1689

E. P. Thomas Brown   2696

EPHELIA. Joan Philips   910

EPHEMERA. Edward Fitzgibbon   248, 1064

EPHRAIM HARDCASTLE. William Henry Pyne   2445, 2688, 2818

EPHRAIM HOLDING. George Mogridge   776

EPSILON. J. Baldwin Brown   1657

E. R. C. Rev. Eustace R. Conder   1198, 1823

ERICK MACKENZIE. Millicent Grogan   2226

ERITH LYNN. Edward Fox   1958

E. R. S. Ernest R. Seymour   1614

E. S. Edward Sharpham   548

E. S. Edward Stephens   464, 1301

E. S. Edward Stillingfleet, D.D.   1385, 2299

E. S. Elkanah Settle   1314, 1714

E. S. Erasmus Saunders, D.D.   2736

E. S. A. Ernest Silvanus Appleyard   719, 2521, 2801

E. S., B. OF D. Edward Sulton   130

ESDRAS BARNIVELT. Alexander Pope   1299

E. S. H. E. S. Pearson, Countess of Harrington   1944

E. S. L. Hon. Elizabeth Sophia Law   1015, 1629

ESSENUS. Rev. John Jones, LL.D.   1733

ESSEX, EARLE OF. Francis Lord Bacon   145

E. S. T. D. Edward S. T. Daunt   2019

ESTIBIUS PSYCALETHES. William Coward, M.D.   2309

E. T. Edmund Tilnay   2448

E. T. Simon Berington   1585

ETA MAWR. Elizabeth Colling   894, 2499

E. T. C. Edward Thomas Cardale   1824

ETCHELL, MABEL. Charlotte Phillips   2551

ETTRICK SHEPHERD, THE. James Hogg   2064

EUGENE. Hugo Arnot   1399

EUGENIUS, JUNIOR. James
  Owen   401
EUGENIUS   PHILALETHES.
  Arthur A. Sykes, D.D.   1225
EUGENIUS   PHILALETHES.
  Thomas Vaughan,   94, 131, 269,
      835, 1225, 1526, 1533, 1538, 2310
EUGENIUS   PHILALETHES,
  Jun., Robert Samber   2638
EUGENIUS THEODIDACTUS.
  John Heydon   2033
EUISTOR, Fr. Henry More   683
EUPATOR. Joseph Mendham
                              309, 575
EUPHEMON. —— Dawson   1190
EUPISTINUS   THEOPHILUS.
  —— Prichard   2149
EUSEBIUS. Edmund Rack   2112
ΕΥΣΕΒΕΙΣ. R. Welton, D.D.   415
EUSEBIUS   EXONIENSIS.
  Richard Polwhele   805
EUSEBIUS, Vicar of Lilliput. - - - -
  Joseph Robertson   1779
EVANDER. J. Bayford   624
E. V. B. Hon. Eleanor Vere Boyle
                        370, 1218, 1716
EVERARD   FLEETWOOD.
  Samuel Burroughs   768
EVERING, KATHERINE   1518
E. V. S. Edward V. Utterston   2317
E. V. U. Edward Vernon Utterson
                                      1495
E. W. Alexander Cooke   1662
E. W. Edmund Wingate
                  842, 1295, 1525, 2491
E. W. Edward Hawarden   2821
E. W. Edward Ward   1670
E. W. Edward Welchman, M.A.   1194
E. W. Edward West·   1768
E. W. Edward Wilson   2460
E. W. Edward Worsley
                  642, 1222, 2084, 2681
E. W. E. Warren   2438
E. W. E. Wood   2281
E. W. A. L. Susan Warner   2261
E. WERNER. Emile Buersten-
  binder   920, 1746, 2081, 2217, 2247,
                              2512, 2707
EXONIENSIS,   EUSEBIUS.
  Richard Polwhele   805
EXPLORABILIS. Eliza Haywood   1248
EX-PUSEYITE. Henry N. Oxen-
  ham   1897

F.

F. A. Francis Atterbury   2777
FABRICIA NUNNERY, Spinster.
  Peter Coxe 104, 2836, Errata, Vol. iv.
FÆNILIGNUM, THO.   Thomas
  Heywood   1898
FAG, FREDERICK.   James
  Johnson, M.D.   2098
FAITH, WORKLESS.   Rev. J.
  Berridge   954
FALCONER, EDMUND. Edmund
  O'Rourke   870, 1597, 1680
FALKLAND.   Francis Perceval
  Eliot   796
FALKLAND. John Robert Scott
                            1861, 2202
FANE, VIOLET. Mrs Singleton
                              602, 975
FANNY, AUNT. Fanny Barrows
              879, 1028, 1497, 1726, 1812
FANNY FERN. Sarah Parton
                  894, 1933, 2228, 2242
FANNY FORRESTER. Emily C.
  Chubbuck   1635
F. ANSTEY. F. Anstey Guthrie   2729
FARMER, A. W. Dr Sam Seabury
                              477, 965
FATHER FITZ-EUSTACE.   W.
  Fraser   824
FATHER   IGNATIUS.   Joseph
  Leycester Lyne 337, 1171, 1203, 1561
FAUSTINUS SCRIBLERUS   2073
F. B. Francis Bragge, A.B.   2823
F. B. OBSERVANT.   Richard
  Britton   1545
F. C. Francis Cradock   2797
F—— C——. Frederick Corfield   1567
F. C. W. F. C. Watley   1723
F. D. C. Frances D. Cartwright   1948
F. DE LUNATICO, K.F.M. G.P.R.
  James   440
F. D., Professor of Divinity. Francis
  Davenport   2187
F. E. Francis Eccles   379
F. E. Francis Ellington   379, 919
FELIX MINUTIUS. Arthur Helps 830
FELIX SUMMERLEY.   Henry
  Cole   1063 (2)
FELTHAM BURGHLEY. C. A.
  Ward   748, 1991, 2389, 2454
FERAGUS. C. H. Williams   2800
FERDINANDO FUNGUS. ——
  Williams   1721

FERN, FANNY. Sarah Parton 894, 1933, 2228, 2242
FERRY, GABRIEL. Louis de la Homière 516
F. F. Francis Fauquier 814
F. G. 2701
F. G. Francis Glanville 2547
F. G. Francis Grant, Lord Cullen 1522
F. G., B. of H. Francis Godwin, Bishop of Hereford 1538
F. G. L. Frederick George Lee 411, 1333
F. G. TRAFFORD. J. H. Riddell 1011, 1561, 1656, 1896, 2841
F. H. Francis Howgil 2009
F. H. —— Hutchinson 447
F. H., KNT. Sir Francis Hubert 602
FIDELIS. Dr Power, Bishop of Waterford 1448
FIDO, PASTOR. Allan Blayney 913
FIELDING, THOMAS. John Wade 2318
FILIUS TERRAE. Robert E. Garnham 1417
FILIUS TERRAE. Stephen Weston 2802
FITZ-ADAM, ADAM. Philip D. Stanhope, Earl of Chesterfield 2841
FITZ-ADAM, ISMAEL. John Macken 1072, 1333
FITZ-EUSTACE, FATHER. W. Fraser 824
FITZ-EUSTACE, RANDOLPH. W. Fraser 256
FITZ-HUGH, FRANCIS. Francis Alexander Mackay 543, 552
FITZ-OSBORNE, SIR THOMAS, Bart. William Melmoth, Jun. 1446
FITZ-VICTOR, JOHN. Percy Bysshe Shelley 1979
FIZLE B'NEY. Robert Hunter 90
F. K. Francis Kirkman 2714
F. K., SIR. Francis Kinaston 1341
FLAGELLUM. William Henry Ireland 68
FLEETWOOD, EVERARD. Samuel Burroughs 768
FLEMING, GEORGE. Julia Fletcher 1076, 1307, 1742
F. L. W. Francis Lodowyck, F.R.S. 443
FLY MAY. Wellington Somerset 499
F. M. Francis Meres 2823
F. M. Sir Frederick Madden 63
F. M. C. Frances Mary Cusack 1205
F. M. F. S. Felicia M. F. Skene 1569

F. M. P. Frances Mary Peard 1818
F. N. Nicholas French 1696
F. N. B. Francesco Nigri Bassanese 353
F. N. B. Franciscus Niger Bassentinus 353
F——N, C. C. Ferguson 1343
F. O. Frederick Oakeley, M.A. 1478
FONTENELLE, B. LE BOVIER DE. W. Gardiner 508
FORREST, GEORGE, M.A. Rev. J. G. Wood 1065
FORRESTER, FANNY. Emily C. Chubbuck 1635
FOSTER, FRANK. D. Pusely 57, 68, 222, 563, 1279 (2), 1686, 1759, 1834, 2614, 2810
FOULEWEATHER, ADAM. Thomas Nash 2829
FOULIS, OLIVER. David Lloyd 295
F. P. Henry More 683
F. P. Thomas Porter 2825
F. P. M. O. P. HIB. William Collins 1634
F. R. Francis Rous 1565, 2592
F. R. Richard Finch 2287
F. R. Robert Ferguson 2062
FRANCIS A SANCTA CLARA. Francis Davenport 862, 2187
FRANCISCO LOPEZ DE ABEDA. Andreas Perez 2462
FRANCISCUS PALÆOPOLITANUS. Henry More 683
FRANCIS FITZ-HUGH. Francis A. Mackay 543, 552
FRANCIS FULLWOOD. Richard Baxter 2247
FRANCIS OLDYS, A.M. George Chalmers 1484
FRANCK CARELESS. Richard Head 935
FRANK FOSTER. D. Pusely 57, 68, 222, 563, 1279 (2), 1686, 1759, 1834, 2614, 2810
FRANK SEAFIELD, M.A. Alexander H. Grant, M.A. 1495
FR. BR. Francesco Bracciolini 2618
FREDERICK FAG. James Johnson, M.D. 2098
FREDERICK SCHLEIRMACHER. C. Thirlwall, D.D. 537
FREEHOLDER, A. Alexander Carlyle, D.D. 2070
FREE LANCE. Alex. Richardson 874, 990

FREEMAN, Dr. J. Russell Endean 1963
FREEMAN, THEOPHILUS.
  William Matthews 999
FR. EUISTOR. Henry More 683
FRIEDRICH HALM. F. von
  Münch-Bellinghausen 1225, 2448
F——R——N. C. Ferguson 1343
F. S. Fabian Steadman 304
F. S. Francis Sabie 1848
F. S. Francis Seager 353, 2271
F. T. Francis Thynn 643
F. T. Francis Trollope 1667
F. T. F. Tanner 1929
F. T. Robert Fleming 1139
F. T. Thomas Fitzherbert 223
F. T. Thomas Francklin 1364
F. THOMAS. J. M. Forster,
  F.R.A.S. 786
FULLWOOD, FRANCIS. Richard
  Baxter 2247
FUME, JOSEPH. W. A. Chatto 1850
FUNGUS FERDINANDO. ——
  Williams 1721
F. W. Ferdinando Warner 2079
F. W. Francis Wrangham 917
F. W. G. F. W. Guidickins 117
F. W. H. F. W. Halfpenny 329, 2463
F—Y, J—N. John Fry 230
F. W., SIR KNT. Sir Francis
  Wortley 2522
F. YRUBSLIPS. Francis Slipsbury 182

G.

G. George Grenville, Lord Nugent 1340
G. L. C. Ghent 887
G. A. George Allan 430
G. A. George Alsop 1830
G. A. Grace Aguilar 1255
GABBLE GRIDIRON. Joseph
  Haslewood 1052
GABRIEL D'EMILLIANNE.
  Antoine Gavin 985, 1770, 2368
GABRIEL FERRY. Louis de la
  Homière 516
GABRIEL, JOHN. Thomas Dur-
  fey 818
GABRIEL SILVERTONGUE.
  James Montgomery 2808
GABRIEL TINTO. G. W. Anthony
  2821
GAFFER GRINDSTONE. Alex-
  ander Hill :964

GAMALIEL SMITH. Jeremy
  Bentham 1751
GAMBADO, GEOFFREY. H.
  Bunbury 10, 100
GANDER, SIR GREGORY, Knt.
  George Ellis 1958
GAOLG, EKAL. J. A. Lake Gloag
  1264
GARAGANTUA PANTAGRUELL.
  William Rufus Chetwood 2494
GAR., BER. Bernard Garter 2063, 2620
GARRETT, EDWARD. Isabella
  Fyvie 294, 307, 545, 1799, 1994
GAY, JOSEPH. Alexander Pope 455
GAY, JOSEPH. Captain John
  Durant de Breval 469, 1176, 1895
G. B. George Brewer 1561
G. B. George Burnett 2276
G. B. Gilbert Burnet, D.D.
  312, 2112, 2837
G. B. John Astley 184
G. B. Sir George Buck 564
G. C. G. Caw 1957
G. C. George Care 1459, 2174
G. C. George Carew 2346
G. C. George Carleton 190
G. C. George Chapman 1938, 2793
G. C. H. H. G. Curran 472
G. D. George Dodd 1156, 1908
G. D. G. Doughty 395
G. D. George Downame 2206
G. D. George Downham 2206
G. D. E. Gabriel d'Emillianne
  958, 1770
G. D. L. M. N. N. G. Delamothe
  967
G. E. Edm. Geyton 2716
GENTLEMAN, CAMBRIDGE.
  —— Rawson 1404
GENTLEMAN COMMONER OF
  OXFORD. Samuel Croxall, D.D. 876
G. E. OF C. G. Mackenzie, Earl
  of Cromarty 2532
GEOFFREY, BARBICAN.
  Richard Thomson 391
GEOFFREY CRAYON. Washing-
  ton Irving 66, 252, 2397, 2540
GEOFFREY GAMBADO. H.
  Bunbury 10, 100
GEOFFREY GREYDRAKE. T.
  E. Hingsall 94
GEOFFRY JARVIS. Elizabeth
  Hamilton 1583
GEOR. CHAP. George Chapman 2813

GEORGE CADWALLADER.
G. B. Doddington   2166
GEORGE CRINE, M.D. Sir John
Hill   1540
GEORGE DOULEY. William
Warford   275, 276
GEORGE ELIOT. Marian Evans
32, 562, 908, 1217, 1338, 1613, 1616,
2226, 2263, 2385, 2461
GEORGE FLEMING. Julia
Fletcher   1076, 1307, 1742
GEORGE FORREST, M.A. Rev.
J. G. Wood   1065
GEORGE HORNE, D.D. W. C.
Oulton   1796, 2457
GEORGE HOWARD. Lieut.
Francis C. Laird, R.N.   1313, 2825
GEORGE PURVES, LL.D.
Simon Gray   67, 1043
GEORGE QUIET. George Frede-
rick Pardon   1296
GEORGE ST. GEORGE. Joseph
Snowe   2260
GEORGE SAND. Armadine, L.
A. Dudevant,   443, 497, 521, 1431,
1560, 1616, 1664, 2386, 2614
GERSHOM. Major Gen. J. E.
Goodwyn   141
GERTRUDE. Jane C. Simpson
née Bell   1912
G. F. George Fox   112, 127, 179,
297, 335, 462 (2), 463 (3), 505, 575 (2),
681, 781, 783 (3), 857, 919, 940, 999 (2),
1034, 1054, 1079, 1086, 1087 (2), 1201,
1236 (2), 1248, 1315, 1489, 1879, 2009
(2), 2293, 2331, 2344 (2), 2345, 2446,
2447, 2571, 2586, 2597 (2), 2598 (3),
2601, 2661, 2666, 2679, 2682, 2773, 2791
(3), 2804, 2832
G. F. P. George Frederick Pardon   992
G. F. Giles Firmin   1499, 1996
G. G. Goddred Gylby   45
G. H.   309
G. H. Gavin Hamilton   1044
G. H. George Hall   854
G. H. George Hay, D.D.   2281
G. H. George Herbert   1836
G. H. George Hughes   2525
G. H. Guy Holland   1041
G. H. D. D. George Hakewell,
D.D.   132, 146, 447, 2334
GHENT W. H. William Hunt   885
G. H. M. George Henry Money   2341
G. H. N. G. H. Noehden.   921

G. I. George Iliff   394
G. I. William Mucklow   2475
GIBBONS, LEE. Thomas Roscoe,
Jun.   343, 1304, 1839
GIBBONS, LEE. William Bennett
    1839
GIFFORD. J. John Richards Green
    1918
GIFFORD, JOHN. John Richards
Green   1131, 1137, 1163, 1395, 1699,
1918, 2125
GIFT, THEO. Dora Havers   1535,
1559, 2007, 2773
GILBERT DALRYMPLE, D.D.
Gerard Legh   1356
GILDEROY, ROLAND. Charles
Rowley   1910
GILLESPIE, MAC-SHINIE.
Archibald Simson   101
GIORGIONE DE CASTEL
CHIUSO. Peter Bailey   2401
G. J. George Jay   2334
G. J. Giles Jacob   1518
G. K. George Keith   2330, 2682
G. L. G. Larkin   2841
G. L. George Lauder   300
G. L. George Lawrence   572
G. L. George Ludlam   1689
G. L. Gerard Langbaine   2199
GLENMORE. Donald Shaw   1097
GLEVA, MARY DE. Mary Roberts   14
G. L. M. Gilbert L. Meason   1317
G. M. George Meriton   1989
G. M. Gervase Markham   175, 1005,
1169, 1175, 2292, 2307, 2456 (2), 2779,
2850
G. M. Giles Morrington   1989
G. M. Gregory Martin   1519
G. M. Guy Miege   599, 1624
G. N. George Nugee, M.A.   1882
G. NAWORTH. George Wharton   1601
GNIMELF, REDNAXELA, A. M.
Alexander Fleming, A.M.   2505
GOOSEQUILL, BENJAMIN. J.
M. Adair, M.D.   91
GOOSEQUILL, TIMOTHY   2096, 2187
GORONVA, CAMLAN. Rowland
Williams   1332, 1825
GOTTINGENSIS, ALETHOPI-
LUS. G. W. Alberti   2444
GOVERNOR. John Inglis   2845
GOVGE, WILLIAM. Sir Henry
Finch   864
G. P. Gabriel Plattes   427

G. P.   George Peele   1814
G. P.   George Petyt   1456 (2)
G. P.   George Philips   1240
G. P.   Sir George Peckham   2675
G. P. T.   G. P. Towry   2578
G. R.   Gilbert Rorison   2584
G. R.   Gilbert Rule, D.D   2675
GRACE GREENWOOD.   Sarah Jane Clarke   942, 1069, 1143, 2845
GRACE RAMSAY.   Kathleen O'Meara   2255, 2572
GRACE WHARTON.   Katherine Thomson   2064, 2823
GRAHAM, ENNIS.   Elizabeth Molesworth   404, 547, 1520, 1751, 2549
GRAY, SIMON.   Sir Alexander Boswell   725
GREENDRAKE, GREGORY.   J. Coad   94
GREENWOOD, GRACE.   Sarah Jane Clarke   942, 1069, 1143, 2845
GREGORY, SIR GANDER, Knt.   George Ellis   1958
GREGORY, GREENDRAKE.   J. Coad   94
GREGORY GRIFFIN.   George Canning, etc.   1612
GREGORY, MISO SARUM.   Jonathan Swift, D.D.   1993
GRÉVILLE, HENRY.   Madame Durand   2797
GREY, HERACLITUS.   Charles Marshall   1303, 1934
GREYDRAKE, GEOFFREY.   T. E. Hingsall   94
GREYE, ARMAR.   Maria Greye   1301
GREYSON, R. E. H.   Henry Rogers   2319
G. R. G.   Rev. George R. Gleig   1485
GRIBALDUS SWAMMERDAM.   W. Mudford   1463
GRIDIRON, GABBLE, GENT.   Joseph Haslewood   1052
GRIFFIN, GREGORY.   George Canning, etc.   1612
GRIFFINHOOF, ANTHONY.   George Colman, Yr.   1555
GRILDRIG, SOLOMON.   Dr Rennell, etc.   1617
GRINDSTONE, GAFFER.   Alexander Hill   1964
G. R. P.   George R. Portal   2245
G. S.   George Sandys   1839, 1859 (2), 2245
G. S.   George Searle.   633
G. S.   George Sewell   1245
G. S.   George Stephens   974
G. S.   George Swinock   1465
G. T.   George Trosse   1870
GUALDI, ABBOT.   Gregorio Letti   1473
GUALTIER, BON.   Theodore Martin   245
GUALTIER, BON.   William E. Aytoun, D.C.L.   245
GUARD, THEODORE DE LA.   Rev N. Ward   2387
GUARDEN, THEODORE DE LA.   Nathaniel Ward   1600
GUATIMOZIN.   Dr Jebb   1056
GUINIAD CHARFY.   George Smeeton   930
GULIELMUS LYDE.   Gulielmus Joyner   2433
G. W.   Christopher Wyvill   351
G. W.   George Chapman   2405
G. W.   George Webbe   276
G. W.   George Whitehead   134, 635, 1510, 2014
G. W.   George Wither   987, 1196, 2186
G. W.   George Woodley   1670
G. W.   Gilbert Wakefield   2171
G. W.   Sir George Wheeler, D.D.   1807
G. W.   Vincent Alsop   1568
G. W. J.   G. W. Jordan   21, 1726
G. W. M.   George W. Marshall   329
G. W. M.   George Wilson Meadley   1583
G——Y, J——S   James Gray   1691
GYPSY.   Grace Courtland   1548

H.

H. A.   Hen. Arthur   2048
H. A.   Henry Ainsworth   180
HABBAKUKIUS DUNDERHEADIUS.   Thomas Jackson   2709
HABERDASHER, O. M.   A. Carlyle, D.D.   1925
HACKLE PALMER.   Robert Blakey   1100
HAD----TON, Right Hon. the Earl of, Thomas Baillie Hamilton, Earl of Haddington   1951
H. A. G.   Hervey Arthington   2014
H. A. L.   H. A. Leverson   1193
H. A. L.   Major H. A. Leverson   748, 941, 1193
HALL, REV. JAMES, A.M.   W. Thomson, LL.D.   2612, 2627

HALL, ROBT. Peter Heylin   1083
HALLIDAY, ANDREW. Andrew
   Halliday Duff   50, 2261 (2), 2348, 2519
HALM, FRIEDRICH. F. von
   Munch-Bellinghausen   1225, 2448
HALSTEAD, ROBERT. Henry,
   Earl of Peterborough   2512
HAMILTON, JOHN. John Hamil-
   ton Reynolds   993
HAMON L'ESTRANGE. Peter
   Heylin   1779
HAMPDEN. Thomas Lister, LL.D.
     1622
HAMST, OLPHAR. Ralph Thomas
     1065, 1553
H. A. PAGE. Alexander H. Japp
    1334, 1571, 1747, 1835, 2572 (2)
HARCOURT, B. J. J. Harcourt
   Bland   155
HARDCASTLE, DANIEL.
   Richard Page   31, 211, 1452
HARDCASTLE, EPHRAIM. W.
   H. Pyne   2445, 2688, 2818
HARGRAVE, JASPER. George
   Hardinge   355
HARLAND, MARION. Mary Vir-
   ginia Hawes   70, 1094, 1665, 1710
HARMER, ANTHONY. Henry
   Wharton   2465
HARRIET. Miss White   2727
HARRIET MARLOW, Right Hon.
   Lady. William Beckford   1642
HARRIET MYRTLE. Lydia F. F.
   Miller   200, 524, 566, 1495, 1539, 1799,
       2498, 2772, 2793
HARRISON, JOHAN. J. Bale,
   Bishop of Ossory   2847
HARRY BEAUMONT, Sir. Rev.
   Joseph Spence   542, 1659, 1865
HARRY COBHAM. Edward Long 136
HARRY HIEOVER. Charles
   Bindley   237, 1193, 1942, 1984, 2479 (3),
       2481, 2508, 2841
HARRY LORREQUER. Charles
   James Lever, M.D.   186, 366, 473
HARRY MORDAUNT, Col.
   George Ogle   1645
HARRY WHITNEY. P. Kennedy 1340
HARRY WHITNEY PHILO-
   MATH. P. Kennedy   1340 (2)
HARRY, UNCLE. John Habberton
     1082
HASOLLE, JAMES. Elias Ash-
   mole   900

HAWORTH, WILL. W. Dimsdale 2060
HAYWARD, THOMAS. W. Oldys 284
H. B. Henry Bewley   2574
H. B. Henry Blackwell   1007
H. B. Henry Blundell   28
H. B. Henry Bold   2821
H. B. Henry Burton   386, 1264, 2683
H. B. Henry Roberts   2679
H. B. Hugh Broughton   2556
H. BENNET, M.A. Morgan Wil-
   liams   2630
H. B. T. James Deacon Hume   1446
H. C. H. Cornwaleys   262, 522
H. C. Henry Care
     95, 564, 703, 1459, 2832
H. C. Henry Cheeke   944
H. C. Henry Chettle
     696, 944, 1301, 1911, 1973
H. C. Henry Cockeran   756
H. C. Henry Constable   625, 944, 2478
H. C. Hercules Collins   135
H—— C——. Hugh Carew   2527
H. C. William Henry Ireland
     930, 2249
H. C. DECANVER. C. H. Cavan-
   der   333
H. D. Hannah Doyle   919
H. D. Mrs Henry Davidson 1489, 2689
H. D. Henry Davies   1181, 2502, 2774
H. D. Henry Drummond, M.P.   595
H. D. Richard Hampden   539
H. D. Seth Ward   2767
H. D. Thomas Ken, D.D.   711
H. D., M.A. John Collinges, D.D. 2410
H. E. Edward Hawarden, D.D. 114, 365
H. E. Sir Henry Charles Englefield 605
KESTHΣ, A. William Smith   916
H. E. B. Sir Henry Edward Bunbury,
   Bart.   1959
HEINFETTER, HERMAN.
   Frederick Parker 203, 515, 691 (2), 773,
   844, 1203 (2), 1416, 1492 (2), 1493 (4),
   1766, 1942, 2190 (2), 2238, 2669, 2678,
       2679
HELIOSTROPOLIS. Daniel Defoe 435
H. E. M. Henry E. Manning, D.D.
     630, 1170
HEN. ARTH. Henry Arthur   2048
HENRIETTA. Henrietta Nether-
   cotte   2625
HENRY AUGUSTUS RAYMOND.
   Sarah Scott   1138
HENRY COXE. John Millard
     1006, 1909, 2625 (2)

HENRY F. R. SOAME, SIR. Sir H. E. Bunbury   1959

HENRY GRÉVILLE. Madame Durand   2797

HENRY HOLBEACH. W. B. Rands   2352

HENRY J. THURSTAN. F. T. Palgrave   1868

HENRY STALBRYDGE. John Bale   779

HENRY STONECASTLE. John Kelly   2712

HENRY THOMAS. Henry Ride   2789

H. E. O. Thomas George Fonnereau   626

H. E. P. Harriet E. Phillimore   2769

H. E. R. H. E. Reynolds   958

HERACLITUS GREY. Charles Marshall   1303, 1934

HERBERT AINSLIE, B.A. Edward Maitland   1913

HERETICUS PARTHENOPÆUS. William Gordon   28, 1972

HERMAN HEINFETTER. Frederick Pardon   203, 515, 691 (2), 773, 844, 1203 (2), 1416, 1492 (2), 1493 (4), 1766, 1942, 2190 (2), 2238, 2669, 2678, 2679

HERMANN KUNST. Walter C. Smith, D.D.   1816

HERMIT OF MARLOW. Percy Bysshe Shelley   2797

HERON, ROBERT. John Pinkerton   1441

HESBA STRETTON. Sarah Smith   416, 533, 565, 689, 875, 973, 1094, 1218, 1306, 1515, 1539, 1611, 1740, 1744, 1814, 1876, 2497, 2573, 2690, 2829, 2843

H. F. Henry Fell   1925

H. F. Henry Foley   762

H. F. B. Henry F. Bland   2457

H. F. C. Henry F. Chorley   707

H. G. Henry Grigg   1485

H. G. Rev. Harry Grey   272

H. G. C. H. G. Clarke   758, 763

H. H. Henry Hammond. D.D.   2087

H. H. Hugh Holland   722, 1655, 2123

H. H. Sir Henry Halford   1758

H. H. A. S. Hely H. A. Smith   708

H. H. B. Henry Burnell   2843

H. I. Anthony Hoskins, S.J.   275

H. I. Henry Jacob   2639

HIBERNICUS. De Witt Clinton   1448

HIB. F. P. M. O. P. William Collins   1634

H. I. B. N. Henry I. B. Nicholson   3

HIEROPHILUS. John MacHale   1432

HIEROPHILUS. John Toland   158

HIEOVER, HARRY. Charles Bindley   237, 1193, 1942, 1984, 2479 (3), 2481, 2508, 2841

HIGH CONSTABLE. William Lee   494

HILARIOUS BENEVOLUS. John Britton   1940

HILTON, DAVID. David Hilton Wheeler   279

HIPPONAX. Rev. Thomas Monro   2480

HISTORICUS. Greville Vernon Harcourt   1424

HISTRIONICUS, ANTI-SCRIBLERUS. John Roberts   117

H. K. Henry Keepe   1655

H. K. Henry Killigrew   2336

H. K. Herbert Kynaston   436

H. K. B. C. Henry King, Bishop of Chichester   2050

H. K. BROWNE. Mrs Hawkshaw   200

H. L. Henry Lok   722

H. L. Peter Heylin   1779

H. L. E. H. L. Empaytaz   2433

H. L. F. Henrietta Louisa Farrer   179

H. L. HOWARD. Charles J. Wells   1273

H. L. L. Jane Borthwick   2499, 2573

H. M. H. Marsh   1729

H. M. Humphrey Mackworth   702

H. M. W. H. Logan   1349

H. M'K. Henry M'Kenzie   1331

H. M., M.A. Henry More, M.A.   2053

H. M. G. H. M. Gunn   1144

H. MYRTLE. Lydia F. Miller   1539

H. N. Henry Nicholas   443, 837, 2033, 2047, 2055

H. N. C. H. N. Coleridge   2465

H. N. D. Horatio N. Dudding   1870

H. N. H. Henry Noel Humphreys   421

H. N. O. J. OXON. Henry Hickman   1942

HOBART PASHA. Augustus Charles Hobart, R. N.   1710

H. O. C. Henry Octavius Coxe   943

HODG TURBERVILL. Edmund Gayton   2784

HOGG CERVANTES, F.S.M. Eaton Stannard Barrett   2217

HOGG, CERVANTES, F.S.M. T. P. Lathy   2217

HOGG, NATHAN. Henry Baird   1431

HOGO-HUNT, J. W. John William Houghton   1020, 1319

HOLBEACH, HENRY. W. B.
  Rands   2352
HOLDING, EPHRAIM. George
  Mogridge   776
HOLME, DARYL. David Herbert
                              1515, 2849
HOLME LEE. Harriet Parr 56, 101,
  214, 219, 224, 503, 525, 939, 1014, 1075,
  1084, 1218, 1297, 1298, 1339, 1560, 1675,
  1677, 1970, (2), 2500, 2531, 2572, 2573,
    2672, 2685, 2730, 2792, 2828, 2843
HOMELY, JOSIAS. John Brad-
  ford   2543
HOMO NOVUS. W. J. Courthope
                                     2553
HONESTUS. Edward Norton   211
HONEYCOMB, WILLIAM.
  Richard Gardner   1146
HONORIA, N. Marguerite A.
  Power   1431
HONORIA SCOTT. Mrs Frazer 2819
HONOURABLE MR——. William
  Combe   198
HOOKANIT, BEE. S. R. Wigram 936
HOPE, ASCOTT R. Robert Hope
  Moncrieff 244, 245, 1091, 1557, 1598,
  1686, 1847, 1879, 2230, 2342, 2472,
    2496 (3), 2497 (2), 2709, 2848
HOPE, CRI IN. John Price   418
HOPE, WRAYTHE. Edith Haw-
  trey   2538
HORACE HORNEM. Lord Byron
                                     2787
HORATIUS. Horace Twiss   2253
HORNE, GEORGE, D.D. W. C.
  Oulton   1796, 2457
HORNEM, HORACE. Lord Byron
                                     2787
HOSEA BIGLOW. James Russell
  Lowell   1567
HOWARD, GEORGE. Lieut.
  Francis C. Laird, R.N.   1313, 2825
HOWARD, H. L. Charles J. Wells
                                     1273
HOWLET, I. Robert Parsons   262
H. P. Henry Parker 71, 1003, 1541,
                  2069, 2274, 2346, 2673
H. P. Henry Parrot 550, 1318, 1662,
                                     1671
H. P. Henry Peacham 183, 712, 1558,
                               1605, 1855
H. P. Hugh Peters   1031
H. P. Hugh Platt   2519
H. P. W. H. P. Wyndham   1909

H. R. Henry Reeve   1043
H. R. Hugh Ross   793
H****, RIGHT HONBL. LADY.
  Lady Hawke   1287
H. ST A. K. H. St. A. Kitching   1658
H. S. Henry Savage, D.D.   616, 2094
H. S. Henry Scobell   1981
H. S. Henry Smith   852
H. S. Henry Stubbe   443, 680 (2)
H. S. N. B. Halhed, R. B. Sheri-
  dan   1518
H.S.H. THE M. OF A. Margravine
  of Anspach   2414
H-----S L-----SHE. Her-
  cules Langrishe   2511
H. S., SIR. Henry Shears   1145
H. T. Henry Timberlake   2127
H. T. Henry Turbervill   6
H. T. Henry Turberville   1544
H. TRUSTA. E. S. Phelps   2519
HUDIBRASTON, ANTI-. William
  Rhinde   2079
HUGHSON DAVID, LL.D. Ed-
  ward Pugh   787, 1506, 2785
HUMPHERY, OLD. George Mog-
  ridge   525, 1342, 1810, 1811, 2279,
                        2539 (2), 2574
HUMPHREY OLDCASTLE.
  Nicholas Amhurst   2149
HUMPHREY RAVELIN. G.
  Procter   1524
HUNT, HOGO-, J. W. J. W.
  Houghton   1319
HVNTLEY, W. William Prynne 256
H. W. Horace Walpole   1534
H. W. John Howe   2100

                I.

IAMES ANNE-SON, M. A. James
  Maxwell   310
IATER. John Davis, M.D.   792
IATPOΣ. G. D. Yeats, M.D.   236
I. B. J. Browne   1599
I. B. John Barclay   1595
I. B. John Barlow   1095
I. B. John Beale   1088
I. B. John Brinsley   300
I——B——, M.D. William Temple 2743
I. C. James Cunningham   821
I. C. J. Can   777
I. C. John Carpenter   1928
I. C. John Colleton   2558
I. C. Joseph Caryl   1893

I. C. Rev. James Clark 2821
I. C. M. D. James Clark 389
ICONOCLAST. Charles Bradlaugh 1724 (3), 2203
ICONOCLAST. J. C. Maclennan 2276
I. D. John Dauney 1139
I. D. John Davidson 557
I. D. John Davies 777, 2277, 2278
I. D. John Davors 2314
I. D. John Dennys 2314
I. D. John Disney, D.D. 2371
I. D. and C. M. John Davies and Christopher Marlowe 777
I. D. Sir John Dodderidge 1330 (3)
I. D. PHIL-IREN-ALETHIUS. John Doughtie 2724
I. D., SIR, KNIGHT. Sir John Davies 1727
IDSTONE. Rev. T. Pearce 696
I. E. John Evelyn 2704
I. E. Matthew Kellison 1736, 2209
I. F. John Fisher 130
I. F. John Fletcher 375
I. G. John Green 2122
I. G., D.D. John Gauden, D.D. 1894
IGNATIUS, FATHER. Joseph Leycester Lyne 337, 1171, 1203, 1561
I. H. James Harrington 2509
I. H. James Hog 2753
I. H. James Howell 60
I. H. John Hall 1954
I. H. John Hart 1831
I. H. John Heath 1182
I. H. John Hewitt 608
I. H. Sir J. Haywarde, D.C.L. 2640
I H. Æ. John Hynd 1622
I. HOWLET. Robert Parsons 262
I. H., MR. of ARTS. Joseph Henshaw 1564
I H. WH. John White 760
I. J. H. Rev. John James Holroyd 1014
I. K. John Kepers 527
I. L. John Lane 734
I. L. John Lilburne 1928
I. L. B. J. L. Bird 1754
ILIAD DOGGREL, SIR. Sir Thomas Burnet 1173
I. M. Jervis Markham 1077
I. M. John Marston 141, 1132
I. M. John Mayer 1875
I. M. John Milton 730
I. M. John Monipenny 5
INCOGNITUS RICHARDUS. Richard Brash 42

INCONOCLAST. Charles Bradlaugh 1254
INDICUS. Major Evans Bell 2075
INDICUS MEDICUS. Dr Skinner 2430
INDIGNATIO. Henry Taylor 475
INDOPHILUS. Sir C. E. Trevelyan, K.C.B. 516, 1432
INGENUUS. Thady Fitzpatrick 772
INGOLDSBY. James Hildyard, B.D. 2175
INGOLDSBY, THOMAS. R. H. Barham 1224, 1259
INSULARUS, THEOPHILUS. —— M'Leod 2646
INVERNESSICUS. L. Mackintosh 1773
IOHN BRERELY. James Anderton 2044
IOTA. John Harland, F.S.A. 2502
I. P. John Penkethman 1819
I. P. John Pym 511
I. R. John Floyd 1839, 2057
I. R. J. Rogers 1674
IRENÆUS JUNIOR. Samuel Snowden 602
IRENÆUS KRANTZOVIUS. B. Stillingfleet 2443
IRENÆUS PHILADELPHUS. Lewis du Moulin 2780
IRONSIDE NESTOR. Rev. Dr. Samuel Croscall 104
I. R. Robert Jenison, S.J. 1846
I. S. Henry Fletcher 1885
I. S. John Statham 335
ISA. Isabella Craig 1947
I S A' $\frac{10}{}$ 2, θ 4 $\frac{1000}{}$. Arise Evans 1303
ISAAC BICKERSTAFF. Jonathan Swift, D.D. 233, 1993, 2744
ISAAC BICKERSTAFF. Sir Richard Steele 1028, 1254, 1524, 1993
ISAAC CREWDSON. Benjamin Dockray 1684
ISAAC RABBOTEM. Philip de Marnix 220
ISAAC TOMKINS. Lord Brougham 2583, 2797
ISMAEL FITZADAM. John Macken 1072, 1333
ISOCRATES. Rev. H. M'Neile 624
I. T. John Taylor 2443
I. T. S. John Talwyn Shewell 2653
I. U. James Usher 416
I. V. C. John Vincent Cane 2599

I. W.   John Wells   2272
I. W.   John Wingate   2272
I. W. L.   —— Warner   43

J.

J. A.   J. Allen   2850
J. A.   James Arderne, D.D.   635
J. A.   James Armour   1995
J. A.   John Aikin, M.D.   2830
J. A.   John Allen   147
J. A.   John Allington   261
JACIA.   John Crane   2140
JACOB ABBOTT.   T. S. Henderson   288
JACOB CURATE.   Robert Calder   2273
JACOB OMNIUM.   Matthew J. Higgins   1253, 1445, 1448, 1485, 2083, 2568, 2588
JACQUETTA AGNETA MARIANA JENKS.   William Beckford   206
J. A. D ***   Jacques A. Dulaure   1960
J. A. M.   J. A. Merryweather   1089
J. A. M.   John A. Murray   1399
JAMBON, JEAN.   J. H. A. Macdonald   1835
J. A., M.D.   John Arbuthnot, M.D.   845
J. A., M.D., F.R.S.   Dr John Trusler   1907
JAMES ANDREW.   Andrew Mackay   190
JAMES B. MANSON.   James Murray   228
JAMES BROWN.   Joseph Robertson   1717
JAMES HALL, REV. A.M.   Rev. W. Thomson, L.L.D.   2612, 2627
JAMES HAMLEY TREGENNA.   R. B. Paul, M.A.   204
JAMES HASOLLE.   Elias Ashmole   900
JAMES WILLIAM WHITECROSS.   Michael Prus de Wiszniewski   2400
JAMES WILSON.   Andrew Park   2385
JANE ANN.   Ann Jane Morgan   65, 1271, 2848
JANUARY SEARLE.   George Philips   357, 524, 1335, 1470, 1580, 1591
JANUARY SERLE.   George Philips   357
JANUS.   Dr Döllinger   1971
JANUS.   Dr Johann Friedrich   1971

JARVIS, GEOFFRY.   Elizabeth Hamilton   1583
J. A. S.   James Alexander Smith   192, 1020
JA. S.   Ja. Smith   1681
J. A. S.   James Smith   2508
JASPER HARGRAVE.   George Hardinge   355
JASPER SMALLSHOT.   Major Ware   2481
JASPER WILSON.   James Currie, M.D.   1344
J. B.   740
J. B.   James Baine   323
J B.   James Beezley   1378
J. B.   James Birdwood   1078
J. B.   James Budd   635
J. B.   James Burgess   1503
J. B.   J. Baxter   2603
J. B.   John Bate   1690
J. B.   John Barrett   1031
J. B.   John Belson   2617
J. B.   John Berisford   173
J. B.   John Blanch   1177
J. B.   John Bridal or Brydall   448
J. B.   John Brown   1822
J. B.   John Brown, M.D.   2823
J. B.   John Bryan, D.D.   1073
J. B.   John Budge   1570
J. B.   John Bulteel   225, 2126
J. B.   John Bunyan   1078
J. B.   Jonathan Barrett   1772, 2090
J. B.   Jonathan Blackwell   1079
J. B.   Joseph Boyse   1806
J. B. N.   John Bowyer Nichols   1467
J. B. SELKIRK.   James Brown   1944
J. B. U.   Sir James B. Urmston   1868
J. BYEFIELD.   John Friend, M.D.   1399
J. C.   James Clark   1292
J. C.   James Clerk   2335
J. C.   James Cobb   1519
J. C.   James Corker   2168
J. C.   James Craig   2477
J. C.   James Hog   2134
J. C.   J. Carrick   1480
J. C.   J. Colbatch   1580
J. C.   J. Cross, D.D.   497
J. C.   Jeremy Collier   120
J. C.   Jodocus Crull, M.D.   140, 602, 1580
J. C.   John Calef   2383
J. C.   John Campbell, LL.D.   322
J. C., M.D.   J. Castro, M.D.   676

J. C.   John Cennick   2246
J. C.   John Cheney   474, 981
J. C.   John Clayton   2607
J. C.   John Cleaveland   358, 1944, 2242
J. C.   John Cleveland   358
J. C.   J. Cockayne   753
J. C.   John Cockburn, D.D.   770
J. C.   John Collard   787
J. C.   John Collens   2833
J. C.   John Collings, D.D.   568, 597, 853, 2798
J. C.   John Collins   2610
J. C.   John Collop, M.D.   1421
J. C.   John Constantine   1240
J. C.   John Cook, M.D.   1732
J. C.   John Corbet   1240, 1961, 2306
J. C.   John Corey   550
J. C.   John Cotgrave   2824
J. C.   John Crackanthorp   1952
J. C.   John Crook   596, 2688
J. C.   John Crown   90
J. C.   John Cruso   328
J. C.   John Currie   2762
J. C.   Joseph Cundall   2453, 2629
J. C.   Rev. John Campbell   2281
J. C.   Sir James Caldwell   571
J. C.   Sir J. Child   269
J. C.   Sir John Cheke   1730
J. CASSANDER.   John Bruckner   541
J. C. B.   John Coxe Boyce   1957
J. C. C.   194
J. C., D.D.   John Collinges, D.D.   1854
J. C., D.D.   J. Cross, D.D.   151
J. C. E.   J. C. Erck   1251
J. C. G.   Julia C. Grimani   2246
J. C. M.   J. C. Mellish   1554
J. C., M.A.   Josiah Chorley   269
J. C., M.D.   John Collop, M.D.   1564
J. COPYWELL.   William Woty   2381
J. C., RECTOR OF W. N.   Jonathan Chapham, of Wrampling-ham, Norfolk   1765
J. C. SCOTUS.   James Cunningham   1621
J. D.   James Dymock   1050
J. D.   J. Dancer   60, 408
J. D.   J. Davies   777, 843
J. D.   J. D. B. de Bow   1963
J. D.   John Dauncy   843
J. D.   John Davenport   2025
J. D. C.   John David Chambers   2052
J. D.   John Davidson   885
J. D.   John Davidson, W.S.   2146
J. D.   John Davies   68, 89, 408, 1132, 1962, 2049

J. D.   John Disney, D.D.   2377
J. D.   John Disturnell   719
J. D.   John Dix   1881
J. D.   John Donne, D.D.   1947
J. D.   John Dove   2154
J. D.   John Drope, M.A.   1195
J. D.   John Dryden   736
J. D.   John Dunton   749
J. D.   John Durie   312
J. D.   John Dury   312, 480
J. D. B.   John Durant de Breval   182
J. D. C.   John David Chambers   444
J. D—N.   John Dean   1007
J. D., SIR.   Sir John Davis, Kt.   2087
J. D., S.J.   John Dormer, S.J.   1896, 2333, 2336, 2813
J. E.   J. Eliot   1505
J. E.   John Eachard   1046, 1673
J. E.   John Eliot   1221, 1952
J. E.   John Elsum   777
J. E.   John Evelyn   367, 2485
JEAN JAMBON.   J. H. A. Macdonald   1835
JEDEDIAH CLEISHBOTHAM.   Sir Walter Scott   2541 (4)
JEDEDIAH PUZZLEPATE.   John Douglas Giles   2709
J. ELAGNITIN.   J. Nightingale   1636
JENKS, JACQUETTA., A.M.   William Beckford   206
JEREMIAH RINGLETUB.   John Styles, D.D.   1815
JEREMY SAVONAROLA, DON.   Francis S. Mahony   874
J. E. S.   James Carnegie, Earl of Southesk   1088
J. E., S.R.S.   John Evelyn   30
JEWEL, JOHN, Lord Bishop of Saresbury.   Degory Whear   155
J. F.   J. Fairfax   568
J. F.   J. Fenton   1304
J. F.   John Dobson   688
J. F.   John Falconer   2238
J. F.   John Fleming   998
J. F.   John Fountaine   2206
J. F.   John Fransham   841
J. F.   John Frith   1687
J. F.   John Fry   1338
J. F.   John W. Fletcher   2293
J. F.   Joseph Fletcher   1125
J. F. SUNAVILL.   J. F. Sullivan   1020, 1319
J. G.   James Glassford   975, 1623
J. G.   James Grant   1230

<table>
<tr><td>J. G.</td><td>John Gay</td><td>2005</td></tr>
<tr><td>J. G.</td><td>John Goodwin</td><td>293</td></tr>
<tr><td>J. G.</td><td>John Gough</td><td>2500</td></tr>
<tr><td>J. G.</td><td>Joseph Glanvil</td><td>242, 2434</td></tr>
<tr><td>J. G. A. F.</td><td>J. G. A. Forster</td><td>393</td></tr>
<tr><td>J. G. H. B.</td><td>John George Hamilton Bourne</td><td>857</td></tr>
<tr><td>J. GIFFORD.</td><td>John Richards Green</td><td>1918</td></tr>
<tr><td>J. H.</td><td>Denis Florence M'Carthy</td><td>1295</td></tr>
<tr><td>J. H.</td><td>James Handley</td><td>432</td></tr>
<tr><td>J. H.</td><td>James Harris</td><td>2591</td></tr>
<tr><td>J. H.</td><td>James Hely</td><td>1648</td></tr>
<tr><td>J. H.</td><td>James Hog</td><td>862, 2434</td></tr>
<tr><td>J. H.</td><td>James Horsburgh</td><td>1015</td></tr>
<tr><td>J. H.</td><td>James Howell</td><td>703</td></tr>
<tr><td>J. H.</td><td>J. Harrington</td><td>1051</td></tr>
<tr><td>J. H.</td><td>J. Harrison</td><td>243</td></tr>
<tr><td>J. H.</td><td>J. Hewlett</td><td>605</td></tr>
<tr><td>J. H.</td><td>J. Hutchinson</td><td>2636</td></tr>
<tr><td>J. H.</td><td>John Hall</td><td>743, 1055, 1188</td></tr>
<tr><td>J. H.</td><td>John Hallet</td><td>1483</td></tr>
<tr><td>J. H.</td><td>John Harris, M.A.</td><td>685</td></tr>
<tr><td>J. H.</td><td>John Hart</td><td>1080</td></tr>
<tr><td>J. H.</td><td>John Hayden</td><td>1362</td></tr>
<tr><td>J. H.</td><td>John Hayward</td><td>1024</td></tr>
<tr><td>J. H.</td><td>John Hoddesdon</td><td>2572</td></tr>
<tr><td>J. H.</td><td>John Harmar</td><td>2339</td></tr>
<tr><td>J. H.</td><td>John Horne</td><td>686</td></tr>
<tr><td>J. H.</td><td>John Howell</td><td>2126</td></tr>
<tr><td>J. H.</td><td>John Hughes, M.A.</td><td>1332</td></tr>
<tr><td>J. H.</td><td>John Humfrey</td><td>1452, 1767</td></tr>
<tr><td>J. H.</td><td>John Humphrey</td><td>204, 1381, 1767, 2510</td></tr>
<tr><td>J. H.</td><td>John Hutchinson</td><td>1019, 1665, 1711, 1769, 2130, 2718</td></tr>
<tr><td>J. H.</td><td>Sir J. Harrington</td><td>63</td></tr>
<tr><td>J. H.</td><td>Sir John Hill, M.D.</td><td>1430</td></tr>
<tr><td>J. H.</td><td>Joseph Highmore</td><td>826</td></tr>
<tr><td>J. H.</td><td>Joshua Hoyle, D.D.</td><td>1262</td></tr>
<tr><td>J. HARCOURT B.</td><td>J. Harcourt Bland</td><td>155</td></tr>
<tr><td>J. H., B.D.</td><td>John Hull</td><td>2714</td></tr>
<tr><td>J—— H——</td><td>C. A—D. S. J. Howardine</td><td>572, 2083</td></tr>
<tr><td>J.... H....</td><td>C. A. D. S. J. Hornihold</td><td>1055, 2083</td></tr>
<tr><td>J. H. CRAIG.</td><td>James Hogg</td><td>1193</td></tr>
<tr><td>J. H. D.</td><td>Rev. J. H. Davies</td><td>1313</td></tr>
<tr><td>J. H., D.D.</td><td>Joseph Hall, D.D., Bishop of Norwich</td><td>255, 2318</td></tr>
<tr><td>J. H. G.</td><td>Joseph H. Gibbs</td><td>2059</td></tr>
<tr><td>J. H. G.</td><td>Rev. J. Hampden Gurney</td><td>2050</td></tr>
<tr><td>J. H.</td><td>John Hoddesdon</td><td>1159</td></tr>
<tr><td>J. H., M.A.</td><td>John Howe, M.A.</td><td>168</td></tr>
<tr><td>J. H. N.</td><td>John Henry Newam</td><td>1344</td></tr>
<tr><td>J. H. S.</td><td>J. H. Shorthouse</td><td>1270</td></tr>
<tr><td>J. H. W.</td><td>John H. Wynne</td><td>2539</td></tr>
<tr><td>J. I.</td><td>Jacob Ilive</td><td>2094</td></tr>
<tr><td>J. I.</td><td>James Ingram</td><td>1597</td></tr>
<tr><td>J. I.</td><td>James Ingram, D.D.</td><td>397</td></tr>
<tr><td>J. J.</td><td>J. Johnson</td><td>73</td></tr>
<tr><td>J. J.</td><td>John Johnson</td><td>2245</td></tr>
<tr><td>J. J. S.</td><td>J. J. Stockdale</td><td>2398</td></tr>
<tr><td>J. K.</td><td>John Keble</td><td>615</td></tr>
<tr><td>J. K.</td><td>John Kersey</td><td>1720</td></tr>
<tr><td>J. K., F.R.S., and S.A.Sc.</td><td>James Keir</td><td>928</td></tr>
<tr><td>J. K. L.</td><td>James Warren Doyle, Bishop of Kildare and Leighlin</td><td>578, 1356, 1448 (2), 1449 (2), 2169, 2763</td></tr>
<tr><td>J. K——T, SIR.</td><td>Sir John Knight</td><td>2470</td></tr>
<tr><td>J. L.</td><td>J. Lake</td><td>416</td></tr>
<tr><td>J. L.</td><td>John Gother</td><td>1852</td></tr>
<tr><td>J. L.</td><td>John Lane</td><td>61</td></tr>
<tr><td>J. L.</td><td>John Lemprière, D.D.</td><td>2743</td></tr>
<tr><td>J. L.</td><td>John Longmuir</td><td>2502</td></tr>
<tr><td>J. L.</td><td>John Love, Jun.</td><td>1282</td></tr>
<tr><td>J. L.</td><td>Rev. James Lukin</td><td>1323</td></tr>
<tr><td>J. L. D. L., LL.D.</td><td>John Louis de Lohne</td><td>1857</td></tr>
<tr><td>J. L. J.</td><td>Rev. J. L. Jackson, M.A.</td><td>389</td></tr>
<tr><td>J. L., S. D.</td><td>J. Lake, S. Drake</td><td>416, 2840</td></tr>
<tr><td>J. L. W.</td><td>Jean L. Watson</td><td>294, 521</td></tr>
<tr><td>J. M'G.</td><td>John M'Gilchrist, M.D.</td><td>367</td></tr>
<tr><td>J. M'N.</td><td>J. M'Naughton</td><td>2109</td></tr>
<tr><td>J. M'S.</td><td>Joseph Macsweeney, M.D.</td><td>795</td></tr>
<tr><td>J. M.</td><td>James Maxwell, M.A.</td><td>1323</td></tr>
<tr><td>J—— M——.</td><td>James Montgomery</td><td>2020</td></tr>
<tr><td>J. M.</td><td>James Mumford</td><td>2165</td></tr>
<tr><td>J. M.</td><td>James Murray</td><td>2628</td></tr>
<tr><td>J. M.</td><td>Jervis Markham</td><td>2548</td></tr>
<tr><td>J. M.</td><td>J. Masson</td><td>1626 (2), 1627 (2)</td></tr>
<tr><td>J. M.</td><td>John Major</td><td>2080</td></tr>
<tr><td>J. M.</td><td>John Marsh, C.L.</td><td>172</td></tr>
<tr><td>J. M.</td><td>John Melton</td><td>2396</td></tr>
<tr><td>J. M.</td><td>John Milton</td><td>11, 1738, 2081, 2396, 2521, 2553, 2675</td></tr>
<tr><td>J. M.</td><td>John Muir</td><td>1220, 1753</td></tr>
<tr><td>J. M.</td><td>Principal James M'Cosh</td><td>2653</td></tr>
<tr><td>J. M.</td><td>Josiah Martin</td><td>1046</td></tr>
<tr><td>J. M.</td><td>Joseph Massie</td><td>1789</td></tr>
<tr><td>J. M.</td><td>Joseph Mitchell</td><td>2388</td></tr>
<tr><td>J. M. D.</td><td>John M. Davenport, F.S.A.</td><td>1591</td></tr>
<tr><td>J. M., D.D.</td><td>Jasper Maine, D.D.</td><td>630</td></tr>
<tr><td>J. M., M.A.</td><td>John Mason, M.A.</td><td>1613</td></tr>
</table>

J. M., Sir.   Sir J. Mennis   1681
J. N.   James Nayler   128, 700
J. N.   John Nalson   1306
J. N.   John Nichols   235, 2417
J. N.   John Nichols, F.A.S.E.   236
J. N.   John Norden   1622
J. N.   J. Nott, D.D.   2317
J—N C——Y.   John Courteney   2137
J. N. D.   John Nelson Darby
   82, 1754, 1755 (2), 1985
J**N D****N, D.D.   John
   Duncan, D.D.   1934
J. N., D.D.   Joseph Naylor, D.D.   1472
J——N F——Y.   John Fry   230
JN. M——D.   Hans Wood   2191
J——N, M. J.   Mary J. Jourdan   1617
JNO. CHAS. O'REID.   Josiah Con-
   der   2204
J. O.   James Owen   1935, 2686
J. O.   John Oldmixon   1468, 1673
J. O.   J. Olde   131, 471
JOBBRY, ARCHIBALD.   John Galt
   1568
JOB CRITHANNAH.   Jonathan
   Birch   922
JOCELYN PEN CLER.   Pierce
   Connelly, M.A.   1971, 2023
JOEL COLLIER.   J. L. Bicknell   1683
JOH. DE LA SALLE.   John Hall   1856
JOHAN HARRISON.   John Bale,
   Bishop of Ossory   2847
JOHANN ABRICHT, A.M.   Jona-
   than Birch   683
JOHANNES CATHOLICUS.   John
   Rutty   815
JOHN ANDREWS ARNETT.
   John Hannett   230, 1230
JOHN A. WITTITTERLEY.   Eliza-
   beth T. Carne   2589
JOHN BEAUFORT, L.L.D. ——
   Thelwall   564
JOHN BRERELY.   James Anderton
   1526, 1530, 2044, 2249
JOHN BUNYAN, Jr.   Rev. William
   Arnot   706
JOHN DANGERFIELD.   Oswald
   John Frederick Crawfurd, H.B.M.
   2627
JOHN EDGAR, Sir.   Sir Richard
   Steele   2558
JOHN FITZVICTOR.   Percy
   Bysshe Shelley   1979
JOHN GABRIEL.   Thomas Durfey
   818

JOHN GIFFORD.   John Richards
   Green   1131, 1137, 1163, 1395, 1699,
   1918, 2125
JOHN HAMILTON.   John Hamil-
   ton Reynolds   993
JOHN JEWEL.   Lord Bishop of
   Saresbury, Degory Whear   155
JOHN KNOKES.   John Frith   45
JOHN LATOUCHE.   Oswald John
   Frederick Crawfurd, H.B.M.   2626
JOHNNY.   Frank Chancellor   2812
JOHN OF MANCHESTER.   John
   Bosworth   2249
JOHN PHOENIX, M.A.   Captain
   Derby   1905
JOHN SCOTT RIPON.   John Scott
   Byerley   244
JOHN SEARCH.   Rev. Thomas
   Binney   484, 1047, 2129
JOHN SMITH.   John D. Lewis   2402
JOHN SMITH.   John Sergeant   1688
JOHNSON ABRAHAM.   Sir John
   Hill, M.D.   1523
JOHN TROTT.   Henry St John,
   Lord Bolingbroke   1377
JONATHAN DAWPLUCKER.
   John Barclay, M.D.   2144
JONATHAN DEAN.   Jonathan
   Swift, D.D.   568
JONATHAN OLD.   David Alfred
   Doudney, D.D.   2683 (2)
JON. B.   Benjamin Johnson   207
JON BEE.   John Badcock
   629, 1504, 2406
JONES, T. PERCY.   William E.
   Aytoun   925
JOSE MACPACKE.   James Pea-
   cock   1808
JOSEPH FUME.   W. A. Chatto   1850
JOSEPH GAY.   Alexander Pope   455
JOSEPH GAY.   Captain John D.
   Breval   469, 1176, 1895
JOSEPH SKILLETT.   Lord John
   Russell   824
JOSEPHUS.   Rev. J. Wolfe   624
JOSEPHUS TELA.   Jos. Webb   1902
JOSHUA ABDIELS.   W. Brooks   3
JOSHUA BOWCHIER, M.A.
   George Trosse   289
JOSIAS HORNELY.   John Brad-
   ford   2543
J. P.   1999
J. P.   John Parrinchieffe   867
J. P.   John Pennyman 9, 437, 2061, 2062

lxi J. P. — J. V. lxii

J. P.	John Perrinchiefe	867
J. P.	John Phillips	756, 2549
J. P. C.	John Payne Collier	620
J. PRIOR BUTLER.	Thomas H. Ward	253
J. Q.	John Quicke	1082, 2555
J. R.	Dr J. Rumsey	2418
J. R.	James Relly	786
J. R.	Job Roys	2476
J. R.	John Ray, M.A.	424
J. R.	John Rhodes	129, 2480
J—— R——.	John Ricketts	1951
J. R.	John Riddell	2255
J. R.	Joseph Ritson	2074
J. R.	Joseph Robertson, LL.D.	2372
J. R.	Joseph Rutter	2350
J. R.	Patrick Delaney	1789
J. R. C.	John Rose Cormack, M.D.	1756
J. R. D.	John Dix	1065
J. R., D.D.	John Ross, D.D.	260
J. R. F.	J. R. Finlay	2726
J. R. H.	James R. Hakewill	194
J. R., M.A.	John Russell, M.A.	2335
J. R. M. L.	James Ramsay	1665
J. R. W.	John Ryle Wood, M.A.	2436
J. R, W. B.	James Rice, Walter Besant	315, 2571
J. S.	Ignatius Brown	2708
J. S.	James Shirley	548
J. S.	John Sage	2018
J. S.	John Sergeant	115, 664, 1361, 1609, 2084, 2526, 2567
J. S.	John Sheppard	2574
J. S.	John Shirley, M.D.	2362
J. S.	John Shurley, M.A.	723
J. S.	John Small	952
J. S.	John Smith	693, 1179
J. S.	John Sowter	2795
J. S.	John Speed	996
J. S.	John Stillingfleet	2414
J. S.	John Stubbs	940, 2666
J. S.	John Studley	1844
J. S.	John Sympson	57
J—— S——.	Joseph Spence	977
J. S.	Joseph Sutton	1486
J. S.	Joseph Sykes, M.A.	611, 1335, 1795
J. S.	J. Sadler	1555
J. S.	J. Singleton	703
J. S.	J. Small	154, 2359
J. S.	J. Stoddart	921
J. S.	Major John Scott	1412, 1452
J. S., A. C.	John Sleech, Archdeacon of Cornwall	1674
J. S. D. S. P.	Jonathan Swift, D.D.	217
J——S G——Y.	James Gray	1691
J. S., M.A.	John Sadler	933
J. S., M.A.	John Slade	2335
J. SMITH.	Charles Baring	1448
J. T.	Jeremy Taylor, D.D.	654
J. T.	John Talbot	1309
J. T.	John Taylor	374, 1759, 2538
J. T.	Jonn Thaddaeus	2100
J. T.	John Toland	79
J. T.	J. Torbuck	429
J. T.	John Toy, M.A.	2831
J. T.	John Troughton	1369
J. T.	Josiah Tucker	1211
J. T. B.	John Trotter Brockett	1536, 2275, 2382
J. T., D.D.	Joseph Trapp, D.D.	1618
J. T. G.	Judith Towers Grant	1511
J. T. W.	J. Talboys Wheeler	80, 81
J. U.	James Usher	1246
J. U.	J. Upton	1627 (2)
JULIA ÆMELIA.	Emily Blacke	294
JULIO.	Joseph Sykes, M.A.	1322, 1947
JULIUS JUNIPER.	Thomas Foster, B.A.	289
JUNIOR, CORIAT.	Samuel Paterson	104, 159
JUNIOR, DEMOCRITUS.	Robert Burton	86
JUNIOR, EUGENIUS.	James Owen	401
JUNIOR, IRENÆUS.	Samuel Snowden	602
JUNIPER, JULIUS.	Thomas Foster, B.A.	289
JUNIUS.		1433-40
JUNIUS BRUTUS.	Charles Blount	156
JUNIUS BRUTUS.	Johannes Crellius	1334
JUNIUS BRUTUS.	Robert Ferguson	156
JUNIUS R.	Richard Younge	2320
JUNIUS SECUNDUS.	Charles Kelsall	494
JUSTIA.	F. Colburn Adams	1835
JUSTITIA, M.	John Frearson	2128, 2712
J. V.	John Veitch	658, 1384
J. V.	J. Verneuil	1748
J. V.	John Vicars	1909

J. V. C.   John Vincent Cane   784, 920
J. V.   John Vizard   1693
J. W.   Isaac Walton   859
J. W.   James Wallace, M.D.   1158
J. W.   James Welwood, M.D.   2096
J. W.   James Wilcock   355
J. W.   John Wade   296
J. W.   John Wauchope   2243
J. W.   John Wesley   867
J. W.   John Whiting   8
J. W.   John Williams   384, 689, 929
J. W.   John Wilson   565, 802, 1682, 2105
J. W.   John Worlidge   2534 (2), 2769
J. W.   Joseph Wyche, M.O.S.B.,   532
J. W.   J. Walker   297
J. W.   J. Warner   587
J. W.   J. White   1857
J. W.   J. Wilcox   2395
J. W.   J. Wybard   2537
J. W. C—T—SS OF R—S—G.   Jane Wynne, Countess of Rosenberg   1656
J. W. D.   John W. Donaldson   266
J. W.   John Worlidge   141
J. W. HOGO-HUNT.   John Williams Houghton   1020, 1319
J. W., M.D.   James Welwood   123
J. W. PRIEST.   John Watson   759
J. W. S.   James W. Slatter   2241
J. Y.   Dr J. Young or Younge   2343
J. Y. A.   John Young Akerman   2495, 2542

K.

KATE, COUSIN.   Catherine D. Bell   178, 1177, 1518, 1520, 1547, 1554, 1710, 2341, 2679, 2795
KATE THORNE.   Miss Gray   1710
KATHERINE EVERING   1518
KEITH LESLIE.   Keith Johnston   1747, 2387, 2526, 2724, 2804
KENNER DEENE.   Charlotte Smith   101, 387, 708, 1497, 2221, 2242, 2271
KERRY, KNIGHT OF.   Maurice Fitzgerald   1387
K. F.   Francis Kirkman   1997
KINGSMAN, A.   Rev. Robert William Essington, M.A.   1838
KIRKE, EDMUND.   J. R. Gilmore   1470, 1686
KIRWAN.   Nicholas Murray   1452, 2224
K. J.   Richard Younge or Young   1849
K. J. F.   K. J. Finlay   294
KNICKERBOCKER DIEDRICH.   Washington Irving   1144

KNIGHT OF KERRY.   Maurice Fitzgerald   1387
KNIGHT OF MORAR.   Sir W. A. Fraser   422
KNOCKDUNDER, ABEL.   Lieut. H. P. A. Shortrede   1355
KNOKES, JOHN.   John Frith   45
KNOTT, EDWARD.   Matthew Wilson   365, 1603
KN-OXONIAN.   Rev. John Allan   920
KOLIADES, CONSTANTINE.   J. P. Le Chevalier   2704
K. P.   Katherine Philips   1945
K. P.   Kenrick Prescott   1614, 2347
KRANTZOVIUS, IRENAEUS.   B. Stillingfleet   2443
KUNST, HERMANN.   Walter C. Smith, D.D.   1816

L.

L.   Catherine Swanwick   1944, 2250, 2545
L. A.   Lombe Atthill   398
L. A.   Louisa Anthony   2621
L. A. D. P.   L. A. du Pouget   2245
L. A. DU P.   Louis A. du Puget   2622
LAICK, WILLIAM.   George Ridpath   125, 501, 2275
LAIRD OF TORFOOT.   Thomas Brownlee   1695
LAMB LEADER.   William Anderson   1916
LANCASHIRE LAD, A.   Thomas Snowden   2383
LANCE, FREE.   Alexander Richardson   874, 990
LANCELOT LANGSTAFF.   J. K. Paulding   2255
LANCELOT TEMPLE.   John Armstrong   2373
LANE, WICKLIFFE.   Mrs Edmund Jennings   1685
LANGDON, MARY.   Sydney A. Story   1201
LANGSTAFF, LANCELOT.   J. K. Paulding   2255
LATOUCHE, JOHN.   Oswald John Frederick Crawford, H.B.M.   2626
LAUNCELOT, DOM CLAUDE.   Mary Anne Shimmelpenninck   169?
LAUNCELOT TEMPLE.   John Armstrong, M.D.   2405
LAYNE PYNGLE.   J. Fox Turner   2365
LAZARUS, EBENEZER.   Robert Mason   1866

L. B. Lord Buckhurst 1711
L. B. Luke de Beaulieu 1171, 2120
L. D. Leonard Digges 1011
L - - D B - - - - - - - - KE. Henry St John, Lord Viscount Bolingbroke 1358, 1512
L. E. —— Hicks 1922
L. E. Hon. Eleanor Eden 720
L. E. L. Edwards 616
LEADER, LAMB. William Anderson 1916
LEADER SCOTT. Lucy Baxter 2168
LEE, ALFRED. John Clark Ferguson 744
LEE GIBBONS. Thomas Roscoe 343, 1304, 1839
LEE GIBBONS. W. Bennett 1839
LEE HOLME. Harriet Parr 56, 101, 214, 219, 224, 503, 525, 939, 1014, 1075, 1084, 1218, 1297, 1298, 1339, 1560, 1675, 1677, 1970 (2), 2500, 2531, 2572, 2573, 2672, 2685, 2730, 2792, 2828, 2843
LEEVIT, DON T. B. James Mudie Spence, F.R.G.S. 1484
L. E. L. Letitia Elizabeth Landon 238, 719, 930, 937, 1026, 1217, 2223 2621, 2659, 2724, 2778
LEO. Lieut. Col. Pemberton 2262
LEONARD LOVECHURCH. Rev. George Smith, M.A. 1398
LESLIE, KEITH. Keith Johnston 1747, 2387, 2526, 2724, 2804
L'ESTRANGE, HAMON. Peter Heylin 1779
LETO POMPONIO. Cardinal Vitelleschi 2723
L. H. Luke Howard 868
LIBERTAS. Hon. Mrs C. Norton 1452
LIEUT. WARNEFORD, R.N. William H. C. Russell 1272, 1895, 2240, 2397, 2542, 2544
LIMNER, LUKE. F. S. Leighton 1532
LIMNER, LUKE. John Leighton 2513
LINDAMOUR. Charles Gildon 1629
LIPSIENSIS PHILELEUTHERUS. Richard Bentley, D.D. 2157
LITTLE, THOMAS. Thomas Moore 1959
L. L. Rev. George Smith, M.A. 1398
L. L. C. Louisa Lane Clarke 524
LL - - -, REV. C. Charles Lloyd, LL.D. 1775
L. M. Daniel Defoe 2372
L. M. Leonard Mascall 2027

L. MARIOTTI. Antonio Gallenga 57, 928, 1118, 1257 (3), 1322, 1984, 2263
L. M. W. M., RIGHT HON. Lady Mary W. Montagu 2395
L. N. R. Ellen Ranyard 228, 245, 1335, 1484, 1634, 1761, 2495, 2670
L. O. Lewis Owen. 341, 2468
LOCHNAGAR. Magnus Mowat 2242
LOCKER, ARTHUR. J. H. Forbes 2389, 2493, 2529
LOG, ABEL. Charles B. Greatrix 2810
LONCARDIENSIS, THEOPHILUS PHILOKURIACES. Thomas Young 1514
LONDINENS, M. N. MED. Marchmont Nedham 1563
LONDINENSIS, ANONYMOUS. Thomas Lewis 1378
LONDINENSIS, PHILELEUTHERUS. Patrick Squire, D.D. 2141
LONDINIENSIS, PHILALETHES. Caleb Fleming, D.D. 407
LONG SILENT. Thomas T. Lynch 833, 2450
LORD B. Lord Belfast 1557, 1692, 2706, 2797
LORD B * * * * * * *. Lord Brougham 894
LORD VI - - - T B - - - - KE. Viscount Bolingbroke 1358, 1512
LORREQUER, HARRY. Charles J. Lever, M.D. 186, 366, 473
LOTHROP, AMY. A. B. Warner 697, 1017, 1684, 2466
LOT, PARSON. Charles Kingsley 367
LOVECHURCH, LEONARD. Rev. George Smith, M.A. 1398
L. P. Lawrence Price 2822
L. S. Lancelot Sharpe, M.A. 83
L. S. Launcelot Sharpe 1952
L. S. E. Michael Augustus Gathercole 1450
L——SHE, H——S. Hercules Langrishe 2511
L. T. Lewis Theobald 1626, 1628
L-TT—N, E—M—D. Edmund Litton 1900
LUCIUS. Dr Samuel Parr 283
LUCIUS. James B. P. Dennis 1383, 1384
LUCIUS M. PISO. W. Ware 2225
LUDOVICUS, M. John Campbell, LL.D. 1866
LUKE LIMNER. F. S. Leighton 1532
LUKE LIMNER. John Leighton 2513

LUMPWITZ, PROFESSOR, S.U.S. H. W. Bunbury   2542

LUNATICO, F. DE, K.F.M. G. P. R. James   440

L. U. P——, A.M. Thomas Edwards   1388

L. W. Laurence Womock, D.D.   475

L. W. Leonard Willan   1825

L. W. T. D. C. William T. Dove   2354

LYDE, GULIELMUS. Gulielmus Joyner   2433

LYNN, ERITH. Edward Fox   1958

LYSIPONIUS CELER, M.D.L. Johann Groenevelt, M.D.   1321

LYVECANUS CLERICUS. C. Otway   106

M.

M. A. Frederick E. Weatherly   1841

MABEL ETCHELL. Charlotte Phillips   2551

MÆVIUS. Dr John Martyn   1590

MAGENTA. Captain Mahon   1066

MAJOR A * * * * *. C. B. Coles   2379

M. A. K. Mary Ann Kelty   1508

MALACHI MALAGROWTHER. Sir Walter Scott, Bart.   1395, 2300, 2568, 2582

MALAGROWTHER, MALACHI. Sir Walter Scott, Bart.   1395, 2300, 2568, 2582

MALCOLM MACGREGOR. William Mason   568, 783, 1802

MALLEUS TREPIDANTIUM. Samuel Young   147, 473, 953, 972, 2182, 2296, 2409, 2817

MALTHUS, PHILO-. George Hancock   507

MANCHESTER, JOHN OF. John Bosworth   2249

MANSON, JAMES B. James Murray   228

MAR., CH. Christopher Marlowe   2620

MARCELLUS. Allan Ramsay, Jr.   1448

MARCLIFFE, THEOPHILUS. William Godwin   1509

MARCUS TULLIUS CICERO. William Melmoth   341

MARGARET DODS. Christina J. Johnston   510

MARGELINA SCRIBELINDRA MACULARIA. W. Kenrick, LL.D.   1815

MARIA DEL OCCIDENTE. Maria Brooks   2854

MARIA R * * * * * * Maria Riddell   2784

MARION HARLAND. Mary Virginia Hawe   70, 1094, 1665, 1710

MARIOTTI, L. Antonio Gallenga   57, 928, 1118, 1257 (3), 1322, 1984, 2263

MARKHAM, MRS. Elizabeth Penrose née Cartwright   1115, 1136, 1137, 1716, 2339

MARK ROCHESTER. William C. M. Kent   603

MARK TWAIN. Samuel Langhorne Clemens   74, 551, 986, 1014, 1224, 1226 (2), 1548 (2), 1727, 1985, 2230

MARLOW, RIGHT HON. LADY HARRIET. William Beckford   1642

MARMADUKE MILTON. Charles Dunster   2250

MARMADUKE MYRTLE. Sir Richard Steele   1520

MAR-PREIST, MARTIN. Henry Robinson   166

MARTEL, CHARLES. Thomas Delf   1519, 1558, 2016, 2017 (2)

MARTIN DOYLE. Ross Hickey   60, 442 (2), 517, 555, 895, 897, 936, 1100 (2), 1251, 1310, 1552, 1984, 2240, 2408, 2738

MARTINGALE. —— White   755, 2479, 2686

MARTIN MAR—PRIEST. Henry Robinson   166

MARTIN PARKER. Amos Strettell   1741

MARTINUS SCRIBLERUS. Rev. Robert Morehead   862

MARY DE GLEVA. Mary Roberts   14

MARY LANGDON. Sydney A. Story   1201

MARY OLD LADY. Margaret O. W. Oliphant   2701

MASSACHUSETTENSIS. Daniel Leonard   1556

MATTHEW STRADLING. M. F. Mahony.   1251

ΜΑΘΟΣ ΘΥΟΣ Thomas South   716

MATILDA, ANNA. Hannah Cowley   1959, 1960

MATILDA, ROSA. Mrs Byrne   118

MATTHEW BROWNE. W. B. Rands   2737

MATTHEW WHITE. William Prynne   1737

MATTHEWS & CO. L. S. Buckingham   58

MATURIN, REV. C. R.   Rev. James Wells   2712

MAWR, ETA.   Elizabeth Colling   894, 2499

MAX ADELER.   Charles H. Clark   1810, 1836

MAY FLY.   Wellington Somerset   499

MAYNARD, WALTER.   William Beale   774

MAXIMUS, SCRIBLERUS. James Love   533

M. B.   James Corker   2222

M. B. DRAPER.   Jonathan Swift, D.D.   1402

M. B. DRAPIER.   Jonathan Swift, D.D.   1415

M. C.   Marmaduke Carver   656

M. C.   Matthew Carter   1668

M. C.   Michael Constable   1700

M. C.   W. Maskell   1800

M. C. M. E.   Cresacre More   1465

M. D.   Matthew Davies   1383

M. D.   Michael Dodson   1732

M——D. JN.   Hans Wood   2191

M. E.   Mathias Earbery   1809

M. E.   Matthias Earbery   738

MEDICO CAMPO, DON RICHARDO DE.   Gabriel Harvey   2655

MEDICUS.   Isaac Pidduck, M.D.   2037

MEDICUS.   John Epps, M.D.   1242

MEDICUS INDICUS.   Dr Skinner   2430

MEGATHYM SPLENE, B.A., OXEN.   Cockburn Thomson   69

MELA BRITANNICUS.   Charles Kelsall   1178, 2157

M----E, LADY M--Y W---Y.   M. W. Montague   1443

MELMONTH.   Samuel Jackson Pratt   1717

MELMOTH, COURTNEY.   Samuel Jackson Pratt   1781, 2057, 2346, 2510, 2548.   Errata Vol. 4

M. E. M. J.   Margaret E. M. Jones   1255, 1281, 2783

MEMORITER.   David Pae   2338

MENALCAS.   Bracy Clarke   2142

MENCIUS PHILALETHES.   Peter Annet   1141

MENENIUS.   Digby P. Starkey   1801

MENIPPUS.   Rev. Thomas Easton   2195

MERCATOR.   James Anderson, LL.D.   2582

MERCHANT, T.   Thomas Dibdin   1531

MERCURIOPHILUS ANGLICUS   Elias Ashmole   900

MERCURIUS ACHERONTICUS   James Howell   2621

MERCURIUS PRAGMATICUS.   Marchamont Nedham   107, 1455, 1936

MERCURIUS RUSTICUS.   Thomas Frognall Dibdin   231

MERCURIUS SPUR.   Cuthbert Shaw   2073

MEREDITH, 'OWEN.   Hon. E. R. Bulwer Lytton   420, 1523, 2216, 2325, 2787

MERRET, CHRISTOPHER.   Henry Stubbe   1564

M. E. S. ACHETA DOMESTICA.   L. M. Budgen   779

METAPHORICUS, ARCHIMA-GIRUS.   William Kenrick, LL.D.   1297

M. F.   Margaret Fell   301, 564, 1522, 2609, 2678, 2827

M. F.   Margaret Fox née Fell   301, 564, 1522, 2609, 2678, 2827

M. F. M.   Mary F Maude   2282

M. G.   Martin Greene   21

M. G.   Martin Grene, S.J.   205

M. G. B.   George Buchanan   612

M. G. B.   Master George Buchanan   45

M. G. D.   George Drummond   2376

M. H.   Matilda Horsburgh   370, 517, 1084, 1310, 1554, 1756, 2073, 2227, 2257, 2498

M. H.   Mrs Hullah   917

MICAH BALWHIDDER, — REV. JOHN GALT   101

MICHAEL ANGELO TITMARSH.   William Makepeace Thackeray   435, 687, 1252, 1300, 1677, 1835, 1860, 2296

MILITIA MEA MULTIPLEX.   William Tooke   2726

MILTONICUS.   —— Henderson   986

MILTON, MARMADUKE.   Charles Dunster   2250

MINOR CALVINUS. SCOTO-BRITANNUS.   Archibald Bruce   965

MINSTREL, MUNGO THE.   —— Darkison   250

MINUTIUS, FELIX.   Arthur Helps   830

MIRA.   Eliza Haywood   2814

MISODIABOLES.   Sir John Harrington   2705

MISO DOLOS.   Charles Leslie   1029

MISOPLANES AND PHILA-LETHES.   —— Wastall   1854

M. J. C. James Clark 653, 1033
M. J. J. Maria J. Jewsbury 1895
M. J. J——N. Mary J. Jourdan 1617
M. J. M * * *. Katherine King 1893
M. J. M. D. Margaret J. M. Dunbar 180
M. JUSTITIA. John Frearson 2128, 2712
M. L. Michael Livingston 62, 1874
M. L. Miguel de Cervantes Saavedra 2628
M. L. B. 370
M. L. L. Martin Llewellyn 1597
M. LUDOVICUS. John Campbell, LL.D. 1866
M. M. M. Marsin 68
M. M. Matthew Montagu 534
M. M. Mungo Murray 570, 571 (2), 2600, 2601
M. M. C. CIRUJANO. George Borlase Childs 64, 212, 699
M * * * * * MONSIEUR. J. Fr. Melon 1965
M. N. James Kennedy, B.D. 2145
M. N. Marchamont Nedham 643
—— M——N. W. Baron 711
M. N. William Camden 2133
MNASON. William P. Smith, D.D. 2277
M. N. MED. LONDINENS. Marchamont Nedham 1563
MOFUSSILITE, THE. John Lang 2606
MONMOUTH, T. DE. Thomas Powell 724
MONSIEUR * * *. Antoine Varillas 2115
MONSIEUR M * * * * *. J. Fr. Melon 1965
MONTAGUE WILLIAMS. —— Wasborough 1358
MONTELION, KNIGHT OF THE ORACLE. John Phillips 699, 1243, 1654
MONTELION. Thomas Flatman 699
MONTGOMERY, BETTY. William Cullen, M.D. 985
MORAR, KNIGHT OF. Sir W. A. Fraser 422
MORGAN DE PEMBROKE. Morgan Evans 1944
MORDAUNT, COL. HARRY. George Ogle 1645
MORDECAI MULLION. Professor J. Wilson 2425
MORETON, ANDREW. Daniel Defoe 838, 1863, 2042, 2309, 2314
MORIARTY, DENIS IGNATIUS. John O'Brien Grant 2814

M. P. Martin Parker 279, 605, 842, 1029, 1072, 2220, 2678, 2788
M. P. Mary Pennington 1690
M. P. Mary Pennyman 2446
M. P. Mary Pope 2635
M. P. Matthew Poole 1350
M. R. Montgomerie Ranking 2059
MR ——, HONOURABLE. William Combe 198
M. R. C. Robert Calder 2307
M. R. L. M. R. Lahee 2593
M. S. John Clutton, M.A. 1378
M. S. Matthew Symson, M.A. 745
M. S. Menella B. Smedley 2499
M. S. Michael Stanhope 1738
M. S. Moses Stringer, M.D. 1820
M. S. Thomas Jeamson 187
M. S. G. S. Machell Stace 543
M. S., REV. Matthew Smith 2672
MSS. H. G. Saville, Marquis of Halifax 359
M. ST. Michael Stanhope 551
M. T. C. M. B. F. L. S. Sir Thomas Charles Morgan 865
M. T. H. Thomas Hutton 2168
M. T. M. Magister Thomas More 1465
MULLION, MORDECAI. Professor J. Wilson 2425
MULTIPLEX, MILITIA MEA. William Tooke 2726
MUNGO THE MINSTREL. —— Darkison 250
MURPHY Errata Vol. 4
MUSAEUS PALATINUS. Richard Brathwait 2695
MUSCIPULA, SEN. John Collier 552
MUSOPHIL, THINE ANONYM. Daniel Tuvill 2719
MUSSEL MOU'D CHARLIE. G. R. Kinloch 209
M. W. Mary Williams 1496
M. W. Sir William Morice 98
M. W. T. William Tennant 1853
MYRTLE, H. Lydia Falconer Miller 1539
MYRTLE, HARRIET. Lydia Falconer Miller 200, 524, 566, 1495, 1539, 1799, 2498, 2772, 2793
MYRTLE, MARMADUKE. Sir Richard Steele 1520
MYSELF. Mrs Purcell 1825
M - - - Y W - - - Y M - - - - E. Lady M. W. Montague 1443
MACARONI, A. —— Taylor 2559

MACCARTE, DUNCAN. Samuel
Squire, D.D. 1383
MACGREGOR, MALCOLM.
William Mason 568, 783, 1802
MACKENZIE, ERICK. Millicent
Grogan 2226
MACPACKE, JOSE. James
Peacock 1808
MACSARCASM, REV. SIR ARCHI-
BALD. William Shaw, D.D. 1474
MACSARCONICA, ARCHY, F.R.S.
Thomas Hastings 248
MACSHINIE, GILLESPIE. Archi-
bald Simson 101
MACULARIA, MARGELINA
SCRIBELINDRA. W. Kenrick,
LL.D. 1815
M'GREGOR, MALCOLM. William
Mason 568, 783, 1802
M'RORY, REV. RORY. J. Cameron
Lees, D.D. 1531

N.

NARJENN, THO. Thomas
Tanner 2412
NASBY, PETROLEUM V. D. R.
Locke 1699
NATHAN, BEN SADDI. Robert
Dodsley 390, 2292
NATHAN HOGG. Henry Baird 1431
NATHAN OLIVER. Robert
Blakey, Ph.D. 916
NATH. CROUCH. Richard Burton 757
NAUFRAGUS. —— Horne 50
NAUTICUS, PHILO-. L. H. Hal-
loran 911
NAWORTH, G. George Wharton 1601
N. B. Nathaniel Baxter 2391
N. B. N. Barbon, M.D. 656
N. B. N. Basely 2338
N. B. Nicholas Baxter 2408
N. B. Nicolas Bear, M.A. 2188
N. B. Nicolas Blaikie 1333
N. B. Nicholas Bretton
894, 923, 935, 1866
N. C. Nathaniel Carpenter 30
N. D. George Cavendish 1466
N. DRALLOC. John Collard 787, 1467
N. D. Robert Parsons 2127, 2196,
2550, 2569, 2640, 2790
NESTOR IRONSIDE. Rev. Dr
Samuel Croxall 104
NEVILLE TEMPLE. Hon. Julian
Charles Henry Fane 2545

N. F. Nathaniel Field 904
N. F. Nathaniel Fiennis 2714
N. F. D. Nicholas Fatio de Duillier 976
N. G. John Dobson 688
N. H. D. D. M. M. S. Nathaniel
Holmes 1034
N. HONORIA. Marguerite A.
Power 1431
NICHOLAS DOLEMAN. Robert
Parsons 2791
NICHOLAS NIPCLOSE, SIR,
BART. David Garrick 2559
NIL. H. J. Whitling 1080
NIMROD. Charles James Apperley
101, 354, 1179, 1193, 1471, 1589,
2148, 2479
NIPCLOSE, SIR NICHOLAS,
BART. David Garrick 2559
N——N T——S. Thomas Newen-
ham 891
N. N. Laurence Anderton 2656
N. N. Charles Leslie 2018
N. N. Charlwood Lawton 407, 2297
N. N. Edmund Calamy, D.D. 647
N. N. Edward Scarisbrook 1481
N. N. Gilbert Burnet, D.D. 858
N. N. John Nalson 2000
N. N. John Sergeant 1609
N. N. Lawrence Anderton 2027, 2656
N. N. Robert South, D.D. 2370
N. N. Samuel Grascome 2139
N. N. Vincent Alsop 140
N. O. Abraham Woodhead 689
N. O. Edward Thompson 600
NOBODY. G. Robinson 1948
NOBODY. James Robertson 1948
NOBODY, JUNR. Thomas Hodg-
son 1947
N. O. M. A. Richard Bentley 2202
NON CLERICUS. —— Cottle 2224
NORFOLCIENSIS, PHILE-
LEUTHERUS. Samuel Parr,
LL.D. 649, 658
NORTH AMERICAN. Thomas B.
Chandler, D.D. 75
NORTH-BRITISH PRO-
TESTANT. Archibald Bruce 1240
NORTH CHRISTOPHER.
Professor John Wilson 2102, 2435
NORVAL. James Scrymgeour
912, 2772
NOVUS HOMO. W. J. Courthope
2553
N. R. John Hunter 1630

N. S. John Wilkins   2767
N. S. John Willis, D.D.   1286
N. S. Nathaniel Stephens   2767
N. S. Sylvester Norris   2053
NUNNERY, FABRICIA, SPINSTER. Peter Coxe.   104, 2836
     Errata Vol. 4
N. W. Nathaniel Ward   638
N. W. Nicholas Wincop   2141
N. W. Nic. Watts   2547
N. W. N. West   1208
N. Y. ——   1334
N. Y. John Dury   659
N. Y. John Fry   1911

O.

O. A. T. H. P. Oliver Plunkett   1290
OBSERVANT, F. B. Richard Britton   1545
OBSERVATOR. Rev. John Evans   1441
OCCIDENTE, MARIA DEL. Maria Brooks   2854
OCTAVIUS. Dr William Hales   2058
O'DOWD, CORNELIUS. Charles James Lever   514
OFELLUS. Francis Squire   2802 (2)
O. H. Oliver Heywood   53, 1256
O'HARA FAMILY, THE. John Banim   239, 252, 904, 1562, 2539
O. L. Octave Delepierre   2229
OLD BOOMERANG. John Richard Houlding   201
OLD BUSHMAN. H. W. Wheelwright   293
OLDCASTLE, HUMPHREY. Nicholas Amhurst   2149
OLD HUMPHREY. George Mogridge   525, 1342, 1810, 1811, 2279, 2539 (2), 2574
OLD JONATHAN. David Alfred Doudney, D.D.   2683, (2)
OLD LADY MARY. Margaret O. W. Oliphant   2701
OLD SAILOR, THE. Matthew Henry Barker, R.N.   1262, 1316, 1478, 2607, 2610, 2790
OLD SHEKARRY, THE. H. A. Leverson   748, 941, 1193
OLD VICAR, THE. John Samuel Bewley Monsell, LL.D.   1487
OLDYS, FRANCIS, A. M. George Chalmers   1484
OLEANDER. David M'Culloch   564

OLIM OXONIENSIS. George Wilmot   1384
OLINTHUS. William J. A. Sheehy   2167
OLIVER FOULIS. David Lloyd   295
OLIVER, NATHAN. Robert Blakey, Ph.D.   916
OLIVER, STEPHEN. William Andrew Chatto   1810, 2076, 2263
OLIVER YORKE. Francis Mahony   2132
OLPHAR HAMST. Ralph Thomas   1065, 1553
O. M. HABERDASHER. Alexander Carlyle, D.D.   1925
OMNIUM, JACOB. Matthew J. Higgins   1253, 1445, 1448, 1485, 2083, 2568, 2588
O. N. Serenus de Cressy   2222
ONE OF THE BOYS. Percy H. Fitzgerald   2268
ONE OF THE 687 F.R.S. —— SSS. Dr A. B. Granville   2271
ONESIMUS. Peter L. Courtier   1589, 2056
ONE, TWO, THREE, FOUR. Daniel Defoe   771
ONE WHO HAS WHISTLED AT THE PLOUGH. Alexander Somerville   204
ONE WHO KNOWS IT WELL. C. R. Lushington   1987
ONTOLOGOS. William Kenrick, LL.D.   1041, 2176
O. P. Oliver Pigge   434, 2340
OPATVS DVCTOR. James Mumford   2069
O'REID, JNO. CHAS. Josiah Conder   2204
ORIELENSIS PHILELEUTHEROS. J. Davison, M.A.   2353
ORINDA. Katherine Philips   1428
ORTHOS, PHIL-. George Johnstone   832
ORWELL. Walter Chalmers Smith   239
OSCAR. Mrs Leman Grimstone   2851
OSCOTIAN. William Charles Mark Kent   339
OTWAY, SYLVESTER. John Oswald   835, 1953
OUIDA. Louisa de La Ramée   175, 345, 356, 696, 937, 974, 1081, 1201, 1218 (2), 1669, 1866, 1916, 2056, 2385, 2502, 2654, 2698, 2707, 2738, 2787

O. W. John Bridle, D.D. 1405
O. W. Obadiah Walker 1051
O——W, A——R. Arthur Onslow 2470
OWEN MEREDITH. Hon. E. R. Bulwer-Lytton 420, 1523, 2216, 2325, 2787
OXONIAN, AN. Stephen Weston 2655
OXONIAN, KN. Rev. John Allan 920
OXONIENSIS, A.M. Nathaniel Tillson Marsh 1832
OXONIENSIS. Henry Brooke, D.C.L. 161
OXONIENSIS. Rev. Francis Trench 2209
OXONIENSIS. Thomas Monro 1898
OXONIENSIS, OLIM. George Wilmot 1384
OXONIENSIS, PHILANTHRO-PUS. Dr Morgan 1407
OXONIENSIS, PHILOMATH. Richard Walker, B.D. 918
OXOS. John Coglan 472
OYSTER FROM HOME, AN. Henry Cobbold 1954
OZIOSI. Robert Merry, &c. 178

P.

II. Rev. Joseph Wasse 1626
P. Robert Kemp Philp 1903
P. Stuart Menteith 1879
P. A. Peter Annet 1283
P. A. Philip Ayres 2355
PACIFICUS. John Payne 2601
P. A., D.D. Peter Allix, D.D. 2115
PADRING, RYRIE BJOLLA. P. V. Fitz Patrick 2558
PAETS, CORNELIUS. Arthur A. Sykes, D.D. 1188
PAGE, H. A. Alexander H. Japp 1334, 1571, 1747, 1835, 2572 (2)
PALÆOPOLITANUS, FRAN-CISCUS. Henry More 683
PALATINUS, MUSÆUS. Richard Brathwait 2695
PALEDONIUS, PHILOGENES. R. Brathwayt 180
PALLET, PETER PAUL. Rev. Richard Warner 2096, 2187
PALMER, HACKLE. Robert Blakey 1100
PAMEACH, RYHEN. Henry Peachman, M.A. 619

PANTAGRUELL, GARAGANTUA. William Rufus Chetwood 2494
P. A. Patricius Aberdonensis. Patrick Forbes, Bishop of Aberdeen 833
PARAGRAPH PETER. James Makillrick Adair, M.D. 91
PARALLAX. Dr Samuel Rowbotham 2853
PARENS. —— Synge 720
PARIAH, CAROLINE. Francis Cornwallis 1902
PARK, ABNER. Rev. Alex. Stevenson Twombly 1605
PARKER, MARTIN. Amos Strettell 1741
PARKER, SAMUEL. Charles Leslie 836
PARLANTE, PRISCILLA. Hon. Mary A. C. Bradshaw 912, 1582
PARLEY, PETER. George Mogridge 2332
PARLEY, PETER. Samuel Griswold Goodrich 1889
PARLEY, PETER. William Martin 1169
PARRESIASTES, PHILOPHILUS. Henry More, D.D. 775
PARRHASI, THEODORUS. John Le Clerc 1863
PARSON LOT. Charles Kingsley 367
PARTHENOPHÆUS HERETI-CUS. William Gordon 28, 1992
PARVUS, CATO. Thomas Frognall Dibdin 231
PASCAL, YR. Pierce Connelly 325, 1658, 2821
PASHA, HOBART. Augustus Charles Hobart, R.N. 1710
PASQUIN, ANTHONY. John Williams 201, 546, 549, 721, 1481, 1715, 1914, 1946, 1954, 1980, 2643
PASQUINUS, PETRUS, C.P.M. Thomas Comber 2277
PASTOR FIDO. Allan Blayney 913
PATRICOLA. John Toland 2307, 2484
PATRIOTICUS. W. P. Russel 1809, 2414
PATRICIUS ABERDONENSIS. Patrick Forbes 833
PATRICIUS WALKER. W. Allingham 2076
PAUL PINDAR. John Yonge Akerman 1507
P. B. P. Bakewell 659
P. B. Peter Belon 1636

P. B. S. Percy Bysshe Shelley 2851
P. C. W. Philip Carteret Webb 2353
2354, 2485
P. COLQUHOUN. R. Shaw 1770
P. D. R. Bentley 979
P. D. M. Matthew Patison 1207
P. D. M. Matthew Pattenson 1207
P. D. M. Peter Du Moulin, D.D. 1375
P····, DR. William Payne, D.D. 1356
PEDESTRIAN, THE. John Aiton, D.D. 730
PEMBROKE, MORGAN DE. Morgan Evans 1944
PEN CLER JOCELYN. Pierce Connelly, M.A. 1971, 2023
PENDENNIS, ARTHUR. W. M. Thackeray 1737
PENDRAGON. Henry Sampson 1639
PENSILVANIAN. William Penn 588
PEN, SILVER. Eliza Meteyard 599, 1497
PENTWEAZLE, EBENEZER. C. Smart 1179
PERCY, JONES, T. William E. Aytoun 925
PERCY, REUBEN. Joseph Clinton Robinson 1508, 1884
PERCY, RUEBEN. Thomas Byerly 1508, 1884
PERCY, SHOLTO. Joseph C. Robertson 1508, 1884
PERCY, SHOLTO. Thomas Byerley 1508, 1884
PEREGRINE SMYTH. William King, LL.D. 1299
P. E., REV. FATHER DOM. Philip Ellis 929
PER PHILANTHROPUM. Mark Hildesley 2128
PETER. William Cockburn, M.A. 1888
PETER BULLCALF. Joseph S. Fry 1140
PETER CORNELIUS. Hugh Peeters 2795
PETER OF PONTEFRACT. Richard Graves 1524
PETER PARAGRAPH. J. M. Adair, M.D. 91
PETER PARLEY. George Mogridge 2332
PETER PARLEY. Samuel G. Goodrich 1889
PETER PARLEY. William Martin 1169

PETER PAUL PALLET. Rev Richard Warner 2096, 2187
PETER PINDAR. John Wolcott, M.D., 53, 143, 225, 252, 287, 346, 440, 460, 506, 865, 894 (2), 902, 1012, 1061, 1237, 1254, 1316, 1460, 1517, 1529 (2), 1661 (2), 1741, 1803 (2), 1804 (3), 1818, 1835, 1845, 1871, 1893(2), 1915 (2), 1955, 1956, 1958, 2165, 2213, 2218 (6), 2234, 2235, 2236, 2255, 2277, 2390, 2510, 2543, 2549, 2657, 2798, 2830, 2840
PETER PINDAR, JUNIOR. John Agg 2218, 2233, 2590, 2686
PETER PLYMLEY. Sidney Smith 1449, 2589, 2696
PETER PONDER, REV. Rev. William Bell 422, 1307
PETER PORCUPINE. William Corbett, 75, 241, 600 (2), 612, 1463, 1497, 1776, 1778, 2651
PETER POSITIVE. James Montgomery 2020
PETER THE PLOWMAN. James Mercer 2024
PETROLEUM V. NASBY. D. R. Locke 1699
PETRUS PASQUINUS, C.P.M. Thomas Comber 2277
P. F. Payne Fisher 1950, 2606
P. F. P. Fuller 1409
P. F. Phineas Fletcher 740, 1916, 2058
P. F. C. Alexander Dunlop 2125
P. F., SERGEANT-MAJOR. Payne Fisher 1950, 2606
P. G. D. Peter Gally de Gaujac 2675
P. H. Peter Heylin 2509
P. H. P. Hardcastle 2061
P. H. Philemon Holland 2123
P. H. Sir Patrick Hume 2030
P. H., D.D. Peter Heylin, D.D. 2781
P. H. ΦΙΛΟΠΟΙΗΤΗΣ. Patrick Hume 102
PHILADELPHUS. Saxe Bannister 2150
PHILADELPHUS, IRENÆUS. Lewis Du Moulin 2780
PHILADELPHUS, THEOPHILUS. John Ley 853
PHILAGATHUS. Edward Pearce 475
PHILAGATHUS. Rev. Samuel Rolle 2411
PHILALETHES. Charles Leslie 324, 2737
PHILALETHES. Colonel Webbe 2348

PHILALETHES. George Turner 1610
PHILALETHES. Hon. Archibald Campbell 1401
PHILALETHES. James Beezley 1378
PHILALETHES. John Jones, LL.D. 785
PHILALETHES. John Swinton, B.D. 536
PHILALETHES. John Wesley, A.M. 1378
PHILALETHES. Joseph Besse 415
PHILALETHES. Joseph Ollive 415
PHILALETHES. Joseph Rogers, M.D. 109
PHILALETHES. Lord Mandeville 624
PHILALETHES. Matthias Earbery 1120, 1210
PHILALETHES. Rev. John Bruce 2145
PHILALETHES. Rev. John Gough 647
PHILALETHES. Rev. Thomas Randall 1780
PHILALETHES. Rev. William Goode, M.A. 831
PHILALETHES. Richard Bentley 1408
PHILALETHES. Robert Findlay, D.D. 2144, 2697
PHILALETHES. Sir James Tyrrell 1872
PHILALETHES. Sir Richard Hill 1403
PHILALETHES. Thomas Delaune 1936
PHILALETHES. T. Twining 657
PHILALETHES-ALAZONOMAS-TIX. Henry More 1788
PHILALETHES, A.M. Robert Fellowes, D.D. 1132
PHILALETHES CANTABRIGI-ENSIS. Bishop Kaye 2141, 2178
PHILALETHES CANTABRIGI-ENSIS. James Jurin, M.D. 165, 1010, 1619
PHILALETHES CANTABRIGI-ENSIS. John Jackson 900, 2141
PHILALETHES CANTABRIGI-ENSIS. Zachary Grey 2267
PHILALETHES, EUGENIUS. Arthur Ashley Sykes 1225
PHILALETHES, EUGENIUS. Thomas Vaughan 94, 131, 269, 835, 1225, 1526, 1533, 1538, 2310
PHILALETHES, EUGENIUS, JUN. Robert Samber 2638

PHILALETHES LONDINIENSIS. Caleb Fleming, D.D. 407
PHILALETHES, MENCIUS. Peter Annet 1141
PHILALETHES, MISOPLANES AND. —— Wastall 1854
PHILALETHES RUSTICANS. Richard Shepherd, D.D. 2109
PHILALETHES RUSTICUS. William Asplin 1214
PHILANDER. Ford, Earl Gray 1519
PHILANDER. Rev. James Wright 307
PHILANAGNOSTES CRITICUS. Thomas Herne 13
PHILANAX. John Norris 1680
PHILANAX, CALVIN. Samuel Young 972
PHIL. ANG. John Pennyman 279
PHIL ANGLUS. Joseph Pennyman 1511
PHIL'ANGLUS. William Penn 751, 1835, 2045
PHILANTHROPES. John Fellowes 1037
PHILANTHROPOS. James Grant 2758
PHILANTHROPOS. John Dove 2080
PHILANTHROPOS. John Forster 2135
PHILANTHROPOS. Rev. James Morrison 2070
PHILANTHROPOS. Thomas Mortimer 839
PHILANTHROPOS, THEOPHI-LUS. David Hall 798
PHILANTHROPOS, THEOPHI-LUS. Robert Poole, M.D. 1907
PHILANTHROPUM, PER. Mark Hildesley 2128
PHILANTHROPUS. John Locke 2297, 2567
PHILANTHROPUS. Joseph Besse 773
PHILANTHROPUS OXONIEN-SIS. D. Morgan 1407
PHILANTIIUS. John Sharp, Jun. 2189
PHILARENVS. James Howell 1601
PHILARET. John Dunton 194
PHILARETES, PHILIPPUS, A. C. C. Thomas Comber 46
PHILARETUS. Thomas Letchworth 799
PHILECCLESIA. Rev. C. H. Davis, M.A. 2514
PHILELEUTHEROS. John Fell 1294
PHILELEUTHEROS ORIEL-ENSIS. J. Davison, M.A. 2353

PHILELEUTHERUS ANGLI-
CANUS. J. W. Donaldson, D.D. 2747
PHILELEUTHERUS BRITAN-
NICUS. John Hildrop, D.D. 2113
PHILELEUTHERUS CANTA-
BRIGIENSIS. Thomas Herne
798, 886, 1405, 2586
PHILELEUTHERUS CHRIST-
IANUS. Rev. T. Broughton 385
PHILELEUTHERUS DUBLIN-
IENSIS. Patrick Delany, D.D. 2113
PHILELEUTHERUS LIPSIEN-
SIS. Richard Bentley, D.D. 2157
PHILELEUTHERUS LONDIN-
IENSIS. Samuel Squire, D.D. 2141
PHILELEUTHERUS NORFOL-
CIENSIS. Samuel Parr, LL.D.
649, 658
PHILELEUTHERUS, TYRO.
John Duncan, D.D. 37
PHILEMON. Rev. C. S. Hawtrey 624
PHILENIA. Mrs Morton 1832
PHILHELLEN, SCOTTISH.
Edward Mason 1897
PHILINDUS. Dr Max Müller 516
PHILIPPUS PHILARETES,
A. C. C. Thomas Comber (1), 46
PHILIP WHARTON. John C.
Thomson 1078, 2823
PHIL-, J. R., EN-ALETHIUS, I. D.
John Doughtie 2724
PHILLIPS, THO. William Drake 1509
PHILO. —— Maitland 2652
PHILO - BASILEUS PHILO-
CLERUS. W. Carpender 1288
PHILOBASILEUS, THEOPHILUS.
Thomas Pierce, D.D. 2033
PHILOBIBLICUS CANTABRIG-
IENSIS. J. Chapman, D.D. 2137
PHILOBIBLOS. Thomas Rodd 596
PHILO-BRITANNUS. C. Dave-
nant, LL.D. 2114
PHILOCHELIDON. Thomas
Forster 1774
PHILO-CHRISTIANUS. William
Brough, D.D. 2247
PHILOCHRISTUS. J. Proast,
Archdeacon of Berks 2300
PHILO-CLERUS, PHILO-BASI-
LEUS. William Carpender 1288
PHILO-CRITICUS. Francis Hare
D.D. 414
PHILOCRITICUS CANTABRI-
GIENSIS. John Jackson 2644

PHILODEMUS. Joseph Clegg 515
PHILOGENES PALEDONIUS. '
Richard Brathwayt 180
PHILOGLOTTUS. Richard Parker 813
PHILOJUVENIS. C. J. Hambro 724
PHILOLOGIST. Rev. Richard
Shepherd 1802
PHILO-MALTHUS. George Han-
cock 507
PHILOMATH. Harry Whitney,
Patrick Kennedy 1340 (2)
PHILOMATH, OXONIENSIS.
Richard Walker, B.D. 918
PHILOMATH, T. N. Jonathan
Swift, D.D. 892
PHILOMIRTH, AARON. John H.
Parr 1684
PHILO-MUSUS. Nicholas Am-
herst 1799
PHILOMUSUS, BASILIUS.
Robert Waring, M.A. 16
PHILOMUSUS, BASILIUS.
Thomas Barlow, D.D. 1880
PHILOMUSUS, BASILIUS.
Thomas Pierce 2566
PHILO-NAUTICUS. L. H.
Halloran 911
PHILONOMUS ELEUTHERUS.
J. Arbuthnot, M.D. 1270
PHILOPARRIUS, THEOPHILUS.
Thomas Paget 2132
PHILOPATER. William Pyrnne 2024
PHILOPATRIA. Rachel Fanny
A. Lee 797
PHILOPATRIS. Bishop of St
David's 1441
PHILOPATRIS. Charles Blount 1294
PHILOPATRIS. Thomas Burgess,
D.D. 1441
ΦΙΛΟΠ'ΑΤΡΙΣ. Sir Josiah Child 2649
PHILOPATRIS, PHILOPHILUS.
Andrew Symson 2709
PHILOPATRIS VARVICENSIS.
Samuel Parr, D.D. 362
PHILOPENES. Jo. Dormer, S.J. 2720
PHILOPHILUS PARRESIASTES.
Henry More, D.D. 775
PHILOPHILUS PHILOPATRIS.
Andrew Symson 2709
PHILOPHRASTES. Sir Ralph
Freeman 1309
ΦΙΛΟΠΟΙΗΤΗΣ, P. H. Patrick Hume 102
ΦΙΛΟΠΟΛΙΤΕΙΟΥΣ. Alexander Skene
1595

PHILOPOLITES. William Petman 1419

PHILOPOLITES, W. P. William Prynne 1818

PHILO-ROSKELYNIS. Robert Forbes, Bishop of Caithness 17

PHIL-ORTHOS. George Johnstone 832

PHILO SCOTUS. Philip B. Ainslie 2166

PHILOSTRATUS. Thomas Forster, F.L.S. 2416

PHILOTHEORUS. Caleb Fleming, D.D. 2129

PHILOTHEOS PHYSIOLOGUS. Thomas Tryon 970, 1654, 2795, 2796

PHILOTHEUS, ABRAHAM. A. Wright 83

PHILOTESIS. Daniel Roberts 2096

PHILO-TRAGICUS. Thady Fitzpatrick 772

PHILUS ADELPHUS. John Ley 642

PHIZ. H. K. Browne 1193

P. H., M.D. Paul Hiffernan, M.D. 2319

PHŒNIX, JOHN, M.A. Captain Derby 1905

PHŒNIX. Sir Henry Martin, Bart. 169

PHOTIUS, JUNIOR. —— Sherlock 1445

PH. TRELERNIE. Peter Heylin 2707

PHYSIOLOGUS, PHILOTHEOS. Thomas Tryon 970, 1654, 2795, 2796

PIERCE, DOD. Dr Barrowby 1403

PIERCE, DOD. Dr Schomberg, Jr. 1403

PIKROMEL, TIMOTHEUS. Thomas Clarke 789

PILEUS QUADRATUS. Stephen Reay 1776

PINDAR, PAUL. John Younge Akerman 1507

PINDAR, PETER. John Wolcott, M.D. 53, 143, 225, 252, 287, 346, 440, 460, 506, 865, 894 (2), 902, 1012, 1061, 1237, 1254, 1316, 1460, 1517, 1529 (2), 1661 (2), 1741, 1803 (2), 1804 (3), 1818, 1835, 1845, 1871, 1893 (2), 1915 (2), 1955, 1956, 1958, 2165, 2213, 2218 (6), 2234, 2235, 2236, 2255, 2277, 2390, 2510, 2543, 2549, 2657, 2798, 2830, 2840

PINDAR, PETER, JUNIOR. John Agg 2218, 2233, 2590, 2686

PISCATOR. Thomas P. Lathy 92

PISISTRATUS, CAXTON. G. E. Bulwer-Lytton 243

PISO, LUCIUS M. W. Ware 2225

PITTS, THOMAS. John Tutchin 1725

PLACE, BENJAMIN. Edward Thring 2577

PLAIN TIMOTHY. G. W. Blaikie 924

PLOWMAN, PETER THE. James Mercer 2024

PLYMLEY, PETER. Sidney Smith 1449, 2589, 2696

P. M. Patrick Middleton 677

P. M. Peter Muffet 438

P. M. Philip Massinger 904, 1981

P. M. Pierre Mathieu 1981

POETASTER. Thomas Dekker 2352

POLEMOPHILUS BROWN. Alexander Geddes, LL.D. 1737

POLYPUS. Eaton Stannard Barrett 68 (2)

POMPONIO, LETO. Cardinal Vitelleschi 2723

PONDER, REV. PETER. Rev. William Bell 422, 1307

PONTEFRACT, PETER OF. Richard Graves 1524

PORCUPINE, PETER. William Corbett 75, 241, 600 (2), 612, 1463, 1497, 1776, 1778, 2651

POSITIVE, PETER. James Montgomery 2020

P—— P——, POET LAUREAT. George Daniel 2525

P. P., REV., M.A. Richard Graves 897

P. R. Patrick Robertson 1335

P. R. Robert Parsons 2648

PRAGMATICUS MERCURIUS. Marchamont Nedham 107, 1455, 1936

PRESBYTER. George Lewthwaite 2386

PRESBYTER ANGLICANUS. J. H. Harris 200, 2390

PRESBYTER CALVANIANUS. Archibald Bruce 103, 2065

PRESBYTER CATHOLICUS. Rev. William Harness 2774

PRESBYTER CICESTRENSIS. Henry Latham 130

PRESBYTERUS. Robert Hussey 1083

PRIMCOCK, A. James Ralph 2547

PRIOR, J. BUTLER. Thomas H. Ward. 253

PRISCILLA * * * *. Priscilla Wakefield 1341

PRISCILLA PARLANTE. Hon. Mary A. Cavendish Bradshaw 912, 1582

PROBUS BRITANICUS. Samuel Johnson, LL.D. 1549
PROMOTION BY MERIT. William Angus 2057
PROTESTANT, NORTH BRITISH. Archibald Bruce 1240
PSYCALETIIES ESTIBIUS. William Coward, M.D. 2309
P. T. Philip Thickness 1287
PUBLICOLA. D. J. Williams 1442
PUBLICOLA. John Adams, LL.D. 1773
PUBLICOLA. Jonathan Swift, D.D. 1402
PUBLICUS. Caleb Fleming 1642
PUBLICUS SEVERUS. Sir John J. Dillon 1178
PUEDE-SER, DON DIEGO. James Mabbe 855, 2460
PUNJABEE. W. D. Arnold 1763
PURVES, GEORGE, LL.D. Simon Gray 67, 1043
PUSEYITE EX-. Henry N. Oxenham 1897
PUZZLEPATE, JEDEDIAH. John Douglas Giles 2709
P. W. Patrick Walker 2438
P. W. P. Wyborne 368
PYNGLE LAYNE. J. Fox Turner 2365
P——Y, WILLIAM. William Pudsey 495

Q.

Q. E. D. F. von Munch Bellinghausen 1054
Q IN THE CORNER. John Harris Vol iv., 2595
QUADRATUS PILEUS. Stephen Reay 1776
QUAKER. Joseph Wyeth 193
QUARTUS, SCRIBLERUS. Thomas Cooke 217
QUEERFELLOW, QUINTIN. Charles Clark 690
QUEVEDO REDIVIVUS. G. G. Byron, Lord Byron 2771
QUID-PRO-QUO. Charles John Smyth, M.A. 584
QUID. Robert Allan Fitzgerald 1263
QUIET GEORGE. George Frederick Pardon 1296
QUINQUAGENARIUS. Godfrey Fausett, D.D. 915

QUINTIN QUEERFELLOW. Charles Clark 690
QUIZ. Edward Caswall 2405
QUIZ, A WONDERFUL. J. R. Lowell 2081
QUORUM UNUS. William Wadd 1758
Q. Z. Dr Ellison 1668

R.

R. Arthur Blennerhasset Rowan 2462
R. Zachary Pearce 1626 (2)
R A. R. Allot 752
R. A. R. Argall 2448
R. A. R. Aston 1918
R. A. Richard Alleine 226, 1022, 1079, 2768, 2841
R. A. Robert Armin 2720
R. A. Robert Aylet 275
R. A. Robert Aylett 2815
RABBOTEM, ISAAC. Philip de Marnix 220
RAG, TAG, AND BOBTAIL. J. Cameron Lees, D.D. 2221 (2)
RALEIGH, W. Henry St John, Lord Bolingbroke 530
R. ALISTER. Alexander Robertson 213, 222, 866
RAMBAND YOELING. Frédéric Gilbert 1498
RAMSAY, GRACE. Kathleen O'Meara 2255, 2572
RAMUS RANDOLPH. Edward N. Dennys 71
RANDALL, ANNE FRANCIS. Mary Robinson 1419
RANDOLP, FITZ-EUSTACE. W. Fraser 256
RANDOLPH, RAMUS. Edward N. Dennys 71
RANGER, CHARLES. Arthur Murphy 1044
RANGER, ENGLISH CONNAUGHT. Edward Cooper 550
RAVELIN, HUMPHREY. G. Procter 1524
RAWDON, CRAWLEY. George F. Pardon 208, 234 (3), 1060, 1066
RAYMOND, HENRY A. Sarah Scott 1138
R. B. Honble. Robert Boyle 962, 1796
R. B. Richard Baddeley 1471
R. B. Richard Barnfield 1052
R. B. Richard Baxter 1654

R. B. Richard Booker 2260
R. B. Richard Brathwait 1683
R. B. Richard Brathwayt 1500, 2050
R. B. Richard Brome 1311
R. B. Richard Broughton 1651
R. B. Richard Burton 44, 599, 752, 756, 757, 870, 1001, 1144, 1156, 1158, 1166, 2709, 2714, 2722, 2828
R. B. Robert Baily 129
R. B. Robert Barclay 2219
R. B. Robert Baron 1623
R. B. Robert Blackwell 513
R. B. Robert Boreman 523
R. B. Robert Bostock 631
R. B. Robert Bragge 1466
R. B. Robert Brett 615, 711, 1806 (2), 2106, 2574
R. B. Robert Brown 1834
R. B. Robert Burton 2709
R. B. Robert Parsons 143
R. B. G. Robert Baillie 2195
R. B. J. R. B. Jones 2771
R. B. K. Robert Baillie 1858
R. B. M. Robert B. Mansfield 2270
R. B. P. Ralph Buckland 2291
R. B. P. Robert B. Paul 1138
R. C. Ralph Cudworth 2709
R. C. Ralph Cudworth, D.D. 648
R. C. R. Chambers 1815
R. C. Richard Carew 843, 1021
R. C. Richard Cattermole 995
R . . . . . . C . . . . . . Richard Challoner, D.D. 340
R. C. Richard Chamberlaine 1495
R. C. Richard Claridge 118
R. C. Richard Corbet 1955
R. C. Richard Crane 546, 1316
R. C. Richard Crashaw 309
R. C. Robert Calder 1326, 2337
R. C. Robert Carruthers 1139
R. C. Robert Cawdrey 1021
R. C. Robert Chambers 1846
R. C. Robert Clark 1027
R. C. Robert Clavel 1103
R. C. Robert Codrington 2033, 2660
R. C. Robert Colvill 299
R. C. Robert Connold 1757
R. C. Robert Crowley 2270
R. C. Roger Cook 2631
R. C. Roger Cotton 177
R. C. C. Richard Charles Coxe 1604
R. C., D.D. Richard Smith, Bishop of Chalcedon 273
R. C. H. Sir Richard Colt Hoare 1102

R - - - - - C - LD - R. Robert Calder 2474
R. C. M. Robert Cotton Money 1275
R. C. M.A. Robert Calder, M.A. 2009
R. C., SIR. Richard Cocks 2391
R. C., SIR. Sir Robert Cotton 2329
R. D. 876
R. D. Richard Day 249
R. D. Richard Duppa 739
R. D. Robert Davenport 544, 1733, 1937
R. D. Robert Dixon, D.D. 306
R. D. Sir Robert Dallington 276
R. DOLEMAN. Robert Parsons 470
R——D S——LE, SIR. Sir Richard Steele 1395
R. E. C. Rachel E. Cresswell 1597, 2459
REDIVIVUS QUEVEDOS. G. E. Byron, Lord Byron 2771
REDMAN WESTCOT. Adam Littleton 2193
REDNAXELA. Hon. Mrs Cropper 1090
REDNAXELA GNIMELF, A.M. Alexander Fleming, M.A. 2505
R. E. E. W. R. E. E. Warburton 1193
REGINALD DE ST LEON, COUNT. Edward du Bois 2250
REGINALDE WOLFE. Thomas F. Dibdin 1283
R. E. H. GREYSON. Henry Rogers 2319
REKATIHW, DRAWDE. Edward Whitaker 1204
REMEMBRANCER, BRITAIN'S. George Wither 2513
RESEARCH. J. Wood Beilby 2678
RETNYW, WERDNA, M.D. Andrew Wynter, M.D. 1800, 1911
REUBEN PERCY. Joseph Clinton Robinson 1508, 1884
REV. * * * * * * * * * *, M.A. James Pycroft, M.A. 431
R. F. Richard Farnworth 132, 382, 1034, 1078, 1172, 2604, 2822
R. F. Richard Frankum 220
R. F. Robert Ferguson 2411
R. F. BRANCASSINE. Hughes R. P. Fraser Halle 540
R. F., D.D. Roger Fenton, D.D. 2337
R—— F——. Robert Forbes 61
R. F., SIR. Sir Richard Fanshaw 2068
R. G. R. Goodrige 1525
R. G. Richard Gough 285, 555, 1149

R. G. Robert Gould   1525, 1998
R. G. Robert Gardiner   1237 (2), 1238 (2), 1239
R. G. Robert Greene   240, 667, 2292, 2570
R. H. Abraham Woodhead   483, 655, 1057
R. H. R. Heath   1856
R. H. R. Henderson   178
R. H. R. Holden   1057
R. H. Richard Harvey   1198, 1896
R. H. Richard Hawkins   654
R. H. Richard Head   1633, 2046, 2103
R. H. Richard Hubberthorne   2447
R. H. Robert Harrison   1498
R. H. Robert Heron   2251
R. H. Robert Hobson   1057
R. H. Robert Hooke   195
R. H. Robert Howlett   93
R—— H——. Thomas Carte   981
R. H. C. Hon. Robert Henry Clive   695
R. H. D., JR. Richard Henry Dana, Junr.   2702
R. H., M.A., Richard Hollinworth, M.A.   849
R. H. S. R. H. Shepperd   2553
R. H. THE E. OF R. John Wilmot, Earl of Rochester   1951
R. I. Richard Johnson   2166
RICHARD BEWLEY, M.A. R. Harrington, M.D.   2641
RICHARD BURTON. Nathaniel Crouch   2709
RICHARD THIMBLEBY. Richard Ashby   2425
RICHARD WALTER. Benjamin Robins   2782
RICHARDE BRIGHTWELL. John Frith   1917
RICHARDUS INCOGNITUS. Richard Brash   42
RICHWORTH, WILLIAM. Thomas White   623
RIC. RO. Richard Robinson   2667
RICTER WODEN VANDYCK. Andrew Coventry Dick   1759
REDCAP. George Frederick Pardon   873
RIGHT HON. EARL OF HAD-······TON. Earl of Haddington   1951
RIGHT HON. LADY H ****. Lady Hawke   1287
RINGLETUB, JEREMIAH. John Styles, D.D.   1815

RIPON, JOHN SCOTT. John Scott Byerly   244
RIVETAS, ANDREW, JR. Andrew Marvell   1675
R. J.   1233
R. J. Richard Johnson   2166
R. J. L. Richard J. Lane   2475
R. JUNINS. Richard Younge   2320
R. J. WOOLLEN DRAPER. Lieut. J. Mackenzie   2831
R. L. Rev. Roger Lawrence   670
R. L. Robert Lawrie   1021
R. L. Sir Roger L'Estrange   406
R. L., SIR. Sir Roger L'Estrange   618
R. L. WESTLAND. Robert W. Lowe   2810
R. M. Professor Robert Manning   2216
R. M. Ralph Maddison   751
R. M. Richard Mayhew   1943
R. M. R. Manerick   2252
R. M. R. Monsey   2262
R. M. Robert Morris   1380
R. ******, MARIA. Maria Riddell   2784
R. M., D.D. R. Mosson, D.D.   1931
R. N. Richard Niccols   986, 2392
R. O. Richard Overton   1543
ROBERT BRAZEN, F.N.S. Colin Maclaurin   1947
ROBERT BURTON. Nathaniel Crouch   2709
ROBERT HALL, GENT. Peter Heylin   1083
ROBERT HALSTEAD. Henry, Earl of Peterborough   2512
ROBERT HERON. John Pinkerton   1441
ROBERT SCOTT. James Robins   1135
ROBERT SEYMOUR. John Motley   29, 2528
ROBERT TURNER COTTON. Mortimer Collins   1672
ROBERT WARNEFORD, LIEUT., R.N. W. H. C. Russell   1272, 1895, 2240, 2397, 2542, 2544
ROBERTS, CAPTAIN. Augustus Charles Hobart, R.N.   1710
POB POI. John Macgregor   1020
ROCHESTER, MARK. William C. M. Kent   603
ROCK, CAPTAIN. Roger O'Connor   1451
ROCKINGHAM, SIR CHARLES. Count de Jarnac   346
ROCKWOOD. Thomas Dykes   2497

RODOLPHUS. Charles Croke   945
ROGER WIDDRINGTON. Roger
    Preston   1736, 2221
ROGER WIDDRINGTON. Thomas
    Preston   1736 (2), 2221
ROLAND GILDEROY. Charles
    Rowley   1910
RO., RIC. Richard Robinson   2667
RORY M'RORY, REV. J. Cameron
    Lees, D.D.   1531
ROSA. Rosa Raine   2064
ROSALIND. Rosalind Davis   993
ROSA MATILDA. Mrs Byrne   1181
ROSKELYNSIS, PHILO. Robert
    Forbes, D.D., Bishop of Caithness 17
POI, POB. John Macgregor   1020
R. P.   927
R. P. Richard Peers   1947
R. P. Richard Perrinchief   2533
R. P. Richard Polwhele   783
R. P. Robert Paltock   1464
R. P. Robert Pricket   1174, 1266
R. P. Robert Pultock   1464
R. P. W. Robert Plumer Ward   1206
R. R. Richard Robinson   199, 240
R. R. Robert Rogers, B.D.   2169
R. R. William Rowley   1605
R. S. Richard Sault   256
R. S. Richard Sheldon   349
R. S. Richard Smith, Bishop of
    Chalcedon   202
R. S. Richard Stanwix, B.D.   1171
R. S. Robert Paltock   1464
R. S. Robert Pultock   1464
R. S. Robert Sempill   1908
R. S. Robert Southwell   1649, 2659
R. S. R. Skinner   388
R. S. R. Stanyhurst   1905
R. S. R. Stapylton   1905
R. S., D.D. Robert Scott, D.D.
                            986, 2338
R. S. H. Robert S. Hunt   1683
R. S. H. Robert Stephen Hawker   2776
R—— S——, SIR. Sir Robert
    Sibbald   1357
R. S. S. J. Richard Strange   1468
R. T. Rebekah Travers   1606
R. T. Richard Tuke   2457
R. T. Robert Tofte   61, 1323, 1829,
                                   2701
R. T. Sir Peter Pett   642
R. THOM. Edward Mayhew   2637
RUDDIMAN, THOMAS, M.A.
    Roger Robertson   1243

RUEBEN PERCY. Thomas
    Byerley   1508, 1884
RURAL D.D. David Esdaile, D.D.   504
RUSTICUS. Edward Newman   1442
RUSTICUS. Frederick Denison
    Maurice, B.A.   2511
RUSTICUS, MERCURIUS.
    Thomas Frognall Dibdin   231
RUSTICANS, PHILALETHES.
    Richard Shepherd, D.D.   2109
RUSTICUS, PHILALETHES.
    William Asplin   1214
RUTH BUCK. Mrs Joseph Lamb
                    1183, 1262, 1939, 2652
RUTH ELLIOTT. Lillie Peck   2776
R. V. Richard Verstegan   622
R. V. Robert Veel   1717
R. V. Robert Verstegan   2342
R—V—D D— T—. William Thom,
    M.A.   1067
R. W. Isaak Walton   1517
R. W. Richard West   348
R. W. Robert Ware   1971
R. W. Robert Whitchall
                        762, 1550, 2549
R. W. Robert Wright   1187
R. W. Robert Wright, D.D.   2098
R. W. R. Wharton   369
R. W. R. Whithall   2600
R. W., B.D. Richard White   404
R. W., D.D. Robert Wilde, D.D.   1816
R. W. D. P. R. Wetham   1731
R. W. S. R. W. Smiles   2788
R. W. S. W. Reginald W. Sackville-
    West   1119
RYHEN PAMEACH. Henry
    Peachman, M.A.   619
RYRIE BJOLLA PADRING.
    P. V. Fitz Patrick   2557

                    S.

S. John Skelton   2557
SADDI, NATHAN BEN. Robert
    Dodsley   390, 2292
SAILOR, THE OLD. Matthew
    Henry Barker, R.N.   1262, 1316, 1478
                        2607, 2610, 2790
ST GEORGE, GEORGE. Joseph
    Snowe   2260
SAINT-JOHN, THEOPHILUS.
    Rev. Samuel Clapham, M.A. 364, 1986
ST LEON, COUNT REGINALD
    DE. Edward du Bois   2250

SALEM, AHAB. Rev. James Murray   1724
SALLE, JOH. DE LA. John Hall   1856
SALOPIENSIS. Job Orton   634
SAMUEL A. BARD. Ephraim G. Squier   51
SAMUEL PARKER. Charles Leslie   836
SANCTA CLARA, FRANCIS A. Francis Davenport   862, 2187
SANDEMANIAN. —— Pike   2051
SAND, GEORGE. Armadine L. A. Dudevant   443, 497, 521, 1431, 1560, 1616, 1664, 2386, 2614
SA. OXON. S. Parker, Bp. of Oxford   2089
SARAH TYTLER. Henrietta Keddie   294, 406, 566, 624, 993, 1014, 1090, 1186, 1317, 1642, 1683, 1747, 1812, 1816, 1851, 2273 (2), 2392, 2453, 2518, 2805
SARESBURY, LORD BISHOP OF. J. Jewel D. Whear   155
SARUM, GREGORY MISO. Jonathan Swift, D.D.   1993
SATIRICUS SCULPTOR. William H. Ireland   354
SAVONAROLA, DON JEREMY. Francis S. Mahony   874
S. B.   Francis Willis and others   80
S. B.   Samuel Barker   1627
S. B.   Samuel Bold   845, 1401, 2296
S. B.   Samuel Bolde   845
S. B.   S. Bredwell   2079
S. C.   Mrs Croft   1033 (2)
S. C.   Sabin Chambers   993
S. C.   Samuel Carter   1324, 1456, 2181
S. C.   Samuel Clarke   750
S. C.   Samuel Colliber   1210
S. C.   Samuel Colvil   1636, 2273
S. C.   Samuel Croxall   2316
S. C.   Hugh Paulin de Cressy   427, 779, 893, 2222
SC., AN. Anthony Scoloker   625
SCARABÆUS. D. Badham, M.D.   2069
SCHLEIERMACHER, DR. Frederick C. Thirlwall, D.D.   537
S. C. L.   S. C. Lampreys   266
SCOTO - BRITANNICO. Miss Webster   1476
SCOTO - BRITANNUS. Thomas M'Crie, D.D.   964
SCOTO-BRITANNUS, CALVINUS MINOR. Archibald Bruce   965

SCOTT, HONORIA. Mrs Frazer   1819
SCOTTISH PHILHELLEN. Edward Mason   1897
SCOTT, LEADER. Lucy Baxter   2168
SCOTT, ROBERT. James Robins   1135
SCOTUS. John Gibson   2304, 2507
SCOTUS. Samuel Raleigh   2117
SCOTUS, J. C. James Cunningham   1621
SCOTUS, PHILO. Philip B. Ainslie   2166
S. C., REV. FATHER. Serenus Cressy   929
SCRIBE, SIMON. Adam Black   1562
SCRIBBLE, TIMOTHY. A. Cowper   1749
SCRIBLERUS, FAUSTINUS.   2073
SCRIBLERUS, MARTINUS Rev. Robert Morehead   862
SCRIBLERUS, MAXIMUS. James Love   533
SCRIBLERUS QUARTUS. Thomas Cooke   217
SCRIBLERUS SECUNDUS. Henry Fielding   204, 1008, 1422
SCRUB, TIMOTHY. John Kelly   884
SCRUTATOR. Charles Jerram, A.M.   1451
SCRUTATOR. Charles Pennell Measor   1252
SCRUTATOR. Charles Rivington   2505
SCRUTATOR. K. W. Horlock   1093 1180, 1448, 1512, 1557, 1985, 2099, 2271, 2481
SCRUTATOR. Rev. John O'Hanlon, M.R.I.A.   1252
SCULPTOR, SATIRICUS. William Henry Ireland   354
S. D.   —— Danforth   191
S. D.   Samuel Downes   6
S. D.   Samuel Lee, M.A.   721
S. D.   S. Drake   416
S. D., J. L.   S. Drake, J. Lake   416, 2840
S. E.   Giles Duncombe   2684
S. E.   Sampson Ever   690
S. E.   Stephen Egerton   1987
SEAFIELD, FRANK, M.A. Alexander H. Grant, M.A.   1495
SEARCH, CHRISTIAN, LL.D. Sir W. C. Smith, Bart.   1607
SEARCH, EDWARD. Abraham Tucker   966, 1486
SEARCH, JOHN. Rev. Thomas Binney   484, 1047, 2129
SEARCH, WARNER CHRISTIAN. Sir Wm. C. Smith, Bart.   104

SEARLE, JANUARY. George Philips 357, 524, 1335, 1470, 1580, 1591

S. E. B. Sir Samuel Egerton Brydges 1589, 1795, 1944, 2391

SECONDSIGHT, SOLOMON. T. B. Greaves 1239

SECUNDUS, AMICUS. Rev. William A. Thomson, D.D. 272, 2090

SECUNDUS, ATTICUS. John M'Diarmid 1432

SECUNDUS, JUNIUS. Charles Kelsall 494

SECUNDUS, SCRIBLERUS. Henry Fielding 204, 1008, 1422

SEEDAIR, STEPHEN. Phineas Seedair 2615

SEGDIRBOEG. George Bridges 1421

SELKIRK, J. B. James Brown 1944

SENEX. Edward Rowland 2051

SENILIS. John Nelson 1915

SENIOR. John Penrose, M.A. 888

SEN MUSCIPULA. John Collier 552

SEPTENTRIONALIS CLERICUS. J. Richardson 2137

SERGEANT, B. Robert Butler 1697

SERGEANT-MAJOR, P. F. Payne Fisher 1950, 2606

SERLE, JANUARY. George Philips 357

SEVERUS, PUBLICUS. Sir John J. Dillon 1178

SEYMAR, WILLIAM. William Ramsey 478

SEYMOUR, ROBERT. John Motley 29, 2528

SEYMOUR, W. Cuthbert Shaw 1804

S. F., M.A. Samuel Felgate 1757

S. F., MRS. Sarah Field née Fyge 1951

S. G. Samuel Grascome 352, 1106, 2267

S. G. S. Groome 1016

S. G. Symon Gunton 1831

S. G. O. Lord Sidney G. Osborne 1447

S. H. James Tidmarsh 1700

S. H. Samuel Harsnett 574, 664

S. H. Samuel Holden 557

S. H. S. Hayes, M.R.I.A. 1986

S. H. S. Hinde 1258

S. H. S. Hynde 1258

S. H. A. B. E C. EN. Samuel Harding 2381

SHAVER, THE. John Macgowan 2008, 2333

SHEKARRY, THE OLD. H. A. Leverson 748, 941, 1193

SHEMAYA, EBN. David Parkes 2483

SHEPHERD, ETTRICK. James Hogg 2064

S. H. F. Sarah H. Fox 1952

SHIRLEY. John Skelton 303, 1758

SHOLTO PERCY. Joseph C. Robertson 1884

SHOLTO PERCY. Thomas Byerley 1508

S. H., SENIOR. Rev. Samuel Hunton 1103

SIDNEY DARYL. Douglas Straight 1072, 2231

SIGMA. J. B. Shaw 2454

SIGMA. Samuel Newington 513 (2), 1725, 2028, 2565

SIL AWL. Ralph Wallis 1662

SILENT, LONG. Thomas T. Lynch 833, 2450

SILLY BILLY. Eustace C. Grenville Murray 2501

SILVANUS URBAN. John Nichols 2231

SILVERCLOUD. G. S. Brown 2509

SILVER PEN. Eliza Meteyard 599, 1497

SILVERTONGUE, GABRIEL. James Montgomery 2808

SILVESTER OTWAY. John Oswald 835, 1953

SILVIA. Countess of Berkeley 1519

SIMEON SOUTH. J. M'Gregor 2386

SIMEON BAXTER. Rev. Samuel Peters 2704

SIMON GRAY. Sir Alexander Boswell, Bart. 725

SIMON SCRIBE. Adam Black 1562

SIMON WAGSTAFF. Jonathan Swift 456

SIMPLEX. John Young 1228

SIRRAHNIO. John Harris 2236

S. I. S. Sir James Sempill 1908

SISTER ANNE. 1518

S. J. Stephen Jay 563

SKETCHLEY, ARTHUR. George Rose 1634, 1675 (5), 1676 (11), 1677 (3), 1835

SKILLETT, JOSEPH. Lord John Russell 824

S. L. Stephen Lobb 1056

S——LE, R——D, SIR. Sir Richard Steele 1395

S. L. ΚΟΣΜΟΠΟΛΙΤΕΣ. S. Lusignan 1165

SLOTH. Robert Thom   790
S. M. Menella Bute Smedley 1332, 1536, 1742, 2718
S. M. Selina Martin   2403
S. M. Shackerley Marmion   548
SMALLSHOT, JASPER. Major Ware   2481
S M E C T Y M N U U S. Edmund Calamy   106, 2749
SMECTYMNUUS. Matthew Newcomen   106, 2749
SMECTYMNUUS. Stephen Marshall   106, 2749
SMECTYMNUUS. Thomas Young   106, 2749
SMECTYMNUUS. William Spurstowe   106, 2749
S. M. H. S. M. Heaton   2581
SMITH, ALEXANDER. Sydney Dobell   2454
SMITH, GAMALIEL. Jeremy Bentham   1751
SMITH, J. Charles Baring   1448
SMITH, JOHN. John D. Lewis   2402
SMITH, JOHN. John Sergeant   1688
SMITH, THE, OF SMITHEDEN. Daniel M'Ivor   2787
S., MR., MR OF ART. John Still, M.A.   2243
SMYTH, PEREGRINE. William King, LL.D.   1299
S. N. Samuel Newman   467
S. N. Thomas Elrington   1232
S. N. Thomas Vaughan   199
S. N. Sylvester Norris, D.D.   135, 163, 1057
SNARLY CHARLEY. Charles Clark   901
S——N, A——W. Andrew Stevenson   1409, 2790
S. O. Sydney Owenson, Lady S. Morgan   2250
. S. O. Thomas Scot   2813
SOAME, SIR HENRY F. R. Sir H. E. Bunbury   1959
SOCRATES, CHRISTIANUS. Edward Stephens or Stevens 158, 1216
SOLOMON ABRABANEL. William Arnall   451
SOLOMON GRILDRIG. Dr Rennell, &c.   1617
SOLOMON SECONDSIGHT. T. B. Greaves   1239
SOMEBODY. William Donaldson   1464

SOPHRON. W. Cunninghame   624
SOUTH, SIMEON. J. M'Gregor   2386
SOUTH, THEOPHILUS. Edward Chitty   1204
S. P. Samuel Page   63
S. P. Samuel Parker   318
S. P. Samuel Pepys   1977
S. P. Samuel Pick   913
S. P. Samuel Pordage   1953
S. P. S. Pennington   1445
S. P. A. M. Jonathan Swift, D.D.   739
SPARKS, TIMOTHY. Charles Dickens   2519
S. P. ARMIG. Samuel Pordage   1678
SP., ED. Edmund Spenser 452, 1678, 2039, 2548
SPLENE, MEGATHYM, B.A., OXON. Cockburn Thomson   69
SPUR, MERCURIUS. Cuthbert Shaw   2073
S. R. Richard Smith   126
S. R. Samuel Rid   182, 1052
S. R. Samuel Rosewell   471
S. R. Samuel Rowlands 227, 373, 527, 533, 601, 688, 1028, 1052, 1082, 1307, 1454, 1552, 1567, 1609, 1661, 1740, 2811
S. R. Samuel Rowley   1747
S. R. Sarah Renou   2738
S. R. Simon Robson   373
S. R. N. I. Thomas Scot   2778, 2779
S. R. W. Sarah R. Whitehead   2228
——S ——S. Charles Lucas   964
S. S. Samuel Shaw   2776
S. S. Samuel Sheppard   2305
S. S. Samuel Starling   126
S. S. Sarah Sheppard   362, 1206
S. S. Thomas Rogers   443
S. S., M.A. Samuel Smith   360
S. T. Samuel Thomas   2152
S. T. Samuel Timmins   1513
S. T. S. Tucker   2458
S. T. Thomas Stonna   2163
S. T. William Fleetwood, D.D.   1406
STALBRYDGE, HENRY. John Bale   779
STAWEL, AUGUSTUS. Alfred O. Legge   1543
S——T, DR. Jonathan Swift, D.D. 243, 251, 296, 1186, 1458, 2036, 2259, 2743
STEADY. Allan Ramsay   1380
STELLA. Estella A. Lewis   2258

STEPHEN COLLET, M.A. John
S. Byerley   2128
STEPHEN OLIVER. W. A.
Chatto   1810, 2076, 2263
STEPHEN SEEDAIR. Phineas
Deseret   2615
STONECASTLE, HENRY. John
Kelly   2712
STONEHENGE. John Henry
Walsh   194, 285, 695, 696, 1053, 1544,
                          2209, 2380
STRADLING, MATHEW. M. F.
Mahony   1251
STRETTON, HESBA. Sarah Smith
416, 533, 565, 689, 875, 973, 1094, 1218,
1306, 1515, 1539, 1611, 1740, 1744,
1814, 1876, 2497, 2573, 2690, 2828,
                               2843
ST——PE, W——M. Sir William
Stanhope   1828
S * * * T, REV. DR. Jonathan
Swift, D.D.   1141, 1313
SUMMERLEY, FELIX. Henry
Cole   1063 (2)
SUNAVILL, J. F. J. F. Sullivan
                         1020, 1319
S. W. John Sergeant   2266
S. W. Rev. Stephen Weston 1989, 2524
S. W. S. Walker   694
SWAMMERDAM, GRIBALDUS.
W. Mudford   1463
SWANSEA, ANN OF. Frances
Ann Kemble   303, 354, 391, 509, 577
1011, 1059, 1520, 2311, 2314, 2706,
                               2826
S. W. E. S. W. Evitt   1838
SW—FT, DR. Jonathan Swift, D.D. 243
SWIFT, DEAN. Benson Earle
Hill   1915
S. W. M. K. Sir William Moore, or
Mure   300
SW—T, DR. Jonathan Swift, D.D.
                         1458, 2259
SYDNEY YENDYS. Sydney
Dobell   2222
SYLVANUS, THEOPHRASTUS.
J. Thelwall   1886
SYLVATICUS. J. F. Pennie   2538
SYLVESTER, C. Lady Wood   2229
SYLVESTER, OTWAY. John
Oswald   835, 1953
SZE, ZADKIEL, TAO. Richard J.
Morrison, R.N.   1064

T.

T. A. Thomas Acheley   1557, 1667
T. A. Thomas Aiton   1826
T. A. Thomas Aldridge   2008
T. A. Thomas Allen, M.D.   368
T. A. Thomas Ashe   310, 1325
T. A., CAPT. LIGHT DRAGOONS.
Capt. Thomas Ashe   1149
TAIL, REV. DR. William Thom 2743
TALVI. Therese Albertina Louisa
Robinson   1123, 2545
TALVI. Thérèse A. L. von Jakob
                         1123, 2545
TAMOC CASPIPINA. Jacob
Duché   326
TAVALTTBOB. —— Graham   625
TAO SZE, ZADKIEL. Richard J.
Morrison, R.N.   1064
TARKARI. Peter Reid   2817
TAYLOR, THEODORE. John C.
Hotten   1026, 2557
TAYLOUR, CHARLES. Henry
Keepe   2664
T. B.   246
T. B. Anthony Brewer   521
T. B. James Shirley   1520
T. B. John Eachard, D.D. 1055, 2432
T. B. Sir Henry Janson   1896
T. B. T. Barker   80
T. B. Thomas Bayly, D.D.   2233
T. B. Thomas Bellamy   1896
T. B. Thomas Beverley   157
T. B. Thomas Boosey   1916
T. B. Thomas Blount   98, 1020, 2343,
                               2345
T. B. Thomas Bowes   1586, 967
T. B. Thomas Bradbury   1678
T. B. Thomas Branch   2015
T. B. Thomas Brett, LL.D. 1048, 1364
T. B. Thomas Brightwell   1275
T. B. Thomas Browne   2233
T. B. Timothy Batt   2794
T. B. Timothy Bright   2648
T. B. Timothy Brown   2680
T. BOBBIN. John Collier   2734
T. C. Christopher Gent   1937
T. C. Sir Thomas Culpepper   1659
T. C. T. Clapham   2336
T. C. T. Corbett   19
T. C. Theophilus Cibber   1871
T. C. Thomas Cartwright   2178
T. C. Thomas Carwell alias Thor-
wold   1311

T. C. Thomas Churchyard
                    2063, 2212, 2667
T. C. Thomas Clarke 1973
T. C. Thomas Crane 2039
T. C. Thomas Crawfurd 1752
T. C. D. John Wilson Croker 887
T. C., D.D. Thomas Comber, D.D. 395
T. CLARK, REV. John Galt 2626, 2787
T. C. TRAUELLER. Sir J. Harrington 84
T. D. Rev. Theophilus Dorrington 2120
T. D. Robert Davenport 241
T. D. T. Dawson 159
T. D. Theophilus Dorrington 852
T. D. Thomas Barker 241
T. D. Thomas Davenport 268
T. D. Thomas Decker 304, 1264
T. D. Thomas De Laune 1207
T. D. Thomas Deloney 304, 993, 1004, 1937, 1938, 2233, 2572
T. D. Thomas Doolittle or Doolitel 907, 2044, 2097
T. D. Thomas Duffet 2053
T. D. Thomas Durfey 431, 931, 2028
T. DE MONMOUTH. Thomas Powell 724
T. E. Anthony Ashley Cooper, Earl of Shaftesbury 1353
T. E. Robert Boyle 2421
T. E. Thomas Edgar 2690
T. E. Thomas Edwards 959
T. E. Thomas Ellwood 20
T. E. Thomas Emes 618
T. E. Thomas Erskine 1014
TELA, JOSEPHUS. Jos. Webb 1902
TELBA. William Ablett 2218, 2493
TEMPLE, LANCELOT. John Armstrong 2373
TEMPLE, LAUNCELOT. John Armstrong, M.D. 2405
TEMPLE, NEVILLE. Hon. J. C. H. Fane 2545
TERRAE FILIUS. Robert E. Garnham 1417
TERRAE FILIUS. Stephen Weston 2802
TER. TISANTHROPE. W. H. Gillespie 1826
T. F. T. Forster 1070
T. F. Thady Fitzpatrick 772
T. F. Thomas Fitzherbert 586, 2523
T. F. Thomas Flatman 1849
T. F. Thomas Ford 460, 2166, 2771
T. F. T. Forde 1526
T. F. Thomas Fuller 1273

T. F. Thomas Fuller, B.D. 437
T. F. Thomas Fuller, D.D. 776
T. F. D. T. F. Dibdin 271
T. F. S. T. F. Salter 1102
T. F., SR. Sir Thomas Fanshaw 1987
T. G. David Dakers Black 2656
T. G. Theophilus Gale 2670
T. G. Thomas Gainsford 1018
T. G. Thomas Godden or Godwin 340
T. G. T. Gripps, E.A.P. 2552
T. G. Thomas Gwin 2426
T. G., M.A. Thomas Goffe 309
T. G. C. T. G. Carroll 412
T. H. Capt. Edward Johnson 1144
T. H. Thomas Hewerdine, M.A. 521
T. H. Thomas Heywood 1003, 1550, 1898, 2667
T. H. Thomas Hicks 456, 617
T. H. Thomas Hodges 2635
T. H. Thomas Hooker 387, 951, 1871, 2456, 2457 (2), 2705
T. H. Thomas Howell 871
Θ 4 1000 I S A'10 2. Arise Evans 1303
THALES. Rev. H. Simonds 624
T. H. C. Chauncey Hare Townshend 609
THEATRICUS, ANTI-. Thady Fitzpatrick 772
THEMANINTHEMOON. Rev. John Eagles 908
THEODIDACTUS, EUGENIUS. John Heydon 2033
THEODORE BASILLE. Thomas Becon 387, 565, 1024, 1738, 1871, 1939, 1980, 2211, 2667
THEODORE DE LA GUARD. Rev. N. Ward 2387
THEODORE DE LA GUARDEN. Nathaniel Ward 1600
THEODORE TAYLOR. John C. Hotten 1026, 2557
THEODORUS PARRHASI. John Le Clerc 1863
THEODORUS VERAX. Clement Walker 83
THEODOSIA. Anne Steel 1951
THEODOSIUS. Rev. W. Marsh 624
THEO GIFT. Dora Havers 1535, 1559, 2007, 2773
THEOLOGUS TYRO-, A.M. —— Stone 2358
THEOPHANES CANTABRIGIENSIS. Samuel Squire, D.D., Bishop of St David's 88

THEOPHILANTHROPIST. William R. Peck   662
THEOPHILUS. Caleb Fleming, D.D.   965, 2563
THEOPHILUS. Patrick Duigenan, LL.D.   40
THEOPHILUS. Rev. J. H. Stewart   624
THEOPHILUS CHRISTIAN. John Owen, M.A.   901
THEOPHILUS CHURCHMAN. H. Hickman   2198
THEOPHILUS CHURCHMAN. Peter Heylin, D.D.   1124, 2198
THEOPHILUS EUPISTINUS. —— Prichard   2149
THEOPHILUS FREEMAN. William Matthews   999
THEOPHILUS INSULANUS. —— M'Leod   2646
THEOPHILUS MARCLIFFE. William Godwin   1509
THEOPHILUS PHILADELPHUS. John Ley   853
THEOPHILUS PHILANTHRO-PUS. David Hall   798
THEOPHILUS PHILANTHRO-POS. Robert Poole, M.D.   1907
THEOPHILUS PHILOBASILEUS. Thomas Pierce, D.D.   2033
THEOPHILUS PHILO-KURIACES LONCARDIENSIS. Thomas Young   1514
THEOPHILUS PHILOPARRIUS. Thomas Paget   2132
THEOPHILUS, SAINT JOHN. Rev. Samuel Clapham   364
THEOPHILUS, ST JOHN, LL.D. Samuel Clapham, M.A.   1986
THEOPHILUS SOUTH. Edward Chitty   1204
THEOPHRASTUS, SYLVANUS. J. Thelwall   1886
THEOPH. VERAX. Clement Walker   2127
THERAPEUTES. David Brodie   1077
THETA. Julia Hyde   2517
THETA. William Thorn   2572
THIMBLEBY, RICHARD. Richard Ashby   2425
THINE ANONYM. MUSOPHIL. Daniel Tuvill   2719
THINKS-I-TO-MYSELF. Edward Nares   1201

THINKS-I-TO-MYSELF, WHO? Edward Nares   2566
THO. FÆNILIGNUM. Thomas Heywood   1898
THOMAS BELLAMY. Sir Henry Janson   1896
THOMAS BROWN. Thomas Moore 872, 976 (2), 1239, 2169, 2207 (2), 2536, 2841
THOMAS BULL. William Jones   1818 (2)
THOMAS CARRE. Miles Pinckney   2530
THOMAS CLERK. Thomas Hartwell Horne   2841
THOMAS CLAYTON. Peter Motteux   180
THOMAS DUFFLE. John Galt   2492
THOMAS FIELDING. John Wade   2318
THOMAS FITZOSBORNE, SIR, BART. W. Melmoth   1446
THOMAS HENRY. Henry Ride   2789
THOMAS HAYWARD. W. Oldys   284
THOMAS INGOLDSBY. R. H. Barham, B.A.   1224, 1259
THOMAS LITTLE. Thomas Moore   1959
THOMAS PITTS. John Tutchin   1725
THOMAS RUDDIMAN, M.A. Roger Robertson   1243
THOMAS, TOBYAS. Thomas Brown   1481
THOMAS WHITE, JUN. T. S. Omond   1948
THOM, R. Edward Mayhew   2637
THO. NARJENN. Thomas Tanner   2412
THO. PHILLIPS. William Drake   1509
THORNE, KATE. Miss Gray   1710
THORNY AILO. John Taylor   978
T. H. R. B. Hon. Robert Boyle   384
T. H. R. B. E. The Right Hon. Robert Boyle   852
T—— H——, SIR, BART. Sir T. Hanmore   2590
T. H., SR. Sir Thomas Hawkins   1170, 2261
ΘΤΟΣΜΑΘΟΣ. Thomas South   716
THURSTAN, HENRY J. F. T. Palgrave   1868
TH. W. Thomas Wright   1868
TI. John Taylor   150
TIM BOBBIN. John Collier 1316, 1630, 1940, 2593, 2734

TIM BOBBIN, THE SECOND.
Robert Walker   1940
TIMON. Thomas Burnet   2665
TIMOTHEUS PIKROMEL.
Thomas Clarke   789
TIMOTHY GOOSEQUILL 2096, 2187
TIMOTHY, PLAIN. G. W.
Blaikie   924
TIMOTHY SCRIBBLE. A.
Cowper   1749
TIMOTHY SCRUB. John Kelly   884
TIMOTHY SPARKS. Charles
Dickens   2519
TIMOTHY TITCOMBE. J. G.
Holland   vol. iv. 2595
TIMOTHY TOUCH'EM. Thomas
Beck   57
TIMOTHY TOUCHSTONE.
—— Oliphant, &c.   2654
TIMOTHY TWIG. Alexander
Campbell   1059
TINCLARIAN, DOCTOR. Dr
Mitchell   2290
TINDALION, ANTI-. Robert
Lyon   1409
TINTO, GABRIEL. G. W. Anthony   2821
TISANTHROPE, TER. W. H.
Gillespie   1826
TITCOMBE, TIMOTHY. J. G.
Holland   vol. iv. 2595
TITMARSH, MICHAEL ANGELO.
William Makepeace Thackeray
435, 687, 1252, 1300, 1677, 1835, 1860, 2296
T. J. Thomas Jolly   2765
T. J. Thomas Jordan   372
T. K. A. Rev. Thomas K. Arnold   1323
T. K. Thomas Kerr, D.D., Bishop
of Bath and Wells   2234
T. K. Thomas Keyworth   2014
T. K. T. Knight   846
T. L. Thomas Lawrence, M.A.   652
T. L. Thomas Lawson   160
T. L. Thomas Letchworth   1664
T. L. Thomas Lewis   1648
T. L. Thomas Lewis, M.A.   761
T. L. Thomas Lodge 337, 682, 922, 1467, 2227
T. L. - - - -. Thomas Lodge, M.D.   835
T. L' W. Th. le Wright   1660
T. M. Christopher Merrett, M.D.   1345
T. M. Clement Walker   1139
T. M. Theodore Martin   2223

T. M. Thomas Mall, M.A.   418
T. M. Thomas Man   2100
T. M. Thomas Manby   2377
T. M. Thomas Markby   2690
T. M. Thomas Meriton   2788
T. M. Thomas Merriott   1039
T. M. Thomas May   2619, 2811
T. M. Thomas Middleton 130, 1125, 1541, 2653
T. M. Thomas Moffat, M.D.   2385
T. M. Thomas Moore   1959
T. M. Thomas Morton, Bishop of
Durham   842
T. M. Thomas Moubray   334
T. M. Thomas Mouffett, M.D.   2385
T. M. Thomas Muffett, M.D.   2385
T. M. Thomas Mun   656
T. MERCHANT. Thomas Dibdin   1531
T. M., SIR. Tobie Mathews, Kt.   1882
T. N. Thomas Norton   1235
T. N. PHILOMATH. Jonathan
Swift, D.D.   892
T. O. Titus Oates   614
TOBY. Jonathan Swift, D.D.   360
TOBY. —— Wagstaffe   360
TOBYAS THOMAS. Thomas
Browne   1481
T. O. D. Titus Oates   618
TOMKINS, ISAAC. Lord Brougham   2583, 2797
TOM-TIT, EBENEZER. Charles
Smith   1343
TOM TYPE   2096
TORFOOT, LAIRD OF. Thomas
Brownlee   1695
TOSSOFFACAN, ASDRYAS-
DUST. Edmund Gayton   2822
TOUCH'EM, TIMOTHY. Thomas
Beck   57
TOUCHSTONE, TIMOTHY.
—— Oliphant, &c.   2654
TOWN, MR. Bonnel Thornton   478
TOWN, MR. George Colman   478
T. P. Thomas Palfreyman   2635
T. P. Thomas Parson   384
T. P. Thomas Porter   967
T. P. Thomas Procter   1032, 1308
T. P. Vincent Alsop   1632
T. P——, A.M. Thomas Pye, A.M.   2823
T. P. A. P. O. A. B. I. T. C. O. S.
Arthur Ashley Sykes, D.D. 769, 2693
T. P. S. C. T. Thomas Phillips   2509
T. R.   404
T. R. Thomas Randolph   79, 1681

T. R.   Thomas Ravenscroft   1567
T. R.   Thomas Reeve, M.D.   550
T. R.   T. Rud   1626, 1627 (3), 1628
T. R.   Thomas Rudyard   79
TRAFFORD, F. G.   J. H. Riddell
     1011, 1561, 1656, 1896. 2841
TRAGICUS, PHILO-.   Thady Fitz-
   patrick   772
T. R. A. M.   Thomas Rogers   1526
TRAUELLER, T. C.   Sir J.
   Harrington   84
T. R. B.   Thomas Squire Barrett   848
T. R. B. M.   Thomas Ravenscroft   1567
T. R. D. J. S. D. O. P. I. I.   Rev. Dr
   Jonathan Swift   1629
TREGENNA, JAMES HAMLEY.
   R. B. Paul, M.A.   204
TRELEINIE, PH.   Peter Heylin   2707
TREPIDANTIUM   MALLEUS.
   Samuel Young   147, 473, 953, 972, 2182,
     2296, 2409. 2817
TREVOR, EDWARD.   E. R.
   Bulwer Lytton   2546
TRINITY-MAN.   —— Wright   69
TROIS-ETOILES.   Eustace C. G.
   Murray   1568
TROTT, JOHN.   Henry St. John,
   Lord Bolingbroke   1377
TROVATO, BEN.   Samuel Lover   2217
TRUEMAN.   William Paine   2299
TRUMAN.   John Farwell   1385
TRUSTA, H.   E. S. Phelps   2519
T. S.   Thomas Burgess, D.D., Bishop
   of Salisbury   857
T. S.   Thomas Comber   852
T. S.   Thomas Scot   2781
T. S.   Thomas Scott   949
T. S.   T. Sherman   2852
T. S.   Thomas Shadwell   477
T. S.   Thomas Shillitoe   7
T. S.   Thomas Stanley   201
T. S.   Thomas Story   2601
T. S.   Thomas Streatfield   1812
T. ST. D.   Thomas Burgess, D.D.   1080
T. S. M.   Thomas S. Muir   609, 1754, 2076
T * * * * S N * * * * * * M.   Thomas
   Newenham   891
T. S. OF V.   Thomas Scot   2308
T—— S——Y.   Richard Finch   477, 579,
     1407, 2301
T. T.   Gilbert Burnet, D.D.   116
T. T.   Thomas Taylor   1678
T. T.   Thomas Tuke   640
T. T.   Thomas Tully   1422

T. T.   T. Tymme   604
T. T. T.   Thomas Henry Sealy   1976
TURBERVILL, HODG.   Edmund
   Gayton   2784
T. V.   Thomas Vincent   1023
T. V., B. OF. D.   T. Vicars   190
T. V. F.   Thomas V. Fosbery, M.A.   1196
T. W.   1291
T. W.   George Saville, Marquis of
   Halifax   1366
T. W.   Thomas Walkington, M.A.
     1821, 2562
T. W.   Thomas Walkley   331, 332
T. W.   Thomas Wall, M.A.   1023
T. W.   Thomas Ward   789, 2435
T. W.   Thomas Waring   269
T. W.   T. Watkins   2535
T. W.   Thomas Watts, M.A.   2286
T. W.   Thomas Weaver   1932, 2449
T. W.   Thomas Wennel   162
T. W.   Thomas Whichcot   1932
T. W.   Thomas Wilcocks   1016, 2379,
     2517, 2728
T. W.   T. Whinnel   226
T. W.   T. White,   vol. iii. 2595
T. W.   Thomas Wood   618, 671
T. W.   T. Woodford   2633
TWAIN, MARK.   Samuel Lang-
   horne Clemens   74, 551, 986, 1014,
   1224, 1226 (2), 1548 (2), 1727, 1985,
     2230
TWIG, TIMOTHY.   Alexander
   Campbell   1059
TWINROCK ELMLICHT.   T. P.
   Mitchell   2562
T. W. P.   Thomas Worthington   2813
T. W., SR.   Sir Thomas Wrothe   4
TYPE, TOM.   2096
TYRO   PHILELEUTHERUS.
   John Duncan, D.D.   37
TYRO-THEOLOGUS, A.M.   ——
   Stone   2358
TYTLER, Sarah.   Henrietta Keddie
   294, 406, 566, 624, 993, 1014, 1090,
   1186, 1317, 1642, 1683, 1747, 1812,
   1816, 1851, 2273 (2), 2392, 2453, 2518,
     2805

U.

U.   Julius, Charles, and William
   Hare   1056
UBIQUE.   Parker Gillmore   1060
ULYSSES.   Samuel C. Graves   1412

UMBRA. Charles C. Clifford, M.P.
                                1181, 2626
UNCLE ADAM. C. A. Wetter-
  burgh   2325
UNCLE ADAM. George Mogridge 371
UNCLE HARRY. John Habberton
                                      1082
UNDA. Thomas S. Muir   912, 1218,
                                      2251
UNUS QUORUM. William Wadd
                                      1758
URBAN, SILVANUS. John Nichols
                                      2231
UVEDALE, CHRISTIAN, M.D.
  Sir John Hill   496

                  V.

V. Mrs Archer Clive   1201, 1663, 1875,
                                2064, 2721
V. Lady Clive   2846
V. A. Vincent Alsop   711
VALENS. Richard Burke   1443
VALERIUS CORVINUS. Thomas
  Blacklock   2151
VANDYCK, RICTER WODEN.
  Andrew Coventry Dick   1759
VARVICENSIS PHILOPATRIS.
  Samuel Parr, D.D.   362
VERAX. George Townsend and
  Robert Blakey, Ph.D.   1745
VERAX. Henry Dunckley, M.A. 1443
VERAX. Morris Moore   9
VERAX. Samuel Alexander   2140
VERAX. Thomas Foster   383, 2748
VERAX THEODORUS. Clement
  Walker   83
VERAX THEOPH. Clement Walker
                                      2127
VERITAS. Andrew MacGeorge
                          400, 2477, 2490
VERUS. John Taylor   552
VERUS. Sir John B. Burges   1431
VIATOR. Thomas D'Oyly   727, 1945
VIATOR. William Beckford   787
VICAR, THE OLD. John S. B.
  Monsell, LL.D.   1487
VICESIMUS BLINKINSOP, LL.D.
  Theodore Hook   2552
VINCENT, WILLIAM. Thomas
  Holcroft   1920
VINDEX. —— Hannay   1419
VINDEX. Joseph Gurney Bevan   849

VIOLET FANE. Mrs Singleton
                                602, 975
VI - - - T. B - - - - KE, LORD.
  Viscount Bolingbroke   1358
VOLUNTAS AMBULATORIA.
  Henry Walker   2547
V. P. Vavasor Powell   684
VUILLYAM WRAGHTON. Wil-
  liam Turner   2183
VV BAS. Richard White   203

                  W.

W. John E. Walsh   2403
W. W. F. Wakeman   2403
W. A.   1743
W. A. William Aglionby   2004
W. A. William Alexander   1566
W. A. William Allen   339, 650, 654,
                                1301, 2486
W. A. William Allen, D.D.   386, 2328
W. A. William Asplin   1392
W. A. William Atwood   1512
W. A. William Austin   1392
W. A. C. William Andrew Chatto 2737
W. A. D. William Abernethy
  Drummond   1327
W. A. F. Lieut.-Col. W. A. Fyers,
  C.B., R.B.   1256
WAGSTAFF, SIMON. Jonathan
  Swift   456
WAGSTAFF, WALTER. W. Oldes-
  worth   102
WALKER, PATRICIUS. W. Alling-
  ham   2076
WALLBRIDGE, ARTHUR. Arthur
  W. Lunn   239, 517, 2608
WALTER BOYD, M.P. William
  Combe   1416
WALTER CLINTON. W. H. Daven-
  port Adams   2530
WALTER MAYNARD. William
  Beale   774
WALTER RICHARD. Benjamin
  Robins   2782
WALTER WAGSTAFF.   W.
  Oldesworth   102
WARD, ARTEMUS. Charles F.
  Browne   185
WARNEFORD, LIEUT. R.N. W.
  H. C. Russell   1272, 1895, 2240, 2397,
                                2542, 2541
WARNER, CHRISTIAN SEARCH.
  Sir William Cusack Smith, Bart.   104

WARWICK, EDEN George Jabet 1699, 1960

WATERS. William Russell 204, 1341, 2023, 2099, 2223, 2397, 2617, 2698, 2708

WAVERLEY, EDWARD BRAD-WARDINE. John Wilson Croker 2696

W. B. Richard Finch 2743
W. B. William Bagwell 2824
W. B. William Barlow, M.A. 2634
W. B. William Bayly 781, 1473
W. B. William Barkstead 2557
W. B. William Basse 2557
W. B. William Basset 514
W. B. William Blair 1931
W. B. William Broomfield 881
W. B. William Brown 1214, 2399
W. B. C. William Bell Crafton 2374
W. B., D.D. Joseph Boyse, D.D. 2767
W. B. F. William B. Flower 2205
W. B. H. William B. Heathcote 2052
W. B., J. R. Walter Besant, James Rice 315, 2571
W. B., M.A. William Barton, M.A. 2732
W. B. P. AND D. William Bishop 667
W. BULL. Ann Jebb 2699
W. C. Bishop Carleton. vol. iv. 2596
W. C. David Garrick 1488
W. C. Sir William Coventry 1422
W. C. Walter Cary 249
W. C. W. Colman 560
W. C. William Carter 751, 2720
W. C. William Caton 1637
W. C. William Chambers 1949
W. C. William Charke 2169
W. C. William Cheyne 974
W. C. William Clarke 470, 1962
W. C. William Clifford 382
W. C. William Cockin 1793
W. C. William Collins 1634
W. C. William Cooper 1902, 1903, 2314
W. C. William Coward, M.D. 1041, 1293
W. C. William Crashaw 621, 1256
W. C. C. William C. Coward 2730
W. C., REV. Rev. William Cole 1300
W. C. S. Warner Christian Search 104
W. C., SIR. Sir William Coventrie 359
W. D. Rev. William Dalton 526
W. D. Wedderburn Dundas 1489
W. D. W. Davidson 1408, 2301
W. D. W. Duncan 279, 2589
W. D. W. Dimsdale 2060
W. D. W. Disney 1741

W. D. William Darrel 1332 (2)
W. D. William Dewsbury 2598, 2835
W. D. William Dickenson 1616
W. D. William Douglas 672, 2515
W. D. William Drummond 1945
W. D. William Dudgeon 2487
W. D. William Duggard 762
W. D. William Durham 1466
W. D., M.A. William Derham, M.A. 187
W. DR George Walker, D.D. 748
W. D., SIR. Sir William Davenant 927, 1711, 2659
W. E. William Emerson 1705
W. E. William Erbury 1259, 1532
WEAVER, THE CHESHIRE. J. D. Latouche 93, 853
W. E. R. William E. Richardson 1362
WERDNA RETNYW, M.D. Andrew Wynter, M.D. 1800, 1911
WERNER, E. Emile Buerstenbinder 920, 1746, 2081, 2217, 2247, 2512, 2707
WESTCOT, REDMAN. Adam Littleton 2193
WESTLAND, R. L. Robert W. Lowe 2810
WETHERELL, ELIZABETH. Susan Warner 741, 2063, 2814
W. F. William Field 1111
W. F. William Flint 2643
W. F. William Freke 947, 1490, 1970
W. F. William Fulke 1665
W. F. B. L. W. F. B. Lawrie 1202
W. F., D.D. William Fulke, D.D. 1608
W. F. OF D. W. Forbes of Disblair 2846
W. F., SIR. Sir W. Fownes 1610
W. G. Walt Godbear 2547
W. G. William Gardner 1329
W. G. W. Geaves 2491
W. G. William Giles 580
W. G. William Goodall 2668
W. G. William Gough 1506
W. G. William Green 10
W. G. William Grey 374
W. G. William Gryndall 1075
W. G. William Wright 2637
W. G. S. William Grant Stewart 1336
W. G. S. William G. Shaw 1596
W. H. 1905
W. H. W. Harris, M.D. 895
W. H. W. Hughes 2473
W. H. William Hammond 1945
W. H. William Hickes 1038
W. H. William Hinde 665

W. H. William Hodson   683
W. H. William Hore   2547
W. H. William Houschone   467
WHARTON, GRACE. Katherine Thomson   2064, 2823
WHARTON, PHILIP. John C. Thomson   1078, 2823
WHATSHISNAME. E. C. Massey 1051
WHATS-YOU-CALL-HIM. Patrick Andrews   511
W. H. D. W. H. Dorman   417
W. H. D. A. W. H. Davenport Adams   1689, 2460, 2682, 2829
W. H. DY. W. H. Darby   211
W. H. H. William Henry Harvey, M.D.   365
WH., IH. John White   760
WHIPEM, BENEDICK. Richard Harris   1726
WHISTLECRAFT, WILLIAM AND ROBERT. John H. Frere 1652
WHITE, BABINGTON. Mary E. Braddon   404
WHITE, MATTHEW. William Prynne   1737
WHITE, THOMAS, JUN. T. S. Omond   1948
WHITECROSS, JAMES WILLIAM. Michael Prus de Wisznicwski   2400
WHITNEY, HARRY PHILO-MATH. Patrick Kennedy   1340 (2)
W. H., JUNR. William Hodgson 1469
W. H. OF EX. IN OX. William Heale   145
W. HVNTLEY. William Prynne   256
WICKLIFFE LANE. Mrs Edmund Jenings   1685
WIDDRINGTON, ROGER. Roger Preston   1736 (2), 2221
WILFRED WOODFALL. Sir Samuel E. Brydges, Bart.   1685
WILKES, MR. Samuel Derrick   1003
WILL HAWORTH. W. Dimsdale 2060
WILLIAM ALLEN. Silus Titus   1301
WILLIAM B——T. William Bisset   1672
WILLIAM CHURNE. Francis E. Paget   1177
WILLIAM DE WOR. FAT. Rev. Hutton Beetham   253
WILLIAM GOVGE. Sir Henry Finch   864
WILLIAM HONEYCOMB. Richard Gardiner   1146

WILLIAM LAICK. George Ridpath   125, 501, 2275
WILLIAM PIKE, CHRISTOPHILUS. Wm. Lucy, Bishop of St David's   1768
WILLIAM P——Y. William Pudsey   495
WILLIAM AND ROBERT WHISTLECRAFT. John Hookham Frere   1652
WILLIAM RICHWORTH. Thomas White   623
WILLIAM SEYMAR. William Ramsey   478
WILLIAM U. COOPER, B.A. James G. Bertram   933
WILLIAM VINCENT. Thomas Holcroft   1920
WILLIAM WRAGHTON. William Turner   1194
WILLIAMS, MONTAGUE. —— Wasborough   1358
WILL WILL. William Williams   1798
WILSON. J. de la Brune   1480
WILSON, JAMES. Andrew Park 2385
WILSON, JASPER. James Currie, M.D.   1344
WITTITTERLY, JOHN A. Elizabeth T. Carne   2589
W. J. D. William John Deane   1529
W. J. F. William John Fitzpatrick 2811
W. J. D. R. W. J. D. Ryder   391
W. J. D. W. J. Duncan   1755
W. K. William Kelly   1754
W. K. William Kenrick   784
W. K. W. Kemp   727
W. K. White Kennett, D.D.   1399
W. K. A. M. White Kennet, Bishop of Peterborough   620
W. L. Robert Laing   905
W. L. William Leybourne   604
W. L. William Lisle   1756, 2770
W. L. William Loddington   2060, 2687
W. L. William Lodge   1845
W. M. Catherine Marsh   2731
W. M. Walter Moyle   660
W. M. William Maskell   1418
W. M. William Mitchell   1700
W. M. C.   370
W. M., M.A. Willoughly Mynors M.A.   2337
W - - M. ST - - PE. Sir William Stanhope   1828
W. N. Nicholas Breton   213

W. N. W. Nelson 758
W. N. William Ney 2639
W. N. William Nind 1012
W. O. William Oldys 679
WOLFE REGINALDE. Thomas F. Dibden 1283
WOODFALL WILFRED. Sir Samuel E. Brydges, Bart 1685
WOOLDEN DRAPER, R. J. Lieut J. Mackenzie 2831
WOR. FAT, WILLIAM DE. Rev. Hutton Beetham 253
WORKLESS, FAITH. Rev. J. Beveridge 954
W. P. Sir William Petty 52
W. P. William Peddelsden 2458
W. P. William Penn 520, 1045, 1360, 1736, 2717
W. P. William Phiston 1867
W. P. William Pinke 851
W. P. William Prynne 1935, vol. iv., 2596
W. P. William Sampson 2771
W. PH. W. Phiston 1315
W. P. J. William Penn 1225
W. P. J. William Penn, Jun. 2257
W. P. PHILOPOLITES. William Prynne 1818
W. P. R. W. P. Russel 917
W. R. William Rathband 277
W. R. William Richards 2786
W. R. William Ross 1714
W. R. William Rowley 1558
WRAGHTON, VUILLYAM. William Turner 2183
WRAGHTON, WILLIAM. William Turner 1194
W. RALEIGH. Henry S. John, Lord Bolingbroke 530
WRAYTHE, HOPE. Edith Hawtrey 2538
W. R. H. W. R. Hawkes 1613
W. S. 405
W ——— S ——— 1331
W. S. John Sergeant 2266
W. S. Sir Walter Scott 2131
W. S. Wentworth Smith 2057
W. S. Whitley Stokes 1933, 2587
W. S. William Salesbury 215
W. S. William Selwyn 2695
W. S. William Sewell, B.D. 1633
W. S. William Shakespeare 2057
W. S. William Sheppard 841, 1864, 2388
W ——— S ———. William Sheppen 2590

W. S. William Sherlock, D.D. 1376
W. S. William Shippen 950
W ——— S ———. William Shippen 2468
W. S. William Slatyer 2050 (2)
W. S. William Smith 239, 780, 1035, 1284, 2420
W. S. William Smythies 56
W. S. William Spalding 1362
W. S. William Stafford 449
W. S. William Stallenge 1236
W. S. William Strachan 2441
W. SEYMOUR. Cuthbert Shaw 1804
W. SH. 925
W. S. M. William Shaw Mason 232
W. S., M.P. William Stewart 1410
W. T. 1159
W. T. William Tomlinson 785, 2342, 2834
W. T. William Tooke 1959
W. T. William Typing 650
W. T. F * * * G * * * * * W. T. Fitzgerald 2653
W. TH. Thomas Wright 1868
W. U. R. William Upton Richards 888, 1050
W. W. 340
W. W. Thady Fitzpatrick 772
W. W. William Walsh 2499
W. W. William Walwyn 2609
W. W. William Watson 620, 1216, 2462
W. W. William W. Hicks 1841
W. W. William West 922
W. W. William Williams 1798
W. W. William Winstanley 1723
W. W. William Wollaston 610
W. W. G. William Wright 2637
W. W. William Wright, S.J. 277
W. W., F.R.S. 846
W. W. W. W. W. Wright 1695
WYKEHAMIST. Dr Blackiston 2172
WYKEHAMIST, A. Frederick Gale 2054
WYSEMAN, DEMETRIUS. Duke Willis 2062

X.

X. William Ware 2397
X. A. P. John Peace 683
X. H. Mrs Brewster Macpherson 1014
X. Y. John Maclaurin, M.A. 1516
X. Y. Z. Thady Fitzpatrick 772
X. Y. Z. W. Purton 1037

Y.

YENDYS, SYDNEY. Sydney Dobell   2222

YORKE, OLIVER. Francis Mahony   2132

YORICK. Laurence Sterne 1431, 2322, 2339

YOUNG, D'URFEY. Frederick Forrest   2080, 2797

YRUBSLIPS, F. Francis Spilsbury 182

YVELING, RAMBAUD. Frédérick Gilbert   1498

Z.

ZACHARY, CRAFT. Charles Kelsall   929

ZADKIEL. Richard James Morrison   1047

ZADKIEL, TAO. SZE. Richard J. Morrison, R.N.   1064

ZENAS. G. Taylor   2279

ZERO. Allan Ramsey, Jun.   2512

ZETA. J. Anthony Froude   2346

Z. S. Thomas Hooker   387

INDEX OF AUTHORS.

ABBOT, —— (1845)   958
ABBOT, Charles, Lord Colchester (1795-1849)   1289, 2431
ABBOT, Charles, Lord Tenterden (1786)   2718
ABBOT, George, Archbishop of Canterbury (1624-1641)   124, 2638
ABBOT, Hon. E. S., Baroness Colchester (1833)   2737
ABBOT, Right Hon. Charles (1829)   2471
ABBOT, Thomas K. (1857)   2205
ABBOTT, Edwin Abbott (1878-1882)   1818, 1898
ABBOTT, Thomas Eastoe (1814)   1876
ABERCORN, Earl of, J. Hamilton (1729)   298
ABERCROMBIE, John, M.D. (1835-1843)   498, 1070, 1607, 2566
ABERCROMBY, David, S.J. (1682)   110
ABERCROMBY, Patrick (1706-1707)   47, 1150
ABERDEEN, Bishop of, Hon. Archibald Campbell (1702-1713)   2067, 2434
ABERDEEN, Bishop of, James Gordon (1700)   2431
ABERDEEN, Bishop of, John Skinner (1792)   422, 1698
ABERDEEN, Bishop of, Patrick Forbes (1627)   833
ABERNETHY, John, M.A. (1722-1762)   1702, 2287, 2340
ABLETT, William (1857, N.D.)   2218, 2493
ACHELEY, Thomas (1567-1602)   1557, 1667
ACHERLEY, Roger (1733)   1289
ACHONRY, Dean of, Edward Honre (1850)   763
ACLAND, Arthur, H. Dyke, M.A. (1849)   559
ACLAND, Henry W., M.D. (1862)   2019
ACLAND, Troyte, Lieut. J. E. (1881)   2592
ACRYSE, Lewis (1702)   395
ACTON, F. Stackhouse (1868)   327

ADAIR, Dr J. W. (1790)   551
ADAIR, James (1768)   1782
ADAIR, James Makittrick, M.D. (1790-1791)   91, 2701
ADAIR, James, M.P. (1798)   1435
ADAIR, Robert (1795)   2806
ADAIR, W. James (1765-1785)   666, 2580
ADAM, —— (1754)   1231
ADAM, William (1707)   1357, 2298
ADAM, William, Lord Chief Commissioner (1819)   1786, 2489, 2490
ADAMS, —— (1790-1791)   753, 2825
ADAMS, Alexander Maxwell, LL.D. (1829)   531
ADAMS, C. P. (1846)   533
ADAMS, F. Colburn (1855)   1835
ADAMS, Francis (1853)   187
ADAMS, J. (1819)   438
ADAMS, James (1726)   1551
ADAMS, John   Errata, vol. iv.
ADAMS, John, LL.D. (1792)   1773
ADAMS, President J. (1805)   662
ADAMS, Rev. —— (1848)   2405
ADAMS, Rev. John (1792-1793)   1147, 1148
ADAMS, T. (1756)   600
ADAMS, William, D.D. (1772-1773)   114, 1869
ADAMS, W. H. Davenport (1868-1872)   609, 1689, 2460, 2530, 2682, 2829
ADAMSON, John (N.D.)   2423
ADDAMS, Dr (1824)   329
ADDINGTON, Henry (1831)   917
ADDINGTON, Mr (1774)   2269
ADDINGTON, Stephen (1787)   1394
ADDINGTON, Stephen, D.D. (1757)   677
ADDISON (1711)   1565
ADDISON, Berkely, A.M. (1843)   717
ADDISON, Joseph (1707-1719)   110, 706, 966, 1322, 1814, 1873, 2005, 2228, 2575, 2599
ADDISON, Lancelot, D.D., Dean of Lichfield (1677-1697)   388, 1009, 1107, 1647

ADOLPHUS, John (1803) 939
ADOLPHUS, John Leycester (1821) 1452
ADOLPHUS, Otto (1852) 450
ADRICHOMIUS, Christian (1654) 604
AGG, John (1812-1813) 2218, 2233, 2590, 2686
AGGAS, E. (1589) 636
AGGAS, Edward (1576, N.D.) 579, 1823
AGLETHORPE, James Edward (1732) 1712
AGLIO, Augustine (1830) 139
AGLIONBY, William (1671) 2004
AGNEW, E. C. (1837-1863) 1011, 1599, 2225, 2251, 2539, 2848
AGNEW, David. C.A. (1853) 870
AGUILAR, Grace (1838) 1255
AÏDÉ, Hamilton (1859-1865) 473, 2217
AIKIN, Dr John (1793-4) 838
AIKIN, John (1772) 827
AIKIN, John, D.D. (1790) 2474
AIKIN, John, M.D. (1790-1815) 38, 2830
AIKEN, P. F. (N.D.) 1883
AIKMAN, James (1825) 637
AINLEY, —— (1862) 2413
AINSLIE, Hew (1822) 1913
AINSLIE, John (1833) 201
AINSLIE, Lieut.-Gen. George Robert (1830) 1206
AINSLIE, ——, M.D. (1799) 1917
AINSLIE, Philip B. (1861) 2166
AINSLIE, Sir Whitelaw, M.D. (1799-1831) 931, 1917
AINSWORTH, Henry (1608-1640) 180, 520
AINSWORTH, William Harrison (1823-1834) 573, 2226, 2390
AITKEN, Andrew (1830) 2586
AITKEN, J. (1825) 295
AITKINSON, Thomas, jun. (1821) 2589
AITON, John, D.D. (1842) 415, 730
AITON, Thomas (1730) 1826
AKENSIDE, Mark (1744) 783, 1940
AKERMAN, John Yonge (1830-1858) 1507, 2495, 2542
ALBERTI, George William (1747) 2444
ALBIN, John (1795) 1717
ALCOCK, John (N.D.) 1
ALCOCK, Sir Rutherford (1861) 1485
ALCOTT, Louisa M. (N.D.-1877) 1031, 1498, 1642
ALDER, Thomas (1804) 1838
ALDERSON, E. H. (1846) 2623
ALDRED, Rev. Ebenezer (1811) 1495

ALDRICH, Henry, D.D. (N.D.-1687) 2178, 2760
ALDRIDGE, Thomas (1717) 2007
ALEXANDER, Ann, née Dillwyn (1858) 994
ALEXANDER, Ann, née Tuke (1812-1846) 2155, 2525, 2793, 2826
ALEXANDER, Cecil Frances (N.D.-1846) 1197, 2726
ALEXANDER, John, Advocate (1835) 796
ALEXANDER, John, D.D. (1839) 2195
ALEXANDER, Rev. John (1761-2) 1461
ALEXANDER, Samuel (1814-1819) 2140, 2332
ALEXANDER, William (N.D.) 267
ALEXANDER, William (1685) 1566
ALEXANDER, William (1811-1877) 1271, 1752, 1776, 1981, 2060, 2385, 2403
ALEXANDER, William, M.D. (1704) 815
ALFORD, Henry, M.A. (1833) 1945
ALFORDS, Mrs (1860) 2166
ALISON, Archibald, Advocate (1825) 2147
ALISON, Sir Archibald, Bart. (1816) 2626
ALLAN, —— (1704) 540
ALLAN, —— (N.D.) 2260
ALLAN, George (1773-1784) 35, 430
ALLAN, Rev. John (1853-1865) 517, 568, 920, 1341, 2027
ALLAN, Robert (1810) 1482
ALLARDYCE, Mrs (1867) 1031
ALLEINE, Joseph (1664) 301
ALLEINE, Richard (1663-1668) 226, 1022, 1079, 1680, 2768, 2841
ALLEN, —— (1788) 2654
ALLEN, Bennet (1764) 1943
ALLEN, C. (1858) 918
ALLEN, Captain —— 1438
ALLEN, Cardinal William (1584-1594) 470, 580, 2676
ALLEN, Dr Thomas (1665) 368
ALLEN, H. (1750) 10
ALLEN, J. (1624) 2850
ALLEN, James (1757) 424
ALLEN, James (1708) 644
ALLEN, John (1641) 147
ALLEN, John (1807-1857) 342, 376, 401, 773, 905, 1395, 1442, 1571, 1589, 2042, 2477, 2513, 2577
ALLEN, John, M.D. (1795) 1206
ALLEN, M. (1846) 1137

ALLEN, R., M.A. (1875)   1484
ALLEN, Rev. G. (1833)   2580
ALLEN, Richard (1704)   235
ALLEN, Robert (1606)   694
ALLEN, Thomas (1753)   2034
ALLEN, William, D.D. (1672-1684)
   96, 339, 386, 560, 650, 654 (2), 970,
     1689, 1891, 2328, 2486
ALLEN, William (1806)   834
ALLEN, William (1798)   1094
ALLEN, William (1820)   2282
ALLEN, William, F.R.S. (1815)   445
ALLESTRY, Dr. (1647)   2023
ALLINGHAM, John Till (1800)
   894, 2596 (vol. iii.)
ALLINGHAM, W. (1873)   2076
ALLINGTON, John (1649, 1655)
   261, 1040
ALLISON, J. (1844)   603
ALLIX, Peter, D.D. (1688-1709)
   96, 225. 248, 642, 645, 851, 1115, 1285,
     2114, 2146
ALLOT. R. (1600)   752
ALLSOP, Thomas (1836)   1425
ALLUM, —— (N.D.)   1408
ALMON, John (1762-1810) 91, 191, 236,
   962, 1160, 1162, 1210, 1345, 1394, 1412,
     1413, 2196 (2), 2202
ALSOP, George (1669)   1830
ALSOP, Vincent (1675-1698) 140, 711,
   856, 883, 1567, 1632, 2177, 2262, 2754
ALTHAM, Michael (1686-1688) 33, 532,
     2435, 2751
AMBLER, Charles (1792)   2202
AMES, Richard (1691-1693) 207, 701,
   900, 909, 1255, 1260, 1320, 1330, 1940,
     2285, 2382
AMES, William (1622)   2172
AMHURST, Nicholas, or Amherst
   (1717-1743) 108, 118, 171, 425 (2), 476,
   529 (2), 780, 985, 1414 (2), 1799, 2042,
   2043, 2149, 2303, 2504, 2554, 2589, 2689
AMNER, Richard (1768)   678
AMORY, Thomas (1681-1769) 138, 622,
     1475, 1577, 1994
AMYOT, Thomas (1812)   23
ANCILLON, Charles (1718)   834
ANDERDON, Christopher, S. J.
   (1692)   335, Errata, vol. iv.
ANDERDON, J.L.(1847,1861) 1607, 2218
ANDERSEN, Hans Christian (1845)
     1819
ANDERSON, —— (1844)   1394
ANDERSON, Adam (1787-9)   1109

ANDERSON, Adam, M.R.I.A.
   (1867)   1267
ANDERSON, Alexander (1821)   1273
ANDERSON, George (1753, 1755) 82, 832
ANDERSON, George (1852)   184
ANDERSON, Henry (1737)   769
ANDERSON, J. (1660)   2833
ANDERSON, James, A.M. (1723)   496
ANDERSON, James, LL.D. (1776,
   1793)   1986, 2582
ANDERSON, John (1615)   85
ANDERSON, John, jun. (1832)   2404
ANDERSON, John L. (1851)   1484
ANDERSON, Patrick (N.D.)   511
ANDERSON, Rev. John (1711-1716)
   121, 521, 549, 575, 617, 1367, 2295
ANDERSON, Rev. Charles (1825)   2489
ANDERSON, Rev. William (1843)   409
ANDERSON, Walter, D.D. (1755) 1133
ANDERSON, William (1850)   890
ANDERSON, William (1831)   1800
ANDERSON, William (1794)   1916
ANDERSON, W. M. (1857)   545
ANDERTON, James (1608-1624)
   1526, 1530, 2044, 2249
ANDERTON, Lawrence (1633-4)
   2027, 2656
ANDERTON, W. (1693)   2163
ANDREWS, Dr E. A. (1853)   326
ANDREWS, Dr Edward (1825)   2769
ANDREWS, John, D.D. (1682, 1735)
     108, 1005
ANDREWS, Lancelot (1630)   1875
ANDREWS, Miles Peter (1780-1788)
   1726, 1960, 2450, 2451
ANGELL, John (1761)   800
ANGLESEY, Earl of, Arthur Annes-
   ley (1659-1688) 750, 1306, 1354, 1361,
     2109, 2681
ANGUS, Joseph, D.D. (N.D.)   2072
ANGUS, William (1878)   2057
ANLEY, Charlotte (1826-1841)
     1621, 2020
ANNALY, Baron, J. Gore (1770)   325
ANNESLEY, Arthur, Earl of Angle-
   sey (1659-1688) 750, 1306, 1354, 1361,
     2109, 2681
ANNET, Peter (1739-1764)   429, 961,
   1129, 1141, 1160, 1283, 2188 (3), 2324,
     2412, 2520
ANSPACH, Margravine, Lady
   Craven (1778-1802)   901, 1617, 1639,
     1939, 2406, 2414, 2451
ANSTED, Professor (1846)   330

ANSTY, Christopher (1767-1797)   279, 732, 776, 1459, 1715, 1873, 1955, 2008, 2466
ANSTEY, John (1796)   1936
ANSTIS, John (1706, 1724)   1450, 2123
ANSTRUTHER, Captain (1725)   1358
ANTHONY, A. (1843)   1253
ANTHONY, G. W. (1853)   2821
ANTHONY, Louisa (1844)   2621
ANTROBUS, Benjamin (1691)   290
ANTROBUS, J. (1849-1854)   556, 2844
APPERLEY, Charles James (1831-1876)   101, 354, 1179, 1193, 1471, 1589, 1742 (2), 2148, 2479
APPLEGARTH, Robert (1776)   2561
APPLETON, Sophia Lousie (1865)   1916
APPLEYARD, Ernest Silvanus (1846-1852)   409, 719, 1051, 2017, 2036, 2521, 2526, 2801
ARBUCKLE, James, A.M. (1734)   1094
ARBUTHNOT, —— (1773)   1228
ARBUTHNOT, Archibald (1746)   259
ARBUTHNOT, John, M.D. (1692-1727)   163, 164, 501, 613, 813, 845, 899, 952, 1248, 1269 (2), 1270, 1300, 1324, 1328, 1455, 1980, 2004, 2202, 2338, 2536
ARBUTHNOT, John (1735)   540
ARCHDEACON, Matthew (1839)   1340
ARCHER, —— (1856)   269
ARCHER, Captain (1861)   1595
ARCHER, Edward (1858)   2407
ARDERNE, James, D.D. (1671)   635
ARGALL, R. (1621)   2448
ARGLES, M. (1877-1878)   1649, 1905
ARGLES, Mrs (1881)   1677
ARGYLE, Duke of, John Campbell (1740)   557
ARGYLE, Duke of, G. D. Campbell (1842)   1402
ARGYLL, Sheriff of, W. Robertson (1867)   1097
ARKLEY, Patrick (N.D.)   2273
ARMAGH, Archbishop of, —— Boulter (1733)   963
ARMAGH, Archbishop of, Dr James Usher (1642, N.D.)   187, 636
ARMAGH, Archbishop of, J. Bramhall (1706)   2791
ARMIN, Robert (1615)   2720
ARMITAGE, Rev. Robert, M.A. (1842-1850)   688 (2), 789, 1885, 2011
ARMSTRONG, F. Claudius (1856, 1857)   1566, 2848
ARMSTRONG, H. (1824)   1554

ARMSTRONG, John (1735-1791)   225, 473, 793, 2373, 2454
ARMSTRONG, John, M.D. (1744-1778)   183, 477, 565, 1805, 2405, 2546
ARMSTRONG, Nicholas (1856-8)   2616
ARMOUR, James (1702)   1995
ARNALL, William (1727-1736)   95, 417, 451, 961, 1404, 1770, 1821, 2149, 2301
ARNOLD, Frederick (1856)   65
ARNOLD, Matthew (1849, 1852)   744, 2503
ARNOLD, Rev. Thomas K. (1836)   1323
ARNOLD, Thomas (1832)   704
ARNOLD, W. D. (1853)   1763
ARNOT, Hugo (1775-1777)   800, 946, 1397, 1399
ARNOT, Rev. William (1842-1853)   706, 1572
ARNWAY, John, D.D. (1645, 1649)   1744, 2537
ARROWSMITH, —— (1673)   2118
ARTHINGTON, Hervey (1607)   2014
ARTHINGTON, Maria (1847)   2066
ARTHUR, Grace (1789)   2550
ARTHUR, Hen. (1797)   2048
ARTHUR, John (1738)   1524
ARTHUR, Professor Archibald (1780)   1827
ARUNDELL, Francis V. J. (1840)   2427
ARWAKER, Edmund, M.A. (1684)   734
ASCHAM, Anthony (1689)   2288
ASCHAM, Roger (1545)   2615
ASGILL, John (1696-1712)   687, 794, 2153, 2618
ASH, Edward, M.D. (1828-1855)   43, 1227, 2091, 2342
ASHBURTON, Lord, J. Dunning (1764)   1402
ASHBY, *alias* Thimbleby, Richard (1672)   2425
ASHE, Captain Thomas (1813, 1868)   1149, 1963
ASHE, Thomas (1682, 1693)   310, 1325
ASHETON, William (1663)   837
ASHHURST, Thomas Henry, D.C.L. (1843-1849)   861, 1715, 2358 (4)
ASHMOLE, Elias (1650, 1660)   900, 2414
ASHMORE, John (1621)   350
ASHTON, Thomas, D.D. (1771)   733, 867, 1405, 2298
ASHURST, Eliza A. (1847)   1431, 1664
ASHWELL, George (1674)   25

ASHWORTH, John Hervey (1851, 1864)   2079, 2261

ASKEW, Miss (1792)   2202

ASPLAND, R. (1846)   2054

ASPLAND, Robert Brooke (1831)   2216

ASPLIN, William (1730, 1739) 1214, 1392

ASPLIN, William M.A. (1728, 1729)   67, 86

ASSHETON, Dr William (1710)   636

ASSHETON, W. (1684, 1685   45, 2233

ASSHETON, William (1663)   837

ASSHETON, William D.D. (1670) 2603

ASTEL, Mary (1695-1722) 315, 381, 765, 795, 878, 1210, 1424, 1638, 2113, 2332

ASTLE, —— (1781)   430

ASTLE, Daniel (1777)   2039

ASTLE, Thomas (1775-1784)   138

ASTLEY, Francis Duckinfield (1809)   1043, 2723

ASTLEY, John (1584)   184

ASTON, Hon. W. (1788)   2654

ASTON, Joseph (1822, N.D.)   1610, 2189

ASTON, Lord (1811)   2318

ASTON, R. (1661)   1918

ASTON, Sir Thomas. Bart. (1642)   428

ATCHESON, Alfred S. (1849)   254

ATCHESON, Nathaniel (1814, 1823)   461, 1133

ATHERSTONE, Edwin (1830)   2284

ATKEY, Rev. Anthony (1745, 1773)   1454, 1536

ATKINS, A. (1843-1863) 432, 1844, 1886, 1905

ATKINS, Henry Martin (1838)   188

ATKINS, J. P. (1853)   1570

ATKINS, Sarah (1822)   976

ATKINSON, Benjamin Andrews (1729, 1730)   340, 2758

ATKINSON, Jasper (1802, 1826)   488, 2485

ATKINSON, Joseph (1785, 1788)   1558, 1684

ATKINSON, Thomas (1798)   1767

ATKINSON, Rev. W. (1801-1802)   305, 1058, 1359

ATKYNS, R. (1669)   1305

ATTERBURY, Francis (1687)   118

ATTERBURY, Francis, Bishop of Rochester (1716, 1722)   174, 2291

ATTERBURY, Francis D.D. (1701-1714)   12, 206, 323, 501 (2), 557, 754, 882, 1365, 1636, 1861, 1981, 2198, 2215, 2298, 2434, 2568, 2601, 2697, 2777

ATTERBURY, Lewis (1706)   112

ATTHILL, Lombe (1820)   398

ATTWOOD, Thomas (1828)   2273

ATTWOOD, W. (1690)   152

ATTWOOD, William (1680-1695) 34, 140, 175, 984, 1202, 1262, 1289, 1361, 1512, 2212, 2248

AUBERT, Mrs (1719)   1070

AUBIN, —— (1703)   367

AUBIN, Mrs (1730)   1605

AUBRY, M. (1795)   218

AUCKLAND, Lord, William Eden (1771-1781)   490, 2017, 2441

AUDLAND, John (1672)   2696

AUDLEY, Lady Eleanor (1633, 1650)   740, 2032

AUSTEN, James (1790)   1506

AUSTEN, Jane (1811-1816)   744, 1543, 2008, 2321

AUSTEN, John (1651)   380

AUSTEN, Mrs (1833)   1501

AUSTIN, Mrs (1850)   343

AUSTIN, Sarah (1825)   1333

AUSTIN, William (1672, 1730) 615, 1392

AVELING, J. H., M.D. (1854)   2803

AVERY, Benjamin, LL.D. (1716-1719) 426

AVISON, Charles (1753)   800

AVILA, Juan D' (1707)   2461

AXON, William E. A. (1868)   2347

AYLET, Robert (1600, 1653)   275, 2815

AYLETT, Robert, LL.D. (1622)   2529

AYLMER, John, D.D. (1559)   1069

AYLOFFE, Sir Joseph (1772)   301

AYRES, James (1742)   2257

AYRES, Philip (1667)   2355

AYRTON, William (1853)   48

AYSCOUGH, Francis, D.D. (1735) 2031

AYSCOUGH, Samuel (1783)   2151

AYTOUN, Roger (of Inchdairnie) (1828)   1791

AYTOUN, William Edmonstoune, D.C.L. (1832-1854) 245, 706, 732, 925, 1835, 1961

B.

BABINGTON, Thomas (1813)   1986

BACHE, Lieut. R. (1827)   1754

BACKWELL, T. (1646)   127

BACON, Anthony (1775)   2357

BACON, Francis, Lord (1601-1663)   145, 263, 351, 576, 1330, 2821

BACON, Matthew (1756)   997

BACON, Nathaniel (1647)   1115

BACON, Phanuel (1729-1758) 1190, 1234, 1307, 1658, 1799, 2410, 2547, 2684

BACON, Thomas (N.D.) 2701
BADCOCK, John (1823) 629, 1504, 2406
BADCOCK, Samuel (1780) 2407
BADDELEY, Richard (1669) 1471
BADGER, Albert, M.A. (1695) 2123
BADHAM, Charles (1835) 270
BADHAM, D., M.D. (1837) 2069
BAGE, Robert (1784-1796) 213, 877, 1090, 1261, 1538, 1670
BAGGE, Henry Theodore James (1852) 994, 2513
BAGNALL, Abraham, M.D. (1826) 149
BAGNALL, John Nock (1854) 1168
BAGOT, Lewis (1772) 584
BAGOT, William, Lord (1824) 1596
BAGSHAW, Christopher (1601) 2674
BAGSHAW, Edward (1660-1683) 133, 314, 1049, 1420, 2302, 2305, 2362, 2688
BAGWELL, William (1664) 2824
BAILEY, Benjamin (1817) 192
BAILEY, Lewis, Bishop of Bangor (1619) 1988
BAILEY, Nathaniel (1704) 628
BAILEY, Peter (1820) 2401
BAILEY, Philip James (1839) 913
BAILEY, Rev. —— 1801) 1211
BAILEY, Samuel (1821-1845) 537, 581, 665, 828 (2), 845, 1375, 1549, 1651, 2071, 2080, 2210
BAILEY, T. (1654) 746
BAILEY, Walter, M.D. (1588) 2365
BAILLIE, —— (1763) 1874
BAILLIE, E. C. C. (1853, N.D.) 2047, 2795
BAILLIE, Hugh, LL.D. (1775, 1776) 162, 2431
BAILLIE, Joanna (1798, 1846) 1797, 2326
BAILLIE, John (1736) 1874
BAILLIE, Mrs (1867) 1181
BAILLIE, Robert (1640, 1649) 1311, 1858, 2195
BAILLIE, Robert, A.M. (1877) 2713
BAILLIE, Sophia, née Denman (1846) 1797
BAILLIE, W. R. (1850) 255
BAILY, Dr Thomas (1671) 2825
BAILY, Joseph (1843) 109
BAILY, Robert (1624) 129
BAILY, Thomas, D.D. (1655) 1466
BAIN, Donald (1806-1841) 1815, 1874, 2392
BAINBRIGG, Dr Th. (1689-90) 2290
BAINE, James (1770) 323
BAIRD, Henry (1847) 1431
BAIRDY, John (1681) 310
BAKER, —— (1786) 2370

BAKER, David Bristow, M.A. (1831) 1704, 2644
BAKER, David Erskine (1764) 444
BAKER, G. (1709) 2146
BAKER, George (1810) 329
BAKER, Henry (1756) 829
BAKER, Henry (1745) 1612
BAKER, H. W. (1854) 559
BAKER, Samuel (1854) 918
BAKER, Thomas (1681-1709) 30, 924, 1062, 1076, 1190, 2113, 2685
BAKER, Thomas (1866) 1924
BAKER, William (1770) 1885
BAKEWELL, P. (1642) 659
BAKEWELL, T. (1805, 1807) 697, 1655
BALBANI NICCOLO (1608, 1612) 1738, 2066, Errata, vol. ii.
BALCARRES, Earl of, Colin Lindsay (1714) 17
BALCOMB, Amelia (1836) 1016
BALDIE, W. D. (1878) 1261
BALDWIN, —— (1776) 35
BALDWIN, —— (1811-13) 246
BALDWIN, A. H. (1853) 2728
BALDWIN, George (1801) 1247
BALDWYN, Rev. Edward (1787-1791) 476, 542, 989
BALE, John, Bishop of Ossory (1543, 1544) 779, 2847
BALFOUR, Alexander (1819-1826) 304, 897, 947, 1097
BALFOUR, Andrew (1834) 2468
BALFOUR, Clara Lucas (1857) 292
BALFOUR, James (1763) 600
BALFOUR, Sir James, Bart., (1834) 210
BALFOUR, John (1772) 563
BALGUY, John, M.A. (1718-1741) 685, 801, 946, 1326, 1366, 2298, 2305, 2386 (3)
BALGUY, T. (1768) 1424
BALL, Gawen, M.D. (1819) 1995
BALL, John (1635) 2376
BALL, Richard (1825-1830) 545, 1187, 1759, 1982, 2153
BALL, Richard (1830) 1982
BALL, Richard (1828) 2153
BALL, William (1827) 545
BALL, William (1828) 1187
BALL, William (1825) 1759
BALLANTYNE, —— (1723) 818
BALLANTYNE, James (1843) 991
BALLANTYNE, John (1813) 2814
BALLANTYNE, Rev. James Errata, vol. iv.

BALLANTYNE, Rev. John (N.D.)   447
BALLANTYNE, Robert Michael
  (1857-1860) 1184, 1635, 1685, 2219, 2777
BALLARD, J. (1851)   917, 2299
BALLINGALL, Sir George, M.D.
  (N.D.)   1742
BALLOW, Thomas (1737)   2634
BAMBRIDGE, Thomas, D.D. (1687) 106
BAMBRIGG, Thomas, D.D. (1687)   106
BAMPFIELD, Francis (1681)   1182
BANCKES, Matthew (1682)   2345
BANCKES, Richard, *or* Banks
  (1688)   2129
BANCROFT, A. (1770)   1133
BANCROFT, Edward, M.D. (1769)
                             808, 2154
BANCROFT, John(1691, 1693) 1084, 1303
BANCROFT, Richard, D.D. (1591,
  1593)   564, 2527
BANDELLO, Matteo (1576)   1667
BANGOR, Bishop of, Lewis Bailey
  (1619)   1988
BANGOR, Dean of, Dr W. Lloyd
  (1676)   1456
BANIM, John (1824-1842) 94, 239, 252,
  543, 602, 904, 1562, 2191, 2409, 2539,
                                 2544
BANIM, Michael (1826, 1828)   252, 543
BANKS, John (1739)   2363
BANKS, Jonathan (1688)   1483
BANKS, Richard Banckes *or* (1688) 2129
BANKS, Thomas Christopher (1816,
  1831)   612, 1415
BANKES, —— (1831)   1641
BANKES, John (1739)   540
BANKTON, Lord, Andrew M'Dowall
  (1747)   818
BANNANTINE, James(1737-1801) 1635
                            1724, 1811
BANNATYNE, George (N.D.)   45
BANNATYNE, John (1703, N.D.)   1354
                                 2435
BANNERMAN, Henry (1832)   1643
BANNERMAN, J. (1816)   623
BANNISTER, James (1780)   2318
BANNISTER, John William (1821) 2398
BANNISTER, Saxe (1822-1842)   388,
                            1099, 2150
BANNISTER, Thomas (1846)   279
BANSLEY, Charles (1841)   2649
BAPTISTE, Jean, Le Chevalier (1829)
                                 2704
BARBA, Albaro A., M.A. (1670)   2292
BARBADOES, Bishop of (1829)   880

BARBAULD, Anna Letitia(1790, 1793)
                              41, 2389
BARBER, John (1819)   2594
BARBOU, N., M.D. (1690)   656
BARBOUR, John (1620)   31
BARBOUR, John Gordon (1824, 1825)
                          1487 (2), 2066
BARBOUR, Mrs (1856)   2794
BARBOUR, Robert (1759)   804
BARBOUR, Robert W. (1879)   1263
BARCA, Mme. Calderon de la (1843)
                                 1470
BARCLAY, —— (1766)   847
BARCLAY, Alexander (1506)   326 (2)
BARCLAY, John, M.D. (1799, 1819) 1563,
                                 2144
BARCLAY, John (1818)   54
BARCLAY, John (1685)   1595
BARCLAY, John (1772)   1905
BARCLAY, Rev. Peter, M.A. (1881)
                                 2729
BARCLAY, Robert (1740)   995
BARCLAY, Robert (1679)   2219
BARCLAY, Sir William (1639)   1516
BANCROFT, Charles (1688-1690)
                            1371, 2119
BARETTI, Joseph (1786)   2605
BARHAM, Francis (1840)   1522
BARHAM, Rev. Richard Harris,
  B.A. (1841-1870) 998, 1224, 1259, 2416
BARHAM, Thomas Foster, M.B.
  (1823-1824)   433, 1008, 2177
BARING, Charles (1810)   1448
BARKER, —— (1766)   847
BARKER, John, M.D. (1742)   1230
BARKER, Matthew Henry, R.N.
  (1835-1867) 1062, 1262, 1316, 1478, 1741,
                        2607, 2610, 2790
BARKER, R. (1663)   852
BARKER, Rev. S., A.M. (1815)   2700
BARKER, Samuel (1731-1732)   1627
BARKER, T. (1693)   80
BARKER, Thomas (1620)   241
BARKER, Thomas (1654)   523
BARKER, Thomas (1780)   1607
BARKER, W. Burckhardt (1854)   1984
BARKHAM, Dr John   Errata, vol. iv.
BARKSDALE, Clement (1651-1685) 200,
  204, 1335, 1420, 1747, 1762, 1810, 2166
BARKSTEAD, William (1617)   2557
BARLEE, C. (1787)   2506
BARLOW, Edward (1715)   1608
BARLOW, Joel (1815)   1074
BARLOW, John (1618)   1095

BARLOW, Thomas, D.D., Bishop of
  Lincoln (1648, 1688)   645, 915, 1880,
                     1988, 2214
BARLOW, William, M.A. (1690)   2634
BARNARD, —— (1642)   783
BARNARD, E. (1757)   2771
BARNARD, John (1641-1660)   84, 87,
                       347, 2378
BARNARD, John (1770)   2130
BARNARD, Mrs (1865)   925
BARNARD, Robert (1809-1816)   1340,
                     1581, 2843
BARNARD, Sir John (1750)   487
BARNAULD, Mrs (1793-1794)   838
BARNES, R. (1817)   1769
BARNES, Rev. Joshua (1716-1719)   428
BARNES, Richard William (1850-
  1865)   162, 1320, 1342
BARNES, Thomas (1815)   1861
BARNFIELD, Richard, or Barne-
  field (1594, 1598)   434, 451, 1052, 1949
BARON, John (N.D.)   313
BARON, Robert (1647)   1623
BARON, W. (1608)   711
BARON, W. (1706)   1106
BARR, James, D.D. (1820)   1407
BARRÉ, Lieut-Col. Isaac, M.P.
  (1848)   1435
BARRETT, Eaton Stannard (1807-
  1817)   68 (2), 434, 1870, 2217, 2396,
                     2539
BARRETT, Francis (1815)   1500
BARRETT, John (1675-1680)   1031,
                     2103
BARRETT, Jonathan (1849-1852)
                 1772, 2090
BARRETT, Richard (1821)   228
BARRETT, Stephen (1747)   2788
BARRETT, Thomas Squire (1869)   848
BARRETT, William (1679)   1749
BARREUL, Abbé (1797-1798)   1577
BARRINGTON, Hon. Daines (1766)
                 1792
BARRINGTON, John Shute, Vis-
  count Barrington (1701-1733)   22, 118,
  680, 821, 1332, 1350, 1386, 1624, 2214,
                     2216
BARRON, Richard (1750)   882
BARRON, William (1777-1780)
                 1152, 1163
BARROW, J. (1735)   627
BARROW, John (1864)   859
BARROW, John (1824-1852)   1570, 1571,
                     2022

BARROW, J. H. (1827)   744
BARROW, Sir John (1831-1832) 838, 891,
                     1573
BARROWBY, Dr (1746)   1403
BARROWE, Henry (N.D.)   1893
BARROWS, Fanny (1868-1870)   879,
          1028, 1497, 1726, 1812
BARTER, Catherine (N.D.)   70, 1173
BARTLETT, William Henry (1849-
  1823)   946, 1017, 1910, 2283
BARTON, Bernard (1812-1818)   1610,
                 1946, 2658
BARTON, Richard (1747)   81
BARTON, Richard (1792)   898
BARTON, William, M.A. (1644-
  1654)   247, 2051, 2732
BARWICK, John, D.D. (1644)   349
BARWIS, Jackson (1776-1779) 625, 2585
BARTY, James S., D.D. (1850)   1892
BASSANESE, Francesco Nigri
  (N.D.)   353
BASELY, N. (1649)   2338
BASIRE, Isaac, D.D. (1659)   1153
BASS, Sarah (1856)   1498
BASSE, William (1617)   2557
BASSENTINUS, Franciscus Niger
  (N.D.)   353
BASSETT, E. B. (1869)   1637
BASSETT, Francis, Lord de Dun-
  stanville (1783-1809)   534, 1785, 2469,
                     2576
BASSETT, Joseph Davie (1813)   1382
BASSETT, Joshua (1687-1704) 816, 2084
BASSETT, William (1670)   514
BASTON, Thomas (1716)   2583
BATE, George (1649)   2122
BATE, Henry (1774)   1084
BATE, John (1634)   1690
BATE, Julius, M.A. (1739-1748) 535, 582,
                  770, 852
BATEMAN, Charles (1758)   765
BATEMAN, James, M.A. (1845)   1840
BATEMAN, J. C. (1858, 1859) 1710, 2810
BATES, Ely (1786)   371
BATES, W. (1695)   2753
BATES, W. R. Gray (1833)   1838
BATEUS, Georgius (1652)   449
BATH, Earl of, William Pulteney
  (1727-1778)   118, 290, 323, 324, 468, 767,
  874, 1187, 1321, 1344, 1351 (3), 1968,
  2032 (2), 2110, 2194, 2200, 2378, 2488,
                     2581
BATH AND WELLS, Bishop of, C.
  Moss, D.D. (1744)   840

BATH AND WELLS, Bishop, G. Hooper, D.D. (1683, 1701)   398, 1698

BATH AND WELLS, Bishop of, Richard Kidder, D.D. (1687-1690)   1369, 1753, 2295, 2570

BATH AND WELLS, Bishop of, Thomas Ken, D.D. (1675-1703)   108, 711, 864, 1389, 1545, 2234

BATHURST, Charles (1854, 1857) 1337, 2149

BATHURST, Dr Richard (1753)   47

BATHURST, Henry, Earl (1761)   2564

BATT, Charles William (1788)   676

BATT, Timothy (1648)   2794

BATTELL, Ralph (1659, 1683) 1886, 2784

BATTELY, Archdeacon John (1774) 140

BATTEN, Sir William (1648)   2675

BATTY, Christopher (1757)   424

BATTY, Rev. Adam (1854)   1073

BATTY, Rev. Richard (1750-1756)   2287, 2334, 2848

BAUDRIER, Sieur de (1711)   1724

BAXTER, Andrew (1740-1750) 164, 770, 1559

BAXTER, J. (1600)   2603

BAXTER, Lucy (1883)   2168

BAXTER, Nathaniel (1606)   2391

BAXTER, Nicholas (1575)   2408

BAXTER, Richard (1652-1696)   1, 654, 1285 (2), 1654, 1748, 1851, 1894, 1988, 2223, 2247, 2831

BAYES, Thomas (1731, 1736) 683, 1244

BAYFORD, —— (1818)   1787

BAYFORD, J. (1828-1829)   624

BAYLEY, R. S. (1835)   2673

BAYLEY, Sir John (1813)   246

BAYLY, Benjamin (1707)   798

BAYLY, Thomas, or Baylie, D.D. (1640-1651)   351, 2233

BAYLY, Thomas Haines (1827, 1828)   206, 2053

BAYLY, Walter, or Bayley (1626)   635

BAYLY, William (1662, 1664) 781, 1473

BAYNE, A. (1717)   1245

BAYNES, John (1776, 1782)   168, 1801

BAYNTON, Captain (1791)   202

BEACONSFIELD, Earl of, Benjamin Disraeli (1826-1880)   497, 747, 1083, 1442, 2483, 2619, 2724, 2774, 2781, 2804, 2829, 2848

BEACH, Phil. (1736)   1419

BEACH, Thomas (1737)   833

BEALE, John (1724)   1088

BEALE, William (1867)   774

BEAMISH, N. Ludlow (1829)   1877

BEAMONT, William (1864)   656

BEAN, J. (1793)   380

BEAN, Rev. James (1808)   2852

BEAR, Nicholas, M.A. (1699)   2188

BEARD, John Relly, D.D. (1839-1849)   228, 1036, 1883, 2282, 2283

BEARE, William (1750)   2686

BEASLEY, —— (1836)   2769

BEATON, John (1708)   2376

BEATS, John (1873)   1679

BEATTIE, Dr (1821)   2227

BEATTIE, James (1771)   1619

BEATTIE, James, LL.D. (1778-1787)   1408, 1492, 2273

BEATTIE, William, M.D. (1829-1839)   1082, 1270, 1969

BEATY, Ann (1845)   2452

BEAUCHAMP, Viscount, F. I. S. Conway (1783)   1396

BEAUFORT, Daniel Augustus (1788)   2354

BEAUFORT, Louis de (1740)   679

BEAUFOY, —— (1828)   2613

BEAUFOY, Henry (1808)   2272

BEAUFROY, —— (1828)   2629

BEAULIEU, Luke de (1649-1687)   411, 659, 1171, 2120

BEAUMELLE, L. A. de la (1753) 2107

BEAUMONT, —— (1683)   2799

BEAUMONT, Francis (1607-1815)   241, 349, 355, 356, 1190, 1308, 1536, 1556, 1599, 2620, 2825

BEAUMONT, Francis, (1602-1620)   349, 1556, 2254

BEAUMONT AND FLETCHER (1607-1815) 241, 349, 355, 356, 1190, 1308, 1536, 1599, 2620, 2825

BEAUMONT, James A. (1849)   1948

BEAUMONT, J. (1602)   1607

BEAUMONT, John (1704)   2005

BEAUMONT, John, T. B. (1816)   1446

BEAVER, Col. (1753)   1431

BEAZELY, Samuel (1828, 1830)   1842, 2230

BECANUS, Rev. Father Martinus, S.J. (1619)   2637

BECK, Baroness Von (1850)   1889

BECK, Joseph (1785)   2726

BECK, Thomas (1795-1811)   57, 1635, 1642

BECKET, Andrew (1786, 1787) 467, 2656

BECKETT, —— (1796)   2140

BECKETT, Andrew (1811)   1522

BECKFORD, Peter (1781-1818)   827, 1269, 2577

BECKFORD, William (1780-1835) 166, 206, 236, 706, 787. 1257, 1642, 1975, 2099, 2498

BECON, Thomas (1541-1543) 387, 565, 1024, 1738, 1871, 1939, 1980, 2211, 2667

BEDDEVOLE, M. (1691)   823

BEDDOES, Thomas, M.D. (1792-1806)   64, 1545

BEDFORD, Archdeacon of, Rev. R. Shepherd (1756)   1802

BEDFORD, Arthur, M.A. (1736, 1738)   847, 1771

BEDFORD, 5th Duke of, Francis Russell (1786)   609

BEDFORD, 6th Duke of, John Russell (1822)   1837

BEDFORD, Grosvenor (1797, 1814)   1423, 1680

BEDFORD, Hilkiah (1710-1724) 586, 1482, 2388, 2751, 2757

BEDFORD, Peter (1839)   1570

BEDFORD, Thomas (1791)   1269

BEDINGFIELD, Philip (1719, N.D.)   247, 1375

BEEKE, Henry, D.D. (1798)   1366

BEER, G. H., M.D. (1813)   184

BEETHAM, Rev. Hutton (1785)   253

BEEVER, Susannah (1870)   1304

BEEZLEY, James (1776)   1378

BEGBIE, James Warburton (1859) 1066

BEHN, APHRA (1677-1693)   77, 572, 1519, (2), 2231

BEILBY, J. Wood (1869)   2678

BEILBY, Ralph (1791)   1001

BEITH, Alexander, D.D. (1839)   2455

BELCHER, W. (1814-1816) 1038(3), 2150

BELDAM, —— (1772)   482

BELDAM, Joseph (1823)   1870

BELFAST, Lord, Hon. F. R. Chichester (1851-1866)   1558, 1692, 2706 2797, Errata, vol. ii., Errata, vol. iv.

BELFOUR, Rev. Hugo John (1822)   1654

BELL, Archibald (1835)   295

BELL, Benjamin (1797)   1774

BELL, Catherine Douglas (1847-1871) 178, 205, 1177, 1520, 1547, 1554, 2341, 2679, 2795

BELL, Charles Dent (1853)   240

BELL, Hon. Charles H. (1880)   1597

BELL, Hugh (1791)   1210

BELL, Jane Cross Simpson née (1836)   1912

BELL, John (1706)   5

BELL, John (N.D.)   2684

BELL, John (1785)   2787

BELL, Major Evans (1865)   2075

BELL, Mrs Henry G. (N.D., 1831)   1131, 2392

BELL, R. (1746-1749)   768, 1997, 2137 2392

BELL, Rev. William (1875, 1876)   422, 1307

BELL, Robert (1827)   1837

BELL, Thomas (1680)   1042

BELL, William B., B.C.L. (1823)   2063

BELL, William, D.D. (1765)   584

BELLAMONT, Earl of, Charles Coote (1783)   1384

BELLAMY, D. (1741)   1886

BELLAMY, Thomas (1663)   1897

BELLEGARDE, J. P. Morvan de (1706-1707)   2117 (2)

BELLENDEN, William (1668)   404

BELLERS, John (1712)   817, 2421

MÜNCH-BELLINGHAUSEN, F. von (1844-1849)   1054, 1225, 2448

BELLOY, —— de (1765)   2382

BELON, Peter (1675)   1636

BELOE, Rev. William (1786, 1798)   1287, 2078

BELOE, William (1773, 1817)   63, 637, 966, 1273, 2346

BELSHAM, Thomas (1808)   1730

BELSHAM, William (1789, 1791)   829, 1105, 1785

BELSON, John (1662)   2617

BELTON, —— (1834, 1840)   92, 2701

BENDELOWE, P. (1769)   96

BENLOWES, Edward (1649)   570

BENLOWES, Philip (1768)   1228

BENGO, John (1797)   1959

BENNET   Errata, vol. iv.

BENNET, A. M. (1785, 1786)   99, 1296

BENNET, John (1683)   495

BENNET, John (1788)   2505

BENNET, Philip (1736)   218

BENNET, William (1875)   2681

BENNETT, —— (1779)   2553

BENNETT, J. W. (1831)   2643

BENNETT, Rev. William J. E., M.A. (1847-1868)   1501, 1808, 1833, 2206, 2540

BENNETT, Thomas   Errata, vol. iv.

BENNETT, Thomas, M.A. (1673) 2371

BENNETT, William (1827-1849) 370, 1368, 1839, Errata, vol. iv. (2)
BENNING, William (1836) 1071
BENOIST, Elie (1694) 1154
BENSON, Auditor (1719) 1940 (2)
BENSON, Edward White (1824) 726
BENSON, Mrs (1864) 1710
BENSON, William (1711) 1169, 1387, 2299
BENSON, William (1725) 2770
BENSON, William, M.A. (1739, 1741) 1424, 1994
BENT, James (1693) 1725
BENTHAM, Edward (N.D., 1773) 349, 1243
BENTHAM, Edward, D.D. (1748) 1376
BENTHAM, Jeremy (1776, 1823) 954, 1751
BENTHAM, Rev. John (1756) 333
BENTINCK, William Henry C. (1825) 1435
BENTLEY, —— (1803, 1804) 914, 2170, 2171
BENTLEY, Dr (1710) 2005
BENTLEY, John (N.D.) 1062
BENTLEY, Joseph (1864-1868) 226, 1656, 1968
BENTLEY, R. (1598) 1279
BENTLEY, R. (1750, 1751) 197, 979
BENTLEY, Richard (1798, 1799) 491, 492 (3)
BENTLEY, Richard (1719, 1721) 1408, 2202
BENTLEY, Richard, D.D. (1713, 1721) 687, 2157
BENTLEY, S. (1833) 853
BENTLEY, Thomas (N.D.) 1898
BERENS, Edward, M.A. (1828) 402
BERENS, Edward, Archdeacon of Berks (1820, 1823) 2409, 2617, 2739
BERENS, Rev. Edward (1821) 1869
BERESFORD, James (1810) 231
BERESFORD, Rev. James (1806) 1632
BERINGTON, Joseph (1780) 2484
BERINGTON, Simon (1737) 1585
BERINGTON, Rev. Joseph (1776) 1445
BERINGTON, Simon (1786) 51
BERISFORD, John (1699) 173
BERKELEY, Countess of (1693) 1519
BERKELEY, George, D.D., Bishop of Cloyne (1721-1786) 51, 63, 83, 581, 639, 817, 1388, 2035, 2091, 2564, 2837
BERKELEY, George, Earl of Berkeley (1680) 1113

BERKELEY, George Monck (1784-1788) 735, 1082, 1547, 1742
BERKELEY, Lady Elizabeth (1780-1781) 901, 1617, 2451
BERKENHEAD, John (N.D.) 948
BERKENHEAD, Sir John (1650) 2690
BERKENHOUT, John (1767) 2237
BERKS, Archdeacon of, Edward Berens (1820, 1823) 2409, 2617, 2739
BERKS, Archdeacon of, Jonas Proast (1691, 1704) 2300, 2567
BERNARD, —— (1798) 2387
BERNARD, Francis E. King née (1800) 2103
BERNARD, Julia Smith née (1809-1813) 1443, 1814, 2020
BERNARD, Richard (1619, 1641) 873, 2378
BERNARD, Sir Thomas (1790, 1813) 1480, 2480
BERNEVILLE, Marie Catherine Juenelle de, Countess D'Aulnoy (1693-1708) 1224, 1589, 1999
BERRIDGE, John (1762) 1295
BERRIDGE, Rev. J. (1760) 954
BERRIMAN, William, D.D. (1719) 35, 2290, 2308
BERRY, Mary (1802-1844) 446, 747, 901, 2413, 2419
BERTIE, Peregrine, Lord Willughby (1589) 2359
BERTRAM, —— (1858) 249
BERTRAM, James G. (N.D.) 933
BERVACK, John (1705) 139
BERWICK, Edward (1819) 580
BESANT, Walter (1882) 2205
BESANT, Walter, and James Rice (1872-1876) 315, 1025, 1685, 2082, 2571, 2823
BESSE, Joseph (1732-1747) 111, 257, 415, 417, 773, 844 (2), 981, 2041, 2136, 2138, 2171, 2740 (3), 2741 (4)
BEST, Henry (1826-1829) 950, 1257, 1889
BEST, John Richard (1826-1841) 1254, 1971, 2622
BETHAM, Sir William, F.S.A. (1831) 2492
BETHEL, Slingsby (1671-1692) 1241, 1525, 1780, 2000, 2048, 2843
BETHUNE, John (1758-1771) 824, 950, 2377
BETHUNE, John Elliot Drinkwater (1829, 1833) 1473, 1501

BETTERLEY, W. (1689)   265

BETTERTON, Thomas (1680, 1741)
   77, 1153, 1477, 2033, 2191

BETTS, Henry John (1854)   1017

BEVAN, George Jones (1821)   524

BEVAN, John (1822)   2749

BEVAN, Joseph Gurney (1802-1805)
   554, 849, 2356

BEVAN, Samuel (1857)   2598

BEVANS, John, Junr. (1802)   2445

BEVERIDGE, W. (1704)   395

BEVERLEY, —— (1685)   669

BEVERLEY, R. M. (1835)   1979

BEVERLEY, Robert (1705, 1722)
   1130, 1168

BEVERLEY, Rev. Thomas (1688)   436

BEVERLEY. T. (1690)   2828

BEVERLEY, Thomas (1695, 1699) 157,
   1033, 2115

BEWLEY, Henry (1829, 1859) 904, 2574

BEXLEY, Lord, Nicholas Vansittart
(1793)   2111

BEYLE, L. Alex Cés (1818)   2225

BEYLE, Marie Henrie (1824)   1584

BEZA, Theodore (1568-1648)   471, 1282
   2768

BEZA, Reverend (1608)   1738

BIBER, George Edward (1848)   1394,
   1850 (2)

BICKERSTAFF, Isaac (1770-1805)
   2102, 2478

BICKERSTAFFE, Isaac (1756-1805)
   7, 308, 563, 688, 776, 1076, 1200, 1455,
   1490, 1518, 1519, 1535, 1844, 2102, 2236,
   2269, 2478, 2514, 2572, 2596 vol. iii.

BICKERSTETH, —— (N.D., 1867)
   4, 370, 389, 532, 973, 1273

BICKERSTETH, C. (1864-1866)   1341,
   1854, 1978, 2497, 2499, 2526

BICKERSTETH, Edward Henry
   Errata, vol. iv. (2)

BICKERTON, ——   1438

BICKNELL, Alexander (1776-1818) 152,
   1134, 1269, 2012

BICKNELL, J. L. (1785)   1683

BICKNELL, John (1773)   714

BIDDLE, John, M.A. (1648-1687)   267,
   471, 2555

BIDDLE, Richard (1830, 1831) 1571, 2195

BIDDULPH, M. A. (N.D.)   1313

BIGG, William (1858)   804

BIGLAND, Ralph (1791)   25

BIGLAND, Richard (1791)   25

BILLAM, Francis T. (1806)   2784

BILLING, Edward (1659, 1664) 884, 2835

BILSTONE, ——, M.A. (1731)   2767

BINCKES, William, D.D., Dean of
Lichfield (1701, 1702)   858, 1994

BINDLEY, Charles (1845-1858)   237,
   1102, 1193, 1942, 1984, 2479 (3), 2481,
   2508, 2841

BINDLEY, James (1775)   428

BINDON, David (1739)   1965

BINGHAM, Frances L. (1845)   1185

BINGHAM, Jane M. (1846, N.D.) 78, 1281

BINGHAM, Rev. George (1772)   2535

BINGHAM, Sir Charles (1767)   813

BINGLEY, William (1814)   1682

BINNEY, Rev. Thomas (1833, 1850)
   484, 1047, 2129

BINNING, John (N.D.)   1371

BINNS, Thomas (1806)   565

BINNS, Wildon H. (1861)   1834

BIRCH, Dr (1759)   429

BIRCH, Rev. Dr Thomas (1741-1743) 193

BIRCH, Jonathan (1832-1838)   683, 922

BIRCH, Mrs Walter (1838)   1267

BIRCH, Samuel (N.D.)   2

BIRCH, Thomas, D.D. (1747)   1232

BIRCH, William (1731)   274

BIRCH, William John, M.A. (1840) 2082

BIRCHLEY, William (1651)   380

BIRD, Isabella L., Mrs Bishop
(1856-1869)   188, 764, 1754

BIRD, James Barry (1794-1819) 1328 (2),
   1329 (2)

BIRD, Robert Montgomery (1834)   298

BIRD, William W. (1823)   2485

BIRDWOOD, James (1691)   1078

BIRKENHEAD, Sir John (1648-1682)
   113, 189, 295, 1601 (2), 1715, 1739, 1876,
   2214, 2690

BIRNIE, Sir Andrew (1702)   447

BIRT, Captain Edward (1755)   1426

BISANI, Alessandro (1793)   1911

BISBIE, Nathaniel (1692)   2710

BISBY, Dr (1691)   114

BISCHOF, Gustav, Ph.D. (1841)   1906

BISCOE, Richard, M.A. (1732-1735) 121,
   1371, 2135, 2299

BISHOP, Dr William (1604, 1614)   667,
   2118

BISHOP, George (1660)   2602

BISHOP, John B. (1870)   1819

BISHOP, Mrs., Isabella L. Bird
(1856-1869)   188, 764, 1754

BISHOP, Rev. Samuel (1762)   1802

BISSET, John (1731, 1732) 1640, 2210

BISSET, William (1711)   1672
BISSITT, Dr (1804)   1926
BLACK, —— (1706)   2421
BLACK, Adam (1852)   1562
BLACK, David (1706)   819
BLACK, David Dakers (1731)   1337
BLACK, David Dakers (1872)   2656
BLACK, Dr John (1824)   583, 2522
BLACK, John (1822)   1846
BLACK, John, LL.D. (1806)   885
BLACK, Lawrence (1839)   991
BLACK, William (1706-1707)   1993,
                    2158, 2376, 2433
BLACK, William (1871)   1674
BLACK, William, Advocate (N.D.)   1345
BLACKBOURNE, Rev. John (1729)
                                        255
BLACKBURNE, Francis, M.A.,
    Archdeacon of Cleveland (1752-
    1780) 150, 471, 797, 1123, 1591, 1745,
    1796 (2), 2110, 2141, 2142, 2154, 2330,
                    2367, 2700
BLACKBURNE, Rev. John (1854-
    1855)   1974
BLACKE, Emily (1855)   294
BLACKHALL, Rev. Samuel, D.D.
    (1772)   1378
BLACKISTON, Dr (1759)   2172
BLACKLOCK, Thomas (1776)   2151
BLACKMORE, Richard Doddridge
    (1864)   410
BLACKMORE, Sir Richard (1699-
    1718)792, 1173, 1307, 1330, 1703, 2260,
                                       2369
BLACKSTONE, Sir William (1750,
    1769)   796, 1391
BLACKWELL, Henry (1730)   1007
BLACKWELL, Jonathan (1644)   1079
BLACKWELL, Miss (1840, 1841)
                                   741, 789
BLACKWELL, Robert (1726)   513
BLACKWELL, Thomas (1735-1747)
                                   769, 2031
BLACKWELL, Thomas, LL.D.
    (1748)   1424
BLACKWOOD, Harriet, Lady
    Dufferin (1863)   1491
BLADEN, Captain (1705)   362
BLAGDEN, Isabella (1865, 1867)
                                  1749, 2826
BLAGDON, Francis William (1805)
                                        914
BLAIKIE, G. W. (1828)   924
BLAIKIE, John (1868)   1814

BLAIKIE, Nicolas (1671)   1333
BLAIKIE, Rev. W. G., D.D., LL.D.
    (1879)   1017
BLAIR, Hugh, D.D. (1736-1763)   537,
                    1765, 1787, 1943
BLAIR, Rev. William (1853)   391
BLAIR, Thomas (1824)   1016
BLAIR, William (1819)   1931
BLAKE, Anthony R. (1828)   2583
BLAKE, Francis (1741)   861
BLAKEY, Robert (1846)   1100
BLAKEY, Robert, Ph.D. (1836-1854)
                    916, 1745, 1966, 1967
BLAKISTON, E. F. (1861)   1046
BLAKISTON, Lieutenant (1829)   2688
BLANCH, John (1714-1725)   219, 1177,
                                       2530
BLAND, Henry F. (1858)   2457
BLAND, J. Harcourt (1854)   155
BLANDFORD, Lord, W. Godol-
    phin (N.D.)   1355, 1762
BLANE, Sir Gilbert, Bart., M.D.
    (1782-1819)   17, 1227, 2327, 2512
BLANE, William, F.R.S. (1781)   826
BLANE, William Newnham (1824)   854
BLANKET, Lieut. (1777)   1429
BLANSHARD, Richard (1826)   2581
BLAYNEY, Allan (1652)   913
BLAZE DE BURY, Baroness Marie
    P. Rose (1868, 1869)   67, 1520
BLECHYNDER, Richard (1685)   2702
BLEECK, Arthur Henry (1854)   1984
BLENMAN, Richard (1742)   2145
BLESARD, John Robert (1835)   2785
BLESSINGTON, Countess of,
    Margaret Gardiner (1822-1846)   1276,
                    1490, 1533, 2076, 2401, 2611
BLESSINGTON, Earl of, Charles
    John Gardiner (1826)   567
BLESSMAN, Jonathan (1715)   1409
BLEW, William (1848-1869)   398, 402,
                                        721
BLEWITT, George (1725)   774
BLISS, Philip, D.D. (1813)   230
BLOME, R. (1660)   893
BLOMFIELD, Charles J., Bishop
    of London (1823)   2167
BLOOMFIELD, Robert (1801)   895
BLORE, Thomas (1815)   1057
BLOUNT, Charles (1679-1695)   156,
                    1047, 1294, 1304, 1619, 2254
BLOUNT, Edw. (1600)   1125
BLOUNT, Edward (1709)   366
BLOUNT, Sir Henry (1672)   655

BLOUNT, Thomas (1656-1674) 98, 300, 1020, 1711, 2343, 2345

BLOUNT, Walter Kirkham (1687) 456

BLOWER, Elizabeth (1780-1788) 907, 1010, 1547, 1864

BLOXAM, J. M. (1844) 635

BLUNDELL, Henry (1803) 28

BLUNDELL, John (1712) 1575

BLUNT, Gregory (1802) 2395

BLUNT, Rev. John Henry, M.A. (1854-1869) 693, 1299, 1833, 1977, 2261, 2566, 2804

BLUNT, Sir Henry (1650) 2781

BLUNT, William (1819) 1960

BOADEN, James (N.D.) 2020

BOASE, Charles William (1876) 19

BOASE, Frederic (1876) 19

BOASE, George Clement (1848-1876) 19, 1194, 2064, 2258

BOASE, Henry (1823, 1826) 266, 1387

BOATE, Dr G. (1726) 1701

BODDINGTON, Mary (1834-1837) 1035, 2402, 2407

BODENHAM, John (1597-1600) 224, 1962, 2824

BODENHAM, John (1722) 2823

BOECKH, Augustus (1828) 2053

BOEHM, Ant. Will (1714) 2031

BOGUE, David, D.D. (1790) 2092

BOHN, H. G. (1813) 912

BOHUN, Edmund (1682-1689) 38, 584, 692, 1152, 2107, 2304

BOHUN, Edward (1683, 1685) 145, 2566

BOHUN, William (1737) 1988

BOID, Captain Edward (1827-1843) 465, 1166, 2629

BOIS, Edward du (1799-1817) 572, 873, 879, 1686, 1812 (2), 1911, 2207, 2250

BOLD, Henry (1657) 2821

BOLD, John (1745) 2387

BOLD, Samuel (1690-1691) 845, 2296

BOLDE, Samuel (1688-1717) 258, 647, 712, 845

BOLES, W. (1731) 1616

BOLINGBROKE, Lord. Henry St. John (1710-1775) 426, 529, 530, (3) 679, 887, 892, 923, 966, 1030, 1358, 1377, 1396, 1448, 1512, 1784, 1797, 1798 (2), 2055, 2149, 2293

BOLLAN, William (1746-1768) 89, 433, 502, 781, 1214, 1215, 1684

BOLLAND, Rev. John (1853) 1831

BOLTON, —— (1707) 2013

BOLTON, Edmund (1610, 1624) 737, 1710

BOLTON, John (N.D.) 1282

BOLTON, Robert (1751-1755) 124, 598

BOLTON, Robert, LL.D., Dean of Carlisle (1748-1762) 744, 1013, 1371, 1376, 1423

BOMBET, L. A. C. (1817) 1474

BONAR, Archibald (1796) 1008

BONAR, John (1765-1767) 488, 1628

BONAR, Rev. Andrew A. (1843) 1693

BONAR, Rev. Andrew Redman (1844-1858) 306, 1171, 1997, Errata, vol. iv.

BONAR, Rev. John (1750-1765) 1628, 1776

BOND, Sir Thomas, Bart. (1799) 1700

BOND, William (1734) 1921

BONE, John (1807) 2238

BONWICKE, Ambrose, B.D. (1729) 1875

BOODLE, E. (1843) 1035

BOOG, Rev. Dr (1835) 854

BOOKER, Luke (1816) 1857

BOOKER, Rev. Daniel (1746) 219

BOOKER, Richard (1689) 2260

BOON, A. (1656) 843

BOONE, James Shergold, M.A. (1819-1834) 1842, 2801

BOORNE, James (1865) 969

BOOSEY, Thomas (1835) 1916

BOOTH, —— (1739) 491

BOOTH, A. (1656) 843

BOOTH, Joshua (1788) 707

BOOTH, Pithie (1863) 834

BOOTHBY, Sir Brooke (1791-1796) 1412, 2455

BORDE, Andrew, M.D. (1630, N.D.) 1605, 2243

BOREMAN, Robert (1651) 523

BOREMAN, T. (1730) 608

BORINGDON, Lord (1807) 1851

BORLAND, Francis (1715) 1580

BORLASE, Edmund (1680-1682) 270, 1153

BORLASE, Rev. Henry (1838) 2188

BORNE, Ignace de (1783) 1271

BOROUGHS, Rev. —— (1773) 825

BORRENSTEIN, —— (1822) 720

BORTHWICK, Jane (1864-1867) 2499, 2573

BORTHWICK, John (1813-1830) 849, 1403, 2356

BOSANQUET, James Whatman (1836) 563

BOSCAWEN, William (1798) 2028

BOSSUET, Jacques Bénigne (1687) 2633
BOSTOCK, R. (1647) 2275
BOSTOCK, Robert (1585) 631
BOSTON, —— (1779) 133
BOSTON, Michael   Errata, vol. iv.
BOSTON, Thomas (1722) 2067
BOSWELL, James (1761-1784) 541, 547, 735, 831, 1800, 2471
BOSWELL, James (1661) 1803
BOSWELL, James (1816) 2452
BOSWELL, John (1750) 2159
BOSWELL, John, M.A. (1758) 323
BOSWELL, John W. (1790) 2514
BOSWELL, Rev. John (1751) 2148
BOSWELL, Robert, W.S. (1784) 247
BOSWELL, Sir Alexander, Bart. (1803-1816) 725, 2449, 2475, 2830
BOSWELL, Thomas Alexander (1825-1826) 1277, 2099
BOSWORTH, John (1853) 2249
BOSWORTH, Joseph, D.D. (1849) 778
BOTFIELD, Beriah (1830) 1276
BOTT, Edmund (1771) 423
BOTT, Thomas (1725-1744) 2014, 2201
BOUCHER, Barton (1818) 705
BOUGHEN, Edward (1644) 1691
BOULTER, ——, Archbishop of Armagh (1733) 963
BOULTON, Richard (1715-1716) 454
BOURN, Samuel (1754-1768) 2280, 2647
BOURNE, John George H. (1833-1835) 857, 1909, 2453
BOW, J. D. B. de (1845) 1963
BOWDEN, —— (1836) 1528
BOWDEN, James (1863) 844
BOWDLER, Harriet M. (1852) 2339
BOWDLER, John (1798) 2117
BOWDLER, Mrs Thomas (1775-1808) 955, 1945, 1985, 2448
BOWDLER, Rev. Thomas (1824) 1573
BOWDLER, Thomas, M.A. (1815) 1459
BOWER, Archibald (1757, 1730) 252, 1104
BOWES, Thomas (1586) 967
BOWLES, Caroline Anne (1826) 2415
BOWLES, Caroline, Mrs Southey (1822-1829) 357, 741, 2544, 2814
BOWLES, Edward (1643) 1928
BOWLES, John (1766-1815) 409, 624, 1980, 2040, 2108, 2697
BOWLES, William Lisle (1789-1820) 1951, 2172, 2322
BOWLKER, —— (1766) 2711
BOWMAN, Anne (1853) 1323

BOWRA, William (1793)
BOWREY, Thomas (1701) 629
BOWRING, John (1823) 611
BOWRING, Sir John, LL.D. (1822) 2419
BOWYER, William (1729-1773) 673, 1336, 1875, 2316
BOXHORN, Mark Zuirius (1701) 168
BOYCE, John Coxe (1842) 1957
BOYCE, Thomas (1752) 2231
BOYD, Andrew Kennedy Hutchison, D.D. (1854-1882) 206, 308, 356, 441, 518, 538, 1043, 1310, 1340, 1342, 1834, 1999, 2102, 2286, 2518
BOYD, Archibald (1850) 707
BOYD, Hugh M'Aulay (1798) 1435
BOYER, Abel (1713-1717) 452, 1587, 1899
BOYER, John B. de, Marquis D'Argens (1765) 372
BOYLE, Charles, Earl of Orrery (1703) 188
BOYLE, Francis Viscount Shannon (1690, 1691) 1422, 1657
BOYLE, Hon. Eleanor Vere (1853-1877) 370, 1218, 1716
BOYLE, Hon. Robert (1663-1698) 384, 795, 852, 962, 1050, 1096, 1105, 1796, 2095, 2112, 2264, 2422
BOYLE, John Magor (1835) 1032
BOYLE, Robert (1675) 2421
BOYLE, Roger, Earl of Orrery (1655-1676) 754, 1865
BOYS, T. (1818) 928
BOYSE, Rev. Joseph, D.D. (1688-1722) 412, 1806, 2138, 2287, 2767
BOYSE, Samuel (1732-1742) 62, 598, 2726
BRAC, Andrew Edmund (1855, 1860) 431, 1494
BRACCIOLINI, Francesco (1638) 2618
BRACEBRIDGE, Charles Holte (1827) 201
BRADBURY, Mrs (1865) 1916
BRADBURY, Thomas (1717-1732) 1678-2138
BRADDICK, Walter (1768) 372
BRADDON, Mary Elizabeth (1863-1885) 237, 366, 404, 419, 567, 568, 912, 1084, 1181, 1270, 1274, 1292, 1314, 1515, 1520, 1523, 1617, 1670, 1819 (2), 1895, 2058, 2075, 2219, 2240 (2), 2390, 2501 (2), 2537, 2599, 2774, 2844
BRADFORD, John (1841) 2543
BRADLAUGH, Charles (1859 ——) 1254, 1724 (3), 2203

BRADLEY, Charles (1822)   1827
BRADLEY, Henry (1733)   2642
BRADLEY, R. (1779)   770
BRADLEY, Rev. Edward, B.A.
    (1853-1866)   50, 431, 549, 878, 1017,
    1068, 1521, 1560, 1670, 1675, 1705, 1834,
        1905, 2226, 2351, 2540, 2611, 2809
BRADSHAW —— (1790)   2278
BRADSHAW, Hon. Mary Ann
    Cavendish (1808, 1810)   912, 1582
BRADSHAW, Rev. William (1703) 2633
BRADSHAW, William (1599-1605)
    762, 1189, 2038, 2045, 2380, 2638, 2652,
                                  2687
BRADY, Dr Nathaniel (1692)   2078
BRADY, John Henry (1824-1835)
                1496, 1919 (2), 1924
BRADY, Robert, M.D. (1681——)
                977, 1048, 1231, 2661
BRAGG, Jane (1839, 1862)   1332, 2726
BRAGG, Dr Robert (1778)   1279
BRAGGE, Francis, B.D. (1712)   978,
                982, 1217 (2), 2822
BRAGGE, Robert (1676)   1466
BRAIDWOOD, William (1792)   1859
BRAMHALL, Archbishop (1643)   2340
BRAMHALL, J., Archbishop of
    Armagh (1706)   2791
BRAMHALL, John, Bishop of Derry
    (1659-1686)   109, 128, 1153, 2752
BRAMHALL, John, D.D. (1649)   877
BRAMLY, Rev. T. J. (1845)   1504
BRAMSTON, John (1733)   1539
BRAMSTON, James (1729)   183
BRAMSTON, James, M.A. (1743)   543
BRAMWELL, George (1823)   1542
BRANCH, Thomas (1753)   2015
BRAND, Sir Alexander (N.D.)   1839
BRAND, John, M.A. (1790)   1965
BRANDRAM, Rev. Andrew (1826)   228
BRANKS, William (1861-1865)   1079,
                1470, 1566, 2537
BRASBRIDGE, Thomas (1574)   3
BRASH, Richard (1825)   42
BRASHER, A. (1882)   2078
BRAITHWAIT, Richard (1640-1655)
                190, 213, 1683, 2695
BRATHWAIT, Richard (1805)   707
BRAITHWAITE, Henry Thomas
    (1851)   2125
BRATHWAITE, Richard (1847)   1882
BRATHWAYT, Richard (1615-1669)
    180, 308, 336, 1030, 1142, 1174, 1500,
    1601, 1849, 2050, 2501, 2502, 2808

BRAY, Anna Eliza (1828)   2041
BRAY, Charles (1838)   727
BRAY, T. (1702)   232
BRAY, Thomas, D.D. (1697)   233
BRAY, Rev. Thomas, D.D. (1712) 1850
BRAY, William (1800)   430
BRAY, William, F.S.A. (1778)   2398
BRAYLEY, E. W. (1806)   465
BRECHIN, Bishop of, Alexander
    Penrose Forbes (1847-1853) 439, 1170,
                1574, 1595, 1622
BRECHIN, Bishop of, J. Raitt (1744) 1235
BRECKNOCK, Timothy (1764)   706
BREDWELL, S. (1588)   2078
BREED, Mr —— (1834)   1504
BREKELL, John (1753-1754)   1844
BREMOND, Gabriel de (1678)   2730
BREMNAR, John (1846)   1218
BREND, William (1662)   2363
BRENT, John (1836)   1333
BRERELY, R. (1632)   1283
BRERETON, Thomas (1719)   542
BRETON, Nicholas (1582-1643)   213,
    514, 753, 894, 923, 935, 1053, 1201 (2),
                1866 (2), 2824
BRETT, Arthur, M.A. (1669)   601
BRETT, Dr (1758)   477
BRETT, Robert (1849-1867)   403, 615,
    693, 711, 916, 1806 (2), 1981, 2106, 2574
BRETT, Thomas, LL.D. (1701-1743)
        14, 378, 424, 687, 949, 1048, 1364
BREVAL, Captain John Durant de
    (1716-1727) 182, 469, 1176, 1895, 2507
BREVITER, Thomas (1728) 1634, 2006
BREWER, Anthony (1617, 1647)
                                521, 1605
BREWER, George (1793)   1561
BREWER, George, M.D. (1843)   1552
BREWER, James Norris (1829)   931
BREWSTER, Margaret Maria (1842)
                                 528
BREWSTER, Rev. J. (1823)   1572
BREWSTER, Samuel (1701-1704)   383,
                                1401
BREWSTER, Sir David (1804-1806)
                                850, 1137
BRICE, Andrew (1755)   2367
BRIDAL or BRYDALL, John (1676) 448
BRIDGE, J. (1843)   1359
BRIDGES, A. M. (1860)   2688
BRIDGES, George (1739)   1421
BRIDGES, James (1823)   1414
BRIDGES, James, W.S. (1812, 1824)
                                158, 2735

BRIDGES, Robert (1876) 1056
BRIDGES, Thomas (1762-1771) 48, 216, 629, 930, 1732
BRIDGEWATER, Benjamin (N.D.) 2128
BRIDGEWATER, Earl of, F. H. Egerston (1793) 1483
BRIDGMAN, J. (1795) 237
BRIDLE, John, D.D. (1758) 1405
BRIGGS, James (1814) 1220
BRIGHT, George, D.D., Dean of St Asaph (1682, 1695) 795, 880
BRIGHT, Timothy (1615) 2648
BRIGHTLAND, J. (1711) 2090
BRIGHTWELL, Thomas (1828) 1275
BRIMLEY, George (1851) 2063
BRINDLEY, J. (1766) 1140
BRINKLOW, Henry (1536) 451
BRINKLOW, R. (1536) 451
BRINSBY, John (1648) 300
BRISBANE, Emily (1850) 2286
BRISCOE, J. (1696) 651
BRISCOE, John Ivatt (1824) 1363
BRISCOE, Sophia (1771, 1772) 924, 1634
BRISTED, —— (1772) 2283
BRISTED, John (1803) 54, 536
BRISTOL, Bishop of, George Smalridge, D.D. (1701) 2441
BRISTOL, Bishop of, Robert Gray, D.D. (1802, 1808) 335, 2564
BRISTOL, Dean of, Dr Simon Robson (1585) 373
BRISTOL, Earl of, George Digby (1667) 742
BRISTOW, John Charles (1835) 2703
BRISTOW, Rev. —— (1756) 1642
BRITAINE, William de (1680) 1187
BRITTON, John (1806, 1807) 465, 1940
BRITTON, John, F.S.A. (1801) 219
BRITTON, Richard (1616) 1545
BROCKETT, John Trotter (1818-1827) 1101, 1536, 2275, 2382, 2537
BRODICK, —— (1768) 372
BRODIE, Alexander (1826) 2033
BRODIE, David (1859) 1077
BRODIE, Sir Benjamin Collins (1854) 2053
BRODRICK, T. (1720) 1104
BROGHILL, Lord, Roger Boyle (1655-1669) 1865
BROKESBY, Francis, B.D. (1708) 2435
BROMDY, J. H. (1822) 1885
BROME, Alexander (1665-1672) 529, 1950, 2101
BROOME, Ralph (1789) 1442

BROME, Richard (1649-1653) 407, 560, 1311
BROMFIELD, William (1755) 2266
BROMLEY, William (1693-1705) 2134 (2), 2345
BRONTË, Anne (1846-1850) 58, 1946, 2552, 2844
BRONTË, Charlotte (1846-1857) 1261, 1946, 2026, 2352, 2740, 2844
BRONTË, Emily Jane (1846, 1850) 1946, 2844
BROOKE, Christopher (1613, 1614) 1013, 2693
BROOKE, Henry (1735-1750) 872, 897, 1716, 2711
BROOKE, Henry, D.C.L. (1740) 161
BROOKE, Frances, née Moore (1754-1788) 60, 1134, 1141, 1812, 2229, 2770
BROOKE, Lord, Fulke Greville (1609, 1651) 2619, 2620
BROOKE, Robert (1641) 658
BROOKE, Robert (1780) 2133
BROOKE, Stopford A. (1880) 2216
BROOKE, T. (N.D.) 722
BROOKES, R., M.D. (1720) 1701
BROOKFIELD, A. M. (1881, 1884) 1978, 2386
BROOKS, Joshua W. (1834) 3
BROOKS, Maria (1833) 2854
BROOME, —— (1717) 2798
BROOMFIELD, William (1725) 881
BROSTER, John, F.S.A. (1799) 726
BROTHERTON, Edward (1869) 2003
BROTHERTON, Mrs (1856) 186
BROUGH, William, D.D. (1650) 2247
BROUGHAM, Henry (1694) 2107
BROUGHAM, Henry, Lord Brougham and Vaux (1804-1854) 62, 466 (2), 525 (2), 655, 894, 1134, 1382, 1572, 1766, 1965, 2583, 2797, 2839
BROUGHTON, Rev. Hugh (1590, 1591) 2378, 2556
BROUGHTON, Rev. Thomas (1732, 1737) 385, 1670
BROUGHTON, Rhoda (1867-1870) 434, 1751, 2103
BROUGHTON, Richard (1655) 1651
BROUN, John Brown or (1665) 144
BROWN, —— (1807) 8
BROWN, —— (1783) 2404
BROWN, A., M.A. (1837) 997
BROWN, Andrew, M.D. (1702-1706) 361, 810, 2266, 2296, 2445
BROWN, Anthony (1739) 903

BROWN, Charles John, D.D. (1832) 1251, 1362
BROWN, Charlotte Elizabeth (1826) 1258
BROWN, Colin (1869, 1870) 1682 (2)
BROWN, David (1826) 586, 2696
BROWN, Edward (1672) 655
BROWN, Edward (1871) 746
BROWN, George (1804) 1383
BROWN, George (1703) 2603
BROWN, George Shaw (1863) 2509
BROWN, Hugh (1832) 790
BROWN, Ignatius (1678) 2708
BROWN, J. (N.D.) 466
BROWN, James (N.D.) 2320
BROWN, James (1824, 1825) 1000, 1774
BROWN, James (1862, 1869) 228, 248, 1944
BROWN, James (1775) 1215
BROWN, James (1703) 2296, 2495
BROWN, James Bryce (1844) 2737
BROWN, James, M.D. (1816) 1035
BROWN, J. Baldwin (1864) 1657
BROWN, John (1678) 1156
BROWN, John (1743, 1779) 1174, 1822
BROWN, John, D.D. (1755-1803) 34, 61, 192, 212, 832, 862, 1405, 2576
BROWN, John, M.D. (1787) 1783
BROWN, John, M.D. (1851) 2823
BROWN, John, or Broun (1665) 144
BROWN, John Taylor (1867, 1869) 230, 1203
BROWN, Robert (1694) 2510
BROWN, Robert (1817-1879) 435, 1084, 1270, 1400, 1555, 1591, 1834
BROWN, Rev. John (1787) 966
BROWN, S. J. (1687) 1876
BROWN, Thomas (1690) 1321
BROWN, Thomas (1701) 1481, 1589
BROWN, Thomas (1691) 1757, 2093 (2)
BROWN, Thomas (1814) 1855
BROWN, Thomas (1688) 2093
BROWN, Thomas (1833) 2167
BROWN, Thomas (1704) 2482
BROWN, Thomas (1813) 2696
BROWN, Thomas Crowther (1862, 1866) 1331, 2513
BROWN, Thomas, M.D. (1808-1817) 252, 2001, 2168
BROWN, Timothy, P.P. (1745) 2680
BROWN, Tom (1687) 2110
BROWN, W. (N.D.) 2399
BROWN, Walter (N.D.) 1332, 1559
BROWN, William (1858) 161
BROWN, William (1710) 1214

BROWN, William (1706) 1987
BROWN, William (1694) 1990
BROWN, William, junior (1843) 934
BROWN, William Laurence, D.D. (1784, 1789) 801, 2727
BROWNE, Capt. John M. (1827) 1123
BROWNE, Charles Farrer (1865) 185, 227
BROWNE, Charlotte E. Tonna née, see Tonna.
BROWNE, Dr Thomas (1645) 1299
BROWNE, Francis (1780) 1428
BROWNE, Halbot K. (N.D.) 1193
BROWNE, Isaac Hawkins (1736, 1815) 829, 1916
BROWNE, J. (1640) 1599
BROWNE, James, LL.D. (1832) 1481
BROWNE, John, LL.D. (1825) 538
BROWNE, Joseph, M.B. (1705) 1655
BROWNE, Joseph, D.D. (1706) 2777
BROWNE, Moses (1723, 1729) 67, 1917
BROWNE, Peter, Bishop of Corke and Rosse (1728, 1733) 2024, 2566
BROWNE, Simon (1721, 1732) 595, 2410
BROWNE, Sir Thomas (1642) 2129
BROWNE, Thomas (1640) 2233
BROWNE, Thomas (1831) 1864
BROWNE, Thomas, B.D. (1690-1691) 115, 311, 2436, 2800
BROWNE, Thomas, D.D. (1683) 1620
BROWNE, William (1613) 2693
BROWNE, William (1768) 2761
BROWNING, Elizabeth Barrett (1826) 799
BROWNLEE, Thomas (1822) 1695
BRUCE, Alexander (1722-1759) 766, 1226, 2276
BRUCE, Archibald (1774-1813) 103, 335, 965, 1240, 1307, 1878, 1952, 2065, 2108
BRUCE, Captain Alexander (1706) 649
BRUCE, George (1820) 1871
BRUCE, James (1840) 239
BRUCE, John (1734-1798) 485, 1123, 2179 (2), 2199
BRUCE, John, F.S.A. (1837) 104, 1334, 2567
BRUCE, Rev. Archibald (1782, 1797) 1882, 2505
BRUCKNER, John (1768, 1790) 541, 1902
BRUHIER D'ABLAINCOURT, Jean Jacques (1746) 2806
BRUNE, J. de la (1691) 1480
BRUNTON, Alex., D.D. (1822) 1838

BRUNTON, Mary (1811, 1814) 637, 2319
BRUTO, Giovanni Michele (1598) 1705
BRUZEAU, Paul (1687) 881
BRYAN, John, D.D. (1674) 1073
BRYANT, Jacob (1775-1793) 36, 1770, 2749, 2768
BRYCE, James, D.D. (1841) 1411, 1917
BRYDALL, John (1580) 1288
BRYDALL, John (1758) 2357
BRYDALL, John Bridal or (1676) 448
BRYDGES, Grey, Lord Chandos (1611, 1620) 639, 1178
BRYDGES, Sir Samuel Egerton, Bart. (1785-1831) 162, 186, 236, 933, 942, 1333, 1457, 1512, 1589, 1639, 1685, 1795, 1942, 1944, 2111, 2391, 2454, 2726
BRYDGES, Thomas (1797) 291
BRYDONE, James (1847) 2090
BUBIER, G. B. (1855) 1197
BUC, Georg (1605) 564
BUCER, Martin (1530, 1566) 2052, 2633
BUCHAN, Alexander (1727) 607
BUCHAN, A. W. (1873) 831
BUCHAN, George (1820) 1697
BUCHAN, Patrick (1870-1873) 1004, 1340
BUCHANAN, —— (1763) 2328
BUCHANAN, C. (1816) 2783
BUCHANAN, David (1645) 2680
BUCHANAN, George (1571-1572) 45, 612
BUCHANAN, George (1642) 2703
BUCHANAN, James, D.D. (1842) 41
BUCHANAN, Professor Robert (1856-1859) 956, 2620, 2785
BUCHANAN, Rev. —— (1753) 722
BUCHANAN, Rev. Thomas (1843) 1618
BUCHANAN, Robert (1817) 1097
BUCHANAN, Robert, D.D. (1839) 1998
BUCK, Sir George (1605) 564
BUCKE, Charles (1813-1819) 78, 1256, 1904
BUCKERIDGE, Lieut.-Col. (1800) 2534
BUCKHAM, Philip W. (1825) 2558
BUCKHURST, Lord, Thomas Sackville (1671) 1711, 2621
BUCKINGHAM, Duke of. George Villers (1623-1682) 355, 787, 1387, 1957, 2124, 2673
BUCKINGHAM, Duke of, John Sheffield (1682) 819
BUCKINGHAM, Leicester-Silk. (1854) 58
BUCKLAND, A. C. (1820) 1447
BUCKLAND, Ralph (N.D.) 2291

BUCKLER, Benjamin' D.D. (1751-1775) 460, 740, 2032, 2111, 2492, 2524
BUCKLER, John Chessell (1823) 1781
BUCKLEY, Sir R. (1690) 97
BUCKLEY, Theodore Alois (1848) 1701
BUCKMINSTER, Eliza Lee née (1849) 1475
BUCKRIDGE, William (1704) 1369
BUDD, James (1701) 635
BUDD, Thomas II. (1871) 2231
BUDGE, Edward (1809-1850) 406, 1786, 2137
BUDGE, Jane (1860, 1866) 757, 1545
BUDGE, John (1845-1857) 1570, 2431, 2432
BUDGELL, Eustace (1733) 2368
BUDGEN, L. M. (1849-1855) 779, 1546, 1561
BUDWORTH, Josiah (1795) 944
BUERSTENBINDER, Emile (1876-1884) 920, 1746, 2081, 2217, 2247, 2512, 2707
BUGG, Francis (1693) 2433
BUGG, Rev. George (1819-1827) 549, 2280
BULKELEY, Richard (1717) 1451
BULKELEY, Charles (1751) 2747
BULL, Henry (1570) 381
BULL, John (1824) 2406
BULLAR, Joseph, M.D. (1850-1868) 838, 2575
BULLOCK, Christopher (1718) 1886, 2629
BULLOCK, Stephen (1716) 50
BULTEEL, John (1644-1675) 77, 225, 2126
BULWER-LYTTON, Edward G. E. L., Lord Lytton (1826-1871) 243, 420, 436, 534, 613, 666 (2), 707 (2), 833, 884, 1022, 1072, 1313, 1319, 1524, 1732, 1740, 1818, 1875, 1881, 1914, 2208, 2212, 2253, 2284, 2799, 2805, 2836
BULWER - LYTTON, Edward Robert (1859-1863) 1523, 2216, 2325, 2546, 2787
BULWER, Sir Henry Lytton (1824) 2602
BUMPSTEAD, William (1739) 1214
BUNBURY, —— (1718) 1048
BUNBURY, H. (1792, 1809) 10, 100
BUNBURY, H. W. (1801) 2542
BUNBURY, Major Thomas (1857, 1861) 1683, 2167
BUNBURY, Sir Henry Edward, Bart. (1833) 1959
BUNCE, C. R. (1791) 2623

BUNN, A. (1819) 2545
BUNNETT, Fanny Elizabeth (1857) 1094, 1316
BUNSEN, Chevalier (1852) 246
BUNYAN, John (1691, 1774) 1078, 1263
BURDETT, C. D. (1827, 1828) 191, 756
BURDETT, Constance (1878) 934
BURDETT, Sir Francis, Bart. (1818) 100
BURDON, Richard (1845) 1840
BURDON, William, M.A. (1797, 1803) 918, 2071
BURFORD, John, M.A. (1727) 174
BURGE, William, Q.C. (1829) 1387
BURGES, Cornelius (1641-1660) 1188, 1745, 2094, 2433, 2759 (2)
BURGES, George, B.A. (1832) 2397
BURGES, James (1840) 2196
BURGESS, James (1754) 1503
BURGESS, Mary Ann (1800) 2029
BURGESS, Rev. George (1824) 341
BURGESS, Samuel W. (1825) 1118
BURGESS, Sir James Bland (1780-1792) 66, 1091, 1431
BURGESS, Thomas, D.D. (1777-1819) 209, 1080, 2095
BURGESS, Thomas, D.D., Bishop of St Davids (1819) 1441
BURGESS, Thomas, D.D., Bishop of Salisbury (1782-1833) 482, 812, 857, 1244
BURGESS, W. H. (1819, 1820) 227 (2)
BURGH, James (1747-1792) 19, 185, 280, 542, 1196, 1652, 1964, 2037, 2576
BURGH, Rev. William, B.A. (1827) 435
BURGH, William (1773, 1776) 1071, 2279
BURGH, William, or De Brugh, D.D. (1839) 764
BURGHLEY, Lord (1677) 1265
BURGOING, Jean-François (1799) 1112
BURGON, John William, M.A. (1855) 1743
BURGOYNE, Col. John Fox (1831) 1250
BURGOYNE, John (1781, 1786) 1513, 2208
BURGOYNE, Lieutenant-General John (1774) 1536
BURGOYNE, Montague (1817) 2491
BURKE, —— (1765) 1845
BURKE, Edmund (1756-1796) 19, 157, 1349, 1770, 1901, 2178, 2353, 2579, 2582, 2747
BURKE, Ed. Plunkett (1833) 1501
BURKE, J. F. (1834-1844) 282, 898, 1316

BURKE, Mrs (1787, 1796) 44, 732, 743
BURKE, Richard (1777) 1443
BURKE, Right Hon. Edmund (1771) 1435
BURKE, William (1859) 1435
BURLEIGH, Lord, William Cecil (1583, 1585) 574, 575, 855
BURN, A. (1789) 381
BURN, Andrew (1789) 2810
BURN, James Dawson (1855-1868) 204, 440, 1017
BURN, R. Scott (1864) 1037
BURNABY, Charles (1700-1703) 1312, 1518, 1649, 2120
BURNAND, F. G. (N.D.) 1184
BURNBY, John (1772) 1115
BURNE, Nicol (1581) 46
BURNELL, Henry (1659) 2842
BURNET, Elizabeth (1708) 1608
BURNET, Gilbert, D.D. (1665-1717) 111, 116, 151, 312, 502, 508, 648, 658, 769, 771, 773, 858, 963, 1346 (2), 1422, 1484, 1644, 1648, 1778, 2013, 2045, 2107, 2108, 2111, 2112, 2113, 2125, 2126, 2225, 2305, 2437, 2515, 2587, 2715, 2720, 2756, 2760, 2837
BURNET, Gilbert, Bishop of Salisbury (1680, 1717) 508, 2515, 2720
BURNET, Gilbert, D.D., Bishop of Sarum (N.D.) 1346
BURNET, Sir Thomas (1712-1777) 361, 1173, 1833, 2164, 2424, 2680, 2727
BURNET, T. (1700) 122
BURNET, Thomas (1812) 1139
BURNET, Thomas (1712-1715) 2309, 2665
BURNET, Thomas, LL.D. (1691-1719) 158, 582, 2363
BURNET, William (1724) 801
BURNETT, Frances H. (1878) 2526
BURNETT, George (1865, 1871) 1974, 2276
BURNETT, James, Lord Monboddo (1773, 1779) 136, 1825
BURNS, Jabez, D.D. (1844, 1845) 381, 2056
BURNS, Robert (1789) 1990
BURNS, Robert, D.D. (1826, 1830) 2176, 2199
BURNEY, C. (1769, 1811) 187, 815
BURNEY, Frances (1793) 270
BURNEY, Frances D'Arblay, née (1782, 1791) 346, 847
BURNEY, Sarah Harriet (1796, 1808) 411, 1011

BURRELL, Lady (1793)   1949
BURROUGH, Edward (1656-1661)
   321, 547, 576, 1185, 1291, 1888, 2190,
   2259, 2447, 2599, 2666, 2760
BURROUGHS, Samuel (1726-1768)
   768, 1150, 1337
BURROW, Sir James (1763)   90, 914
BURSCOUGH, Robert (1702)   2766
BURSCOUGH, William (1732)   2068
BURT, Captain Edward (1755)   1426
BURT, William (1810)   611
BURTON, Dr J. (1540)   1245
BURTON, Edward, B.D. (1829)   2571
BURTON, Edward, D.D. (1820)   36
BURTON, Henry (1632-1660)   186, 686,
   1264, 2045, 2169, 2683
BURTON, John (1764)   2003
BURTON, John Hill, D.C.L. (1865)   509
BURTON, John, M.D. (1749, 1769)
   91, 1008
BURTON, Mrs John Hill, née Innes
   (1865, 1874)   1570, 1835
BURTON, Philip (1778, 1791)   325, 2467
BURTON, Richard (1682-1732)   44,
   373, 599, 752, 756, 757, 870, 1001, 1144,
   1156, 1158, 1167, 2695, 2709, 2714, 2722,
   2828
BURTON, Robert (1632, 1687)   86, 757
BURTON, Robert (1710)   2709
BURTON, William (1652)   927
BURY, Arthur, D.D. (1690, 1691)   313,
   588, 1691
BURY, Baroness Blaze de, Marie P.
   Rose (1868, 1869)   67, 1520
BURY, James (1859)   1908
BURY, Lady Charlotte Maria (1822-
   1842)   69, 468, 614, 626, 666, 853, 935,
   1130, 1278, 1517, 1542, 1549, 1578, 1990,
   2323, 2529
BUSH, Edward (1576)   2335
BUSHBY, Henry Jeffreys (1855)   1654
BUSHE, Gervase Parker (1769)   314
BUSHNAN, John S., M.D. (1860)
   1834
BUSK, Hans (1819)   211, 610
BUSK, Mrs (1825)   2540
BUSK, R. H. (1870, 1873)   1183, 1872,
   2249
BUTLER, Alban (1754)   2155
BUTLER, Alfred (1842)   1086
BUTLER, Charles (1777-1815)   23, 807,
   1112, 1732, 2367
BUTLER, J. (1747)   865
BUTLER, John (1847)   2398

BUTLER, John, D.D., Bishop of
   Hereford (1762-1814)   37, 497, 1402,
   1435, 2329, 2417
BUTLER, John, Bishop of Oxford
   (1772)   1402
BUTLER, Josephine (1871)   496
BUTLER, Joseph, LL.D., Bishop of
   Durham (1716, 1719)   1361, 2344
BUTLER, Richard, Dean of Clon-
   maconis (1837, 1840)   2427 (2)
BUTLER, Robert (1823)   · 1697
BUTLER, Samuel (1643-1691)   31, 1185,
   1356, 1601, 1918, 2037, 2696
BUTLER, Samuel (1872)   788
BUTLER, W. (1781)   369
BUTT, Beatrice May (1877, 1879)
   599, 833
BUTT, Isaac (1848)   993
BUTT, Nathan (1832)   2074
BUTT, Rev. J. M. (1824)   2066
BUTTER, Alfred (1842)   1613
BUTTERWORTH, Henry (1818)   330
BUXTON, B. H. (1876)   1263
BUXTON, H. J. W. (1865, 1866)
   1688, 1944
BUXTON, Sir Thomas F. Errata, vol. iv.
BUXTON, Sir Thomas P. (1837)
   2164, Errata, vol. iv.
BYERLEY, John Scott (1803, 1823)
   244, 2128
BYERLEY, Thomas (1823, 1824)
   1508, 1884
BYFIELD, A. (1645)   273
BYLES, Sir John Barnard (1850)   2455
BYNG, —— (1852)   2580
BYRNE, Mrs William Pitt (1805-
   1869)   221, 913, 934, 1013, 1016, 1181,
   1910, 2083, 2104, 2707, 2854
BYROM, Dr John (1726-1751)   774, 782,
   2685
BYRON, George G. N., Lord Byron
   (1807-1823)   56, 698, 755, 1318, 1458,
   1653, 1952, 1954, 2382, 2771, 2787
BYSSHE, Edward (1707)   428

C.

CABANEL, Daniel (1811)   285, 2602
CADDELL, Cecilia Mary (1825,
   1832)   1557, 1709, 2120
CADENHEAD, William (1811)   1490
CADWALADER, Thomas (1745)   813
CAESAR, Charles (1689)   1759
CAESAR, Sir Julius (1597)   90

CAITHNESS, Bishop of, R. Forbes, D.D. (1774)   17
CALAMY, Benjamin, D.D. (1683, 1684)   638, 2420
CALAMY, Dr Edmund (1714)   2066
CALAMY, Edmund (1641)   106, 2749
CALAMY, Edmund, B.D. (1645)   700
CALAMY, Edmund, D.D. (1699)   647
CALCUTTA, Bishop of, Daniel Wilson, D.D. (1818)   586
CALDECOTT, Thomas (1819)   1062
CALDER, Rev. Robert (N.D., 1705)   133, 686
CALDER, Robert (1692-1717)   110, 117, 523, 1326, 1374, 2009, 2067, 2089, 2273, 2307, 2337, 2360, 2474
CALDER, William (1838)   1949
CALDERON DE LA BARCA, Mme. (1843)   1470
CALDERWOOD, David (1602-1636)   71, 525, 583, 621, 668, 782, 856, 1869, 1892, 2059, 2105 (2), 2415, 2462
CALDWELL, J. (1810)   2612
CALDWELL, Sir James (1766)   571
CALEF, John (1781)   2383
CALFHILL, James (1565)   199
CALLAGHAN, —— (1819)   1353
CALLANDER, —— (1763)   1196
CALLANDER, John (1779, 1782)   598, 816
CALLAWAY, Henry (1841)   1209
CALLENDER, James Thomson (1792)   1966
CALPRENEDE, Seigneur de la, Gauthier de Costes (1676)   326
CALTON, Calvin (1833)   76
CALTHROP, Sir Henry (1642)   1459
CALTHROPE, Hon. Somerset J. G. (1857)   1427
CALVERLEY, Charles Stuart (1862, 1872)   937, 2726
CALVERT, Dr (1838)   1569
CALVIN, John (N.D.)   45
CAMBRIDGE, Richard Owen (1756)   884
CAMDEN, Lord Charles (1794)   1435
CAMDEN, William (1730)   1125
CAMDEN, William (1614)   2132
CAMERON, Alexander, Bishop of Maximianopolis (1798)   1408
CAMERON, John (1626, N.D.)   851, 2845
CAMERON, John Alexander (1849)   1653
CAMERON, Rev. William (1796)   1801
CAMERON, Richard (1708)   815
CAMFIELD, Benjamin (1668)   2330

CAMP, Maria Thérèse de, Mrs C. Kemble née (1808)   565
CAMPANELLA, Thomas (1654)   660
CAMPBELL, —— (1740)   474
CAMPBELL, Alexander (1726-1797)   712, 846, 1059, 1803
CAMPBELL, Archibald (1825)   991
CAMPBELL, Archibald (1703-1767)   1160, 1406, 1457, 2068, 2254, 2564
CAMPBELL, Archibald, Bishop of Aberdeen (1702, 1713)   2067, 2434
CAMPBELL, Archibald, D.D. (1728)   170
CAMPBELL, Dr (1738)   284
CAMPBELL, Dr John (1744)   2350
CAMPBELL, Dr Thomas (1777)   1902
CAMPBELL, Dr William (1709)   2665
CAMPBELL, Dugald (1707)   2174
CAMPBELL, Duncan (N.D.)   161
CAMPBELL, George D., Duke of Argyle (1842)   1402
CAMPBELL, George D., Marquis of Lorne (1842)   1402
CAMPBELL, G. L. (1744)   2127
CAMPBELL, Harriette (1839)   1819
CAMPBELL, Hon. Archibald (1738)   1401
CAMPBELL, Hugh H., Earl of Marchmont (1739)   2488
CAMPBELL, John (1833)   2069
CAMPBELL, John, B.A. (1823)   1100
CAMPBELL, John, Duke of Argyle (1740)   557
CAMPBELL, John Francis (1863-1869)   1470, 2357, 2440
CAMPBELL, John, LL.D. (1736-1771)   304, 321, 322, 459, 465, 841, 1089, 1097, 1358, 1368, 1615, 1702, 1866, 2002, 2079, 2124, 2322, 2461, 2628
CAMPBELL, John, W.S. (1795)   38
CAMPBELL, Lady Charlotte (1812)   2320
CAMPBELL, Mrs (1810)   2379
CAMPBELL, Peter Colin, D.D. (1873)   18
CAMPBELL, Peter, S.S.C. (1825)   1766
CAMPBELL, Rev. John (1801)   2280
CAMPBELL, Robert (1846)   717
CAMPBELL, Sir Ilay (1809)   1103
CAMPBELL, Thomas (1807, 1843)   100, 1145
CAMPBELL, Walter F.   Errata, vol. iv.
CAMPBELL, William (1778)   1294
CAMPE, Joachim Heinrich (1822)   1729
CAN, J. (1604)   777
CAN, John (1765)   788
CANCELLER, James (1626)   1
CANDLER, —— (1824)   2517

clxv   CAN —

CANDLER, John (1812)   2177
CANDLISH, Robert Smith, D.D.
(1839-1841)   969, 2296, 2485
CANE, John Vincent (1661-1672)   14,
625, 784, 920, 2599
CANNE, John (1641)   2532
CANNING, —— (1740, 1749) 2138, 2359
CANNING, —— (1802, 1807) 740, 2269
CANNING, George (1762, 1790)   1178,
1612
CANNING, Mr (1805)   1617
CANNING, W. (1688)   1013
CANT, Andrew (1711-1714) 2334 (3),
2337
CANTERBURY, Archbishop of,
George Abbot (1624, 1641)   124, 2638
CANTERBURY, Archbishop John
Whitgift (1589)   1666
CANTERBURY, Archbishop of,
Matthew Parker (1557-1564) 145, 584,
1022, 2811
CANTERBURY, Archbishop of,
T. Cranmer (1547)   353
CANTERBURY, Archbishop of,
Thomas Tenison, D.D. (1670-1688)
171, 532, 631, 971, 1753, 2003, 2393,
2552, 2649
CANTERBURY, Archbishop of,
W. Fleetwood (N.D.)   584
CANTERBURY, Archbishop of,
William Juxon (1662, 1694)   364, 2510
CANTERBURY, Archbishop of,
William Wake, D.D. (1682-1716) 263,
400, 448, 502, 589, 640, 646, 653, 864,
1123, 1347, 1995, 2003, 2294, 2525, 2692,
2762
CANTERBURY, Canon of, George
Thorpe, D.D. (1687, 1688)   921, 1753
CANTERBURY, Dean of (1860)   2166
CAPEL, Arthur, Lord Capel (1654) 349,
558
CAPEL, Edward (N.D.)   1752
CAPELL, Edward (1760)   2030
CAPES, John Moore, M.D. (1871) 2092
CAPPE, Newman (1786)   2319
CAPPER, Ed. (1731-1732)   1626
CAPPER, F. (1829)   880
CAPPER, Joseph, (N.D.)   1709
CAPPER, Samuel, jun. (1855)   915
CARACCIOLI, Charles (1766)   139
CARBUTT, Dr Edward (1829)   1443
CARDALE, Edward Thomas (1866) 1824
CARDALE, J. (1854)   648
CARDALE, J. B. (N.D.)   1362

CAR   clxvi

CARDALE, Paul (1758-1774) 437, 1726,
2642, 2668
CARDIGAN, Archdeacon of, E.
Yardley, B.D. (1762)   1904
CARGILL, William (1841)   940
CARE, Dr Henry (1678-9)   1843
CARE, George (1685, 1689)   1459, 2174
CARE, Henry (1679-1688)   95, 564, 703,
758, 1152, 1338, 1459, 1646, 1770, 2761,
2800, 2832
CAREW, George (1675)   2346
CAREW, Hugh (1723)   2527
CAREW, J. P. (1834)   1887
CAREW, Lady Elizabeth (1613)   2618
CAREW, Richard (1616, N.D.) 843, 1021
CAREW, Thomas (1616, 1634)   421, 843,
CAREY, David (1824)   958
CAREY, George Saville (1770)   1533,
1747, 1815
CAREY, Henry (1715-1773)   73, 394,
504, 703 (2), 1547, 2619, 2827
CAREY, N. (1676)   2423
CAREY, Patrick (1651)   2659
CAREY, Peter (1810, 1811)   1419, 2083
CAREY, Rosa Nouchette (1869-
1871)   212, 2220, 2799
CAREY, W. (1667)   754
CARLELL, Lodowicke (1639)   188
CARLETON, Bishop (1662)   2596,
vol. iv.
CARLETON, Capt. John W. (1844,
1846)   1195, 2101
CARLETON, George, Bishop of
Chichester (1624)   190
CARLETON, William (1833)   2621
CARLILE, Christopher (1572)   661
CARLISLE, Alexander (1846)   408
CARLISLE, Archdeacon of, William
Paley (1774)   587
CARLISLE, Bishop of, Edmund
Law, D.D. (1769-1774) 488, 582, 1769
CARLISLE, Dean of, R. Bolton,
LL.D. (1748-1762)   744, 1013, 1371,
1376, 1423
CARLISLE, Earl of, Frederick
Howard (1798, 1808)   2583, 2710
CARLISLE, Nicholas (1826, 1837)   429
1572
CARLISLE, Nicholas, F.S.A. (1825) 1101
CARLYLE, Alexander (1829)   697
CARLYLE, Alexander, D.D. (1757-
1769)   174, 820, 873, 980, 1925, 2070
CARLYLE, Thomas (1824-1838)   1012,
1473, 2258, 2816

CARLYLE, Thomas, Advocate (1827-1860) 156, 690, 699 (2), 786, 815, 929, 1266, 1395, 1411, 1806, 1817, 2043, 2511, 2531, 2833
CARLYON, Edward Augustus (1851) 1327
CARMALT, Rev. William (1823) 1412
CARMENT, Rev. David (1843) 921, 2699
CARMICHAEL, Archibald N. (1842, 1845) 996, 2236
CARMICHAEL, James (1678) 821
CARMICHAEL, John (1807) 2642
CARNARVON, Earl of, H. J. G. Herbert (1836) 1977
CARNE, Elizabeth T. (1860, 1868) 525, 2589
CARNE, John (1820-1831) 857, 1948, 2502, 2544
CARNEGIE, James, Earl of Southesk (1862) 1088
CARNEGIE, Mrs (N.D.) 710
CAROLINA, Governor of, J. Pownall (1795) 1239
CARROLL, William (1705, 1706) 2160, 2265
CARON, R. (1660) 2764
CARPANI, Guiseppe (1817) 1474
CARPENDER, William (1661) 1288
CARPENTER, Elias (1815) 870
CARPENTER, John (1607) 1928
CARPENTER, Mary (1847-1864) 910, 1581, 1663
CARPENTER, Nathaniel (1629) 30
CARPENTER, T. C. (1809) 1586
CARPENTER, William (1824-1827) 535
CARPIO, Lope Felix de Vega (1623) 1914
CARR, —— (1817) 287
CARR, Frank (1873) 293
CARR, John (1764) 923
CARR, John, LL.D. (N.D.) 603
CARR, Rev. William (1828) 616
CARR, William, B.D. (1824) 1178
CARRICK, J. (1849) 1480
CARRINGTON, E. (1828) 472
CARRINGTON, George, B.A. (1871, 1873) 433, 1053
CARROLL, Bishop John (1784) 43
CARROLL, T. G. (1825) 412
CARROL, William (1709) 2472
CARRUTHERS, Robert (1824, 1827) 1139, 1959
CARSTAIRS, Charlotte (1786, 1835) 1185, 1828
CARSTAIRS, William (1712) 2277

CARSTAIRS, William, D.D., (1712) 318
CARSTAIRES, William, D.D. (1710) 2276, 2435
CARSTARES, William, Principal Errata, vol. iv. (2)
CARTE, Rev. Thomas (1704) 2765
CARTE, Thomas (1715-1743) 978, 981, 1252
CARTER, Elizabeth (1832) 857
CARTER, F. Hayne (1845) 2476
CARTER, Isaac (1800) 2060
CARTER, John (1845) 1579
CARTER, Matthew (1650) 1668
CARTER, Robert (1852) 1193
CARTER, Samuel (1688-1710) 1324, 1337, 1456, 1457, 2181, 2632
CARTER, Thomas (1845) 1579
CARTER, W. (1672) 260
CARTER, William (1671, 1695) 751, 2720
CARTERET, Lord (1747) 2488
CARTWRIGHT, Chr. (1652) 352
CARTWRIGHT, Edmund (1768-1783) 494, 2013, 2454
CARTWRIGHT, Elizabeth Penrose née (1824-1853) 78, 1115, 1136, 1716, 2339
CARTWRIGHT, Frances D. (1835) 1948
CARTWRIGHT, John (1775) 75, 1380
CARTWRIGHT, Major John (1778, 1802) 1593, 2654
CARTWRIGHT, Mrs Robert (1850) 1316
CARTWRIGHT, Rev. E. (N.D.) 177
CARTWRIGHT, Rev. W. (1854, 1874) 874, 2076
CARTWRIGHT, Robert, M.D. (1864) 2348
CARTWRIGHT, Thomas (1599, N.D.) 380, 2178
CARTWRIGHT, Thomas, Bishop of Chester (1687) 105
CARTWRIGHT, W. (N.D.) 395
CARTWRIGHT, William (1671) 1757
CARTWRIGHT, William, M.A. (1639) 2236
CARVER, Marmaduke (1666) 656
CARWELL, alias Thorold Thomas (1658) 1311
CARY, H. (1823) 1804
CARY, Henry, Lord Vis. Falkland (1680) 1160
CARY, J. (1700) 27
CARY, Walter (1541, 1552) 244, 249
CARYL, John (1674) 761
CARYL, John, Baron Dartford (1700) 2050

CARYL, John Earl (1700) 2050
CARYL, Joseph (1659) 1893
CARYLL, John (1671) 2391
CARYSFORT, Lord (1786) 2191
CASANUOVO, Leonard (1855) 1094
CASAUBON, Meric (1638, 1641) 2640, 2718
CASE, —— (1820) 1116
CASE, John, M.D. (1586) 1989
CASEY, Elizabeth (1876-1879) 1207, 1649, 2796, 2826
CASHEL, Archbishop of, Richard Laurence (1823, 1829) 2159, 2162
CASSANDRA, Lady Hawke (1788) 1287
CASSELL, John (1852) 743
CASSELS, —— (1874) 2520
CASSELS, Walter Gibson (1836) 2149
CASTLE, A. (1719) 639
CASTLE, G. (1658) 1693
CASTLEMAIN, Earl of, Roger Palmer (1667-1679) 341, 450, 980, 1320, 2174
CASTLEY, J. (1793) 1823
CASTRO, J., M.D. (1721) 676
CASWALL, Edward (1836, 1838) 1941, 2405
CATESBY, Thomas, Lord Paget (1738) 784
CATHCART, Miss (1833) 44, 1081
CATON, William (1660) 1637
CATTERMOLE, Richard (1832, 1841) 220, 995
CATTON, Charles, R.A. (1790) 760
CAULFIELD, James (1795, 1814) 240, 355
CAULFIELD, Mrs Edwin T.(1825) 1225
CAUNTER, Rev. John Hobart (1814-1836) 297, 908, 2257
CAURTIER, Peter L. (1806) 1529
CAUSSIN, Nicholas (1678) 1170
CAVALLI, Stephen (1667) 2355
CAVAN, Lord (1773) 1730
CAVE, John (1679) 2336
CAVE, William (1683) 2331
CAVE, William, D.D. (1684) 656
CAVENDER, C. H. (1846) 333
CAVENDISH, George (1641-1706) 1466, 1585, 1709
CAVENDISH, Georgiana, Duchess of Devonshire (1799) 1592
CAVENDISH, Gilbert (1620) 1178
CAVENDISH, W., Duke of Devonshire (1681) 2091

CAVENDISH, William, Duke of Newcastle (1649) 522, 2723
CAVENDISH, William Spencer Duke of Devonshire (1844) 1064
CAW, G. (1784) 1957
CAWDREY, Daniel (1641, 1658) 12, 2520
CAWDREY, Robert (1600) 1021
CAWDREY, Zachary (1681) 1995
CAWDWELL, Thomas (1719, 1720) 866, 1824
CAWLEY, John, D.D. (N.D.) 313
CAWOOD, John (1829, 1830) 398, 2196
CAWTHORNE, Joseph (1782) 885
CAZOTTE, Jacques (1794) 613
CECIL, Robert, Earl of Salisbury (1606) 129
CECIL, Sir Edward (1626) 1036
CECIL, William, Lord Burleigh (1583-1585) 574, 575, 855
CECYL, Robert Cecil or, Earl of Salisbury (1606) 129
CELISIA, Mrs, née Mallet (1771, 1772) 69, 1221
CENE, Charles le (1702) 793
CENNICK, John (1742, 1752) 426, 2246
CENTLIVRE, Susanna (1703-1707) 214, 992, 1521, 1933, 2494
CERVANTES, Saavedra Miguel de (1619) 2628
CÉS, Beyle L. Alex. (1818) 2225
CHAIGNEAU, William (1752) 1140
CHALCEDON, Bishop of, Richard Smith, D.D. (1609-1655) 203, 273, 682, 2049
CHALKHILL, John (1683) 2558
CHALLICE, A. E. (1859) 2815
CHALLICE, Dr (1863, 1864) 967, 1091
CHALLONER, Richard, D.D., Bishop of Debra (1729-1748) 280, 340, 1503, 1583, 2368, 2609
CHALMERS, Alexander (1811-1826) 1570, 2030
CHALMERS, George (1762-1825) 105, 150, 218, 490, 598, 612, 875, 1472, 1484, 1821, 2211, 2310, 2607
CHALMERS, Patrick (1848) 89
CHALMERS, Thomas, D.D. (1805) 1771
CHALMERS, William, A.M. (1843) 401 (3)
CHALONER, Captain John (1821-1823) 410, 2224, 2719
CHALONER, Sir T. (1584) 2380

CHALONER, Thomas (1657)   2662
CHAMBERLAIN, Thomas (1871)   1571
CHAMBERLAINE, Frances Sheridan *née* (1673-1772) 664, 710, 1144, 1583
CHAMBERLAINE, Richard (1698) 1495
CHAMBERLAYN, —— (1702)   1044
CHAMBERLAYNE, Edward, LL.D. (1761)   10
CHAMBERLAYNE, Edward, LL.D. (1647-1683)   508, 754, 2001, 2005
CHAMBERLAYNE, John (1720-1723)   1164
CHAMBERLEN, Dr (1717)   1901
CHAMBERS, E. (1781)   1987
CHAMBERS, John David (1852, 1853)   444, 2052
CHAMBERS, John, D.D. (1751)   1226
CHAMBERS, Mrs Robert (N.D.)   49
CHAMBERS, Robert (1600-1612)   1815, 1846
CHAMBERS, Robert, LL.D. (1833-1862)   88, 725, 916, 1618, 2224, 2399, 2728
CHAMBERS, William (1821-1851)   863, 1949
CHAMEROVZOW, Louis Alexis (1845, 1847)   392, 743
CHAMIER, Frederick (1832)   1471
CHAMPION, Richard (1784)   487
CHAMPNEY, Anthony (1614)   1544
CHANCELLOR, Frank (1871)   2812
CHANCELLOR, William (1772)   2419
CHANDLER, Benjamin (1720)   155
CHANDLER, John (1729)   647
CHANDLER, John (1836)   1749
CHANDLER, Richard, D.D. (1802) 1139
CHANDLER, Samuel, D.D., (1730-1745)   668, 1045, 1400, 1814, 1924
CHANDLER, Thomas B., D.D. (1774)   75
CHANDOS, Lord, Grey Bridges (1611, 1620)   639, 1178
CHAPHAM, Jonathan (1683)   1765
CHAPMAN, —— (1740)   763
CHAPMAN, Alexander (1606)   380
CHAPMAN, George (1594-1631)   293, 777, 1746, 1839, 1938, 2405, 2702, 2793, 2813
CHAPMAN, John (1732-1747) 88, 1264, 2135 (2)
CHAPMAN, John, D.D. (1728-1752)   483, 988, 1232, 1765, 2137
CHAPMAN, L. (1661)   178
CHAPMAN, Rev. John (N.D.)   2732

CHAPMAN, Thomas, D.D. (1751)   565
CHAPONE, Hester (1774)   1447
CLARKE, William (1603)   2169
CHARLES, Elizabeth (1850-1877) 56, 225, 392, 478, 516, 627 (2), 705, 1318, 1553, 1817, 2319, 2403, 2539, 2591, 2731, 2776, 2788, 2819, 2827
CHARLES, George Drummond (1868)   2564
CHARLES, Mitchell Charles (1851)   1062
CHARLESWORTH, John (1787-1833)   2048, 2365, 2590
CHARLESWORTH, Maria Louisa (1850-1856)   55, 516, 1486, 1618, 2519
CHARLETON, Walter, M.D. (1661-1674)   776, 1213, 1701
CHARLEVILLE, Lady (1796-1797) 2055
CHARLTON, Mary (1824)   1868
CHARLTON, William Henry (1847)   2448
CHARNOCK, John (1792)   2213
CHARPENTIER, Francois (1664) 2648
CHARTERS, Samuel, D.D. (1815)   796
CHASE, Drummond Percy, M.A. (1854, 1857)   1935, 2091
CHATEAUBRIAND, Viscount de (1816)   1650
CHATER, John (1767, 1773)   103, 1168
CHATHAM, Earl of, William Pitt (1809)   1435
CHATTERTON, Thomas (1770)   736
CHATTO, William Andrew (1834-1839)   93, 1810, 1850, 2076, 2263, 2737
CHAUNCY, Isaac, *or* Chauncey (1692)   843
CHEADLE, Eliza (N.D.)   1542
CHEEKE, Henry (N.D , 1579)   353, 944
CHEKE, Sir John (1536, 1550)   1730, 2165
CHELSUM, James, D.D. (1776, 1786)   1149, 2155
CHENEY, John (1680)   474, 981
CHEPMELL, Charles William, B.A. (1849)   357
CHESNEY, Lieut. Col. Charles C., R.E. (1876-1881)   633, 1727, 2022
CHESNEY, Lieut. Col. Francis Rawdon, R.A. (1873)   2673
CHESTER, Bishop of, Francis Gastrell, D.D. (1696-1746)   584, 1658, 2016, 2160, 2374, 2421
CHESTER, Bishop of, George Hall (1655)   2658

CHESTER, Bishop of, J. Pearson, D.D. (1668)   2031

CHESTER, Bishop of, Nicholas Stratford, D.D. (1657-1688)   646, 951, 1330, 1707, 1754, 1883

CHESTER, Bishop of, T. Cartwright (1687)   105

CHESTER, Bishop of, William Cleaver (1808)   1491

CHESTERFIELD, Earl of, Philip D. Stanhope (1743-1821)   146, 319, 900, 1435, 1805, 2742, 2841

CHESTLIN, —— (1648)   1888

CHETTLE, Henry (1567-1631)   570, 696, 752, 944, 1301, 1911, 1937, 1938, 1973, 2619

CHETWOOD, J. R. (1750)   2316

CHETWOOD, William Rufus (1720-1778)   285, 1004, 2458, 2494, 2783 (2)

CHEVALIER, Jean Baptiste le (1829)   2704

CHEVALIER Pierre (1672)   655

CHEYNE, George, M.D. (1701)   1731

CHEYNE, William (1718)   32, 974

CHEYNELL, Francis (1645-1652)   12, 199, 217, 2531

CHICHESTER, Bishop of, George Carleton (1624)   190

CHICHESTER, Bishop of, Dr. P. Gunning (1676)   1456

CHICHESTER, Bishop of, Francis Hare (1730)   1387

CHICHESTER, Bishop of, Henry King (1649-1657)   578, 1949, 2050

CHICHESTER, Bishop of, John Williams, D.D. (1686-1694)   108, 263, 630, 1155, 1753, 1852, 2044, 2056, 2338, 2569

CHICHESTER, Bishop of, Robert Grove, D.D. (1683-1688)   117, 921, 1754, 1891

CHICHESTER, Bishop of, T. Mannington (1685)   2378

CHICHESTER, F. R., Lord Belfast (1851-1866)   1558, 1692, 2706, 2787, Errata, vol. ii., Errata, vol. iv.

CHICKER, Edward (1815)   435

CHIDLEY, —— (1652)   546

CHILD, Robert (1652)   2256

CHILD, Sir Josiah (1668-1694)   269, 639, 654, 2356, 2649

CHILDS, George Borlase (1862, 1863)   64, 212, 699

CHILDS, Miss (1845)   1526

CHILLINGWORTH, William (1644)   156

CHILMEAD, Edmund (1654)   660

CHISHOLM, —— (1859)   2219

CHITTY, Edward (1841)   1204

CHOLMONDELEY, Rev. ——, M.A. (1836)   948

CHOPPIN, Rev. R. (1722)   2287

CHORLEY, Henry F. (1839-1854)   365, 707, 1490, 1812

CHORLEY, Josiah (1688)   269

CHRISTCHURCH, Dean of, J. Fell, D.D. (1647)   2023

CHRISTIAN, Edward (1791)   848

CHRISTIE, Fyfe (1865)   1867

CHRISTIE, James (1801, 1806)   669, 1227

CHRISTIE, John (1819)   2431

CHRISTIE, Rev. James (1865)   1755

CHRISTIE, Rev. William (1860)   270

CHRISTIE, Thomas (1792)   1631

CHRISTIE, T. W. (1851)   1398

CHRISTIE, William (1792)   797

CHRISTISON, Robert, M.D. (1821)   2377

CHUBB, Thomas (1730)   445

CHUBBUCK, Emily C. (1848)   1635

CHUDLEIGH, Lady Mary (N.D.)   910

CHURCH, —— (1817)   2492

CHURCH, Thomas, D.D. (1737-1755)   83, 818, 2176, 2328, 2375

CHURCHILL, Charles (1761-1804)   1013, 1740, 1959, 2228, 2594

CHURCHILL, W. (1770)   2550

CHURCHYARD, Thomas (N.D)   2063

CHURCHYARD, Thomas (1740)   2212

CHURCHYARD, Thomas (1602)   2667

CHURTON, Dr (1830)   2133

CIBBER, Colley (1707-1745)   404, 435, 560, 2268, 2550

CIBBER, Theophilus (1731),   1871

CLACY, Helen (1858-1863)   200, 1867, 1875, 2789

CLAGGET, Nicholas (1688)   124

CLAGGET, Nicholas, D.D., Archdeacon of Sudbury (1685)   1891

CLAGGET, William, D.D. (1681-1688) 7, 122, 124, 631, 646, 648, 1753 (2), 1859, 2003, 2066, 2171, 2270, 2297, 2343, 2486, 2687, 2737

CLAPHAM, H. (1609)   393

CLAPHAM, John (1602, 1606)   1124, 1134

CLAPHAM, Rev. Samuel, M.A. (1805, 1812)   364, 1986

CLAPHAM, T. (1704)   2336
CLAPPERTON, William (1809)   1869
CLARA, Franciscus Sancta (1659)   413
CLARENDON, Earl of, Edward Hyde (1648-1674)   97, 981, 1354, 1364, 2310
CLARIDGE, John (1744)   2350
CLARIDGE, Richard (1697, 1713)   118, 681
CLARIS, John Chalk (1814-1820)   710, 2189, 2573
CLARK, Benjamin (1682)   389
CLARK, Bracy, F.L.S. (1820-1842)   865, 1721, 1828, 2142, 2368, 2417, 2730
CLARK, Charles (1837-1861)   234, 690, 901, 919
CLARK, Charles Heber (N.D.)   1810, 1836
CLARK, David (1821)   515
CLARK, Dr John (N.D.)   985
CLARK, Hewson (1823, 1828)   907, 1093
CLARK, Hugh (N.D.)   1648
CLARK, Isaac (1817)   413
CLARK, James (1699-1722)   52, 389, 544, 653, 1033, 1292, 1293, 1373, 1568, 1737, 1923, 1982, 2320
CLARK, James, A.M. (1691, 1703)   1557, 1996
CLARK, John (1845)   926
CLARK, John (1778)   2840
CLARK, Mrs Crespigny *née* (1796)   1876
CLARK, Rev. James (1703)   2821
CLARK, Robert (1875)   1027
CLARK, S. (1653)   1257
CLARK, Thomas, M.D. (1853)   2210
CLARK, W. B., A.M. (1836)   2203
CLARKE, Adam, LL.D. (1802-1808)   830 (2), 1697
CLARKE, Alured, D.D. (1738)   817
CLARKE, Anne (1808)   2408
CLARKE, Captain, R.M. (1839)   92
CLARKE, Dr Howson (1811)   1457
CLARKE, Edward Daniel, LL.D. (1793, 1803)   2555, 2613
CLARKE, Edward, M.A. (1755)   1368
CLARKE, George (1685)   2641
CLARKE, H. G. (1841)   758, 763
CLARKE, James (1788)   512
CLARKE, John (1826)   579
CLARKE, John, D.D. (1732)   580
CLARKE, Louisa Jane (1841, 1842)   524, 2104
CLARKE, Rev. Richard (1759)   810
CLARKE, R. F. (1833)   2533
CLARKE, S. (1820-1822)   281, 1180

CLARKE, Samuel (1643-1707)   597, 750, 1105
CLARKE, Samuel, D.D. (1699-1724)   1388, 1646, 1772, 2437
CLARKE, Sarah Jane (1853-1856)   942, 1069, 1143, 2845
CLARKE, Thomas (1840)   789
CLARKE, Thomas (1850)   1151
CLARKE, Thomas (1621)   1973
CLARKE, William (1580, 1595)   252, 470, 1962
CLARKE, William (1742)   1336
CLARKE, William (1788)   2268
CLARKE, William (1819)   2169
CLARKE, William (1850)   2584
CLARKSON, Andrew (1731)   1924
CLARKSON, Christopher (1814)   1146
CLARKSON, David, B.D. (1676, 1682)   633, 1944, 1984, 2677
CLASON, —— (1672)   161
CLASON, Patrick (1769)   828
CLAUDE, Jean (1686, 1707)   25, 2354
CLAUGHTON, T. L. (1841)   2729
CLAVEL, Robert (1665)   1103
CLAVERING, Sir William A. (1845-1849)   439, 1820, 2546
CLAVERS, Mary Kirkland, *née* (1842)   941
CLAVIS DE FLORIAN, J. P. (1827)   732
CLAYTON, David (1717)   2361
CLAYTON, John (1646)   2607
CLAYTON, Robert, Bishop of Clogher (1751, 1761)   695, 773, 802, 1188
CLAYTON, Thomas (1707)   180
CLEAVER, W. (1761)   734
CLEAVER, William, Bishop of Chester (1808)   1491
GLEGG, Joseph (1757)   515
CLEGHORN, George (1824, 1837)   2139, 2150
CLEGHORN, Robert, M.D. (1796)   2399
CLELAND, John (1751-1771)   33, 1539, 1578, 2464, 2596 vol. iv., 2606, 2796
CLEMENS, Samuel Langhorne (1872-1876)   74, 551, 986, 1014, 1224, 1226 (2), 1548 (2), 1727, 1985, 2230
CLEMENT, Simon (1695)   653
CLEMENT, W. (1741)   1990
CLEMENTS, —— (1710)   2754
CLERC, John le (1690, 1700)   932, 1863
CLERK, James (1690, 1705)   1987, 2335
CLERK, John (1785)   1295
CLERK, John (1706)   1368
CLERK, ——, probationer (1712)   1764
CLERKE, William (1663)   1546

clxxvii   CLE — COG   clxxviii

CLEVELAND, Archdeacon of, Francis Blackburne, M.A. (1752-1780) 150, 471, 797, 1123, 1591, 1745, 1796 (2), 2110, 2141, 2142, 2154, 2330, 2367, 2700

CLEVELAND, John, *or* Cleaveland (1646, 1658), 358 (2), 1202, 1305, 1536, 1613, 1944, 2242

CLIFFORD, Charles Cavendish, M.P. (1865, 1866) 1181, 2626

CLIFFORD, Edmund (1860, 1872) 1050, 1468

CLIFFORD, Hon. Robert (1797, 1798) 166, 1577

CLIFFORD, Martin (1675) 2635

CLIFFORD, William (1665) 382

CLELAND, James, LL.D. (1819) 1397

CLINCH, —— (1812) 1444

CLINTON, De Witt (1822) 1448

CLINTON, H. F., M.A. (1807) 2416

CLISSOLD, Rev. Augustus (1856) 1411

CLISSOLD, Stephen (1820, 1838) 489, 1807

CLIVE, Hon. Robert Henry (1841) 695

CLIVE, Lady Archer (1836-1864) 920, 1201, 1270, 1663, 1875, 1947, 2064, 2721, 2812, 2846

CLOGHER, Bishop of, Robert Clayton (1751-1761) 695, 773, 802, 1188

CLOGHER, Dean of, J. Smedley (1721) 1950

CLONMACONIS, Dean of, Very Rev. Richard Butler (1837, 1840) 2427 (2)

CLOVET, M. (1671) 1653

CLOWES, Rev. John, M.A. (N.D., 1813) 55, 1027

CLOYNE, Bishop of, George Berkeley, D.D. (1725-1749) 51, 63, 581, 639, 817, 1388, 2035, 2091, 2564, 2837

CLUBBE, Rev. John (1758-1765) 1126, 1369, 1907

CLUBBE, W. (1812) 1923

CLUNES, John (1833) 1122

CLUNY, Alexander (1769) 76

CLUTTON, John, M.A. (1787-1825) 397, 743, 1378

COAD, J. (1832) 94

COADE, George, jun. (1746, 1747) 1365, 1397

COATES, H. (1832) 2793

COATES, James (1724) 666

COATES, W. (1831) 1523

COATS, James (1725) 1718

COBB, Gerard Francis (1867) 1307

COBB, James (1786-1798) 369, 686, 762, 927, 1074, 1519, 2382, 2450, 2451, 2452, 2502

COBBE, Francis Mary   Erratta, vol. iv.

COBBE, M. (1855) 798

COBBETT, William (1795-1798) 1497, 1776, 1778

COBBIN, Ingram (1819) 28

COBBOLD, Rev. Spencer (1835) 712

COBBOLD, Robert Henry (1832) 1954

COBDEN, Richard (1835) 748

COCHRANE, Alexander (1838) 1943

COCHRANE, Alexander Baillie, M.P. (1849, 1864) 1523, 2847

COCHRANE, Archibald, Earl of Dundonald (1784) 28

COCHRANE, Charles (1830) 1276

COCHRANE, James (1813) 324

COCHRANE, Mrs Dr (1844) 934

COCKAYNE, J. (1644) 753

COCKBURN, Captain George W. (N.D.) 1814

COCKBURN, Catherine Trotter *or* (1696-1747) 58, 582, 1518, 2163, 2205

COCKBURN, Henry (1822-1826) 490, 861, 1780

COCKBURN, Henry, Lord (1822) 1397

COCKBURN, John, D.D., (1691-1712) 501, 770, 1120, 2369

COCKBURN, Patrick (1721) 1882

COCKBURN, Sir A. J. E. (1843) 2496

COCKBURN, William, M.A. (1723) 1888

COCKBURN, William, M.D. (1730) 560

COCKERAN, Henry (1632) 756

COCKERELL, Mr —— (1831) 2153

COCKIN, William (1775, 1785) 181, 885, 1793, 2564

COCKINGS, George (1781) 76

COCKMAN, Thomas, D.D. (1763) 963

COCKS, Richard (1722) 2391

CODRINGTON, Robert (1644, 1652) 2033, 2660

COETLOGAN, Charles Edward de (1788, 1807) 2104, 2551, 2668

COFFEY, Charles (1729, 1733) 614, 1896

COFFIN, —— (1801) 742

COFFIN, Edward (1619, 1622) 2124, 2674

COGAN, Thomas, M.D. (1776, 1779) 1270, 1453

COGHLAN, Charles (1857) 1517

COGLAN, John (1877) 477

COGLAN, Thomas (1833)

COHAUSEN, J. H. (1771) 1089
COIGNET, Pierre (1611) 132
COLBATCH, J. (1700) 18, 1580
COLBATCH, John, D.D. (1722-1739) 1289, 2089, 2758
COLCHESTER, Archdeacon of, John Hansley (1662) 2773
COLCHESTER, Lord, Charles Abbot (1795, 1849) 1289, 2431
COLCHESTER, Baroness, Hon. E. S. Abbot (1833) 2737
COLCHESTER, Lady, Elizabeth S. Law Errata, vol. ii. (2)
COLE, Benjamin, T. H. (1829) 2819
COLE, Francis Edward Baston (1854) 1610
COLE, Henry, C.B. (1841-1851) 908 (2), 1063 (3), 2349
COLE, J. (1829) 138
COLE, Rev. William (1788) 1300
COLE, Thomas (1756) 167
COLEBROKE, H. D. (1823) 2485
COLEBROOKE, Henry Thomas (1804) 2150
COLEBROOKE, Sir George, Bart. (1790, 1791) 1374, 2394
COLERIDGE, Christabel (N.D.) 1063
COLERIDGE, Henry Nelson, M.A. (1826-1835) 1245, 2395, 2465
COLERIDGE, Samuel Taylor (1795, 1812) 1529, 1817
COLERIDGE, Sara (1822-1830) 17, 1245, 2210
COLERIDGE, William H., D.D. (1829) 880
COLERAINE, Lord, Henry Hare (1683) 2393
COLES, C. B. (1835) 2379
COLES, Elisha (1673, 1677) 1747, 1983
COLES, Gilbert, D.D. (1688) 947
COLET, J. A. (1792) 1411
COLMAN, George (1750-1788) 478, 540, 612, 879, 1683, 1842, 1968, 1976, 2333, 2508, 2595, 2845
COLMAN, George, yr. (1782-1819) 1020, 1539, 1555
COLMAN, W. (1633) 560
COLLARD, John (1794, 1795) 787, 1467
COLLENS, John (1660) 2833
COLLET, S. (1737) 1858
COLLETON, John (1620) 2558
COLLIBER, Samuel (1718) 1210
COLLIER, J. (1713, 1717) 491, 1302
— — ER, Jane (1753, 1754) 546, 803

COLLIER, Jeremy (1688-1720) 99, 120, 264, 343, 593, 610, 689, 899, 1370, 1806, 1891, 2092, 2763 (2), 2768
COLLIER, John (1746-1775) 552, 1316, 1630, 2734
COLLIER, John (1828) 2593
COLLIER, John Dye (1808) 1472
COLLIER, John Payne, F.S.A. (1819-1842) 544, 620, 1960, 2057, 2316, 2649
COLLIER, Sir George (1776, 1784) 2321, 2451
COLLIER, Sir Robert Porrett (1842) 2693
COLLING, Elizabeth (1838-1870) 894, 1726, 2499
COLLINGES, John, D.D. (1661-1723) 568, 597, 853, 1854, 2086, 2410, 2521, 2745, 2798 (2)
COLLINGRIDGE, Augustus (1844) 1461
COLLINS, Anthony (1707-1729) 116, 643, 651, 653, 674, 793, 1110, 1399, 1405, 1901, 2009, 2107, 2108, 2173, 2266
COLLINS, Arthur (1713, 1720) 213, 899, 1880
COLLINS, Hercules (1693) 135
COLLINS, John (1660) 2610
COLLINS, Mortimer (1871, 1873) 1672, 2313
COLLINS, Rev. John (1777) 1380
COLLINS, Samuel, M.D. (1671) 2003
COLLINS, T. (1725, 1737) 1267, 2236
COLLINS, William (1675) 1634
COLLINS, William (1742-1757) 1825, 1889, 2727
COLLINS, William (1834) 2034
COLLOP, John (1656, 1661) 1421, 1564
COLLS, J. H. (1805) 1174
COLLYER, Mrs (1750) 1427
COLLYER, William Bengo, D.D., (1808) 160
COLQUHON, John Campbell (1824-1847) 40, 409, 496, 2854
COLQUHOUN, Lady Janet (1834, 1835) 1217, 1305
COLQUHOUN, MacChombaich de (1857) 444
COLQUHOUN, Patrick, LL.D. (1796, 1819) 485, 2645
COLQUITT, Anthony (1682) 1643
COLRIDGE, Sara (1837) 1895
COLTMAN, Eliza (1811, N.D.) 888, 2791
COLTON, Caleb C., M.A. (1819) 2134
COLVIL, Samuel (1681, 1692) 1636, 2273
COLVILLE, Robert (1775) 541

COLVILL, Rev. Robert (1757-1771) 299, 729, 904, Errata vol. i.

COLVILLE, Margaret Agnes (1856-1860) 567, 700, 1085, 2493

COMB, William (1790) 483

COMBE, Taylor (1810) 607

COMBE, Thomas (1844) 1205

COMBE, William (1678-1779) 34, 133, 616 (3), 2841

COMBE, William (1789-1790) 483, 1347, 2234

COMBE, William (1812-1821) 560, 755, 1140, 1438, 2310, 2570, 2611

COMBE, William (1727-1777) 707, 708, 928, 1092, 1381, 2299

COMBE, William (1787-1821) 1109, 1141, 1149, 1151, 1165, 1167

COMBE, William (1775-1813) 198, 416. 621, 902, 1092 (2), 1375, 1416, 1443, 1827, 1870, 1899, 1927, 1956, 2233, 2395, 2702, 2833

COMBE DE VRIGNEY, M. de la (1707) 2628

COMBER, Thomas (1810) 46, 2277

COMBER, Thomas (1691-1693) 852, 2042

COMBER, Thomas (1677) 2211

COMBER, Thomas, D.D., Dean of Durham (1678-1689) 96, 385, 386, 395, 428, 647, 650, 970, 1365, 1933, 2584

COMBES, De, —— (1768) 2648

COMBRUNE, Michael (1757, 1768) 772, 2419

COMENIUS, J. A. (1650, 1670) 1003, 1149

COMPENDIOUSE 1086

COMPTON, Dr Henry (1677) 2637

COMPTON, Henry (1669) 1265

COMPTON, Henry, Bishop of London (1667) 1473

COMPTON, Theodore (N.D., 1840) 207, 1419

COMYN, Rev. Henry (1850) 1860

CONCANON, Matthew (1721) 1558

CONDER, Josiah (1811-1850) 785, 1494, 2148, 2204

CONDER, Rev. Eustace R. (1854, 1856) 1198, 1823

CONESTAGGIO, Girolamo (1600) 1125

CONGREVE, William (1698, 1700) 74, 1219

CONINGESBY, George, D.D. (1753) 1267

CONINGHAM, James (1704) 537

CONNECTICUT, Bishop of, Dr Samuel Seabury (1774, 1775) 477, 965, 2733

CONNELLY, Pierce, M.A. (1851-1856) 325, 1658, 1971, 2023, 2821

CONNOLD, Robert (1676) 1757

CONNOR, Bishop of Down and, —— Leslie (1640) 779

CONNOR, Bishop of Down and, Richard Mant, D.D. (1808, 1830) 1407, 2058, 2301

CONOLLY, —— (1736) 478

CONQUEST, J. T., M.D. (1841) 1170

CONSTABLE, —— (1741) 2464

CONSTABLE, Archibald (1822) 1581

CONSTABLE, Henry (1579, 1592) 625, 944, 2478

CONSTABLE, John (N.D.) 2160, Erratta, vol. iv.

CONSTABLE, John, S.J. Errata, vol. iv.

CONSTABLE, Michael (1848) 1700, 1831

CONSTANTINE, J. (1265) 1240

CONYBEARE, John Josias (1809) 2224

CONYBEARE, William John, M.A. (1854, 1856) 401, 1663, 1892

CONYNGHAM, Right Hon. Wm. (1787) 689

CONWAY, Francis I. S., Viscount Beauchamp (1783) 1396

COOK, Captain James (1771) 1277

COOK, Captain S. E., R.N. (1838) 1783

COOK, Edward (1689) 2290

COOK, George, D.D. (1842) 1594

COOK, James (1839) 2155

COOK, John, M.D. (1762) 1732

COOK, Millicent W. 1874, (1876) 1184 (2), 2536

COOK, Richard (1827) 1841

COOK, Roger (1696) 2631

COOKE, —— (1694) 1154

COOKE, —— (1807) 1423

COOKE, Alexander (1617-1630) 1662, 2798, 2839 (2)

COOKE, Anne (N.D.) 951

COOKE, C. (1854) 1936

COOKE, E. (1819) 2083

COOKE, Edward (1798) 174

COOKE, Edward (1682, 1685) 175, 390

COOKE, John (1614) 1938

COOKE, John, M.D. (1762) 1732

COOKE, Rev. William (1858) 2051

COOKE, Shadrach (1691) 383

COOKE, Sir George (1747) 2180, 2239

COOKE, Thomas (1724-1734)   62, 216, 217, 434, 488, 1881, 2553
COOKE, William (1776)   35
COOKE, William (1783)   308
COOKWORTHY, William (1751)   684
COOLE, Benjamin (1696-1712)   1349, 1631, 2061, 2129
COOLEY, William D. (1830)   1141
COOMBE, William (1790)   614
COOPER, Anthony Ashley, Earl of Shaftesbury (1675-1716)   363, 599, 1353, 1354, 1658, 2290, 2304, 2344, 2415, 2700, 2701
COOPER, Charles Purton, Q.C. (1831-1847)   312, 1775, 2054, 2101, 2121, 2164, 2239
COOPER, Dr Myles (1774)   969
COOPER, Edward (1850)   550
COOPER, Elizabeth (1737)   1681
COOPER, G. S. (1851)   1277
COOPER, James Fenimore (1821-1850)   220, 250, 254, 1077, 1319, 1490, 1652, 1757, 1914, 1915, 1989, 1991, 2103, 2794
COOPER, John Gilbert (1745-1764)   301, 786, 1004, 1424, 1951, 1981
COOPER, M. G. (1837)   2557
COOPER, Rev. Samuel (1766-1773)   983, 1393, 1418
COOPER, Rev. W. (1765)   2816
COOPER, Samuel (1843)   948
COOPER, Sir Grey (1765)   1604, 1845
COOPER, Susan F. (1850)   2240
COOPER, Thomas (1856)   2658
COOPER, Thomas, Bishop of Winchester (1589)   46
COOPER, William (1669, 1673)   1903, 2314
COOTE, Charles, Earl of Bellamont (1783)   1384
COOTE, Charles, LL.D. (1804)   2404
COOTE, J. (1818)   2317
COPE, Arthur Cleaveland (1842)   192
COPE, Harriet (1811, N.D.)   2658, 2794
COPELAND, Henry (1848)   1197
COPELAND, Thomas (1842)   1653
COPELAND, W. J. (1848)   1197
COPLAND, Alexander, Advocate (1833)   1664
COPLAND, Robert (N.D.)   2242
COPLESTON, Edward, D.D. Bishop of Llanduff (1803-1819)   53, 852, 1414, 2175, 2302, 2308, 2353, 2570
COPLESTON, John Gay (1832, 1835)   572, 1528

COPLEY, A. C. (1602)   104
COPLEY, Anthony (1596, 1601)   128, 922
CORBET, John (1640-1679)   655, 779, 1240, 1961, 2306
CORBET, John, B.A. (1688)   2295
CORBET, Misses, or Corbett (1826-1835)   293, 742, 1800 (2), 2392, 2539
CORBET, Richard, Bishop of Norwich (1648)   1955
CORBETT, Charles Henry (1851)   2651
CORBETT, T. (1739)   19
CORBETT, William (1795-1801)   75, 241, 244, 600 (2), 612, 1397, 1463, 2651
CORDER, Susanna (1839)   2095
CORDEROY, Jeremiah (1604)   2364
COREY, John (1701)   550
CORFIELD, Frederick (1819)   1567
CORKE AND ROSSE, Bishop of, Peter Browne, D.D. (1728, 1733)   2024, 2566
CORKER, James (1680, 1683)   2168, 2222, 2482
CORMACK, John Rose, M.D. (1844, 1858)   1756, 2712
CORMARTIN, —— (1809)   2628
CORNEILLE, —— (1805)   338
CORNEILLE, —— (1664)   1969
CORNEILLE, P. (1637-1640)   404
CORNISH, Joseph (1772-1777)   242, 260, 1417, 2327
CORNWALEYS, H. (1693)   262, 522
CORNWALL, Archdeacon of, John Sleech (1762)   1674
CORNWALL, Ebenezer (1848)   2716
CORNWALLIS, Caroline Frances (1841-1854)   273, 377, 1001, 1244, 1886, 1902, 1904, 2485
CORNWALLIS, Sir William (1604)   1621
CORP, Harriet (1809-1849)   136, 420, 517, 2538, 2625
CORPE, John (1758)   2445
CORRANUS, Ant. (1586)   2415
CORRIE, Edgar (1791)   483
CORRY, John (1798-1801)   1873, 2259
CORY, Robert, junr. (N.D.)   1696
CORYATE, G. (1763)   603
COSENS, Rev. Dr. (1772)   1805
COSENS, Rev. W. B. (1852)   2600
COSIN, James (1745)   1692
COSIN, John, D.D., Bishop of Durham (1672)   426
COSIN, Richard, LL.D. (1584-1593)   126, 145, 493

COSIO, Telesforo de Trueba y (1834) 2255
COSTA, G. de (1627) 2620
COSTARD, Rev. George (1733) 2463
COSTES, Gauthier de, Seigneur de La Calprenède (1676) 326
COTA, Rodrigo (1707) 2461
COTES, —— (1808) 2414
COTES, Humphrey (1766) 767
COTGRAVE, John (1671) 2824
COTTERILL, Sir Charles (1676) 326
COTTIN, Sophie Ristand (1825) 741
COTTLE, —— (1852) 2224
COTTON, Calvin (1839) 2775
COTTON, Charles (1667-1694) 292, 454, 1160, 1590, 2262
COTTON, Clement (1674) 877
COTTON, E. (1751) 2772
COTTON, Henry, D.C.L. (1817) 1755
COTTON, John, B.D. (1630) 1932
COTTON, Joseph (1818) 1573
COTTON, Roger (1596) 177
COTTON, Sir Robert (1627-1642) 276, 2329, 2378, 2660
COTTON, Sir Robert Bruce (1628-1642) 562, 943
COULTON, Miss (1860, 1870) 975, 1833
COUPAR, Patrick (1724) 1260
COUPAR, Robert, M.D. (1789) 2466
COUPER, Simon (1704, 1705) 871, 1211, 1657, 2586
COURAYER, Pierre Francois Le (1728) 587
COURTAREY, Rev. John (1810) 1359
COURTENAY, George (1773) 825
COURTENAY, John, M.P. (1768, 1809) 362, 1955, 2004, 2137
COURTENAY, Peregrine (1803) 1920
COURTHOPE, William John (1864) 2553
COURTIER, Peter L. (1798-1813) 1529, 1589, 2056, 2728, 2792
COURTILZ DE SANDRAS, Gatien (1695) 1481, 1967
COURTLAND, Grace (1879) 1548
COURTNEY, —— (1808) 2689
COVE, Morgan (1795) 811
COVENTRIE, Sir William (1688) 359
COVENTRY, Francis (1750, 1751) 1145, 1883
COVENTRY, Henry (1736, 1743) 193, 1897
COVENTRY, Sir William (1673, 1685) 749, 1422
COVENTRY, Thomas, Lord (1641) 1885

COVERDALE, Miles (1539-1547) 375 (2), 856, 1032
COWAN, Charles (1840) 81
COWAN, David (1849) 1108
COWAN, Malcolm (1830) 1461
COWARD, William C. (1843) 2730
COWARD, William, M.D. (1702-1706) 4, 644, 900, 1040, 1293, 2309
COWIE, John (N.D.) 2436
COWLEY, Abraham (1633-1683) 32, 80, 947, 1955, 2260
COWLEY, Hannah (1776-1788) 1959, 1960, 2240
COWPER, A. (1744) 1749
COWPER, Earl, Sir William Cowper (1710) 1382
COWPER, Hon. Spencer, Dean of Durham (1766) 2645
COWPER, John (1732) 814
COWPER, Lady Amabel (1876) 2715
COWPER, W., M.D. (1749) 2516
COWTAN, Robert (1866) 1867
COX, Edward W. (1829) 1819
COX, George, M.A. (1834, 1837) 239, 1262
COX, John Edward, D.D. (1872) 1683
COX, Mrs, née Wight (N.D.) 293
COX, Nicholas (1686) 1006
COX, Rev. Thomas (1720-1731) 1534
COX, Robert (1661) 1605
COX, Robert, W.S. (1847) 1573
COX, Sir Richard, Bart. (1711-1762) 766, 1227, 2002, 2024, 2328, 2432
COXE, Arthur Cleaveland (1840, 1845) 375, 2260
COXE, Dr Thomas (1669) 662
COXE, Henry Octavius (1840) 943
COXE, Miss (1802) 1902
COXE, Peter (1807, 1809) 104, 863, 2836
COXE, Rev. William, Archdeacon of Wilts (1823) 2404
COXE, Richard Charles (1844) 1604
COXE, Tench (1792) 265
COXE, William (1799) 90
COYER, L'Abbé (1771) 1222
COZENS, Zachariah (1793) 2613
CRAB, Roger (1657) 558
CRABB, George (1780) 306
CRABBE, George (1781) 1460
CRACKANTHORP, John (1736) 1952
CRADOCK, Francis (1661) 2797
CRADOCK, Hon. Harriet née Lister (1860) 1186
CRADOCK, Joseph (1770-1815) 948, 1429, 2738

CRAFTON, William Bell (N.D.)   2374
CRAGGS, Robert, Lord Nugent
  (1739-1774)   880, 1803
CRAGHEAD, Robert (1696)   1645
CRAIG, Isabella, Mrs Knox (1856-
  1881)   1210, 1218, 1947
CRAIG, James (1727)   2477
CRAIG, Miss (1859)   292
CRAIK, —— (1849)   1807
CRAIK, George Lillie (1833)   2058
CRAIK, Henry (1831)   720
CRAIK, Mrs (1866, 1875)   1746, 2340
CRAMER, Joannes, Fredericus (1714) 985
CRAMER, John Anthony, D.D. (1820) 676
CRAMP, John Mockett, D.D. (1844) 2118
CRAMP, William (1821, 1822)   203, 408
CRAMPTON, Sir Philip, Sur. Gen.
  (1823)   195
CRANE, John (1800-1859)   35, 286 (2)
    2140, 2207
CRANE, Richard (1662, 1665)   546, 1316
CRANE, Thomas (1672)   2039
CRANMER, Thomas, Archbishop of
  Canterbury (1547)   353
CRASHAW, Richard (1652)   309
CRASHAW, William (1621, 1628) 621, 930
CRAUFURD, David (1681, 1714)
    1155, 1300
CRAUFURD, James (1681)   1155
CRAUFURD, Quintin (1790, 1815)
    1886, 2401
CRAVEN, Charles Audley, A. (1853)   48
CRAVEN, Lady, Margravine of
  Anspach (1778-1802)   901, 1617, 1639,
    1939, 2406, 2414, 2451
CRAWFORD, John (N.D.)   2034
CRAWFORD, Mr (1707)   1150
CRAWFORD, Rev. Francis, LL.D.
  (1875)   788
CRAWFORD, Thomas, D.D. (1844) 2093
CRAWFURD, Archibald (1819, 1825)
    2250, 2541
CRAWFURD, James (1682)   2231
CRAWFURD, John (1829, 1830)   371
    1227, 2735
CRAWFURD, Oswald John
  Frederick, H.B.M. (1875)   2626
CRAWFURD, Thomas (1708)   1752
CRAWLEY, George John Lloyd
  (1853)   747
CRAWSHAW, William (1608-1677)
    1256, 1738, 2006
CREASE, J. (1849)   2243
CREBILLON, —— (1735)   2406

CREBILLON, Cl. Prosp. Jolyot de
  (1749)   77
CREECH, William (1788, 1791)   28, 725
CREEDE, William (1660)   2122
CRELLIUS, Johannes (1646)   1334
CRELLIUS, John (1646)   860
CRÉQUINIÈRE, —— de La (1705)   59
CRESPIGNY, Mrs, née Clark (1796) 1876
CRESSY, Hugh Paulin de, or Cressey
  (1661-1672)   1748, 2059, 2117, 2222
CRESSY, Serenus de, or Cressey
  (1661-1686)   118, 427, 689, 779, 893,
    929, 2117, 2222 (2)
CRESSWELL, Rachael E. (1845,
  1849)   1597, 2459
CRESTADORO, Prof. Andrea (1856) 183
CREWDSON, Ellen, née Fox (18—)   521
CRICHTON, Andrew, LL.D. (1828) 2204
CRISP, Edward, M.D. (1851)   1193
CRISP, Henry (1754)   2770
CRISP, J. (1821)   509
CRISP, Mrs (1769)   909
CRISP, S. (1681)   1715
CRISP, Stephen (1711)   2368
CRISP, Thomas (1695, 1697)   817, 1291
CROFT, Herbert, D.D. (1675)   1691
CROFT, John, F.A.S. (1792)   2278, 2316
CROFT, Mrs (1878, N.D.)   1033 (2)
CROFT, Sir Herbert (1775, 1780)
    2, 287, 1517
CROGGAN, Lucy (1836)   2703
CROKATT, Rev. Gilbert (1708)   493
CROKE, Charles (1667)   945
CROKE, Sir Alexander (1838)   1874
CROKER, Crofton (1850)   2099
CROKER, Mr and Mrs Crofton (1834)1223
CROKER, Right Hon. John Wilson,
  D.C.L. (1804-1826)   73, 216, 887, 1134,
  1441, 1451, 1650, 2234, 2298, 2400, 2559,
    2696
CROKER, Thomas Crofton (1825-
  1853)   328, 879, 1223, 1687, 2099
CROLY, George, LL.D. (1817, 1832)
    1860, 2008, 2253, 2543, 2846
CROMARTY, Earl of, George
  Mackenzie (1695-1712)   9, 34, 291,
  500, 914, 1356, 1372, 1635, 1856, 2279,
    2344, 2532, 2652
CROMARTY, Earl of, Sir G.
  Mackenzie (1829)   996
CROMMELIN, May (1874-1881)   1267,
    1633, 1685, 1822, 2064
CROMPTON, William (1624, 1667)
    2165, 2249

CROOK, John (1659, 1667) 596, 2688
CROOK, J. (1807, 1819) 1711, 2776
CROPPER, Hon. Mrs (1858) 1090
CROSBIE, Andrew (1769) 2575
CROSCALL, Rev Dr Samuel (1714) 104
CROSE, J. D. de la (1687) 2711
CROSS, —— (1755) 114
CROSS, —— (1851) 2720
CROSS, James C. (1806) 2450
CROSS, J. C., D.D. (1685, 1687) 151, 497
CROSS, Mrs Marian Evans (1861) 2385
CROSS, W. (1846) 669
CROSS, William Sharp (1849) 2090
CROSSE, John, F.S.A. (1822) 333
CROSTHWAIT, Dr Thomas (1704) 2677
CROSTHWAITE, Rev. John Clarke (1844-1845) 1641
CROUCH, Nath. (1687, 1710) 757, 2709
CROWE, Catherine (1838, 1844) 51, 176, 1597
CROWE, Eyre Evans (1825, 1853) 366, 2602, 2847
CROWE, William (1668) 329
CROWE, William, LL.D. (1788) 1455
CROWLEY, Robert (N.D.) 2270
CROWLEY, Thomas (1782) 1423
CROWN, John (1674) 1752
CROWNE, John (1674, 1692) 90, 558, 1752
CROXALL, Samuel, D.D. (1714-1720) 876, 1826, 2316
CROZE-MAIGNAN, S. C. (1817) 82
CRUDEN, Alexander (1739) 1507
CRUISE, Richard (1861) 1689
CRUISE, W. (1783) 808
CRULL, Jodocus, M.D. (1694-1711) 140, 602, 1580, 1999
CRUMPE, Miss (1829) 1011
CRUSO, John (1642) 328
CRUTTWELL, C. J. (1842) 1249
CRUTTWELL, Rev. Richard, LL.B. (1824) 1243
CUBIÈRES DE PALMEZEAUX, Michael (1791) 1633
CUDWORTH, Ralph, D.D. (1642) 648, 2709
CUDWORTH, William (1765) 141
CULHAM, B. P. (1805) 922
CULLEN, Lord, Sir Francis Grant (1689-1716) 259, 644, 794, 1300, 1347, 1351, 1522, 1874, 2092, 2369, 2744
CULLEN, Margaret (1802) 1172
CULLEN, William, M.D. (N.D.) 985

CULLUM, Mrs (1775) 366
CULPEPER, Sir Thomas, or Culpepper, K.T. (1623, 1673) 823, 1659, 1923, 2615
CULROSS, Lady (1603) 1021
CULTON, W. C. (1796) 2778
CULVERWELL, J. P. (1844) 1541
CUMBERLAND, Richard (1757-1795) 73, 287, 554, 737, 901, 1084, 1751, 1792, 2449, 2452, 2518, 2802
CUMBERLAND, Richard, LL.D. (1767) 1418
CUMMING, Alexander (1705) 2338
CUMMING, John, D.D. (1825-1864) 220, 2375, 2482
CUMMING, John, M.A., D.D. (1716, 1717) 2112, 2140
CUMMINS, Maria S. (1863-1868) 1074, 1316, 1530
CUNDALL, Joseph (1849-1856) 2453, 2629
CUNDELL, John (1824) 2239
CUNINGHAME, W. (1828-1829) 624
CUNNINGHAM, Alexander, M.A. (1689, 1690) 791, 2436
CUNNINGHAM, H. S. (1861, 1875) 391, 1321, 2805
CUNNINGHAM, J. (1770-1774) 814, 2505
CUNNINGHAM, James (1678, 1683) 821, 1621
CUNNINGHAM, John (1747) 1518
CUNNINGHAM, Rev. John William, M.A. (1814-1856) 1664, 2257, 2724, 2842
CUNNINGHAM, Peter (1783, 1787) 367, 2242
CUNNINGHAM, Rev. Gabriel (1689, 1690) 686, 2436
CUNNINGHAM, Sir Alex. (1714) 2370
CUNNINGHAM, T. (1766, 1768) 1325, 2180
CUNNINGHAM, Timothy (1761, 1780) 1128, 1129, 1145, 1600, 2159
CUNNINGHAM, W. (1810) 2159
CUNNINGHAM, William, D.D. (1836) 2015
CUNNINGHAME, W. (1802) 2687
CURLING, Henry (1851) 968
CURLL, Edmund (1727) 154
CURRAN, H. G. (1844) 472
CURRIE, James, M.D. (1793) 1344
CURRIE, John (1727-1734) 1290, 2151, 2286

CURRIE, John (1740)   2762
CURRIE, Rev. A. (1854)   1023
CURRY, John, M.D. (1767-1775)   1111, 1118, 1782,
CURSHAM, M. A. (1825)   1552
CURTEIS, Thomas, D.D. (1798)   2335
CURTIS, —— (1798, 1834),   211, 2191
CURTIS, George William (1851)   1741
CURTIS, William (1771)   1236
CURWEN, Thomas (1843)   2388
CUSACK, Frances Mary (1868)   1205
CUST, Hon. Elizabeth (1829)   246
CUSTRIN, Charles F. Necker de (1745)   495
CUTHBERTSON, Misses (1823, 1830)   1194, 2389
CUTTS, John Lord (1685)   1681

D.

D'ABLAINCOURT, Jean Jacques Bruhier (1746)   2706
D'AGUILAR, Rose (1795)   1024
D'ANCEMONT, R. (1819)   1113
D'ANVERS, Alicia (1716)   10
D'ARBLAY, Francis, *née* Burney (1782, 1791)   346, 837
D'ARGENS, Marquis, John B. de Boyer (1765)   372
D'ARGENVILLE, A. J. Dezallier (1712)   2563
D'AULNOY, Countess, M. C. J. de Berneville (1693, 1708)   1224, 1589, 1999
D'AVILA, Juan (1707)   2461
DACRE, Lady (1833)   2099
DADDO, Rev. William, A.M. (1750)   2596, vol. iv.
DEAR, Lord, Thomas Douglas (1790)   2211
DAGGE, Henry (1774)   483
DAGLEY, E. F. (1869)   879
DAGLEY, Richard (1804)   995
DALE, Rev. Thomas (1841)   712
DALE, Thomas, M.A. (1819, 1821)   1250, 2814
DALE, W. (1772)   299
DALGLEISH, William, D.D. (1776, 1777)   2320, 2676
DALLAS, Alexander, M.A. (1827)   2688
DALLAS, Alexander Robert Charles (1822, 1840)   522, 2829

DALLAS, Mrs Thomas (1836)   2192
DALLAS, Rev. Alexander (1844)   1684
DALLAS, Sir George (1815)   236
DALLAWAY, Rev. T. (N.D.)   2817
DALLINGER, J. (1821)   1002
DALLINGTON, Sir Robert (1629)   276
DALLINGTON, Sir Thomas (1604)   2732
DALLISON, Charles (1648)   2235
DALRYMPLE, Alexander, F.R.S. (1771-1788)   481, 483, 487, 808, 1003, 1369, 1562, 1782, 2111, 2198, 2487, 2575
DALRYMPLE, H. E. (1851)   1504
DALRYMPLE, Hugh (1761-1770)   2221, 2830
DALRYMPLE, James (1796)   424
DALRYMPLE, James, Earl of Stair (1695)   2753
DALRYMPLE, John (1763)   158
DALRYMPLE, John, Earl of Stair (1781)   489
DALRYMPLE, Sir David (1712)   15
DALRYMPLE, Sir David (N.D.)   2593
DALRYMPLE, Sir David, Lord Hailes (1714-1790)   15, 26, 34, 89, 332, 669, 1327, 1474, 1496, 1576, 1592, 1629, 1774, 1799, 1821, 2036, 2246, 2338, 2339, 2399 (2), 2400 (2), 2463, 2464, 2593, 2840
DALRYMPLE, Sir James, Bart. (1714)   2753
DALRYMPLE, Sir John (1775, 1776)   41, 2213
DALTON, —— (1831-1836)   367, 1005, 1248, 1812, 2217, 2219
DALTON, Cornelius N., B.A. (1868, 1884)   1952, 2257
DALTON, John, D.D. (1738)   462
DALTON, Rev. William (1841)   526
DALY, Rev. Robert (1826)   1790
DALYELL, Sir John Graham (1798-1801)   955, 2273
DALZEL, Professor (1785)   2367
DAMPIER, Henry (1799)   2162
DANA, Richard Henry, jun. (1841)   2702
DANCE, James (1767)   2739
DANCE, James, *or* Love (1742)   1847
DANCER, John (1664-1675)   60, 408, 447, 1286
DANETT, Thomas (1591)   608
DANFORTH, S. (1665)   191
DANIEL, —— (1820)   1277

DANIEL, Gabriel (1692, 1704) 662, 2782

DANIEL, George (1811-1852) 601, 1534, 1640, 1961, 2407, 2525, 2594, 2770, 2845

DANIEL, Henry John (N.D.) 137

DANIEL, Mrs Robert M. (1846) 1970

DANIEL, Robert Mackenzie, *or* Daniels (1843-1846), 1043, 1970, 2276, 2847, 2850

DANIEL, Samuel (1606) 2063

DANKS, John (1674) 573

DANSEY, Rev. William (1831) 179

DANSON, Thomas (1678) 567

DARBY, Rev. Charles (1680) 207

DARBY, John Nelson (1853-1877) 82, 624, 687, 1075, 1253, 1727, 1754, 1755 (3), 1985

DARBY, Rev. Samuel, M.A. (1785) 1410

DARBY, W. H. (1859) 211

DARELL, John (1652) 1673

DARELL, William (1687) 1332

DARKISON, —— (1868) 250

DARLEY, —— (1842) 1941

DARLING, Charles John (1877) 2271

DARLING, Rev. T. (1857) 1197

DARLINGTON, Sir Robert (1605) 2528

DARRELL, William (1687, 1704) 1005, 1332

DART, —— (1721) 2840

DART, John (1721) 2803

DARTFORD, Baron, John Caryl (1700) 2050

DARWIN, Erasmus, M.D. (1791) 250

DASENT, George Webbe (1870) 99

DASHWOOD, Rev. George H. (1847) 2384

DASHWOOD, Sir Francis, Bart. (1773) 6

DAUBENTON, Mad. Marguérite (1789) 2852

DAUNEY, John (1660) 843, 1139

DAUNT, Edward Synge T. (1861) 2019

DAVAL, Peter (1761) 2750

DAVENANT, Charles, LL.D. (1677-1710) 660, 662, 663, 805, 822 (2), 823, 830 (2), 1718, 2114, 2391, 2452, 2605, 2672

DAVENANT, Sir William (1634-1671) 421, 545, 927, 1148, 1711, 2217, 2254, 2383, 2658

DAVENPORT, Christopher (1655) 745

DAVENPORT, E. (1827) 779

DAVENPORT, Francis (1659, 1670) 413, 862

DAVENPORT, John (1642) 2026

DAVENPORT, John Marriott, F.S.A. (1873) 1591

DAVENPORT, Professor Francis (N.D.) 2187

DAVENPORT, Richard Alfred (1832) 1573

DAVENPORT, Robert (1620, 1639) 241, 544, 1733, 1937

DAVENPORT, Thomas (1664) 268

DAVÉSIÉS DE PONTÈS, L. (1847, 1850) 1739, 2318

DAVIDOFF, M. (1854) 157

DAVIDSON, Benjamin (1851) 2533

DAVIDSON, G. (1866) 1750

DAVIDSON, John (N.D.) 1497

DAVIDSON, John (N.D.) 1784

DAVIDSON, John (1769) 511

DAVIDSON, John (1590) 557

DAVIDSON, John (1852) 885

DAVIDSON, John, W.S. (1792) 2146

DAVIDSON, Mrs Henry, *née* Harriet Miller (1857, 1859) 1489, 2689

DAVIDSON, Rev. John (1869) 222

DAVIDSON, W. (1851) 1408, 2301

DAVIE, C. H. (1850) 1156

DAVIES, Edward (1795) 741

DAVIES, Henry (1832-1846) 1181, 2502, 2774

DAVIES, John (1617-1679) 68, 89, 408, 777, 843, 1132, 1150, 1856, 1962, 2049, 2277, 2278, 2823

DAVIES, John, D.D. (1830) 2478

DAVIES, Myles (1715) 731

DAVIES, Rev. J. H. (1875) 1313

DAVIES, Rev. John (1822) 1183

DAVIES, Robert, F.S.A. (1850) 906

DAVIES, Sir John, *or* Davis (1596-1653) 663, 1727, 1823, 2087, 2838

DAVIES, Thomas (1777-1789) 362, 804, 1808, 2419, 2840

DAVIS, —— (1731) 860

DAVIS, Ellis (1875, 1876) 512, 2060

DAVIS, John (1687) 2633

DAVIS, John, M.D. (1748, 1754) 792, 1829

DAVIS, Rev. C. H., M.A. (1870) 2514

DAVIS, Rosalind (1860) 993

DAVIS, Thomas (1843) 2451

DAVIS, W. (1797) 444

DAVISON, J., M.A. (1803) 2353

DAVORS, John (1613) 2314

DAVY, Martin (1858) 1789

DAVY, Rev. Charles (1772) 477

DAVY, Sir Humphrey, Bart. (1807, 1828) 637, 2255

DAVYS, John (1711, 1739)   411, 2455
DAWBENY, H. (1659)   1124
DAWE, Anne (1770)   2850
DAWES, Matthew (1776)   1383
DAWES, Richard (1767)   1826
DAWES, Sir William, D.D., Archbishop of York (1731)   85
DAWSON, —— (1781-1794)   692, 1190
DAWSON, Benjamin, LL.D. (1735, 1771)   99, 540, 845, 958, 1406
DAWSON, J. (1769)   949
DAWSON, T. (1730)   159
DAWSON, William (1805)   2578
DAY, Hon. Robert (1700)   964
DAY, J. (1605, 1607)   878, 2625
DAY, J. (1856)   1871
DAY, Richard (1581)   249
DAY, Samuel (1796)   270
DAY, Thomas (1773-1818)   610, 614, 714, 1147, 1269, 1683
D'ELEY, Count (1721)   2003
D'EPINARY, Madame de la Live (1815)   507
D'ERBIGNY, Henri-Lambert, M. de Thibouville (1770)   561
D'ERMONONVILLE, Viscomte, R. L. Gerardin (1783)   799
D'EWES, Sir Symond (1640)   276
D'HAPPONCOURT, F. d'Issembourg, Dame de Graffigny (1749)   2324
D'HAPPONVILLE, F. d'I., Dame de Graffigny (1774)   1892
D'HAUTEFEUILLE, M. la Contesse E. (1852)   857
D'HOLBACH, Baron, Paul Thyry (1813)   721
DE BEAUFORT, Louis (1740)   679
DE BEAULIEU, Luke (1649-1687)   411, 659, 1171, 2120
DE BELLOY, —— (1765)   2382
DE BERNEVILLE, Marie C. J., Countess d'Aulnoy (1693-1708)   1224, 1589, 1999
DE BOW, J. D. B. (1845)   1963
DE BREMOND, Gabriel (1678)   2730
DE BREVAL, John Durant (1716-1727)   182, 469, 1176, 1895, 2507
DE BURGH, William, D.D. (1839)   764
DE BURY, Baroness Blaze, Marie P. Rose (1868-1869)   67, 1520
DE CHASTELLUX, Marquis F. J. (1774)   801

DE CHATEAUBRIAND, Viscount (1816)   1650
DE COETLOGON, Charles Edward (1788-1807)   255, 2104, 2668
DE COMBES (1768)   2648
DE COSTA, G. (1627)   2620
DE CRESSEY, Hugh Paulin (1661-1672)   1748, 2059, 2117
DE CRESSEY, Serenus (1661-1674)   118, 427, 689, 779, 893, 929, 2117, 2222 (2)
DE GAUJAC, Peter Gally (1698)   2675
DE GRAFFIGNY, Dame, F. d'I. d'Happoncourt (1749)   2324
DE GRAFFIGNY, Dame, F. d'I. d'Happonville (1774)   1892
DE HAVILLAND, C. (1835)   2322
DE JARNAC, Count (1849, 1851)   1517, 2220
DE LOHNE, John Lewis (1772, 1807)   1435, 1857
DE MANDEVILLE, Bernard (1702-1732)   771, 871, 964, 1377, 1632, 2423, 2766
DE MORSAN, Lefevre (1740)   1542
DE OCCHAN, Gulielmus (N.D.)   620
DE PASCUAL, Antonio D. (1852)   2693
DE PASSERAN, Albert, Count de (1732)   1901
DE POUILLY, Louis J. Levesque (1749)   2564
DE POWIS, T. J. (1857, 1859)   1948, 2717
DE QUELUS, —— (1720)   1701
DE QUINCEY, Thomas (1822, 1832)   472, 1307
DE ROJAS, Fernando (1707)   2461
DE SAINT-MARNE (1725)   1724
DE SANDRAS, Gatien Courtliz (1695)   1481, 1967
DE SOULIGNÉ, —— (1701, 1710)   446, 1507, 1814
DE SPINOZA, Benedict (1689)   2 47
DE VESLE, Count Pont (1778)   2406
DE VILLEMAREST, Charles Maxime (1834-1836)   1478
DE VOLTAIRE, F. Arouet (1869)   2071
DE VRIGNY, M. de la (1707)   2628
DE WISZNIEWSKI, Michael Prus (1853)   2400
DE WITT, John (1703)   873
DE LA BEAUMELLE, L. (1753)   2107
DE LA MOTTE, Philip (1803)   2014
DES MAISEAUX, Pierre (1719-1723)   1110, 2527

DEACON, John (1656) 1040
DEACON, Thomas (1722, 1748) 440, 453
DEACON, U. (1747) 2732
DEACON, William Frederick (1824, 1835) 857, 2792
DEALE, —— (1828, 1833) 531, 542
DEAN, John (1740) 1007
DEAN, Samuel (1726) 2514
DEAN, Sir R. (1766) 618
DEAN, Thomas (1704) 816
DEANE, A. (1823) 2613
DEANE, Thomas (1688) 2130
DEANE, William John (1850) 1528
DEBRA, Bishop of, Richard Challoner, D.D. (1729-1748) 340, 1503, 1583, 2368, 2609
DECK, P. (1792) 46
DECKER, Sir Matthew (1744) 803, 2329
DECKER, Thomas, or Dekker (1598-1621) 304, 1053, 1264, 1937
DEE, John, D.C.L. (1577) 997
DEEBLE, Joseph Harry (1853) 1266
DEFOE, Daniel (1682-1824) 17, 18, 53 (2), 54, 72, 85, 90, 111, 112, 173 (2), 177, 191, 198, 210, 221, 265, 355, 365, 371, 377, 386, 421, 425, 435, 458 (2), 468, 493, 502, 561, 577 (2), 628, 670 (4), 671, 689, 701, 709 (2), 713, 723, 735, 736, 739, 766, 768, 770, 771, 772, 791 (2), 806 (2), 812, 813, 819 (2), 820 (2), 822, 830, 838, 840, 860, 874, 889, 898, 909, 921, 933, 944, 945, 951, 952, 962, 971, 972, 973, 1001, 1015, 1048, 1067, 1095 (2), 1107, 1151, 1155, 1157, 1159, 1161, 1163, 1164, 1167, 1189, 1196 (3), 1211, 1237, 1278, 1280, 1286, 1288, 1304, 1332, 1340 (3) 1346, 1352, 1355, 1357, 1358, 1368, 1385, 1394 (2), 1460, 1462 (2), 1463, 1469, 1577, 1579, 1584, 1585, 1586, 1587, 1602 (3), 1604, 1615, 1619, 1636, 1648 (2), 1662, 1672, 1694, 1698, 1719, 1721, 1730 (2), 1735, 1736, 1778, 1802, 1828 (2), 1843, 1848, 1858, 1863, 1866, 1878, 1887, 1930, 1965, 1970, 1997, 2002, 2003, 2041, 2042, 2062, 2088 (2), 2089, 2091, 2095, 2096, 2111, 2118, 2131, 2141, 2147, 2158, 2165, 2171 (2), 2182, 2196, 2234, 2275 (2), 2289, 2290, 2309, 2310, 2311, 2312, 2313 (2), 2314, 2331, 2332, 2341, 2349, 2372, 2378, 2380 (2), 2388, 2393, 2418, 2420, 2422, 2424, 2437, 2461, 2467, 2469, 2470, 2480, 2487, 2498, 2503, 2520, 2524, 2533, 2613, 2616, 2617, 2632, 2665, 2666, 2674, 2694 (3), 2709, 2710, 2712, 2736,

2739, 2754, 2756, 2776, 2781, 2782, 2799, 2804, 2807, 2809, 2831
DEKKER, Thomas (1600-1618) 208, 223, 701, 1053, 1763, 1937 (2), 2352, 2739, 2
DELACOURT, J. (1725) 3
DELAMOTHE, N. G. (1595) 967
DELANY, Patrick, D.D., Bishop of Down (1729-1754) 488, 691, 1108, 1188, 1371, 1377, 1789, 2113, 2190, 2652
DELAP, John, D.D. (1762-1786) 308, 1080
DELAUNE, Thomas (1684-1712) 1207, 1936
DELAUNEY, —— (1779) 1130
DELEPIERRE, Octave (1836) 2229
DELF, Thomas (1856-1859) 1519, 1558, 2016, 2017 (2)
DELL, Henry (1756-1757) 968, 1619, 1622, 2480
DELOLME, John Louis, or Delome (1784, N.D.) 1154, 1595
DELONEY, Thomas (1598) 304
DELONEY, Thomas (1619-1672) 993, 1667, 1938, 2233, 2572
DELONEY, Thomas (1652-1737) 1004, 1746, 1937, 2352
DEMPSTER, —— (1763) 541
DEMPSTER, Charlotte L. H. (1869-1875) 824, 1181, 1254, 2725
DENHAM, Sir John (1642-1684) 86, 510, 611, 992, 1848, 2125
DENHAM, Thomas (1788) 2551
DENIS, Charles (1765) 2382
DENISON, Edmund B., LL.D. (1855) 417
DENISON, Joseph, M.P. (1840-1846) 162, 438, 637, 771, 1248, 1724, 1729, 1733, 1855, 2394, 2725
DENISON, Mary Andrews (1877), 2557
DENMAN, Sophia Baillie, née (1846) 1797
DENNANT, Edward (N.D.) 2513
DENNE, Samuel (1772) 1126
DENNIS, James B. P. (1848, 1850) 1383, 1384
DENNIS Jeffrey (1813, 1818) 38, 39
DENNIS, John (1692-1720), 361, 561, 1830, 1949, 2009, 2035, 2666
DENNIS, Jonas, B.C.L. (1830) 355
DENNIS, Thomasine (1806) 2454
DENNISTOUN, James, Advocate (1832-1834) 1399, 1505
DENNY, Sir W. (1653) 1881

DENNYS, Edward N. (1851)   70
DENNYS, John (1613)   2314
DENT, John (1783)   2098
DENTON, Thomas (1754)   1209
DENTON, William, M.D. (N.D., 1664)   1178, 2440
DENZIL, Lord Hollis (1669-1679)   324, 1042, 1359, 1384, 1509, 2423
DERBY, Captain (1866)   1905
DERBY, Earl of, Charles Stanley (1671, 1678)   1265, 2681
DERBY, Earl of, Edward G. Stanley (1828)   508
DERHAM, William, M.A. (1700)   187
DERING, Edward (N.D.)   1022
DERING, Sir Edward (1641)   479
DERODON, David (1673)   985
DERRICK, Francis (1869-1875)   224, 890, 942, 1301, 1872, 2386
DERRICK, Samuel (1759, 1769)   443, 1003
DERRY, Bishop of, John Bramhall (1659-1686)   109, 128, 1153, 2752
DESERET, Phineas (1856)   2615
DESPENCER, Baroness de., R. F. A. Lee (1808-1828)   4, 787, 2139
DESPRÉAUX, Nicholas B. (1695)   558
DESVOEUX, A. V. (1734)   453
DEUCHAR, Alexander (1839)   466
DEVERELL, Robert P. (1794)   72
DEVONSHIRE, Charles (1836)   410
DEVONSHIRE, Duchess of, G. Cavendish (1799)   1592
DEVONSHIRE, Duke of, W. Cavendish (1681)   2091
DEVONSHIRE, Duke of, William Spencer Cavendish (1844)   1064
DEWHURST, C. (1833)   801
DEWSBURY, William (1661-1664)   2598, 2835 (2)
DEZALLIER D'Argenville, A. J. (1712)   2563
D'ISOLA, Baron (1671)   2000
DIBDIN, Charles (1774-1792)   369, 1014, 1067, 1459, 1549, 1622, 1971, 2059, 2325, 2351, 2451 (2), 2452, 2794
DIBDIN, Edward R. V. (N.D.)   569
DIBDIN, Thomas (1795, 1805)   1531, 1805
DIBDIN, Thomas Frognall, D.D., (1803-1839)   223, 230, 231, 249, 271, 531, 637, 955, 1133, 1283, 2464, 2833
DICK, Andrew, Coventry (1859)   1759
DICK, John (1871)   1086
DICK, Robert, M.D. (1846)   1712

DICKENS, Charles (1836-1840)   1582, 1816, 2401, 2405, (2) 2500, 2519
DICKENSON, John (1598)   1052
DICKENSON, William (1628)   1616
DICKIE, H. D. (1828)   2153
DICKINSON, Charles (1820)   555
DICKINSON, Charles, D.D., Bishop of Meath (1836, 1838)   720, 1870
DICKINSON, F. H. (1850)   1491
DICKINSON, John (1766, 1774)   1322, 1720
DICKINSON, William (1819)   941
DICKSON, Adam (1762)   2633
DICKSON, David, M.D. (1711)   1409
DICKSON, M. F. (1837-1845)   2243, 2263, 2458
DICKSON, Professor David (1684)   2683
DICKSON, Rev. Adam (1773)   804
DICKSON, Robert, M.D. (1836)   2194
DICKSON, Samuel, M.D. (N.D., 1837)   940, 1906
DICKSON, William (1804)   1122
DIGBY, George, Earl of Bristol (1667)   742
DIGBY, J. (1663)   1620
DIGBY, Kenelm Henry (1822-1848)   286, 450, 1662, 1664
DIGBY, Sir Kenelm (1638, 1648)   471, 2235
DIGBY, Lord George (1643)   2664
DIGGES, Dudley (1642, 1643)   112, 2201, 2714
DIGGES, Leonard (1653)   1011
DIGGES, Sir Dudley (1611)   902
DILKE, Charles Wentworth (1814-1815)   1809
DILKE, Charles Wentworth (1716)   1813
DILKE, Sir Charles Wentworth, Bart. (1874)   884
DILLINGHAM, William, D.D. 1689)   2041
DILLON, John J. (N.D.)   1099
DILLON, Sir John Joseph (N.D., 1801)   1178, 2069
DILLON, John Talbot (1781)   1427
DILLON, Robert Crawford, D.D. (1826)   1513
DILLON-LEE, Henry Augustus, Viscount Dillon (1817-1824)   661, 1468, 2227
DILLWYN, Ann Alexander, née (1858)   994
DILLWYN, Lewis Weston (1829)   1591
DIMSDALE, W. (1673)   2060
DINMORE, Richard (1793)   259
DINNIE —— (1876)   2449

DINSDALE, Frederick P., LL.D. (1849)   1019

DISNEY, John (1711-1810)   932, 972, 2140, 2158

DISNEY, John, M.A. (1710)   36

DISNEY, John, D.D. (1774-1814) 37, 179, 488, 617, 1401, 1590, 1732, 1779, 2140, 2371 (3), 2377, 2393, 2580

DISNEY, W. (1681)   1741

DISRAELI, Benjamin, Earl of Beaconsfield (1826-1880) 497, 747, 1083, 1442, 2483, 2619, 2724, 2774, 2781, 2804, 2829, 2848

DISRAELI, Isaac (1791-1838) 298, 551, 610, 673, 697, 740, 747, 934, 1004, 1207, 1382, 1493, 2062, 2724

DISTURNELL, John (1848)   719

DIX, John, or Ross (1846-1857) 1047, 1065, 1504, 1881 (3)

DIXON, Henry Hall (1856-1862)   1978, 2276, 2385

DIXON, Mrs (1740)   1950

DIXON, Robert, D.D., Vice-dean of Rochester (1683)   306

D'OSTERVALD, Jean F. (1715, 1825)   7, 1911

D'OYLEY, Samuel, M.A. (1718)   378

D'OYLY, Sir Charles (1828)   2606

D'OYLY, Thomas (1843)   727, 1945

DOBELL, Sydney (1850-1854)   209, 2222, 2454

DOBIE, James (1831)   849

DOBREE, Samuel (1819)   246

DOBSON, John (N.D., 1663)   688 (2)

DOBSON, John (1815)   738

DOBSON, Susannah (1779-1796)   1113, 1494, 1580

DOBSON, William (1757)   137

DOCKRAY, Benjamin (1835)   1684

DODD, Charles (1742)   150

DODD, Charles Edward (1818)   205

DODD, George (1856, 1859)   1156, 1908

DODD, George William (1859)   250

DODD, Philip Stanhope, M.A. (1807)   1102

DODD, W. (1751)   566

DODD, William, LL.D. (1747-1870) 55, 395, 470, 509, 717, 782, 1715, 1870, 2393, 2680, 2851

DODDRIDGE, Philip (1730)   964

DODERIDGE, Sir John (1629)   1330 (3)

DODINGTON, George Bubb, Lord Melcombe (1726-1761) 785, 1135, 1794, 2166

DODS, Marcia (1872)   1649

DODSLEY, Robert (1729-1825) 390, 425, 1568, 1805, 1992, 2292, 2316, 2341, 2390, 2559

DODSON, Jeremiah, M.A. (1665)   1991·

DODSON, Michael (1790)   1732

DODSWORTH, Rev. William (1835)   2291

DODWELL, Henry (1662-1743)   311, 385, 464, 597, 693, 989, 2421, 2696, 2752

DODWELL, William (1755)   1390

DOLBY, Thomas (1839)   936

DÖLLINGER, Dr (1869)   1971

DOMVILLE, Sir William, Bart. (1849, 1850)   1665, 2244

DONALDSON, Capt. (1706)   481

DONALDSON, J. (1827)   838

DONALDSON, James (1698, 1706) 1357, 1652, 1980

DONALDSON, John William, D.D. (1827-1855) 266, 2173, 2506, 2558, 2747

DONALDSON, William (1768)   1464

DONATTI, Louis (1841)   1829

DONKIN, Lieut.-Gen. Sir R. (1829) 1403

DONLEVY, ——   Errata, vol. iv.

DONNE, John, D.D. (1611-1633)   85, 1203, 1947, 2028

DOOLITTLE, Thomas, or Doolitel (1667-1688)   907, 2044, 2097

DORMAN, W. H. (1866)   417

DORMER, John, S.J. (1679-1696) 1727, 1896, 2333, 2336, 2720, 2813

DORR, Benjamin (1839)   1131

DORRINGTON, Theophilus, M.A. (1687-1710)   671, 852, 2120

DORSET, —— (1775, 1782)   467, 1899

DORSET AND MIDDLESEX, Earl of (1664)   1969

DORSET, Captain (1782)   797

DORSET, Duke of, Charles Sackville (1752)   2631

DORSET, Mrs (1807)   1878

DOSSIE, Robert (1758, 1768) 732, 1066, 1234, 2490

DOUBLEDAY, Thomas (1818, 1852)   512, 2397

DOUCE, Francis (1811, 1822)   342, 555, 1762

DOUCET, N. B. (1840)   984

DOUCIN, Louis (1703)   257

DOUDNEY, David Alfred, D.D. (1856-1864)   2239, 2683 (2)

DOUGHTIE, John (1651)   2724

DOUGHTY, G. (1703)   395

DOUGHTY, John (1644)   1305
DOUGLAS, —— (1868)   1509
DOUGLAS, Christiana Jane (1850-1879) 101, 185, 904, 1081, 1138, 1672, 1819, 2227, 2390
DOUGLAS, D. (1782)   235
DOUGLAS, Francis (1755-1773) 888, 1164, 1475, 1777, 2108, 2241
DOUGLAS, George (1724)   1323
DOUGLAS, James (1782)   2625
DOUGLAS, James, M.D. (1741)   536
DOUGLAS, John (1756-1775) 151, 611, 2289
DOUGLAS, John, D.D., Bishop of Salisbury (1754-1760) 252, 456, 468, 535, 982, 1344, 2330, 2394
DOUGLAS, Lady Eleanor (1650)   740
DOUGLAS, Lieut. (1781)   999
DOUGLAS, Neil (1792)   55, 1652
DOUGLAS, Robert (1746)   2419
DOUGLAS, Sir John Skynner, Kt. (1604)   2078
DOUGLAS, Sylvester, Lord Glenbervie (1800, 1821)   2189, 2622
DOUGLAS, Thomas, Lord Daer (1790)   2211
DOUGLAS, William (1747, 1750) 2513, 2746
DOUGLASS, —— (1733)   1904
DOUGLASS, William (1736   672
DOULEVY, Rev. Andrew (1742)   336
DOVE, John   Errata, vol. iv.
DOVE, John (N.D., 1758)   2080, 2154
DOVE, John D.D. (1746)   1215
DOVE, Patrick Edward (1850)   2564
DOVE, William T. (1755)   2354
DOVER, Thomas (1733)   746
DOVER, William (1739)   2718
DOW, Alexander (1768)   2545
DOWELL, John, M.A. (1683)   2657
DOWELL, Thomas (1849)   895
DOWLING, Frank L. (1855)   923
DOWLING, W. (1857)   1960
DOWN, Bishop of, Richard Mant, D.D. (1808-1830)   1407, 2058, 2301
DOWN AND CONNOR, Bishop of, H. Leslie (1639-1649) 779, 1553, 2468
DOWN, Dean of, Patrick Delany, D.D. (1729-1754) 488, 691, 1108, 1188, 1371, 1377, 1789, 2113, 2190, 2652
DOWNES, Captain (1733)   68
DOWNES, Robert (1708)   2228
DOWNES, Samuel (1722)   6

DOWNES, Theophilus, M.A. (N.D.) 1691)   647, 849
DOWNES, William James (1833)   1120
DOWNHAM, George, or Downame (1643)   2206
DOWNIE, John (1810)   2511
DOWNING, George (1780)   2777
DOWNING, Rev. Colybute (1644)   413
DOWNLEY AND DUNNING, (1769)   2323
DOWNMAN, Hugh, M.D. (1775, 1781)   703, 737, 1953, 2415
DOYLE, Hannah (1860)   919
DOYLE, J. (1820)   2035
DOYLE, James Warren, Bishop of Kildare and Leighlin (1822-1827) 578, 1356, 1448, 1449, 2169, 2763
DRAGE, —— (1748)   13
DRAKE, —— (1718)   1225
DRAKE, James, D.D. (1699)   136
DRAKE, James, M.D. (1699-1702) 792, 1158, 1593, 2364, 2369, 2426
DRAKE, S. (1677, 1687)   416, 2840
DRAKE, Thomas, M.D. (1697)   2349
DRAKE, William (1661)   1509
DRANE, Augusta Theodisia (1858-1864) 1135, 1308, 2250, 2584, Errata, vol. iv.
DRAPE, Miss (1867)   383
DRAPER, Elizabeth (1775)   1427
DRAPER, William (1833)   1501
DRAYTON, Michael (1620, 1630) 349, 1746
DREGHORN, Lord, Colin Maclaurin (1816)   2452
DREGHORN, Lord, John Maclaurin (1757-1769) 154, 485, 488, 825, 1298, 1774, 1899
DRENNAN, William, M.D. (1785) 1441
DREW, Mrs (1857)   1320
DREWE, Patrick (1710)   399
DREWITT, Thomas (1800)   2812
DRING, Thomas (1655)   332
DROMORE, Bishop of, George Rust, (1661)   1361
DROMORE, Bishop of, Thomas Percy, D.D. (1761-1779) 933, 948, 1074, 1090, 1300, 1472, 1750, 2448
DROPE, John, M.A. (1662, 1664) 1195, 2717
DRUE, Thomas (1631)   1481
DRUMMOND, Dr Abernethy (1752-1771) 163, 305, 2097, 2159, 2164

DRUMMOND, George (1708) 2376
DRUMMOND, George W. A. H. (1804) 2615
DRUMMOND, Henry (1825) 367
DRUMMOND, Henry (1822-1858) 624 (2), 1658, 1775, 2616
DRUMMOND, Henry, M.P. (1828-1857) 141, 258, 398, 595, 867, 1126, 2016, 2080, 2214, 2291, 2472, 2522, 2616
DRUMMOND, Mrs (1735) 911
DRUMMOND, Rev. Dr (1822) 417
DRUMMOND, Sir William (1821) 1574
DRUMMOND, Thomas, D.D. (1743) 1370
DRUMMOND, William (1616, 1617) 944, 1945
DRUMMOND, W. Abernethie (1577) 108
DRUMMOND, William Abernethy, D.D. (1759, 1778) 334, 1327
DRUMMOND, William H., D.D. (1826) 288
DRURY, Robert (1732, 1733) 613, 893, 1531
DRY, J. (1717) 1606
DRYDEN, John (1674-1691) 7, 62, 592, 621, 736, 1098, 1103, 1531, 1563, 1752, 1943, 2302, 2390
DRYDEN, Mrs Anne R. Lamb (1844) 304
DRYSDALE, William (1798) 2247
D'UFFIEUX, M. (1781) 2382
DUBOIS, —— (1799) 879
DUBOIS, Edward (1804) 572
DUBOIS, Edward (1817) 873
DUBOIS, Edward (1808) 1686
DU BOIS, Edward (1801) 1812
DU BOIS, Edward (1808) 1812
DU BOIS, Edward (1799) 1911
DU BOIS, M. (1805) 2207
DU BOIS, Edward (1800) 2250
DU BOIS, Edward (1799-1817) 572, 873, 879, 1686, 1812 (2), 1911, 2207, 2250
DU FOSSE, Pierre Thomas (1694) 1590
DU MOULIN, Lewis (1641-1680) 1653, 2359, 2780
DU MOULIN, Peter, D.D. (1668, 1680) 302, 1375, 2359
DU PERRON, Jacques Davy, Cardinal (1623) 340
DU PRÉ, James (1732, 1745) 475, 2222
DU PAGET, Louis Albert (1852, 1863) 2245, 2622

DU RANCHIN, —— (1638) 2199
DUBLIN, Archbishop of, Richard Whately, D.D. (1819-1860) 473, 720, 1105 (2), 1247 (2), 1336 (2), 1337, 1342, 1446, 2736
DUBOIS, Fontanelle J. Gasp (1788) 728
DUBREUIL, Jean (1781) 1987
DUCAREL, Andrew Coltee, LL.D. (1754-1779) 1165, 2417, 2612
DUCHAL, Dr James (1762) 2340
DUCHÉ, Rev. Jacob (1777, 1791) 325, 1771
DUCKETT, —— (1715) 1173
DUCKETT, George (1717) 2515
DUDDING, Horatio Nelson (N.D.) 1870
DUDEVANT, Armandine L. A. (1847-1881) 443, 497, 521, 1431, 1560, 1617, 1664, 2386, 2614
DUDGEON, William (1732, 1734) 1391, 2436, 2487
DUDLEY, Howard (1836) 1126
DUDLEY, Sir Henry Bate (1782, N.D.) 704, 1867
DUFF, —— (1815) 547
DUFF, Andrew Halliday (1860-1873) 50, 2261 (2), 2348, 2519
DUFF, William, M.A. (1749, 1767) 800, 1712
DUFFERIN, Lady Harriet Blackwood (1863) 1491
DUFFET, Thomas (1674, 1678) 77, 744, 2053
DUFOUR DE LONGUERNE, Abbé L. (1687) 1123, 2649
DUGARD, Samuel, M.A. (1673, 1695) 1550, 1885
DUGARD, William (1665) 762
DUGDALE, Sir Wm. (1655, 1681) 332, 2377
DUICK, J. (1734) 498
DUIGENAN, Patrick, LL.D. (1786) 40
DUILLIER, Nicholas Fatio de (1699) 976
DUKE, John (1649) 2023
DULANEY, Daniel (1766) 488
DULAURE, Jacques Antoine (1786) 1960
DUMAY, —— (1772, 1773) 1360, 1712
DUMONT, Fr. (1713) 2458
DUNBAR, George (1842) 1749
DUNBAR, Margaret J. M. (1852) 180
DUNBAR, Thomas, M.A. (1811) 254
DUNBLANE, Bishop of, J. Gillane (1714) 1482, 2161, 2441
DUNCAN, Andrew, M.D. (1786) 2355

DUNCAN, Dr John (1783) 1657
DUNCAN, Henry, D.D. (1826) 2816
DUNCAN, Isabella (1860) 1990
DUNCAN, James (1816) 1035
DUNCAN, John (1815) 431
DUNCAN, John, D.D. (1762-1804) 37, 798, 1934
DUNCAN, John Shute, M.A. (1808, 1825) 251, 1102
DUNCAN, Mary G. Lundie (1832-1852) 74, 370, 1146, 1573
DUNCAN, P. (N.D.) 798
DUNCAN, Philip Bury (1822-1840) 801, 824, 1614
DUNCAN, W. (1794) 279, 2589
DUNCAN, William (1837) 607
DUNCAN, W. J. (1877-1880) 1755, 1834
DUNCKLEY, Henry, M.A. (1878) 1443
DUNCOMBE, Giles (1665) 2684
DUNCOMBE, Rev. John, M.A. (1774-1783) 140, 837, 1115, 1863
DUNCOMBE, William (1728) 1385
DUNCON, Rev. John (1648-1653) 2190, 2727
DUNDAS, Henry, Lord Melville (1793, 1796) 1123, 2199
DUNDAS, James (1796) 2734
DUNDAS, John (1709, 1710) 1609, 2517
DUNDAS, Wedderburn (1838) 1489
DUNDONALD, Earl of, A. Cochrane (1784) 28
DUNGWORTH, —— (N.D.) 398
DUNHAM, Samuel Astley, LL.D. (1831-1838) 65, 1136, 1145, 1148, 1502, 1722, 2643
DUNKELD, Bishop of, Thomas Rattray, D.D. (1728, 1744) 89, 809
DUNLOP, —— (1818, 1829) 1816, 1827
DUNLOP, Alexander (1847-1867) 47, 472 (2), 743, 1325, 2125, 2243
DUNLOP, Alexander Murray (N.D.) 2806 (2)
DUNLOP, Andrew (1828) 1184
DUNLOP, John Errata, vol. iv.
DUNLOP, M. and W. R. (1858-1860) 1185, 2594
DUNLOP, William (1719-1720) 423, 983
DUNLOP, William, M.D. (1832) 2491
DUNLOP, Professor William (1720) 1993
DUNLOP, Samuel (N.D.) 24
DUNN, —— (1776) 606
DUNN, D. (1775) 1826
DUNN, H. (1867) 1458
DUNN, Henry (1862) 2509

DUNNING, —— (1848) 1435
DUNNING AND DORONLEY (1769) 2323
DUNNING, J., Lord Ashburton (1764) 1402
DUNSAY, Baron, Edward Plunkett (1859) 1834
DUNSTANVILLE, Lord de, Francis Basset (1783, 1809) 534, 1785, 2469, 2576
DUNSTER, Charles, M.A. (1804-1812) 484, 665 (2), 1381, 1418, 1961, 2532
DUNSTER, Charles (1790) 2250
DUNSTER, Samuel (?) (1777) 2259
DUNTON, John (1692-1728) 193, 194, 2772
DUNTON, John (1692-1771) 749, 1076, 1286, 1671, 1708, 2056, 2369, 2782
DUPIN, Louis Ellies (1693) 1723
DUPPA, B., Bishop of Winchester (1673) 558
DUPPA, Richard (1809, 1816) 739, 1478, 1578
DUPPA, Richard, B.C.L. (1813-1814) 41, 1226
DURAND, David (1730) 1477
DURAND, Madame (1880) 2797
DURANT DE BREVAL, John (1716-1727) 182, 469, 1176, 1895, 2507
DURFEY, Thomas (1678, 1690) 293, 431, 818, 939, 2028
DURHAM, Bishop of, Edward Malty (1809) 2112
DURHAM, Bishop of, Joseph Butler, LL.D. (1716-1719) 1361, 2344
DURHAM, Bishop of, John Cosin, D.D. (1672) 426
DURHAM, Bishop of, J. Pilkington (1563) 292
DURHAM, Bishop of, Richard Neile (1624) 1529
DURHAM, Bishop of, Thomas Morton, D.D. (1605-1643) 842, 1706
DURHAM, Bishop of, W. V. Mildert, D.D. (1805) 1418
DURHAM, Dean of, Hon. S. Cowper (1766) 2645
DURHAM, Dean of, Thomas Comber, D.D. (1678-1689) 96, 385, 386, 395, 428, 647, 650, 970, 1365, 1932, 2584
DURHAM, William (1660) 1466
DURIE, William (1848) 1515
DURY, John (1649-1661) 312 (2), 480, 659, 2796
DUTTON, A. (1734) 1693

DUTTON, Rev. Thomas (1740)   660
DWARRIS, Sir Fortunatus (1832)   61
DYCE, Rev. Alexander (1856)   2100
DYER, George, B.A. (1793)   452
DYER, John, LL.B. (1740)   2237
DYER, Samuel (1772)   1436
DYER, Sir Edward (1585)   1990
DYKES, Thomas (1881)   2497
DYMOCK, —— (1602)   1869
DYMOCK, James (1676)   1049
DYMOND, Jonathan (1823)   766
DYSON, Jeremiah (1744, N.D.)   321, 784
DYSON, Mrs Charles (1833)   1595

E.

EACHARD, John, D.D. (1648-1672)
   960, 1046, 1055, 1673, 2432
EAGLES, John (1815)   1278
EAGLES, Rev. John (1826)   908
EAMES, W. (1716-1719)   428
EARBERY, Matthias (1716-1724)   738,
   1120, 1216, 1378, 1809, 2007
EARDLEY WILMOT, John (1778)   2364
EARLE, John, Bishop of Salisbury
   (1628)   1612
EASBY, J. (1843)   1541
EAST, Timothy (1824-1857)   569, 836,
   1641, 2350
EASTLAKE, Lady Elizabeth Rigby
   (1841-1855) 1065, 1267, 1431, 1504, 1682,
   2184
EASTON, Rev Thomas (1818)   2195
EASTWICK, J. B. (1849)   707
EATON, Charlotte Ann, née Waldie
   (1817-1827)   1693, 2225, 2774
EATON, Joseph (N.D.)   2069
EATON, Mrs (1853)   566
EBER, General (1862)   2551
ECCLES, Ambrose (1794-1805)   434,
   1599, 1934
ECCLES, Francis (1664)   379
ECHARD, Lawrence, M.A. (1691)   934
ECKHARDT, Juluis (1880)   2241
EDEN, Charles Page (1835)   2320
EDEN, Hon. Eleanor (1858)   720
EDEN, Hon. Emily (1859, 1860) 2321 (2)
EDEN, Right Hon. William, Lord
   Auckland (1771-1781)   490, 2017, 2441
EDEN, Sir Frederick Morton, Bart.
   (1807)   1548
EDGAR, J. G. (1853)   252
EDGAR, Thomas (1650)   2690
EDGECUMBE, Richard, Earl of
   Mount Edgecumbe (1827)   1683

EDGE, W. J. (1841)   915
EDGEWORTH, Maria (1800)   327
EDINBURGH, Bishop of, G.
   Wishart (1648)   1158
EDINBURGH, Lord Provost of, P.
   Lindesay (1733)   1241
EDISON, John Sibbald (1839-1850)
   810, 1303, 1452, 2250
EDMUNDS, Rev. John (1761)   1205
EDMUNDSON, Joseph (1766)   1112
EDMUNDS, Henry, LL.D. (1741)   868
EDMUNDSON, Henry (1658)   908
EDWARD, Andrew (N.D.)   560, 710
EDWARD, Rev Daniel (1877)   2837
EDWARDS, Annie, or Edwardes
   (1858-1869) 1659, 1823, 1961, 2529, 2843
EDWARDS, Bryan (1796)   1957
EDWARDS, Edward (1837)   262, 1050
EDWARDS, George (1795)   658
EDWARDS, John, D.D. (1710)   2753
EDWARDS, Jonathan, A.M. (1778)   809
EDWARDS, Jonathan, D.D. (1695,
   1702)   863, 2157
EDWARDS, L. (1858)   616
EDWARDS, Matilda Bentham
   (1862-1868)   687, 688, 1269, 1491, 2815
EDWARDS, Miss (1781)   1832
EDWARDS, Rev. —— (1715)   388
EDWARDS, Thomas (1748-1761)
   306, 959, 1388, 2522
EFFINGHAM, Earl of, Thomas
   Howard (1782)   809
EGAN, Anthony, or Egane (1678)   1853
EGAN, Pierce (1821-1822)   2083
EGERTON, Francis, Earl Ellesmere
   (1826, 1843) 252, 699, 1616, 1859, 2614
EGERTON, Francis Henry, Earl of
   Bridgewater (1793)   1483
EGERTON, Sarah, née Fyges (N.D.) 1951
EGERTON, Stephen (1613, 1618)
   1219, 1987
EGLETON, John (1714)   2757
EGMONT, Earl of, John Perceval
   (1733-1763)   486, 506, 850, 874, 2069,
   2308
EISENMENGER, Dr J. A. (1742)   2618
EIZAT, Dr (1699)   1568
EIZAT, Sir Edward (1695)   142
ELEY, Count D' (1721)   2003
ELDERFIELD, Christopher (1650) 407
ELFORD, —— (1786)   2366
ELIBANK, Lord, Patrick Murray
   (1754-1775) 487, 730, 828, 1230, 1397,
   2067, 2577

ELIOT, Francis Perceval (1791)   796
ELIOT, John (1658-1672) 1221, 1505, 1952
ELKING, Henry (1720)   1240
ELLABY, James, A.M. (1837)   137
ELLESMERE, Earl of, Francis Egerton (1826-1843)   252, 699, 1616, 1859, 2614
ELLINGTON, Francis (1662, 1665)   379, 412, 919
ELLIOT, Charlotte (1863)   1181
ELLIOT, Ebenezer, *or* Elliott (1801-1850)   513, 1662, 1740, 1892, 2725
ELLIOT, John Lettsom (1847-1850)   933, 1396 (3), 2591
ELLIOT, Miss (1781)   1155
ELLIOT, Sir Gilbert, Lord Minto (1752)   2036
ELLIOTT, Miss (1781-1783) 1556, 1829, 1976
ELLIS, —— (N.D.)   2322
ELLIS, Alexander John (1844)   1905
ELLIS, Arthur (1855)   1253
ELLIS, Clement, M.A. (1658-1688)   1369, 1908, 2043, 2106, 2722
ELLIS, Daniel, F.R.S.E. (1828)   490
ELLIS, Edmund (1655, 1696)   616, 2279
ELLIS, George (1778-1790) 1159, 1568, 1958, 2465
ELLIS, Harriet Warner (1868)   1833
ELLIS, John (1739, 1758)   307, 2526
ELLIS, John, D.D. (1743)   1309, 2422
ELLIS, John, F.R.S. (1771)   635
ELLIS, Mrs William, *née* Sarah Stickney (1843)   1669, 2776
ELLIS, Philip (1686)   929
ELLIS, Rev. Thomas (1819)   2416
ELLIS, Sir Henry (1811, 1833) 329, 1461
ELLIS, Thomas (1661)   2629
ELLIS, W. (1772)   2516
ELLIS, William (1848-1852)   916, 1246, 2029, 2804
ELLISON, Dr (1726)   1668
ELLWOOD, Thomas (N.D., 1699)   29, 2412
ELLYS, Anthony, Bishop of St Davids (1736)   1936
ELLYS, Anthony, D.D. (1752)   2139
ELLYS, Sir Richard, Bart. (1736)   2756
ELPHINSTONE, Sir Howard (1833)   1501
ELRINGTON, Thomas (1822)   1232
ELSDALE, Annie F. (1844)   2543
ELSLEY, J. (1799)   102
ELSTOB, William, M.A. (1703)   806

ELSUM, John (1700)   777
ELTON, Sir Arthur Hallam (1855)   1227
ELWIN, Hastings (N.D.)   2347
ELY, Bishop of, Benjamin Laney (1668)   2351
ELY, Bishop, Dr P. Gunning (1676)   1456
ELY, Bishop of, Matthew Wren, M.A. (1657)   481
ELY, Bishop of, Simon Patrick, D.D. (1686-1688)   1753, 2636
ELY, Bishop of, Thomas Greene (1726)   2018
ELY, Bishop of, Thomas Turton, D.D. (1827, 1829)   2161, 2758
ELY, Bishop of, William Fleetwood (1707-1720)   392, 583, 1468
ELY, Dean of, George Peacock, M.A. (1831)   1782, 2153
ELY, Humphrey (N.D.)   350
ELYS, Edmund (1654-1692) 71, 98, 616, 685, 717, 1420, 2756
EMERSON, George B. (1846)   2179
EMES, Thomas (1698)   618
EMERSON, John Swift (1823)   1818
EMERSON, William (1743-1770)   691 (2), 1705, 2029
EMLYN, Thomas (1702-1718)   274, 687, 847, 982, 1188, 2008, 2143, 2197, 2763, 2766
EMPAYTAY, H. L. (1830)   2433
EMRA, Elizabeth Holmes, *née* (1830)   2263
ENDEAN, J. Russell (1868-1880)   559, 1963 (2), 2291
ENFIELD, William, LL.D. (1770-1784)   426, 760, 1991
ENGALL, Thulia S. (1852)   1076
ENGLEFIELD, Sir Francis (1594)   470
ENGLEFIELD, Sir Henry Charles, Bart. (N.D., 1814)   605, 2553
ENGLISH, Francis Mary (1858)   2684
ENGLISH, George B. (1822)   1696
ENGLISH, Henry Scale (1830)   88
ENSOR, George (1816)   1262
ENTY, Rev. John (1732)   1391
EPINAY, Mme. de la Live d' (1815) 507
EPPS, John, M.D. (1827)   1242
ERBERY, William (1653)   1532
ERBURY, Baron, Lord Robert Grosvenor (1852)   1335
ERBURY, William (1654)   1259
ERCK, J. C. (1817)   1251
ERNDTEL, Christian H. (1711)   2125

ERSKINE, David (N.D.)   849
ERSKINE, E. (1765)   189
ERSKINE, Ebenezer (1722, 1733)   1054, 2677
ERSKINE, Hon. Andrew (1763, 1764)   541, 2350
ERSKINE, John, D.D. (1742-1780)   18, 876, 1564, 2116, 2349, 2385, 2760
ERSKINE, Lady Francis (1772)   1591
ERSKINE, Mr (1780)   568
ERSKINE, Ralph (1720)   1033
ERSKINE, Ralph, M.A. (1747)   1327, 1698
ERSKINE, Thomas (1830)   1014
ERSKINE, Thomas, Lord Erskine (1817-1819)   177, 897, 2303
ERSKINE, William, W.S. (1798)   780
ERSKINE OF GRANGE, Hon. James (1736)   903
ESDAILE, David, D.D. (1865)   504
ESPIARD, François J. de la Borde (1753)   2473
ESPINASSE, Isaac (1810)   1356
ESPRIT, Jacques (1691)   886
ESSEX, Earle of (1603)   145
ESSINGTON, Robert William (1846-1872)   1337, 1839
ESTWICK, Samuel, LL.D. (1772)   486
ETON, William (1805)   465
ETOUGH, Rev. Henry (1743)   1389
ETTINGSALL, Thomas (1832)   94
EUDES, Morton (1609)   341
EUSTACE, Rev. John Chetwode (1810, 1814)   1963, 2031
EVANS, Abel (1710, 1713)   156, 2727
EVANS, Arise (1654)   1303
EVANS, John, A.M. (1683)   315
EVANS, John, D.D. (1716-1719)   428
EVANS, Lewis (1830)   1939
EVANS, Mary Ann (1846-1879) 32, 562, 908, 1217, 1338, 1475, 1613, 1616, 2226, 2263, 2385, 2461, Errata, vol. iv.
EVANS, Morgan (1860)   1944
EVANS, Rev. John (1837)   1441
EVANS, Theophilus (1757)   1142
EVANSON, Edward (1772)   695
EVELEIGH, Josiah (1719)   585
EVELYN, John (1649-1738) 30, 360, 367, 777, 1166, 1321, 1459, 1679 (2), 2485, 2704
EVER, Sampson (1677)   690
EVERARD, W. (1765)   1599
EVERETT, Alexander Hill (1822, 1828)   74, 836

EVERETT, Edward (1824, 1831)   1051, 2039
EVERS, —— (1784)   1274
EVITT, S. W. (1839)   1838
EWES, Sir Symonds d' (1640)   276
EWINGTON, H. (1805)   168
EXETER, Bishop of, George Lavington (1749, 1759)   774, 1659
EXETER, Bishop of, H. Phillpots (1827)   1428
EXETER, Bishop of, John Gauden, D.D. (1661)   1914
EXETER, Dean of, William Holmes, D.D. (1742)   524
EYRE, —— (1690)   2758
EYRE, Francis (1778-1799) 917, 2360, 2366
EYSTON, Charles (1722)   1126

F.

FABER, Frederick William (1843-1846)   240, 845, 2071
FAIRBAIRN, John (1835)   1820
FAIRFAX, Henry (1688)   1212
FAIRFAX, J. (1679)   568
FAIRHOLT, Frederick William (1853)   1053
FALCONER, Edwin (1856)   297
FALCONER, John (1692)   2238
FALCONER, Rev. Dr Thomas (1805) 179
FALCONER, Rev. Thomas (1798, 1799)   2146, 2188
FALCONER, Rev. Thomas, A.M., M.D. (1804)   1411
FALCONER, Thomas (1834)   1168
FALCONER, Thomas M.A. (1802) 2251
FALCONER, William (1808-1817) 674, 1786
FALCONER, William, M.D. (1771)   36
FALKLAND, Lord Viscount Henry Cary (1680)   1160
FALLOWFIELD, John (N.D.)   1858
FANE, Hon. Julian C. H. (1861)   2546
FANE, John, Earl of Westmoreland (1820, 1822)   1572, 1573
FANE, Mildmay, Earl of Westmoreland (164-)   1832
FANNANT, Edward (1680)   1160
FANNANT, Thomas (1641)   2674
FANSHAWE, Sir Richard (1652, 1670)   921, 2068, 2317, 2699
FANSHAW, Sir Thomas (1658)   1987
FANQUE, Mlle. (1759)   1
FANQUIER, Francis (1756)   814

FAREWELL, James (1589)   1252
FARINGTON, —— (1707)   2130
FARMER, Ralph (1657)   2258
FARNIE, H. B. (1864)   1892
FARNIE, Henry (1857)   1027
FARNWORTH, Richard (1655-1665) 132, 254, 382, 383, 1034, 1078, 1172, 2604, 2822
FARQUHAR, Barbara H. (1848, 1850)   1879, 2083
FARQUHAR, George (1705)   2482
FARWELL, John (1682)   1385
FARRAH, Benjamin (1692)   1624
FARRAR, Rev. Frederick W. (1862)   2253
FARRER, —— (1790)   2651
FARRER, Henrietta Louisa (1847-1877) 58, 66, 179, 199, 528, 698, 905, 911, 1170, 1477, 1486, 1501, 1833, 2082, 2205, 2206, 2250, 2319, 2540, 2541
FATIO DE DUILLIER, Nicholas (1699)   976
FAUCHEUR, Michel le (N.D.)   821
FAULKNER, T. (N.D.)   1111
FAUSETT, Godfrey, D.D. (1835)   915
FAUSSET, A. R. (1858)   876
FAVART, C. S. (1770)   2084
FAWCETT, Millicent Garrett (1878)   1261
FAWKES, Francis (1780, N.D.) 170, 253
FAWKES, Mrs (1852)   1312
FAY, Theodore S. (1832)   706
FEA, James (1750)   1000
FEARN, John (1814)   798
FEATLEY, Daniel (1626, 1644) 1881, 2245
FEIJO, Father (1760)   1175
FEILDE, Edward (1844, 1847) 558, 2051
FEILDE, John (1617)   46
FEIST, Charles (1825)   2575
FELGATE, Samuel (1682)   1757
FELL, Henry (1661)   1925
FELL, Dr John (1673-1684)   1858, 2288
FELL, J., Bishop of Oxford (1674)   2722
FELL, John (1774)   1294
FELL, John, D.D. (1659)   1240
FELL, John, D.D., Dean of Christ-church (1647)   2023
FELL, Rev. John (1784, N.D.) 816, 1782
FELL, Margaret Fox *née* (1657-1677) 302, 564, 1522, 2609, 2678, 2694, 2827
FELL, Rev. Philip (1676)   1456
FELLOWES, Robert, D.D. (1817) 1133
FELLTHAM, Owen (1659, 1686) 215, 261

FELTON, Samuel (1787-1792) 1213 (2), 2556
FENNELL, James H. (1839)   450
FENNER, Dudley (1584-1602) 140, 185, 520, 589, 593
FENTON, Elijah (N.D.)   1800
FENTON, J. (1603)   1304
FENTON, Richard (1811, 1815) 1579, 2611
FENTON, Roger, D.D. (1615)   2337
FENWICK, George, B.D. (1759)   2052
FENWICK, Mrs (1795)   2311
FERGUS, Henry (1830-1832)   1167
FERGUSON, —— (1689)   1322
FERGUSON, Adam, LL.D. (1757-1776) 82, 1163, 1659, 2138, 2151
FERGUSON, C. (1738)   1343
FERGUSON, Charles (1833)   716
FERGUSON, J., Lord Pitfour (1764) 853
FERGUSON, John Clark (1849)   744
FERGUSON, Robert (1673-1711) 24, 156, 238, 258, 268, 610, 618, 765, 870, 1291, 1318, 1374 (2), 1385, 1414, 1695, 1745, 2062, 2181, 2304, 2411, 2570, 2806
FERGUSS, Miss (1777)   2573
FERMOY Col. Philip Roche (1828)   439
FERNE, Henry, D.D. (1643, 1644) 303, 778
FERNYHOUGH, Captain Thomas (1829)   1615
FERRAR, Nicholas (1634)   1195
FERRERS, Edmund (1816, 1817) 412, 1206
FERRERS, G. (1820)   1556
FERRIER, Jas. Frederick, LL.D. (1848)   1771
FERRIER, Susan (1818-1821) 611, 1225, 1549
FERRIER, Walter (1831)   1396
FERRIER, William (1801)   2171
FERRYMAN, —— (1843)   2333
FESSENDEN, Thomas Green (1803)   1957
FESSEY, H. (1654)   604
FETHERSTONE, Christopher (1586)   289
FFOULKES, Edmund S., B.D. (1853)   2024
FIELD, Barron (1815)   1102
FIELD, E. (1854)   1545
FIELD, Henry (1820)   1577
FIELD, J. E., M.A. (N.D.)   1312
FIELD, John (1700)   532, 2432
FIELD, Nathaniel (1632)   904
FIELD, Sarah, *née* Fyge (1771)   1951

FIELD, William (1815)   1111
FIELDING, —— (1780)   1092
FIELDING, Henry (1730-1771) 49, 152,
    204, 355, 529 (2), 534, 1008, 1120, 1422,
    1516, 1633, 1636, 1808, 2078, 2606, 2620
FIELDING, Sarah (1744-1760) 49, 546,
            888, 1036, 1144, 1501
FIENNES, Nathaniel, (1642, 1660) 1650,
                        2714
FIENNES, William, Viscount Say
    and Sele (1659)   938
FILLINGHAM, William (1806)   1220
FILMER, Sir Robert, Knt. (1647-
    1653) 52, 84, 962, 1707, 1768, 1788, 2059
FINCH, Anne, Countess of Winchel-
    sea (1713)   1631
FINCH, Daniel, Earl of Nottingham
    (1713)   1791
FINCH, Emily (1841)   1318
FINCH, George (1831, 1841)   272, 922
                        2176, 2177
FINCH, Heneage, Earl of Notting-
    ham (N.D., 1660)   134, 841
FINCH, Henry (1621)   2842
FINCH, Richard (1739-1746) 477, 579, 594,
    960, 1407, 1409, 1703, 2287, 2301, 2743
FINCH, Sir Henry (1615)   864
FINDLAY, Dr (1773)   196
FINDLAY, Robert (1778)   1409
FINDLAY, Robert, D.D. (1762-1781)
            1890, 2144, 2697
FINLAY, Alexander S. (1837)   1444
FINLAY, John (1802)   2786
FINLAY, J. R. (1874)   2725
FINLAY, K. J. (1866)   294
FINLAYSON, J. (1771)   1546
FIREBRACE, Rev. John (1771, 1772)
            987, 1408, 1936
FIRMAN, Giles (1660, 1661) 1499, 1996
FIRMIN, Thomas (1787)   425
FISHER, —— (1798)   2269
FISHER, Admiral William (1850,
    1851)   1894, 2075
FISHER, Edward, B.A. (N.D.)   162
FISHER, Edward (1644-1722) 118, 376,
                907, 1551, 2306
FISHER, Gregory Mushet alias
    (1623)   238
FISHER, J. (1765)   189
FISHER, Jasper, D.D. (1633)   977
FISHER, Joane (N.D.)   613
FISHER, John (1692)   1977
FISHER, John (1821)   2183
FISHER, John, S.J. (1626)   130

FISHER, John, or Piercy (1623)   110
                Errata, vol. iv.
FISHER, Lydia J. (1847)   1430
FISHER, Miss (1849)   889
FISHER, Payne (1663, 1683) 1950, 2532,
                        2606
FISHER, Richard Trott (1836)   739
FISHER, Thomas (1776)   1298
FISHER, Thomas (1825)   1709
FISK, G. (1847)   1830
FISON, Margaret (1846)   1015
FITZGEFFREY, Henry (1620)   349
FITZ-GEOFFREY, Charles (1648) 1022
FITZGERALD, Edward (1851-
    1852)   834, 1969
FITZGERALD, Maurice (1771-
    1845)   1387, 2006, 2098
FITZGERALD, Percy H., M.A.
    (1861-1869)   204, 1968, 2222, 2268
FITZGERALD, Rev. —— (1809)   103
FITZGERALD, Robert Allan (1866) 1263
FITZGERALD, W. T. (1793)   2653
FITZGIBBON, Edward (1847-1850)
                248, 1064, 1671
FITZHARDINGE, Elizabeth (1781) 1639
FITZHARRIS, Viscount, James
    Howard (1837)   2177
FITZ-HERBERT, Sir Anthony
    (1515)   244 (2)
FITZ-HERBERT, Sir William
    (1779)   2365
FITZHERBERT, Thomas (1602-
    1614)   223, 586, 2170, 2523
FITZPATRICK, Patrick V. (1828) 2558
FITZPATRICK, Right Hon. Richard
    (1775)   700
FITZPATRICK, Thady (1760)   772
FITZPATRICK, William John (1856,
    1859)   973, 2811
FITZROY, Augustus H., Duke of
    Grafton (1790)   1099
FITZWILLIAM, Viscount (1811)   1451
FITZWILLIAM, Earl of, —— Went-
    worth (1795)   1354
FLAMANK, James (1834)   1694
FLAMSTEED, J. (1680)   694
FLANNIGAN, Mrs (1844)   137
FLATMAN, Thomas (1658, 1682) 699,
                1085, 1693, 1849
FLEETWOOD, William (1687)   23
FLEETWOOD, William (1717)   1357
FLEETWOOD, William (1710)   2570
FLEETWOOD, Wm., Archbishop
    of Canterbury (N.D.)   584

FLEETWOOD, William, Bishop of Ely (1707-1720)   392, 583, 1468

FLEETWOOD, William, Bishop of St Asaph (1713)   986

FLEETWOOD, William, D.D. (1712-1719) 549, 1285, 1376, 1406, 1853, 2306, 2333

FLEMING, Abraham (1589, 1618) 290, 2633

FLEMING, Caleb, D.D. (1730-1773) 103, 122, 134, 143, 146, 160, 165, 338, 354, 361, 407, 409, 598, 615, 814, 815, 847, 899, 965, 974, 984, 1209, 1264, 1354, 1398, 1404, 1543, 1604, 1642, 1700, 1706, 1805, 1847, 1935, 1941, 2085, 2129, 2145, 2162, 2252, 2563, 2587

FLEMING, John (1771)   998

FLEMING, Rev. Alexander, M.A. (1808-1840)   130, 1451, 2505

FLEMING, Robert (1675-1693) 403, 650, 977, 1138, 1998, 2358, 2527, 2676

FLETCHER, Beaumont and (1607-1815) 241, 349, 355, 356, 1190, 1308, 1536, 1599, 2620, 2825

FLETCHER, Andrew (1698-1706) 12, 651, 2274, 2470, 2471 (2), 2486, 2691

FLETCHER, E. (1825)   739

FLETCHER, Giles (N.D.)   1461

FLETCHER, Henry (1660)   1885

FLETCHER, John (1640-1815) 514, 1599, 2567, 2852

FLETCHER, John William (1771) 2293, 2764

FLETCHER, Joseph (1613, 1629) 375, 1125

FLETCHER, Julia (1877, 1880) 1076, 1742

FLETCHER, Martha (1825)   449

FLETCHER, Phineas (1631-1633) 740, 1916, 2058, 2381

FLETCHER, Rev. William (1833-1841)   402, 1487, 2119

FLEURY, C. (1749)   1542

FLEXMAN, Roger, D.D. (1752)   2148

FLINDERS, Anne (1840, 1842) 472, 907

FLINT, T. (1828)   1462

FLINT, William (1815)   2643

FLITCROFT, H. (1768)   2559

FLOOD, Henry (1814)   1436

FLOOD, Right Hon. Henry (1783)   212

FLORES, Jean de (1556)   1124

FLORIAN, J. P. Clavis de (1827)   732

FLOUNDERS, Jonathan (1814, 1822) 377, 2431

FLOWER, Benjamin (1792)   2018

FLOWER, William B. (1849)   2205

FLOWERDEW, Rev. John (1839)   1767

FLOYD, John, S.J. (1612-1639) 394, 1839, 2057, 2608

FOARD, J. F. (1861)   1465

FOLEY, Henry (1873, 1875)   762, 1472

FOLEY, R. (1756)   997

FONBLANQUE, John (N.D.)   2330

FONNEREAU, Thomas George (1849)   626

FONTANELLE, J. Gasp Dubois (1788)   728

FONTENELLE, Bernard le Bovier de (1688)   1162

FOORD, Emanuel (1633)   892

FOORD, James J. (1788)   1299

FOOTE, Samuel (1778)   529, 1535, 2645

FORBES, ——, Bishop of Leith (1765) 1921

FORBES, Alexander, Baron Forbes (1734)   826

FORBES, ——, Bishop of Leith (1765, 1767)   809, 1921

FORBES, Alexander Penrose, D.C.L., Bishop of Brechin (1847-1853) 439, 1170, 1574, 1595, 1622

FORBES, D. (1725)   511

FORBES, Duncan (1735, 1747) 1365, 2444

FORBES, Duncan, Lord President (1737, 1750)   2116, 2630

FORBES, Duncan, of Culloden (1730-1767)   492, 1588, 2422

FORBES, G. H. D. (1828)   1754

FORBES, Granville H. (1863)   2739

FORBES, J. (1800)   252

FORBES, James (1813, 1824)   626, 2209

FORBES, John Hay, Lord Medwyn (1815-1871)   40, 2354, 2389, 2493, 2529

FORBES, Murray (1786)   2648

FORBES, Patrick Bishop of Aberdeen (1627)   833

FORBES, Robert, D.D., Bishop of Caithness (1774)   17

FORBES, Robert (1755)   61

FORBES, William, of Disblair (1704-1728) 211, 819, 1531, 1914, 2080, 2168, 2441, 2846

FORD, —— (1641)   610

FORD, Charles (1859)   1896

FORD, James (1815, 1816)   615, 1718

FORD, John (1732)   264

FORD, Rev. James, D.D. (1825)   1574

FORD, Richard (1837)   1116

FORD, Simon, D.D. (1667-1669)   474, 1506, 1508

FORD, Thomas (1854, 1855)   460, 2166
FORD, Thomas (1794)   476
FORD, Thomas (1660)   2771
FORDE, Thomas (1647, 1649) 1526, 2594
FORDYCE, David (1745)   623
FORDYCE, James, D.D. (1766)   2340
FORMBY, Henry (1851, 1856) 711, 929,
                                1908, 2270
FORREST, Frederick (1761, 1766)
                                2080, 2797
FORRESTER, A. (1741)   325
FORRESTER, Alfred Henry (1827-
    1859) 9, 65, 291, 879, 880, 984, 1024, 1256,
    1302, 1497, 1895, 1908, 1909, 2386, 2541,
                                      2686
FORRESTER, David (1679)   631
FORRESTER, Lieut.-Col. James
    (1734)   1962
FORRESTER, T. (1843)   1070
FORRESTER, Thomas (1706) 342, 2193
FORRESTER, Thomas (1684, 1692)
                                519, 2103
FORSAGETH, J., D.D. (1782)   2581
FORSAITH, Thomas S. (1856)   1063
FORSHALL, Josiah (1851)   155
FORSTER, E. (1809)   1793
FORSTER, J. G. A (1767)   393
FORSTER, John (1807, 1852) 626, 2135,
                                      2206
FORSTER, John, of Lincoln's Inn
    (1828-1833)   1773 (3), 1774, 1778
FORSTER, Josiah (1789)   2061
FORSTER, Nathaniel B. D., D.D.
    (1743-1767)   679, 767, 211
FORSTER, Rev Charles (1830)   2766
FORSTER, Samuel (1726)   1672
FORSTER, Thomas, (1807, 1809)
                                637, 1774
FORSTER, Thomas, F.L.S. (1823) 2416
FORSTER, Thomas I. M., F.R.A.S.
    (1845-1850)   786 (2)
FORSTER, Thomas, M.D. (1832)   1564
FORSTER, W. (1633)   33
FORSYTH, Ebenezer (1867)   2348
FORSYTH, William, M.A. (1850)   920
FORSYTH, William (1861, N.D.)
                                1552, 1613
FORTESCUE, James, D.D. (1754)   1969
FORTESCUE, J. F. (1857)   1246
FOSBERY, Thomas V., M.A. (1844) 1196
FOSBROOKE, Thomas Dudley,
    M.A. (1833)   2643
FOSS, Henry (1827)   330
FOSS, Payne and (1825)   332 (2)

FOSSE, Pierre Thomas du (1694)   1590
FOSTER, Catherine (1838)   1726
FOSTER, Francis (1779)   2583
FOSTER, Hugh Ker (1828)   1862
FOSTER, James (1755)   2154
FOSTER, Rev. Benjamin (1786)   2417
FOSTER, Sir Michael (1720-1759)
                        320, 489, 851, 1360
FOSTER, T. (N.D.)   2818
FOSTER, Thomas (1808, 1810) 383, 2748
FOSTER, Thomas, B.A. (1789)   289
FOTHERGILL, Jessie (1878, 1879)
                                929, 2024
FOTHERGILL, John, M.D. (1765,
    1770)   490, 2418
FOULIS, Sir James, Bart. (1775)   1783
FOUNTAINE, John (1661)   1422, 2206
FOWKE, Mrs (1720)   1672
FOWLER, Edward, D.D., Bishop of
    Gloucester (1671-1709)   350, 593, 637,
    952, 971, 1753, 2015, 2112, 2185, 2294,
                                2556, 2742
FOWLER, Eliza Heywood née (1744-
    1788) 785, 911, 944, 1140, 1141, 1142,
                                      1194
FOWLER, John (1759)   1319
FOWLER, Thomas, D.D. (1678)   2754
FOWNES, Joseph (1772)   772
FOWNES, Sir W. (1725)   1610
FOX, Charles James (N.D., 1806) 823, 2488
FOX, Edward (1854)   1958
FOX, Ellen Crewdson née (18—)   521
FOX, Francis, M.A. (N.D.)   1767
FOX, George (1654-1706) 112, 127, 179,
    297, 306, 335, 462 (2), 463 (3), 505, 546,
    574, 575 (2), 681, 781, 783 (3), 857, 919,
    939, 999 (2), 1034, 1054, 1079, 1086,
    1087 (2), 1201, 1236, (2), 1248, 1315,
    1489, 1879, 2009 (2), 2293, 2331, 2344,
    (2), 2345, 2445, 2446 (2), 2447, 2548,
    2571, 2586, 2597 (2), 2598 (3), 2601,
    2661, 2666, 2670, 2679, 2682, 2773, 2791
                                (3), 2804, 2832
FOX, G., jun. (1681)   1715
FOX, Henry R. V., Lord Holland
    (1807-1818)   705, 1373, 2584
FOX, Margaret, née Fell (1657-1677)
    302, 564, 1522, 2609, 2678, 2694, 2827
FOX, Sarah (1852)   1610
FOX, Sarah H. (1863)   1952
FOX, William (1792-1796)   41, 969
FOXE, John (1580)   1971
FRAME, Robert (N.D.)   2397
FRAMPTON, Dr Josiah (1796)   2585

FRAMPTON, John (1579)   1667
FRANCIS, Sir Philip (1798-1818)
                 664, 1120, 1436, 2068
FRANCKEN, Christian (1580)   470
FRANCKLIN, Thomas (1751)   202
FRANCKLIN, Thomas, D.D. (1766-
   1776)   348, 503, 715, 1364, 1559
FRANCKLYN, Gilbert (1792-1793)
                              305, 419
FRANK, Arnee (1820)   271
FRANCKLAND, Thomas, M.D.
   (1679-1681)   100, 1176
FRANKLIN, A. (1800)   2450
FRANKLIN, Benjamin (1759, 1761)
                             1121, 1241
FRANKLIN, John (1683)   2185
FRANKLIN, T. (1721)   581
FRANKUM, Richard (1861)   220
FRANSHAM, John (1720)   841
FRASER, Archibald C. (1800)   2375
FRASER, James Baillie (1828, 1832)
                             1097, 1310
FRASER, P. (1835)   35
FRASER, Patrick, LL.D. (1848,1855)
                             697, 2704
FRASER, Rev. P. (1829)   2704
FRASER, Simon (1811)   734
FRASER, Sir William A. (1869)   422
FRASER, W. (1822, 1824)   256, 824
FRAZER, Mrs (1822)   2819
FREARSON, John (1855, 1858) 2128, 2712
FREE, John, D.D. (1755, 1764) 1559, 1654
FREEBAIRN, David (N.D.)   2067
FREKE, William (1703-1709)   21, 947,
                             1490, 1970
FREEKE, William C. (1687)   829
FREEMAN, Samuel, D.D. (1684-
   1688)   223, 315, 641, 1753, 1919
FREEMAN, Sir Ralph (1635, 1655)
                             1213, 1309
FREIND, John, M.D. (1707, 1719)
                              18, 1399
FRENCH, —— (1836)   741
FRENCH, Annie Hector née (1873) 2831
FRENCH, M. (1865)   615
FRENCH, Nicholas (1668)   1696
FRENCH, Robert (1770)   496
FREND, William (1787)   486, 1003
FRERE, B. (1813)   48
FRERE, George (1768)   2368
FRERE, John Hookman (1790-1842) 30,
   237, 624, 974, 1308, 1612, 1652, 2040,
                                 2561
FRERE, Mary (1869)   1521

FRERE, R. L. (1831)   916
FRESHFIELD, Mrs Henry (1861)   71
FRESTON, Rev. Anthony (1784-
   1796)   41, 2048
FRIEDRICH, Dr Johann (1869)   1971
FRISWELL, James Hain (1864-1875)
         4, 227, 826, 956, 1004, 2478
FRITH, John (1429-1641) 45, 714, 1687,
                                 1917
FROUDE, J. A. (1847)   2346
FROUDE, R. Hurrell (1836)   1528
FRY, Caroline (1830-1860) 375, 558, 994,
      1034, 1046, 1492, 1990, 2518, 2535
FRY, Edmund (1859)   2413
FRY, Henrietta Joan (1845, 1847) 1198,
                             2207, 2801
FRY, John (1738-1816)   230, 796, 1338,
                       1911, 2318, 2439
FRY, Joseph Storrs (1816, 1829)   1140,
                             1446, 1706
FRY, Rev. Thomas (1839)   905
FRY, Sarah (1826)   875
FRY, Sarah Maria (N.D., 1856) 1516, 1547
FRYER, Michael (1810, 1842) 1244, 2650
FULKE, William (1563)   1666
FULKE, William, D.D. (1670)   1608
FULLER, —— (1611)   2840
FULLER, Francis, M.A. (N.D.)   1564
FULLER, James Franklin (1878)   1270
FULLER, John (1829)   1694
FULLER, P. (1718)   1409
FULLER, Thomas (1640-1660) 61, 1273,
                                 2594
FULLER, Thomas, B.D. (1654)   437
FULLER, Thomas, D.D. (1654)   776
FULLER, Thomas, M.D. (N.D.)   1564
FULLERTON, Lady Georgiana
   (1868)   506
FULLOM, Stephen Watson (1849) 1302
FULLWOOD, Francis, D.D. (1661-
   1689)   59, 692, 1039, 1765, 2200, 2426,
                                 2604
FURLONG, W. (1834)   2466
FURLY, Benjamin (1663)   2842
FUSELI, Henri (1767)   2156
FYERS, Lieut.-Col. W. A., C.B., R.B.
   (1859)   1256
FYFFE, Charles Ann, M.A. (N.D.)   2154
FYGE, Sarah Field née (N.D.)   1951
FYGES, Sarah Egerton née (N.D.)   1951
FYLER, Fanny (1850)   1971
FYSHE, Symon (1845)   2524
FYVIE, Isabella (1868-1876)   294, 307,
         543, 545, 1799, 1994, 2315

G.

GADBURY, John (1680)   1700
GAINSFORD, Thomas (1619) 1018, 2669
GAIRDNER, Andrew (1735, 1736)   8, 259, 987
GALE, Frederick (1867)   2054
GALE, John (1711)   2108
GALE, Robert (1697)   1310
GALE, S. (1784)   808
GALE, Theophilus (1669, 1673) 1465, 2670
GALL, James (1827, 1844) 926, 961, 2343
GALL, R. (1796)   2687
GALL, Rev. James (1868, 1871) 2010, 2395
GALLENGA, Antonio (1841-1853)   57, 928, 1118, 1257 (3), 1322, 1984, 2263
GALLOWAY, Joseph (1775-1783) 305, 491, 510, 846, 873, 1113, 1413, 1450, 1778, 1928, 1966, 2172, 2176
GALT, John (1818-1839) 101, 156, 206, 626, 718, 774, 1319, 1568, 1817, 2049, 2074, 2216, 2229, 2389, 2460, 2483, 2492, 2626, 2787
GALT, William (1844)   2075
GALLY DE GAUJAC, Peter (1698) 2675
GALLY, Henry (1763)   2295
GALLY, Henry, D.D. (1731, 1754) 672, 2087
GAMBLE, John (1811)   2403
GAMBOLD, John (1754)   1921
GANDER, Joseph (1703)   1847
GANDY, Edward (1827)   1655
GANDY, Henry (1700-1712) 37, 118, 470, 713, 1223, 1288, 1359, 1809, 2143, 2440
GARBETT, —— (1784)   2644
GARBRAND, John (1680)   1041
GARDEN, Dr James (1752)   445
GARDEN, Francis, Lord Gardenstone (1780)   1402
GARDEN, George, D.D. (1669)   148
GARDEN, George, D.D. (1703) 319, 2010
GARDEN, George, D.D. (1603)   1396
GARDENSTONE, Lord, Francis Garden (1780)   1402
GARDINER, Bernard, LL.D. (1717) 1925
GARDINER, Charles John, Earl of Blessington (1826)   567
GARDINER, Dr Samuel (1689)   265
GARDINER, Margaret, Countess of Blessington (1822-1846)   1276, 1490, 1533, 2076, 2401, 2611
GARDINER, Richard (1754, 1780) 1146, 2323

GARDINER, Robert (1713-1724) 1237 (2), 1238 (2), 1239
GARDINER, Thomas (1817)   1474
GARDINER, W. (1762)   508
GARDNER, —— (1696)   2436
GARDNER, Andrew (1727)   1510
GARDNER, Archibald (1851, 1852) 581, 1663
GARDNER, W. A. (1845)   2244
GARDNER, William (1771)   1329
GARLAND, Richard (1813)   2611
GARLICK, Thomas (1719)   1562
GARNETT, Richard (1858)   2012
GARNHAM, Robert Edward (1789-1790)   844, 1416, 1417, 2194
GARNIER, Robert (1594, 1595) 513, 2618
GARRET, W. (1818)   20
GARRETT, Annie (1847)   2341
GARRETT, Ellen Amelia (1847)   2341
GARRETT, Walter (1706-1707)   2556
GARRICK, David (1747-1778) 62, 244, 337, 356, 388, 523, 555, 704, 745, 839, 878, 880, 897, 968, 992, 1056, 1096, 1253, 1488, 1535, 1537, 1561, 1633, 1707, 1719, 1803, 1880, 2381, 2449 (3), 2550, 2559
GARTER, Bernard (1565-1579) 1281, 1736, 2063, 2620
GARTER, Sir Charles G. Young (1841) 18
GARTSHORE, Mrs Murray (1847)   416
GARTH, Sir Samuel, M.D. (1699-1715) 410, 455, 666
GARVEY, Michael A. (1850)   1889
GASCOIGNE, Mrs (1839-1855) 751, 837, 1739, 2551
GASKELL, Elizabeth Cleghorn (1848-1860) 531, 1504, 1553, 1655, 1750, 2209, 2242
GASPEY, Thomas (1820-1859) 302, 705, 1137, 1506, 1690, 1832, 2208, 2319, 2822
GASTON, Rev. Hugh (1813)   441
GASTRELL, Francis, D.D., Bishop of Chester (1696-1746) 584, 1658, 2016, 2160, 2374, 2421
GATAKER, Charles (1673)   931
GATFORD, —— (N.D.)   1212
GATHERCOLE, Michael A. (1834) 1450
GATSON, A. F. (1866)   1834
GATTY, Alfred (1833, 1847)   222, 893
GAUDEN, John, Bishop of Worcester (1644-1662)   351, 649 (2)
GAUDEN, John, D.D. (1659-1660) 543, 1894
GAUDEN John, D.D., Bishop of Exeter (1661)   1914

GAUJAC, Peter Gally de (1698)   2675
GAUNTLETT, Rev. H. (1810)   1453
GAVIN, Antoine (1691-1693)   958, 1770, 2368
GAY, John (1711-1732)   30, 1649, 2005, 2586
GAYTON, Edmund (1645-1660)   366, 2784, 2822
GEALE, H. (1849)   789
GEARING, William (1676)   723
GEAVES, George (1675, 1676) 1151, 2491
GEAVES, W. (1675, 1676)   1151, 2491
GEDDES, —— (1767)   800
GEDDES, Alexander (1790, 1792)   120, 926
GEDDES, Alexander, LL.D. (1787-1807) 150, 212, 216, 746, 1372, 1417, 1645, 1732, 1737, 1749
GELLIE, Mrs William (1878)   2592
GEE, Edward, D.D. (1687-1688)   121, 329, 1380, 1418, 2011, 2299, 2568, 2729, 2761
GENEST, Rev. John (1832)   2417
GENTLEMEN, Francis (1764-1777) 548, 704, 997, 1649, 1850, 2348, 2502, 2514, 2602
GEORGE III., King   1438
GEORGE, Sampson (1808)   2107
GEORGIRENES, Joseph, Archbishop of Samos (1657)   2662
GERARD, Abbé Louis Philippe (1806)   518
GERARD TROPHIME, Marquis de Lally-Tollendall (1793)   705
GERARDIN, R. L., Vicomte D'Ermenonville (1783)   799
GERMAIN, Christopher Saint (1580) 616
GERMAINE, Lord, G. Sackville   1437
GERMANO, Christopherus de Sancto (1532, 1538)   33, 2254
GERBIER D'OUVILLY, George (1657)   886
GEREE, John, M.A. (1647)   2608
GEYTON, Edm. (1662)   2716
GHENT, L. C.   887
GHIKA, Princess Koltzoff Massalsky née Helena (1861)   2827
GIB, Rev. Adam (1766-1780)   667, 863, 2536, 2716
GIBB Miss (1872)   1656
GIBB, Sir George Duncan, Bart., (1870)   1800
GIBBES, Phebe (1764)   1462
GIBBON, Charles (1840)   1344

GIBBON, Edmund (1770, 1819) 540, 1436
GIBBON, J. (1686)   566
GIBBON, John (1682)   2013
GIBBS, Joseph H. (1865)   2059
GIBERNE, Agnes (1864-1869)   77, 220, 1488, 1529, 1614
GIBNEY, Captain (1858)   1684
GIBSON, —— (1729)   1584
GIBSON, Atkinson F. (1826)   2653
GIBSON, Charles Philip (1875)   368
GIBSON, Edmund, Bishop of London (1701-1738) 26, 311, 342, 451 (2), 454 668, 889, 1050, 1166, 1171, 1368, 1478 (2), 1549, 1790, 1857, 2006, 2007, 2116 2145, 2211, 2265, 2327, 2375, 2516, 2532
GIBSON, John (1817)   2304, 2507
GIBSON, John, M.D. (1768)   976
GIBSON, Rev. Charles B., M.R.I.A. (1854)   1319
GIBSON, Thomas (1682)   86
GIBSON, William (1717)   1348, 2297
GIFFARD, —— (1736)   1604
GIFFORD, Andrew (1751)   678
GIFFORD, Arthur (1785)   1817
GIFFORD, Richard (1753)   497
GIFFORD, William (1789-1800) 217, 720, 784, 1532
GILBART, James William, F.R.S. (1851)   1505
GILBERT, Frédérick (1875)   1498
GILBERT, G. or J. (1738)   1123
GILBERT, G. A., Capt. R.A. (1847) 356
GILBERT, John (1686-1706)   130, 400, 2108
GILBERT, John T. (1864)   1169
GILBERT, Sir Geoffrey (1717-1756) 997, 1108, 1324
GILBERT, Sir Jeffrey (1717-1758) 1324, 2180, 2643
GILBERT, Thomas (1787)   425
GILBERT, Thomas 1679)   2592
GILBERT, William (1858-1873)   503, 682, 2352, 2798
GILBY, Anthony (1547, 1581) 121, 1939
GILCHRIST, Ebenezer, M.D. (1770) 13
GILCHRIST, James (1814)   2085
GILCHRIST, Octavius (1805)   2207
GILDON, Charles (1694-1719) 446, 1026, 1477, 1500, 1521, 1562, 1625, 1629, 1729, 1874, 1895, 1978 (2), 2222, 2665
GILES, John Allen, D.C.L. (1829) 2172
GILES, John Douglas (1833)   2709
GILES, William (1688)   580
GILL, John, D.D. (1729, 1753)   211, 810

GILL, Rev. J. (1860)   1494
GILL, Thomas H. (1871)   2192
GILLAN, Mary (1777)   2599
GILLAN, John, Bishop of Dunblane (1714)   1482, 2161, 2441
GILLAN, John (1713)   2755
GILLESPIE, George (1637-1645)   189, 350, 668, 2812
GILLESPIE, Patrick (1661, 1677) 177 (2)
GILLESPIE, William H. (1873)   1826
GILLIES, J. (1760)   2380
GILLIES, John (1769)   1233
GILLIES, Mary (1864)   1661
GILLIES, Robert Pierce (1813-1839)   370, 473, 1059, 1205, 1489, 1831, 1847, 2215, 2540, 2593
GILLMORE, Parker (1869)   1060
GILMORE, J. R. (1863)   1470, 1686
GILPIN, Elizabeth (1860)   883
GILPIN, George (1636)   220
GILPIN, Joseph (1812)   1913
GILPIN, Rev. William (1796)   2585
GILPIN, W. (1798)   861
GILPIN, William, M.A. (1747-1768) .   208, 622, 820
GIMINGHAM, Miss (1884)   2703
GIRDLESTONE, —— (1808)   2092
GIRDLESTONE, E. D. (1850)   2812
GIRDLESTONE, Rev. Charles, M.A. (1823, 1857)   2071, 2342, 2413
GIRARD, Guillaume (1670)   1160
GISBERT, Blaise (1718)   378
GISBORNE, Dr (1815)   2229
GLADSTONE, John (1836)   1294
GLANVIL, Joseph (1662-1678)   242, 792, 1505, 1526, 2434
GLANVILLE, Francis (1658)   2547
GLANVILLE, John, T. (1847)   2340
GLAS, John (1736, 1738) 1043, 2718, 2719
GLASCOCK, William Nugent (1826-1834)   1704, 1705, 1722, 2249, 2540
GLASS, H. (1856)   518
GLASS, John, M.A. (1728)   862, 1350
GLASSE, Dr (1784)   1533
GLASSE, Hannah (1747)   181
GLASSFORD, James, Advocate (1818-1835) 733, 975, 1623, 1754, 2471
GLAUBER, John R. (1669)   1902
GLEIG, Rev. George Robert (1821-1870) 69, 369, 392, 522, 1072, 1485, 1696, 1819, 2510, 2566, 2728
GLEN, William (1856)   2167
GLENBERVIE, Lord, Sylvester Douglas (1800, 1821)   2189, 2622

GLENIE, James, M.A. (1785-1805)   1777, 2174, 2366
GLOAG, J. A. Lake (1876)   1264
GLOUCESTER, Bishop of, William Warburton, D.D. (1727-1809) 69, 428, 536, 769, 1355, 1400, 1426, 2732, 2746
GLOUCESTER, Bishop of, Edward Fowler, D.D. (1671-1709)   350, 593, 637, 952, 971, 1753, 2015, 2112, 2185, 2294, 2556, 2742
GLOUCESTER, Bishop of, John Hooper (1553)   2086
GLOVER, Cornelius (1659)   2795
GLOVER, J. H. (1845)   608
GLOVER, Philip (1734, 1751) 1226, 1407
GLOVER, Rev. Frederick A. (1829, 1838)   402, 1873
GLOVER, Richard (1787-1813)   192, 1436, 1575
GLOVER, T. A. (1840)   976
GLOVER, William, M.D. (1851)   1381
GOAD, John, D.D. (1687)   205
GOADBY, Robert (1759, 1775) 152, 1205
GODBEAR, Walt. (1658)   2547
GODDEN, Thomas, or Godwin (1672, 1677)   340, 1292
GODFREY, Michael (1694)   258
GODOLPHIN, Mr (1664)   1969
GODOLPHIN, William, Marquis of Blandford (N.D.)   1355
GODWIN, Francis, Bishop of Hereford (1657)   1538
GODWIN, Mary W. Shelley née (1788-1838)   884, 945, 957, 1131, 1319, 1502, 1505, 1829, 2721
GODWIN, Mrs (1788)   1553
GODWIN, William (1805-1862)   418, 872, 1136, 1138, 1146, 1509, 1687, 1713, 1838, 1849
GODWYN, Morgan (1676)   1164
GOFFE, Thomas (1656)   309
GOLDEN, William (1791)   2657
GOLDING, Arthur (1571-1580) 660, 2050
GODSMID, Isabel (8139-1852)   2346, 2596 vol. iii., 2769
GOLDSMITH, Dr (1762)   183
GOLDSMITH, Lewis (1804-1806)   911, 1580, 2206, 2312
GOLDSMITH, Oliver (1758-1772)   220, 405, 771, 1136, 1474, 1479, 1578, 1690, 1949, 1956
GOLDWIN, —— (1753)   259
GOLIGHTLY, Charles P., M.A., (1841-1867)   1977, 2505

GOMPERTZ, J. (1813)   1639
GOOCH, Barnaby (1577)   1839
GOOD, Thomas, D.D. (1677)   264
GOODAL, Walter (1769)   1244
GOODALL, Charles (1689)   1946
GOODALL, William (1740)   2668
GOODE, Rev. William, M.A. (1834-
    1848)   109, 831, 2148
GOODENOUGH, Richard J. (1768,
    1779)   517, 2816
GOODHUGH, William (1828, 1839)
                              993, 1670
GOODMAN, John, D.D. (1684-1688)
                  640, 1026, 1813, 2327
GOODRICH, Henry (1776)   1772
GOODRICH, H. Newton (1856)   1201
GOODRICH, Samuel   Griswold
    (1836-1864)   926, 1889, 2292, 2576
GOODRICKE, Henry (1776)   1772
GOODRIDGE, R. (1675)   1525
GOODWIN, —— (1688)   2624
GOODWIN, C. W. (1859)   551
GOODWIN, Dr Timothy (1710)   1464
GOODWIN, John (1642)   293
GOODWIN, Thomas (1666)   1871
GOODWYN, Henry (1796-1823)   256,
                            2535, 2537
GOODWYN, Major-General J. E.
    (1866)   141
GOOGE, Barnaby (1579)   1736
GOOLD, Rev. W. H., D.D. (1870)   1819
GORDON, —— (1756)   1725
GORDON, ——, or Gourdon (1687) 2183
GORDON, Francis (1712)   820
GORDON, Harriet M. Yorick Smythies
    née (1835-1860)   254, 256, 528 (2), 931,
    1177, 1267, 1471, 1521, 1550, 1551, 1558,
                              2792
GORDON, James (1679)   2119
GORDON, James (1706)   2420
GORDON, James (1732)   2484
GORDON, James   Errata, vol. iv. (2)
GORDON, James, Advocate (1806)   729
GORDON, James, Bishop of Aber-
    deen (1700)   2431
GORDON, John, D.D. (1760)   1720
GORDON, John, D.D., Archdeacon
    of Lincoln (1769)   1797
GORDON, John, D.D., Dean of
    Sarum (1613)   2246
GORDON, John, M.D. (1689)   1922
GORDON, Joseph (1825)   1958
GORDON, Mrs, née Margaret Maria
    Brewster (1842)   528

GORDON, P. (1834)   382
GORDON, Sir Thomas (1732-1733) 578,
                              769, 2151
GORDON, Thomas (1718-1725) 152, 577,
                          1191 (2), 1644
GORDON, Thomas (1721, 1733) 341, 423
GORDON, Thomas (1720-1722) 360, 481,
                      532, 1219, 2474
GORDON, Thomas (1763-1776)   771,
            1231, 1334, Errata, vol. iv.
GORDON, Thomas (1733, 1750)   1360,
                              2333
GORDON, Thomas (1720-1750) 161, 512,
                  530, 956, 2373, 2684
GORDON, William (1718-1719) 28, 1384,
                              1972
GORDONE, James (1732)   2484
GORE, Catherine Frances (1827-1845)
    1062, 1081, 1193, 1454, 1578, 1639, 1669,
    1675, 1819, 1829, 1914, 1962, 2224, 2319,
        2397, 2494, 2685, 2826, 2827
GORE, Catherine Grace (1832-1844)   56,
                296, 345, 346, 626, 877
GORE, J., Baron Annaly (1770)   325
GORE, Leslie (1871)   1186
GORE, Montague (1821)   357
GORING, Henry (1835)   377
GORST, Gilpin (1826)   1694
GORTON, John (1833)   1501
GOSSIP, Robert (1881)   2548
GOSTRICK, Joseph (N.D.)   1064
GOSYNHYLL, Edward (1544)   1990
GOTHER, John (1685-1700) 59, 76, 107,
    338, 656, 1028, 1236, 1758, 1851, 1852,
    1853, 1971, 1974, 2011, 2016, 2056, 2084,
                      2113, 2174, 2624
GOTT, Samuel (1670)   684
GOUGE, William, D.D. (1615)   2361
GOUGH, —— (1781)   430
GOUGH, Henry (1847)   1019
GOUGH, James (1767-1773)   280, 1472,
                          1476, 2317
GOUGH, John (1640)   10, 2500
GOUGH, John (1816, 1827)   764, 1542
GOUGH, Rev. John (1788)   647
GOUGH, Richard (1768-1803)   90, 285,
    331, 446, 555, 1126, 1132, 1149, 1392,
                      1491, 1784, 2417
GOUGH, Richard, F.R.S. (1786-1796) 2323
GOUGH, Strickland, A.M. (1730-
    1735)   592, 767, 899
GOUGH, William (1682)   1506
GOULD, Rev. S. Baring (1880)   1567
GOULD, Robert (1675, 1683) 1525, 1998

GOULD, Sir Nathaniel (1726, 1727) 579, 811

GOULD, William (1744) 1393

GOULDNEY, Henry (N.D.) 1735

GOURAND, —— (1870) 2849

GOURDON, Gordon, ——, or (1687) 2183

COWER, Foote, M.D. (1771) 2400

GOWER, Lord Francis Leveson (1830) 2786

GOWER, Richard Hall (1793) 2646

GOWLAND, T. S. (1856) 1057

GOZLAN, Léon (1873) 1537

GRACIAN, Balthasar (1652) 1091

GRACIE, John B. (1830) 8

GRAFFIGNY, Dame de, F. d'I. d'Happonville (1774) 1892

GRAFFIGNY, Dame de, F. d'I. d'Happoncourt (1749) 2324

GRAFTON, Duke of, A. H. Fitzroy (1790) 1099

GRAHAM, —— (1756) 625

GRAHAM, Dougald (1850) 1163

GRAHAM, George (1764) 2549

GRAHAM, James, M.D. (1782) 509

GRAHAM, Mary Jane (1831) 966, 2555

GRAHAM, Mrs (1767) 1511

GRAHAM, Rev. John (1843) 1749

GRAHAM, Sir James (1828) 966

GRAHAM, Thos. J., M.D. (1848) 913

GRAHAM, William (1769, N.D.) 196, 2101

GRAHAME, James (1795-1817) 104, 1016, 1199, 1554, 1949, 1980, 2583, 2697, 2699, 2765, 2785

GRAHAME, Sir Richard (1670) 94

GRAILE, John, A.M. (1683) 2664

GRAINGER, James, M.D. (1764) 807

GRAND, M. le (1786, 1790) 1749, 2544

GRANT, —— (1777) 2236

GRANT, Alexander H., M.A. (1865) 1495

GRANT, Anne, née Macvicar (1809-1811) 829, 1430, 1579

GRANT, Colesworth (1853, 1860) 2230, 2240

GRANT, Francis (1698) 2671

GRANT, G. (1828) 812

GRANT, Henry (1850, 1851) 1251, 2070

GRANT, Horace (1852) 738

GRANT, James (1858-1873) 286, 434, 714, 937, 1018, 1021, 1024, 1036, 1834, 2458, 2493, 2682

GRANT, James (1836-1855) 224, 285, 1048, 1217, 1273, 1487, 1611, 1860, 1910 (2), 1976, 2077 (2), 2627, 2785

RANT, James (1810) 1230

GRANT, James (1840) 1324

GRANT, James (1849) 1575

GRANT, James (1749) 2758

GRANT, James G. (1838) 2237

GRANT, James M. (1805) 554

GRANT, John O'Brien (1838) 2815

GRANT, Judith Towers (1854) 1511

GRANT, Maria M. (1874-1878) 1342, 1685, 2518

GRANT, Rev. Johnson, M.A. (1837) 1274

GRANT, Sir Francis, Lord Cullen (1689-1716) 259, 644, 794, 1300, 1347, 1351, 1522, 1874, 2092, 2369, 2744

GRANT, Thomas, Bishop of Southwark (1855) 1095

GRANT, William, Lord Prestongrange (1745) 1798

GRANTHAM, Sir Thomas (1650) 2020

GRANVILL, William (1695) 1967

GRANVILLE, Augustus, K.B. (N.D.) 1184

GRANVILLE, Dr Augustus B. (N.D.) 2271

GRANVILLE, Denis, D.D. (1663) 186

GRANVILLE, George, Lord Lansdowne (1696-1722) 282, 1009, 1266, 1353, 2349

GRASCOME, Samuel (1688-1705) 157, 158, 260, 352, 359, 467, 491, 898, 1106, 1368, 1555, 1717, 1793, 2139, 2172, 2185, 2267, 2698

GRATTAN, Right Hon. Henry (1781-1861) 212, 1436, 1781

GRATTAN, Thomas Colley (1823, 1829) 1096, 2621

GRAVE, John (1662) 2448

GRAVES, Lord (1814) 1343

GRAVES, Richard (1766-1804) 420, 433, 833, 835, 897, 912, 1247, 1519, 1524, 1941, 2100, 2192, 2230, 2477

GRAVES, Samuel Colleton (1814) 1412

GRAY, Alice (1865) 1496

GRAY, Captain Charles (1747) 210

GRAY, J. (1821) 1227

GRAY, James (1816) 462

GRAY, James (1729) 1691

GRAY, J. B. (1878) 2393

GRAY, John (1777) 689

GRAY, John (1792) 802

GRAY, John (1797) 831

GRAY, John (1785) 1929

GRAY, Jonathan (1819, 1825) 1277, 1454

GRAY, Miss (N.D.) 1710

GRAY, Rev. Andrew (1834-1845) 356, 689, 2071

GRAY, Rev. James (1712) 2423

GRAY, Robert, D.D., Bishop of Bristol (1802-1808)   335, 2564
GRAY, Simon (1817, 1818)   67, 1043
GRAY, Thomas (1773)   330
GRAY, Thomas (1751)   737
GRAY, Thomas (1867)   1686
GRAY, Thomas (1747, 1769)   1801 (2)
GRAY, W. (1833)   1122
GRAY, W. (1858)   1553
GRAY, ——   Errata, vol. iv.
GRAY, —— (1721)   1577
GRAY, —— of Carse (1818)   2145
GRAYDON, Alexander (1822)   1578
GREAM, R. (1852)   890
GREATRAKES, William (1825)   1436
GREATREX, Charles Butler (1854)   2810
GREAVES, Edward, M.D. (1643)   1659
GREAVES, Richard (1783)   2477
GREAVES, Thomas B. (1824)   1239
GREEN, Francis (1783)   2779
GREEN, George Smith (1752-1756)   1753, 1816, 1865
GREEN, J. (1736)   1278
GREEN, John (1745-1747)   1722
GREEN, John (1780)   1929
GREEN, John (1650)   2122
GREEN, John, D.D., Bishop of Lincoln (1741-1761)   10, 192, 483, 2015 (2)
GREEN, John Richard (1792-1859)   1131, 1137, 1163, 1395, 1699, 1841, 1918, 2125, 2183
GREEN, S. (1808-1815)   976, 2021, 2121, 2224, 2273, 2543
GREEN, Thomas (1788-1810)   849, 868, 1612
GREEN, William (1676)   10
GREENAWAY, Stephen (1762)   36
GREENE, Edward Burnaby (1756-1780)   170, 303, 464, 538, 582, 974, 1090, 1324, 1957, 1967, 2259 (2), 2506, 2552, 2839
GREENE, Martin (1661)   21
GREENE, Robert (1585-1631)   182, 240, 579, 667, 878, 1124, 1614, 1668, 1822, 1846, 1937, 1938, 2292, 2570
GREENE, Thomas, Bishop of Ely (1726)   2018
GREENFIELD, William (1827)   461
GREENFIELD, William, D.D. (1809)   828
GREENHALGH, Thomas (1852)   2730
GREENHOW, T. M. (1863)   2507
GREENSHIELDS, J. B. (1806)   1172
GREENWELL, Dora (1860-1862)   1872, 1945, 2000

GREENWOOD, Col. George (1839)   1100
GREENWOOD, Frederick (1854, 1864)   1521, 1547
GREENWOOD, James (1866)   1740, 2670
GREER, Maria (1871)   1301
GREG, J. R. (1842)   1784
GREG, William Rathbone (1833)   2402
GREGORY, A. T. (1856, 1864)   1984, 1986
GREGORY, Dr James (N.D.)   116
GREGORY, Dr Olinthus (1817)   678
GREGORY, George, D.D. (1785)   825
GREGORY, James, M.D. (1808, 1810)   1525, 2565
GREGORY, John, Bishop of Salisbury (1649)   778
GREGORY, John, M.D. (1766, 1770)   466, 1777
GREGORY, Sir William Henry, K.C.M.G. (1881)   1362
GREGSON, John Stanley (1833)   1014
GREIG, —— (1855)   1696
GRENE, Martin, S.J. (1679)   205
GRENVILLE, George (1766-1807)   489, 492, 2004
GRENVILLE, George (1770)   1436
GRENVILLE, George (1727)   2468
GRENVILLE, George, Lord Nugent (1832, 1847)   1340, 2615
GRENVILLE, James (1783)   1436
GRENVILLE, Lord, William Wyndham Greville (1824)   1758
GRENVILLE, Right Hon. George (1769)   165, 2469
GRESWELL, Rev. Richard (1834)   1195
GRESSWELL, William Parr (1823)   1650
GREVILLE, —— (1795)   283
GREVILLE, C. C. (1845)   1868
GREVILLE, Fulke (1757-1790)   1561, 2160, 2415
GREVILLE, Fulke, Lord Brooke (1609-1651)   2619, 2620
GREVILLE, Hon. Robert F. (1825)   1838
GREVILLE, Robert Kaye, LL.D. (1842)   704, 2244
GREVILLE, William Wyndham, Lord Grenville (1824)   1758
GREW, N. (1684)   1721
GREY, Elizabeth C. (1828-1859)   66, 67, 223, 567, 1195, 1808, 1809, 2531, 2652
GREY, Ford, Earl of Tankerville (1693)   77, 1519
GREY, George (1770)   2686
GREY, Hon. Colonel (1852)   1384
GREY, Hon. Mrs (1845)   250

GREY, J. E. (1854)   573
GREY, Rev. Harry (1855)   272
GREY, Richard, D.D. (1730, 1736) 1592, 1632
GREY, Sir George (1851)   1277
GREY, William (1649)   374
GREY, Zachary, LL.D. (1720-1750) 114, 197, 344, 345, 348, 393, 761, 848, 959, 1308, 1361, 1510 (2), 1618, 1845, 1972, 1993, 1998, 2059, 2158, 2267, 2326, 2473, 2672, 2751, 2835
GRIBBLE, Thomas (1870)   1282
GRICE, Rev. C. P. Le (1804)   563
GRIERSON, Miss (1826) 1263, 1488, 1911
GRIFFEN, G. A. (1615)   2379
GRIFFIN, Benjamin (1715)   460
GRIFFIN, Gerald (1827-1836) 381, 431, 708, 1247, 2217, 2541, 2544
GRIFFIN, Rev. —— (1754)   2280
GRIFFITH, Acton Frederick (1815) 231
GRIFFITH, Alexander (1652, 1654) 1601, 2503
GRIFFITH, Dr (1682)   2428
GRIFFITH, Elizabeth (1765-1782) 212, 701, 824, 1933, 2269, 2326, 2699
GRIFFITH, Matthew, D.D. (1642) 2336
GRIFFITH, Richard (1762-1782) 1979, 2447, 2659, 2699, 2723
GRIFFITHS, John, M.A. (1867)   2593
GRIGG, Henry (1672)   1485
GRIMANI, Julia C. (1849)   2246
GRIMSTON, Hon. Charlotte (1827) 942
GRIMSTON, William, Viscount Grimston (N.D.)   1329
GRIMSTONE, Leman (1820)   2851
GRINFIELD, C. V. (1850)   1913
GRINFIELD, Rev. Edward W. (1834-1851)   1265, 1392
GRINGOIRE, P. (1506)   326
GRIPPS, T., E.A.P. (1696)   2552
GROAT, Alexander G. (1831)   2577
GROENEVELT, Johann, M.D. (1698)   1321
GROGAN, Millicent (1857)   2226
GROOME, S. (1676)   1016
GROSE, Francis (1765-1792) 100, 138, 216, 411, 1057, 1815, 2238, Errata, vol. iv.
GROSE, Francis, F.A.S. (1793)   1815
GROSE, Sir Francis (1809)   10
GROSSETT, Walter (N.D.)   24
GROSVENOR, Lord Robert, Baron Erbury (1852)   1335
GROSVENOR, Rev. Benjamin, D.D. (1716-1719)   428, 2418

GROTE, Mrs (1850)   321
GROVE, —— (1708)   2124
GROVE, Henry (1730-1734)   839, 2820
GROVE, Joseph (1748, 1758)   116, 1474, 2175
GROVE, Mrs (N.D.)   2325
GROVE, Robert (1689)   2041
GROVE, Robert, D.D. (1676-1685) 2287, 2363, 2752
GROVE, Robert, D.D., Bishop of Chichester (1683-1688) 117, 921, 1754, 1891
GROVE, William (1782)   883
GROVER, Albert (1878)   1652
GRUBB, Sarah (1792)   2418
GRUNSTON, Viscount, William Grimston (N.D.)   1329
GRYNDALL, William (1596)   1075
GUARINI, Batista (1602)   1869
GUÉNÉE, Abbé A. (1777)   1432
GUEST, John (1862)   2516
GUIBERT, J. Anth Hypol (1781)   999
GUIBERT, P. le Pesant de Bois (1725)   1477
GUIDICKINS, F. W. (1768)   117
GUIDOT, Thomas (1694)   787
GUIFTHAILE, Henry (1648)   464
GUIGNARD, Mary (1857)   2715
GUILD, William (1608)   262
GUILDFORD, Lord, Francis North (1677)   1901
GUILPIN, Edward (1598)   2405
GUIZOT, M. François (1850)   343
GULIELMUS, Lyde, *alias* Joyner (1686)   2433
GULLAND, Charles (1867)   2531
GUNN, Barbara (1863)   936
GUNN, H. (1834)   1454
GUNN, H. M. (1853)   1144
GUNN, Miss (1833)   507
GUNN, W. (1803)   867
GUNNING, Dr Peter, Bishop of Chichester (1676)   1456
GUNNING, Dr Peter, Bishop of Ely (1676)   1456
GUNNING, Mrs (1764)   890
GUNTON, Symon (1659)   1831
GURDON, Thornhagh (1728)   803
GURNEY, Anna (1819)   1493
GURNEY, Eliza P. (1845)   1736
GURNEY, Hudson (1800-1831) 548, 1077, 1573
GURNEY, Joseph John (1843, 1844) 1850, 2577

GURNEY, Priscilla Hannah (1816, 1818)   461, 1198
GURNEY, Rev. J. Hampden (N.D.) 2050
GUTCH, Robert, M.A. (1836)   2463
GUTHRIE, F. Anstey (1883)   2739
GUTHRIE, James (1653, 1658) 343, 2045
GUTHRIE, James Cargill (1850)   3739
GUTHRIE, William (1754)   973
GUYNN, Albinia (1785)   1155
GUYSE, John, D.D. (1735)   2135
GWATKIN, Thomas (1768)   2162, 2164
GWIN, Thomas (1718)   2426
GWINNE, Matthew (1633)   2620
GWINNET, Richard (1732)   524
GYLBY, Goddred (N.D.)   45

H.

HABBERTON, John (1877)   214, 1082, 1832
HABINGTON, Thomas (1638)   782
HABINGTON, William (1640) 326, 2063
HACKETT, Maria (1816-1833) 257, 268, 515, 1974, 2124
HADDINGTON, Earl of, T. B. Hamilton (1761-1764) 1951, 2644, 2771
HADDO, James (1704, 1730) 690 (2), 765
HADGES, James (1706)   823
HADLEY, George (1734)   605
HADOW, James, D.D. (1703-1731)   319, 2161, 2527, 2758
HAERING, Wilhelm (1825)   2786
HAGGETT, J. (1810)   169
HAGGIT, Rev. John (1794)   518
HAGGITT, George, M.A. (1790)   1786
HAILES, Lord, Sir David Dalrymple (1714-1790) 15, 26, 34, 89, 332, 669, 1327, 1474, 1496, 1576, 1592, 1629, 1774, 1799, 1821, 2036, 2246, 2338, 2339, 2399 (2), 2400 (2), 2463, 2464, 2593, 2840
HAINES, Herbert (1848)   1544
HAKE, Lucy (1828)   2447
HAKEWELL, George, D.D. (1611-1632) 132, 146, 447, 2334, Errata vol. i.
HAKEWELL, James Ridgway (1871)   194, Errata vol. i.
HAKEWILL, William (1641) 1334, 1542
HALDANE, James (1818, 1825)   2697, 2761
HALDANE, John (1757)   1933
HALDANE, Patrick (1718)   319, 1175
HALE, —— (1807)   1054
HALE, Nathan (1828)   75
HALE, Sir Matthew (1673-1713) 497, 631,

660, 815, 1071, 1087, 1152, 1465, 1787, 2512, 2637, 2647
HALE, Thomas (1791)   16
HALE, William, M.A., Archdeacon of London (1854)   2417
HALES, John (1641-1653) 240, 667, 2615, 2796
HALES, Stephen (1734)   969
HALES, William, D.D. (1799)   1234, 1252, 2058
HALFORD, Sir Henry (1839)   1758
HALFPENNY, F. W. (1847, 1849)   329, 2463
HALHED, Nathaniel Brassey (1771-1794)   1208, 1518, 2374
HALIBURTON, Simon (1761)   1582
HALIBURTON, Thomas Chandler (1837-1855) 76, 195, 289, 417, 757, 1344, 1703, 1811, 2256, 2621
HALIFAX, Earl of, Charles Montague (1710, 1787)   1098, 2289
HALIFAX, Marquis of, George Saville (1681-1694) 85, 359, 360, 788, 1119, 1314, 1353, 1366, 2230, 2286
HALIFAX, William, D.D. (1685)   738
HALKERSTON, Helenus (N.D., 1764)   90, 481
HALKETT, J. (1817)   2490 (2)
HALKETT, Lady Anne (1771)   1565
HALL, Amanda H. (1878)   2823
HALL, Anna Maria (1832, 1837)   289, 1836, 2706
HALL, Capt. (1780)   1151
HALL, Captain Basil (1825)   1574
HALL, Chambers (1837)   1909
HALL, David (1742)   798
HALL, George (1852)   854
HALL, George, Bishop of Chester (1655)   2658
HALL, Herbert Byng (1850-1868)   2261, 2479 (2)
HALL, James (1780)   186
HALL, James (1839)   1274
HALL, John (1694)   119
HALL, John (1648)   743
HALL, John (1651, 1653) 1055, 1188, 1856
HALL, John (1816)   1944
HALL, John (1563)   1954
HALL, John Vine (N.D.)   2388
HALL, Joseph (1720)   2412
HALL, Joseph (1597, 1598)   2769, 2770
HALL, Joseph, D.D., Bishop of Norwich (1640-1648) 255, 590, 1190, 1645, 2318, 2360

HALL, Newman, B.A. (N.D.)   135, 938
HALL, Rev. Peter, M.A. (1824-1831) 547, 917, 2549
HALL, Richard, D.D. (1655)   1466
HALL, Robert (1715)   950
HALL, Robert (1642)   1645
HALL, Robert (1825)   2204
HALL, Rev. Robert (1809)   2504
HALL, Thomas (1845, 1848)   728, 2231
HALL, Thomas (1651-1655)   2253, 2279, 2820
HALLARD, Frederick (1858, 1872)   334, 2578
HALLARD, John (1831-1834)   2646
HALLE, Hughes R. P. Fraser (1842) 540
HALLET, J. H. (1840)   2723
HALLET, John (1714)   1483
HALLET, Joseph (1720, 1737) 1209, 1401, 2101, 2173, 2710
HALLEY, Edmund (1679)   1922
HALLIBURTON, Brenton (1825)   1790
HALLIDAY, William (1808)   2717
HALLIWELL, James Orchard (1851, 1859)   1073, 1244
HALLORAN, L. H. (1801)   911
HALL-STEVENSON, John (1760-1783)   822, 872 (2), 1196, 1529, 1537, 1658, 1751, 1870 (2), 2698
HALLYWELL, Henry (1668, 1679) 612, 653, 2664
HALS, William (1750)   459
HAMBRO, C. J. (1847)   724
HAMERTON, Philip Gilbert (1878)   1549
HAMILTON, —— (1787)   1535
HAMILTON, Alexander (1705)   2332
HAMILTON, Alexander, W.S. (1820-1836)   699, 726, 1299
HAMILTON, Andrew (1790)   772
HAMILTON, Captain Thomas (1827-1833)   101, 1597, 2850
HAMILTON, C. G. (1845-1857) 78, 494, 549, 857, 1547, 1749, 2706
HAMILTON, Col. Ralph (1817)   2450
HAMILTON, David (1697, 1701) 1249, 2021
HAMILTON, Elizabeth (1800)   1583
HAMILTON, G.   1712, 1293 (2)
HAMILTON, Gavin (1877)   1044
HAMILTON, Harris, D.D. (1819)   695
HAMILTON, J., Earl of Abercorn (1729)   298
HAMILTON, James, D.D. (1843, 1855) 895, 1068

HAMILTON, John (1839-1842) 1594, 2001, 2490
HAMILTON, Lady Anne (1807, 1832) 202, 777
HAMILTON, Partick (1641)   714
HAMILTON, Professor R. D. (1817) 531
HAMILTON, Robert (1796)   2487
HAMILTON, Sarah (1825, 1829) 65, 2454
HAMILTON, Sir David, M.D., Errata vol. iv.
HAMILTON, Thomas B., Earl of Haddington (1761-1764)   1951, 2644, 2771
HAMILTON, W. (1713)   778
HAMILTON, W. (1810)   1592
HAMILTON, William (1874)   882
HAMILTON, William (1747, 1749) 497, 1950
HAMILTON, William G. (1771)   1436
HAMILTON, Wm., M.A. (1788)   284
HAMILTOUN, Alexander (1696)   512
HAMMON, William (1782)   115
HAMMOND, Anthony (1662, 1721) 1006, 1645
HAMMOND, George (1702)   1646
HAMMOND, Henry, D.D. (1644-1660) 479 (2), 481, 858, 1203, 1321, 1689, 1981, 1982, 2021, 2087, 2184, 2388, 2521, 2732, 2734, 2816
HAMMOND, James (1757)   1518
HAMMOND, William (1816)   1795
HAMMOND, William (1655)   1945
HAMPDEN, Richard (1682)   539
HAMPER, William (1820, 1822) 1556, 2691
HANBURY, Cornelius (1866)   2351
HANBURY, Mrs (1828)   1029
HANCOCK, Charles (N.D.)   1061
HANCOCK, George (1832)   507
HANCOCK, John, D.D. (1705-1709) 119, 1522, 1872
HANCOCK, John, M.D. (1818, 1819) 736, 1325
HANDLEY, James (1705)   432
HANMER, Sir Thomas, Bart., F.R.S. (1807)   2599
HANMORE, Sir T. (1718)   2590
HANNAY, —— (1836)   1419
HANNAY, John (1821)   43
HANNAY, Robert (1823)   1393
HANNET, John (1835, 1837) 230, 1230
HANSLEY, John, Archdeacon of Colchester (1662)   2773
HANSON, A. C. (1810)   2114

HANSON, Sir Levett (N.D.) 29
HANSON, Sir Richard (1869) 1266
HANSON, Sir Richard Davis (1873) 1451
HANSTED, Pet. (1644) 32
HANWAY, Jonas (1753-1760) 730, 1278, 1352, 1664, 1929, 2202, 2322, 2580
HANWAY, Mary Anne (1777) 1279
HANWAY, William (1745) 1953
HAPPONCOURT, F. d'I. de, Dame de Graffigny (1749) 2324
HAPPONVILLE, F. d'I. de, Dame de Graffigny (1774) 1892
HARBIN, George (1772) 1369
HARBIN, Rev. George (1713) 1088
HARCOURT, Greville Vernon (1863) 1424
HARCOURT, Rev. William Vernon (N.D.) 699
HARCOURT, William G. G. V. (N.D.) 1251
HARDCASTLE, P. (1661) 2061
HARDHAM, John (N D.) 945
HARDING, H. (1846) 442
HARDING, Mrs (1818-1858) 515, 573, 680, 859, 2121
HARDING, Samuel (1640) 2381
HARDINGE, George (1800-1813) 103, 355, 804, 830, 923, 2241, 2340
HARDMAN, Frederick (1847-1849) 1882, 2508
HARDWICKE, Earl of, Charles Yorke (1770) 2701
HARDWICKE, Earl of, Philip Yorke (1727-1783) 192, 6354, 1629, 2701, 2786
HARDY, Iza (1872) 1751
HARDY, John S. (1820) 2326
HARDY, Miss (1849, 1854) 473, 2326
HARDY, Thomas (1871, 1872) 610, 2707
HARDY, Thomas, D.D. (1793) 1873
HARE, Augustus William (1822, 1827) 1056, 1332, 1377
HARE, E. (1807) 1008
HARE, Francis, Bishop of Chichester (1730) 1387
HARE, Francis, D.D. (1711-1720) 69, 213, 251, 414, 468, 500, 631, 958, 1540 (2), 1708 (2), 1717, 2098
HARE, Henry, Lord Coleraine (1683) 2393
HARE, James (1794) 809
HARE, Julius Charles (1824, 1827) 1056, 1332
HARGRAVE, Francis (1791) 422

HARGROVE, Ely (1769) 1150
HARINGTON, Dr Edward (1786, 1763) 854, 2267
HARINGTON, James (1684, 1693) 1051, 2756
HARLAN, John, F.S.A. (1843) 2502
HARLEY, Edward (1732) 794
HARLEY, Sir Edward (1681) 818, 1188
HARLEY, James (1822) 2006
HARLEY, Robert, Earl of Oxford (1710-1711) 819, 820, 2095
HARLEY, Richard (1710) 905, 2754
HARLOW, Elizabeth (1789) 763
HARMAN, Thomas (1575) 957
HARMAR, John (1579) 2339
HARMER, Jonathan (N.D.) 2731
HARMER, Rev. Thomas (1765-1777) 1772, 1837, 2147, 2418
HARNESS, Rev. William (1837, 1844) 927, 2774, 2801
HARPER, Alexander (1843) 2517
HARPER, Samuel Brown (1850) 339 917, 2775
HARPER, W. (1775) 2448
HARPER, W. (1752) 2635
HARPER, William (N.D.) 52
HARRINGTON, Countess of, E. S. Pearsall (1874) 1944
HARRINGTON, James (1658-1692) 28, 224, 262, 592, 594, 2092, 2229, 2435, 2438, 2509, 2746, 2747
HARRINGTON, Robert, M.D. (1785-1796) 1730, 2582, 2641
HARRINGTON, Sir J. H. (1628) 63
HARRINGTON, Sir John (1596) 84, 1719, 2705
HARRIS, —— (1706) 644
HARRIS, —— (1737) 1388
HARRIS, Alexander (1847, 1849) 743, 2341, 2556
HARRIS, Dr (1665) 369
HARRIS, E. F. S. (1847-1848) 975, 2186, 2729
HARRIS, Emily Marion (1854-1878) 78, 831, 1599
HARRIS, George, D.C.L. (N.D.) 1790
HARRIS, James (1744, 1760) 563, 2591
HARRIS, James, 1st Earl of Malmsbury (1788) 1245
HARRIS, J. H. (1862) 2390
HARRIS, John (1647) 2236
HARRIS, John (1830) 2595 vol. iv
HARRIS, John, M.A. (1676) 685
HARRIS, John, D.D. (1719) 1396

HARRIS, John, D.D., Bishop of Llandaff (1715)   2648
HARRIS, John Tindall (1852)   2209
HARRIS, Joseph (1757, 1758)   819 (2)
HARRIS, Joseph (1702)   1527
HARRIS, Joseph Hemington (1852)   200
HARRIS, Miriam (1865, 1866) 1516, 2242, 2529
HARRIS, Rev. David (1847)   1333
HARRIS, Richard (1867)   1726
HARRIS, W., M.D. (1679)   895
HARRIS, William, D.D. (1728-1767) 15, 271, 318, 1109, 1773, 2150, 2155, 2373
HARRISON, George (1792-1834) 43, 955, 1756, 2291, 2439
HARRISON, Sir George, K.C.H. (1832)   1769
HARRISON, J. (1620)   243
HARRISON, John (1763)   26
HARRISON, Joseph (1735)   2280
HARRISON, Robert (1853)   1498
HARRISON, Robert (1682)   2501
HARRISON, Thomas (1727)   224
HARRISON, W., M.A. (1862)   473
HARSNET, Samuel, Archbishop of York (1599-1605)   574, 664
HART, Charles (1754)   1089
HART, Cheyney (1761)   376
HART, J. (1666)   750
HART, James (1703)   2528
HART, John (1678)   1080
HART, John (1569)   1831
HART, John, D.D. (1656)   389
HART, Miss (1827)   1430
HART, Mrs, née Fanny Wheeler (1868, 1878)   363, 958, 1677, 2240, 2852
HART, Robert (1754)   1089
HART, T. (1733)   2735
HARTCLIFFE, John, B.D. (1685)   640
HARTE, Walter (1735, 1767) 73, 801, 826
HARTLEY, David, M.P. (1763-1765) 290, 2210, 2488
HARTLEY, Mrs (1877)   1304
HARTLEY, Rev. John (1714, 1716) 596, 2747
HARTLIB, Samuel (1644, 1648) 987, 1707
HARTSHORNE, B. F. (1864)   560
HARTSHORNE, Rev. C. H. (1825) 1060
HARTWELL, Abraham (1624)   2277
HARVEY, Alexander, M.D. (1865) 1543
HARVEY, Christopher, M.A. (1647) 2267, 2532
HARVEY, Gabriel (1597)   2655
HARVEY, John (1769)   288

HARVEY, Richard (1734)   1198
HARVEY, Richard (1593)   1896
HARVEY, Thomas (1647)   2267
HARVEY, Wallace (1843)   392
HARVEY, William Henry, M.D. (1862)   365
HARWOOD, John (1851, 1852) 256, 2483
HARWOOD, John Berwick (1864-1877) 1312, 1313 (2), 1513, 1800, 1924
HASCARD, Gregory (1683, 1685) 638, 639
HASKOLL, Rev. Joseph (1846, 1853) 1129, 1595
HASLET, —— (1774)   1186
HASLEWOOD, J. (1790)   2312
HASLEWOOD, John (1706)   2252
HASLEWOOD, Joseph (1809, 1818) 213, 1052
HASSAL, Miss (1808)   2312
HASTINGS, Thomas (1784, 1793) 248, 2122
HASTLER, J. D. (1827)   739
HATCHETT, William (1731-1741) 372, 884, 1820
HATFIELD, C. W. (N.D.)   2739
HATFIELD, John (1797)   1729
HATTON, Christopher, Lord (1644, 1658)   425, 2052
HATTON, Edward (1708)   1734
HATTON, Father (1826)   1590
HAUGHTON, William (1631)   1937
HAUKINS, T. (1733)   2735
HAUSTED, Pet.   Errata vol. i.
HAUTEFEUILLE, Contess E. d' (1852)   856
HAVARD, William (1737)   1302
HAVERS, Dora (1874-1881) 1535, 1559, 2007, 2679, 2773
HAVILLAND, C. de (1835)   2322
HAWARDEN, Edward (1720-1735) 114, 365, 1979, 2238, 2821
HAWARDINE, J. (1715, 1749) 2083, 2666
HAWES, Mary Virginia (1855-1860) 70, 1665, 1710
HAWES, Stephen (N.D.)   1086
HAWES, William, M.D. (1787)   2337
HAWKE, Cassandra, Lady (1788)   1287
HAWKE, Lord (1782)   2285
HAWKER, Captain (1810)   1275
HAWKER, Charles (1857)   1147
HAWKER, Charlotte E. (1844)   938
HAWKER, Essex (1729)   525
HAWKER, R., D.D. (1794)   160
HAWKER, Rear-Admiral (1838, 1840)   1381, 1394

HAWKER, Robert Stephen (1849) 2776
HAWKES, W. R. (1816) 1613
HAWKESBURY, Earl of, Charles Jenkinson (1798) 2486
HAWKESWORTH, John (1761) 724
HAWKESWORTH, John, LL.D. (1753) 47
HAWKESWORTH, John, LL.D. (1656) 78
HAWKINS, Edward, D.D. (1835) 1395, 1841, 2511
HAWKINS, Miss (1824) 99
HAWKINS, Rev. Charles (1790) 1379
HAWKINS, Rev. W., B.L. (1840) 2403
HAWKINS, Richard (1658) 654
HAWKINS, Sir John (1771) 2015
HAWKINS, Sir Thomas (1634) 2261
HAWKINS, Thomas (1678) 1170
HAWKINS, William (1711) 6
HAWKINS, William (1626) 143
HAWKSHAM, Mrs (1852, 1854) 200 (2)
HAWLES, Sir John (1680) 764
HAWLING, Francis (1723) 1214
HAWORTH, Euphrasia F. (1827) 1915
HAWTHORNE, Rainey (1858) 2207
HAWTREY, Edith (1878) 2538
HAWTREY, Rev. C. D. (1830) 1703
HAWTREY, Rev. Charles, M.A. (1786-1790) 840, 964, 1379
HAWTREY, Rev. C. S. (1828-9) 624
HAWTREY, Rev. Dr (1845-7) 1336
HAY, Colonel Leith (1818) 1586
HAY, Dr (1703) 1209, 2319
HAY, Dr John (1703) 2457
HAY, John, D.D. Errata, vol. iv.
HAY, W. (1728, 1735) 796, 2150
HAY, William (1821) 1243
HAYDEN, John (N.D.) 1362
HAYES, Charles (1710-1747) 538, 675, 1655, 1712, 2523, 2756
HAYES, Henry (1859) 2804
HAYES, S., M.R.I.A. (1794) 1986
HAYES, Thomas (1753, 1784) 2143, 2328
HAYLEY, Mrs (1796) 2657
HAYLEY, William (1778-1834) 702, 735, 782, 783, 834, 1901, 1950, 1956, 2691, 2851
HAYNES, Henry (1728) 264
HAYNES, Hopton (1749) 2280
HAYS —— (1744) 1215
HAYS, Matilda M. (1847) 1431, 1560, 1617, 1664, 2386
HAYTER, T. (1741, 1755) 807, 844

HAYWARD, Abraham, Q.C. (1833-1854) 182, 906, 2416
HAYWARD, John (1603) 1024
HAYWARD, S. (1756) 1398
HAYWARD, Sir John (1606) 2180
HAYWARDE, Sir John, D.C.L. (1604) 2640
HAYWOOD, Eliza (1727-1759) 1248, 1820, 1864, 2000, 2312, 2814
HAYWOOD, Francis 82
HAYWOOD, Thomas (1721) 2011
HAZLITT, William (1805-1826) 742, 810, 1458, 1713, 1753, 1926, 2175, 2404, 2474, 2545
HEAD, Miss (1829) 2242
HEAD, Richard (1666-1679) 185, 307, 935, 1143, 1259, 1633, 1763, 2046, 2103
HEAD, Sir Edmund (1833) 918
HEAD, Sir Francis Bond, Bart. (1833-1852) 289, 876, 1097, 2494
HEADLEY, Henry (1785) 976
HEALE, William (1609) 145
HEARD, William (1770, 1776) 2684, 2720
HEARNE, Thomas (1725, 1731) 1345, 2767
HEARNE, Thomas, M.A. (1703) 2132
HEATH, Benjamin (1763) 319
HEATH, Benjamin, D.C.L. (1765) 2204
HEATH, G. (1796) 1716
HEATH, James (1662, 1672) 261, 934
HEATH, John (1619) 1182
HEATH, John (1747) 2646
HEATH, R. (1764) 997
HEATH, R. (1659) 1856
HEATH, Sir Robert (1694) 1990
HEATHCOTE, Ralph, D.D. (1752-1786) 552, 1251, 1397, 1412, 2439, 2531
HEATHCOTE, William Beadon (1845) 2052
HEATON, Rev. Henry, or John (1741-1743) 192
HEATON, S. M. (1840) 2581
HEAVYSEEGE, Charles (1859) 2260
HEBERDEN, Dr (1741-1743) 193
HEBERDEN, William, M.D. (1759) 429
HECKFORD, Reyner (1775) 657
HECTOR, Annie, née French (1873) 2831
HEDWORTH, Henry (1672, 1673) 506, 2475
HEEREN, A. H. L. (1832, 1833) 1120, 1121
HEGGE, Robert (1663) 1339
HEIGHWAY, Osborn W. Trenery (1854) 1663

HEINRICK, Herman Ludwg P. von
    Puckler Muskaw (1832)   2610
HELLEN, —— (1770)   1771
HELME, Elizabeth (1787)   409, 1516
HELMONT, F. M. van (1682)   295
HELMORE, Thomas, M.A. (N.D.)   2838
HELPS, Arthur (1835-1875)   255, 325,
    337, 408, 445, 478, 508, 830, 973, 1258,
    1303, 1357, 1825, 1833, 2083, 2413, 2443,
                                     2575
HELTON, John (1797)   1239
HELVETIUS, Dr Frederick (1673) 1902
HELY, James (1672)   1648
HEMANS, Felicia (1817-1831)   1641,
                              2392, 2623
HEMPHILL, Barbara (1846, 1855) 1490,
                                     2010
HEMPHILL, Samuel, M.A. (1722) 2425
HENDERSON, —— (1754)   986
HENDERSON, Alexander (1810)   22
HENDERSON, Alexander (1641)   1036
HENDERSON, Andrew (1768, N.D.)
                              1374, 1476
HENDERSON, Andrew, M.A. (1748)
                                     1164
HENDERSON, Ebenezer, D.D.
    (1818)   1013
HENDERSON, H. B. (1829)   225
HENDERSON, Mrs (1831-1833)   209,
              739, 1640, Errata, vol. i.
HENDERSON, R. (1631)   178
HENDERSON, Thulia Susannah
    (1852-1855)   288, 1076, 1815
HENDERSON, William (N.D.)   2342
HENDRIKES, Rose H. Temple née
    (1847)   1965
HENDRY, John, W.S. (1861)   2510
HENLEY, Anthony (1712)   1565
HENLEY, J. (1748)   2730
HENLEY, Samuel, D.D. (1786, 1792)
                                166, 816
HENNINGSEN, C. F. (1844-1848) 81,
              719, 2191, 2397, 2809
HENRY, —— (1827)   385
HENRY, David (1772-1774)   457, 1106
HENRY, Matthew (1690-1710)   23, 264,
                                     2356
HENRY, Robert, D.D. (1775)   1826
HENRY VIII., King (1542)   573
HENRY, Walter (1838)   2654
HENSHAW, Joseph (1639)   1564
HEPBURN, ——, of Bairford
    (1716)   641
HEPBURN, John (1713)   1189

HEPBURN, Thomas (1760, 1761) 1370,
                                     1582
HERAND, John Abraham (1830,
    1843)   603, 1469, 2771
HERBERT, David (1870)   1515, 2849
HERBERT, George (1817)   873
HERBERT, George (1640)   1836
HERBERT, George R. C., Earl of
    Pembroke (1872)   2458
HERBERT, Henry J. G., Earl of
    Carnarvon (1836)   1977
HERBERT, Henry William (1840) 1816
HERBERT, Hon. Algernon, M.A.
    (1828-1838)   280, 810, 1742
HERBERT, Sir William Fitz (1779) 2365
HERBERT, W. (1806, 1830)   465, 1207
HEREFORD, Bishop of, Francis
    Godwin (1657)   1538
HEREFORD, Bishop of, G.I. Hunt-
    ingford (1789-1802) 268, 1343, 2297, 2371
HEREFORD, Bishop of, John
    Butler, D.D. (1762-1814) 37, 497, 1402,
                         1435, 2329, 2417
HEREFORD, Rev. Charles (1790-
    1795)   1134, 1137, 1147, 1148
HERIOT, John (1787, 1788) 1061, 2455
HERLE, Charles (1642, 1650)   116, 856
HERNE, Thomas, M.A. (1718-1720) 13
    (2), 500, 798, 886, 1404, 1405. 1411, 2586
HERON, —— (1751)   1212
HERON, Mrs, née Emily Manning
    (1877)   209
HERON, Rt. Hon. Sir Richard (1797) 995
HERON, Robert (1797, 1807)   434, 1357
                                     2251
HERRIES, —— (1811)   2198
HERRIES, Walter (1700)   595
HERVEY, Hon. Thomas (1746)   1420
HERVEY, Lord John (1727-1743) 87, 121,
    123, 469, 899, 1393, 1629, 1786, 2062,
        2070, 2149, 2259, 2315, 2323, 2440
HESELTINE, William (1829)   1320
HESKETT, Henry (1683)   363
HEUGH, Hugh, D.D. (N.D., 1841) 672,
                                     973
HEWATT, Alexander (1779)   1108
HEWERDINE, Francis (1707)   560
HEWERDINE, Thomas, M.A.
    (1701-1702)   521, 2291, 2326
HEWETSON, William (1732)   1393
HEWETSON, W. B. (1808)   241
HEWETSON, William (1826)   499
HEWITT, John (1847)   608
HEWLETT, J. (1665)   605

HEWLETT, John Grigg, Ph.D., D.D. (1843, 1854)   875, 2580, 2583
HEWLETT, James *or* Joseph T., M.A. (1841-1846) 1050, 1860, 1864, 1892
HEXT, Gertrude Parsons *née* (1859-1878) 55, 219, 744, 1011, 1078, 1341, 1519, 1536, 1547, 1677, 2242, 2518, 2539, 2573, 2688, 2707, 2717
HEY, Mrs William (1833, 1841)   1657, 2100, 2475
HEY, William (1774, 1790)   2363 (2)
HEYDON, John (1655)   2033
HEYLIN, Peter, D.D. (1636-1673) 199, 277 (2), 420, 689, 956, 1083, 1124, 1370, 1512, 1779, 1862, 2097, 2198, 2377, 2509, 2560, 2661, 2707, 2781
HEYRICK, Elizabeth (1824)   1208
HEYWOOD, Eliza, *née* Fowler (1744-1788) 785, 911, 944, 1140, 1141, 1142, 1194
HEYWOOD, John (1533)   1606
HEYWOOD, Oliver (1683, 1693) 53, 1256
HEYWOOD, Samuel (1790, 1812)   2211, 1775
HEYWOOD, Thomas (1601-1657) 554, 571, 907, 926, 1003, 1203, 1531, 1550, 1898, 1996, 2303, 2304, 2667
HIBBERT, George (1821)   2542
HIBBERT, Lieutenant Edward (1824)   1693
HICKERINGILL, Edmund (1680-1682)   953, 1682, 1691, 2107, 2569
HICKES, George, D.D. (1680-1714) 143, 153, 314, 346, 683, 692, 806, 1071, 1281, 1284, 1364, 1389, 1635, 2081, 2143, 2423, 2466, 2473, 2748
HICKES, T. (1703)   456
HICKES, William (1682)   1038
HICKEY, Rev. William   Errata, vol. iv.
HICKEY, Ross (1830-1870) 60, 442 (2), 517, 555, 895, 897, 936, 1100 (2), 1251, 1310, 1552, 1984, 2240, 2408, 2738
HICKFORD, Raynor (N.D.)   1782
HICKMAN, Henry, B.D. (1659-1674)   222, 244, 1942, 2198, 2468
HICKS —— (1687-1689) 591, 1635, 1922
HICKS, John (1671)   2662
HICKS, Thomas (1673)   617
HICKS, William W. (1684)   1841
HIERON, Samuel (1607, 1608) 591, 2305
HIFFERMAN, Paul, M.D. (1750-1774)   715, 1899, 2319, 2821
HIGDEN, William, D.D. (1705)   317
HIGGINS, Matthew J. (1847-1857) 1253, 1445, 1448, 1485, 2083, 2568, 2588

HIGGINS, N. (1768)   372
HIGHMORE, John (1780)   2497
HIGHMORE, Joseph (1765, 1766)   826, 1770
HIGMAN —— (1825)   2531
HILDERSAM, Arthur (N.D.)   2638
HILDESLEY, Mark (1685)   1329, 2128
HILDROP, John, D.D. (1713-1754) 166, 344, 498, 794, 798, 966, 1023, 1371, 1644, 2113
HILDYARD, Christopher (1664)   1492
HILDYARD, J. (1755)   29
HILDYARD, James, B.D. (1858, 1862)   1225, 2175
HILL, Aaron (1734, 1750)   31, 769, 893, 1921
HILL, Alexander (1817)   1964
HILL, Benson Earle (1840)   1915
HILL, Dr John (1753)   1778
HILL, F. H. (1873)   1966
HILL, Henry (1709)   21
HILL, Henry, D.D. (1696)   619
HILL, Joseph, B.D. (1673)   1242
HILL, Rowland (1801)   2476
HILL, Samuel, Archdeacon of Wells (1687-1697)   337, 1679, 1707, 2415
HILL, Sir John, M.D. (1750-1758 50, 468, 496, 1131, 1234, 1430, 1523, 1540, 1704, 2230
HILL, Sir Richard (1768-1804)   37, 45, 932, 1027, 1054, 1403, 1405, 1912 (2), 2136, 2195, 2439
HILL, Thomas Wright (1822)   1931
HINCKLEY, John, M.A. (1617)   1917
HINCKS, Edward, D.D. (1833)   745
HINDE, S. (1662)   1258
HINDE, William (1614)   665
HINDLEY, Anne (1850)   1471
HINE, John Green (1860)   2475
HINTON, Edward (1643)   2722
HINTON, James (1859, 1866) 1538, 1699
HIPPISLEY —— (1838)   2729
HIPPISLEY, John (1729-1767) 478, 935, 2325
HIPPISLEY, Sir John C., Bart. (1799)   1430
HISLOP, A. (1855)   1657
HISTORICAL   1116
HITCHCOCK, Robert (1773-1777)   512, 1530
HITCHCOCK, Robert (1590)   2073
HITCHING, Charles (1718)   2124
HOADLY, Benjamin, D.D. (1702-1735) 143, 274, 568, 588, 592, 732, 773,

907, 967, 1260, 1365, 1368, 1384, 1404,
1918, 2067, 2088, 2301, 2327, 2330, 2443,
2575, 2669, 2743, 2776
HOADLY, Dr John (1711-1748) 1535,
1904, 2376
HOARD, Samuel, B.D. (1633) 1023
HOARE, Archdeacon (1837-8) 1991
HOARE, Edward N., Dean of Achonry (1850) 763
HOARE, Louisa (1819-1826) 970, 1100,
1426
HOARE, Mary (1826) 1235
HOARE, Prince (1792-1825) 308, 629, 719
HOARE, Sarah (N.D.) 1943
HOARE, Sir Richard Colt, Bart.
(1815-1827) 1101, 1102, 1364, 1651, 2098
HOBART, Augustus Charles, R.N.
(1867) 1710
HOBART, Hon. Mrs Charles (1874) 356
HOBHOUSE, Sir Benjamin, Bart.
(1792) 2641
HOBHOUSE, Sir John C. (1816,
1819) 2511, 2654
HOBHOUSE, Thomas (1784) 1306
HOBSON, John (1790) 159
HOBSON, Robert (1841) 1057
HOBSON, Samuel (1825, 1846) 525, 1702,
2849
HOCKLEY, William Brown (1826-
1843) 1577, 1848, 2774, Errata, vol. iv.
HODDESDON, John (1652, 1662) 1159,
2572
HODGE, —— (1699) 1291
HODGES, Dr Walter (1743) 1629, 2115
HODGES, James (1700-1706) 594, 2212,
Errata, vol iv.
HODGES, Thomas (1673) 2635
HODGKINSON, —— (1794) 1445
HODGSON, Abigail (1827) 2247
HODGSON, Thomas (N.D.) 1947
HODGSON, W. B. (1854) 411
HODGSON, William (1844) 1469
HODSHON, Ralph (1768) 666
HODSON, Mrs (1809, 1831) 2392, 2785
HODSON, Principal Dr Bernard
(1795) 1650
HODSON, William (1620) 683
HODSON, William (1775, 1783) 48, 180,
2854
HODY, Edward (1753) 196
HODY, Humphrey (1696, 1699) 97, 2115,
2444
HOFLAND, Barbara, née Wreaks
(1813-1828) 1297, 1559, 1600, 1872

HOFFMAN, E. T. W. (1852) 2500
HOG, James (1705-1731) 328, 470, 505
(2), 815, 862, 1345, 1367, 1421, 2134, 2272,
2434, 2438, 2443, 2698, 2753, Errata,
vol. iv.
HOG, James Maitland (1827) 273
HOG, Robert (1800) 1950
HOGAN, Rev. Edmond, S.J. (1873)
1167
HOGG, James (1707) 528
HOGG, James (1814-1832) 704, 1193,
1508, 1953, 2022, 2064, 2449,
HOGG, John (1693) 113
HOHENLOHE, Prince of, A. Leopold,
Bishop of Sardica (1823) 865
HOLBACH, Baron d', Paul Thyry
(1813) 721
HOLBOURNE, Sir Robert (1647) 962
HOLCROFT, Thomas (1780-1801) 72,
568, 609, 1093, 1233, 1920
HOLDEN, G. (1826) 1234
HOLDEN, R. (1667, 1685) 257, 1057
HOLDEN, Rev. George, M.A. (1855)
861
HOLDEN, Samuel (1662) 557
HOLDICH, Benjamin (1816) 1134
HOLDSWORTH, T. W. E. (1840) 303
HOLE, Archdeacon (1761) 1829
HOLE, Matthew, D.D. (1702, 1717)
133, 134
HOLE, Samuel Reynolds (1859) 1498
HOLFORD, George (1799) 343, 2497
HOLFORD, George Peter, M.P. (1805)
611
HOLFORD, Margaret (1809) 2785
HOLLAND, J. G. (1873) 2595, vol. iv.
HOLLAND, George C., M.D. (1839)
1230
HOLLAND, Guy (1653) 1041
HOLLAND, Hugh (1614, 1653) 722,
1655, 2123
HOLLAND, H. W. (1864) 2802
HOLLAND, John (1837-1841) 1129,
2612
HOLLAND, Lord Henry, R. V. Fox
(1807-1818) 705, 1373, 2584
HOLLAND, Philemon (1649) 2123
HOLLAND, Samuel (1719) 2460
HOLLAND, T. A. (1824) 433
HOLLES, Lord (1676) 2423
HOLLES, Thomas Pelham, Duke of
Newcastle (1756) 2184
HOLLIDAY, John (1800) 284
HOLLINGBERY, R. H. (1878) 1064

HOLLINGSWORTH, Nathaniel John, M.A. (1812)   595
HOLLINGSWORTH, S. (1786, 1787)   25, 2003
HOLLINGWORTH, R. (1643)   114
HOLLINGWORTH, Richard, D.D. (1692)   2767
HOLLINS, James (1866)   1869
HOLLINWORTH, Richard, M.A. (1645, 1650)   849, 856
HOLLIS, James (1772)   1436
HOLLIS, John (1775, 1799)   152, 825, 1099
HOLLIS, Lord Denzil (1669-1679)   324, 1042, 1359, 1384, 1509, 2423
HOLLIS, Thomas (1745, 1825)   1436, 1798, 2676
HOLLIS, William (1851)   1624
HOLMES, Cecil Frederick (1862)   2775
HOLMES, Dalkeith (1842)   2209
HOLMES, Edward (1828)   2075
HOLMES, Elizabeth, *née* Emra (1830)   2263
HOLMES, Nathaniel (1644)   1034
HOLMES, Oliver Wendell (1876)   986
HOLMES, W. (1785)   2622
HOLMES, William (1800)   2616
HOLMES, William, D.D., Dean of Exeter (1742)   524
HOLROYD, John Baker, Lord Sheffield (1783-1790)   439, 1783
HOLROYD, Rev. John James (1839)   1014
HOLT, Dorothy (1757)   40
HOLT, John (1749, 1750)   197, 2155
HOLWELL, J. J.   Errata, vol i.
HOLWELL, J. T. (1764)   42
HOLWELL, John Zephaniah (1764)   1216
HOLYOAKE, G. J. (1842)   1478
HOME, Henry, Lord Kames (1732-1774)   828, 830 (2), 1765, 2017, 2028, 2404
HOME, John (1757-1778) 58, 65, 70, 702, 903, 2382
HOME, M. J. (1776)   1355
HOMER, A. (1789)   231
HOMER, Philip Bracebridge, B.D. (1804)   1771
HOMER, Rev. Henry (1766)   808
HOMIÈRE, Louis de la (1857)   516
HOND, —— (1819)   833
HONE, William (1820-1822) 943, 1621, 1748, 1966 (2), 2064, 2472

HONYMAN, Andrew (1662, 1669)   2288, 2527, 2528
HONEYMAN, Andrew, Bishop of Orkney (1710)   251
HOOD, Thomas (1825, 1838)   216, 1803, 2479
HOOK, James, D.D. (1824)   1884
HOOK, James, LL.D. (1822)   1881
HOOK, Mrs (1784)   701
HOOK, Theodore (1820-1841) 238, 1473, 1517, 1561, 1860, 1864, 1892, 2552
HOOK, Theodore Edward (1805-1824)   853, 1539, 2261, 2414
HOOK, Walter Farquhar, D.D. (1846, 1872)   364, 2726
HOOKE, —— D.D. (1684)   2233
HOOKE, Nathaniel (1742)   18
HOOKE, Robert (1661)   195
HOOKE, Robert, F.R.S. (1679-1682)   1900
HOOKER, Sir William J. (1840)   511
HOOKER, Thomas (1632-1640) 387, 951, 1871, 2456 (2), 2457 (3), 2705
HOOKER, William (1805)   1855
HOOKES, Ellis (1667-1706)   179, 1236
HOOKES, Elias (1664)   2475
HOOKES, Nathaniel (1620)   349
HOOLE, John (1760)   1653
HOOLE, Rev. Samuel (1782, 1783)   200, 1641
HOOPER, Francis Bodfield (1851, 1853)   1847, 2073
HOOPER, George, D.D. (1689-1721)   641, 876, 1232, 1697, 1864
HOOPER, George, D.D., Bishop of Bath and Wells (1683-1701)   398, 1698
HOOPER, John, Bishop of Gloucester (1553)   2806
HOOTON, Charles (1836)   49
HOPE, Charles, Lord President (1826)   1752
HOPE, George (1761)   125
HOPE, John (1769)   1793
HOPE, Sir Wm., Bart. (1692)   911
HOPE, Thomas (1807, 1819)   84, 637
HOPKINS, Charles (1700)   183
HOPKINS, Ellice (1870)   2838
HOPKINS, Stephen (1765)   1053
HOPKINS, William (1760, 1784)   972, 2655
HOPKINS, William, B.A. (1754-1763)   159, 1499
HOPKINS, William, B.D. (1691)   96
HOPKINS, William, D.D. (1688)   225
HOPTON, Susanna (1687)   2120

HOPTON, Miss (1854, 1856)   78, 2694
HORBERY, Matthew (1735)   98
HORE, William (1658)   2547
HORLOCK, K. W. (1852-1868)   1093,
    1180, 1448, 1512, 1557, 1985, 2099,
                    2271, 2481
HORNBECK, Anthony (1678)   1354
HORNBLOWER, Mrs (1820)   1947
HORNBY, Charles (1701-1738) 345, 952,
        2291, 2305, 2408, 2570, 2587
HORNE, —— (1827-1833)   50, 2851
HORNE, —— (1797)   1168
HORNE, John (1673)   686
HORNE, Richard Henry (1833, 1850)
                    864, 1970
HORNE, Right Rev. George, D.D.,
    Bishop of Norwich (1751-1798)   615
        1376, 1445, 1775, 2471, 2562
HORNE, Thomas, D.D. (1795)   2116
HORNE, Thomas Hartwell, D.D.
    (1803-1848) 82, 232, 332, 374, 439, 448,
    459, 508, 541, 634, 1101, 1119, 1122,
    1202, 1205, 1499, 1548, 1837, 1972, 1973,
    2017, 2082, 2399, 2641, 2658, 2786, 2841
HORNECK, Anthony, D.D. (1688-
    1694)   133, 2071, 2670
HORNECK, Philip (1719)   1096
HORNIHOLD, J. (1771)   1055
HORNIHOLD, Rev. John (1749)   2083
HORSBURGH, James (1851)   1015
HORSBURGH, Matilda (1862-1869)
    370, 517, 1084, 1274, 1310, 1554, 1756,
            2073, 2227, 2257, 2498
HORSLEY, John, M.A. (1730)   768
HORSLEY, Samuel (1790-1796)   2039,
                    2197
HORSLEY, Samuel, D.D. (1784-
    1792)   202, 422
HORSLEY, Samuel, D.D., Bishop
    of St David's (1790)   153
HORSLEY, W. (1748)   938
HORSMAN, Nicholas (1823)   868
HORSMAN, Nicholas (1662)   2476
HORT, Lieut.-Col. John Josiah (1849-
    1850)   567, 1179, 2809
HORWELL, T. E. (1841)   1800
HOSKINS, Anthony, S.J. (1611)   275
HOSKYNS, Chandos W. (1852)   2545
HOTOMANUS, Franciscus (1586)   289
HOTTEN, John Camden (1864-1874)
            366, 1026, 2406, 2557
HOUGH, John, D.D., Bishop of
    Worcester (1688)   1212
HOUGHTON, G. (1800)   740
HOUGHTON, John William (N.D.) 1020,
                    1319
HOUGHTON, Lord, R. M. Milnes
    (1841)   1818
HOUGHTON, Thomas (1740)   427
HOULDING, John Richard (1868)   201
HOULDBROOKE, —— (1792)   2357
HOUSEHONE, William (1690)   467
HOUSTON, —— (1813)   721
HOUSTOUN, Mrs (1862-1882)   212,
    556, 559, 699, 928, 1051, 1076, 1488,
    1515, 2100, 2537, 2813, 2854, Errata
                    vol. iv. (2)
HOUSTON, R. (1720)   95
HOWARD, Charles (1751)   615
HOWARD, Edward (1836, 1857)   289,
                    2080, 2390
HOWARD, Edward, Earl of Suffolk
    (1725-1728)   1630, 1681
HOWARD, Frederick, Earl of Carlisle
    (1798-1808)   2583, 2710
HOWARD, George E. (1770)   2436
HOWARD, Hon. Edward (1671-1689)
            310, 1945, 2393, 2827
HOWARD, James (1848)   840
HOWARD, James, Vis. Fitzharris,
    Earl of Malmesbury (1837)   2177
HOWARD, Lady (1839, 1844) 237, 1013,
                    1274
HOWARD, Lieut. Edward (1837-
    1840)   1259, 1579, 1808, 1838
HOWARD, Luke (1808-1837)   36, 261,
    472, 868, 915, 1574, 2576, 2836, 2847
HOWARD, Martin (1765)   590, 1348
HOWARD, Mary Matilda (1845-
    1860) 253, 461, 1063, 1073, 2837, 2851
HOWARD, Sir Robert (1689-1696)
            1119, 1146, 2703
HOWARD, Thomas, Earl of Effing-
    ham (1782)   809
HOWARD, W. (1733)   1711
HOWARDINE, J. (1750)   572
HOWE, Charles (1751)   615
HOWE, J. (1695)   2753
HOWE, John (1677-1689) 322, 1422, 2100
HOWE, John, A.M. (1680)   116
HOWE, John, M.A. (1677)   168
HOWEL, James (1654-1659) 1760, 1885,
                    2443
HOWEL, William, LL.D. (1687)   1566
HOWELL, J. (N.D.)   2731
HOWELL, James (1643-1662) 60, 223,
    259, 653, 703, 753, 936, 1233, 1395, 1601,
    1855, 1885, 2252, 2443, 2621, 2772, 2819

HOWELL, John (1822, 1833)   465, 1462
HOWELL, John (1656)   2126
HOWELL, Laurence (1712-1716)   316,
                              1830, 2557
HOWELL, Richard (1856)   2401
HOWELL, Thomas (1560)   871
HOWELL, William (1689-1712)   442,
                      1877, 1990, 2833
HOWES, —— (N.D.)   1499
HOWES, Rev. Thomas (1776)   540
HOWGILL, Francis (1657)   2009
HOWISON, William (1826, 1829)   499,
                                   1902
HOWITT, Mary (1845)   1819
HOWITT, William (1818, 1835)   436,
                                   2585
HOWLETT, —— (1782)   1779
HOWLETT, Robert (1706)   93
HOY, Thomas, M.D. (1683)   56
HOYLAND, J. (1812)   787
HOYLE, Joshua, D.D. (1645)   1262
HOYLE, Rev. Charles (1828, 1830) 1913,
                                   2584
HUBBARD, Rev. John Clarke (1801) 1260
HUBBERTHORNE, Richard (1660)
                                   2447
HUBER, Mary (1736, 1738)   1425, 2842
HUBERT, Sir Francis (1628)   602
HUBERT, Sir Francis (1721)   1473
HUDDART, Sir Joseph (1821),   1572
HUDDERSTY, Z. (1850)   2040
HUDDESFORD, George, M.A.
  (1791-1799)   289, 531, 2255, 2607
HUDDESFORD, William (1772)   1503
HUDSON, —— (1790)   1781
HUDSON, Joseph (1785)   2162
HUET, —— (1700)   1586
HUGESSEN, Edward H. K. (1850)   2040
HUGGINS, William (1756)   1792
HUGHES, Benjamin (1774)   784
HUGHES, George (1846)   2207
HUGHES, George (1668)   2525
HUGHES, George, M.A. (1817)   744
HUGHES, John (1713, 1716)   142, 1330,
                                   1802
HUGHES, John (1802)   2030
HUGHES, John, M.A. (1850)   1332
HUGHES, Michael (1747)   1401
HUGHES, Mrs (1787, 1788)   310, 1084
HUGHES, Rev. George (1648)   1272
HUGHES, Thomas (1857-1859)   234,
                             2278, 2605
HUGHES, T. M. (1845)   2191
HUGHES, Thomas, Q.C. (1861)   2605

HUGHES, William (1767-1680) 651, 746,
                             1539, 2473
HUGHES, William (1779)   2335
HUIE, James A. (1840)   1157
HUISH, G. (1668)   2525
HUISH, R. (1832)   930
HULBERT, Charles Augustus (1823)
                                   2843
HULL, John, B.D. (1602)   2714
HULL, Thomas (1766-1771)   879, 1148,
                      1887, 2234, 2461
HULLAH, Mrs (1851)   917
HUMBERT, P. H. (1853)   379
HUMBLE, Michael Morgan, B.A.
  (1852)   1610
HUMBOLDS, Wilhelm von (1849) 2573
HUME, —— (1791)   1346
HUME, David (1739-1748) 826, 2635 (2),
                                   2660
HUME, Hugh, Earl of Marchmont
  (1740)   2331
HUME, James Deacon (1801, 1835)
                            1446, 2579
HUME, Patrick (1695)   102
HUME, Rev. Charles (N.D.)   1929
HUME, Sir Patrick (1580)   2030
HUMFRED, Joh. (1681)   1558
HUMPHREY, —— (1780)   464
HUMFREY, John (1701-1703) 52, 1452,
                             2288, 2591
HUMFREY, John (1668-1714) 116, 461,
  592, 705, 963, 1558, 1767, 1851, 1878,
                             2510, 2710
HUMFREY, John, M.A. (1667)   2038
HUMFREY, John, or Humphrey
  (1671)   1767
HUMFREYS, Mr (1680)   1878
HUMPHREY, Mr (1680)   1878
HUMPHREY, John (1672, 1700)   204,
                             1077, 1381
HUMPHREY, Laurence (1581)   2736
HUMPHREYS, —— (1707)   2725
HUMPHREYS, Edward Rupert,
  LL.D. (1855, 1856)   750, 1427, 2792
HUMPHREYS, Eliza (1856)   1610
HUMPHREYS, Henry Noel (1846,
  1856)   421, 625, 2496
HUMPHREYS, S. (1701)   831
HUMPHREYS, Samuel (1733)   2466
HUMFRYS, John (1675)   1878
HUNT, A. W. (1872, 1874)   1532, 2573,
                                   2707
HUNT, Brian (1722)   1863
HUNT, Christ. (1594)   1021

HUNT, James Henry Leigh (1807-
1832) 196, 384, 538, 907, 1458, 1494,
2391
HUNT, Robert S. (1878) 1683
HUNT, Rowland (1806) 964
HUNT, Thomas (1679, 1682) 171, 1045,
1176, 1673
HUNT, Thomas (1682) 1673
HUNT, Thomas (1679) 1176
HUNT, Thomas (N.D.) 1045
HUNT, William (1713) 885
HUNTER, —— (1810) 209
HUNTER, —— (1728) 693
HUNTER, Alexander, M.D. (1761) 2644
HUNTER, Christopher (1733-1736)
1150, 1205
HUNTER, J. (1731) 846
HUNTER, James (1867) 2166
HUNTER, John (1843) 1630
HUNTER, Joseph (1814) 2810
HUNTER, Rev. Joseph, F.S.A. (1847,
1848) 138, 1753
HUNTER, Robert (1708, 1714) 90, 1345
HUNTINGFORD, George J., D.D.,
Bishop of Hereford (1789-1802 268,
1343, 2297, 2371
HUNTINGFORD, Thomas (1777)
1760
HUNTINGTON, George (1867) 205
HUNTINGTON, Jedediah V. (1849,
1851) 61, 1312
HUNTLEY, Sir H. V. (1856) 301
HUNTON, Philip (1643, 1644) 2636,
2766
HUNTON, Rev. Samuel (1654) 1103
HIND, Richard, D.D., Bishop of
Worcester (1746-1794) 152, 599, 624 (2),
640, 676, 1385, 1407, 1444, 1656, 1820,
2136, 2140
HURDIS, James, D.D. (1790-1797)
46, 1947, 2391, 2738, 2836
HUSSEY, Edward Law (1873) 868
HUSSEY, Robert (1839) 1083
HUSSEY, William (1809-1830) 159,
161, 1427, 1652
HUSTLER, John (1767, 1783) 1793,
2486
HUTCHESON, Archibald (1720,
1722) 832, 1390, 2420, 2442, 2469
HUTCHESON, Francis, LL.D. (1725,
1728) 808, 1231
HUTCHESON, T. S. (1858) 233
HUTCHINSON, —— (1831) 117
HUTCHINSON, —— (1716) 447

HUTCHINSON, C. (1687) 203
HUTCHINSON, Francis, D.D.
(1734) 585
HUTCHINSON, John (1706-1749) 528
1019, 1665 (2), 1711, 1769, 2130, 2163,
2636, 2718
HUTCHINSON, John Hely (1779) 440
HUTCHINSON, Rev. Benjamin
(1765) 1301, 1549
HUTCHINSON, Right Hon. J. H.
(N.D.) 16
HUTCHINSON, Thomas (1776) 2507
HUTCHINSON, William (1772-1789)
701, 855, 1090, 2013, 2799
HUTCHISON, William (1865) 2545
HUTTON, Luke (1612) 664
HUTTON, Rev. John (1781) 2614
HUTTON, R. N. (1848, 1849) 1262, 2099
HUTTON, William (1789) 605
HUTTON, Wyndham M. (1851) 1944
HYDE, Catherine, Marchioness
Broglio Solari (1824-1827) 2020, 2313,
2725
HYDE, Edward, Earl of Clarendon
(1648-1674) 97, 981, 1354, 1364, 2310
HYDE, Julia (1856) 2517
HYDE, Laurence, Earl of Rochester
(1679) 764
HYDE, Lord, and Cornburgh (1758) 1635
HYDE, Rev. John (1864) 1833
HYND, John (1603) 1622
HYNDE, S. (1662) 1258
HYNDMAN, John (1753) 1293

I.

IÄNSON, Sir Hen. (1663, 1672) 1272
1897
IBBETSON, James (1777) 675
ILIFF, George (1855) 394
ILIVE, Jacob (1757) 2094
INATULLA, of Delhi (1768) 2545
INCHBALD, Elizabeth, née Simpson
(1785-1788) 99, 162, 1649, 2814
INCLE 1225
INGELOW, Jean (1864, 1868) 2392, 2508
INGLIS, Charles, Bishop of Nova
Scotia (1779) 1441
INGLIS, Henry David (1825-1831)
1890, 2415, 2530, 2540
INGLIS, J. B. (1832) 1898
INGLIS, John (1811) 439
INGLIS, John (1879) 2845

INGLIS, John, D.D. (1806)   847
INGLIS, Right Hon. John (1839, 1842)   1594, 2000
INGRAM, James, D.D. (1825-1844)   144, 397, 1597, 1774
INGRAM, Robert (1780)   861
INNES, ——, M.P. (1791)   2406
INNES, Alexander, D.D. (1728)   170
INNES, Cosmo, P.C.S. (1860, 1865)   463, 1753
INNES, Dr Robert (1795)   1785
INNES, Duncan (1749, 1750) 1350, 1979
INNES, Mrs John Hill Burton, née (1865-1874)   1570, 1835
INNES, William (1811)   833
INSKIP, Thomas (1843)   306
IRELAND, John, D.D. (1801)   1760
IRELAND, Lord Chancellor of, Richard West (1726)   1080
IRELAND, Thomas (1654)   1649
IRELAND, William Henry (1799-1853) 68, 92, 354, 729, 930, 1259, 1581, 1582, 1643, 2249, 2279, 2349, 2509, 2777
IRELAND, W. H. C. (1811)   1955
IRELAND, William W., M.D. (1861)   1165
IRONS, William Josiah, B.D. (1847-1853)   125, 383, 787, 1991
IRVINE, A. (1824)   415
IRVINE, Mary Catherine (1857, 1859)   188, 972
IRVING, Edward, M.A. (1830)   690
IRVING, Rev. E. (1828-9)   624
IRVING, Robert (1840)   709
IRVING, Robert (1704)   2748
IRVING, Washington (1811-1850) 3, 66, 252, 1144, 1630, 2255, 2397, 2540, 2611
IRWIN, Eyles (1774-1780) 220, 719, 2253
ISAACSON, Henry (1650)   843
ISAACSON, S. (1844-5)   214
ISHAM, John (1694)   558
ISHAM, Rev. Zachary, D.D. (1699) 615
ISOLA, Baron d' (1671)   2000
IVORY, James, Advocate (1819)   1752
IVORY, James, Lord Ivory (1815-18) 943

J.

JABET, George (1847, 1848) 1699, 1960, Erratta, vol. iv.
JACKMAN, Isaac (1777-1787) 68, 686, 1614, 2232
JACKMAN, John (1717)   2079

JACKSON, Bishop John (1732)   2307
JACKSON, Helen (1876)   1604
JACKSON, Henry (1870, 1871) 562, 1078
JACKSON, John (1714-1749) 106, 380, 426, 579, 597, 900, 1587, 2141, 2588, 2644, Errata vol. iv.
JACKSON, John (1654, 1657) 1180, 2412
JACKSON, John, M.A. (1714-1722) 659, 2172
JACKSON, ——, M.P. (1768)   2089
JACKSON, Rev. John (1731-1738) 302, 476, 1934
JACKSON, Rev. J. L., M.A. (1834) 389
JACKSON, Rowland, M.D. (1746)   1906, 1984
JACKSON, Thomas (1833)   2709
JACKSON, Thomas, M.A. (1835) 1545
JACKSON, William (1733)   23
JACKSON, William (1784)   2571
JACOB, George Andrew (1845-1851)   286 (2)
JACOB, Giles (1714-1733)   1108, 1518, 1622, 1957
JACOB, H. (1586)   593
JACOB, Henry (N.D.)   520
JACOB, Henry (1598)   2639
JACOB, Hilderbrand (1738)   1710
JACOB, John (1699)   2690
JACOB, Thomas Greer (1832)   271
JACQUE, Rev. George (1849-1866)   419, 2539
JAFFRAY, A. (1797)   726
JAKOB, Thérèse A. L. von (1850) 1123
JAMES I. (1619)   1877
JAMES VI., King (1603)   2671
JAMES, Charles (1780)   1956
JAMES, George P. Rainsford (1829-1853) 440, 564, 567, 598, 1554, 1684, 2208, 2507
JAMES, Henry (1835)   2487
JAMES, James Henry (1856, 1862) 211, 2028
JAMES, Marian (1857)   1513, 2392
JAMES, R. (1785)   581
JAMES, Rev. Dr (1769)   15
JAMES, Richard, B.D. (1629)   2332
JAMES, Thomas Andrew (1838)   518
JAMES, Thomas, D.D. (1612)   1265
JAMESON, —— (1815)   2656
JAMESON, A. (N.D.)   1623
JAMESON, Anne (1826, 1829) 626, 1521
JAMESON, ——, LL.D. (1748)   536
JAMESON, Robert W., W.S. (1830, 1848)   1225, 1742

JAMIESON, Alex. (1819)   1093
JAMIESON John, D.D. (1790-1828)
     476, 619, 1715, 2413
JAMIESON Professor Alexander
   (1677)   149
JAMIESON, William (1814)   1413
JANE, Joseph (1651)   730
JANE, William (1678, 1689)   1367, 2001
JANNEY, Samuel M. (1860)   76
JANSON, Sir Henry (1663)   1896
JANSSEN, Sir S. T., Bart., M.P.
   (1763)   2409
JAPP, Alexander H. (1872-1880)   1334,
     1571, 1747, 1835, 2572 (2)
JARDINE, David (1833)   1501
JARDINE, J. (1846)   2373
JARDINE, Major Alex. (1788)   1427
JARDINE, Sir Henry (1821)   2180
JARMAN, E. (N.D.)   1247
JARNAC, Count de (1849-1853)   346, 733,
     1517, 2220
JAY, George (1642)   2334
JAY, Harriet (1875, 1879)   1532, 2063
JAY, Stephen (1682)   563
JEAMSON, Thomas (1665)   187
JEBB, Anne (1774, 1793)   1391, 2699
JEBB, Dr (1779)   1056
JEBB, Frederick (N.D.)   1432
JEBB, John (1772)   1387
JEBB, John, M.A. (1774)   1929
JEBB, John, M.D., F.R.S. (1772)   1449
JEBB, John, D.D., Bishop of Limerick
   (1824, 1828)   308, 1983
JEBB, Samuel, M.D. (1725-1727)   1159,
     1479
JEFFERIES, —— (1726)   2198
JEFFERIES, Thomas, *or* Jeffery
     Errata, vol. iv.
JEFFERSON, J. B. (1821)   1168
JEFFERSON, S. (1838)   1126
JEFFERSON, Thomas (1774)   2517
JEFFREY, Dr John, Archdeacon of
   Norwich (1703)   1656
JEFFREY, Francis, Lord Jeffrey
   (1810)   2379
JEFFREYS, M. E. (1851)   2482
JEFFRYS, E. (1718)   2590
JEKYLL, Joseph (1811)   875
JELF, William Edward, B.D. (1873)
     2074, 2291
JENINGS, Mrs Edmund (N.D.)   1685
JENISON, Robert, S.J. (1631)   1846
JENKIN, C. (1858-1865)   1817, 2769,
     2810

JENKIN, Rev. Robert (1688)   1117
JENKIN, Robert (1709)   2146
JENKIN, Robert, D.D. (1690)   592
JENKINS, David (1649)   1020
JENKINS, Dr (1691)   2596, vol. iv.
JENKINS, Edward (1870-1876)   241,
     510, 1014, 1511
JENKINS, Joseph, M.A. (1775)   1830
JENKINS, Mary (1861)   1058
JENKINS, Mrs (1841-1846)   1515, 2409,
     2798
JENKINSON, Anne (1609)   1565
JENKINSON, Charles, Earl of Liver-
   pool (1757-1801)   657, 658, 2197, 2486,
     2752
JENKINSON, Charles, Earl of
   Hawkesbury (1798)   2486
JENKINSON, C., Earl of Liverpool
   (1757-1801)   657, 658, 2197, 2487, 2752
JENKINSON, James (1762)   2256
JENKS, —— (1797)   206
JENKS, Silvester (1693-1710)   241, 504,
     2373
JENNINS, Charles (1770-1774)   2347,
     2619 (2)
JENNER, David (1718)   1996
JENNER, Rev. Charles (1764-1771)
     1426, 1428, 1539, 1917
JENNINGS, David (1792)   1075
JENNINGS, Henry Constantine
   (1779-1785)   747, 961, 1656, 1907
     1980, 2514
JENNINGS, Rev. David (1740)   2765
JENOUR, Joshua (1778, 1798)   1785,
     1860
JENYNS, Soame (1729-1784)   181, 669,
   962, 1628, 1641, 1766, 1800, 1944, 2265,
     2361, 2481, 2576, 2579, 2734
JEPHSON, Robert (1768-1794)   473,
     491, 825
JERDAN, William (1818, 1829)   1890,
     2396
JEREMY, Henry (1818)   83
JERMYN, J. (1818, 1847)   737, 1905,
     2600
JERNINGHAM, Edward (1763-1809)
   64, 632, 736, 1174, 1323, 1533, 1614
     1760, 1879, 1952, 2318, 2845
JERRAM, Charles, A.M. (1802)   1451
JERRARD, Paul (1852)   247
JERVISE, Andrew (1855)   94
JEWEL, J., Bishop of Salisbury
   (1562)   145
JEWELL, Joseph (1821)   36

JEWRY, Laura (1847)   1307
JEWSBURY, Marie Jane (1825, 1831)   1895, 2392
JOBERT, Louis (1697)   1310
JOCELYN, —— (1718)   799
JODRELL, Sir Richard Paul, M.D. (1786, 1787)   1817, 2315, 2810
JOHN, Frederick, 5th Lord Monson (1839-1842)   949, 1275
JOHNES, Thomas (1806)   331
JOHNS, Rev. Charles Alex., F.L.S. (1854, 1855)   393, 1036
JOHNS, William (1678)   2621
JOHNSON, Arthur (1819)   1841
JOHNSON, Benjamin (1604)   207
JOHNSON, Ben, *or* Jonson (1617-1621)   372, 944, 1521, 1556, 1710
JOHNSON, Capt. Edward (1654)   1144
JOHNSON, Charles (1702, 1733)   297, 945, 1005
JOHNSON, Francis (1608)   353
JOHNSON, Dr Samuel (1753-1790)   47, 1873, 2339, 2347
JOHNSON, J. (1664)   73
JOHNSON, J. (1729)   2245
JOHNSON, James, M.D. (1834)   2098
JOHNSON, John (1709)   414 (2)
JOHNSON, John, M.A. (1710)   2034
JOHNSON, Joseph (1860, 1861)   1093, 1243, 2556
JOHNSON, Rev. John (1706)   1171
JOHNSON, Rev. Samuel (1682-1697)   173, 1287, 1820, 2057, 2160, 2671
JOHNSON, Richard (1612-1755)   892, 1668, 2166, 2169
JOHNSON, Robert (1828)   439
JOHNSON, Samuel, (1688-1777)   7, 476, 509, 1348, 2683, 2796
JOHNSON, Samuel, LL.D. (1738-1790)   14, 23, 456, 885, 1202, 1280, 1506, 1549, 1873, 1967, 2013, 2076, 2547, 2581
JOHNSON, Thomas (1731)   800
JOHNSON, Thomas, A.M. (1736)   2515
JOHNSON, W. (1830)   836
JOHNSON, William (1873)   1249
JOHNSON, William (1798)   1383
JOHNSON, William (1858) Errata, vol. iv.
JOHNSTON, —— (1858)   1249
JOHNSTON, Andrew Gregory (1816)   1450
JOHNSTON, Charles (1760-1786)   49, 394, 1132, 1140, 1913, 2192
JOHNSTON, Dr (1737)   1175

JOHNSTON, Ebenezer (N.D.)   722
JOHNSTON, James (1731)   1660
JOHNSTON, Joseph (1685-1687)   864, 981, 1358, 2175, 2750
JOHNSTON, Keith (1878-1884)   1747, 2387, 2526, 2724, 2804
JOHNSTON, Nathaniel (N.D.)   569
JOHNSTONE, —— (1840)   2536
JOHNSTONE, Christina Jane (1815-1832)   409, 510, 682, 741, 1741
JOHNSTONE, George (1732)   832
JOHNSTONE, George, M.P. (1771)   2578
JOHNSTONE, Rev. John (1841)   2505
JOHNSTONE, Robert W. (1871)   2064
JOLIFFE, Thomas R. (1819-1827)   1428, 1694
JOLLY, Emily (1856-1874)   288, 326, 433, 548, 1297, 1671, 1686, 1879, 2248, 2769, 2815
JOLLY, Thomas (1698)   2765
JOLYOT DE CREBILLON, Bl. Prosp. (1749)   77
JONES, —— (1841)   70
JONES, —— (1771)   965
JONES, C. (1775)   2459
JONES, C. A. (1858-1871)   1833, 2082, 2251, 2499, 2518
JONES, Captain (1646)   1923
JONES, Capt. William, R.N. (1830)   1776
JONES, David (1716)   1161
JONES, David (1790-1794)   1417, 2092, 2504, 2582, 2800 (2),
JONES, David (1702)   1475
JONES, David (1817)   2014
JONES, Dr R. (1659)   2188
JONES, Elizabeth (N.D.)   727
JONES, Erasmus (1735)   1527
JONES, Ernest (1841)   2830
JONES, Griffith (1744)   1932
JONES, Henry (1875-1878)   1327, 1328
JONES, Henry (1746-1761)   1467, 1903, 2128
JONES, Henry (N.D.)   1942
JONES, H. M. (1827)   2227
JONES, J. (1769)   2358
JONES, John (1642, 1643)   390, 850
JONES, John (1750, 1755)   338, 669
JONES, Margaret E. M. (1837, 1839)   1255, 1281, 2783
JONES, Mr (N.D.)   1438
JONES, R. B. (1856)   2771
JONES, Rev. John (1749)   959

JONES, Rev. John, LL.D. (1819-1827)   785, 1733, 2178, 2587, 2663
JONES, Rev. John Pike (1820, 1828)   250, 722
JONES, Sarah L. (1863)   1470, 2495
JONES, Sir William (1772-1825)   618, 842, 1229, 1291, 1374, 1436, 1948
JONES, Stephen (1795, 1812)   1145, 1199
JONES, W., B.D. (1612)   1917
JONES, William (1752-1795)   496, 677, 1335, 1382, 1818 (2), 2110, 2267, 2408
JONES, William (1679)   2838
JONES, William, F.R.S. (1777-1798)   1392, 1426, 1768
JORDAN, C. W. (1799)   1769
JORDAN, G. W. (1799, 1800)   21, 1726
JORDAN, J. W. (1824)   265
JORDAN, Tho. (1649)   570
JORDAN, Thomas (1665)   372
JORTIN, John, D.D. (1731-1753)   800, 1625, 2146
JOSSELIN, John (1574)   1484
JOURDAN, Mary J. (1836, 1856)   72, 1617
JOY, George (1534, 1535)   1031, 2049
JOY, Henry H. (1838)   1412
JOYCE, Jeremiah (1803)   82
JOYNER, *alias* Lyde Gulielmus (1686)   2433
JOYNER, William (1686)   1790
JUDD, J. (1856)   518
JUDD, Sylvester (1850)   2208
JUDSON, Mrs (1848)   1635
JULLIEN, A. (1824)   2607
JURIN, James, M.D. (1734-1757)   165, 1010, 1619
JUSTAMOND, J., M.A. (1776)   1900
JUSTAMOND, John Obadiah (1758)   2143
JUSTICE, Alexander (1707)   1002
JUXON, William, Archbishop of Canterbury (1662, 1694)   364, 2510

K

KAMES, Lord, Henry Home (1732-1774)   828, 830 (2), 1765, 2017, 2028, 2404
KAMPE, Joachim H. (1852)   2530
KAUFFMAN, C. H. (1803)   629
KAY, Robert (1816)   1035
KAYE, Bishop (1834, 1838)   2141, 2178
KAYE, John William (1844)   1885

KEACH, Benjamin (1675-1692)   163, 1018, 1040, 2389, 2789
KEARY, Annie (1857-1863)   1091, 1261, 2382
KEARY, E. (1857)   1091
KEATE, George, F.R.S. (1760-1766)   87, 1943, 2551
KEATE, Rev. William (1790)   35
KEBLE, John, M.A. (1827-1865)   384, 615, 1528 (2), 2052
KEBLE, Joseph, LL.B. (1707)   795
KECK, T. (1656)   2129
KEDDIE, Henrietta (1852-1882)   294, 406, 566, 624, 702, 993, 1014, 1090, 1093, 1187, 1306, 1312, 1317, 1566, 1642, 1683, 1747, 1762, 1812, 1816, 1851, 1896, 2273 (2), 2392, 2433, 2518, 2529, 2798, 2805
KEDDIE, William (N.D.)   2482
KEEPE, Henry (1683, 1688)   1655, 2664
KEIGHTLEY, Thomas (1828, 1837)   879, 2313
KEILL, John, M.A. (1701)   813
KEIR, James (1789)   928
KEIR, James, F.R.S. (1771)   628
KEIR, Mrs (1786)   1242
KEIRN, —— (1714)   1646
KEITH, Charles, of Montrose (1776)   896
KEITH, Duncan (1882)   1758
KEITH, George (1682-1699)   718, 2330, 2682
KEITH, G. Skene (1797)   40
KEITH, William (1730)   805
KEITH, Sir William, Bart. (1729)   817
KELHAM, Robert (1758)   71
KELLISON, Matthew (1617-1672)   273, 981, 1736, 2229
KELLY, Dennis Burrowes (1839)   1542
KELLY, Hugh (1766-1774)   207, 413, 1578, 2269, 2565
KELLY, John (1732-1756)   884, 1455, 1550, 1941, 2594, 2712
KELLY, P. (1826)   1287
KELLY, W. (1834)   1887
KELLY, William (1876)   1754
KELSALL, Charles (1812-1836)   494, 929, 1178, 1355, 2157
KELTY, Mary Ann (1821-1866)   614, 906, 1469, 1508, 1831, 2082, 2167, 2499, 2652, 2773, 2794
KEMBLE, Frances Ann (1814-1831)   303, 354, 391, 509, 577, 1011, 1027, 1059, 1520, 2311, 2314, 2706, 2826, Errata vol. iv.

KEMBLE, John Philip (1786-1789) 1531, 1849, 2452
KEMBLE, Mrs Charles, née M. T. de Camp (1808) 565
KEMP, Anne (N.D.) 497
KEMP, W. (1588) 727
KEN, Thomas, D.D., Bishop of Bath and Wells (1675-1703) 108, 711, 864, 1389, 1545, 2234
KENDALL, A. (1798) 327
KENDALL, Edward Augustus (1798-1835) 291, 755, 1298, 2462
KENDALL, Francis (1816) 608
KENNAWAY, Charles Edward (1854) 1884
KENNEDY, —— (1826) 567
KENNEDY, Archibald (1749, 1752) 1215, 1779
KENNEDY, Benjamin Hall, D.D. (1844-1871) 1323, 2054, (2), 2595, vol. iii.
KENNEDY, Edward S. (1871) 2054
KENNEDY, Gilbert (1721-22) 1724
KENNEDY, Grace (1725 1897
KENNEDY, Grace (1823, 1825) 709, 2025
KENNEDY, James (1786) 607
KENNEDY, James, B.D. (1876) 2145
KENNEDY, James, M.D. (1762) 172
KENNEDY, John (1756) 989, 1406, 2693
KENNEDY, John, D.M. (1751) 678
KENNEDY, Mr —— (1831) 2392
KENNEDY, Mrs (1831) 2392
KENNEDY, Patrick (1855, 1856) 1340 (2)
KENNETT, White, D.D., Bishop of Peterborough (1681-1718) 26, 322, 620, 689, 902, 1152, 1343, 1354, 1399, 1565, 1594, 1794, 2001, 2101, 2440, 2599, 2664, 2750, 2772, 2820
KENNICOTT, Benjamin, D.D. (1747-1772) 1369, 1943, 2836
KENNY, Arthur H., D.D. (1822) 1445
KENNY, Mary (1822, 1823) 365, 1446
KENRICK, William, D.D., LL.D (1751-1773) 582, 784, 786, 984, 1041, 1245, 1297, 1698, 1815, 1867, 2176, 2284, 2811
KENT, John (1772) 1436
KENT, William Charles Mark (1847-1869) 339, 603, 1015, 1501
KENYON, John (1833) 2206
KEPERS, John (N.D.) 527
KER, Henry Bellenden (1819, 1833) 1501, 2753
KER, John (1721) 1376
KER, William (1689) 2411

KER, William T., M.A. (1879) 2187
KERR, Charles (1788) 1296
KERR, Lady Amabel (1876) 2715
KERR, William S. R., Marquis of Lothian (1863) 953
KERSEY, John (1702) 1720
KETTILBY, —— (1765) 718
KETTLE, Mary Rosa Stewart (1852, 1860) 716, 871
KETTLE, Rose Mackenzie (1851-1854) 1455, 2389, 2409, Errata, vol. ii.
KETTLEWELL, Rev. John (1688-1693) 377, 381, 384, 712, 1982
KEYNES, F. John, S.J. (1675) 689
KEYWORTH, Thomas (1817) 2014
KIDD, Rev. J., M.D. (1835) 333
KIDDER, Rev. Richard, D.D., Bishop of Bath and Wells (1687-1690) 1369, 1753, 2295, 2570
KIDGELL, John (1755) 308
KILDARE AND LEIGHLIN, Bp. of, James Warren Doyle (1822-1827) 578, 1356, 1448, 1449 (2), 2170, 2763
KILLALA, Bishop of, John Maxwell (1640) 779
KILLALA, Bishop of, Joseph Stock (1800) 1699
KILLIGREW, Henry (1643) 2336
KILLIGREW, Sir William (1664, 1669) 1213, 1848
KILLIGREW, Thomas (1720) 1624
KILNER, Joseph (N.D.) 16
KILPATRICK, James (1731) 821, 2333
KILVERT, Adelaide S. (1841) 1172
KILVERT, R. (1644) 649
KIMBALL, Richard B. (1850) 2251
KIMBER, Isaac (1731, 1746) 1136, 1478
KINASTON, Sir Francis (1636, 1642) 496, 1341
KINDERLY, Nathaniel (1721) 2004
KING, Charles (1705) 25
KING, Counsellor (1771) 968
KING, Daniel (1656) 337
KING, David, LL.D. (1832) 849
KING, Dr William (1754, 1771) 113, 705
KING, Dr William, M.A. (1750) 742
KING, Edward (1795) 1198
KING, Edward, F.R.S. (1785, 1803) 1174, 2037
KING, E., Earl of Kingsborough (1830) 139
KING, Frances E., née Bernard (1800) 2103
KING, Gregory (1684, 1685) 1824 (2)

KING, Harriet E. Hamilton (1869)   189

KING, Henry, D.D., Bishop of Chichester (1649-1657) 578, 1949, 2050

KING, John, D.D. (1701)   95

KING, John, D.D., Bishop of London (1611)   2335

KING, John Myers (1849)   1864

KING, Katherine (1870, 1872) 832, 1893

KING, Lord, Peter King (1691)   767

KING, Mrs (1813)   911

KING, Peter, Lord King (1691)   767

KING, Philip, D.D. (1656)   2526

KING, Richard (1808)   286

KING, R. J. (1840)   2695

KING, Robert (1844)   2253

KING, Rufus (1807)   1878

KING, Sir Peter, Lord Chancellor, Ockham (1703)   1149

KING, Thomas (1763)   1518

KING, Walter William (1841)   1038

KING, William, D.D. (1691, 1754) 2488, 2623

KING, William, Earl of Lovelace (1848)   2197, 2203

KING, William, LL.D. (1694-1751) 95, 181, 369, 623, 972, 1279, 1299, 1672, 1802, 1955, 2035, 2237, 2298, 2440, 2602, 2621, 2719, 2763

KINGESBY, George (1760)   87

KINGLAKE, Alexander W. (1844)   776

KINLOCH, George R. (1827-1829) 89, 209, 1759, 1851

KINLOCH, Lord William Penny (1833-1866)   404, 2069, 2594, 2615

KINGSBOROUGH, Earl of, E. King (1830)   139

KINGSLEY, Charles (1850-1851)   72, 367, 2846

KINGSLEY, Dr (1872)   2458

KINGSLEY, Jeffreys (1838)   2483

KINGSMAN, William (1811)   1414

KINGSTON, Dr Richard (1707-1709) 775, 1212

KIPPIS, Andrew, D.D. (1761-1795) 488, 728, 1461, 1472

KIRKBY, John (1745)   307, 1472

KIRKE, Thomas (1679)   1638

KIRKLAND, Mary, née Clavers (1842)   941

KIRKMAN, Francis (1661-1675) 1997, 2047, 2714, 2824

KIRKPATRICK, James (1713, 1721) 1117, 2760

KIRKPATRICK, J., M.D. (1750)   2284

KIRKTON, James (1703)   1143

KIRKWAN, A. V. (1841)   1977

KIRKWOOD, James (1692)   2670

KISMET, George Fleming (N.D.)   1307

KITCHIN, John (1605)   1824

KITCHINER, William, M.D. (1811-1822) 142, 182, 445, 510, 1939, 1985

KITCHING, H. St A. (1832)   1658

KITTO, John (N.D.)   88

KITTO, John, D.D. (1799)   1641

KNAPP, John Leonard (1818, 1829) 186, 1275

KNIGHT, Charles (1836)   1739, 1908

KNIGHT, Ellis Cornelia (1790-1812) 392, 606, 633, 2623

KNIGHT, George (1837)   2157

KNIGHT, Henry Gally (1816)   1204

KNIGHT, James, D.D. (1711-1715) 482, 1403, 2010, 2281, 2676

KNIGHT, J. C. (1854)   665

KNIGHT, Mr (1805)   1617

KNIGHT, Sir John (1694)   2470

KNIGHT, T. (1809)   846

KNIGHT, Thomas (1725)   812

KNIGHTON, William (1855)   2022

KNOTT, Edward (1636, 1654)   635, 1223, 2040

KNOTT, Rev. Robert Rowe, M.A. (1839)   1711

KNOWLES, Mary (N.D.)   449

KNOWLES, Sir Charles (1765)   804

KNOX, —— (N.D.)   2591

KNOX, Alexander (1824)   1232

KNOX, Captain Charles (1841, 1842) 1069, 2413

KNOX, Isabella Craig (1856-1881) 1210, 1218, 1947

KNOX, John (1558, 1581)   926, 998

KNOX, John (1784)   2733

KNOX, J. Spencer (1840)   1869

KNOX, Thomas (1856)   628

KNOX, Vicesimus, D.D. (1778-1821) 137, 733, 825, 890, 1890, 2472, 2819

KNOX, William (1765, 1796) 409, 489, 505, 866, 1791, 2004

KNOX, William (1824)   2772

KOLTZOFF-MASSALSKY, Princess, née Helena Ghika (1861)   2827

KOOPS, Matthias (1800)   1109

KRASINSKI, Count Valerian (1852) 1650

KYD, Thomas (1594-1605)   513, 928, 2462, 2618

KYFFIN, Maurice (1587)   589

KYLE, Rev. Robert Wood (1842)   1417

KYNASTON, Herbert (1852)   436
KYNASTON, Sir Francis (1636)   496
KYNASTON, Thomas (1785)   1419

L.

LA BRUNE, J. de (1691)   1480
LA CALPRENÈDE, Seigneur
   Gauthier de Costes (1676)   326
LA CRÉQUINIERE, —— de (1705) 59
LA CROSE, J. D. de (1687)   2711
LA HOMIERE, Louis de (1857)   516
LA MARCHE, Oliver de (1594)   2186
LA PLACETTE, Jean de (1687,
   1688)   1219, 2393
LA ROCHE, Charles F. T. de (1753), 77
LA ROCHE, Michael de (1722, 1730)
     1494, 1582
LA RAMÉ, Louisa de (1863-1883)   175,
   345, 356, 696, 937, 974, 1081, 1201, 1218
   (2), 1669, 1866, 1916, 2056, 2384, 2502,
     2654, 2698, 2707, 2738, 2787
LA VALÉE, Joseph (1790)   1709
LABELLIÈRE, P. (1789)   2600
LABOUCHERE, Henry (1871)   627
LACEY, William (1639)   1284
LACY, John (1707-1713)   546, 998
LACY, Katherine (N.D.)   1173
LAFFAN, May (1876-1879)   935, 1169,
     1176
LAHEE, M. R. (1860)   2593
LAING, Alexander (1827-1846)   169,
     255, 419, 2074, 2402
LAING, David (1821-1852)   996, 1757,
     1946, 2464
LAING, David, LL.D. (1833-1858)   268,
     331, 1840
LAING, Malcolm (1804)   1124
LAING, Robert (1726)   905
LAIRD, Lieut. Francis C., R.N.
   (1822-1824)   1313, 2825
LAKE, ——, D.D. (1811)   1364
LAKE, J., (1677, 1687)   416, 2840
LALLY-TOLLENDALL, Marquis
   de, T. Gerard (1793)   705
LAMB, ——, (1672)   2496
LAMB, Anne R., Mrs Dryden (1844)   304
LAMB, Charles (1796-1831)   739, 1677,
     1827, 2258
LAMB, E. (1860)   2262
LAMB, Hon. W. (1799)   811
LAMB, Lady Caroline (1816, 1823)
     32, 1017, 1037

LAMB, Mary (1809, 1814)   1677, 1959
LAMB, Mrs Joseph (1861-1862)   1183,
     1262, 1939, 2652
LAMBE, Robert (1765)   1133
LAMBE, Thomas (1762)   1528
LAMBE, William (N.D.)   2763
LAMBERT, —— (1774)   1389
LAMBERT, C. E. (1836)   214
LAMBERT, Henry (1851)   1570
LAMPE, John F. (1732)   73
LAMPREYS, S. C. (1834)   266
LANCASTER, J. (1821)   863
LANCASTER, Joseph (1801)   2748
LANCASTER, Nathaniel (1767)   1609
LANCASTER, Rev. T. (1797)   1930
LANCASTER, William P., M.A.
   (1866)   1898
LANDELS, Rev. W. (1857)   2715
LANDON, James, T. B. (1851-1853)
     835 (2), 1042
LANDON, Letitia Elizabeth (1737-
   1838)   238, 719, 832, 930, 937, 956,
   1026, 1217, 2223, 2621, 2659, 2724,
     2778
LANDON, T. B., M.A. (N.D.)   2831
LANDOR, Robert Eyres (1846)   907
LANDOR, Walter Savage (1798-
   1859)   405, 439, 994, 1080, 1883, 1949,
     1959, 2386
LANE, Bartholomew (1684)   159
LANE, John (1648)   61
LANE, John (1603)   734
LANE, Richard J. (1855)   2475
LANEY, Benjamin, Bishop of Ely
   (1668)   2351
LANEHAM, Robert (N.D.)   1421
LANG, John (1853)   2606
LANGBAINE, Gerard, D.D. (1638-
   1678)   106, 594, 778, 946, 947, 2023,
     2199, 2678
LANGFORD, Dr (1809)   887
LANGHORNE, John, D.D. (1762-
   1784)   523, 632, 729, 1004, 1447, 1449,
     2729
LANGLAND, Robert (1550)   2771
LANGLAND, Robert, or Longland
   (1814)   1911
LANGLEY, D. B. (1854)   2535
LANGLEY, Rev. Samuel (1777)   994
LANGRISHE, Sir Hercules, Bart.
   (1772, 1783)   212, 2511
LANGTON, Zachary (1753)   792
LANGIUS, John (1669)   2314
LANKESTER, Dr Edwin (1846)   2724

LANSDOWNE, Lord, George Gran-
ville (1696-1722) 282, 1009, 1266, 1353,
2349
LANTAFFE, T. (1816) 859
LARDNER, Nathaniel, D.D. (1753-
1764) 807, 1383, 1422, 1772
LARDNER, Rev. Dionysius, LL.D.
(1833) 2643
LARKEN, Rev. Edmund R., M.A.
(1847) 1617
LARKIN, G. (1711) 2841
LARPENT, Sir George (1823) 2040
LARWOOD, Joshua (1809) 789
LASCELLES, Rowley (1816-1831)
1442, 1444, 2703
LATERRIÈRE, Dr Salles (1830) 1962
LATEY, John Lash (1841) 1453
LATHAM, Henry (1846) 130
LATHY, Thomas P. (1807-1819) 92, 2217
LATOUCHE, James De (1727-1760)
93, 953, 2361
LATROBE, Charles Joseph (1837) 2414
LATTA, T. A. (1862) 1830
LATTIN, Patrick (1799) 315
LAUDER, Alexander (1712) 2758
LAUDER, George (1641) 300, 2687
LAUDER, Sir Thomas Dick, Bart.
(1825) 1505
LAUDER, William, M.A. (1754) 1302
LAUGHTON, Rev. William (1841) 2192
LAUNDY, Edwin (1832) 2105
LAUNE, Thomas de (1712) 1207
LAURENCE, —— (1828) 247, Errata,
vol. iv.
LAURENCE, H. (1825) 1507
LAURENCE, James, Chevalier de
Laurence (1810) 1910
LAURENCE, Richard (1821) 2173
LAURENCE, Richard, Archbishop
of Cashel (1823-1829) 2159, 2162
LAURENCE, Roger (1712-1734)
238, 670, 1221, 1674, 2244, 2304, 2524
LAURENCE, Thomas (N.D.) 2727
LAURENCE, Thomas, M.A. (1668) 652
LAURIE, James (1836-1838) 916, 2157
LAURIE, William A., W.S. (1850) 1570
LAVINGTON, George, Bishop of
Exeter (1749, 1755) 774, 1659
LAW, —— (1813) 2309
LAW, E. (1854) 2236
LAW, Elizabeth Susan, Lady Col-
chester   Errata, vol. ii. (2)
LAW, Edmund, D.D., Bishop of
Carlisle (1769-1774) 488, 582, 1769

LAW, Hon. Elizabeth Sophia (1832-
1833) 1015, 1629
LAW, J. (1757) 866
LAW, John (1705) 1652
LAW, Lady E. (1853) 1622
LAW, W. (1754) 382
LAWRENCE, Frederick (1841, 1857)
548, 1251
LAWRENCE, George (1642) 572
LAWRENCE, George Alfred (1863-
1874) 130, 213, 249, 253, 255, 291, 1060,
1561, 1560, 2257, 2385, 2530
LAWRENCE, Herbert (1769) 1462
LAWRENCE, John (1714-1747) 64, 148,
1855
LAWRENCE, Mrs Rose (1828) 1318
LAWRENCE, Richard, LL.D. (1820,
1821) 2161, 2173
LAWRENCE, Roger (1708) 1330
LAWRIE, Robert (1660) 1021
LAWRIE, W. F. B. (1851) 1202
LAWRY, Rev. John (1741-3) 193
LAWSON, John, B.D. (1764-1774) 176,
675, 1797
LAWSON, John Parker, M.A. (1827-
1839) 237, 994, 1122, 1474, 1478, 1480,
1500
LAWSON, Rev. J. (1839) 1883
LAWSON, Thomas (1660) 160
LAWTON, Charlwood (1705, 1706)
407, 2297
LAYTON, Henry (1670-1704) 174, 1787
(3), 1788, 1789, 2285, 2302
L'ESTRANGE, Hammond (1655) 2124
L'ESTRANGE, Joseph (1825) 1934
L'ESTRANGE, Sir Roger (1583-
1760) 21, 38, 120, 153, 155, 157, 324,
345, 406, 448, 490, 529, 618, 1056, 1284,
1329, 1342, 1743, 1792, 1934, 2119 (2),
2149, 2233, 2289, 2304, 2565, 2566, 2603,
2704
LE CHEVALIER, Jean Baptiste
(1829) 2704
LE CLERC, Jean (1690, 1700) 932, 1863
LE COURAYER, Pierre François
(1728) 587
LE FAUCHEUR, Michel (N.D.) 821
LE FREEKE, William (1687) 829
LE GRAND, M. (1786, 1790) 1749, 2544
LE GRICE, Rev. C. P. (1804) 563
LE MESURIER, Thomas, B.D.
(1795-1819) 1412, 1948, 2623
LE NEVE, John (1711, 1716) 902, 1500
LE NOIR, Jean (1678) 1727, 2224

LE VAYER, Sieur de la Nothe (1649) 1459
LEACH, Thomas (1791) 485
LEADBEATER, Mary (1794) 867
LEAHY, David (1845) 2201
LEAKE, John (1733) 2268
LEAKE, Stephen Martin (1626) 1760
LEAKE, W. Martin (1825) 1119
LEANERD, John (1678, 1679) 520, 2077
LEAR, Mrs Sydney (1871) 2319
LEAR, S. H. (1858) 2082
LEASK, William, D.D. (1854) 2508
LEATHES, Mr Stanley (1869) 2414
LEBLICH, Domingo Badia y (1816) 2627
LECAMUS, Antoine (1754) 3
LECHMERE, Edmund, D.D. (1632, 1770) 668, 1945
LECKY, William E. H., M.A. (1861) 1334
LEDWICH, Edward (1771) 139
LEE, Arthur (1764-1775) 159, 795, 1784, 2292, 2469
LEE, Eliza, née Buckminster (1849) 1475
LEE, Francis, M.D. (1690-1718) 480, 1142, 1310, 1588
LEE, Frederick George (1851-1865) 411, 1333
LEE, General Charles (1803) 1436
LEE, Hannah F. (1848) 2586
LEE, Harriet (1786) 789
LEE, Henry A. Dillon, Viscount Dillon (1817-1824) 661, 1468, 2227
LEE, John (1753) 1122
LEE, Mrs George (1839, 1841) 1469 (2)
LEE, P. (1840) 434 (2)
LEE, Principal (1824, 1832) 1278, 1592
LEE, Rachel F. A., Baroness de Despencer (1808, 1828) 4, 797, 2139
LEE, R. E. (1833) 1537
LEE, Robert, D.D. (1844) 1972
LEE, Samuel, M.A. (1659, 1677) 721, 1823
LEE, Sophia (1785, 1787) 1090, 2098
LEE, William (1795, 1846) 87, 494, 2466
LEECH, J. (1845, 1847) 396 (2)
LEEDS, Duke of, F. G. Osborne (1775) 2367
LEES, James Cameron, D.D. (1877-1881) 1531, 2221 (2), 2507
LEFEVRE, Mrs (1808) 867
LEFEVRE, Sir George William, M.D. (1843) 1471

LEGER, Barry St (1824) 2419
LEGGE, Alfred Owen (1876) 1543
LEGH, George, LL.D. (1718, 1719) 312, 1409
LEGH, Gerard (1718) 1356
LEICESTER, C. (1848, 1857) 893, 1537
LEICESTER, Peter (1830) 186, 250, 2550
LEIGH, Chandois (1818, 1832) 1954, 2617
LEIGH, Edward (1652) 1899
LEIGH, John (1861) 2390
LEIGH, P. B. (1827) 1326
LEIGH, Richard (1673, 1675) 347, 1953, 2624
LEIGHLIN, Bishop of Kildare, and James Warren Doyle (1824, 1827) 578, 1356, 1448, 2169, 2763
LEIGHTON, Alexander (1624, 1628) 160, 2467
LEIGHTON, Francis (1769) 1681
LEIGHTON, F. S. (1870) 1532
LEIGHTON, John (1853) 2513
LEISURE, Rob Mart (1764) 2261
LEITCH, Alexander (1857) 378
LEITH, Bishop of, —— Forbes 1765-1767) 809, 1921
LEJANU, Miss (1805) 1508
LEJANU, Rev. Philip, D.D. (1777) 1432
LELAND, Thomas, D.D. (1762-1772) 849, 1509
LEMAISTRE, J. G. (1799, 1803) 958, 2230
LEMNIUS, Levinus (1587) 1085
LEMON, Robert (1830-32) 2489
LEMPRIÈRE, John, D.D. (1818) 2743
LENNOX, Charles, Duke of Richmond (1785) 113
LENNOX, Charlotte, née Ramsay (1747-1758) 910, 1083, 1586, 1897, 1951, 2347
LENNOX, Mr Charles (1760-1) 1312
LENNY, C. (1847) 2348
LEONARD, Daniel (1776) 1556
LEOPOLD, Alexander, Prince of Hohenlohe, Bishop of Sardica (1823) 865
LEOTIUS, Jacobus (1715) 2059
LESLIE, Charles (1692-1714) 107, 121, 206, 218, 226 (2), 238 (2), 259, 316, 317, 323, 324 (2), 326, 363, 578, 659 (2), 672, 684, 792, 836, 924, 991, 1029 (2), 1136,

1147, 1348, 1349, 1557, 1713, 1714, 1758, 1857, 1980, 2011, 2018, 2131 2170, 2210, 2255, 2258, 2308, 2357, 2369, 2409, 2442, 2737, 2791, 2825

LESLIE, Charles (1808)   1373
LESLIE, Charles (1750)   2065
LESLIE, Charles, M.A. (1755)   320
LESLIE, Henry, Bishop of Down and Connor (1639-1649) 779, 1553, 2468
LESLIE, Rev. Charles (1714)   1809
LESLIE, Sir John, W.S. (1818)   478
LETCHWORTH, Thomas (N.D., 1765)   799, 1664
LETI, Gregorio (1667, 1670)   309, 1743
LETSOME, Sampson, M.A. (1734) 1220
LETTSOM, John Coakley, M.D. (1772-1804) 1055, 1099, 1100, 1101 (2), 1102, 1702, 2109, 2110
LETTSOM, W. Nanson (1856)   2448
LEVER, Charles James (1837-1864) 186, 366, 473 (2), 514, 626, 1560, 2390
LEVERSON, Major H. A. (1860-1871)   748, 941, 1193, 2844, Errata, vol. iv.
LEVESON, Gower, Lord Francis (1830)   2786
LEVESQUE DE POUILLY, Louis J. (1749)   2564
LEWES, George Henry (1847)   2078
LEWGAR, John (1662)   788
LEWIN, Ross (1834)   1471
LEWIS, David, M.A. (1842)   2023
LEWIS, E. (1730)   2093
LEWIS, Estella A. (1875)   2258
LEWIS, George (1834)   2274
LEWIS, Harold (1876)   402
LEWIS, James, D.D. (1830)   580
LEWIS, John (1717, 1755) 53, 914, 1127, 2324
LEWIS, John, D.D. (N.D.)   2764
LEWIS, John Delaware (1849, 1851) 30, 2402
LEWIS, John, M.A. (1716)   2142
LEWIS, Lady Theresa (1859)   2321
LEWIS, Matthew Gregory (1796-1878)   1652, 2451, 2542, 2739
LEWIS, M. G. (1825, 1850)   73, 1267
LEWIS, Rev. George (1834)   732
LEWIS, Rev. John (1721, 1740)   674, 2288
LEWIS, Sir George Cornwall (1828-1839)   1019, 1088, 2053
LEWIS, Thomas (1709-1726)   86, 403, 413, 561, 1378, 1648, 2029

LEWIS Thomas, M.A. (1817)   2278
LEWIS, Thomas, M.A. (1720)   761
LEWIS, William, M.D. (N.D.)   126
LEWKENOR, John (1693)   1608
LEWKENOR, Lewes (1594)   2186
LEWTHWAITE, George, M.A. (1865)   2386
LEY, John (1641, 1653)   642, 853
LEYBOURN, William (1685)   604
LEYDEN, John (1799)   1112
LICHFIELD, Bishop of, John Lonsdale (1824)   2419
LICHFIELD, Dean of, J. C. Woodhouse (1818)   2353
LICHFIELD, Dean of, Launcelot Addison, D.D. (1677-1697) 388, 1009, 1107, 1647
LICHFIELD, Dean of, William Binckes, D.D. (1701-1702)   858, 1994
LIEBERKAUN, —— (1771)   31
LIGHTBODIE, George (1638)   55
LILBURNE, John (1645-1650) 598, 749, 1186, 1928, 2303, 2700, 2708
LILLO, George (1731)   2386
LILLY, John (1591-1632) 991, 1562, 1669, 2258
LILLY, William (1676)   2425
LIMERICK, Bishop of, John Jebb, D.D. (1824-1828)   308, 1983
LIN, Thomas (N.D.)   2528
LIN, Thomas, Junr. (1711)   971
LINCOLN, Archdeacon of, J. Gordon, D.D. (1769)   1797
LINCOLN, Bishop of, C. Wordsworth (1862)   1172
LINCOLN, Bishop of, John Green, D.D. (1741-1761) 10, 192, 483, 2015 (2)
LINCOLN, Bishop of, R. Sanderson, D.D. (1647-1670)   32, 2094
LINCOLN, Bishop of, Thomas Barlow, D.D. (1680-1682)   645, 1988, 2214
LIND, —— (1776)   121
LIND, Dr (1778)   1416
LIND, James, M.D. (1757-1769)   827, 2588
LIND, John, M.D. (1773, 1775)   1424, 2152
LIND, John, F.R.S. (1776)   2588
LINDESAY, P., Lord Provost of Edinburgh (1733)   1241
LINDLEY, Benjamin (1700, 1708)   348, 2634
LINDLEY, J. (1827)   2724

LINDSAY, Coiin, Earl of Balcarres
(1714)   17
LINDSAY, G (1737)   2432
LINDSAY, John (1716, 1759) 1039, 1069,
2367, 2369
LINDSAY, Lord (1838)   1945
LINDSAY, Patrick (1735)   2090
LINDSAY, Theophilus, M.A. (1785-
1813)   195, 246, 848
LINELF, William (1843)   287
LINFIELD, Thomas (1718)   112
LINFORD, Thomas, D.D. (1687,
1688)   1753, 2423
LING, Nicholas (1597, 1598)   175, 1962
LINGARD, John, D.D. (1807-1836) 845,
1365, 1733, 1779, 2136 (2), 2154, 2194
LINNING, Thomas (N.D.)   1348
LINTON, Anthonie (1609)   1738
LINTON, E. Lynn (1872)   2670
LIPPINCOTT, Mrs (1853)   1143
LISLE, William (1603, 1628)   1756, 2770
LISTER, Hon. Harriet Cradock née
(1860)   1186
LISTER, John (1870)   777
LISTER, Thomas Henry (1826-1834)
101, 177, 777, 1039, 1085
LISTER, Thomas, LL.D. (1797)   1622
LITTLEJOHN, P. (1791, 1793)   556,
1083
LITTLETON, Adam (1662, 1682)
2193, 2415
LITTLETON, Edward, M.A. (1689,
1691)   1054, 1540, 1792, 2029
LITTON, Edmund (1747)   1900
LIVE D'EPINAY, Madame de la
(1815)   507
LIVERPOOL, Earl of, C. Jenkinson
(1757-1801), 657, 658, 2197, 2487, 2752
LIVINGSTON, Edward (1827)   943
LIVINGSTON, Michael (1680, 1682)
62, 1874
LIVINGSTON, William (1757)   2201
LIZARS, D. (1831)   725
LLANDAFF, Bishop of, J. Harris,
D.D. (1715)   2648
LLANDAFF, Bishop of, Rev. Edward
Copleston, D.D. (1803-1819)   53, 852,
1414, 2175, 2302, 2308, 2353, 2570
LLANOS, Valentin (1825, 1826)   698,
2257   Errata, vol iv.
LLEWELLIN, Edward (1650)   684
LLEWELLYN, Martin (1646, 1672)
1597, 2813
LLOYD, —— (N.D.)   1086

LLOYD, Albany Rossendale (1873)   399
LLOYD, Charles (1764-1767)   468, 540,
590, 850, 1174, 2148, 2669
LLOYD, Charles, LL.D. (1812-1814)
785, 1437, 1775, 1866, 2626
LLOYD, Charles, Bishop of Oxford
(1825)   943
LLOYD, David (1664)   295
LLOYD, David, D.D. (1648)   1338
LLYOD, David, M.A. (1822)   2829
LLYOD, Dr William, Dean of Bangor
(1676)   1456
LLOYD, Evan (1766)   1982
LLOYD, Lodowick (1610)   1824
LLOYD, née Charlotte Rees (1808,
1811)   42, 561
LLOYD, Robert (1760-1761)   31, 167,
2347
LLOYD, Thomas (1779)   812
LLOYD, William, Bishop of St
Asaph (1667-1677)   490, 1512
LLOYD, William, D.D. (1679-1691)
120, 1379, 1853
LLOYD, William, D.D., Bishop of
Worcester (1667-1692) 630, 1320, 2006,
2086, 2288
LLWYD, Richard (1800)   218
LOARTES, Gasper, D.D. (1582)   927
LOBB, Richard (1800)   497
LOBB, Stephen (1685-1698)   987, 1056,
2179, 2667, 2754
LOBB, Theophilus, M.D. (1750, 1757)
119, 2245
LOBO, Jeronymo (1669)   2373
LOCKE, D. R. (1865)   1699
LOCKE, John (1675-1708)   54, 172,
441, 795, 984, 1145, 1345, 1354, 1858 (5),
2084, 2087, 2297, 2310, 2372, 2421, 2567
2702, 2762
LOCKER, J. (1734, 1736)   1423, 1827
LOCKHART, George (1714)   1576
LOCKHART, John Gibson (1819-
1852)   1141, 1143, 1892, 2123, 2434,
2453, 2560, 2720
LOCKHART, Laurence, D.D. (1845,
1846)   124, 875
LOCKWOOD, Rev. Richard (1816) 2095
LOCKYER, Nicholas, M.A. (1670)   2442
LODDINGTON, William (1674)   2060
LODDINGTON, William (1764)   2687
LODEVE, Guill., E. J. G. de Clermont
(1802)   1165
LODGE, A. (1845)   570
LODGE, Edmund (1810)   1480

LODGE, John (1770)   2717
LODGE, Thomas, M.D. (1590-1602)
     337, 682, 835, 922, 1467, 1856, 2227
LODGE, William (1679)   1845
LODOWYCK, Francis, F.R.S.(1647) 443
LOFFT, Capel (1776-1812) 141, 258, 265,
     895, 2211, 2736, 2765
LOFFT, Captain (1785, 1837)   807, 2320
LOGAN, —— (1726)   523
LOGAN, Allan (1712-1730)   766, 1707,
     1764, 2068
LOGAN, David (1844)   1782, 2831
LOGAN, Eliza (1823-1829)   2187, 2251
LOGAN, George, A.M. (1732-1737)
     24, 109, 501, 1188, 1326, 1644, 2055
LOGAN, John (1788)   2201, 2731
LOGAN, Rev. John (1783, 1787)   676
     2240
LOGAN, William (1721)   1376
LOGAN, William Hugh (1834-1841)
     214, 420, 726, 954, 1185, 1349, 1569,
     Errata, vol. iv.
LOGIE, William (1844)   397
LOHNE, John Lewis de (1807)   1435
LOHNE, John Louis de (1772)   1857
LOK, Henry (1597)   722
LONDON, Archdeacon of, W. Hale,
   M.A. (1854)   2417
LONDON, Bishop of, Beilby Porteous
   (1799-1808)   259, 2329
LONDON, Bishop of, C. J. Blom-
   field (1826)   2167
LONDON, Bishop of, Edmund Gib-
   son, D.D. (1701-1738) 26, 311, 342, 451
   (2), 454, 668, 889, 1050, 1166, 1171, 1368,
   1478 (2), 1549, 1790, 1857, 2006, 2007,
   2116, 2145, 2211, 2265, 2327, 2375, 2516,
     2532
LONDON, Bishop of, Henry Comp-
   ton (1667)   1473
LONDON, Bishop of, John King,
   D.D. (1611)   2335
LONDON, Bishop of, J. Randolph,
   D.D. (1807)   414
LONDON, Bishop of, J. Williams
   (1673)   1172
LONDON, Bishop of, Robert Lowth
   (1762)   2371
LONG, —— (1803)   1920
LONG, Charles Edward (1825-1830)
     484, 1709
LONG, Charles, M.P. (1800)   2549
LONG, Edward (1757, 1778)   136, 306,
     757, 1140, 2322, 2651

LONG, George, A.M. (1832)   1461
LONG, Henry Lawes (1836)   1788
LONG, Professor (1830)   1067
LONG, Roger, D.D. (1731)   2213
LONG, Thomas, B.D. (1680-1690)
     499, 980, 1077, 1104, 1745, 1748, 2112,
     2185, 2715, 2778
LONGFELLOW, Henry Wadsworth
   (1847)   832
LONGLAND, Robert Langland or
   (1814)   1911
LONGLANDS, Miss (1857)   1320
LONGMUIR, John, D.D. (1825)   431
LONGMUIR, John, LL.D. (1869,
   1870)   2502, 2792
LONGUERNE, Abbé de, Louis
   Dufour (1687)   1123, 2649
LONSDALE, John, Bishop of Lich-
   field (1824)   2419
LORD, E. (1841)   665
LORDAN, C. J. (1844)   432
LORIMER, John Gordon, D.D. (1833)
     396, 2293
LORIMER, William (1694, 1713)   153,
     2337
LORNE, Marquis of, G. D. Campbell
   (1842)   1402
LOTHIAN, —— (1771)   1932
LOTHIAN, Marquis of, William S.
   R. Kerr (1863)   953
LOTHIAN, Maurice (1834)   858
LOUDON, Jane Webb (1827)   243
LOUDON, J. C., née Webb (1811-
   1829)   25, 1052, 1678, 2496, 2542
LOUDON, John (1750-1808)   1208, 2266
LOUDON, Margaret (1830)   928
LOUDON, Margracia (1832, 1833)
     633, 945
LOUGHBOROUGH, Lord, A.
   Wedderburn (1805)   1437
LOUISA, Augusta, Lady Lyons
   (1848, 1853)   1520, 1816, 2391
LOUVEL, Rob. Mart. (1764)   2261
LOVE, Benjamin (1839)   1541
LOVE, Christopher (1642)   572
LOVE, James (1740-1742)   533, 1847
LOVE, James (1767)   2739
LOVE, John (1749)   2746
LOVE, John, jun. (1704)   1282
LOVELACE, Earl of, William King
   (1848)   2197, 2203
LOVELING, William (1741)   1323
LOVELL —— (1686)   1854
LOVELL, G. W. (1836, 1841) 2049, 2679

LOVER, Samuel (1859)   2217
LOWE, Helen (1844-1864)   2546, 2715, 2851
LOWE, Right Hon. Robert (N.D.)   1943
LOWE, Robert (1841)   186
LOWE, Robert W. (1881)   2810
LOWE, Solomon (1716, 1729)   135, 2041, 2745
LOWELL, J. (1808)   666
LOWELL, James Russell (1848)   1567
LOWELL, John (1813)   1887
LOWELL, J. R. (1748)   281
LOWMAN, Moses (1716-1733)   171, 174, 317, 428, 595, 1795, 2016
LOWNDES, William (1695)   988
LOWRIE, —— (1833)   2811
LOWTH, Robert, Bishop of London (1762)   2371
LOWTH, Robert, D.D. (1729, 1766)   996, 1416
LOWTH, Simon (1696-1713)   731, 1114(2)
LOWTHER, G. (1840)   1556
LOUVEL, Rob. Mart. (1764)   2261
LUCAS, Charles (1796, 1798)   327, 964
LUCAS, Henry (1777)   2548
LUCAS, Mrs Martin (1848)   2629
LUCAS, Richard, D.D. (1685-1705)   383, 765, 1187, 1924, 1983
LUCAS, Samuel (1859-1864)   237, 557, 743, 1664
LUCAS, William (1750)   933
LUCKOMBE, Philip (1780)   2612
LUCY, Henry (1874)   1597
LUCY, William, Bishop of St Davids (1657)   1768
LUDKIN, Dr (1694)   2428
LUDLAM, George (1817)   1689
LUKE, —— (1548)   1269
LUKE, S. (1851, 1859)   286, 910
LUKIN, Rev. James (N.D., 1871)   1323 2849, Errata, vol. iv.
LUKIN, Robert (1822)   2642
LUMISDEN, Charles (1600)   864
LUND, —— (1710)   2239
LUND, John (1788)   707
LUNN, Arthur Wallbridge (1842, 1848)   239, 517, 2608
LUNN, James (1790)   824
LUPTON, Donald (1637, 1640)   1018, 1161
LUSHINGTON, C. R. (1847)   1987
LUSHINGTON, R. (1659)   2188
LUSHINGTON, Thomas (1646, 1650)   860, 1295

LUSIGNAN, S. (1783)   1165
LUTHER, Charles W., M.D. (1845)   466
LUTTRELL, Henry (1819-1827)   53, 531, 542, 1490
LUX, William (1719)   1951
LYALL, Alfred (1830, 1856)   30, 2201
LYALL, William, LL.D. (1842)   2506
LYDE, Gulielmus Joyner, alias (1686)   2433
LYDE, William (1686)   1790
LYDEOTT, E. (1684)   2025
LYDGATE, John (1510)   527
LYLLY, John (1589, 1591)   304, 1854
LYMAN, Theodore (1826)   635
LYNCH, Thomas T. (1856)   833, 2450
LYNE, Joseph Leycester (N.D., 1870)   337, 1171, 1203, 1561
LYNFORD, Thomas, M.A. (1687)   1743
LYNN, E. (1847)   206
LYNTON, Anthonie (1609)   1738
LYON, George (1821)   2516
LYON, Rev. John (1787)   266
LYON, Robert (1734)   1409
LYON, Sir James Balfour (1706)   1162
LYONS, Lady Augusta Louisa (1848-1853)   1520, 1816, 2391
LYONS, Robert D., M.D. (1856)   2179
LYTTELTON, George, Lord Lyttelton (1728-1772)   34, 240, 491, 623, 898, 949, 1136, 1426, 1718, 1776, 1780, 1889, 2028, 2600
LYTTELTON, Henry, Lord Lyttelton (1803)   2654
LYTTELTON, Thomas, Lord Lyttelton (1780)   1437, 1946
LYTTLETON, Hon. W. H., Lord Lyttleton (1836)   16
LYTTON, Edward Robert Bulwer (1859-1863)   1523, 2216, 2325, 2546, 2787
LYTTON, E. G. E. Lytton Bulwer, Lord Lytton (1826-1871)   243, 420, 436, 534, 613, 666 (2), 707 (2), 833, 884, 1022, 1072, 1313, 1319, 1524, 1732, 1740, 1818, 1875, 1881, 1914, 2208, 2212, 2253, 2284, 2799, 2805, 2836

M.

MACARDY, Joseph (1842)   2244
M'ARTHUR, John (1801)   924
MACARTHUR, Samuel (1780)   708
MACARTNEY, Sir George, Earl Macartney (1773)   15
MACAULAY, Auley, M.A. (1780)   829

MACAULAY, Catherine (1767-1790)
1511, 1784
MACAULAY, Dr (1831)   1183
MACAULAY, John (1780)   2705
MACAULAY, Zachary (1823) 719, 1420
MACBRIDE, John (1697, 1713) 96, 2256,
2745
MACBRIDE, John David, D.C.L.
(1824-1837)   627, 1335
MACCARTHY, D. C. (1858)   1906
M'CARTHY, Denis Florence (1848)
1295, Errata, vol. iv.
M'CARTHY, Justin (1866-1867)   1876,
2794
M'CAUL, Alexander, D.D. (1845)   1263
M'CHEYNE, Rev. Robert Murray
(1843)   1693
M'CLATCHIE, Patrick Miller (1823) 702
M'CLELLAN, James Crighton (1852)
2806
MACCLESFIELD, Earl of, Lord
Polwarth (1744)   2718
M'COMBIE, William (1838)   376
M'CONECHY, James (1821)   764
MACCORMAC. Dr (1870)   2276
MACCORMICK, C. (1792)   2312
M'COSH, J., M.D. (1872)   1760
M'COSH, Principal James, D.D.
(1847)   2653
M'CRIE, Thomas, D.D. (1798-1827) 506,
964, 1530, 2567, 2759, 2765. 2805
MACCULLOCH, —— (1823)   608
M'CULLOCH, David (1876)   564
M'CULLOCH, James M., D.D. (1828)
2680
M'CULLOCH, James Ramsay (1831-
1855)   1121, 1768, 1777, 1779, 2399,
2490
M'DIARMID, John (1822)   1432
MACDONALD, Andrew (1782-1784)
1219, 2724
MACDONALD, George (1851)   1945
MACDONALD, John H. A. (1877) 1835
MACDONALD, Thomas (1788)   2200
M'DONALD, W. Bell (1842)   906
M'DONNEL, —— (1812)   1783
M'DONOUGH, Captain Felix (1819-
1826)   1089 (4), 1092, 1097
M'DOUGALL, Henry (1799)   2403
M'DOWAL, Charles (1835)   2820
M'DOWALL, Andrew, Lord Bank-
ton (1747)   818
M'DUFF, John Ross, D.D. (1841-
1874)   72, 251, 374, 405, 417, 837, 857,

883, 890, 939, 994, 1026, 1043, 1047,
1485, 1495, 1597, 1617, 1664, 1741, 1941,
2499 (2), 2576, 2615, 2801, 2837
MACFAITE, Ebenezer (1760)   2151
MACFARLANE, Charles (1844-1845)
303, 711, 1339
MACFARLANE, Mr (1831)   2392
M'FIE, Mrs (1836)   2495
MACFARLANE, William (1856)   713
M'GAURAN, —— (1844-1852)   239,
1024, 1529, 2786, 2816
M'GAVIN, James Reid (1852)   2249
M'GAVIN, William (1831)   267
MACGEORGE, Andrew (1870-1875)
114, 400 (2), 831, 961, 2037, 2477, 2490
M'GHEE, Robert J. (1833)   1302, 1926
M'GIBBON, Alexander (1809)   125
M'GILCHRIST, John, M.D. (1852)   367
M'GILL, Jacob W. (1861)   1817
M'GILL, John (1866)   229, 688
MACGILL, R., M.A. (1815)   2073
MACGILL, Sir John D. II., Bart.
(1778)   2114
MACGOWAN, J. (1852-1854)   200, 936
MACGOWAN, J. (1803)   1476
MACGOWAN, John (1761-1788)   175,
888, 987, 2008, 2333
MACGOWAN, Rev. John (1772)   1223
MACGREGOR, Alexander (1856)   2319
M'GREGOR, J. (1834)   2386
MACGREGOR, John (1855)   1030
M'GRUGAR, Thomas (1783)   1444
MACHALE, John, D.D. (1821, 1822)
1432, 2439
MACKARNESS, Matilda Anne
(1845-1870)   79, 371, 416, 418, 852,
1026, 1042, 1497, 1605, 1618, 1716, 1811,
2081, 2325, 2381, 2483, 2503, 2518, 2592,
2624
MACKARNESS, John Fielder, M.A.,
Bishop of Oxford (1847, 1878) 920, 2393
MACKAY, Andrew (1805)   190
MACKAY, Charles, LL.D. (1841)   1509
MACKAY, Francis Alexander (1853,
1857)   543, 552
MACKAY, James (1860)   975
MACKEN, John (1818, 1821) 1072, 1333
MACKENNA, Theobald (1800, 1801)
171, 1345
MACKENZIE, Alexander (1790)   2735
MACKENZIE, Anne (1857)   2315
MACKENZIE, Anne Maria (1791)   563
MACKENZIE, Captain A. S. (1834-
1836)   74, 2284, 2460, 2846

MACKENZIE, Colin (1818, 1825) 1756, 2547

MACKENZIE, E. (1816) 24

MACKENZIE, George (1824) 258

MACKENZIE, George, Earl of Cromarty (1695-1712) 9, 34, 291, 500, 914, 1356, 1372, 1635, 1856, 2279, 2344, 2532, 2652

MACKENZIE, Georgiana Muir (1865) 1755

MACKENZIE, George, Viscount Tarbat (1689) 1592

MACKENZIE, Henry (1771-1793) 1287, 1331, 1432, 1539, 1540, 1948, 2013, 2058

MACKENZIE, James (1734-1812) 824, 827, 2631

MACKENZIE, J. W. (1829) 996

MACKENZIE, Lieut. J. (1786) 1217, 2831

MACKENZIE, Mary Jane (1820-1829) 1011, 1335 (2), 2022

M'KENZIE, Peter (1816) 1035

M'KENZIE, Rev. Donald (1812) 1318

MACKENZIE, Sir George (1660-1710) 170, 1592, 1657, 2129, 2472, 2744

MACKENZIE, Sir George, Earl of Cromarty (1829) 996

MACKENZIE, Sir G. Stewart, Bart. (1815) 1420

MACKENZIE, William (1810, 1868) 2059, 2455

M'KIE, James (1874) 292

MACKINNON, Charles (1865) 2059

MACKINNON, William A. (1828) 2217

MACKLIN, Charles (1746) 1383

MACKNIGHT, Thomas (1854, 1855) 2210, 2571

MACKWORTH, Sir Digby (1823) 626

MACKWORTH, Sir Humphrey (1704-1720) 259, 702, 1351, 1678, 2035

MACKY, John (1723, 1724) 1280 (2)

M'INTOSH, Hugh, M.A. (N.D.) 2689

MACINTOSH, Lachlan (1814) 1773

MACINTOSH, William (1724-1782) 806, 814, 2626, 2631

M'IVOR, Daniel (1857) 2787

M'LAGGAN, Alexander (1737) 1349

MACLAGAN, David (1869) 2219

MACLAGAN, Douglas, M.D. (1850) 1758

M'LAGAN, James, D.D. (1829) 38

MACLAREN, Archibald (1857) 878

MACLAREN, Charles (1825, 1830) 2075, 2276

MACLAREN, John (1844) 610

MACLAREN, Miss (1869-1873) 706, 2592, 2716

M'LAREN, William (1815) 1482

M'LAUCHLAN, Thomas, D.D. (1849) 603

MACLAURIN, —— (1754) 1231, Errata, vol. iv.

MACLAURIN, Colin (1801) 1947

MACLAURIN, Colin, Lord Dreghorn (1816) 2452

MACLAURIN, John (1747) 1373

MACLAURIN, John (1754) 1703

MACLAURIN, John (1753) 2554

MACLAURIN, John, Lord Dreghorn (1757-1769) 154, 485, 488, 825, 1298, 1774, 1899

MACLAURIN, John, M.A. (1753) 1516

MACLEAN, Alexander Walker (1835) 34

M'LEAN, Charles (1879) 710

M'LEAN, ——, D.D. (1800) 408

MACLEAN, Lachlan (1838) 1112

M'LEAN, Mrs (1824, 1825) 1217, 2659

MACLEAN, Rev. Archibald (1797) 2579

MACLEANE, Laughlin (1777) 1437

MACLEAR, Thomas, F.R.A.S. (1837) 2853

MACLELLAN, Francis (1835, 1836) 838, 2403

M'LELLAND, George (1842) 765

MACLENNAN, J. C. (1860) 2276

M'LENNAN, Malcolm (1869, 1871) 225, 1879

M'LEOD, —— (1763) 2646

MACLEOD, —— (1832) 1011

MACLEOD, A. (1841) 2708

MACLEOD, Malcolm (1866) 1984

MACLEOD, Norman, D.D. (1862-1866) 229, 529, 1811, 2293, 2567

MACLEOD, William (1879) 1491

MACMAHON, Joseph P. (1782) 1860

M'MAIN, John (1727) 2194

MACMICHAEL, William (1830) 1500

MACMICHAEL, William, M.D. (1827) 1024

MACMULLEN, John (1846) 303

MACNALLY, Leonard (1776-1788) 156, 535, 1091

M'NAUGHTON, J. (1826) 2109

M'NEIL, —— (1804) 2695

M'NEILL, Alexander (1816) 1035

M'NEILL, Archibald, W.S. (1868) 1755

MACNEIL, Hector (1796-1811) 294, 1587 (2), 1968, 2615, 2783

M'NEILE, Rev. H. (1828-9)   624
MACNISH, Robert (1834)   245
M'NEILL, Sir John (1836)   2028
M'NICOLL, Thomas (1852)   2809
MACONOCHIE, Alexander (1845) 1572
MACONOCHIE, Allan, Lord Mea-
    dowbank (1814)   484
MACPHERSON, James (1758-1779)
                955, 1097, 2213, 2369
MACPHERSON, James, M.D.
    (1779)   1130
MACPHERSON, Mrs Brewster
    (1870-1878)   1014, 1854
MACQUEEN, Daniel, D.D. (1748-
    1756)   1445, 1772
MACQUER, Prof. Pierre J. (1771) 628
MACQUIN, Abbé Ange-Denis (1820)
                                       2535
MACQUOID, Katherine S. (1873) 1910,
                                       2606
MACRAE, David (1798, 1799)   1242,
                                       2204
MACRAY, John (1827, 1870) 2367, 2503
MACRAY, William Dunn, M.A.
    (1850)   331 (2)
MACSWEENY, Joseph, M.D. (1824)
                                        795
MACSWINEY, Owen (1706)   303
M'TAGGART, Mrs (1830)   1578
M'VICAR, —— (1840) 339, Errata, vol. iv.
MACVICAR, Anne Grant née (1809-
    1811)   829, 1430, 1579
M'WARD, Robert (1671-1681) 210, 317,
                           755, 1970, 2672
MABBE, James (1630-1640)   855, 2221,
                                       2460
MABERLEY, Joseph (1844)   2019
MACE, William (1729)   1731
MADAN, Spencer, M.A. (N.D.)   2014
MADAN, Rev. Martin (1780, 1785)
                                2560, 2577
MADDEN, D. Owen (1843, 1844) 1214,
                                       1250
MADDEN, J. (1737)   1593
MADDEN, Samuel, D.D. (1729-1738)
                        1590, 2106, 2560
MADDEN, Sir Frederick (1836)   63
MADDISON, Ralph (1640)   751
MADOX, Isaac, D.D. (1733, 1734)   313,
                                       2755
MAGEE, William (1837)   661
MAGENS, Magens Dorrien (1798) 2583
MAGINN, William, LL.D. (1827-
    1829)   1616, 2103, 2541, 2810

MAGNALL, Miss (1802)   1112
MAHON, Captain (1865, 1868) 1066, 2649
MAHON, Lord Viscount (1834)   1430
MAHONY, Francis (1836)   2132
MAHONY, Francis Sylvester (1847) 874
MAHONY, M. F. (1872)   1251
MAIDMENT, James (1828-1859)   8, 80,
    175, 210, 1059, 1117, 1185, 1715, 1750,
      1759, 1956, 2022, 2132, 2232, 2550
MAIN, —— (1809)   2493
MAINE, —— (1809)   2493
MAINE, Jasper, D.D. (1639-1648) 77,
                        407, 630, 2332
MAINWARING, John, B.D. (1760-
    1798)   1588, 2153
MAIR, E. H. (1877)   2100
MAIR, Thomas (1747)   2792
MAISEAUX, Pierre des (1719, 1723)
                            1110, 2527
MAISTRE, Le (1799)   958
MAITLAND, —— (1832)   2652
MAITLAND, Agnes C. (1875, 1876)
                             742, 2826
MAITLAND, Edward (1868-1872)
                      1097, 1267, 1913
MAITLAND, Henry (1876)   2099
MAITLAND, John (N.D.)   1964
MAITLAND, Julia Charlotte (1843-
    1854)   328, 1113, 1428
MAITLAND, Samuel Roffey, D.D.
    (1817-1835)   677, 790, 2622, 2777
MAJOR, John (N.D.)   2080
MALARD, Michael (1718)   968
MALCOLM, Mr —— (1831)   2392
MALCOLM, Sir John (1814, 1827)
                           1889, 2404
MALCOLME, David, D.D. (1738)   802
MALCOLME, John, M.A. (1721-22)
                                       1661
MALDEN, Henry (1769)   15
MALESON, Col. George Bruce
                          Errata, vol. iv.
MALET, —— (1839)   330
MALING, E. A. (1862)   937, 1035
MALKIN, A. T. (1829, 1831) 1119, 1138
MALL, Thomas, M.A. (1665)   418
MALLET, David (1728-1763) 64, 79, 280,
                728, 742, 836, 854, 2725
MALLET, Mrs Celisia née (1771-1772)
                               69, 1221
MALLOCK, William Hurrell (1872) 839
MALLORY, John (1734)   1640
MALMSBURY, 1st Earl of, James
    Harris (1788)   1245

MALMESBURY, Earl of, James Howard (1837) 2177
MALONE, —— (1770) 2181
MALONE, Edmund (1780-1810) 236, 553, 2523, Errata, vol. iv.
MALTBY, Edward, Bishop of Durham (1809) 2112
MALTBY, William (1856) 2100
MALTHUS, Daniel (1779-1789) 799, 1875, 2455
MALTHUS, Rev. T. R. (1798, 1800) 810, 1247
MAN, Henry (1775) 416, 1672
MAN, James (1753) 347
MAN, Thomas (1662) 2101
MANBY, George William (1806) 1117
MANCHESTER, Duke of, G. Montague (1854) 357
MANDEVILLE, Bernard de (1702-1732) 771, 871, 964, 1377, 1632, 2423, 2766
MANDEVILLE, Lord (1828-9) 624
MANERICK, R. (1596) 2252
MANFIELD, Charles (1790) 1242
MANGIN, Arthur (1868) 1689
MANGIN, Rev. Edward, M.A. (1805-1833) 828, 1011, 1388, 1419, 1480, 1486, 1800, 1916, 2720
MANGIN, W. (1833) 1916
MANLEY, Mrs de la Riviere (1707-1733) 70, 526 (2), 1581, 2313
MANLEY, Thomas (1661) 2377
MANN, Emily (N.D.) 2548
MANN, Henry (1776-7) 2654
MANN, James (1817) 1531
MANN, Nicholas (1747) 540
MANNERS, John Henry, Duke of Rutland (1805-1822) 1276 (3), 2612
MANNERS, Lord John (1841) 2804
MANNING, —— (1781) 430
MANNING, Anne (1850-1874) 51, 221, 225, 369, 390, 391, 432, 461, 517, 566, 572, 625, 705, 707, 756, 890, 1029, 1081, 1098, 1183, 1242, 1259, 1261, 1312, 1313, 1488, 1501, 1512, 1536, 1555, 1561, 1633, 1653, 1747, 1808, 1818, 1974, 2048, 2243, 2321, 2416, 2460, 2499, 2546, 2614, 2719, 2738, 2799, 2846
MANNING, Charles Robert, M.A. (1858) 307
MANNING, Edward (1665) 190
MANNING, Emily, Mrs Heron née (1877) 209
MANNING, Francis (1703) 67

MANNING, Henry E., D.D. (1844, 1855) 630, 1170
MANNING, Owen (1754-1774) 489, 1229, 2485
MANNING, Professor Robert (1731) 2216
MANNING, Robert (1716-1725) 750, 1639, 1920, 2120, 2380
MANNING, Samuel, D.D. (N.D. 1870) 1256, 2462
MANNINGHAM, Thomas, Bishop of Chichester (1685) 2378
MANNINGHAM, Thomas, D.D. (1721) 1361
MANNINGS, John S. (1806) 543
MANNINGTON, A. (1863) 939
MANNOCK, Rev. John (1752) 1970
MANSEL, Henry L. (1852) 2263
MANSFIELD, Earl of, W. Murray (N.D. 1722) 1009, 2572
MANSFIELD, Robert B. (1852-1870) 1505, 2270, 2793
MANT, Richard, D.D., Bishop of Down and Connor (1808-1830) 1407, 2058, 2301
MANT, Walter Bishop, M.A. (1831) 966
MANTI, Thomas (1781-1782) 1523, 2382
MANUCHE, Cosmo (1652) 214
MANWARING, —— (N.D.) 2731
MAPLETOFT, Rev. John, D.D. (1707, 1714) 2317, 2820
MARANA, John Paul (1770) 1453
MARAT, J. P. (1772-1776) 354, 806, 1901
MARBECK, John (1550) 249
MARBURY, Edward (1652) 437
MARCET, Jane (1816-1833) 507 (3), 508, 1270
MARCH, —— (1833) 1272
MARCHE, Oliver de la (1594) 2186
MARCHMONT, Earl, H. H. Campbell (1739) 2488
MARCHMONT, Earl of, Hugh Hume (1740) 2331
MARCUS, Moses (1731) 123
MARCY, John N. (N.D.) 1326
MARDELEY, John (N.D.) 576
MARGOLIOUTH, M. (1856) 94
MARGRAVINE OF ANSPACH, Lady Craven (1778-1802) 901, 1617, 1639, 1939, 2406, 2414, 2451
MARISHALL, Jean (1767) 1132
MARJORIBANKS, Alex. (1830) 1381
MARJORIBANKS, Capt. John (1792) 2406

MARKBY, Thomas (1852)　2690
MARKET, Harborough　1234
MARKHAM, Gervase (1595-1635)　175,
　1005, 1077, 1169, 1175, 1233, 1667, 1940,
　1942, 2292, 2307, 2456 (2), 2779, 2850
MARKHAM, Jervis (1600)　2548
MARKLAND, James H., D.C.L.
　(1845)　2192
MARKS, Richard (1816-1848)　837, 1663,
　1704, 1799, 1916, 2072, 2189, 2739
MARLOWE, Christopher (1605-
　1631)　68, 777, 2545, 2620
MARMION, Shackerley (1666)　548
MARNIX, Philip de (1636)　220
MARRIOTT, Charles, B.D. (1835)　1561
MARRIOTT, Charles, M.A. (1852)　2361
MARRIOTT, George W., B.C.L.
　(1812)　2603
MARRIOTT, John (1623)　351
MARRIOTT, Sir James (1759-1762)
　171, 1394, 1953, 1964
MARRYATT, Thomas, D.D. (1790) 1904
MARRYAT, Captain Frederick
　(1829-1836)　1259, 1262, 1306, 1704,
　1739, 1843, 1893, 2080
MARRYATT, Joseph (1816)　2578
MARSAM, Dame Dameris (1705)　1797
MARSDEN, John (1842)　1899
MARSH, Anne (1834-1863)　44, 91,
　198, 327, 525, 743, 837, 904, 1079, 1081,
　1454, 1659, 1670, 1750, 2043, 2080, 2229,
　2543, 2544, 2593, 2659, 2699, 2817
MARSH, Catherine (1855-1875)　254,
　569, 757, 975, 1025, 1075, 1485, 1595,
　2073, 2352, 2731
MARSH, Charles (1766, 1828)　419,
　1443, 1460
MARSH, H. (1664)　1729
MARSH, John (1808)　1591
MARSH, John C. L. (1642)　172
MARSH, Mrs (1856-1876)　247, 1312,
　1313, 1514, 1546, 1671, 1881, 2063, 2592,
　2721, 2826
MARSH, Nathaniel Tilson (1843)　1832
MARSH, Rev. W. (1828-9)　624
MARSHALL, —— (1788, 1790) 329, 1012
MARSHALL, Charles (N.D., 1879)
　1303, 1934
MARSHALL, Frederick (1873)　967
MARSHALL, George W. (1867)　329
MARSHALL, James (1860)　1523
MARSHALL, Jane (1765-1772)　1132,
　1142, 2390
MARSHALL, John (1817)　1965

MARSHALL, Miss (1844)　934
MARSHALL, Nathaniel (1722)　319
MARSHALL, Nathaniel, D.D.
　(1714)　1882
MARSHALL, Rev. Edmond　1438
MARSHALL, Stephen (1641)　106, 2749
MARSHALL, Thomas (1875)　94
MARSHALL, Thomas, D.D. (1679)　336
MARSHALL, Thomas W. (1873,
　1874)　1222, 1808, 2041
MARSHALL, William (1785, 1796)
　1932 (2), 2200
MARSIN, M. (1697)　68
MARSTERS, Rev. Samuel (1689)　311
MARSTON, John (1598-1616) 141, 1132,
　1233, 1607, 2278
MARTEN, Henry (1646, 1649) 515, 2836
MARTIN, Benjamin (1733)　2091
MARTIN, David (1746)　1149
MARTIN, George (1740, 1811)　850, 1740
MARTIN, Gregory (1619)　1519
MARTIN, H. (1801, 1802)　1082, 2144
MARTIN, Henry (1835-1836)　591, 716,
　1383, 1897, 2681
MARTIN, John (1620)　621
MARTIN, John (1852)　766
MARTIN, John (1674)　1020
MARTIN, John (1798)　2576
MARTIN, Josiah (1714-1730) 1046, 2138
MARTIN, Major W. (1857)　1592
MARTIN, Miss (1835, 1848)　356, 1562
MARTIN, Mrs (1823)　2169
MARTIN, Rev. David (N.D.)　537
MARTIN, Rev. Frederick (1835-
　1838)　1755, 2465
MARTIN, Robert Montgomery
　(1832-1852)　285, 1868, 1963
MARTIN, Selina (1828-1844)　378, 444
　1693, 2393, 2403
MARTIN, T. (1659)　1554
MARTIN, Sir Henry, Bart. (1848) 169
MARTIN, Theodore (1838-1855)
　245, 667, 1532, 2223
MARTIN, Thomas (1795)　2356
MARTIN, T. D. (1853)　14
MARTIN, William (1865)　1169
MARTINEAU, Harriet (1844-1853)
　1470, 2381
MARTYN, Benjamin (1789)　1472
MARTYN, Dr John (1737)　1590
MARTYN, Henry (1701)　491
MARTYN, Thomas (1770, 1787)
　393, 1006, 2398
MARTYN, Thomas, F.R.S. (1766)　755

MARTYN, Rev. Thomas (N.D.) 705
MARVELL, Andrew (1672-1689) 21, 52,
    425, 1675, 1711, 1922, 2124, 2157, 2288,
               2569
MASCALL, Leonard (1588) 2027
MASERES, Baron (1772) 2034
MASERES, Francis (1775-1809) 27, 34,
         304, 768, 1637, 1794
MASKELL, Rev. William (1816-1845)
         1418, 1800, 2318, 2524
MASON, —— (1802) 2269
MASON, Francis (1743, 1747) 498, 1132
MASON, George (1768) 797
MASON, John (1725-1748) 797 (2), 1919,
               2478
MASON, John, M.A. (1691) 1613
MASON, John Monk (1758) 2161
MASON, Rev. William (1782) 168
MASON, Robert (1789) 1866
MASON, William (1747-1782) 568, 783,
    1092 (2), 1304, 1530, 1609, 1623, 1681,
               1802
MASON, Wiliam Shaw (1823) 232
MASSARD, Jacques (1690) 2162
MASSARY, Isabel (1861) 2413
MASSALSKY, Princess Koltzoff,
    née Helena Ghika (1861) 2827
MASSEY, E. C. (1854) 1051
MASSIE, J. (1757) 485
MASSIE, John (1756) 299
MASSIE, Joseph (1750-1757) 299, 805,
        1377, 1789, 2034
MASSIE, Rev. J. W. (1835) 2276
MASSIE, W. (1831-1840) 66, 931, 1490, 2531
MASSINGER, Philip (1628-1632)
          904, 1981
MASSON, Edward (1852) 1897
MASSON, Francis (1743, 1747) 498, 1132
MASSON, J. (1731-1732) 1626 (2), 1627 (2)
MASTERS, Rev. Samuel Errata, vol. iv.
MASTERS, Robert, B.D. (1795) 2356
MATHER, Cotton, D.D. (1700-1711)
      741, 1813, 2131, 2563
MATHER, Increase (1694, 1700) 263, 1359
MATHER, Samuel (1672, 1721) 593, 646,
               1372
MATHERS, M. Patrick (1672) 1044
MATHERS, Helen (1875-1882) 188, 435,
           1316, 2498
MATHESON, George, B.D. (1874) 60
MATHESON, Rev. J., D.D. (1835) 2071
MATHEW, John (1680) 349
MATHEWS, Sir Tobie (1622-1663)
           1882, 2126

MATHIAS, Thomas James (1796-
    1802) 43, 165, 1213, 1389, 1400, 1845,
    1848, 1964, 2038, 2058, 2149, 2232, 2269,
             2346, 2623
MATHIESON, James E. (1879) 2212
MATHIEU, Pierre (1628) 1981
MATHIESON, Thomas (1743) 1024
MATILDA, Rosa, Mrs Byrne (1805-
    1869) 221, 913, 934, 1013, 1016, 1181,
       1910, 2083, 2104, 2707, 2854
MATTHEW, Rev. J. C. (1860) 387
MATTHEWS, John (1801) 742
MATTHEWS, William (1779-1808)
        482, 812, 999, 1713
MATURIN, Charles Robert (1812-
    1824) 62, 903, 1545, 1568, 1614, 2827
MATY, Matthew, M.D. (1755) 202
MAUDE, Mary Fawley (1847-1849)
         2282, 2283 (3)
MAUDE, Thomas (1780, 1791) 1248,
        2725, 2729, 2801
MAUDUIT, Israel (1757-1781) 486
    1414, 1790, 1797, 1856, 2160, 2377,
               2588
MAUGHAN, Janet (1860-1863) 366, 421,
          2208, 2249
MAULE, Henry (1706) 1162
MAUNDER, Samuel (1825) 1496
MAUPERTIUS, Marquis de (1769) 816
MAURICE, Frederick Denison, B.A.
    (1834) 836, 1305, 2511
MAURICE, Henry, D.D. (1682-
    1700) 141, 580, 720, 1363, 1372, 2134,
               2761
MAURICE, Priscilla (1845, 1853) 1082,
      1101, 1990, 2246, 2381
MAURICE, Thomas (1775-1813) 534,
    2268, 2308, 2759, 2790, 2803
MAURICE, Rev. Thomas (1777-
    1812) 253, 1055, 1061, 2208
MAURICE, Rev. Thomas, M.A.
    (1778) 1842
MAURY, Sarah Mytton (1859) 188
MAVOR, Rev. William, LL.D. (1792-
    1809) 606, 1717, 2768
MAW, Mary (1778) 856
MAWBREY, Thomas (1711) 154
MAWER, John, M.A. (1731, 1732)
          1331, 2727
MAWERS, —— (1758) 1431
MAWHOOD, —— (1775) 2582
MAWYER, John, M.A. (N.D.) 782
MAXIMIANOPOLIS, Bishop of,
    A. Cameron (1798) 1408

MAXWELL, Bishop John (1644, 1703)				1998, 2248
MAXWELL, George Clerk (1736)		1780
MAXWELL, Henry (1730)		1592
MAXWELL, Hugh, M.A. (1721)		219
MAXWELL, James (1614)		310
MAXWELL, James, M.A. (1612)		1323, 2471
MAXWELL, John (1646)		292
MAXWELL, John (1781)		823
MAXWELL, John (1739)		2351, 2650
MAXWELL, John, Bishop of Killala (1640)		779
MAXWELL, John, Bishop of Ross (1641, 1646)		105, 778
MAXWELL, Mrs (1883)		1895
MAXWELL, Patrick (1849)		1058
MAXWELL, Peter Benson (1855)		2812
MAXWELL, Sir William Stirling (1848)		2453
MAXWELL, William Hamilton (1825-1848)		256, 920, 1685, 1808, 2497, 2730, 2816
MAY, Richard (1780)		256
MAY, Thomas (1639-1688)		647, 855, 2619, 2811
MAY, William (1852)		9
MAYER, Brantz (1854)		2191
MAYER, John, B.D. (1619)		1875
MAYHEW, Edward (1608)		2637
MAYHEW, Richard (1679)		1943
MAYNE, Charles (1733)		792
MAYNE, Jasper, D.D. (1639-1648)		77, 407, 630, 2332
MAYNE, Lady (1770)		7
MAYNE, Miss (1854)		1261
MAYNE, Zachary (1694, 1728)		2409, 2692
MAYNWARING, Arthur (1711)		1565
MAYNWARING, Everard, M.D. (1684, 1691)		338, 1204
MAYO, Charles (1860)		1168
MAYO, Isabella (1868)		1799
MAYO, Richard (1699-1754)		1926, 2690, 2692
MEAD, —— (1717)		496
MEADLEY, George Wilson (1812-1816)		1392, 1583, 2300
MEADOWBANK, Lord, A. Maconochie (1814)		484
MEARE, Dr (1672)		2429
MEARS, John (1731, 1760)		336, 2367
MEASON, Gilbert Laing (1828)		1317
MEASOR, Charles Pennel (N.D.)		1252

MEATH, Bishop of, C. Dickinson (1836, 1838)		720, 1870
MEATH, Bishop of, Thomas Lewis O'Beirne, D.D. (1780-1813)		484, 487, 1004, 1016, 1355, 1394, 2369
MEDCALF, William (1849)		1935
MEDINA POMAR, The Duke de (1876)		901
MEDWAY, Lewis (1706)		1231
MEDWIN, Thomas (1823, 1827)		60, 2030
MEEK, Robert (1805)		236
MEEN, Henry (1780)		170
MEGGET, Thomas (1830)		1837
MEGGISON, Holkar (1831)		2479
MEILHAN, Senac de (1788)		492
MEIN, Robert (1760, 1764)		406, 726
MELCOMBE, Lord, G. B. Dodington (1726-1761)		785, 1135, 1794, 2166
MELDRUM, George (1690, 1705)		561, 1348, 2021, 2336, 2740
MELLISH, J. C. (1801)		1554
MELMOTH, William (1711, 1773)		341, 1047
MELMOTH, William, Jr. (1748)		1446
MELON, J. Fr. (1739)		1965
MELTON, John (1609)		2396
MELVIL, Elizabeth, Lady Culross (1603)		1021
MELVILLE, George John Whyte (1862)		1548
MELVILLE, Lord Henry Dundas (1793, 1796)		1123, 2199
MELVILLE, W. Lesle (1840)		915
MEMES, Mrs Dr John Smythe, née Ann Ritchie (1824)		1501
MENDEZ, Moses (1751-1759)		216, 357, 2220, 2390, 2351
MENDHAM, Rev. Joseph (1822-1850)		309, 400, 575, 778, 1513, 2038, 2077, 2417, 2478, 2547
MENDOZA, Diego H. de (1639)		1938
MENDOZA, Don Antonio de (1654)		2068
MENDOZA, Juan G. de (1588)		1125
MENNIS, Sir J. (1656)		1681
MENTEITH, Stuart (1843)		1879
MENZIES, John (1705)		1786
MERBECK, Roger (1550)		249
MERCER, Edward Smyth (1866)		1599
MERCER, James (1813)		2024
MERCER, Thomas (1772-1774)		1947, 2322
MERCER, William (1785)		1353

MEREDITH, E. (1687)   1378
MEREDITH, Edward (1682)   2442
MEREDITH, G. W. (1825)   2614
MEREDITH, Sir William, Bart. (1765-1778)   1120, 2070, 2175
MERES, Francis, M.A. (1634)   2823
MEREWEATHER, F. (1812)   582
MERIMÉE, Prosper (1825)   1934
MERITON, George (1685)   1989
MERITON, Thomas (1658)   2788
MERIVALE, John (1811)   272
MERLE, —— (1838)   1568
MERRETT, Christopher, M.D. (1665-1670)   11, 1345
MERREY, Walter (1789)   2148
MERRIOTT, Thomas (1660)   1039
MERRITT, Henry (1865)   2219
MERRY, Robert (1784, 1788)   178, 682, 1960
MERRYWEATHER, —— (1681)   636
MERRYWEATHER, J. A. (1833)   1089
MESSINK, Mr —— (1781, 1782) 373, 2451
MESTON, William (1720-1738)   1308, 1636, 1812, 1895
MESURIER, Thomas le, B.D. (1795-1819)   1412, 1948, 2623
METERANUS, Emanuel (1602)   2667
METEYARD, Eliza (1863, 1866)   599, 1497
METHUEN, —— (1819)   1732
METHUEN, Paul, Baron (1810)   2845
MEYRICK, Frederick, M.A. (1855) 851, 1658
MIALL, Edward (1842)   1748
MIALL, W. H. (1846)   768
MICE, Edward (1674)   1278
MICHELBORNE, John (1738-1739) 1250
MICKLE, William Julius (1762-1782)   305, 467, 1385, 1968, 2033, 2047, 2777
MIDDLEHAM, Dean of, Rev. B. Nicholls (1814)   1992
MIDDLESEX, Earl of Dorset and (1664)   1969
MIDDLETON, Conyers, D.D. (1719-1748)   590, 978, 1246, 1379, 2146, 2156, 2157, 2305, 2439, 2441, 2661
MIDDLETON, Marmaduke (1822) 1958
MIDDLETON, Patrick (1733-1741) 311, 677, 769
MIDDLETON, R. (1819)   1511
MIDDLETON, Thomas (1604)   130
MIDDLETON, Thomas (1646, 1677)   164, 1125
MIDDLETON, Thomas (1602-1668)
240, 243, 356, 408, 519, 889, 1541, 1611, 1904, 2653
MIDDLETON, Thomas (N.D.)   992
MIDDLETON, Thomas (1579)   1612
MIDGLEY, Dr Samuel (N.D.)   1062
MIDGLEY, Robert (1687)   1732
MIEGE, Guy (1669-1697) 599, 1624, 2127
MILBOURN, Luke (1688, 1713)   1390, 1637, 2364
MILDERT, William V., D.D., Bishop of Durham (1805)   1418
MILDMAY, —— (1763)   1962
MILDMAY, Sir W. (1765)   1327
MILES, William A. (1790-1794) 533, 1394
MILEY, John, D.D. (1743)   2225
MILL, —— (1804)   1929
MILL, James (1804-1835)   807, 954
MILLAR, David, A.M. (1738)   189
MILLAR, James (1814)   1058
MILLAR, John (1812)   102
MILLAR, John (1796)   1432
MILLAR, John, M.D. (1807)   2643
MILLAR, M. (1776)   1428
MILLARD, James, M.A. (1847)   1254
MILLARD, John (1812, 1817) 1006, 1713, 1909, 2625
MILLER, Edmund (1727)   174
MILLER, George (1819-1826) 1524, 1975, 2726
MILLER, Hugh (1829-1844) 1447, 1954, 2216, 2529 (2), 2699
MILLER, Hariet, Mrs Henry Davidson née (1851-1859)   1489, 2689
MILLER, James (1731-1744)   169, 180, 421, 1070, 1539, 1669, 1962, 2711
MILLER, James, S.S.C. (1843)   1791
MILLER, John (1848)   2565
MILLER, John, M.A. (1837)   2573
MILLER, Lydia Falconer (1845-1867)   200, 524, 566, 1495, 1539, 1799, 1867, 2498, 2773, 2793
MILLER, Rev. James (1730-1744)   1180, 1192, 1535
MILLER, Rev. Joseph Augustus (1851)   785
MILLER, Thomas (1827)   1768
MILLER, Thomas (N.D.)   1836
MILLER, William Haig (1871, N.D.)   547, 1621
MILLES, Thomas (1613-19)   2629
MILLES, Thomas, Bishop of Waterford (1721)   22
MILLINGEN, John Gideon, M.D. (1811-1845)   49, 220, 1259, 2497

MILLS, Andrew Hervey (1767)   422
MILLS, George (1866, 1878)   220, 530
MILLS, J., F.R.S. (1772)   826
MILMAN, Henry H. (1829)   1157
MILNE, Rev. Adam (1743)   608
MILNE, Robert, M.A. (1865)   1785
MILNE, Sir David (1829)   2133
MILNE, William (1720)   2594
MILNER, J. (1740)   1984
MILNER, John, B.D. (1689-1700)   15, 2365, 2733
MILNER, John, S.T.B. (1690)   592
MILNER, Thomas, M.A. (1859)   1834
MILNES, Richard Monkton, Lord Houghton (1841)   1818
MILTIE, Baron Karl von (1831)   2687
MILTON, John (1637-1700)   11, 99, 146, 169, 690, 727, 730, 1039, 1283, 1468, 1555, 1738, 1816, 1994, 2081, 2119, 2378, 2521, 2553, 2675, 2703
MILTON, John (1609)   2396
MINIFIE, Miss (1764-1783)   212, 510, 890
MINOT, Laurence (1795)   1950
MINTO, Lord, Sir Gilbert Elliot (1752)   2036
MISSON, M. (1707)   546
MITCHELL, Dr (1713-1767)   2002, 2290
MITCHELL, Dr John (1757)   499
MITCHELL, J. (1877)   4
MITCHELL, John (1859)   1545
MITCHELL, Joseph (1725)   788, 2388
MITCHELL, Mrs Lawers (1867)   2707
MITCHELL, Thomas Peter (1857)   2562
MITCHELL, W. (1853, 1873)   60, 380, 1030, 1269, 1559
MITCHELL, William (1875)   1700
MITFORD, John, Lord Redesdale (1780)   2645
MITFORD, John, R.N. (1818)   50
MITFORD, Miss (1831)   2392
MITFORD, Rev. J. (1811)   1382
MITFORD, William (1774)   806, 821
MOBERLEY, Arthur (1849)   2723
MOFFATT, Thomas, M.D. (1599)   2385
MOGRIDGE, George (1829-1871)   371, 525, 746, 776, 1061, 1296, 1342, 1506, 1810 (4), 1811 (2), 1961, 2279, 2332, 2539 (2), 2574
MOINGIN, Arthur (1869)   609
MOIR, Andrew (1768)   1221
MOIR, David Macbeth, M.D. (1825-1843)   698, 1338, 1477, 1958
MOIR, George (1827-1852)   162, 955, 1533, 2536

MOIR, John (1786)   2622
MOIR, Rev. John (1776, 1783)   1163, 1765
MOISES, Edward (N.D.)   1358
MOLESWORTH, Elizabeth (1870-1877)   404, 547, 1520, 1751, 2350, 2549
MOLESWORTH, Robert, Viscount Molesworth (1694-1719)   14, 956, 1352
MOLLOY, Charles (1715-1732)   1061, 1887, 2317
MOLORY, Sir Thomas (1634)   1666
MOMERIE, A. W. (1879)   1826
MONBODDO, Lord, James Burnett (1773, 1779)   136, 1825
MONCRIEF, John (1748)   303
MONCRIEFF, —— (1759)   2560
MONCRIEFF, Alexander (1729, 1730)   2032, 2145
MONCRIEFF, James (1837)   2833
MONCRIEFF, Rev. Alexander (1747)   2792
MONCRIEFF, Robert Hope (1868-1881)   244, 245, 1091, 1557, 1598, 1686, 1848, 1879, 2230, 2342, 2472, 2496 (2), 2497 (3), 2848
MONCRIEFF, W. D. Scott, C.E. (1872)   1554
MONER, D. (1829)   1344
MONEY, A. (1856)   2341
MONEY, G. Henry (1856)   2341
MONEY, Robert Cotton (1828)   1275
MONFRIES, Alexander (1879)   395
MONIPENNY, John (1603-1633)   5, 353
MONK, Edwin (1846)   2051
MONK, Hon. Mary (1716)   1548
MONKLAND, Mrs (1834, 1837)   1691, 2739
MONRO, Alexander, D.D. (1691-1696)   22, 151, 422, 770, 1147, 1368, 1997, 2472
MONRO, Alexander, M.D., F.R.S. (1744)   796
MONRO, Edward, M.A. (1845-1854)   214, 394, 1072, 1813, 1860, 2677, 2786, 2788
MONRO, Halbert (1732)   769
MONRO, Thomas (1791, 1795)   63, 1898
MONRO, Rev. Thomas (1793)   2480
MONSELL, John, S.B., LL.D. (1870)   1487
MONSEY, R. (1665)   2262
MONSON, Frederick John, 5th Lord Monson (1839, 1842)   949, 1275
MONSON, Sir John (1647, 1680)   643, 2360, 2366

MONTAGU, Basil (1814-1830)   2023, 2423, 2577

MONTAGU, Capt. Matthew, R.N. (1854)   918

MONTAGU, Capt. Montagu, R.N. (1826)   2629

MONTAGU, Charles, Earl of Halifax (1687, 1710)   1098, 2289

MONTAGU, Elizabeth (1770)   813

MONTAGU, M. (1796)   973

MONTAGU, Matthew (1856)   533

MONTAGU, Matt. Robinson (1777)   1877

MONTAGUE, Charles (1690)   785

MONTAGUE, Edward, Earl of Sandwich (1670-1740)   426, 926, 2292

MONTAGUE, Elizabeth (1760)   623

MONTAGUE, George, Duke of Manchester (1854)   357

MONTAGUE, Lady Mary W. (1747-1763)   1443, 2395

MONTALVAN, Inan Perez de (1631)   2460

MONTEFIORE, Charlotte (1853)   920

MONTEFIORE, Lady (1844)   1752

MONTESQUIEU, —— (1722)   1889

MONTGOMERY, Charles Montague (1825)   1505

MONTGOMERY, Florence (1867-1875)   1880, 2592, 2593, 2728, 2815

MONTGOMERY, Jemima, Baroness Tautphocus (1850, 1853)   556, 1225

MONTGOMERY, James (1797-1837)   1502, 2020, 2038, 2808

MONTGOMERY, John (1852-1878)   845, 2026, 2577

MONTGOMERY, Mrs Alfred (1842)   2682

MONTGOMERY (Robert) 1827   57

MONTGOMERY, Rev. Robert (1828)   2056

MONTGOMERY, Sir James (1692)   1045

MONTI, V. (1845)   570

MOOR, Major Edward (1825)   1447

MOOR, William (1747)   647

MOORE, —— (1773)   2051

MOORE, Edward (1744, 1748)   872, 2651

MOORE, Frances Brooke née (1754-1788)   60, 1134, 1141, 1812, 2229, 2770

MOORE, Henry (1781)   2836

MOORE, James J. (1875)   1908

MOORE, John, M.D. (1779-1810)   728, 1659, 1978, 2732, 2853

MOORE, Morris (1847)   9

MOORE, Rev. William (1882)   2725

MOORE, Sir John Henry (1778)   1958

MOORE, Sir William (N.D.)   300

MOORE, Thomas (1806-1835)   516, 872, 976 (2), 1239, 1580, 1804, 1959, 2169, 2207 (2), 2264, 2536, 2605, 2627, 2841

MOORE, Thomas (1752)   1785

MORANT, Rev. Philip, M.A. (1728-1747)   5, 545

MORAY, Robert (N.D., 1682)   51, 515

MORDAUNT, Charles, Earl of Peterborough (1719)   2138

MORDEN, Lord, Charles Yorke (1746)   2422

MORE, Cresacre (1627)   1465

MORE, Hannah (1777-1808)   238, 421, 832, 1103, 1802, 1883, 2580

MORE, Dr Henry (1651)   2297

MORE, Henry (1650-1672)   683, 1788, 2170

MORE, Henry, D.D. (1656-1686)   102, 263, 775

MORE, Henry, M.A. (1642)   2053

MORE, Magister Thomas (1627)   1465

MORE, Sir Thomas (N.D., 1685)   1606, 2244, 2720

MOREHEAD, Rev. Robert (1813, 1814)   862, 1956, 2465

MOREHEAD, William (1713)   2459

MORELL, Sir Charles (1764)   503

MORELL, Thomas, D.D. (1739, N.D.)   307, 2281

MORER, Rev. Thomas (1702)   2354

MORESON, John (1515-24)   1223

MORGAN, Ann Jane (N.D.)   65, 1271, 2848

MORGAN, Dr (1722)   1407

MORGAN, James (1678)   2730

MORGAN, John (1732, 1736)   1901, 2345

MORGAN, John, Minister (1826-1837)   432, 542, 1062, 2182, 2205

MORGAN, Lady Sydney, S. Owenson (1803)   2250

MORGAN, Matthew, D.C.L. (1692)   735

MORGAN, Maurice (1758, 1794)   487, 765, 804, 1386

MORGAN, Rev. Samuel (1791)   441

MORGAN, Sir Thomas Charles (1808)   865

MORGAN, Thomas (1737, 1742)   265, 591

MORGAN, Thomas, M.D. (1725, 1737)   948, 1658, 1702

MORGES, Adrian Roux de (1690)   1575

MORIARTY, Dennis J. (1838) 2814
MORICE, James (N.D.) 278
MORICE, Sir William (1659) 98, 1380
MORIER, James (1837, 1849) 206, 350, 1552
MORISON, James (1807) 1731
MORISON, John (1867) 201
MORISON, Rev. James, D.D. Errata, vol. iv.
MORLEY, Dowager Countess of (1832) 937, 2234
MORLEY, George, Bishop of Winchester (1641, 1660) 360, 1644
MORLEY, George, Bishop of Worcester (1670) 1376
MORLEY, Henry (1850, 1851) 581, 1184
MORNAY, A. (1841) 1906
MORRELL, Thomas, S.T.P. (1771) 334
MORRES, Hervey Redmond, Viscount Mount-Morres (1780, 1794) 484, 534
MORRICE, Matthias (1759) 2413
MORRINGTON, Giles (1685) 1989
MORRIS, Corbyn, F.R.S. (1741-1751) 817, 1346, 1410, 1781
MORRIS, Edward (1790) 47
MORRIS, G. (1806) 1755
MORRIS, Gouverneur (1806) 128
MORRIS, Lewis (1878) 777, 2453
MORRIS, R. (1739) 818
MORRIS, Rev. Francis Orphen, B.A. (1850, 1858) 1377, 1977, 1986
MORRIS, Richard (1659) 1380
MORRIS, Robert (1742, 1768) 148, 903
MORRISON, Colonel (1843) 2038
MORRISON, James, M.A. (N.D.) 42
MORRISON, R. (1816) 623
MORRISON, Rev. James (1840) 2070
MORRISON, Richard James, R.N. (1861, 1867) 1047, 1064
MORSAN, Lefevre de (1740) 1542
MORTHLAND, Charles (1708) 20
MORTIMER, —— (1761) 682, 2622
MORTIMER, Mrs Thomas (1838-1872) 517, 894, 1306, 1485, 1489, 1660, 1705, 1740, 1880, 1992, 2081, 2082
MORTIMER, Rev. Thomas, B.D. (1846) 1486
MORTIMER, T. (1758) 629
MORTIMER, Thomas (1761) 839
MORTON, C. (1696) 640
MORTON, Mrs (1790) 1832
MORTON, P. (1830) 1010
MORTON, Rev. Thomas (1596) 2639
MORTON, Thomas (1796) 370

MORTON, Thomas (1599, 1613) 2638, 2649
MORTON, Thomas, D.D., Bishop of Durham (1605, 1643) 842, 1706
MORVAN DE BELLEGRADE, J. B. (1706, 1707) 2117 (2)
MOSELEY, A. (1753) 553
MOSELEY, Richard (1750, 1752) 1391, 1417
MOSER, George E. (1878) 2005
MOSER, Joseph (1793) 1523
MOSS, Charles, D.D., Bishop of Bath and Wells (1744) 840
MOSS, Charles, D.D. (1749) 2324
MOSS, Robert, D.D., Dean of Ely (1717) 2180
MOSS, Thomas (1770) 1950
MOSSE, —— (1814) 745
MOSSOM, R., D.D. (1660) 1931
MOTHE LE VAYER, Sieur de la (1649) 1459
MOTHERWELL, William (1824) 2168
MOTTE, Philip de la (1803) 2014
MOTTEUX, Peter Anthony (1705-1723) 30, 77, 180, 2482
MOTTLEY, John (1728-1800) 29, 530, 1268, 1811, 1881, 2262, 2528, 2814
MOUBRAY, John (1770) 2089
MOUBRAY, Thomas (1712) 334
MOUFFETT, Thomas, M.D. (1599) 2385
MOULE, Joseph (1842-1843) 1400, 1979
MOULE, Thomas (1818-1828) 605, 2738
MOULIN, —— Du (1671) 1653
MOULIN, Lewis du (1641-1681) 2359, 2780
MOULIN, Peter du, D.D. (1668-1680) 302, 1375, 2359
MOULIN, Thomas du (1680) 2359
MOULINE, —— de, Sieur du Parc (1727) 435
MOULTON, Thomas, D.D. (N.D.) 1687, 2571
MOULTRIE, John, M.A. (1850) 2251
MOULTRU, Rev. —— (1797) 886
MOUNSON, Sir John (1647) 2366
MOUNTACUTE, Walter (1649) 1263
MOUNT EDGECOMBE, Earl of, Richard Edgecombe (1827) 1683
MOUNTENEY, Barcley De (1839) 1383
MOUNTIFORT, William (1705) 2852
MOUNTMORRES, Viscount, Hervey Redmond Morres (1780, 1794) 484, 534
MOWAT, Magnus (1862) 2242

MOWER, Arthur (1817, 1837) 2809, 2854
MOYLE, John (1702) 2000
MOYLE, Walter (1697) 173, 660, 1357, 2303
MOZEEN, Thomas (1751) 2850
MOZLEY, H. (1841, 1852) 878, 889, 1515, 1516
MOZLEY, James Bowling, D.D. (1845) 1784
MUCKLOW, William (1673) 2475
MUDFORD, William (1802, 1840) 539, 932, 1463, 1758, 1994, 2493
MUDIE, Alexander (1682) 2273
MUDIE, Charles Edward (1872) 2502
MUDIE, Peter (1822-1830) 207, 284, 458, 1017, 1106, 1639, 2297
MUDIE, W. R. (1825) 198
MUFFET, Robert (1592) 437
MUFFETT, Thomas, M.D. (1599) 2385
MUILMAN, Peter (1772) 793
MUIR, John (N.D.) 1220, 1753
MUIR, John, D.C.L. (1842-1874) 265, 482, 2520
MUIR, Thomas S. (1843-1877) 213, 298, 362, 609, 912, 1218, 1254, 1487, 1754, 1892, 2076, 2251, 2351 (2), 2701
MUIR, William, S.S.C. (1833) 1398
MULGRAVE, Lord Constantine, John Phipps (1769) 1351
MULLEN, Allen (1682) 84
MÜLLER, Dr Max (1858) 516
MULOCK, Dinah Maria (1849-1882) 48, 56, 66, 206, 254, 255, 386, 422, 698, 877, 878, 1067, 1076, 1090, 1103, 1253, 1270, 1324, 1470, 1496, 1498, 1636, 1685, 1737, 1746, 1756, 1807, 1815, 1835, 1947, 2224, 2340, 2453, 2508, 2571, 2689, 2698, 2713, 2826 (2), 2849
MUMFORD, James, S.J. (1652-1686) 339, 2069, 2165, 2747
MUMFORD, Joseph, S.J. (1686) 339
MUN, Thomas (1621) 656
MÜNCH-BELLINGHAUSEN, Freyhar von (1844-1849) 1054, 1225, 2448
MUNDAY, Anthony (1582-1619) 255, 570, 579, 663, 703, 891, 1611, 2527, 2793
MUNDELL, A. (1830) 2187
MUNDY, Francis Noel Clark (1767, 1776) 1708, 1944
MUNRO, —— (1843) 2812
MURALT, Béat Louis (1726) 1425
MURALT, L. de (1751) 684
MURDOCH, Rev. J. (1831) 2387
MURE, Sir William (N.D.) 300

MURRAY, A. (1773) 413
MURRAY, Archibald (1805) 707
MURRAY, Eustace Clare Grenville (1854-1882) 251, 743, 968, 1568, 1910, 2231 (2), 2501, 2848
MURRAY, General (1782) 2466
MURRAY, George (1802) 840
MURRAY, Hamilton (1849, 1851) 884, 1342
MURRAY, Hugh (1804, 1814) 512, 2530
MURRAY, J. (1838) 724
MURRAY, James (1768-1773) 482, 731, 1151, 1729, 2340 (2), 2628
MURRAY, James (1852, 1861) 228, 2453
MURRAY, John (1831, 1839) 1063, 2680
MURRAY, John A., Lord Murray (1850) 1399
MURRAY, John, M.D. (1802) 446
MURRAY, Lady C. (1799) 282
MURRAY, Lindley, (1792) 2418
MURRAY, Lord George (1749) 17
MURRAY, Lord J. A. Murray (1850) 1399
MURRAY, Mungo (1679-1681) 569, 570, 571 (2), 2600, 2601
MURRAY, Nicholas (1851, 1852) 1452, 2224
MURRAY, Patrick, Lord Elibank (1754-1773) 487, 730, 828, 1230, 1397, 2067, 2577
MURRAY, Rev. David (1844) 229
MURRAY, Rev. James (1764, 1778) 1146, 1724, 2340
MURRAY, Sir Thomas, F.A.S.E. (1827) 1479
MURRAY, William, Earl of Mansfield (N.D., 1752) 1009, 2572
MURPHY, Arthur (1753-1778) 609, 1044, 1050, 1308, 1744, 2269, 2480, 2592, 2716, 2795, 2805, 2853
MURPHY, Edward W. (1851) 40
MURPHY, Serjeant (1844) 2775
MUSGRAVE, Agnes (1795) 404
MUSGRAVE, Sir Richard, Bart., M.P. (1798, 1804) 2507, 2600
MUSKAU, H. L. H., Prinz von Pückler (1832) 2610
MUSKET alias Fisher, Gregory (1623) 238
MUSSARD, Pierre (1667, 1732) 475, 2222
MUTEL, Charles (1702) 2630
MUZZEY, A. B. (1841) 758, 763
MYLES, James (1848) 366

MYLNE, Robert (1712)   1764
MYLNE, William (1720)   2594
MYNORS, Willoughby, M.A. (1717, 1718)   2337, 2512
MYNSHULL, Richard (N.D.)   2731

N.

NAGHTEN, Frederick, B.A. (1845) 1611
NAISH, William (1845, 1859) 1010, 2402
NALSON, John (1683, 1684) 1306, 2000
NALSON, John, LL.D. (1677-1680) 520, 953, 2029, 2671
NAPIER, Admiral Sir Charles (1838) 1705
NAPIER, E. H. D. E. (1849) 1868
NAPIER, Macvey (1840) 1469
NAPLETON, John, D.D. (1773) 488
NARES, Edward, D.D. (1812, 1823) 1085, 1201, 2566
NARES, Robert (1789) 2152
NARY, Cornelius (1718-19) 1731
NASH, —— (1589) 1854
NASH, Rev. Treadway, D.D. (1781) 430
NASH, Thomas (1589-1636) 70, 519, 928, 1546, 1553, 1928, 2063, 2189 (2), 2829
NASH, Thomas (1869) 63, 1080, 1563
NAUSE, Frederick, Bishop of Vienna (1618) 2633
NAYLER, James (1655-1667) 128, 221, 700, 1184, 1315, 1606
NAYLOR, B. S. (1854) 2593
NAYLOR, Joseph, D.D. (1669) 1473
NAYLOR, Sir George (1792) 423
NEADE, William (1625) 701
NEAL, Alice (1853) 67
NEAL, Jonathan (1825) 287
NEAL, Nathaniel (1746) 960
NEAL, Rev. Daniel (1733) 1347
NEALE, Erskine, M.A. (1827-1850) 239, 417, 564, 1469, 1503 (2), 2264, 2321, 2813
NEALE, John Mason, M.A., D.D. (1843-1848) 1129, 1197, 2063, 2497, 2716
NEALE, Rev. G. P. (1843) 2342
NEALE, T. (1696) 2034
NEALE, William Johnson (1833-1842) 1161, 1324, 1976, 2019
NEATE, Charles, M.A. (1830, 1838) 1927, 2155, 2489
NEAVES, Lord (1869) 2449
NECKER DE CUSTRIN, Charles Frederick (1745) 495

NEDHAM, Marchamont (1644-1678) 107, 321, 368, 384, 632, 643, 1329, 1455, 1563, 1602, 1603, 1738, 1843, 1935, 2302, 2665
NEILE, Richard, Bishop of Durham (1624) 1529
NEILL, Pat. (1832) 2806
NEILSON, Mrs Andrew (1855) 533
NELSON, John (1866) 1915
NELSON, Rev. —— (N.D.) 1166
NELSON, Robert (1688-1714) 718, 2281, 2624, 2811
NELSON, W. (1719) 758
NELSON, William (1725) 2180
NESS, Bertha (1878) 2247
NESSE, Christopher (1666-1683) 190, 544, 614, 665 (2), 1300, 1877, 2500, 2661
NETHERCOTT, Henrietta (1858) 2625
NETTLETON, Thomas (1729) 2444
NEVE, John le (1711, 1716) 902, 1500
NEVE, Philip (1789) 554
NEVIL, Henry (1716) 1942
NEVILL, Henry (1647, 1659) 1861, 2381
NEVILLE, —— (1779) 1942
NEVILLE, Henry (1647-1681) 842, 1255, 1311, 1933
NEVILLE, Hon. Richard C. (1848) 2323
NEVILLE, O. (1811) 1331
NEVILLE, Thomas (1752) 2144
NEWBY, C. J. (1864-1869) 1297, 1550, 2829
NEWBERY, —— (1762) 183
NEWBERY, Francis (1798) 2578
NEWCASTLE, Duke of, K.G., Henry Pelham (1810) 1802
NEWCASTLE, Duke of, T. P. Holles (1756) 2184
NEWCASTLE, Duke of, William Cavendish (1649) 522, 2723
NEWCOMB, George (1843) 1150
NEWCOMB, T. (1762) 798
NEWCOME, Henry, M.A. (1671) 883
NEWCOME, Mrs (1728) 768
NEWCOME, Susannah, née Squire (1738) 1918
NEWCOME, Thomas (1712) 231
NEW-COMEN, Matthew (1641) 106, 2741
NEWENHAM, Thomas (N.D.) 891
NEWINGTON, Samuel (1856-1858) 513 (2), 1725, 2028, 2565
NEWMAN, Arthur (1607) 227
NEWMAN, Edward (1849-1857) 1234, 1442

NEWMAN, Francis W. (1847)   1155
NEWMAN, Jeremiah W. (1805-7)   1516
NEWMAN, John Henry (1836-1856)
    302, 401, 723, 742, 1336, 1344, 1515,
            1528, 1641, 2037
NEWMAN, Samuel (1682)   467
NEWMARCH, William (N.D.)   2381
NEWNHAM, Francis (1815)   1939
NEWTE, Thomas (1788)   2610
NEWTON, Benjamin (1756)   1189
NEWTON, Bishop (1775)   675
NEWTON, Emma (1844)   631
NEWTON, Rev. John (1789, 1793) 1450,
            1732
NEWTON, Rev. William (1730)   1483
NEWTON, Richard, D.D. (1733,
    1755)   859, 1941, 2019
NEWTON, Samuel (1767)   1389
NEWTON, Sir Isaac (1704)   1822
NEWTON, Thomas (1587)   1085
NEWTON, William (1741)   2147
NIBBS, Rev. —— (1829)   2096
NIBLOCK, Joseph White, D.D.
    (1835)   1912, 2557
NICCOLS, Richard (1614, 1627)   221,
           986, 2392
NICHOL, John P., LL.D. (1852)   1595
NICHOLAS, Henry (1574-1575)   443,
       627, 837, 2033, 2047, 2055
NICHOLL, Whitlock, M.D. (1819-
    1822)   83, 1156, 2400
NICHOLLS, Frank, M.D. (1751)   1894
NICHOLLS, Rev. Boucher, Dean of
    Middleham (1814)   1992
NICHOLS, Anne Susanna (1804)   1276
NICHOLS, Francis (1719)   281
NICHOLS, John (1763-1809)   90, 103,
    235, 290, 423, 437, 1128, 1255, 1934,
           2231, 2417
NICHOLS, John Bowyer (1818)   1467
NICHOLS, John, F.A.S.E. (1819)   236
NICHOLS, N. (1731)   1212
NICHOLS, Philip (1763)   328
NICHOLSON, Francis, M.A. (1682)   448
NICHOLSON, Henry (1705)   470
NICHOLSON, Henry I. B. (1851)   3
NICHOLSON, John (1809)   1844
NICOL, Erskine, A.R.A. (1867)   1267
NICOL, Martha (1856)   1255
NICOLAS, Lady Nicholas Harris
    (1846)   298
NICOLAS, Sir Nicholas Harris (1820-
    1830)   390, 1582, 2022, 2189, 2492 (2),
           2773

NICOLE, Pierre (1710)   494
NICOLE, Pierre (1834)   1887
NICOLL, James (1840)   1111
NICOLL, Joseph (1735, N.D.)   173, 2323
NICOLSON, Alexander (1867)   1330
NIEBUHR, B. G. (1843)   2496
NIGHTINGALE, J. (1822)   1636
NIND, William (1856)   1012
NISBET, E. (1601)   297
NISBET, Mrs (1848)   1342
NISBET, Patrick (1762)   2286
NIXON, Anthony (1612)   632
NIXON, Rev. Edward J. (1844)   875
NOAKE, Dorothy (1735)   1464
NOBLE, C. J. (1762)   2782
NOBLE, R. G. (N.D.)   1131
NODIER, Charles (1815)   1165
NOEHDEN, G. H. (1796)   921
NOEL, Antoine Abbè de la Pluche
    (1733)   2466
NOEL, Hon. Gerard T. (1826)   187
NOEL, Lady Augusta (1875)   1840
NOIR, Jean le (1678)   1727, 2224
NOKES, William (1710)   1647
NOLAN, Edward (1168, 1868)   56, 1249,
           2225
NOLAN, F. (1804, 1826)   955, 1386
NOLAN, Rev. Frederick, LL.D.
    (1810)   1230
NOORTHOUCK, John (1764)   1160
NORDEN, John (1586, 1624) 1208, 1622
NORMAN, John, J. C. (1850)   2270
NORMANBY, Marquis Constantine,
    H. Phipps (1825-1832)   503, 758, 1559,
           1847
NORRIS, Edwin (1853)   623, 1037
NORRIS, H. H. (1815-1839) 1544, 2018,
           2205
NORRIS, John (1682, 1683)   1095, 1680
NORRIS, John, M.A. (1691)   363
NORRIS, Mrs (1808)   1287
NORRIS, Rev. John (1694)   2476
NORRIS, Sylvester, D.D. (1615-1623)
         135, 163, 1057, 2093
NORTH, —— (1844)   132
NORTH, Francis, Lord Guildford
    (1677)   1901
NORTH, George (1741)   113
NORTH, Hon. Roger (1713)   651
NORTH, Dudley, 3rd Baron North
    (1659)   941
NORTH, Dudley, 4th Lord North
    (1969, 1670)   1695, 1767
NORTH, Sir Dudley (1691, 1701) 491, 663

NORTHCOTE, Sir Stafford H., Bart. (1849)   2374

NORTHLEIGH, John, M.D. (1688)   687, 1862

NORTHUMBERLAND, Archdeacon of, T. Sharp, D.D. (1733)   2742

NORTHUMBERLAND, Duchess of (1775)   2375

NORTON, Edward (1857)   211

NORTON, Hon. Caroline E. S. (1829, 1836)   2455, 2775

NORTON, Hon. Mrs. C. (1848)   1452

NORTON, Mrs (1835)   2814

NORTON, Richard (1696)   1876

NORTON, Robert (1852)   2090

NORTON, Thomas (N.D.)   33, 291, 638, 2621

NORTON, Thomas (1562, 1569) 1235, 2791

NOURSE, Timothy (1691)   651

NOVA-SCOTIA, Bishop of, Charles Inglis (1779)   1441

NOVICE, G. W. (1865)   1487

NOWELL, Alexander (1609)   336

NOWELL, Thomas, D.D. (1760)   679

NOY, William (1641)   2639

NORWICH, Archdeacon of, Dr John Jeffrey (1703)   1656

NORWICH, Bishop of, Dr A. Sparrow (1661)   423

NORWICH, Bishop of, E. Reynolds (1669)   102

NORWICH, Bishop of, George Horne, D.D. (1751-1798) 615, 1376, 1445, 1775, 2471, 2562

NORWICH, Bishop of, Joseph Hall, D.D. (1640-1648) 255, 590, 1190, 1645, 2318, 2360

NORWICH, Bishop of, R. Corbet (1648)   1955

NORWOOD, Cornelius (1694)   683

NORWOOD, Richard (1665)   2652

NORWOOD, Samuel (1871)   1184

NOTT, George Frederick, D.D. (1795-1808),   1530, 1894, 1950

NOTT, John, M.D. (1772-1810) 70, 1091, 1307, 1342, 2317

NOTTINGHAM, Earl of (1692)   2006

NOTTINGHAM, Earl of, Daniel Finch (1713)   1791

NOTTINGHAM, Earl of, Henege Finch (N.D., 1660) ·   134, 841

NUGEE, George, M.A. (1857)   1882

NUGENT, Lord George Grenville (1832-1847)   1340, 2615

NUGENT, Robert (1749-1751) 490, 898

NUGENT, Robert Craggs, Lord Nugent (1739, 1774)   880, 1803

NUGENT, Robert, M.P. (1739)   785

NUNN, Lorenzo, N. (1852)   1616

NUTT, F. (1789)   457

NUTTALL, Mr (1679)   1557

NUTTING, H. (1856)   915

NYE, Philip (1651-1677)   217, 314, 1674

NYE, Stephen (1692, 1700)   29, 1105

O

O'BEIRNE, Thomas Lewis, D.D., Bishop of Meath (1780-1813) 484, 487, 1004, 1016, 1355, 1394, 2369

O'BRIEN, Dennis (1787)   2737

O'BRIEN, J. (1768)   937

O'BRIEN, William (1772, 1773) 544, 707

O'BRYEN, Denis (1783, 1795) 594, 1016, 2039

O'CONNELL, Edmond (1808)   2717

O'CONNELL, Daniel (1811)   1107

O'CONOR, Charles, D.D. (1810-16)   433

O'CONOR, Charles, M.R.I.A. (1771)   1782

O'CONOR, Charles (1753)   680

O'CONOR, Dr (1818-19)   232

O'CONOR, E. (1818)   1038

O'CONOR, Roger (1799, 1828) 41, 1451

O'HANLON, Rev. John, M.R.I.A. (1871)   1252

O'HARA, —— (1817)   1144

O'HARA, Kane (1764-1777)   166, 1026, 1613, 2698

O'KEEFE, John (1767-1784)   327, 2349, 2451 (2), 2850

O'LEARY, Arthur (1801)   1593

O'MEARA, Kathleen (1873, 1874) 2255, 2572

O'ROURKE, Edmund (1852-1865)   61, 870, 1543, 1597, 1680

O'SULLIVAN, —— (1824)   308

OAKELEY, Frederick, M.A. (1842, 1844)   861, 1478

OAKES, Abraham, LL.D. (1751)   2498

OAKESHOTT, J. (1848)   2616

OAKLEY, Benjamin (1812)   1445

OATES, Titus, D.D. (1683, 1689)   614, 618, 667

OCCHAM, Gulielmus de (N.D.)   620

OCKHAM, Lord Chancellor, Sir P. King (1703)   1149

OCKLEY, Simon (1712)   1208
ODELL, Thomas (1721)   371
OFFOR, John (1823)   2098
OGILVIE, Henry (1833)   2513
OGILVIE, Jane (1840)   1063
OGILVIE, John (1787, 1789)   893 (2)
OGILVIE, John, D.D. (1769)   1855
OGILVIE, William (1781)   812
OGILVY, Dorothea (1868)   2817
OGILVY, George (1834)   398
OGLE, George (1740)   1645
OGLE, Nath. (1821)   1207
OLDE, J. (1556)   113, 471
OLDFIELD, Thomas Henton B. (1792, 1794)   459, 775
OLDHAM, John (1683)   80
OLDISWORTH, William (1709-1711)   102, 619, 2092, 2764
OLDMIXON, John (1709-1730)   143, 167, 282, 410, 527, 539, 582, 796, 1131 (2), 1135, 1418, 1468, 1565, 1584, 1673, 2108, 2195
OLDYS, William (1732-1746)   283, 284, 424, 679, 1069, 1153, 1583, 1681
OLIPHANT, —— (1788)   2654
OLIPHANT, Charles, M.D. (1702)   2360
OLIPHANT, Margaret C. W. (1849-1885)   299, 391 (3), 566, 1072, 1077, 1182, 1298, 1314, 1319, 1488, 1525, 1532, 1547, 1575, 1604, 1830, 1867, 2072, 2701, 2731
OLIVER, George, D.D. (1828)   722
OLIVER, Rev. George (1827)   416
OLIVER, Rev. Peter (1787)   2282
OLLIVE, Joseph (1737)   415
OLLYFEE, John (1702)   581
OMOND, Thomas Stewart (1876)   1948
ONGLEY, Robert Henry (1757)   809
ONLEY, W. (1827)   2220
ONSLOW, Arthur (1740)   2470
OPENSHAW, Robert (1591)   2373
OPIE, Mrs (1790)   562
ORD, Craven (1798)   2719
ORD, John Walker (1833)   2787
ORDE, Mrs (1837)   186
ORFORD, Earl of, Horace Walpole (1741-1791) 20, 91, 327, 518, 1073, 1092, 1095, 1359, 1534, 1563, 2109, 2407
ORFORD, Earl of, Sir Robert Walpole (1710-1735) 480, 1347, 1351, 1792, 2311, 2369, 2421, 2425, 2437, 2575
ORIEL, Provost of, E. Hawkins, D.D. (1835)   1395
ORKNEY, Bishop, A. Honeyman (1710)   251

ORME, Rev. William (1826, 1830)   506, 1572
ORRERY, Earl of (1772)   1136
ORRERY, Earl of, Charles Boyle (1703)   188
ORRERY, Earl of, Roger Boyle (1655, 1676)   754, 1865
ORSON, B. (1809)   874
ORTON, J. (1830)   2585
ORTON, James (1852)   853
ORTON, Job (1770)   634 (2)
OSBORNE, Francis (1652-1715)   52, 1118, 1890, 1967, 2289
OSBORNE, Francis G., Duke of Leeds (1775)   2367
OSBORNE, G., Lord Sidney (1866)   1447
OSBURN, William (1841, 1854)   139, 1255
OSGOODE, William (1779)   2150
OSSORY, Bishop of, Griffiths William, D.D. (1644)   848
OSSORY, Bishop of, John Bale (1543, 1544)   779, 2847
OSSORY, Bishop of, John Parry (1660)   313
OSTERVALD, Jean F. (1702, 1715)   7, 2630
OSWALD, James (1766)   158
OSWALD, James, D.D. (1791)   1199
OSWALD, John (1781, 1789)   61, 284, 835, 1953, 2077
OSWALD, Margaret (1808)   2400
OSWALD, Rev. Dr (1767)   1424
OTIS, James (1765)   271, 2750
OTWAY, Cæsar (1823, 1847)   106, 2402 (2), 2610
OULTON, Walley Chamberlaine (1789, 1795)   188, 1796, 2457
OUTRAM, George (1851)   1337
OVERAL, —— (1741)   380
OVERBURY, Sir Thomas (1614)   2815
OVERTON, Richard (1644)   1543
OWEN, —— (1836, 1854)   407, 2054
OWEN, —— (1642)   1891
OWEN, Charles, D.D. (1716-1721)   561, 670, 1922, 2747
OWEN, E. (1762)   1707
OWEN, Henry, D.D. (1748, 1774)   535, 1070
OWEN, Hugh, M.A. (1808)   2417
OWEN, James (1694-1704)   401, 671, 1638 (2), 1935, 2686
OWEN, John (1669-1680)   177, 2421, 2680
OWEN, John (1825)   1366

OWEN, John, D.D. (1662-1682) 95, 260
267, 274, 636, 641, 642, 1221, 1704, 1877,
2748
OWEN, John, M.A. (1804)   901
OWEN, Josiah (1738)   2156
OWEN, Lewis (1609, 1629)   341, 2468
OWEN, Nicholas (1775, 1792) 297, 1157
OWEN, Robert (1813, 1847) 1643, 1735
OWENSON, Sydney, Lady S. Mor-
gan (1803)   2250
OXENHAM, Henry N. (1858)   1897
OXFORD, Bishop of (1825)   943
OXFORD, Bishop of, J. Butler, D.D.
(1772)   1402
OXFORD, Bishop of, J. Fell (1674) 2722
OXFORD, Bishop of, John F. Mack-
arness, M.A. (1847, 1878)   920, 2393
OXFORD, Bishop of, John Ran-
dolph, D.D. (1792, 1802)   745, 2142
OXFORD, Bishop of, Samuel Par-
ker (1670, 1688)   650, 2089
OXFORD, Earl of, Robert Harley
(1710-1711)   819, 820, 2095
OZELL, John (1722, 1734)   1889, 2481

P.

PACE, Rev. William (1835)   1528
PACKINGTON, Sir John (N.D.)   2469
PAE, David (1853-1866)   436 (2), 957,
1011, 1018, 1064, 1263, 1525, 1634, 1982,
2005, 2338, 2522, 2702
PAGE, James R. (1849)   2072
PAGE, R. (1841, 1843)   3, 1211
PAGE, Richard (1826)   1452
PAGE, Samuel (1619)   63
PAGET, —— (1853)   2616
PAGET, E. (1586)   1022
PAGET, Eusebius (N.D.)   1022
PAGET, Lord Alfred (1857)   1428
PAGET, Francis Edward (1833-1873)
299, 549, 1177, 1524, 1840, 2436
PAGET, Thomas Catesby, Lord
Paget, M.P. (1738-1741) 784, 1630, 2437
PAGET, T. C. (1736)   798
PAGET, Thomas (1649)   2132
PAGET, W. (1749)   1192
PAINE, Robert T., Jun. (1815)   1074
PAINE, Thomas (1772-1794)   34, 321,
442, 1814, 2039, 2079
PAINE, William (1682)   2299
PAINTER, John (1756   1684
PAISLEY, James, Lord (1731)   2641
PALEARIUS, Aonius (1638)   224

PALEY, William, Archdeacon of
Carlisle (1774)   587
PALFREYMAN, Thomas (1578)   2635
PALGRAVE, Francis Turner (1858) 1868
PALGRAVE, Sir Francis (1832)   2178
PALLAVICINO, Ferrante (1644)   2252
PALMER, —— (1776)   949
PALMER, Alicia Tindal (1809)   1194
PALMER, Edward (1667)   735
PALMER, Herbert, D.D. (1645)   980
PALMER, J. F. (1837)   621
PALMER, John (1772)   962
PALMER, Josiah (1795)   944
PALMER, Mrs (1837)   621
PALMER, R. (1840)   2489
PALMER, Roger, Earl of Castle-
maine (1667-1679)
341, 540, 980, 1320, 2174
PALMER, Samuel (1703)   587
PALMER, Thomas (1606)   795
PALMER, William, M.A. (1832-1846)
191, 845, 1069, 1070
PALMERSTON, Viscount, H. J.
Temple (1819)   1735
PALMEZEAUX, Michael Cubières
de (1791)   1633
PALTOCK or PULTOCK, Robert
(1751)   1464
PANIZZI, Antonio (1839)   333
PANTON, —— (1812)   676
PARC, Sieur de, —— de Mouline
(1727)   435
PARDOE, Julia H. (1834, 1835)
1546, 2466
PARDON, George Frederick (1849-
1869) 208, 234 (3), 388, 873, 992, 1060
1066, 1296
PARFECT, Rev. —— (1760, 1762)
494, 1346
PARIS, John Ayrton, M.D. (1824,
1827)   1058, 1904
PARIS, Thomas Clifton (1850)   1064
PARISH, H. H. (1838)   281
PARK, Andrew (1845-1853)   219, 2385
PARK, J. (1664)   2694
PARK, John James, LL.D. (1830)   1288
PARK, Mr (1815)   231
PARK, Thomas (1817)   873
PARKE, Robert (1588)   1125
PARKER, —— (1809)   195
PARKER, Frederick (1847-1862)   203,
515, 691, 692, 773, 844, 1203 (2), 1416,
1492 (2), 1493 (4), 1766, 1942, 2190 (2),
2238, 2669, 2678, 2679

PARKER, Harriett (1851)   1956
PARKER, Henry (1493)   449
PARKER, Henry (1640-1651)   71, 95, 316, 503, 513, 562, 642, 1003, 1290, 1541, 1765, 1789, 1963, 2069, 2274, 2346, 2659, 2669
PARKER, Henry (1688)   2673
PARK, Hon. Justice (1808)   717
PARKER, James (1877)   928
PARKER, John (N.D., 1650)   995, 1036
PARKER, John Henry (1840, 1853)   1019, 1243, 2416
PARKER, Joseph, D.D. (1867-1874)   720, 1855
PARKER, M. (N.D.)   279, 605
PARKER, Martin (1635-1640)   479, 842, 1029, 1072, 2220, 2678, 2788
PARKER, Matthew, Archbishop of Canterbury (1557-1564)   145, 584, 1022, 2811
PARKER, Rev. W. (1753)   1375
PARKER, Richard (1739)   813
PARKER, Robert, M.A. (1607)   2268
PARKER, Samuel (1681-1717)   232, 318, 347, 672, 821
PARKER, Samuel, Bishop of Oxford (1688-1670)   650, 2089
PARKER, Samuel, D.D. (1673, 1771)   578, 2182
PARKER, T. L. (1815)   606
PARKER, William (1651)   1320
PARKES, David (1839)   2483
PARKHURST, John (N.D.)   1609, 2362
PARKINSON, A. (1726)   422
PARKINSON, James (N.D.)   924
PARKINSON, James, M.A. (1689)   16
PARKINS, C. (1776)   1138
PARNELL, Dr Thomas (1737)   804
PARKS, Mr (1705)   2215
PARNELL, Sir H., Bart., M.P. (1832)   1927
PARNELL, Thomas (1717)   1173
PARNELL, William (1804, 1819)   1228, 1560
PARR, Harriet (1854-1882)   56, 101, 214, 219, 224, 503, 525, 939, 1014, 1075, 1084, 1218, 1297, 1298, 1339, 1560, 1675, 1677, 1970, 1971, 2500, 2531, 2572, 2573, 2672, 2685, 2730, 2792, 2828, 2843
PARR, John Hamilton (1821)   1684
PARR, Samuel, D.D., LL.D. (1781-1809)   283, 362, 486, 649, 1356, 2155, 2616
PARRINCHIEFFE, John (1572)   867

PARROT, Henry (1606-1626)   550, 1318, 1662, 1671
PARRY, Charles Henry, M.D. (1837)   1571
PARRY, John, Bishop of Ossory (1660)   313
PARRY, Thomas (1751)   2671
PARSONS, —— (1602)   572
PARSONS, Daniel (1860)   2688
PARSONS, Gertrude, née Hext (1859-1878)   55, 219, 744, 1011, 1078, 1341, 1519, 1536, 1547, 1677, 2242, 2518, 2539, 2573, 2688, 2707, 2717
PARSONS, Philip (N.D., 1771)   824, 1725
PARSON, Rev. Philip (1766, 1779)   624, 1222
PARSONS, Robert (1580-1641)   129, 143, 223, 262, 275 (2), 470, 512, 586, 696, 940, 1284, 1458, 2127, 2196, 2313, 2550, 2569, 2640, 2648, 2675, 2790
PARSONS, Robert, S.J. (1592)   577
PARSONS, Thomas (1804)   384
PARSONS, William (1787)   1958
PARTON, Sarah P. (1853-1865)   893, 912, 1933, 2228, 2242, 2346
PARTRIDGE, —— (1774)   1109
PARTRIDGE, John (1680)   1700
PARTRIDGE, Rev. Samuel, M.A. (1813, N.D.)   2207, 2575
PASCAL, Blaise (1658, 1679)   1690, 2048
PASCUAL, Antonio D. de (1852)   2693
PASQUIN, Anthony (N.D.)   2232
PASSERAN, Albert, Count de (1732)   1901
PATCHING or PHATCHEN, Resta (1757)   950
PATERSON, Adam (N.D.)   1756
PATERSON, George (1852)   2351
PATERSON, James (1747)   210
PATERSON, James (1840)   498
PATERSON, Nathaniel, D.D. (1836)   1543
PATERSON, Samuel (1767, 1788)   104, 159, 1271, 2466
PATERSON, W. (1819)   2263
PATERSON, William (1695-1717)   471, 773, 1231, 2037
PATISON, Matthew (1623)   1207
PATMORE, Coventry, K.D. (1854, 1877)   91, 2713
PATMORE, Peter George (1824-1844)   282, 367, 2125
PATON, —— (1780)   2816
PATON, Andrew Archibald (1844)   1643
PATON, James, D.D. (1773, 1796)   196, 1425

PATON, Sir J. Noel (1861)   1946
PATRICK, Bishop (1643)   2097
PATRICK, F. C. (1798, 1799) 1264, 1661
PATRICK, John, D.D. (1674-1688) 983, 2117, 2624, 2770
PATRICK, Symon, D.D. (1669-1687) 93, 165, 501, 639, 652, 886, 971, 987, 1598, 1914, 2286, 2338
PATRICK, Simon, D.D., Bishop of Ely (1686, 1688)   1753, 2636
PATRICK, Symon, D.D., Dean of Peterborough (1687)   2302
PATRIDGE, Rev. Samuel (1811)   2355
PATTEN, Thomas, D.D. (1834)   1415
PATTEN, William (1575)   301
PATTENSON, Matthew (1623)   1207
PATTESON, Rev. Edward (1803)   969
PATTISON, Mark, M.A. (1840)   311
PAUL, Charles Kegan (1861)   2554
PAUL, Margaret Agnew (1878)   2722
PAUL, Mrs (1856, 1857)   567, 700, 2493
PAUL, Rev. James (N.D.)   733
PAUL, Robert Bateman, M.A. (1829-1872)   82 (2), 204, 1137
PAUL, Sir John Dean, Bart. (1821-1828)   1540, 2230
PAULDING, Dr (1832)   2529
PAULDING, James (1825)   1269
PAULDING, James Kirke (1811-1831) 711, 1310, 1331, 1431, 2255, 2398, Errata, vol. iv.
PAULDING, J. P. (1835)   1179
PAYBODY, Thomas (1629)   1292
PAYN, James (1864-1874) 191, 346, 419, 946, 1060, 1487, 1488, 1516, 1550, 1560, 1622, 1680, 1751, 1883, 1885, 2826
PAYNE and FOSS, Messrs (1825)   332 (2)
PAYNE, E. W. (N.D.)   1706
PAYNE, Henry (1687)   113
PAYNE, Isaac (1805)   1837
PAYNE, J. (1837)   719
PAYNE, John (1771, 1802) 1373, 2505, 2601
PAYNE, Nevil (1673, 1675) 903, 1663, 2382
PAYNE, William (1685, 1687) 643, 2397
PAYNE, William, D.D. (1687-1696) 128, 652, 655, 1356, 1753
PAYNTER, Thomas, M.A. (N.D.)   1986
PEACE, John (1841, 1842)   603 (2)
PEACH, William (1852)   2560
PEACHMAN, Henry, M.A. (1615-1642) 183, 619, 712, 1558, 1605, 1855, 2481

PEACOCK, George, M.A., Dean of Ely (1831)   1782, 2153
PEACOCK, James (1785)   1808
PEACOCK, Lucy (1786-1799) 51, 1496, 2772
PEACOCK, Thomas Love (1816-1861) 544, 1056, 1076, 1535, 1567, 1632, 1741, 2206
PEAKE, Eliza (1844)   1174
PEAPS, William (1649)   1518
PEARCE, Edward (1681, 1682)   474, 475 (2)
PEARCE, Rev. T. (N.D.)   696
PEARCE, William (1795)   2818
PEARCE, Zachary, D.D., Bishop of Rochester (1722-1733) 963, 973, 1393, 1620 (4), 1625, 1626, 1627, 1628, 2175, 2176, 2203, 2300
PEARD, Frances Mary (1869-1875) 1818, 2228, 2573, 2705, 2820
PEARSALL, Elizabeth S., Countess of Harrington (1874)   1944
PEARSON, Albert H., M.A., (1868) 2258
PEARSON, C. (1842)   369
PEARSON, Edward, B.D. (1799)   1372
PEARSON, John, D.D., Bishop of Chester (1668)   2031
PEARSON, Richard, M.D. (1794, 1798)   25, 2565
PEART, Emily (1869)   245
PEART, S. (1778)   500
PEASGOOD, Fr. (N.D.)   923
PECHALL or PESHALL, Sir John (1772, 1773)   1167 (2)
PECHEL, Samuel (1781)   1108
PECHY, John, M.D. (1682-1695) 2427 (2), 2428 (4), 2429 (5), 2430 (4)
PECK, Francis, M.A. (1719) 2384, 2602
PECK, Lillie (1876, 1808)   2776, 2800
PECK, William R. (N.D.)   662
PECKHAM, Sir George (1583)   2675
PECKWELL, Henry, D.D. (N.D., 1778)   14, 1030
PEDDLE, Mrs (1789)   2236
PEDELSDEN, William (1657)   2458
PEEBLES, William (1803, 1811) 292, 535
PEEL, Sir Robert (1846)   954
PEELE, George (1584, 1595) 167, 215, 613, 1814
PEER, J. W. (1826)   2773
PEERS, Richard, M.A. (1667, 1715) 360, 1947
PEETERS, Hugh (1659)   2795

PEGGE, Samuel, LL.D. (1772, 1797) 931, 943, 1207

PEIRCE, Rev. James (1712-1721) 120, 345, 771, 1241, 1921 (3), 2038, 2173, 2721

PELHAM, Henry, Duke of New-castle, K.G. (1810) 1802

PELL, John (1664) 719

PELLING, Edward, D.D. (1687-1688) 140 (2), 952, 2568

PEMBERTON, Benjamin (1822) 1401

PEMBERTON, Lieut.-Col. (1869) 2262

PEMBERTON, Thomas (1812) 195

PEMBROKE, Earl of, G. R. C. Herbert (1872) 2458

PENALUNA, William (1819, 1834) 404, 855

PENDLEBURY, Henry (1687) 1926

PENGELLY, Sir Thomas 1731) 1478

PENHOUET, Monsieur (1797) 1425

PENINGTON, Isaac (N.D.) 258

PENKETHMAN, John (1628) 1819

PENLEY, S. (N.D.) 2407

PENN, Granville (1810-1841) 237, 248, 387, 1768, 1827, 2524

PENN, John (1792) 216

PENN, Richard (1794) 166

PENN, Richard, F.R.S. (1833) 1560

PENN, William (1662-1699) 96, 439, 483, 503, 520, 588, 751, 752, 817, 1028, 1044, 1045, 1049, 1224, 1225, 1292, 1298, 1360, 1662, 1714, 1736, 1835, 1891, 2037, 2045, 2305, 2356, 2476, 2570, 2717

PENN, William (1718-1794) 301, 2424, 2767

PENN, William (1823) 868

PENN, William, Jun. (1668) 2257

PENNANT, —— (1781) 430

PENNANT, Thomas (1763) 861

PENNECK, Rev. Henry, M.A. (1842) 156

PENNECUIK, Alexander, M.D. (1699, 1715) 1009, 1849

PENNEFATHER, John (1871) 923

PENNY, William, Lord Kinloch (1833-1866) 404, 2069, 2594, 2615

PENNIE, J. F. (1827) 2538

PENNINGTON, Mary (1649) 1690

PENNINGTON, Mrs S. (1766) 1445

PENNY, A. J. (1858) Errata, vol. iv. (2)

PENNY, Anne (1771) 1954

PENNY, John (1831) 2607

PENNY, Mrs S. J. (1857-1861) 55, 1663, 2223

PENNYMAN, Joseph (1680-1700) 9, 279, 427, 2061, 2062

PENNYMAN, Joseph (1689) 1511

PENNYMAN, Mary (1676) 2446

PENROSE, Elizabeth, née Cart-wright (1824-1853) 78, 1115, 1136, 1137, 1716, 2339

PENROSE, John, M.A. (1831-1849) 888, 1021, 1068

PENROSE, Thomas, D.C.L. (1790) 2400

PENROSE, Vice-Ad. Sir Charles V. (1820) 969

PENNY, John (1587-1590) 276, 1189, 1807, 2633, 2649

PENTON, Stephen (1682, 1688) 648, 1056

PENTYCROSS, Thomas (1777) 2823

PEPPERELL, W. (1746) 1214

PEPYS, Samuel (1677, 1690) 1575, 1977

PERCEVAL, Dudley M. (1849) 715

PERCEVAL, Hon. and Rev. Arthur Philip, B.C.L. (1832-1849) 38, 40, 74, 234, 395, 403, 408, 1119, 1302, 1379, 1400, 1412, 2161, 2513 (2), 2653, 2777, 2839

PERCEVAL, Hon. and Rev. G. C. (1825, 1831) 1926, 2326

PERCEVAL, John, Earl of Egmont (1733-1763) 486, 506, 850, 874, 2069, 2308

PERCIVAL, Margaret (1847, 1849) 1251, 2227

PERCIVAL, Right Hon. Spencer (1791, 1792) 711, 2197

PERCIVAL, Thomas, M.D. (1777) 1768

PERCY, T. (1762) 1628

PERCY, Thomas, D.D., Bishop of Dromore (1761-1779) 933, 948, 1074, 1090, 1300, 1472, 1750, 2448

PERCY, Thomas, LL.D. (1785) 2726

PERCY, William (1594) 2454

PEREIRA, Jonathan, M.D. (1843) 1336

PEREZ, Andreas (1707) 2461

PEREZ DE MONTALVAN, Juan (1631) 2460

PERKINS, Eliza (1834) 250

PERKINS, Henry (1853) 1981

PERNETTI, Abbé (1751) 1902

PERRAULT, Nicolas (1570) 1266

PERRIER, Anna (1866) 1253

PERRINCHIEF, Richard (1661-1668) 656, 1221, 2533

PERRINCHIEFE, John (1572) 867

PERRON, Cardinal Jacques Davy du (1623) 340

PERROT, Sir James (1600) 480

PERRY, —— (1750) 2647

PERRY, James (1778-1779) 780, 1617

PERRY, William, M.D. (1807) 2618

PERY, Edm. Sexton (1757) 1427

PESHALL *or* PECHALL, Sir John (1772, 1773) 1167 (2)

PETER, Rev. Samuel (1782) 2704

PETER, William, M.A. (1834) 2247

PETERBOROUGH, Bishop of, White Kennet, D.D. (1681-1718) 26, 322, 620, 902, 1152, 1343, 1354, 1399, 1565, 1594, 1794, 2001, 2101, 2440, 2599, 2664, 2750, 2772, 2820

PETERBOROUGH, Dean of, Simon Patrick, D.D. (1687) 2302

PETERBOROUGH, Earl of (1685) 1681, 2512

PETERBOROUGH, Earl of, Charles Mordaunt (1719) 2138

PETERKIN, Alexander (1828-1839) 403, 1332, 1415, 2125, 2153

PETERKIN, Rev. W. (1779) 855

PETERS, Charles, M.A. (1760) 164

PETERS, Dr Samuel A. (1781) 1000

PETERS, Hugh (1651) 1031

PETHERAM, John (1843) 2091

PETT, Sir Peter (1661-1688) 642, 1068

PETTIGREW, Thomas L. (1833) 1523

PETTMAN, William (1786, 1810) 1386, 1419, 1706, 2475, 2576

PETTY, Sir William (1647-1683) 52 (2), 1790, 2636

PETVIN, John (1753) 1345

PETYT, George (1690) 1456

PETYT, William (1680) 280

PEYRERIUS, Isaac (1655, 1656) 1597, 2561

PHAYER, Thomas (1543) 1715

PHELAN, Mrs, *née* Tonna, *see* Tonna

PHELAN, William, D.D. (1823, 1824) 2300, 2398

PHELPS, Elizabeth S. (1854, N.D.) 2346, 2519

PHIBBS, Mary (1855) 66

PHILIP, —— (1870) 2845

PHILIP, Rev. Robert (1835) 1744

PHILIPOT, John (1629-1674) 331, 405 (2)

PHILIPPART, Sir John (1823-1824) 719

PHILIPPES, Henry (1656) 494

PHILIPPS, Fabian (1649, 1669) 1302, 2007

PHILIPPS, John (1660, 1679) 1268, 1654

PHILIPS, George (1850, 1852) 357, 524, 1580, 1591

PHILIPS, George (1689) 1240

PHILIPS, Joan (1689) 910

PHILIPS, John (1705, 1708) 240, 555

PHILIPS, Katherine (1663, 1705) 1428, 1969

PHILIPS, Mr (1720) 1672

PHILLIMORE, Harriet E. (1878, 1879) 1081, 2769

PHILLIPPS, Mary Charlotte (1868) 545

PHILLIPPS, Miss (1860, 1862) 1685, 2102

PHILLIPS, Ambrose (1723, 1733) 425, 963

PHILLIPS, Charles (1854) 1692

PHILLIPS, Charlotte (N.D.) 2551

PHILLIPS, Constantia (1735) 1067

PHILLIPS, Edward (1685-1730) 355, 1500, 1689

PHILLIPS, George (1850) 1335

PHILLIPS, George S. (1850) 1470

PHILLIPS, John (1655-1703) 358 (2), 699, 756, 1243, 1549, 1603, 2256, 2260, 2467 (2), 2549, 2750

PHILLIPS, Katharine (1664) 1945

PHILLIPS, Miss (1869) 2507

PHILLIPS, Rev. T. (1854) 245

PHILLIPS, Rev. Thomas (1761) 1897

PHILLIPS, Richard (1802, 1808) 756, 1099, 1641

PHILLIPS, Samuel, LL.D. (1851-1859) 299, 743, 825, 2308, 2797

PHILLIPS, Sir Richard (1803, 1823) 33, 1884

PHILLIPS, Sir T. (1821) 2607

PHILLIPS, Thomas (1758, 1767) 1159, 2509

PHILLIPS, W. (1722) 1094

PHILLIPS, William (1824) 158

PHILLPOTS, Henry, Bishop of Exeter (1827) 1428

PHILLPOTTS, Henry, D.D. (1807) 1390

PHILLPOTTS, Mary Charlotte (1864, 1865) 1012, 1067, 1876

PHILP, Robert Kemp (1851-1870) 226, 229, 514, 602, 628, 629, 698, 764, 890, 891, 938, 1066, 1120, 1183 (2), 1242, 1279, 1314, 1470, 1721, 1903, 1985, 2085 (5), 2415, 2557, 2785, 2849

PHILPOT, Charles (1798) 1245

PHILPOT, John, Archdeacon of Winchester (1554) 2650

PHILPOT, Stephen (1746) 802

PHIPPS, Constantine Henry, Marquis of Normandy (1825-1832) 503, 758, 1559, 1847

PHIPPS, Constantine John, Lord Mulgrave (1769) 1351

PHIPPS, Joseph (1763)   2820
PHISTON, William (N.D., 1550)   1315, 1867
PICHON, Thomas (1760)   1008
PICHOT, Amédée (1825)   1112
PICK, Samuel (1639)   913
PICKEN, Andrew (1829, 1834) 240, 419, 698, 2315
PICKERING, E. K. (1851)   1973
PICKERING, Ellen (1833-1859) 59, 974, 1081, 1599, 1692, 2012, 2481
PICKERING, Roger (1752, 1755) 2109, 2115
PICKERSGILL, Lieut. (1782)   465
PICTET, Bernardus (1694)   133
PIDDINGTON, Rose (1859, 1866) 991, 1319
PIDDUCK, Isaac, M.D. (1848)   2037
PIERRE, Charles I., Castel Saint (1728)   652
PIERCE, Thomas (1648)   2566
PIERCE, Thomas, Dean of Salisbury (1683)   2757
PIERCE, Thomas, D.D. (1663-1688) 569, 688, 2033, 2696
PIERCY, John Fisher or (1623)   110, Errata, vol. iv.
PIGGE, Oliver (1582, 1591)   434, 2340
PIGOT, Charles (1792)   1268
PIGOT, Miss (1832)   2021
PIGOTT, Rev. John Dryden (1839)   443
PIKE, —— (1751)   2051
PIKE, Frances W. A. (1867)   1306
PIKE, John Gregory (1839, 1841) 921, 1859
PIKE, Samuel (1766) 1919, Errata, vol. iv.
PIKE, William P. (N.D.)   2404 (2)
PILKINGTON, James, Bishop of Durham (1563)   292
PILKINGTON, M. (1748)   2287
PINCHARD, Mrs (1794, 1796) 241, 2691
PINCKNEY, Miles (1665)   2530
PINKE, William (1626)   851
PINKERTON, John (1776-1790)   531, 799, 1441, 1563, 1831, 2215, 2630, 2786
PINKNEY, Jane V. (1848-1853)   1312, 2389, 2816, 2848
PIPER, Henry Hunt (1852)   246
PIRIE, Alexander (1766)   800
PIRIE, James (1877)   2784
PISANI, Madame (1836, 1840)   211, 2722
PITCAIRN, Alexander (1828)   2132
PITCAIRN, Robert (1822)   431
PITCAIRNE, Archibald, M.D. (1712, 1722)   189, 1029

PITFOUR, Lord, J. Ferguson (1764) 853
PITMAN, A. (1780)   833
PITMAN, J. (1847)   266
PITT, Robert, M.D. (1707)   298
PITT, Thomas (1751)   2488
PITT, William, Earl of Chatham (1809)   1435
PITTIS, John (1709)   359
PITTIS, Thomas, D.D. (1670)   2021
PITTIS, W. (1736)   1468
PITTS, Joseph (1708)   364, 1209
PITTS, Thomas (1705)   2803
PIX, Mary (1700-1709) 47, 218, 479, 556
PLACE, Francis (1831)   1373
PLACE, William Henry (1854)   1753
PLACETTE, Jean de la (1687, 1688)   1219, 2393
PLAIX, César de (1611)   132
PLANTA, Joseph (1804)   8
PLAT, Sir Hugh (1640)   600
PLATT, Hugh (1596)   2519
PLATTES, Gabriel (1740)   427
PLATTS, John (1715-1719)   794, 1109, 1113
PLAYER, John (1772)   486
PLAYFERE, Thomas, D.D. (1595) 1666
PLAYFORD, John (1667)   334
PLAYFORD, Matthew (1659)   1153
PLOT, R. (1676)   764
PLOWDEN, Francis (1784)   1247
PLOWMAN, Richard (1824)   806
PLOWMAN, Thomas Foster (1869)   30
PLUCHE, Abbé de la, Antoine Noel (1733)   2466
PLUMPTRE, Annabella (1801-1810) 698, 2802
PLUMPTRE, James (1793, 1798)   529, 1315
PLUMPTRE, John (1795)   1919
PLUMPTRE, Rev. John (1795, 1807)   466, 734
PLUMPTREE, J. (1816)   859
PLUNKETT, Edward, Baron Dunsany (1859)   1834
PLUNKETT, Oliver (1672)   1290
POCOCK, Dr (N.D.)   125
POCOCK, Robert (1790, 1802) 394, 1586
POINCY, Louis de (1666)   1150
POLETIKA, M. (1826)   2399
POLGLASE, Ann Eaton (1827)   2352
POLIDORI, J. W. (1819)   2723
POLLARD, Matilda M. (1872)   1173
POLLEXFEN, John (1697)   747
POLLOCK, John (1792)   1239

POLLOCK, Rev. John (1717) 122
POLWARTH, Lord, Earl Maccles-
field (1744) 2718
POLWHEELE, Dig. (1658) 2547
POLWHELE, Richard (1778-1831) 182,
609, 780, 783, 805, 877, 890, 904, 938,
1223, 1365, 1910, 1955, 2241, 2402, 2473,
2716
POMAR, The Duke de Medina
(1876) 901, 2592
POMFRET, John (1700) 372
PONET, Bishop (1753) 2633
PONET, Dr John, Bishop of Roches-
ter and Winchester (1556) 2380
PONSONBY, Lady Emily (1848-
1859) 410, 637, 728, 1554, 1669, 2008,
2519, 2690, 2849
PONTES, L. Davésiés de (1847,
1850) 1739, 2318
POOLE, —— (1822, 1830) 229, 411
POOLE, Dr Richard (1843, 1854) 1040,
2817
POOLE, G. A. (1842) 622
POOLE, John (1811, 1819) 1062, 2699
POOLE, Matthew (1659) 1350
POOLE, Robert, M.D. (1741) 1907
POOLEY, —— (1756) 997
POOLEY, H. (1705) 1593
POPE, Alexander (1711-1776) 35, 455,
709, 796, 799, 927, 979, 1299, 1694, 1720,
1784, 2332, 2343, 2684, 2712
POPE, Mary (1647) 2635
POPE, Walter, M.D. (1670-1679) 339,
1575, 2226
POPPLE —— (1689) 1345
PORDAGE, Dr John (1661) 1678
PORDAGE, Samuel (1660-1682), 206,
1090, 1563, 1678, 1953, Errata, vol. iv.
PORTAL, —— (1755) 2280
PORTAL, Abraham (1760, 1778) 1377,
2450
PORTAL, George R. (1855) 2245
PORTEOUS, —— (1763) 539
PORTEOUS, Beilby, Bishop of
London (1799, 1808) 259, 2329
PORTER —— (1863) 549
PORTER, Anna Maria (N.D.) 1828
PORTER, Commodore (1835) 495
PORTER, George R. (1831, 1841) 1546,
2645
PORTER, John Leech, D.D., LL.D.
(1858) 1064
PORTER, Sir James (1768) 1784
PORTER, Sir Robert Ker (1809) 1429

PORTER, Thomas (1663, 1678) 967, 2825
PORTERFIELD, James (1721) 1982
PORTSMOUTH, Henry (1779) 812
PORTLAND, William, Duke of Port-
land (1816) 1437
POSTLETHWAYT, Malachy (1749) 677
POTE, B. E. (1826, 1831) 1, 189
POTE, Joseph (1749) 1128
POTENGER, John (1691) 1870
POTT, Joseph Holden (1783-1818)
799, 1367, 2156, 2504, 2612
POTTER, Christopher (1621) 1291
POTTER, Henry (1773) 577
POTTER, John (1767-1780) 1169, 1682,
2559, 2838
POTTER, John Philips (1830, 1832)
828, 1690, 2131
POTTER, Robert (1789) 181
POTTER, Thomas (1763) 814
POTTER, W. (1659) 2617
POTTINGER, Henry (1853) 286
POTTINGER, Israel (1761-1776)
708, 1190, 1609
POTTS, Ethelinda Margaretta (1833)
1655 (2)
POTTS, Rev. T. (1790) 1229
POUGET, L. A. du (1863) 2245
POUILLY, Louis J. Levesque de (1749)
2564
POVEY, Charles (1703-1723) 760, 832,
1172, 1229, 1565, 1594, 2770, 2772
POWELL, —— (1772) 2732
POWELL, Baden (1827, 1829) 737, 2376
POWELL, Gabriel (1603) 341
POWELL, John (1825) 2491
POWELL, Rev. Henry Townsend,
M.A. (1847) 337
POWELL, Thomas (1635) 185
POWELL, Thomas (1805) 370
POWELL, Thomas (179-) 724
POWELL, Thomas, D.D. (1661) 1186
POWELL, Navasor (1677) 684
POWELL, William, D.D., Dean of
St Asaph (N.D.) 2329
POWELL, William Samuel, D.D.,
(1760-1774) 1767, 1778
POWER, David (1849) 2186
POWER, Dr, Bishop of Waterford
(1809) 1448
POWER, Marguerite A. (1858) 1431
POWER, Tyrone (1830, 1831) 1306, 1515
POWIS, —— (1759) 2537
POWIS, Mr (1783) 622
POWIS, T. J. de (1857, 1859) 1948, 2717

POWNALL, Governor T. (1854)   1437
POWNALL, H. (1825)   2433
POWNALL, Mary F. B. (1869)   1299
POWNALL, Thomas (1765-1795)   44, 484, 1239
POYNDER, John (1816, 1818) 1157, 1973
POYNET, Dr John, Bishop of Roches-
ter and Winchester (1556)   2380
POYNTER, Eleanor Frances (1871,
1876)   790, 1685
PRAED, William M. (1833)   2624
PRAT, Daniel (1714, 1718)   1706, 2344
PRATT, Rev. Joseph (1829)   2587
PRATT, Samuel Jackson (1774-1790)
744, 877, 1317, 1717, 1781, 2057, 2346,
2350, 2510, 2531, 2548, 2657, 2686
PRÉ, James du (1732, 1745)   475, 2222
PRENTISS, E. (1859-1871)   1498, 2132, 2493, 2500
PRESCOTT, Kenrick (1771, 1774) 1614, 2347
PREST, Thomas (1842)   1553
PRESTON, H. W. (1877)   1253
PRESTON, Roger (1619)   2221
PRESTON, T. (1784)   2600
PRESTON, Thomas (1620)   1736
PRESTON, William (1794)   2382
PRESTONGRANGE, Lord, William
Grant (1745)   1798
PRESTWICK, Mrs (1874)   1069
PREVOST, Antoine François (1780) 568
PREVOST, Sir George, Bart. (1846) 1545
PRICE, Captain Joseph (1782-1783)
932, 1380, 1387, 1402, 2248, 2302, 2326, 2569
PRICE, E. C. (1874, 1880)   1677, 1818
PRICE, John (N.D., 1650)   407, 418
PRICE, Lawrence (1655)   2822
PRICE, Miss (1878)   1515
PRICE, Owen, M.A. (1668)   759
PRICE, Rose Lambart (1824) 1250, 2623
PRICE, Richard (1830)   438
PRICE, Richard, D.D. (1783)   488
PRICE, William (1815)   1145
PRICHARD, —— (1732)   2149
PRICKET, Robert (1604-1607)   1174, 1266
PRIDEAUX, Humphrey, D.D. (1688-
1703)   312, 1295, 1369, 2721
PRIESTLEY, Joseph, LL.D. (1771-
1788)   37, 39, 161, 805, 888, 958, 1371, 2561, 2658
PRING, John (1939-1843) 1616, 1860, 2016, 2394

PRINSEP, John (1793)   24
PRIOR, H. (1870)   2395
PRIOR, Matthew (1687-1717)   309, 702, 754, 872, 1098
PRIOR, Thomas (1729)   1491, 1772
PRITCHARD, Marion (1878)   2013
PROAST, John (1690)   172
PROAST, Jonas, Archdeacon of
Berks (1691, 1704)   2300, 2567
PROBERT, W. (N.D.)   1022
PROCTOR, Bryan Waller (1820-
1850) 704, 728, 763, 935, 1473, 1546,
1569, 1573, 1621, 1958, 2099, 2381, 2839
PROCTOR, G. (1823)   1524
PROCTOR, Thomas (1578)   1032, 1308
PROWER, —— (1857)   1616
PROWETT, Miss (1845)   1946
PROWETT, Rev. J. A. (1845)   1946
PRYNNE, William (1636-1661)   221 (2)
256, 260, 267, 269, 270, 575, 634, 730,
982, 983, 1200, 1511 (2), 1514, 1714,
1728, 1737, 1743 (2), 1818, 1935, 2023,
2024, 2055, 2065, 2204, 2226, 2341, 2394,
2459, 2516, 2590, 2596, vol. iv., 2608,
2663, 2669, 2705, 2757
PSALMANAZAR, George (1753)   828
PÜCKLER-MUSKAN, H. L. H.
Prinz von (1832)   2610
PUDDICOMBE, —— (N.D.)   282
PUDDICOMBE, J. N. (1784)   1253
PUDSEY, William (1701)   495
PUGET, Louis Albert du (1852-1863)
2245, 2622
PUGH, Dr R. (1806, 1817)   1506, 2785
PUGH, Edward (1816)   787
PUGH, Robert (1668)   2174
PUILLY, Louis Jean Levesque de,
Errata, vol. iv.
PULLEN, Henry William, M.A.
(N.D., 1874)   415, 683, 923, 1054, 1183, 2074, 2605
PULLEN, William Henry, M.A.
(N.D.)   1639
PULSFORD, Rev. John (1877)   2525
PULTENEY, —— (1731-7)   529
PULTENEY, Right Hon. William
(1731)   108
PULTENEY, William, Earl of Bath
(1727-1778) 118, 290, 323, 324, 468, 767,
874, 1187, 1321, 1344, 1351 (3), 1968,
2032 (2), 2110, 2194, 2200, 2378, 2488, 2581
PULTOCK, Robert Paltock or
(1751)   1464

PULTON, Andrew (N.D.)   977
PUMPHREY, Thomas (1828)   274
PURBECK, Miss (1790)   2081
PURCELL, Mrs (1820)   1825
PURGE, William (1844)   374
PURTON, W. (1861, 1862)   709, 1037
PURVES, D. Laing (N.D.)   1324
PUSELEY, D. (1857-1876)   57, 68, 222, 563, 1279, 1686, 1759, 1834, 2216, 2614, 2810
PUSEY, Edward Bouverie, D.D. (1835-1855)   687, 694, 1808, 2072, 2476, 2511
PUTTENHAM, George (1589)   185
PYCROFT, James (1837)   2508
PYCROFT, James, M.A. (1845, 1865)   431, 533 (3)
PYE, Henry James (1766-1799)   176, 219, 600, 734, 895, 2353, 2395, 2405, 2657, 2846
PYE, J. Henrietta (1760-1767)   1944, 2356, 2378
PYE, Thomas, A.M. (1777)   2823
PYLKYNGTON, James (1562)   58
PYM, John (1641)   511
PYNE, William Henry (1823, 1825)   2445, 2688, 2818

Q.

QUARLES, Francis (1643, 1645)   1522, 1719, 2808
QUELUS, —— de (1720)   1701
QUICK, John (1682)   2555
QUICKE, John (1676)   1082
QUILLINAN, Alfred (1831, 1834)   1631, 1632
QUILLINAN, Dora, née Wordsworth (1847)   1274
QUIN, Michael J. (1823)   2311
QUINAULT, Monsieur (1675)   60
QUINCEY, Thomas de (1822, 1832)   472, 1307

R

RACK, Edmund (1771, 1774)   753, 2112
RADCLIFF, E. (1773)   2695
RADCLIFFE, Ann (1789)   327
RADCLIFFE, Mrs, née Anne Ward (1791)   2224
RADCLIFFE, Noell (1854, 1859)   66, 1337, 2311, Errata, vol. iv.
RADFORD, Dan (1856)   2704

RAE, W. F. (1873)   1598
RAE, William (1835)   670
RAIKES, J. (1806)   482
RAINE, J. (1833)   257
RAINE, Rev. James (1818)   714
RAINE, Rosa (1849)   2064
RAINFORD, Edward (1843)   1740
RAITHBY, John (N.D., 1798)   600, 2508
RAITT, J., Bishop of Brechin (1744)   1235
RALEIGH, Carew (1656)   1789
RALEIGH, Samuel (1852)   2117
RALEIGH, Sir Walter (1591, 1592)   2179, 2285
RALEIGH, Walter S. (N.D.)   2265
RALPH, James (1728-1758)   190, 312, 316, 541, 885, 1135, 1832, 2546, 2609, 2718
RAM, R. (1684)   2456
RAMÉ, Louisa de la (1863-1883)   175, 345, 356, 696, 937, 1081, 1201, 1218 (2), 1669, 1866, 1916, 2056, 2384, 2502, 2654, 2698, 2707, 2738, 2787
RAMESAY, William, M.D. (1676)   1005
RAMPINI, Charles J. G. (1873)   1428
RAMSAY, A. (1720)   726
RAMSAY, Alla (N.D.)   734
RAMSAY, Allan (1722-1783)   35, 811, 2424, 2538, 2771
RAMSAY, Allan (1769-1780)   1116, 1380, 1448, 1791, 1930, 2512, 2581
RAMSAY, Andrew M., LL.D. (1741)   1930
RAMSAY, Charlotte Lennox née (1747-1758)   910, 1083, 1897, 1951, 2347
RAMSAY, Chevalier, André Michel (1722)   818
RAMSAY, James (1703)   851, 1349, 2604
RAMSAY, James (1660)   1665
RAMSAY, James (1800)   2326
RAMSAY, Rev. James (1765, 1811)   20, 804
RAMSAY, Rev. James, M.A. (1778)   2128
RAMSAY, William (1684)   478
RAMSBOTTOM, Dorning (1774)   420
RAMUS, Peter (1574)   2589
RANCHIN, —— du (1638)   2199
RANDALL, Rev. John (1718)   1111
RANDALL, Rev. Thomas (1767)   1780
RANDOLP, —— (1719)   2434
RANDOLPH, John, D.D. (1804)   2522
RANDOLPH, John, D.D., Bishop of London (1807)   414
RANDOLP, John, Bishop of Oxford (1792, 1802)   745, 2142
RANDOLPH, Thomas (1630-1643)   79, 176, 1681
RANDOLPH, Thomas (1774)   110

RANDOLPH, Thomas, D.D. (1753, 1772)   110, 2753
RANDS, W. B. (1864-1872)   1084, 1488 (3), 2352, 2737
RANKING, Montgomerie (1865)   2059
RANS, Rev. —— (1685)   2512
RANSOM, Jane (1864)   1962
RANYARD, Ellen (1854-1875)   228, 245, 1335, 1484, 1634, 1761, 2495, 2670
RAPIN, Réné, S.J. (1672, 1673)   446, 447, 1286
RASTALL, William (1579)   863
RATHBAND, William (1644)   277
RATHBONE, Hannah Mary (1844-1848)   2410, 2425
RATHBONE, William (1804)   1694
RATTENBURG, John (1837)   1578
RATTRAY, Thomas, D.D. (1728, 1744)   89, 809
RAUPACH, Ernest (1847)   1739
RAVEN, Mathilde (1850)   2690
RAVENHILL, William (1686)   318
RAVENSCROFT, —— (1848)   1596
RAVENSCROFT, Thomas (1611)   1567
RAWLETT, John (1685)   621
RAWLINS, Thomas (1677, 1678)   2605, 2685
RAWLINSON, Richard, LL.D. (1711-1728)   469, 763, 979, 1127 (2), 1148, 1233, 1477, 1631
RAWSON, Dr —— (1710, 1711)   1404, 2837
RAWSTON, George (1841)   1685
RAY, John, M.A. (1670, 1693)   424, 2328
RAYMUND, —— (1667)   938
RAYNAL, Abbe T. G. François (1749, 1787)   1162, 1166
RAYNAL, William T. F. (1776)   1900
RAYNER, John (1780)   1128
RAYNHAM, Viscount, M.P. (1859)   2047
READ, Alexander (1652)   1666
READ, T. (1795)   282
READE, Alfred Arthur (1878)   1686
READE, John Edmund (1829)   298
READE, T. S. B. (1832, 1855)   378, 380, 382
REAY, Stephen, B.D. (1818)   1776
REDDING, Cyrus (1839)   839
REED, Andrew (1822)   2584
REED, Isaac (1777, 1782)   235, 1118
REED, Joseph (1756, 1786)   284, 2227, 2253, 2454
REES, —— (1811)   374

REES, Charlotte Lloyd née (1808, 1811)   42, 561
REES, William Jenkins (1806)   1088
REEVE, Clara, or Reeves (1769-1819)   904, 1828, 1905, 2028, 2698
REEVE, Henry (1838)   1043
REEVE, Rev. Joseph (1776)   2703
REEVE, Sophia (1828)   555
REEVE, Thomas, M.D. (1744)   550
REEVES, —— (1814)   2702
REEVES, John (1789-1807)   1337, 1786, 2580
REEVES, John, M.A., F.R.S. (1779)   770
REICHEL, Oswald Joseph (1866)   713
REID, Christopher (1835)   1301
REID, Daniel (1862)   683
REID, J. (1835)   2057
REID, Mrs (1817)   2785
REID, Peter (1879)   2817
REID, William Hamilton (1817)   2785
REILLY, Hugh (1695)   1250
RELLY, James (1776)   786
RENNELL, Dr (1805)   1617
RENNELL, James (1794)   2789
RENNELL, Thomas (1811)   97
RENNIE, James (1830-1848)   169, 697, 1233, 1234 (2), 1598
RENNIE, James, M.A. (1835)   876
RENNIE, Professor (1826)   1554
RENNY, J. H. (1832)   1101
RENOU, Sarah (1815)   2738
RENOUF, Peter Le Page (1843)   361
RENWICK, James (1707)   1224
REPTON, Humphrey (1788)   2723
REPTON, John Adey (1820)   2650
RESBURY, Nathaniel, D.D. (1685-1688)   319, 739, 1753
RESTA, —— (1694)   2668
RETTIE, James (1868)   4
REYNARDSON, Samuel (1765)   898
REYNELL, Thomas (1792)   1784
REYNOLDS, —— (1716, 1726)   1069, 2130
REYNOLDS, Edward, Bishop of Norwich (1669)   102
REYNOLDS, Edward, D.D. (1650)   1190
REYNOLDS, Frederick Mansell (1834-1836)   512, 1632, 1864
REYNOLDS, H. E. (1868)   958
REYNOLDS, Henry Revell (1796)   40
REYNOLDS, James (1855, 1861)   713, 837, 2064
REYNOLDS, John (1713)   571
REYNOLDS, John Hamilton (1816-1838)   893, 993, 1691, 1803, 1892, 2479

REYNOLDS, Sir Joshua (1750-1816) 1271, 1426
RHINDE, William (1807) 2079
RHODES, Ebenezer (1789) 65
RHODES, G. A. (1818) 1005
RHODES, Henrietta (1811) 2227
RHODES, J. (1628) 2480
RHODES, John (1602) 129
RHODES, Richard (1677) 936
RHODES, William Barnes (1808) 721
RICCALTOUN, Robert (1721, 1769) 505 (2), 675, 1232, 1968, 2411
RICE, James, and W. Besant (1872-1876) 315, 1025, 1685, 2082, 2571, 2823
RICH, —— (1837) 2804
RICH, Barnaby (1584) 892
RICH, Henry, M.P. (1858) 1861
RICH, Lieut.-Col. Sir Robert, Bart. (1853) 1437
RICHARDS, Alfred Bate (1845, 1846) 542, 569
RICHARDS, John, M.P. (1835) 2835
RICHARDS, William (1682) 2786
RICHARDS, William Upton (1843-1862) 888, 1050, 2357
RICHARDSON, —— (1691) 2047
RICHARDSON, Alex. (1870, 1871) 874, 990
RICHARDSON, James (1829, 1862) 2137, 2196, 2509
RICHARDSON, Major John (1829, 1832) 720, 2783
RICHARDSON, Mrs (1862-1866) 420, 1035, 1496, 2498
RICHARDSON, Professor William (1774, 1790) 296, 554, 1221, 1827
RICHARDSON, Richard (N.D.) 573
RICHARDSON, Robert (1739) 198
RICHARDSON, Samuel (1754-1761) 428, 1147, 1847, 2608
RICHARDSON, W. (1784) 91
RICHARDSON, William (1744) 803
RICHARDSON, William E. (1852) 1362
RICHELOT, G. (1857) 1050
RICHER, Adrien (1828) 1480
RICHERIUS, Edmundus (1612) 2634
RICHIE, James, M.D. (1761) 541
RICHINGS, Benjamin (1840) 1003
RICHMOND, Duke of, C. Lennox (1785) 113
RICHMOND, James C. (1849) 2772
RICHMOND, Legh, M.A. (N.D.) 1709, 2848
RICHMOND, Rev. John (1818) 1953

RICKETTS, John (1770, 1771) 1179, 1951
RICKMAN, Edward (1841) 1532
RICKMAN, E. S. (1835) 626
RICKMANN, John (1829) 2471
RID, Samuel (1612) 182
RIDDEL, James (1868) 4
RIDDELL, James, M.D. (1780) 1828
RIDDELL, John (1821, 1840) 317, 2255, 2752
RIDDELL, Maria (1792) 2784
RIDDELL, J. H. (1864-1866) 1011, 1561, 1896
RIDDELL, J. R. (1863) 2841
RIDE, Henry (1828) 2789
RIDER, William, B.A. (1762) 1110
RIDPATH, George (1693-1714) 27, 125, 151, 316, 492, 501, 621, 661, 1049, 1106, 1367, 1557, 1764, 1862, 1886, 2025, 2066, 2105, 2232, 2274, 2275 (2), 2276, 2444
REDESDALE, Lord John., Mitford (1780) 2645
RIDLEY, Gloucester, L.L.B. (1745-1768) 1280, 1390, 2299, 2568, 2588
RIDLEY, Rev. James (1761, 1764) 1140, 2260, 2543
RIGAUD, John, B.D. (1846) 1138
RIGBY, Edward, M.D. (1783) 364
RIGBY, Elizabeth, Lady Eastlake (1841-1855) 1065, 1267, 1431, 1504, 1682, 2184
RIGBY, Miss (1845) 1682
RILEY, —— (1752) 727
RILEY, Athelstan (1878) 2049
RING, John (1786) 436
RITCHIE, Ann, Mrs Dr John Smythe Memes née (1824) 1501
RITCHIE, Wm. (1826) 1774
RITCHIE, James Ewing (N.D.) 1479
RITSON, Isaac (1788) 511
RITSON, Joseph (1781-1810) 89, 229, 239, 553, 632, 754, 992, 1289, 1751, 1785, 1806, 1911, 1950, 2074, 2134, 2220, 2274, 2316, 2462, 2494
RIVERS, David (1798) 1494
RIVERS, George, Lord Rivers (1791) 201
RIVERS, —— Jesuit (1718) 2629
RIVINGTON, Charles (1860) 2505
RIVINGTON, William (1853-1855) 396, 865, 1321
ROACH, R., B.D. (1725) 1046
ROBB, William (1793) 1874
ROBE, James (1723, 1742) 903, 2372
ROBE, T. (1726) 2796

ROBERSON, George (1859) 1841
ROBERT, Robert (1751) 2486
ROBERTON, Mrs (1829) 936
ROBERTS, Daniel (1804) 489, 2096
ROBERTS, Emma (1819) 69
ROBERTS, George Edward (1863) 549
ROBERTS, Henry (1595) 2675
ROBERTS, John (1729, 1772) 117, 1437
ROBERTS, Margaret (1805-1877) 191,
724, 877, 1532, 2531, 2544, 2549, 2827
ROBERTS, Mary (1821-1832) 14, 100,
464, 2317, 2829
ROBERTS, R. (1770-1779) 1537, 1892,
2340
ROBERTS, Rev. George (1848, 1850)
1927 (2), 2467
ROBERTS, Rev. John (1867) 2575
ROBERTS, Samuel (1822-1854) 634,
2233
ROBERTS, Sir Walter (1641) 116
ROBERTS, W. (1829) 1976
ROBERTS, William (1784, 1795) 1609,
1955
ROBERTS, William Hayward, D.D.
(1773) 1956
ROBERTSON, —— (1778) 1092
ROBERTSON, —— (1840) 1558
ROBERTSON, Alexander (1853, 1854)
213, 222, 866, 2508
ROBERTSON, Alexander, M.P. (1820)
2115
ROBERTSON, Bartholomew (1620) 1489
ROBERTSON, G. (1830) 827
ROBERTSON, George Home Errata,
vol. iv.
ROBERTSON, George P. (1825) 2155
ROBERTSON, H. (1848) 1398
ROBERTSON, James (1770) 1948
ROBERTSON, James, D.D. (1841) 124
ROBERTSON, Janet (1850) 55
ROBERTSON, Joseph (1776-1840)
245, 599, 797, 801, 805, 809, 1502, 1717,
1775, 1779, 1859
ROBERTSON, Joseph, LL.D. (1837)
2372
ROBERTSON, Lord, Patrick Robert-
son (1844) 1335
ROBERTSON, Major Henry D.
(1829) 850
ROBERTSON, Margaret M. (1867,
1870) 209, 387, 1830
ROBERTSON, Patrick, Lord Robert-
son (1844) 1335
ROBERTSON, Principal (1768) 1594

ROBERTSON, Rev. Joseph (1775) 1385
ROBERTSON, Roger (1773) 1243
ROBERTSON, William (1865, 1876)
941, 1097, 2350
ROBERTSON, William (1782) 2147
ROBERTSON, William, D.D. (1766) 195
ROBERTSON, William, M.A. (1713)
1460
ROBINS, Benjamin, F.R.S. (1692-
1748) 38, 1699, 1782, 2782 (2)
ROBINS, James (1820-24) 1135
ROBINS, John Radcliffe (1833) 2719
ROBINS, Rev. Arthur (1860, 1862) 1621,
2001
ROBINSON, Christopher (1754) 484
ROBINSON, Dr (1731) 1627
ROBINSON, Dr J. (1646) 1883
ROBINSON, Edward, D.D., LL.D.
(1850) 1123
ROBINSON, Emma (1848) 2205
ROBINSON, F. K. (1855) 1019
ROBINSON, Frederick William
(1855-1870) 227, 310, 387, 394, 1042,
1095, 1182, 1560, 1617, 1743, 1817, 1840,
1970, 2406, 2493, 2707, 2816, 2830
ROBINSON, G. (1770) 1948
ROBINSON, Gregory J. (1879) 2844
ROBINSON, Henry (1644, 1645) 117, 167
ROBINSON, Jane (1844-1868) 297, 387,
406, 555, 700, 787, 1024, 1532, 1535,
1559, 1560, 1840, 2029, 2205, 2803, 2806,
2808, 2809, 2810
ROBINSON, John (1604) 146
ROBINSON, John, D.D. (1694) 17
ROBINSON, Joseph (1844-1848) 297,
2205, 2809, 2810
ROBINSON, Major Edward (1864) 656
ROBINSON, Mary (1799) 1419
ROBINSON, Mrs (1778, 1850) 1123, 2449
ROBINSON, Matthew, Lord Roke-
by (1774, 1776) 485, 988
ROBINSON, ——, of Kendal (1740) 1243
ROBINSON, R. (1776) 1935
ROBINSON, Richard (1583, 1602) 199,
240, 2667
ROBINSON, Rev. John (1806) 414
ROBINSON, Rev. Robert (1777) 1130
ROBINSON, Robert (1736-1782) 168,
645, 1963
ROBINSON, T. (1791, 1799) 426, 2672
ROBINSON, Therese A. L. (1851) 2545
ROBINSON, William (1700, 1733) 1045,
2034
ROBLEY, John (1808) 1887

ROBSON, Isaac (1845)   1682
ROBSON, D. Simon, Dean of Bristol (1585)   373
ROBY, John (1813, 1814)   1272, 1331
ROCHE, Charles F. T. de la (1753)   77
ROCHE, James (1850-1851)   535
ROCHE, Michael de la (1722-1730) 1494, 1582
ROCHE, Miss (1814)   1508
ROCHE, Regina Maria (1807)   72
ROCHEFORT, Charles C. de (1666) 1150
ROCHESTER and Winchester, Bishop of, Dr J. Ponet (1556)   2380
ROCHESTER, Bishop of, Francis Atterbury (1716, 1722)   174, 2291
ROCHESTER, Bishop of, J. Warner (1648)   398
ROCHESTER, Bishop of, Thomas Spratt, D.D. (1685)   2660
ROCHESTER, Bishop of, Zachary Pearce, D.D. (1722-1733)   963, 973, 1620 (4), 1625, 1626, 1627, 1628, 2175, 2176, 2203, 2300
ROCHESTER, Earl of, John Wilmot (1679-1701) 764, 1756, 1951, 2260, 2716
ROCHESTER, Earl of, Laurence Hyde (1679)   764
ROCHESTER, Lord (1677)   572
ROCHESTER, Vice-dean of, R. Dixon, D.D. (1683)   306
ROCHELLE, D. Raoul (1825)   1911
RODD, Horace (1839)   1821
RODD, Thomas (1820, 1826)   330, 596, 2565
RODERIGO, —— (1579)   1667
ROEBUCK, John Arthur, M.P. (1833)   1501
ROEBUCK, John, M.D. (1776)   774
ROGERS, Daniel, B.D. (1633, 1636)   1983, 2639
ROGERS, Henry (1852-1857)   588, 724, 2319
ROGERS, J. (1847, 1857)   72, 2606
ROGERS, J. (1659)   1674
ROGERS, J. (1579)   2517
ROGERS, Joseph, M.D. (1748)   109
ROGERS, J. R. (1852)   402
ROGERS, Major Robert (1766)   1969
ROGERS, Robert, B.D. (1680)   2169
ROGERS, Samuel (1786-1856)   782, 1261, 1318, 1802, 1940, 2100, 2781
ROGERS, Thomas (1689, 1694)   443, 1526, 2673
ROGERSON, Thomas (1719)   505

ROJAS, Fernando de (1707)   2461
ROKEBY, Lord (1811)   795
ROKEBY, Lord, Matthew Robinson (1774, 1776)   485, 988
ROLLAND, —— (1603)   2592
ROLLE, Rev. Samuel (1669)   2411
ROLLESTON, Francis (1858, 1859) 245, 1755
ROLLESTON, Samuel, M.A. (1750, 1751)   1808, 1900
ROLLO, John, M.D. (1783)   1780
ROLLOK, M. Robert (1600)   864
ROLT, Elizabeth (1768)   1629
ROMAINE, W. (1757)   713
ROMILLY, Sir Samuel (1785, 1813)   954, 1373, 1766, 1770
RONEY, C. P. (1842)   1825
ROOKE, John (1819)   2151
ROOKE, Rev. George Henry, D.D. (1741-1743)   192
ROOPER, George (1867)   205, 953
ROPER, Dr (1740)   2133
RORISON, Gilbert (1861, 1865)   504, 2584
ROSCOE, —— (1784)   178
ROSCOE, Henry (1824, 1826) 658, 1503, 2803
ROSCOE, Jane Elizabeth (1820)   1947
ROSCOE, Thomas 1825-1854) 293, 1501, 2803
ROSCOE, Thomas, Jun. (1821-1823)   343, 1304
ROSCOE, W. C. (1851)   2769
ROSCOE, William (1854)   293
ROSCOE, William (1787-1788)   2844
ROSCOMMON, Earl of (1710)   216
ROSE, George (1867)   1634
ROSE, George (N.D.) 1675 (5), 1676 (10), 1677 (4), 1835
ROSE, George (1785)   2038
ROSE, Henry John (N.D.)   1722
ROSE, Henry, M.A. (1675)   1903
ROSE, John (1788, 1793)   297, 2062
ROSE, Marie P., Baroness Blaze de Bury (1868, 1869)   67, 1520
ROSE, Rev. Hugh James, B.D. (N.D.)   1722
ROSE, Rev. John (N.D.)   2020
ROSE, Rev. W. William, LL.D. (1762)   1985
ROSE, Right Hon. George (1793)   264
ROSE, William (1751)   2254
ROSE, William Stewart (1819-1825) 146, 1430, 2574

ROSENBERG, Countess of, Jane Wynne (1785) 1656
ROSENHAGEN, Rev. Philip (1814) 1437
ROSEWELL, Samuel (1706) 471
ROSS, Alexander (1839) 2321
ROSS, Alexander (1656) 2734
ROSS, Bishop of, John Maxwell (1641, 1646) 105, 778
ROSS, Hugh (1702) 793
ROSS, John, D.D. (1711) 260
ROSS, John, M.A. (N.D.) 673
ROSS, John Wilson (1878) 2537
ROSS, née J. Dix (1846-1851) 1504, 1881 (2)
ROSS, Sir John (1825) 2642
ROSS, Walter, W.S. (1778) 1108
ROSS, William (1735) 1714
ROSSE, Bishop of Corke and, P. Browne (1728) 2024
ROSSER, Archibald (1823) 532
ROSSLYN, Earl of, Alexander Wedderburn (1805, N.D.) 1437, 1594
ROTHERAM, John (1757) 797
ROTHERAM, John, M.A. (1760) 150
ROTHSCHILD, Baroness Lionel de (1859) 144
ROUGH, William (1800) 493
ROUS, Francis (1598-1649) 251, 1327, 1565, 2592
ROUS, George (1769-1784) 305, 807, 1398
ROUSE, Rev. E., B.D. (1742) 791
ROUTH, —— (1842) 1785
ROUX, de Morges Adrian (1690) 1575
ROW, Rev. C. A. (1850) 1413
ROW, Richard (1871, 1874) 208, 779, 973
ROWAN, Arthur Blennerhassett, D.D. (1837-1856) 1016, 1314, 2462
ROWBOTHAM, Dr Samuel (1849) 2853
ROWE, Elizabeth (1736, 1737) 974, 1140
ROWE, Peter (1703) 2671
ROWLAND, David (1639) 1938
ROWLAND, Edward (1826) 2051
ROWLANDS, Richard (1722) 1160
ROWLANDS, Samuel (1585-1663) 227, 373, 514, 527, 533, 601, 688, 939, 1028, 1052, 1082, 1307 (2), 1454, 1552, 1567, 1609, 1661, 1740, 2596, vol. iii., 2801, 2811
ROWLATT, Rev. H. (1845) 332
ROWLATT, Rev. William Henry (1821, 1833) 333 (2)
ROWLEY, Alexander (1649) 2268
ROWLEY, Charles (1878) 1911
ROWLEY, Mrs (1668) 356
ROWLEY, Samuel (1634) 1747

ROWLEY, William (1607, 1638) 1558, 1605, 2625
ROWNTREE, William (1848) 158
ROXBY (1809) 1331
ROY, Henry, M.D. (1860) 2494
ROY, Reuben (N.D.) 11
ROY, William (N.D.) 2104
ROYS, Job (1657) 2476
RUD, T. (1731-1732) 1626, 1627, 1628
RUDDER, Samuel (1765, 1768) 1137, 1162
RUDYARD, Thomas (1672) 79
RUDYERD, Sir Benjamin (1660) 2012
RUFF, H. (1803) 1133
RUFFHEAD, Owen, LL.D. (1760, 1763) 486, 2095
RUFFINI, Giovanni (1853-1867) 687, 1324, 1515, 1856, 2073
RUGGLES, Thomas (1792) 214
RULE, Gilbert (1680, 1691) 596, 1644, 2310, 2675, 2751
RUMBALL, Charles (1851, 1857) 1553, 1879
RUMSEY, Dr J. (1826) 2418
RUMSEY, Eliza (1853) 2104
RUMSEY, James (N.D.) 464
RUNDELL, Mrs (1824) 1729
RUSHER, Philip (1789) 544
RUSHTON, Edward (1783, 1787) 666, 2802
RUSHTON, Thomas (1770) 1866
RUSHWORTH, John (1645) 2538
RUSKIN, John (1843-1855) 1304, 1642 (2), 1754
RUSSEL, —— (1781) 808
RUSSEL, Alexander (1856) 865
RUSSEL, W. P. (1807, 1812) 1216, 1809, 2414
RUSSELL, —— (1782, 1828) 335, 2789
RUSSELL, Dr Richard (1737) 1590
RUSSELL, Francis, Duke of Bedford (1786) 609
RUSSELL, Francis, F.R.S. (1793) 2368
RUSSELL, John (1750, 1824) 1426, 2610
RUSSELL, John, Duke of Bedford (1822) 1837
RUSSELL, John, M.A. (1694) 2335
RUSSELL, Lord George William (1830) 298
RUSSELL, Lord John (1819, 1832) 343, 824, 831, 1163, 1413, 1585, 1760, 1804
RUSSELL, Richard, M.A. (1716) 645, 1767

RUSSELL, Sambroke Nicolas (1776) 1513

RUSSELL, W. H. C. (1856-1863) 2240, 2542, 2544

RUSSELL, William (1859-1865) 204, 1081, 1272, 1341, 1895, 2023, 2099, 2223, 2397, 2617, 2698, 2708

RUSSELL, William Clark (1865-1878) 1267, 1270, 2397, 2844

RUSSELL, William, LL.D. (1771, 1779) 1142, 1286, 2322

RUSSELL, W. P. (1806-1812) 99, 103, 283, 917, 1967

RUST, George, Bishop of Dromore (1661) 1361

RUTHERFORD, Samuel (1644, 1703) 1318 (2), 1456

RUTHERFORD, William, D.D. (1788) 2731

RUTLAND, Duke of, John Henry Manners (1805-1822) 1276 (3), 2612

RUTLIDGE, Sir John James (1777) 764

RUTTER, J. (1637-40) 404

RUTTER, John, M.A. (1717) 227

RUTTER, Joseph (1635) 2350

RUTTY, John (1739, 1771) 815, 2294

RUTTY, John, M.D. (1776) 883

RYALL, H. T. (1836-46) 1976

RYAN, Lacy (1729) 420

RYDER, W. J. D. (1847) 391

RYLAND, John (1766) 1462

RYLAND, John, Yr. (N.D.) 1918

RYMER, Thomas (1681-1706) 999, 1453, 2601 (2)

RYVES, Bruno, D.D. (1646-1648) 1603 (3), 1612, 2065

RYVES, Eliza (1789) 1090

S.

ST AMAND, George (1724) 97

ST ANDREWS, Bishop of, C. Wordsworth, D.C.L. (1848) 431

ST ANDREWS, Dean of, J. Torry (1839) 1841

ST ASAPH, Bishop, William Fleetwood (1713) 986

ST ASAPH, Bishop of, William Lloyd (1667-1677) 490, 1512

ST ASAPH, Dean of, George Bright, D.D. (1682-1695) 795, 880

ST ASAPH, Dean of, W. Stanley, D.D. (1688) 880

ST ASAPH, Dean of, William Powell, D.D. (N.D.) 2329

ST AUBYN, J. H. (1834, 1838) 742, 2220

ST CLAIR, John (1874) 882

ST CLAIR, Rosalind (1835) 1552

ST CLAIR, William (1840) 1975

ST DAVID, Bishop of, A. Ellys (1736) 1936

ST DAVID'S, Bishop of, Lawrence Womack, D.D. (1681) 2725

ST DAVID'S, Bishop of, S. Horsley, D.D. (1790) 153

ST DAVID'S, Bishop of, S. Squire, D.D. (1741, 1748) 88, 1117

ST DAVID'S, Bishop of, William Lucy (1657) 1768

ST DAVID'S, Bishop of, T. Burgess, D.D. (1819) 1441

ST GERMAIN, Christopher (1533-1580) 129, 616, 2630 (2)

ST GERMAIN, G. (1668) 2691

SAINT JOHN, B. (1852) 945

ST JOHN, Henry, Lord Bolingbroke (1710-1775) 426, 529, 530 (3), 679, 887, 892, 923, 966, 1030, 1358, 1377, 1396, 1448, 1512, 1784, 1797, 1798 (2), 2055, 2149, 2293

ST JOHN, Honble. John (1790) 1254

ST JOHN, John, M.A. (1787) 1779

ST LEGER, Barry (1824, 1826) 1672, 2419

ST LEGER, Francis B. B. (1829) 2542

ST LEGER, Sir John (1710) 1540

ST MARIA, Simon A. (1637-8) 2771

SAINT MAURE, Charles de (1725) 1724

ST PALAYE, M. de la Curne de (1784) 1579

ST PATRICK'S, Dean of, Jonathan Swift, D.D. (1720) 1629

ST PAUL'S, Dean of, Henry Soames, M.A. (1823) 2751

SAINT PIERRE, Charles J. Castel (1728) 652

SAINT REAL, C. V. de (1676, 1685) 297, 698

SAINTE CROIX, Baron de (1802) 1165

SAALFIELD, Rev. —— (1764) 1900

SAAVEDRA, Miguel de Cervantes (1619) 2628

SABIE, Francis (1595) 1848

SABINE, Joseph (1815) 26

SABRAN, Lewis S. J. (1688) 115

SACHEVERELL, Henry (1705, 1710) 359, 221

SACKVILLE, Charles, Duke of Dorset (1752) 2631
SACKVILLE, George, Lord Germaine (1822) 1437
SACKVILLE, George, Lord Sackville (1822) 1437
SACKVILLE, Thomas, Lord Buckhurst (1671, N.D.) 1711, 2621
SACKVILLE - WEST, Reginald Windsor (1857) 1119
SADLEIR, Sir Edward (1692) 1670
SADLER, John (1640-1664) 375, 933, 1555, 1808, 2215, 2833
SADLER, Michael, F. (1851) 2245
SADLER, Thomas (1766) 1605
SAGE, Bishop John (1690-1704) 22, 322, 984, 2018, 2086, 2440, 2742
SALA, George Augustus (1865) 185
SALES, Sir W. (1655) 2562
SALESBURY, William (1550) 215
SALGADO, J. (1680) 262
SALISBURY, Bishop of, Gilbert Burnet (1680-1717) 508, 2515, 2720
SALISBURY, Bishop of, J. Gregory (1649) 778
SALISBURY, Bishop of, J. Jewel (1562) 145
SALISBURY, Bishop of, John Douglas, D.D. (1754-1760) 252, 456, 468, 535, 982, 1344, 2330, 2394
SALISBURY, Bishop of, John Earle (1628) 1612
SALISBURY, Bishop of, Thomas Burgess, D.D., LL.D. (1782-1835) 482, 812, 857, 1244
SALISBURY, Dean of, Thomas Pierce (1683) 2757
SALISBURY, Earl of, R. Cecil or Cecyl (1606) 129
SALISBURY, Richard Anthony (1805) 1855
SALISBURY, W. (N.D.) 779
SALISBURY, William, B.D. (1768) 2694
SALKELD, John (1617) 2636
SALLON, Rosalie (1877) 46
SALMON, Nathaniel (1733) 1502
SALMON, Thomas (1706, 1724) 537, 1115
SALMON, William (1701, 1710) 672 (3)
SALMON, William, M.D. (1700) 680
SALMOND, —— (1879) 1017
SALNAR, —— (1586) 1071
SALT, Henry (1824) 729
SALTER, Rev. Dr Samuel (1741-3) 193

SALTER, T. F. (1808) 1102
SALTERN, George (1606) 1124
SAMBER, Robert (1721, 1723) 2222, 2638
SAMPSON, —— (1571) 660
SAMOS, Archbishop of, Joseph Georgirenes (1657) 2662
SAMPSON, Marmaduke B. (1849) 2682
SAMPSON, William (1636) 2771
SAMPSON, Henry (1878) 1639
SAMPSON, Marmaduke B. (1858) 552
SAMWAIES, Richard (1653) 751
SANCROFT, Henricus (1814) 1992
SANCROFT, William, D.D. (1690) 1643
SANCTA CLARA, Francisus (1615, 1670) 413, 862
SANCTO GERMANO, Christopherus de (1532, 1538) 33, 2254
SANDBACK, Mrs Henry Roscoe (1845) 76
SANDEMAN, Robert (1762, 1763) 801, 1449
SANDEN, Thomas, M.D. (1802) 2585
SANDERS, Robert (1773) 1524
SANDERS, William (1672) 1044
SANDERSON, Robert, D.D. (1636, 1666) 932, 2459
SANDERSON, Robert, D.D., Bishop of Lincoln (1647-1670) 32, 2094
SANDFORD, —— (1724) 909
SANDHAM, Elizabeth (1809) 2689
SANDRAS, Gatien Courtilz de (1695) 1481, 1967
SANDWICH, Earl of, Edward Montague (1670-1740) 426, 926, 2292
SANDWITH, Humphrey, C.B. (1865) 1755
SANDYS, George (1625-1684) 94, 1839 (2), 1859, 2245
SANDYS, Sir Edwin (1605, 1615) 835, 922, 2126
SANDYS, William (1831) 2465
SANDYS, William, F.S.A. (1867) 2622
SANKEY, —— (1818) 272
SARDICA, Bishop of, Prince of Hohenhole (1823) 865
SARGENT, Richard (1839) 2019
SARTORIS, Adelaide (1868) 1566
SARUM, Bishop of, Gilbert Burnett, D.D. (N.D.) 1346
SARUM, Bishop of, J. Gordon, D.D. (1613) 2246
SATCHELL, S. A. (1806) 2573
SATIS, George (1795) 737
SAULT, Richard (1699) 256

SAUMAREZ, R., B.A. (1848)   227
SAUNDERS, Erasmus, D.D. (1721) 2736
SAUNDERS, Frederick (1853, 1856)
    2253 (2)
SAUNDERS, John (1875)   1490
SAUNDERS, Katherine (1875)   1490
SAUNDERS, R. (1682)   2736
SAUNDERS, Richard, M.A. (1701)
    58, 649
SAUNDERS, Samuel (1719)   1410
SAUNDERSON, William (1650)   199
SAURIN, Benjamin Joseph (1754) 1623
SAVAGE, Henry, D.D. (1660, 1663)
    616, 2094
SAVAGE, John, D.D. (1702)   87
SAVAGE, Marmion W. (1845-1856)
    208, 419, 884, 1687
SAVAGE, Samuel (1719)   2513
SAVARY, Henry (1830)   2073
SAVILLE, George, Marquis of Hali-
   fax (1681-1694) 85, 359, 360, 788, 1119,
     1314, 1353, 1366, 2230, 2286
SAVILLE, Sir George (1762)   171
SAWERS, Rev. Peter (1856)   939
SAWYER, Thomas (1691)   137
SAXBY, Elizabeth M.A.F. (1880) 1855 (2)
SAY AND SELE, Viscount, W.
   Fiennis (1659)   938
SAYER, Benjamin (1833)   197
SAYER, Edward (1790)   1772
SAYWELL, William (1688)   2119
SAYERS, James (1807)   740
SCAFE, John (1820)   1010, 1303
SCANTLEBURY, Thomas (1794-
   1813)   394, 1510, 2214, 2331, 2711
SCARGILL, Sir William (1827)   2660
SCARGILL, William Pitt (1827-1835)
   194, 243, 741, 1882, 2048, 2058, 2077,
     2540, 2542, 2719
SCARISBROOK, Edward (1696)   1481
SCARLETT, Thomas (1595)   831
SCAWEN, John (1790)   1729
SCHILLER, Frederick (1801)   1554
SCHIMMELPENNINCK, Mary
   Ann (1813, 1830)   1693, 2433
SCHMID, J. C. von (1853)   388
SCHOMBERG, A. C. (1777, 1779)
    209, 1801
SCHOMBERG, Dr, Jr. (1746)   1403
SCHOMBERG, Ralph, M.D. (1765,
   1783)   570, 1285, 2226
SCHUBERT, Professor (1838)   1569
SCHWARZ, Madame (1860)   2099
SCLATER, J. (1717)   1826

SCLATER, William (1717)   1826
SCOBELL, Henry (1680, 1689)   1596,
    1981
SCOLOKER, Anthony (1604)   625
SCOT, John, D.D. (1687)   730
SCOT, Patrick (1622)   299
SCOT, Thomas (1622-1624)   222, 351,
   1738, 2308, 2460, 2606, 2778, 2779 (2),
     2780, 2781, 2813
SCOT, Thomas, B.D. (N.D., 1624)   632,
    751
SCOT, William (1602)   525
SCOT, William (1718, 1719)   1729, 1744
SCOTT, —— (1838)   2384
SCOTT, A. J., A.M. (1841)   2058
SCOTT, Daniel, LL.D. (1738)   815
SCOTT, David (1870)   1013
SCOTT, David Dundas (1867)   242
SCOTT, Dr (1758)   92
SCOTT, George (1832)   466
SCOTT, Helenus (1782)   48
SCOTT, Hon. Caroline Lucy (1828,
   1856)   1549, 1810
SCOTT, Hugh (1847, 1850)   403, 533
SCOTT, John (1770, 1775)   495, 2152
SCOTT, John (1773, 1778)   1656, 1783
SCOTT, John, D.D. (1683, 1688)   348,
    1753
SCOTT, John Robert (1789, 1790) 1861,
    2201
SCOTT, Lady Lydia (1834-1850)   1083,
    1195, 1529, 2650
SCOTT, Major John (1774, 1783)   780,
    1412, 1452, 2297
SCOTT, Michael (1836)   545
SCOTT, Mrs (1856, 1857)   1273, 1554
SCOTT, Sarah (1750-1772) 59, 606, 1133,
   1138, 1141, 1148, 1280, 1483, 2554
SCOTT, Rev. —— (1728)   161
SCOTT, Rev. James (1785)   1994
SCOTT, Robert (1820-24)   1135
SCOTT, Robert B. (1810)   1615
SCOTT, Robert, D.D. (1699, 1701)   986,
    2338
SCOTT, Sir Claude Edward, Bart.
    (N.D.) 434
SCOTT, Sir Walter, Bart. (1810-1836)   3
   101, 138, 256, 392, 759, 945, 1060, 1071,
   1258, 1298, 1395, 1478, 1596, 1650, 1876,
   1895, 1916, 2065, 2104, 2131, 2219, 2253,
   2254, 2300, 2312, 2541 (4), 2542, 2568,
     2582, 2659, 2794, 2830
SCOTT, Sir William, Lord Stowell
   (1811-1813)   1447, 2432

SCOTT, Sybil (1849)   2230
SCOTT, T. (1648)   1845
SCOTT, Thomas (1602-1642)   222, 949, 1979, 2220, 2304, 2460
SCOTT, Thomas, B.D. (1622, 1659) 222, 373, 860
SCOTT, W. (1765)   805
SCOUGAL, Henry (1707)   1474
SCOUGALL, J. (1691)   823
SCRYMGEOUR, James (N.D.) 912, 2772
SCUDAMORE, Viscount James (1665)   1173
SCUDAMORE, William E. (1846) 2493
SEABURY, Dr Samuel, Bishop of Connecticut (1774, 1775) 477, 965, 2733
SEACOME, John (1767)   1576
SEAGER, Charles, M.A. (1838, 1842) 200, 559
SEAGER, Francis (1553, 1557) 353, 2271
SEALE, John Barlow (1783)   734
SEALY, J. Hungerford, M.D. (1834) 2229
SEALY, Thomas Henry (1841)   1976
SEARLE, George (1660)   633
SEATON, William (1833)   2388
SEBASTIANUS, Francken (1640)   940
SECKER, Archbishop (1768)   2588
SECKER, Thomas, LL.D. (1764)   115
SEELEY, John Robert, M.A. (1865, 1882)   720, 1694
SEDGWICK, Catherine M. (1824-1830)   410, 1177, 2105, 2625
SEDGWICK, James (1806, 1812) 1102, 1386
SEDGWICK, Rev. J. (1852)   1825
SEDLEY, Sir Charles (1648, 1678) 716, 1711, 1969, 2685
SEEBRIGHT —— (1731)   2168
SEELEY, Robert B. (1823-1869) 194, 321, 398, 827 (3), 1253, 1477, 1574, 1588, 1886, 2000, 2164
SEGAR, Sir William (1590)   249
SELDEN, —— (1640)   276
SELDEN, John (1610-1632)   136, 708
SELLER, Abednego (1680-1695)   501, 864, 942, 1145, 1920, 2163, 2164
SELLON, Lydia (1852)   2171
SELLON, Rev. Walter (1771)   399
SELWYN, William (1815, 1856) 2254, 2695
SEMPIL, Robert Lord (1573)   2316
SEMPILL, Robert (1695)   1908
SEMPILL, Sir James (1695)   1908
SENHOUSE, John (1718)   1838
SENIOR, Nassau William, A.M. (1835)   1700

SERGEANT, —— (1688)   2267
SERGEANT, John (1655-1696)   115, 664, 790, 882, 1361, 1378, 1393, 1609 (2), 1688, 2084, 2266, 2267, 2292, 2567
SERGEANT, Mrs (1843, 1855)   789, 2503
SERGEANT, R. A. (1843)   2263
SERGEANT, John (1665)   2526
SERLE, Ambrose (1775-1810)   43, 76, 364, 379, 381, 382, 400, 1717, 2314
SERRES, Olivia Wilmot (1817)   1287
SETON, William, Jun. (1700-1706) 1241, 2274, 2445
SETON, Sir William (1700, 1703)   500, 914, 2374
SETTLE, Elkanah (1677-1791)   797, 206, 358 (3), 406, 910, 1314, 1714, 1915, 2030, 2139, 2383
SEWALL, Jonathan (1776)   1556
SEWARD, William, F.R.S. (1788-1799)   91, 235, 2099, 2522
SEWELL, Elizabeth Missing (1844-1870) 78, 371, 415, 716, 859, 927, 1012, 1017, 1075, 1152, 1217, 1258, 1274, 1297, 1317, 1547, 1740, 1868, 1995, 2017, 2082 (2), 2320, 2405, 2574 (2), 2717, 2793
SEWELL, George, M.D. (1713-1720) 1245, 1716, 2158, 2184 (2), 2660
SEWELL, John (1793)   542
SEWELL, Rev. W. (1829)   405
SEWELL, Rev. William, B.D. (1831-1850)   414, 716, 1633, 2405, Errata, vol. iv.
SEWELL, William, D.D. (1850)   2712
SEYMOUR, —— (1682)   54
SEYMOUR, Ernest R. (1858)   1614
SEYMOUR, Henry Danby, M.P. (1860)   868
SEYMOUR, John (1752)   1588
SHACKLETON, Abraham (1815)   527
SHADWELL, Charles (1710)   877
SHADWELL, Thomas (1674, 1689) 477, 1563, 1752, 2260, 2437
SHAFTE, J. (1673)   1047
SHAFTESBURY, Earl of (N.D., 1708) 984, 1345
SHAFTESBURY, Earl of, Anthony A. Cooper (1675, 1716) 363, 599, 1353, 1354, 1658, 2290, 2304, 2344, 2415, 2700, 2701
SHAKESPEARE, William (1581-1607)   261, 449, 2057
SHAND, Alexander (1817)   861
SHANNON, Edward N. (1826)   531

SHANNON, Viscount, Francis
   Boyle (1690, 1691)   1422, 1657
SHARP, —— (1706, 1713)   157, 762
SHARP, Abraham (1717-1718)   1010
SHARP, Granville (1765-1810)   41, 409,
         754, 2133, 2139, 2151, 2376
SHARP, Hercules (1825)   995
SHARP, John, D.D. (1684, 1685) 641, 650
SHARP, John, Jun. (1790)   2189
SHARP, Richard (1790, 1834) 1403, 1423
SHARP, Richard, M.P. (1828)   785
SHARP, Sir Cuthbert (1819-1841)
   239, 273, 392, 708, 1491, 1597, 2285,
                                   2843
SHARP, Thomas (1817, 1820) 1844, 2416
SHARP, Thomas, D.D., Archdeacon
   of Northumberland (1733)   2742
SHARP, William (1769, 1770) 163, 2648
SHARPE, —— (1713)   2124
SHARPE, Charles Kirkpatrick(1823-
   1834)   209, 1593, 1865, 1976, 2825
SHARPE, Lancelot, M.A. (1846)   83
SHARPE, Launcelot (1794)   1952
SHARPE, Gregory, LL.D. (1739-
   1795) 590, 1418, 1472, 2198, 2365, 2373
SHARPHAM, Edward (1607)   548
SHARROCK, Robert (1663-71)   2422
SHAW, C. (1849)   526
SHAW, Cuthbert (1760-1768)   516, 948,
                      1653, 1804, 2073
SHAW, Donald (1859)   1097
SHAW, Duncan, D.D. (1769)   675
SHAW, Ferdinando (1713)   2721
SHAW J. (1709)   1450
SHAW, J. B. (1863)   2454
SHAW, Lieutenant (1849)   2773
SHAW, Peter, M.D. (1724-1750)   675,
                   1286, 1900, 2115
SHAW, R. (1800)   1770
SHAW, Samuel (1668, 1679) 2776, 2837
SHAW, Stebbing (N.D.)   2611
SHAW, T. B., M.A. (1857)   11
SHAW, W. (1738)   678
SHAW, William, D.D. (1802)   1474
SHAW, William G. (1868)   1596
SHEARS, Henry (1693-8)   1145
SHEBBEARE, John, M.D. (1754-
   1783) 124, 165, 202, 305, 921, 952, 1153,
   1402, 1447, 1528, 1549, 1794, 1961, 2300,
                   2343, 2396, 2568
SHEBBEARE, John (1855-1856)   949
SHEE, Sir Martin Archer (1829-1835)
                   345, 1072, 1815
SHEEHY, William, J. A. (1838)   2167

SHEERE, Sir Henry (1698)   804
SHEERS, Sir H. (1700)   652
SHEFFIELD, John, Duke of Bucking-
   ham (1682)   819
SHEFFIELD, Lord (1783)   1775
SHEFFIELD, Lord, John B. Hol-
   royd (1783-1790)   439, 1783
SHELBURNE, Lord (1848)   1435
SHELDON, Richard (1611)   349
SHELLEY, Mary W., née Godwin (1788-
   1838) 884, 945, 957, 1131, 1319, 1502,
                   1505, 1829, 2721
SHELLEY, Percy Bysshe(1810-1822)778,
   1131, 1458, 1706, 1805, 1979, 2250, 2797,
                                   2851
SHELTON, Maurice (1718)   1111
SHENSTONE, William (1734-1742)
                   1284, 1954, 2270
SHEPHERD, —— (1773)   1323
SHEPHERD, Henry John (N.D.)   1571
SHEPHERD, Lady Mary (1819, 1824)
                             773, 822
SHEPHERD, R. (1771)   2183
SHEPHERD, Rev. Richard, Arch-
   deacon of Bedford (1756)   1802
SHEPHERD, Rev. Richard, D.D.
   (1759, 1779)   1080, 2109, 2194
SHEPHERD, Rev. Richard (1858) 1873
SHEPHERD, Richard (1761, 1762)
                         1761, 1803
SHEPHERD, W. (1829)   419
SHEPPARD, Elizabeth Sarah (1853-
   1859)   70, 365, 520, 701, 2239
SHEPPARD, John (1862, 1865)2574, 2837
SHEPPARD, Samuel (1647-1651)   440,
                   1281, 2305
SHEPPARD, Sarah (1837, 1841)   362,
                                   1206
SHEPPARD, William (1653-1658)   841,
                   1864, 2388
SHEPPEN, William (1718)   2590
SHEPPERD, R. H. (1866)   2553
SHERER, Moyle (1821-1838)   286, 1208,
   1752, 2100, 2263, 2403, 2498, 2544
SHERIDAN, —— (1781)   2203
SHERIDAN, —— (1802)   2269
SHERIDAN, Charles (1779)   1777
SHERIDAN, Charles F. (1797)   2431
SHERIDAN, Frances, née Chamber-
   laine (1763-1772) 664, 710, 1144, 1583
SHERIDAN, Miss (1839)   626
SHERIDAN, Mr (1721)   243
SHERIDAN, Mrs Thomas (1830,
   1833)   60, 310

SHERIDAN, Richard Brinsley (1771-
  1786)   708, 1518, 2217, 2269, 2451
SHERIDAN, Thomas (1677-1755) 513,
             655, 1239
SHERLOCK, —— (1836)   1445
SHERLOCK, Richard, D.D. (1674) 1253
SHERLOCK, Thomas (1729)   2684
SHERLOCK, Thomas, D.D. (1717-
  1756)   311, 524, 1166, 1822, 2163
SHERLOCK, William, D.D. (1681-
  1719) 107, 108, 119, 125, 263, 499, 587,
  638, 640, 646, 681, 1367 (2), 1372, 1376,
  1717, 1753, 1852, 1914, 2006, 2025, 2042,
    2043 (2), 2185, 2298, 2375, 2750
SHERMAN, J. (1661)   14
SHERMAN, T. (1671, 1680) 2851, 2852
SHEWELL, John Talwyn (1808) 2653
SHIELDS, Alexander (1687, 1690) 1099,
             2372
SHIELDS, Mr (1692)   1147
SHIELS —— (1707)   1224
SHIELS, Alexander, or Shields,
      Errata, vol. iv.
SHIERS, William (1700)   887
SHILLABER, B. P. (N.D.)   1677
SHILLITO, Charles (1788, 1790) 521, 2453
SHILLITOE, Thomas (N.D.)   7
SHIPLEY, Jonathan, D.D. (1774) 2469
SHIPPEN, R. (1712)   2237
SHIPPEN, William (1704-1732) 874, 950,
    1638, 2324, 2468, 2469
SHIPTON, Joseph (1830)   2655
SHIRLEY, James (1640, 1661) 514, 548,
             1520
SHIRLEY, John, A.M. (1677)   1483
SHIRLEY, John, M.D. (1678)   2362
SHIRLEY, T. (1784)   92
SHIRLEY, William (1758)   271
SHIRRA, Robert (1781)   131
SHITTLER, Robert (N.D.)   697 (2)
SHOBERL, Frederic (1816, 1828) 235,
             2544
SHORE, A. and L. (1855)   2788
SHORE, Frederick John (1852)   2147
SHORE, John, Lord Teignmouth
  (1808, 1834)   486, 2582
SHORE, Louisa (1861)   1067
SHORT, J. (1780)   2213
SHORT, Thomas, M.D. (1749)   998
SHORTHOUSE, J. H. (1882)   1270
SHORTREDE, Andrew (1840)   1355
SHOWER, Sir Bartholomew (1679-
  1735) 325, 454, 1366, 1533, 1557, 2089,
             2310, 2566

SHOWERS, Capt. Charles (1853) 2036
SHUCKBURGH, Charles (1740) 137
SHURLEY, John, M.A. (1682) 723
SHUTE, Hardwicke, M.A. (N.D.) 547
SHUTTE, Christopher (1577) 2555
SHUTTLEWORTH, Sir John K.
  (1847)   2269
SIBBALD, Sir Robert (1693-1709) 126,
          793, 1357
SIDEY, James A., M.D. (1869, 1877) 72,
          1636
SIDNEY, Algernon (1744)   2718
SIDNEY, Lord, G. Osborne (1866) 1447
SIEUR DU BAUDRIÈR (1711) 1724
SIGERSON, George, M.D. (1868) 1641
SIKES, George (1662)   1465
SIKES, Thomas, M.A. (1805)   37
SILL, Richard (1797)   2146
SIM, Robert (1852, 1865)   244, 1811
SIME, James (1854)   1664
SIME, James, M.A. (1877)   612
SIME, William (1829, 1830) 1151, 1152
SIMEON, Rev. —— (1811)   1220
SIMMONDS, —— (1790)   1721
SIMMONS, Thomas F. (1819)   2153
SIMMS, W. G. (1841)   471
SIMON, Richard (1685)   1162
SIMON, Thomas Collyns (1847) 1703
SIMOND, Louis (1815)   1275
SIMONDS, Rev. H. (1828-9)   624
SIMPSON, Elizabeth Inchbald née
  (1785-1788)   99, 162, 1649, 2814
SIMPSON, J. (N.D.)   199
SIMPSON, J. (1822)   1101
SIMPSON, James (N.D., 1822) 75, 1452
SIMPSON, Jane Cross, née Bell
  (1836)   1912
SIMPSON, John (1764)   2111
SIMPSON, Joseph (1785)   1873
SIMPSON, J. Palgrave (1846-1847) 1014,
          1430, 2302
SIMPSON, Rev. —— (1783)   212
SIMPSON, Sydrach (1647)   627
SIMPSON, William, M.D. (1680) 2430
SIMPSON, Wolley (1843)   2026
SIMSON, Archibald (1795)   101
SIMSON, David (1723)   2663
SIMSON, Mathias (1703)   2362
SINCLAR, George (1684)   2683
SINCLAIR, J. L. (1864)   1823
SINCLAIR, John (1835)   796
SINCLAIR, John, Master of (1716) 2661
SINCLAIR, Sir Archibald (1703) 2444,
          2487, 2574

SINCLAIR, Sir George, Bart. (1828, 1854)   180, 1972
SINCLAIR, Sir John (1782-1796)   25, 1524, 2581
SINCLAIR, William (1772)   907
SINGER, Samuel Weller (1817, 1818)   625, 702
SINGLETON, J. (1615)   703
SINGLETON, Mrs (1872, 1875) 602, 975
SINGLETON, William (1814, 1824) 1343, 1598
SIRR, Rev. Joseph D'Arcy, B.A. (1815)   1472
SISSON, John (1848)   1827
SKEFFINGTON, John, Kt. and Bart. (1652)   1091
SKELTON, John, Advocate (1862, 1865)   303, 1086, 1758, 2557
SKELTON, Philip (1736, 1751) 598, 1820, 2764
SKELTON, Philip, B.A. (1736)   2435
SKELTON, Rev. Philip (1744, 1755)   305, 662
SKENE, Alexander (1685)   1595
SKENE, Alexander (1833)   2512
SKENE, Felicia M. F. (1847-1876) 684, 1225, 1569, 1882, 2249, 2687, 2718, 2796
SKENE, G. (1797)   40
SKENE, Harriet (1853)   627
SKENE, J. (1703)   978, 1922
SKENE, James Henry (1853, 1854) 80, 563, 975
SKIDMORE, Emmett (1836)   1424
SKIDMORE, Joseph (1713, 1714)   821, 2012
SKINNER, Dr (1694)   2430
SKINNER, John (1757)   674
SKINNER, John, Bishop of Aberdeen (1792)   422, 1698
SKINNER, John, D.D. (1822)   336
SKINNER, R. (N.D.)   388
SKINNER, Rev. —— (1801)   919
SKINNER, Rev. John (N.D.)   1386
SKYNNER-DOUGLAS, Sir John, Kt. (1604)   2078
SLADE, John, M.A. (1676)   986, 2335
SLADEN, John (1732, 1733)   95, 2094
SLATIUS, Henricus (1814)   1992
SLATTER, James W. (1825)   2241
SLATYER, William (1642, 1643) 2050 (2)
SLEECH, John, Archdeacon of Cornwall (1762)   1674
SLEEMAN, R. (1833)   1363
SLIDELL, Alexander (1836)   74

SMALBROKE, Richard, D.D. (1711)   1713, 2109
SMALL, John (1713-1719) 154, 952, 2359, 2437
SMALLBROOKE, Richard, D.D. (1722)   766
SMALLWOOD, Edward (1837, 1840)   556, 1545
SMALRIDGE, George, D.D. (1687)   97, 2110
SMALRIDGE, George, D.D., Bishop of Bristol (1701)   2441
SMART, Benjamin H. (1831-1857) 1379, 1569, 1607, 1837, 2325
SMART, Christopher (1750, 1751) 1179, 2508 (2)
SMEDLEY, Edward, M.A. (1818, 1832)   403, 1527, 1864, 2128, 2402
SMEDLEY, Francis E. (1850)   956
SMEDLEY, J. (1710)   692
SMEDLEY, Jonathan (1728)   1059
SMEDLEY, Jonathan, Dean of Clogher (1721)   1950
SMEDLEY, Menella Bute (1852-1863) 1332, 1490, 1536, 1604, 1742, 2499, 2689, 2718
SMEETON, George (1812)   930
SMELLIE, Alexander (1784)   41
SMILES, R. W. (185—, 1869) 727, 2788
SMIRKE, Robert, R.A. (1815-16)   283
SMITH, Adam (1744)   803
SMITH, Arthur (1847)   2075
SMITH, Caleb (1735)   604
SMITH, Captain (1771-1773) 1001, 1562, 1782
SMITH, Charles (1744)   136
SMITH, Charles (1798)   566
SMITH, Charles (1824)   1343
SMITH, Charles (1758-1766) 2366, 2591
SMITH, Charles Manby (N.D.)   2839
SMITH, Charles Roach (1854)   906
SMITH, Charlotte (1862-1868)   101, 387, 708, 1497, 2221, 2242, 2271
SMITH, C. Lesingham (1835)   1275
SMITH, Dr (1776)   1927
SMITH, Eaglesfield (1796)   2816
SMITH, Edward, M.D. (1865)   1184
SMITH, E. J. (1798)   2390
SMITH, Elisha, M.A. (1719-1736)   550, 1325
SMITH, Elizabeth (1808, 1853) 357, 955, 1581
SMITH, Frederick (1809-1814)   13, 162, 970

SMITH, G. E. (1823)   2495

SMITH, George (1718-1754) 92, 165, 266, 285, 587, 786, 2163, 2692, 2744

SMITH, George (1833)   875

SMITH, George Barnett (1878)   2838

SMITH, Godwin, M.A. (1861)   462, 2525

SMITH, H. (1681)   1715

SMITH, Hannah, *see* Sarah

SMITH, Hely H. A. (N.D.)   708

SMITH, Henry (1591)   852, 2590, 2637

SMITH, Horace (1812-1844) 32, 73, 186, 253, 991 (2), 1261, 1613, 1721, 1816, 2190, 2543, 2607, 2786, 2854

SMITH, Horace and James (1812-1836)   1177, 2125, 2594

SMITH, J. (1724)   1370

SMITH, Ja. (1656)   1681

SMITH, James (1784)   182

SMITH, James (1687, 1712)   620, 2295

SMITH, James Alexander (1856-1861)   192, 744, 1020, 2508

SMITH, John (1683)   693

SMITH, John (1675)   1179

SMITH, John (1813)   1610

SMITH, John (1790)   1612

SMITH, John Gordon, M.D. (1830)   754

SMITH, John Stores (1848)   1619

SMITH, Joseph, D.D. (1754)   412

SMITH, Julia, *née* Bernard (1809-1813)   1443, 1814, 2020

SMITH, Leweson (1827)   2159

SMITH, ——, M.A. (1752)   1388

SMITH, Matthew (1700)   2672

SMITH, Nich. (1652)   1223

SMITH, Parson, probably William (1755)   272

SMITH, Rev. George, M.A. (1799) 1398

SMITH, Rev. Samuel, M.A. (1856) 1505

SMITH, Rev. William (1756, 1766) 274, 1107

SMITH, Richard (1606)   126

SMITH, Richard, Bishop of Chalcedon (1609-1655)   202, 273, 682, 2049

SMITH, Robert (1790)   1612

SMITH, Robert Angus (1879)   1504

SMITH, Samuel (1675)   360

SMITH, Samuel (1746)   2054

SMITH, Samuel, M.A. (1849)   2832

SMITH, Sarah (1864-1880)   416, 533, 565, 689, 875, 973, 1094, 1218, 1263, 1306, 1515, 1539, 1560, 1611, 1710, 1740, 1745, 1814, 1876, 1913, 2498, 2573, 2690, 2828, 2843, Errata, vol. iv.

SMITH, Seba (1834)   1432

SMITH, Sydney (1807-1808) 1449, 2589, 2696, Errata, vol. iv.

SMITH, Sir William Cusack (1803-1836)   104, 1416, 1607, 2076, 2846

SMITH, Thomas (1804)   2083

SMITH, Thomas, D.D. (1688, 1693) 638, 641, 1843

SMITH, Thomas, S.T.B. (1687)   1479

SMITH, Thomas, S.T.P. (1705)   767

SMITH, Walter Chalmers, D.D. (1861-1878)   239, 250, 1098, 1816

SMITH, Wentworth (1607)   2057

SMITH, William (1606)   239

SMITH, William (1803)   344

SMITH, William (1847)   916

SMITH, William (1662, 1685)   504, 780, 1035, 1281, 2420

SMITH, William (1756-1766) 1211, 1348, 1877

SMITH, William, LL.D. (1808)   2561

SMITH, William P., D.D. (1880)   2277

SMITH, W. S. (1849)   331

SMITHURST, Benjamin (1696)   755

SMITHIES, William (1706)   421

SMOLLETT, Tobias George (1749-1783)   50 (3), 51, 859, 2123

SOMOLLETT, Tobias, M.D. (1747-1769)   52, 1126, 1750, 2182 (2)

SMYTH, A. Gillespie (1832-1835) 1817, 2024, 2321

SMYTH, Charles John, M.A. (N.D.) 584

SMYTH, John (1692)   2262

SMYTH, John, M.A. (1691)   2817

SMYTH, Philip (1802)   2206

SMYTH, Philip, LL.D. (1795)   421

SMYTH, Professor (1840)   1571

SMYTHIES, Harriet M. Yorick, *née* Gordon (1835-1869)   254, 256, 528 (2), 931, 1177, 1267, 1471, 1521, 1550, 1551, 1558, 2792

SMYTHIES, William (1671)   56

SNAPE, Andrew (1736)   1993

SNAPE, Rev. Andrew, D.D. (1717) 467

SNART, Charles (1801)   1985

SNELL, —— (1833)   2181

SNELLING, Thomas (1762, 1763) 2734, 2736

SNETT, —— (N.D.)   1438

SNODGRASS, John, D.D. (1770)   728

SNOW, Robert (1842)   1275, 1774

SNOWDEN, Samuel (1693)   602

SNOWE, Joseph (1836)   2260

SOAMES, Henry, A.M., Dean of St Paul's (1823)   2751

SOANE, George (1826, 1834)   974, 2465
SOLARI, Marchioness Broglio, Catherine Hyde (1824-1827) 2020, 2313, 2725
SOMERS, John, Lord Somers (1681-1771) 267, 1286, 1288, 1304, 2315, 2761
SOMERSET, Wellington (1871)   499
SOMERVILLE, —— (1718)   2088
SOMERVILLE, —— (1751)   2508
SOMERVILLE, Alexander (1863)   204
SOMERVILLE, J. (1824)   2177
SOMMERDYCK, Aarsens de (1670) 1279
SOMNER, William, (N.D.)   975
SOULIGNE, —— de (1701-1710)   446, 1507, 1814
SOUTER, Joseph (1816)   1035
SOUTH, Robert, D.D. (1693-1716)   98, 460, 2337, 2370, 2657
SOUTH, Thomas (1846)   716
SOUTHERN, Henry (1820-1838) 1783, 2189, 2324
SOUTHESK, Earl of, J. Carnegie (1862)   1088
SOUTHEY, Mrs, *née* Caroline Bowles (1820-1829)   357, 741, 2415, 2544, 2814
SOUTHEY, Robert (1807-1847)   686, 1382, 1427, 1817, 2516
SOUTHEY, Robert, LL.D. (1803-1817)   73, 2793
SOUTHWARK, Bishop, T. Grant (1855)   1095
SOUTHWELL, Robert (1594-1605) 782, 1547, 1649, 2252, 2374, 2659
SOWDEN, Thomas (1857)   2383
SOWTER, John (1716)   2795
SPADEMAN, Edwin (N.D.)   923
SPALDING, Thomas (1845)   1611
SPALDING, William (1833)   1362
SPARROW, Dr Anthony, Bishop of Norwich (1661)   423
SPATEMAN, Thomas (1742)   2268
SPEARMAN, Alexander (1775)   1826
SPEARMAN, Robert (1753-1759) 7, 765, 1450
SPEED, John (1611-15)   996
SPEED, John, M.D. (1706, 1759)   215, 1210
SPELMAN, Clement (1647, 1648)   1388, 2096
SPELMAN, Edward (1743)   954
SPELMAN, Sir Henry (1642)   2044
SPELMAN, Sir John, Bart. (1642-1643)   316, 348, 663, 2731
SPENCE, Catherine Ellen (1854, 1856)   410, 2552

SPENCE, David (1721)   176
SPENCE, Elizabeth (1827)   559
SPENCE, Elizabeth I. (1799)   1082
SPENCE, F. (1795)   746
SPENCE, James Mudie, F.R.G.S. (1877)   1484
SPENCE, Joseph (1731, 1752) 977, 1865
SPENCE, Joseph, A.M. (1727)   800
SPENCE, Professor John (1753)   1659
SPENCE, Rev. Joseph (1748, 1752) 542, 1924
SPENCE, T. (1793-5)   1913
SPENCE, Thomas (1707)   2555
SPENCER, Capt. Edmund (1836)   2403
SPENCER, Dr A. (1745)   813
SPENCER, John (1657)   2072
SPENCER, Rev. Frederick Charles (1816)   1276
SPENS, Hary, D.D. (1751)   1226
SPENS, J. (1836)   1572
SPENSER, Edmund (1590, 1591)   452, 1678, 2039, 2350, 2548
SPIER, John (1752)   386
SPILSBURY, Francis (1794)   182
SPINCKES, Mr (1710)   1464
SPINCKES, Nathaniel, M.A. (1713-1720)   324, 1744, 1745 (2), 1746, 2178
SPINDLER, C. (1832)   1264, 1266
SPINK, William, S.S.C. (1873)   2263
SPINOZA, Benedict de (1689)   2647
SPOTISWOODE, J. (N.D.)   2470
SPOTSWOOD, Sir John (1706)   2655
SPRAT, Bp. (1658)   1693
SPRAT, Thomas, D.D. Bishop of Rochester (1685)   2660
SPRIGGE, William, M.A. (1657-1660) 1903, 2232
SPRIGGS, William, M.A. (1659)   1646
SPURSTOWE, Dr William (1847)   2615
SPURSTOWE, William (1641) 106, 2749
SQUIBB, William (1827)   1012
SQUIER, Ephraim George (1856)   51
SQUIRE, Francis (1740, N.D.) 883, 2802 (2)
SQUIRE, Samuel, D.D. (1746-1751) 1376, 1383, 2141, 2147, 2160
SQUIRE, Samuel, D.D., Bishop of St David's (1741, 1748)   88, 1117
SQUIRE, Susannah Newcome *née* (1738)   1918
SQUIRE, William (1670)   2715
STACE, Machell (1810)   543
STACE, Michael (1829)   71
STACEY, Mary (1836)   1362
STACKHOUSE, Thomas (1722)   1632

STACKHOUSE, Thomas (1822)　　2246
STAFFORD, James Charles, B.D.
　(1840)　　　　　　　　　　718
STAFFORD, Richard, B.A. (1693)　2444
STAFFORD, William (1581)　261, 449
STAIR, Earl of, James Dalrymple
　(1695)　　　　　　　　　　2753
STAIR, Earl of, John Dalrymple
　(1781)　　　　　　　　　　489
STALLENGE, William (1609)　　1236
STALLYBRASS, —— (1872)　　1081
STANBRIDGE, John (N.D.)　　　1892
STANDISH, Arthur (1613)　　　1719
STANGER, John (1774)　　　　735
STANHOPE, Captain (1720)　　1672
STANHOPE, Dean (1692)　　　583
STANHOPE, Michael (1627, 1633)　551,
　　　　　　　　　　　　　1738
STANHOPE, Philip (1743)　　　900
STANHOPE, Philip Dormer, Earl
　of Chesterfield (1743-1821)　146, 319,
　　　　　　900, 1435, 1805, 2742, 2841
STANHOPE, Philip, Earl of Stan-
　hope (1734)　　　　　　　2489
STANHOPE, Philip Henry, Earl
　Stanhope (1833, 1834)　1429, 1513
STANHOPE, Sir William (1748)　1828
STANLEY, Charles, Earl of Derby
　(1671, 1678)　　　　　1265, 2681
STANLEY, Edward Geoffrey, Earl
　of Derby (1828)　　　　　508
STANLEY, Hon. Alethea Maud
　(1878)　　　　　　　　　2838
STANLEY, Louisa Dorothea (1854)　2788
STANLEY, Mary (1873)　　　2679
STANLEY, Miss (1855)　　　　1180
STANLEY, Rev. Arthur P. (1845)　1630
STANLEY, Right Hon. Lord (1850)　2396
STANLEY, Thomas (1647-1685)　80, 201,
　　　　　　　　　　　　　644
STANLEY, William, D.D. (1674,
　1688)　　　　　　　　880, 2226
STANNUS, Beauchamp W. (N.D.)　1226
STANSFIELD, David (1760)　　306
STANWIX, Richard, B.D. (1652)　1171
STANYAN, Temple (1714)　　　17
STANYHURST, R. (1593)　　　1905
STAPYLTON, Miles, D.D. (1736)　2700
STAPYLTON, R. (1593)　　　　1905
STAPYLTON, Sir Robert (1663,
　1664)　　　　　　　　2407, 2492
STARK, Adam (1823)　　　　2495
STARK, James, M.D., F.R.S.E.
　(1878)　　　　　　　　　2252

STARKE, James (1832)　　　　1246
STARKEY, Digby P. (1853, 1858)　86,
　　　　　　　　　　　　　1801
STARLING, Elizabeth (1835)　　1746
STARLING, Samuel (1670)　　　126
STATHAM, John (1650)　　　　335
STAUNTON, Sir George, Bart.
　(1824)　　　　　　　　　1753
STAUNTON, W. (1642)　　　2501
STAUNTON, William (1719, 1722)
　　　　　　　　　　2084, 2388
STAVELY, Thomas (1674)　　　2226
STAYLEY, George (1759)　　　2217
STEADMAN, Fabian (1677)　　304
STEBBING, Henry, D.D., Arch-
　deacon of Wilts (1718-1757)　103, 589,
　595, 657, 692, 768, 848, 953, 1769,
　　　　　　　　　　　　　1842
STEDMAN, John, M.D. (1782-
　1784)　　　　　　　1314, 1657
STEEDMAN, John, M.D. (1765-
　1784)　　　　　　　1130, 1178
STEEL, A. (1796)　　　　　2687
STEEL, Anne (1760)　　　　1951
STEEL, D. (1794)　　　　　737
STEEL, Rev. —— (1821)　　　764
STEEL, Robert (N.D.)　　　　1500
STEELE, —— (1712)　　　　1565
STEELE, Rev. Henry (1733)　　963
STEELE, Sir Richard (1695-1746)　134,
　135, 379, 568, 1028, 1037, 1229, 1254,
　1395, 1520, 1524, 1921, 1940, 1993, 2025,
　　　　　　　　2055, 2472, 2558
STEER, George (1734)　　　　456
STEEVENS, George (1779)　　2395
STEHELIN, Rev. John Peter,
　F.R.S. (1742)　　　　　　2618
STEILL, David (1603)　　　　2592
STEINMETZ, Andrew (N.D.)　　913
STEPHEN, James (1802-1807)　534, 562,
　　　　　　1728, 1821, 2470, 2788
STEPHEN, James Fitzjames, Q.C.
　(1862)　　　　　　　　　824
STEPHEN, Sir George (1835, 1844)
　　　　　　　　　48, 49, 1057
STEPHENS, Ann S. (1854)　　2851
STEPHENS, David (1746)　　　2576
STEPHENS, E. (1601)　　　　1606
STEPHENS, Edward (1675-1704)　8,
　45, 46, 147, 149, 188, 203, 221, 260, 322,
　344, 464, 480, 1028, 1190, 1216, 1294,
　1301, 1373, 1392, 1633, 1661, 1705, 1788,
　1809, 1926, 1980, 2066, 2071, 2114, 2128,
　　　　2349, 2474, 2561, 2668, 2827

STEPHENS, Edward, of Chering-
ton (1674-1706) 1370, 1479, 1499, 1668,
1974, 2463, 2705
STEPHENS *or* STEVENS, Edward
(1691) 158
STEPHENS, Frederic G. (1869) 717
STEPHENS, George (1821, 1839) 974,
2722
STEPHENS, J. (1661) 2025
STEPHENS, Jeremy (1660) 150
STEPHENS, John (1661) 1116
STEPHENS, John Lloyd (1838) 1218
STEPHENS, Mr —— (1676) 497
STEPHENS, Nathaniel (1654) 2767
STEPHENS, R. (N.D.) 9
STEPHENS, W. (1864) 2519
STEPHENS, William (1709) 20
STEPHENS, William, B.D. (1699,
1705) 1381, 1391
STEPHENSON, —— (1833) 1501
STEPNEY, George (1701) 822
STERLING, John (1833, 1841) 186, 732,
931
STERLING, Sir Anthony C. (N.D.) 1429
STERNE, Lawrence, D.D. (1760-
1775) 1431, 1468, 2322, 2339
STERNE, Richard (1649) 261
STEUART, Adam (1644) 2427
STEUART, Sir Henry, Bart., LL.D.
(1799) 996
STEVENS, —— (1723) 724
STEVENS, Captain John (1707,
1722) 1651, 2461
STEVENS, Edward Stephens *or*
(1691) 158
STEVENS, George Alexander (1760-
1785) 346, 527, 704, 967, 1168, 2656
STEVENS, Grace Buchanan (1818) 1504
STEVENS, John (1725) 2235
STEVENS, M. (1826) 2131
STEVENS, William (1773-1800) 553,
658, 2202, 2205, 2504, 2644
STEVENS, William, F.S.A. (1773) 1712
STEVENSON, —— (1867) 1071
STEVENSON, Andrew (1743, 1747)
1409, 1680, 2790
STEVENSON, John (1779, 1780) 39, 1366
STEVENSON, John Hall (1760-
1783) 822, 1529, 1537, 1658, 1751,
1870 (2), 2698
STEVENSON, Miss (1870) 1173
STEVENSON, W. F. (1846) 1667
STEVENSON, William, D.D.
(1872) 1339

STEWARD, T. F. (1834-1840) 1239,
1555, 1992
STEWARD, Richard, D.D. (1688) 261
STEWARD, Richard (LL.D. (1647) 109
STEWARD, Richard, LL.D., Dean
of Westminster (1682) 1813
STEWART, Adam (1644) 2427
STEWART, Agnes M. (1870, N.D.) 70,
1470
STEWART, Alexander P., M.D.
(1843, 1859) 682, 2015
STEWART, Andrew (1858) 417
STEWART, Charles (1801, 1808) 366, 739
STEWART, Charles Edward (1801,
1803) 171, 867
STEWART, Elizabeth M. (1845,
1850) 1015, 2221, 2235
STEWART, George (1787) 2106
STEWART, J. (1818) 247
STEWART, John (N.D.) 142, 1658, 2628
STEWART, John (1793) 249
STEWART, Professor Balfour
(1875) 2715
STEWART, Professor John (1790) 2399
STEWART, Rev. J. H. (1828-9) 624
STEWART, Richard, LL.D., Dean
of Westminster (1682) 1813
STEWART, Sir James (1669, 1712) 1290,
1764
STEWART, Sir James (1830) 1471
STEWART, William (1731) 1410
STEWART, William Grant (1860) 1336(2)
STHALBERG, George (1776) 1159
STICKNEY, Sarah, Mrs William
Ellis *née* (1843) 1669, 2776
STILEMAN, John (1662) 654
STILL, John, M.A. (1575) 2243
STILLINGFLEET, —— (1691) 2741
STILLINGFLEET, Benjamin (1738,
1760) 1175, 2443
STILLINGFLEET, Edward, D.D.
(1677-1693) 118, 123, 312, 518, 645, 648,
694 (2), 695, 1041, 1266, 1366, 1385,
2299, 2343, 2749, 2766
STILLINGFLEET, John (1697) 2414
STIRLING, John (1717) 2158
STIRLING, Mrs (1849, 1865) 894, 2315
STIRLING, Rev. James (1667) 1692
STIRLING, William, M.P. (1847,
1851) 516, 1341
STIRLING - MAXWELL, Sir W.
(1848) 2453
STOCK, Joseph, Bishop of Killala
(1800) 1699

STOCK, Simon (1637-8)   2771
STOCKDALE, J. J. (1803, 1812)   2398, 2401
STOCKDALE, Mary (1821)   1471
STOCKDALE, Percival (1765, 1773)   403, 1954
STOCKER, Richard (1824)   900
STODDART, Dr (1853)   326
STODDART, J. (1796)   921
STOGDON, H. (1719)   2286
STOKES, George (1826, 1841)   228, 439, 1157
STOKES, Henry Sewell (1871)   2207
STOKES, Rev. George (1818)   1943
STOKES, Whitley (1862)   1933, 2587
STONA, Rev. Thomas, M.A. (1758, 1759)   1401, 2163
STONE, ——, A.M. (1768)   2358
STONE, Cecil Percival (1858)   1903, Errata, vol. iv.
STONE, F. (1841)   183
STONE, George, D.D. (1770)   2181
STONE, John (1798)   1137
STONECASTLE, Henry (1756)   2712
STONEHOUSE, —— (1762)   389
STONEHOUSE, James (1762)   2712
STONEHOUSE, Sir James, M.D. (1776)   1102
STONEHOUSE, William B. (1828)   545
STORY, George (1691)   2663
STORY, Jonathan (1721)   1241
STORY, Robert Herbert, D.D. (1863)   1946
STORY, Sydney A. (1854)   1201
STORY, Thomas (1740)   2601
STOTHERT, James Augustine (1843-1845)   1296 (2), 2374
STOTHERT, Rev. William (1850)   1924
STOW, John (1809-1850)   229, 2110, 2318, 2579, 2727
STOWE, Archdeacon of, John Fowne (1766)   2141
STOWE, Harriet Beecher (1855)   2410
STOWELL, Lord, Sir William Scott (1811, 1813)   1447, 2432
STRACHAN, William (1694)   2440
STRACHAN, W. N. (1879)   1122
STRACHEY, —— (1739)   1220
STRAHAN, William, LL.D. (1712)   2603
STRAIGHT, Douglas (1867, 1868)   1072, 2231
STRANG, John, LL.D. (1863)   2625
STRANGE, Richard, S.J. (1674)   1278, 1468

STRANGE, Sir John (1754)   427
STRATFORD, —— (1784)   926
STRATFORD, Edmund, D.D. (1632)   668
STRATFORD, Nicholas (1688)   655
STRATFORD, Nicholas, Bishop of Chester (1657-1688)   646, 951, 1330, 1707, 1754, 1883
STRATHMORE, Countess of (1774)   2382
STREATFIELD, Thomas (1838)   1528, 1812
STRETSER or STRETZER, Thomas (1741)   1718
STRETTELL, Amos (1632)   1741
STRINGER, Moses, M.D. (N.D.)   1820
STRONACH, George, M.A. (1879-1880)   1458, 1661, 1723
STRONG, Charles, M.A. (1827)   2465
STRONG, Martin (1701)   813
STRUTT, —— (1803)   1129
STRUTT, Elizabeth (1833-1835)   356, 2396
STRUTT, Joseph (1782)   733
STRUTT, S. (1732)   1901
STRYPE, John (1698)   1482
STUART, Andrew (1766-1784)   487, 2024
STUART, Betty (1810)   1314
STUART, C. (1856)   2164
STUART, Charles (1779, 1808)   420, 2755
STUART, Dr Charles (1765)   1628
STUART, Gilbert, LL.D. (1768-1799)   1116, 1437, 1965
STUART, James (1771)   540
STUART, James, LL.D. (1825)   2041
STUART, Peter (1812)   2582
STUART, Richard, LL.D., Dean of Westminster (1682)   1813
STUART, Sir James (1667)   1692
STUBBE, Henry (1659-1672)   443, 680, 1295, 1486, 1564, 1796, 2229, 2464
STUBBES, George (1731)   1711
STUBBE or STUBBES, Henry (1659)   1796
STUBBES, Henry (1675)   680
STUBBES, John (1579)   663
STUBBS, G. (1731)   622
STUBBS, John (1579)   663
STUBBS, John (1670)   2666
STUBBS, Rev. George (1733)   963
STUCKLEY, J. (1667)   1033
STUDLEY, John (1574)   1844
STURCH, William (1799)   141
STURGES, John, LL.D. (1772)   1365
STURGIS, Julian Russell (1878)   1269
STURGIS, Robert S. (1859)   941

STURMY, John (1723)   461

STYLES, John, D.D. (1815, 1839)   1339, 2057

SUCKLING, Sir John (1638, 1641)   58, 511 (2)

SUDBURY, Archdeacon of, N. Clagett, D.D. (1685)   1891

SUFFIELD, Rev. Robert Rodolph (1844-1867)   1496, 1833, 2228, 2705

SUFFOLK, Archdeacon of, Dr L. Womock (1682)   2696

SUFFOLK, Earl of, Edward Hyde (1725, 1728)   1630, 1681

SULIVAN or SULLIVAN, Richard J. (1779)   83

SULIVAN, Sir Rich. J. (1780) 1769, 2613

SULLIVAN, Arabella (1833)   2098

SULLIVAN, James Frank (N.D.)   1020, 1319

SULLIVAN, Richard J. Sulivan or (1779)   83

SULTON, Edward (1624)   130

SUMNER, John Bird, D.D. (1815)   156

SURR, Thomas Skinner (1796, 1807) 479, 1555

SURTEES, Richard (1818)   714

SURTEES, Robert Smith (1838-1865) 188, 1065, 1075, 1098, 1272, 1673, 1675, 1924

SUTCLIFFE, J. (1825)   755

SUTCLIFFE, Joseph   Errata, vol. iv.

SUTCLIFFE, M. (1600)   278

SUTHERLAND, Alexander (1703, 1704)   1986, 2465

SUTHERLAND, Alexander (1819, 1827)   2104, 2518, 2540

SUTHERLAND, Duchess of (N.D.) 2737

SUTTON, —— (1847)   2353

SUTTON, John, M.D. (1764)   1588

SUTTON, Joseph (1835)   1486

SWADLIN, Thomas, D.D. (1645, 1648)   1360, 1600

SWAINE, Edward (1839)   1063

SWANWICK, Catherine (1858-1864)   1944, 2250, 2545, 2586

SWATE, Rev. J. (1811)   374

SWIFT, Edmund Lenthal (1814)   724

SWIFT, Jonathan, D.D. (1704-1754) 52, 111, 216, 217, 234, 243, 251, 257, 289, 296, 360, 468, 469, 456, 499, 553, 557, 568, 633, 645, 734, 739, 774, 783, 791, 825, 872, 892, 928, 957, 1023, 1094, 1141, 1186, 1216, 1222, 1239, 1313, 1334, 1345, 1352, 1361, 1371, 1376, 1402, 1415, 1458, 1540, 1564, 1579, 1629, 1630, 1646, 1647, 1669, 1671, 1673, 1724, 1726, 1735, 1865, 1993 (2), 2029, 2036, 2055, 2210, 2259, 2328, 2362, 2379, 2420, 2424, 2439, 2441, 2481, 2538, 2596, vol. iv., 2627, 2671, 2674, 2743, 2744

SWIFT, Thophilus (1777)   992

SWIFTE, Edmund Lenthal (1814)   80

SWINBURNE, Algernon Charles (1880)   1641

SWINFEN, John (1710)   1766, 2093

SWINNEY, Sidney (1769)   1801

SWINNOCK, George, M.A. (1672)   1465 (2)

SWINTON, John (1765, 1779) 961, 2035

SWINTON, John, B.D. (1738)   536

SWINTON, John, Lord Swinton (1765, 1789)   480, 2067

SYDNEY, Algernon (1689)   610

SYKES, Arthur Ashley, D.D. (1712-1783) 119, 123 (2), 124, 173, 313, 317, 514, 585, 765, 769, 809, 866, 947, 988, 1188, 1225, 1367, 1406, 1411, 1414, 1647, 2079, 2086, 2087, 2088, 2160, 2173, 2248, 2424, 2529, 2557, 2669, 2693, 2700 (2), 2748

SYKES, Joseph, M.A. (1863-1871)   611, 1322, 1335, 1795, 1947

SYLVESTER, Joshua (1612)   1311

SYLVESTER, Matthew (1696)   1654

SYMINGTON, Andrew James (1878)   2572

SYMMONDS, Rev. Charles (1796) 1222

SYMMONS, Edward (1648)   1305

SYMMONS, John (1800)   2581

SYMONDS, Sir William (1840)   1704

SYMONS, B. P., D.D. (N.D.)   1374

SYMONS, J., B.D. (1807)   1413

SYMPSON, —— (1685)   2478

SYMPSON, John (1707)   57

SYMSON, Andrew (1702, 1706)   1856, 2709

SYMSON, David (1703)   1942

SYMSON, Matthew, M.A. (1704)   745

SYNGE, —— (1815-1831) 237, 720, 2398

SYNGE, Edward, D.D., Archbishop of Tuam (1698-1733) 22, 203, 364, 963, 1007, 2365, 2387

T.

TAAFE, Count (1822)   430

TABOR, Miss (1863-1881) 63, 190, 242, 633, 729, 1061, 1094, 1177, 1262 (2),

1319, 1497, 1543, 1607, 1743, 2252, 2321, 2806

TAIT, John, W.S. (1774-1776) 343, 706, 1317, 1957

TAIT, Professor Peter Guthrie (1875) 2715

TAIT, William (N.D.) 1032

TAITT, Alexander (1746) 2211

TALBOT, Catherine (1741-1772) 193, 829, 2112

TALBOT, J. (1686) 1309

TALBOT, Peter (1662) 788

TALBOYS, D. A. (1829, 1833) 675, 1121 (3), 1544

TALFOURD, Sir Thomas Noon (1839-1858) 326, 1017, 1952

TANKERVILLE, Earl of, Ford Grey (1693) 77, 1519

TANNER, Dr (1857) 372

TANNER, F. (1712) 1929

TANNER, Thomas (1658, 1665) 775, 2412

TARBAT, Viscount, George Mackenzie (1689) 1592

TARBAT, William (1833) 2143

TARBET, Lord (1702) 1856

TARBET, William (1852) 2384

TASKER, Rev. William (1778-1860) 309, 477, 735, 1803, 2167

TATE, Thomas (1844) 855

TATHAM, Dr Edward (1773) 1842

TAUNTON, —— (1788) 2654

TAUNTON, Sir William Elias (1819) 1102

TAUTPHOEUS, Baroness, née J. Montgomery (1850, 1853) 556, 1225

TAVEL, Duret de (1832) 298

TAVERNER, William (1704, 1713) 882, 909, 1536

TAYLER, Charles Benjamin, M.A. (1823-1854) 473, 924, 1254, 1561

TAYLOR, —— (1774, 1856) 696, Errata, vol. iv.

TAYLOR, Abraham (1726) 2281

TAYLOR, Ann (1843) 1828, 2207

TAYLOR, Charles (1803-1824) 212, 874, 1009, 2282

TAYLOR, Christopher (1656) 2808

TAYLOR, Dr (1858) 727

TAYLOR, Dr (1731-2) 1626 (2)

TAYLOR, Edgar (1825) 1333

TAYLOR, Edgar, F.S.A. (1840) 1731

TAYLOR, Edward (1774) 554

TAYLOR, Edward F. (1880) 2241

TAYLOR, Elias (1870) 73

TAYLOR, Elizabeth (1868, 1873) 241, 2074

TAYLOR, Frederick (1861) 472

TAYLOR, G. (1818) 2279

TAYLOR, George Watson (1820) 2027

TAYLOR, G. H. (1827) 854

TAYLOR, Henry (1766-1777) 155, 475, 1230, 2108

TAYLOR, Isaac (1829-1842) 88, 209, 739, 892, 1173, 1701, 1726, 1907, 2187, 2260, 2476, 2550

TAYLOR, J. (1777, 1792) 108, 803

TAYLOR, J. (1810, 1833) 299, 552

TAYLOR, James (1687, 1689) 122, 1369, 1400

TAYLOR, Jane (1824-1843) 1828, 2207, 2388

TAYLOR, Jefferys (1844) 1218

TAYLOR, Jeremy, D.D. (1644-1697) 377, 425, 642, 649, 654, 776, 1025, 2052, 2361, 2672

TAYLOR, John (1641-1652) 87, 150, 288 (2), 749, 978, 1077, 1212, 1250, 1252, 1458, 1600, 1728, 1759, 1840, 2007, 2078, 2289, 2538, 2721

TAYLOR, John (1811, 1817) 374, 664, 1202, 2522

TAYLOR, John (1833-1875) 138, 552, 1973, 2483, 2798

TAYLOR, John (1530) 2443

TAYLOR, John (1751) 2721

TAYLOR, John Brough (1816) 1339

TAYLOR, J. R. (N.D.) 557

TAYLOR, Manton Robert (1852) 509

TAYLOR, Rev. Henry (1777) 980

TAYLOR, Rev. James W. (1843-1844) 480, 1100, 2805

TAYLOR, Sir Henry (1827) 1254

TAYLOR, T. (1692) 2782

TAYLOR, Thomas (1791, 1794) 6, 675

TAYLOR, Thomas (1830, 1831) 175, 2576

TAYLOR, Thomas (1663, 1695) 1260, 1678

TAYLOR, Watson (1815) 544

TAYLOR, William (1792, 1793) 1249, 1460

TAYLOR, William Cooke (1838, 1842) 238, 357, 2063

TAYLOR, Zachary, M.A. (1690-1699) 1765, 2121, 2742

TAYLOUR, —— (1704) 1028

TAYLOUR, Robert (1615) 922

TAYLOUR, S. (1658) 1693

TIEGNMOUTH, Lord, John Shore (1808, 1834) 486, 2582

TEMPLE, Anthony (1776)   1766
TEMPLE, A., M.A. (1775)   2136
TEMPLE, Henry John, Viscount Palmerston (1819)   1735
TEMPLE, Richard, Earl Temple (1765-1831)   1437, 2018
TEMPLE, Rose Ellen, née Hendriks (1847)   1965
TEMPLE, Sir J. (1646)   1829
TEMPLE, Sir William, Bart. (1680, 1693)   820, 1591, 1623
TEMPEST, Stephen (1764)   2128
TEMPLE, William (1758)   2743
TEMPLE, William Johnstone (1778)   9
TENISON, Archdeacon (1716)   2666
TENISON, Thomas (1683-1689)   123, 208, 640, 644
TENISON, Thomas, D.D., Archbishop of Canterbury (1670-1688)   171, 532, 631, 971, 1753, 2003, 2393, 2552, 2649
TENNANT, Charles (1858)   956
TENNANT, William (1812, 1827)   105, 1853
TENNYSON, Alfred (1850)   1218
TENNYSON, Alfred and Charles (1827)   1945
TENTERDEN, Lord Charles Abbott (1786)   2718
TERNE, Dr Christopher (1670)   2433
TERRAIL, Pierre (1825)   2210
TERRASSON, Jean (1732)   1480
TERROT, Charles Hughes (1819, 1839)   442, 2090
TETHERINGTON, —— (1783)   2485
TEW, Edward (1776)   2184
THACKERAY, Anne E. (1863-1868)   933, 2499, 2738
THACKERAY, William M. (1840-1854)   435, 687, 1252, 1300, 1677, 1737, 1835, 1860, 2296
THADDAEUS, John (1662)   2100
THANE, John (N.D.)   281
THARIN, Joseph (N.D.)   1719
THEAKSTON, Michael (1854)   1491
THELWALL, —— (1801)   564
THELWALL, A. S., A.M. (1837)   137
THELWALL, John (1790, 1793)   1886, 2506
THEOBALD, Lewis (1713-1752)   346, 460, 704, 1070, 1464, 1626, 1628, 1889, 2775
THEUBET, Colonel von (1842)   608
THIBOUVILLE, Marquis de, H. L. D'Erbigny (1770)   561

THICKNESSE, Philip (1768-1778)   19, 1287, 1538, 1728
THIMBLEBY, Richard Ashly alias (1672)   2425
THIRLBY, Styan (1710-1741)   88, 2713
THIRLWALL, Connop, D.D. (1825)   537
THIRLWALL, Thomas (1804)   302
THOM, —— (1805)   776
THOM, Robert (1840)   790
THOM, William (1762-1799)   586, 1067, 1360, 1669, 2158, 2265, 2287, 2743
THOMAS, Benjamin (1774)   1416
THOMAS, Caddy (1846)   2401
THOMAS, Elizabeth (1726-1762)   704, 1607, 1951
THOMAS, J. (1775)   1157
THOMAS, Lynall (1856)   2209
THOMAS, Ralph (1867-1868)   1065, 1553
THOMAS, Samuel, B.A. (1676-1683)   98, 1998, 2152
THOMAS, Simon (1742)   177
THOMAS, Sir E. (1737)   2733
THOMAS, Timothy (1721)   2840
THOMAS, Vaughan (1831-1847)   44, 209, 1338, 1415, 1596, 2579, 2707
THOMAS, William (1721)   2840
THOMPSON, Captain C. W. (1835)   2687
THOMPSON, Captain Edward (1764)   2414
THOMPSON, Colonel Perronet (1827-1863)   335, 513, 1221
THOMPSON, Dr William (1785)   1965
THOMPSON, E. (1837)   2103
THOMPSON, Francis, B.D. (1704)   2677
THOMPSON, Edward (1756-1770)   527 (2), 600, 1604, 2551 (2), 2655
THOMPSON, Mrs (1856)   1498
THOMPSON, Thomas (1792, 1802)   756, 2596, vol. iv.
THOMPSON, Thomas, F.A.S. (1824)   1799
THOMPSON, William (1827)   1309
THOMPSON, William, M.A. (1751)   1027
THOMS, P. P. (N.D.)   1469
THOMSON, Th. (1833)   2775
THOMSON, —— (1797, 1802)   623, 2269
THOMSON, A. (1788)   372
THOMSON, Adam (1738)   637
THOMSON, Adam (1834)   1614
THOMSON, Adam, D.D. (1834)   156
THOMSON, A. E. (1833)   1501
THOMSON, Alexander (1791, 1848)   2273, 2809

THOMSON, Andrew, D.D. (1805-1820) 1405, 1410, 2301, 2759
THOMSON, A. T. (1833-1837) 494, 1312, 2227
THOMSON, Charles (1829) 289
THOMSON, Cockburn (1858) 69
THOMSON, E. Healy (1858) 1308
THOMSON, George (1807) 2489
THOMSON, George O. L. (1870) 629
THOMSON, James (1730, 1799) 64, 591, 2216
THOMSON, J., M.D. (1816) 2490
THOMSON, John (1841) 2644
THOMSON, John C. (1860, 1864) 1078, 2823
THOMSON, John E. H. (1881) 2716
THOMSON, J. T. (1864) 2425
THOMSON, Katherine (1860) 2064, 2823
THOMSON, Mrs (18—, 1826) 889, 1985
THOMSON, Professor William (1847) 1756
THOMSON, Rev. William Aird (1826) 2090
THOMSON, Rev. William, A.M. (1810) 2137
THOMSON, Richard (1820-1832) 247, 391, 1340, 2540
THOMSON, Robert (N.D., 1834) 1066, 2645
THOMSON, R. W. (N.D.) 2213
THOMSON, Thomas (1809-1815) 424, 450, 1247
THOMSON, William A., D.D. (1826) 272
THOMSON, William, D.D., Archbishop of York (1842) 1837
THOMSON, William, LL.D. (1754-1796) 1429, 1537, 1538, 1587 (2), 2612, 2627 (2)
THORBURN, David (1841) 685
THORBURN, Walter Millar, B.A. (1875) 1047
THORKELIN, Grúnur Jónsson, LL.D. (1788) 812
THORN, Major William (1816) 1571
THORN, William (1863) 2573
THORN, William (1768) 2650
THORNHILL, John (1805) 250
THORNTHWAITE, J. A. (1837) 2848
THORNTON, Bonnell (1750-1767) 478, 1074, 1923, 2508
THORNTON, James (1818) 632
THORNTON, Robert John, M.D. (1799) 1968

THORNTON, William (1702) 2766
THOROLD, Thomas Carwell *alias* (1658) 1311
THORP, Dr (1684) 656
THORPE, George, D.D., Canon of Canterbury (1687, 1688) 921, 1753
THREEPLAND, Moncrieff (1800) 1449
THRING, Edward (1869) 2577
THROSBY, John (1793) 1395
THRUSTON, Capt. Charles T., R.N. (1834) 2393
THURLOW, Lord (1760) 2122
THYNNE, Francis (1652-1667) 643, 1851, 1885
THYRY, Paul, Baron d'Holbach (1813) 721
TICHBORNE, Thomas (1840) 74
TICHET, Eleanor (1650) 740
TICKELL, —— (1802) 2269
TICKELL, Richard (1778, 1780) 132, 441, 780, 1051, 2029, 2843
TICKELL, Thomas (1717) 779
TIDMARSH, James (1852) 1700
TIERNEY, Right Hon. G. (1791) 1413
TIGHE, Mrs (1805) 2053
TIGHE, William (1816) 1780
TILLARD, J. (1742) 990
TILLARD, T. (1742) 2173
TILLOCH, Alexander, LL.D. (1819) 680
TILLOTSON, —— (1685) 640
TILLOTSON, J. (1853) 388
TILLOTSON, John, D.D. (1684, 1685) 640, 1890
TILNAY, Edmund (N.D.) 2448
TILT, Charles (1847) 243
TIMBERLAKE, Henry (1631) 2127
TIMBS, John (1834) 1311
TIMMINS, Samuel (N.D.) 1513
TIMMS, Samuel (1846) 1109
TIMPERLEY, C. H. (1833) 2453
TINCKER, Miss (1800) 2384
TINDAL, Matthew (1697-1730) 39, 385, 578, 583, 594, 767, 793, 948, 1284, 1600, 1699, 2009, 2214, 2294
TINDAL, Matthew, LL.D. (1694, 1709) 729, 1723, 2088
TINDAL, William (1782) 448, 2140
TINGSTADIUS, John Adams, D.D. (1794) 2051
TINMOUTH, William (1846) 548
TIPHAIGNE, de la Roche, C. F. (1753, 1761) 77, 1014
TIPECROFT, J., Earl of Worcester (1530) 2685

TISDAL, William, D.D. (1709)   2664
TISSINGTON, Anthony (1766)   1369
TITE, Sir W. (1845)   993
TITUS, Silus (1659)   1301
TITUS, Silus (1804)   2206
TOBIN, —— (1785)   554
TOD, Rev. George (1820)   1382
TODD, James Henthorn, D.D. (1836) 2257
TODD, Rev. Henry John (1802-1823)
     11, 15, 330
TODD, Thomas, M.A. (1854)   2280
TOFTE, Robert (1597-1598)   61, 1323,
     1829, 2701
TOLAND, —— (1713)   2459
TOLAND, John (1696-1753) 79, 158, 182,
   184, 386, 424, 561, 574, 606, 710, 1041,
   1084, 1199, 1260, 1285, 1476, 1580, 1594,
     1856, 2038, 2093, 2307, 2368, 2484
TOLAND, Matthew, LL.D. (1704)   2088
TOLL, Rev. Frederick (1753)   1920
TOMKIS, —— (1773)   62
TOMKIS, —— (1615)   63
TOMKINS, Martin (1722, 1732) 1266, 2411
TOMKINS, Thomas (1660-1680)   1219,
     1719, 2097
TOMKINS, Thomas, M.A. (1675)   1643
TOMLINS, Elizabeth S. (1787, 1797)
     2653, 2730
TOMLINS, Thomas E. (1785)   889
TOMLINSON, W. (1657)   2342
TOMLINSON, William (1660-1674)
     785, 2834
TONGE, E., D.D. (1570)   1266
TONGUE, Cornelius (1851-1864)   1100,
     1179, 1194, 2101, 2481, 2508
TONNA, Charlotte Elizabeth, *née*
   Browne (1825-1862)   66, 227, 357, 379,
   402, 475, 493, 562, 603, 609, 759, 886,
   918, 1018, 1082, 1258, 1281, 1282, 1302,
   1428, 1570, 1618, 1831, 1868, 1880, 1890,
   1978, 2014, 2073, 2221, 2292, 2375, 2403,
     2533, 2539, 2789, 2844, 2851
TOOKE, —— (1790)   1656
TOOKE, John Horne (N.D., 1789)   1287,
     1437
TOOKE, William (1780-1804) 1959, 2241,
     2723
TOOKE, William (1860)   2726
TOOTLE, Hugh (1724) 352, Errata, vol.
     iv. (2)
TOOVEY, Alfred Dixon (1847)   1641
TOPHAM, Capt. Edward (1776)   1427
TOPLADY, Augustus Montague (1769)
     399, 691

TORBUCK, J. (N.D.)   429
TORRENS, Colonel Robert (1841)   290
TORRENS, Henry (1848)   1532
TORRENS, Lieut.-Col. (1851)   2394
TORRIANO, Gio. (1664)   2126
TORRY, John, Dean of St Andrews
   (1839)   1841
TOTNESS, Archdeacon of (1662)   1039
TOTTLE, Rev. Hugh (1737)   397
TOUCHET, George (1686)   1114
TOUGH, Miss (1840, 1842)   509, 1924
TOULMIN, J. (1773, 1781)   960, 1983
TOULMIN, Joshua, D.D. (1789) 856, 1392
TOURNAY, Thomas (1776)   343
TOURNEUR, Cyril (1608)   2192
TOVEY, Principal Thomas, D.D.
   (1738)   2818
TOWER, Richard (N.D.)   2605
TOWERS, Joseph, LL.D. (1764-
   1797) 38, 281, 618, 620, 623, 772, 807,
     1118, 1379, 1773, 2148, 2577, 2692
TOWERS, Joseph Lomax (1796)   1206
TOWERS, William, B.D. (1654)   192
TOWGOOD, Micaiah (1734-1774) 302,
   401, 671, 672 (2), 816, 1096, 2102, 2328,
     2461
TOWNE, —— (1748)   2139
TOWNE, John (1748-1766)   172, 539,
     674, 959
TOWNE, John, Archdeacon of Stowe
   (1766)   2141
TOWNLEY, Charles (1678)   2774
TOWNLEY, Rev. James (1759)   1096
TOWNSEND, —— (1832)   565
TOWNSEND, Aurelian (1631)   62
TOWNSEND, George (1854)   1745
TOWNSEND, George, D.D. (1842) 1467
TOWNSEND, G. H. (1857)   2347, 2817
TOWNSEND, J. (1806)   2326
TOWNSEND, Joseph (1781-1786)
     677, 964, 1907
TOWNSEND, Luther Tracy, D.D.
   (1869)   532
TOWNSEND, Rev. Charles (1835)
     2818
TOWNSHEND, Charles (1764)   591,
     1700
TOWNSHEND, Charles (N.D.)   1700
TOWNSHEND, Chauncey Hare (1840)
     609
TOWNSHEND, Right Hon. Charles
   (1760)   2150
TOWNSON, Thomas (1767, 1768)   588,
     702

TOWNSON, Thomas, D.D (1768)　618
TOWRY, G. P. (1785)　2578
TOY, John, M.A. (1638)　2831
TRACEY, Richard (1627)　2780
TRACY, John (1796)　2371
TRACY, Richard (1627)　2780
TRAGETT, Rev. T. H. (1857)　2455
TRAHERNE, Thomas, B.D. (1673)　2223
TRAIL, Professor William (N.D.)　737
TRAIL, Rev. James　Errata, vol. iv.
TRAILL, Catharine Parr (1836)　208
TRAILL, Rev. R. (1796)　608
TRAILL, Robert, M.A. (1692)　2762
TRANT, Captain Thomas A. (1827)　2702
TRAPHAM, Dr Thomas (1694)　2428
TRAVERS, Joseph (1703-1722)　57, 321, 1364, 1666, 2619
TRAPP, J., A.M. (1791)　534
TRAPP, Joseph, D.D. (1704-1740) 4, 358, 1618, 1825, 1876, 2360, 2583, 2669, 2677
TRAVERS, Benjamin (1806)　609
TRAVERS, Walter (1574, 1588) 588, 979
TREBY, Sir George (1681)　2681
TREFFRY, Joseph (1836)　2504
TREGELLES, Anna R. (1858)　2797
TREGELLES, S. Prideaux, LL.D. (1847)　130
TRELAWNEY, E. J. (1831)　Errata, vol. iv.
TRELAWNEY, W. H. (1831)　48
TRELAWNY, Sir J. S. (1842)　2693
TREMELLIER, —— (1708)　685
TRENCH, M. (1865, 1875)　615, 1479
TRENCH, Mrs (1816-1820)　189, 1323
TRENCH, Rev. Francis (1851)　2209
TRENCH, Rev. R. C., M.A. (1846) 2246
TRENCHARD, John (1698-1733)　341, 423, 502, 1701, 2368
TRESHAM, Henry (1802)　2102
TRESHAM, Henry, R.A. (1796)　2284
TREVELYAN, George Otto (1862) 1177
TREVELYAN, Sir Charles E., K.C.B. (1857, 1858)　516, 1432
TREVELYAN, W. C. (1829)　1183
TRIGGE, Francis (1589)　146
TRIMNELL, Charles (1702)　2761
TRIMNELL, Charles, Bishop of Winchester (1708)　1865
TRIMNELL, Charles, D.D. (1701-1714)　26, 110, 113, 1322 (2)
TROLLOPE, Anthony (1867)　1742

TROLLOPE, Francis (1833)　2, 1667
TROLLOPE, Francis Milton (1867)　1530
TROSSE, George (1693, 1702)　578, 652, 1870
TROTTER, Alexander (1825)　2626
TROTTER, Catherine, or Cockburn (1696-1747)　58, 1518, 2163, 2205
TROTTER, John (1825)　2626
TROUGHTON, John (1678)　1369
TROYTE, Lieut. J. E. Acland (1881)　2592
TRUEBA Y COSIO, Telesforo de (1834)　2255
TRUMAN, Joseph, B.D. (1669-1671)　651, 747, 1049
TRUMBULL, John (1792)　1531
TRUSLER, John, LL.D. (1766-1783)　522, 630, 736, 1643, 1907, 1987, 2047, 2840
TRUSLER, Nathaniel (1876)　1484
TRYON, Thomas (1683-1688) 970, 1654, 2795, 2796
TUAM, Archbishop, Edward Synge (1698-1733)　22, 203, 364, 963, 1007, 2365, 2387
TUCKER, Abraham (1755-1777)　523, 966, 1486, 1538
TUCKER, Charlotte (1854-1877) 1, 253, 327, 371, 386, 406, 410, 411, 544, 556, 724, 726, 838, 857, 879, 936, 969, 989, 1013, 1018, 1025, 1028, 1074, 1080, 1169, 1181, 1196, 1203, 1313, 1315, 1477, 1486, 1503, 1516, 1606, 1617, 1620, 1685, 1708, 1736, 1737, 1810, 1835, 1861, 1992, 2008, 2076, 2183, 2220, 2350, 2351, 2385 (2), 2461, 2496, 2498, 2500, 2519, 2658, 2717, 2731, 2787, 2788, 2804, 2819, 2843, 2844, 2849, 2851
TUCKER, John Kinsman (1849)　335
TUCKER, Josiah (1750-1810)　264, 314, 342, 1211, 1352, 2016
TUCKER, Mrs Charles (1868)　2143
TUCKER, Nathaniel (1776)　87
TUCKER, S. (1842)　2458
TUDOR, —— (1840)　729
TUFTON, Col. Sackville (1705)　1136
TUKE, Ann Alexander née (1812-1846)　2155, 2525, 2793, 2826
TUKE, Colonel Sir Samuel (1660)　360
TUKE, Richard (1672)　2457
TUKE, Samuel (1806)　2152
TUKE, Thomas (1616)　640

TULLY, George, A.M. (1687, 1688) 107, 587
TULLY, Thomas (1645, 1688) 277, 1422,
                                    1483
TUPLING, John (1854)   937
TUPPER, Ellin-Isabelle (1864)   1948
TUPPER, Margaret-Eleonora (1864)
                                   1948
TUPPER, Martin Farquhar (1845-
    1856)   703, 1870, 2023, 2584
TUPPER, Mary Frances (1864)   1948
TURBERVILL, Henry (1676)   6
TURBERVILLE, George (1575)   1746
TURBERVILLE, Henry (1654)   1544
TURNBULL, George (1731, 1732)   385,
                                   1901
TURNBULL, George, LL.D. (1740)   1210
TURNBULL, Gordon (1785-1796)   149,
                     1450, 1698, 1968
TURNBULL, Rev. Alexander (1806)
                                   1811
TURNBULL, William B., D.D.
    (1837-1844)   954, 1147, 1339, 1840,
                           2150, 2277
TURNER, —— (1701)   2749
TURNER, Daniel (1774, 1781) 901, 2370
TURNER, Dawson (1832-1846) 88, 333,
                     868, 1454, 2031
TURNER, Francis, D.D. (1676)   98
TURNER, George (1858)   1610
TURNER, J. (1684)   2456
TURNER, J. Fox (1855)   2365
TURNER, John (1686)   33
TURNER, John, D.D. (1712-1714)   378,
                     588, 1717, 2484
TURNER, Rev. Baptist N. (1791)   1223
TURNER, Sharon (1811)   2246
TURNER, Sir E. (1739)   1208
TURNER, Sir James (1669)   649
TURNER, T. (1734-5)   1624
TURNER, Thomas (1680)   2214
TURNER, William (1545)   2183
TURNER, William, M.D. (1543)   1194
TURNOR, Edmund (1779)   393
TURNOR, Thomas (1674)   317
TURTON, Sir Thomas (1800)   39
TURTON, Thomas, D.D., Bishop of
    Ely (1827-1829)   2161, 2758
TUTCHIN, John (1691-1703) 941, 1725,
                           2652, 2808
TUVILL, Daniel (1608, 1629) 791, 2719
TWEDDELL, G. (1850)   1881
TWEDDIE, William King, D.D.
    (1854)   1034
TWINING, Henry (1847)   738

TWINING, T. (1723, 1788)   206, 657
TWISS, Horace (1807, 1814) 1979, 2253
TWISS, Richard (1787)   369
TWISS, Richard (1776)   2611
TWISS, Richard (1792)   2656
TWISS, Travers, D.C.L. (1850)   1193
TWISSE, William, D.D. (N.D.)   694
TWOMBLY, Rev. Alexander Steven-
    son (1873)   1605
TWORT, Charles William (1829, 1830)
                              377, 460
TWYCROSS, Rev. J. (N.D.)   1722
TWYNE, Thomas (1576)   2271
TWYSDEN, John (1662)   668, 2364
TWYSDEN, Sir R. (1648)   443
TYE, Christopher (N.D.)   1937
TYERS, Thomas (1780-1784)   508, 704,
                     1116, 1121, 1964
TYLER, Bennet, D.D. (1837)   1448
TYLER, Rev. Alexander (1684)   2384
TYMME, T. (1654)   604
TYMME, Thomas (1574)   2589
TYNDAL, William (1530, 1533)   1988,
                                   2521
TYNDAL, Mrs (1870)   2680
TYPE, Tom (1808)   2096
TYPING, William (1633)   650
TYRELL, Christina (1876-1884)   1746,
                     2081, 2512, 2707
TYRRELL, James (1716)   1104
TYRRELL, Sir James (1681, 1694)   233,
                                   1872
TYRWHITT, Richard, M.A. (1861)   462
TYRWHITT, Thomas (1749-1766)   783
                     1767, 2024, 2623
TYTLER, Alexander Fraser, Lord
    Woodhouselee (1771-1835)   538, 807,
               811, 1110, 1904, 1949, 2219
TYTLER, Anne Fraser (1835)   1553
TYTLER, James (1791)   2195
TYTLER, Margaret F. (1838)   2543
TYTLER, Patrick Fraser (1816-1845)
               211, 1476, 1715, 1976, 2626
TYTLER, William (1769, 1783)   1244,
                                   1957
TYTLER, William, W.S. (1760, 1772)
                              1110, 1226

U

UDALL, Ephraim (1641, N.D.) 1031, 1748
UDALL, John (1593) 438, 601, 1316, 2486
UDALL, Nicolas (1818)   2075
UFFINGTON, Thomas (1760)   2280

UNDERWOOD, —— (1659)   427
UNDERWOOD, T. (1767)   2410
UNDERWOOD, T. R. (1825)   1695
UPCOTT, W. (1814)   244
UPHAM, Edward (1822, 1827)   1297, 1591, 2077
UPTON, J. (1731-32)   1627 (2)
UPTON, James (1749)   2156
URMSTON, Sir James B. (1843)   1868
URQUHART, David (1836-1841)   1976, 2174
URQUHART, Miss (1866)   1081, 1485
URQUHART, Thomas (1652)   732
URQUHART, W. Pollard (1860)   552
USBORNE, T. H. (1852)   2542
USHER, Charles (1699)   1372
USHER, James (1766, 1772)   416, 962, 1246
USHER, Dr James, Archbishop of Armagh (N.D., 1642)   187, 636
UTTERSON, Mrs (1813)   2542
UTTERSTON, Edward Vernon (1812-1836)   1495, 2317, 2770

V

VALLANCY, Charles, LL.D. (1772, 1786)   803, 817
VALLANS, W. (1615)   1176
VALLÉE, Joseph La (1790)   1709
VALPY, Dr A. J. (1821)   2239
VALPY, Rev. E., B.D. (1827)   1731
VALPY, Richard (1818)   738
VAN DYK, Henry Stoe (1827)   1027
VANBURGH, Sir John (1697-1715)   54, 469, 523, 886, 1635, 2048, 2125, 2379
VANDERSTEGEN, William (N.D.)   42
VANCE, Alexander (1858)   203
VANE, Sir Henry (1656, N.D.)   1354, 1708
VANSITTART, Nicholas, Lord Bexley (1793)   2111
VANSITTART, William, D.D. (N.D.)   777
VARILLAS, Antoine (1688, 1717)   2007, 2115
VANDONCOURT, Guillaume de (1815, 1825)   541, 1447
VAUGHAN, Benjamin (1793)   1449
VAUGHAN, David James (1852)   918
VAUGHAN, T. (1781)   901
VAUGHAN, Thomas (1650-1761)   94, 131, 199, 269, 835, 886, 1526, 1533, 1538, 2189, 2310
VAUGHAN, T. Wright (1816)   903
VAUGHAN, William (1626)   1025

VAUX, Francis (N.D.)   736
VAUX, Henry, Lord Brougham (1842, 1844)   62, 1965
VAYER, Sieur de la Mothe le (1649)   1459
VEAL, George (1785, 1818)   1269, 1683
VEEL, Robert (1672)   1717
VEESON, George (1810)   202
VEITCH, J. (1825, 1831)   551, 1384
VEITCH, John (1843, 1850)   658, 1564
VENABLES, Colonel Robert (1662)   859
VENABLES, George (1830)   294
VENN, Rev. H., M.A. (1825)   2153
VENTUM, Harry (1794)   2321
VERGY, Treysac de (1770)   581
VERNEUIL, J. (1637)   1748
VERNEY, Lady (1868, 1871)   912, 1454, 2495
VERNON, —— (1839)   1036
VERNON, Admiral (1746, 1749)   492, 2442
VERNON, George (1670, 1677)   191, 1367
VERNON, John Richard, M.A. (N.D., 1872)   1073, 1974, 2077
VERSTEGAN, Richard (1603)   622
VERSTEGAN, Robert (1601   2342
VERULAM, Lord of, Francis Bacon (1603)   263
VESLE, Count Pont de (1778)   2406
VICARS, John (1819)   754
VICARS, John (1645)   1909
VICARS, T. (1624, 1627)   190, 2530
VICARS, W. (1721)   444
VICKARIS, A. (1696)   794
VICOMTERIE, Louis la (1791)   534
VICTOR, Benjamin (1755, 1778)   2783, 2814
VIDAL, M. T. (1856)   936
VIENNA, Bishop of, Frederick Nause (1618)   2633
VIGNE, —— (1682)   2525
VIGOR, Mrs (1775)   1426
VILANT, William (1681)   2193
VILLARS, Abbé de Montfaucon de (1680)   518
VILLEMAREST, Charles Maxime de (1834-6)   1478
VILLIERS, George, Duke of Buckingham (1623-1682)   355, 787, 1387, 1957, 2124, 2673
VILLIERS, Right Hon. John Charles (1789)   367, 2612
VILLIERS, Sir George (1837, 1838)   1783, 2324
VILVAIN, Robert (1654)   745

VINCENT, Benjamin (1848)　　1220
VINCENT, Thomas (1667)　　1023
VINCENT, William, D.D., Dean of
　Westminster (1780, 1799)　1405, 2196
VITELLESCHI, Cardinal (1876)　2723
VITELLESCHI, Marchese (1876)　2723
VIVIAN, J. H. (1839)　　1619
VIVIAN, John (N.D.)　　1942
VIZARD, John (1872)　　1693
VOITURE, Vincent (1789)　　1131
VOLTAIRE, F. Arouet de (1869)　2071
VRIGNY, Mde. la Combe de (1707)
　　　　　　　　　2628

W.

WADD, William (1810, 1827)　553, 1758
WADDEL, George (1733)　　2143
WADDELL, Peter Hately (1843)　1831
WADDINGTON, John (1856)　　1471
WADDINGTON, Julia Rattray
　(1838, 1839)　　1261, 1633
WADDINGTON, Samuel Ferrand
　(1812)　　　　66, 1299
WADE, John (1824-1853)　16, 296 (2),
　　　　　　　　　2318
WAGSTAFF, T. (1694)　　22
WAGSTAFFE, —— (1713, 1720)　360,
　　　　　　　　　2086
WAGSTAFFE, John (1669, 1764)　736,
　　　　　　　　　2070
WAGSTAFFE, Thomas, M.A. (1690-
　1706) 27, 108, 109, 115, 315, 596, 1103,
　1363, 1370, 1391, 2002, 2146, 2212, 2521,
　　　　　2744, Errata, vol. iv.
WAGSTAFFE, William, M.D. (1711-
　1725)　437, 460, 535, 1358, 2181, 2484,
　　　　　　　　2500, 2555
WAINEWRIGHT, Jeremiah (1722)　84
WAKE, William, D.D., Archbishop
　of Canterbury (1682-1716)　263, 400,
　448, 502, 589, 640, 646, 653, 864, 1123,
　1347, 1995, 2003, 2294, 2525, 2692,
　　　　　　　　　2762
WAKEFIELD, David (1800)　　875
WAKEFIELD, Edward Gibbon
　(1833)　　　　747
WAKEFIELD, Gilbert (1788-1801) 283,
　　　　　　　　949, 2171
WAKEFIELD, Priscilla (1794)　1341
WAKEMAN, W. F. (1847)　　2403
WALBRAN, John Richard (1837,
　1850)　　　1204, 2614

WALDIE, Charlotte Ann (1831,
　1853)　　　　191, 566
WALDIE, Charlotte A. Eaton, née
　(1817, 1827)　　1693, 2225, 2774
WALDIE, Jane (1820)　　2401
WALDO, P. (1772)　　1982
WALDRON, Francis Godolphin
　(1778-1794)　1080, 1303, 1535, 2248
WALDRON, George (1744)　　1129
WALFORD, Beatrice (1871)　　2689
WALFORD, E. (1833)　　2279
WALKER, —— (1776-1825)　432, 441,
　　　　　　　　1430, 2207
WALKER, A. (1790)　　2803
WALKER, Alexander (1833)　　1972
WALKER, Clement (1647-1660)　83,
　　　1096, 1139 (2), 1688, 2127
WALKER, G. (1645)　　287
WALKER, G., M.D. (1851)　　571
WALKER, George (1794)　　1074
WALKER, George, D.D. (N.D.)　748
WALKER, Henry (1641)　　2547
WALKER, J. (1685)　　297
WALKER, J. (1731-2)　1627 (3), 1628
WALKER, James (1810)　　2750
WALKER, James Barr (N.D)　1904
WALKER, John, F.T.C.D. (1796)　397
WALKER, John, LL.D. (1822)　　551
WALKER, Lady M. (1778)　　1680
WALKER, Mary Ann (1861)　　1335
WALKER, Maynard Chamberlaine
　(1796)　　　　788
WALKER, Obadiah (1656-1692)　225,
　257, 448, 649, 726, 881, 1051, 1236, 1858,
　　　　2038, 2261, 2426 (2)
WALKER, Patrick (1724)　　2438
WALKER, Peter (1827)　　233
WALKER, Rev. James (N.D.)　710
WALKER, Rev. John, B.C.L. (N.D.) 1842
WALKER, Rev. Thomas (1771)　61
WALKER, Rev. Thomas, M.A.
　(1767)　　　　1780
WALKER, Richard (1852)　　2239
WALKER, Richard, B.D. (1832-
　1869)　415, 534, 918, 1621, 1841, 1853,
　　　　　　　　　2561
WALKER, Robert (1796)　　1940
WALKER, S. (1720)　　694
WALKER, Sir Edward (1660)　　1258
WALKER, Sir Patrick (1822)　　695
WALKER, Thomas (1705, 1778)　904,
　　　　　　　　2061, 2822
WALKER, William (1704)　　1551
WALKER, William (1648)　　2768

WALKER, W., M.A. (1874) 1574
WALKINGTON, Thomas (1615) 2562
WALKINGTON, Thomas, M.A. (1639) 1821
WALKLEY, T. (1630) 332
WALKLEY, Thomas (1647) 331
WALL, John, M.D. (1763-1806) 860, 1454, 1537
WALL, Martin, M.D. (1806) 1537
WALL, Thomas, M.A. (1658) 1023
WALLACE, —— (1795) 997
WALLACE, Ellen (1844-1849) 494, 1305, 1546, 1675
WALLACE, George (1754) 955
WALLACE, James (1816) 1035
WALLACE, James, M.D. (1724) 1158
WALLACE, Rev. Dr (N.D.) 2309
WALLACE, R. G. (1822) 921
WALLACE, Robert (1737) 1398
WALLACE, Robert, D.D. (1753-1761) 362, 676, 1000, 2723
WALLACE, Thomas (1835) 2587
WALLACE, Thomas, LL.D. (1823, 1827) 1822, 2199
WALLACE, William (1836) 2506
WALLER, Edmund (1655-1743) 319, 1849, 1969, 2599
WALLER, General Sir William (1788) 1959
WALLER, John Francis (1852) 2407
WALLER, Sir William (1682) 684
WALLIS, Dr John (1657) 2094
WALLIS, George (1774) 1296
WALLIS, John, D.D. (1671-1696) 115, 127
WALLIS, Ralph (1666) 1662, 2227
WALLIS, Stamford (1730) 673
WALMSLEY, Charles, D.D. (1812) 1001
WALPOLE, Horace, Earl of Orford (1741-1791) 20, 91, 327, 518, 1073, 1092, 1095, 1359, 1534, 1563, 2109, 2407
WALPOLE, Horatio, Lord (1731-1805) 320, 506, 1042, 1241, 1437, 1689, 2167
WALPOLE, Sir Robert, Earl of Orford (1710-1735) 480, 1347, 1351, 1792, 2311, 2369, 2421, 2425, 2437, 2575
WALROND, John (1720) 2556
WALSH, John Edward (1847) 2403
WALSH, John Henry, F.R.C.S. (1856-1872) 194, 285, 695, 696, 1053, 1544, 2209, 2231, 2380
WALSH, Miss (1810) 1806
WALSH, Peter (1661-1678) 128, 505, 2424

WALSH, Robert (1810-1825) 22, 1231, 1362
WALSH, William (1876) 2499
WALSINGHAM, —— (1681) 266
WALSINGHAM, Edward (1644, 1645) 72, 281
WALTER, Henry (1828-39) 1136
WALTER, Thomas (1679) 854
WALTHER, David (1832) 381, 2767
WALTON, Bryan, D.D. (1641) 2631
WALTON, Isaac (1683) 2558
WALTON, Isaak (1680) 1517
WALTON, W. (1829, 1852) 1697, 2178, 2670
WALTON, William (1778) 636
WALWYN, B. (1783) 790
WALWYN, William (1667) 2609
WANLEY, Humphrey (1732) 1055
WARBURTON, Capt. George (1853) 1569
WARBURTON, Elliot (1851) 1581
WARBURTON, John (1779) 2416
WARBURTON, Major G. (1846) 1169
WARBURTON, Major T. (1849) 478
WARBURTON, R. E. E. (1834) 1193
WARBURTON, W., A.M. (1743) 799
WARBURTON, William, D.D., Bishop of Gloucester (1727-1809) 69, 428, 536, 769, 1355, 1400, 1426, 2732, 2746
WARD, Ann, Mrs Radcliffe née (1791) 2224
WARD, C. A. (1855, 1859) 748, 1991, 2389, 2454
WARD, E. (1853) 252
WARD, Edward (1692-1756) 452, 560, 600, 682, 710, 721, 910, 920, 942, 974, 1083, 1155, 1174, 1185, 1191, 1508 (2), 1552, 1606, 1620, 1643, 1644, 1670, 1750, 2077, 2120, 2182, 2252, 2311 (2), 2456, 2493, 2595, vol. iii., 2608, 2656, 2784, 2807, 2808, 2819, 2830
WARD, Harriet (1848, 1849) 1082, 1868
WARD, Miss (N.D.) 291
WARD, Mrs R. (1828) 371
WARD, Nathaniel (1647-1650) 638, 1600, 2132, 2387, 2600, 2836
WARD, Plumer (1839) 2203
WARD, R. (1844) 804
WARD, Rev. Geo. Ambrose (1846) 937
WARD, Rev. William (1810) 1363
WARD, Robert (1805) 1229
WARD, Robert Plumer (1804-1844) 367, 567 (2), 1206, 1910, 2650, 2735
WARD, Seth, D.D. (1652, 1654) 1903, 2767

WARD, Thomas (1687-1688) 789, 1653, 2435, 2467
WARD, Thomas Humphrey (1878) 253
WARD, W. (1735) 604
WARD, William George, M.A., (1841, 1845) 918, 2420
WARDEN, John (1721) 2814
WARE, Major (1812) 2481
WARE, Rev. William (1844, 1860) 1287, 2853
WARE, W. (1861) 2225
WARE, William (1832-1838) 1318, 1429, 2397
WARE, Robert (1682-1707) 953, 1971, 2118
WARE, Samuel (1809) 2156
WARFORD, William (1616) 275, 276
WARING, Henry (1693) 2238
WARING, Jeremiah (1797) 2587
WARING, Robert, M.A. (1646, 1648) 16, 2055
WARING, S. (1827) 2815
WARING, Thomas (1650) 269
WARNE, Jonathan (1739, 1740) 207, 399
WARNER, —— (1730) 43
WARNER, Anna B. (1852-1868) 388, 697, 741, 1017, 1025, 1069, 1297, 1684, 2466
WARNER, Charles Dudley (1874) 1014
WARNER, Ferdinand, LL.D. (1755) 960
WARNER, Ferdinando (1752) 2079
WARNER, J. (1688) 587
WARNER, J., Bishop of Rochester (1648) 398
WARNER, John (N.D.) 343
WARNER, John, D.D. (1797) 1611
WARNER, R. (1848) 626
WARNER, Rev. Richard (1808, 1809) 2096, 2187
WARNER, Susan (1853-1883) 325, 388, 559, 726, 741, 746, 1015, 1025, 1098, 1181, 1297, 1305, 1324, 1495, 1552, 1567, 1810, 1915, 2013, 2063, 2228, 2261, 2265, 2493, 2617, 2805, 2814, 2817, 2831, 2844
WARR, —— (1686) 573
WARREN, E. (1803) 1960
WARREN, E. (1692) 2438
WARREN, John C., M.D. (1848) 1908
WARREN, Samuel (1839-1841) 49, 1821, 2551
WARREN, Samuel, LL.D. (1832) 1867
WARREN, Sir John Borlase (1791) 2734
WARRINGTON, Rev. William (1813) 71, 303
WARTON, Joseph (1753-1762) 47, 805

WARTON, Joseph, D.D. (1756) 813
WARTON, Thomas (1747-1782) 1940, 2657, 2709, 2726, 2831
WARTON, Thomas, B.D. (1751-1780) 444, 607, 1725, 2818
WARTON, Thomas, D.D. (1777,1782) 1841, 2463
WARWICK, Sir Philip (1646) 1386
WARWICK, Thomas (1784, 1785) 3, 728
WASBOROUGH, —— (1820) 1358
WASE, Charles (1649) 733
WASHINGTON, Joseph (1691) 313
WASHINGTON, Robert (1689) 2432
WASSE, Rev. Joseph (1731-2) 1626 (8), 1627 (6), 1628 (6)
WASTALL, —— (1679) 1854
WATERFORD, Bishop of, Dr Power (1809) 1448
WATERFORD, Bishop of, Thomas Milles (1721) 22
WATERHOUS, Edward (1667) 2372
WATERLAND, Daniel, D.D. (1730-1734) 53, 679, 1703, 2159, 2283 (3), 2524
WATERLAND, Joseph (1702) 2087
WATKINS, John (1816, 1848) 235, 1255, 1588, 2240
WATKINS, Richard (1651) 1739
WATKINS, T. (1717) 2535
WATKINS, William (1778) 192
WATLEY, F.C. (N.D.) 1723
WATSON, Alexander (1794, 1821) 137, 829
WATSON, James (1799, 1821) 1722, 1858
WATSON, Jean L. (1864-1875) 294 (2), 521, 1040, 2453
WATSON, John (1608) 759
WATSON, John (1879) 2000
WATSON, Richard (1782, 1790) 122, 483
WATSON, Richard, S.T.P. (1659) 1849
WATSON, W. (1677) 1265
WATSON, William (1601-1602) 572, 620, 1216, 2462
WATT, Robert, M.D. (1814) 2239
WATTS, Isaac, D.D. (1736-1739) 1720, 2104, 2504
WATTS, Mrs (1820) 2401
WATTS, Nic. (1658) 2547
WATTS, Robert, LL.B. (1710-1714) 1326, 2237, 2679, 2697
WATTS, Susanna (1804) 2785
WATTS, Thomas (1688) 623
WATTS, Thomas, M.A. (1703) 2286
WAUCHOPE, John (1853) 2243

WAUGH, Richard (1805)   250
WAY, Rev. Lewis (1824-1830) 1846, 2433
WAYER, William (1605)   2571
WAYLAND, John (1807)   2371
WEAMYS, Anna (1651)   500
WEATHERHEAD, G. H., M.D. (1834)   1902
WEATHERLY, Frederick E., M.A. (1879)   1841
WEAVER, Robert (1837, 1844)   670, 1079, 2100
WEAVER, Thomas (1649-1654)   1932, 2449
WEBB, Daniel (1744)   814
WEBB, Francis (1739, 1772)   1549, 2580
WEBB, J. B. (1867)   1816
WEBB, J. C. Loudon *née* (1811-1829)   25, 1052, 1678, 2496, 2542
WEBB, Jos. (1818)   1902
WEBB, Joseph (1813)   721
WEBB, Mrs (1855)   528
WEBB, Philip Carteret (1742-1769)   511, 1410, 2070, 2152 (2), 2353, 2354, 2432, 2485
WEBBE, Colonel (1796)   2348
WEBBE, George (1612, 1653)   276, 1988
WEBBE, J. (1600)   887
WEBBER, Francis (1754)   593
WEBBER, Samuel (1741)   823
WEBSTER, Alexander (N.D.)   2152
WEBSTER, David (1807)   1051
WEBSTER, George (1858)   2509
WEBSTER, Grace (1835)   725
WEBSTER, James (1703-1707) 203, 823, 1326, 1348, 1357, 2294, 2590
WEBSTER, James (N.D.)   1909
WEBSTER, Miss (1879)   1476
WEBSTER, Mr (1692)   2710
WEBSTER, William, D.D. (1736-1740)   479, 705, 2799
WEDDELL, —— (1737, 1738) 406, 2783, Errata, vol iv.
WEDDERBURN, —— (1742)   1219
WEDDERBURN, Alexander (1757) 2448
WEDDERBURN, Alexander, Earl of Rosslyn (1805, N.D.)   1437, 1594
WEDDERBURN, Alexander, Lord Loughborough (1805)   1437
WEIMAR, Miss (1808)   72
WEIR, G. (1813)   2607
WEIR, Marion E. (1856)   1170
WELCHMAN, Edward, M.A. (1698-1724)   471, 1194, 2293
WELD, Rev. Nath. (1722)   2287

WELDE, Thomas (1692)   2375 (2)
WELDON, Robert (1651)   131
WELDON, Sir Anthony (1650, 1652)   328, 526
WELL, G. (1687)   2711
WELLER, Rev. Samuel (1740)   2651
WELLESLEY, Richard, Marquis of Wellesley (1804, 1840)   1756, 2010
WELLS, Archdeacon of, Samuel Wells (1692, 1697)   1679, 2415
WELLS, Benjamin (1667)   1953
WELLS, Bishop of Bath and, Charles Moss, D.D. (1744)   840
WELLS, Bishop of Bath and, G. Hooper (1683)   398
WELLS, Bishop of Bath and, Thomas Ken (1686)   864
WELLS, Charles J. (1822, 1824)   1273, 2496
WELLS, Edward, D.D. (1706-1712) 441, 1353, 2443
WELLS, Helen (1798)   2492
WELLS, John (1635)   2272
WELSH, —— (1691, 1692)   621, 1423
WELSH, James (1834)   1100
WELSH, James Jacob (1831)   269
WELSHMAN, Edward (1691)   586
WELTON, R., D.D. (1715)   415
WELWOOD, James, M.D. (1689, 1693)   123 (2)
WELWOOD, James, M.D. (1789) 2096
WENNELL, Thomas (N.D.)   162
WENTWORTH, Earl of, Fitzwilliam (1795)   1354
WENTWORTH, Sir Peter (1641) 1843
WENTWORTH, Thomas (1641)   1806
WESLEY, Charles (1744-1759)   985 (2), 1197 (5), 1198 (4), 2317
WESLEY, John, M.A. (1744-1810)   18, 53, 242, 479, 498, 636 (2), 692, 866, 867, 1374, 1375, 1378, 1404, 1542, 2012, 2016, 2066, 2165, 2256, 2317, 2327, 2329 (2), 2355, 2367, 2408, 2418, 2529, 2574, 2836
WESLEY, Mr —— (1713)   2025
WESLEY, Samuel (1685-1723) 216, 1347, 1533, 1707
WESLEY, Samuel, jun. (1729)   2020
WESLEY, Samuel, M.A. (1730, 1732)   1860, 2696
WEST, Edward (1835)   1768
WEST, Edward, M.A. (1815)   803
WEST, Gilbert (1742)   1235, 2449
WEST, Jane (1799-1827)   47, 67, 1035, 1223, 1522, 2121, 2216, 2279, 2538, 2730

WEST, N. (1676)　　1208
WEST, Richard (1608)　　348
WEST, Richard (1717-1726)　648, 1080, 1229
WEST, Richard, Archdeacon of Westminster (1699)　2444
WEST, Richard, D.D. (N.D., 1701) 2017, 2665
WEST, Rt. Hon. Richard (1733)　963
WEST, Robert (1658, 1672)　559, 2784
WEST, Samuel (N.D.)　2327
WEST, Thomas (1812)　1058
WEST, William (1835)　922
WESTMACOTT, Charles Molloy (1825)　763, 930
WESTMINSTER, Dean of, R. Stuart, LL.D. (1682)　1813
WESTMINSTER, Archdeacon, R. West, D.D. (1699)　2444
WESTMINSTER, Dean of, W. Vincent, D.D. (1799)　2196
WESTMORELAND, Earl of, John Fane (1820, 1822)　1572, 1573
WESTMORELAND, Earl of, Mildmay Fane (164—)　1832
WESTON, Ambrose (1798-1799)　1608
WESTON, Edward (1740)　763
WESTON, Joseph (1824)　2133
WESTON, Richard (1769)　2616
WESTON, Right Hon. Edward (1755, 1768)　522 (2), 889
WESTON, Sir R. (1645)　658
WESTON, Stephen, B.D. (1776-1829)　867, 902, 953, 1309, 1429, 1989, 2355, 2407, 2524, 2655, 2701, 2729, 2773, 2802
WESTON, William (1762)　1718
WETENHALL, Edward, D.D. (1670-1694)　130, 217, 320, 335, 717, 774, 1283, 1369, 1891, 2692
WETHAM, R. (1730-33)　1731
WETTERBURGH, C. A. (1854)　2325
WEYER, Silvain V. de (1831)　1362
WEYLAND, John (1807)　2371
WHALLEY, John (1763)　1236
WHALLEY, Rev. T. S. (1779-1781)　728, 903
WHALLY, John (1752)　1931
WHARTON, George (1644)　1601
WHARTON, Henry (1688-1693)　123, 583, 775, 1156, 1848, 2465, 2636
WHARTON, Philip, Duke of (1723-1724)　2665
WHARTON, R. (1817)　369

WHARTON, Thomas (1750-1751)　2508
WHARTON, Thomas, Marquis of Wharton (N.D.)　1739
WHATELEY, Solomon (1699)　107
WHATELY, Mrs (1846, 1847) 758, 2193
WHATELY, Richard, D.D., Archbishop of Dublin (1819-1860)　473, 720 1105 (2), 1247 (2), 1336 (2), 1337, 1342, 1446, 2736
WHATELY, Robert (1715)　1419
WHATELY, Thomas (1765-1773)　489, 505, 1773, 2148
WHATLEY, George (1769-1774)　2019, 2111
WHATLEY, S. (1741)　2353
WHATLEY, Stephen (1726-1727)　31
WHEAR, Degory (1685)　155
WHEATLEY, —— (1768, 1769) 165, 2004
WHEATLEY, Benjamin Robert (1846, 1848)　330, 332
WHEATLEY, Charles (1736)　378
WHEATLEY, Thomas (1785)　2146
WHEELWRIGHT, Horace W. (1861-1865)　293, 2480, 2551
WHEELER, —— (1695)　2233
WHEELER, David Hilton (1864)　279
WHEELER, Fanny, Mrs Hart née (1868-1878)　363, 958, 1677, 2240, 2852
WHEELER, H. (1790)　2803
WHEELER, J. Talboys (1848, 1851)　80 (2), 81
WHELER, Sir George, D.D. (1720) 1807
WHETSTONE, George (1587)　347
WHEWELL, William (1830-1854)　169, 622, 1941, 2173
WHICHCOT, Thomas (1649)　1932
WHICHCOTE, Benjamin, D.D. (1703)　1656
WHINNEL, T. (1699)　226
WHISTON, D. (1718)　2010
WHISTON, John (1740)　2133
WHISTON, W. (1718, 1745)　2010, 2011
WHISTON, William (1698)　2759
WHITAKER, Edward (1681)　1204
WHITAKER, Edward (1872)　1525
WHITAKER, J., B.D. (1804)　2523
WHITBY, Daniel, D.D. (1682-1714) 59, 601, 645 (2), 659, 680, 885, 1106, 1346, 2042, 2376, 2633, 2640 (2)
WHITCHEAR, Robert (1758)　2426
WHITCOMBE, Samuel (N.D.)　2122
WHITE, —— (1840-1851),　755, 2479, 2686
WHITE, Charles (1829, 1837) 48, 69, 1550

WHITE, Dorothy (1660) 2773
WHITE, Henry, B.A. (1856) 1058
WHITE, J. (1660) 1857
WHITE, James (1789-1847) 51, 715, 913, 1827
WHITE, John (1612) 760
WHITE, John, B.D. (1751) 959
WHITE, Joseph B., M.A. (1817-1833) 1429, 1996, 2310
WHITE, Matthew (1636) 1737
WHITE, Miss (1853) 2727
WHITE, Rev. James (1846, 1847) 1271, 2389
WHITE, Rev. William (1840) 2805
WHITE, R. G. (1746) 969
WHITE, Richard (1621) 203
WHITE, Richard (1694) 404
WHITE, Robert, Advocate (1704-1705) 985, 2495
WHITE, Thomas (1662, 1668) 2595, 2617
WHITE, Thomas (1640) 623
WHITE, Thomas E. (1802) 1165
WHITE, William (1852) 2682
WHITER, Rev. Walter (1794) 2463
WHITFIELD, Edmund, B.D. (1688) 591
WHITFIELD, Henry (1804) 1342
WHITFIELD, W. (1688) 591
WHITFORD, Mrs (1798) 2492
WHITFORD, Richard (1532) 2250
WHITGIFT, John, Archbishop of Canterbury (1589) 1666
WHITEHALL, R. (N.D.) 762
WHITEHALL, Robert (1651, 1652) 1550, 2549
WHITEHEAD, George (1672-1707) 29, 134, 635, 1510, 2014, 2330
WHITEHEAD, John, M.D. (N.D.) 799
WHITEHEAD, Paul (1733-1754) 320, 1132, 2484
WHITEHEAD, Sarah R. (1851-1853) 1710, 2228, 2693
WHITEHEAD, William (1752-1776) 839, 1020, 2656, 2723
WHITELAW, J. M., LL.D. (1861, 1877) 2284, 2722
WHITELOCK, Sir Bulstrode (1682) 1596
WHITHALL, R. (1674) 2600
WHITING, John (1684) 8
WHITING, Sydney (1848-1855) 54, 1082, 1579
WHITLING, H. J. (1845) 1080
WHITMORE, John (1828) 37
WHITNEY, Adelina D. Train (1866) 880, 994, 1872, 2518

WHITTINGHAM, William (1574) 278
WHITTINGTON, Rev. —— (1808) 2629
WHITTY, —— (1824, 1828) 1451, 2540
WHITY, Daniel (1689) 480
WHYTE, Adam (1851) 504
WHYTE, Rev. Thomas (1778) 1112
WHYTE, Rev. William (1841) 35
WHYTE, Robert (1704) 871
WHYTE, William (N.D.) 734
WHYTECHURCHE, E. (1543) 1715
WHYTOCK, Rev George (1798, 1799) 507, 2567
WIDDRINGTON, Roger (1620) 1736
WIDENFELT, Adam (1687) 2812
WIEMAR, Miss (1808) 72
WIGGINS, John (1843-1844) 1214, 1250
WIGGLESWORTH, Rev. W. (1673) 566
WIGHT, Henry (1841) 1663
WIGHT, John (1833) 2519
WIGHT, Mrs Cox née (N.D.) 293
WIGHTMAN, O. G. R. (1788) 2464
WIGHTMAN, Rev. Robert (1736) 2022
WIGHTWICK, George (1828, 1845) 290, 1469
WIGRAM, Joseph C. (1832) 1009
WIGRAM, S. R. (1853) 936
WILBERFORCE, C. (1867) 2228
WILBERFORCE, H. (1836) 1528
WILBERFORCE, Rev. Henry William (1835) 946
WILBERFORCE, Samuel (1833) 1751
WILCOCK, James (1641) 355
WILCOCKS, Joseph (1759, 1792) 2223, 2246
WILCOCKS, Thomas (1581-1597) 1016, 2379, 2517, 2702, 2728
WILCOX, J. (1641) 2395
WILCOX, Rev. Daniel (1717, 1719) 712, 1747
WILD, James (1803) 937
WILD, John (1665) 1043
WILD, Robert, D.D. (1660) 1257, 2618
WILDASH, W. (1772) 1126
WILDE, Robert, D.D. (N.D.) 1816
WILDMAN, Major John (1653) 2315
WILKES, John (1762-1796) 814, 955, 1381, 1386, 1438, 1781, 2524
WILKIE, ——, of Ladythorn (1836) 1483
WILKIE, William, D.D. (1757) 777
WILKIE, William Patrick (1865) 633
WILKINS, George (1822-1830) 243, 508, 2651
WILKINS, George (1607) 1264, 2625

WILKINS, George, D.D. (1823-1838)   375, 2700, 2738, 2775
WILKINS, John (1638, 1654)   664, 2767
WILKINSON, —— (1761-74)   1074
WILKINSON, Edward (1774)   992, 1056
WILKINSON, Edward, M.D. (1798)   2820
WILKINSON, Robert (1615)   1599
WILKINSON, Sir J. Gardner (1840)   2588
WILKINSON, W. F., M.A. (1843)   2103
WILKS, Lieut.-Col. Mark (N.D.)   1119
WILLAN, Leonard (1658)   1825
WILLCOX, C. B. (1842)   1959
WILLEMONT, Thomas (1852)   17
WILLES, John (1688, 1696)   3, 2713
WILLES, John, D.D. (1695)   2135
WILLES, John, D.C.L. (1713)   2470
WILLES, John, LL.B. (1714)   1999
WILLET, Thomas (1778)   294
WILLIAM, David (N.D.)   1670
WILLIAM, John (1642)   1862
WILLIAM, John, D.D. (1683)   314
WILLIAMS, —— (1790, 1812)   1639, 1721
WILLIAMS, Albert (1849)   1771, 2595, vol. iv.
WILLIAMS, Bishop (1704)   395
WILLIAMS, C. H. (1852)   2880
WILLIAMS, Charles, D.D. (1870)   1574
WILLIAMS, David (1771-1791)   164, 827, 1342, 1377, 1445, 1499, 1899, 1929
WILLIAMS, D. J. (1840)   1442
WILLIAMS, Griffith, D.D., Bishop of Ossory (1644)   848
WILLIAMS, Helen Maria (1782, 1783)   728, 1801
WILLIAMS, Isaac (1836-1850)   71, 88, 211, 337, 382, 916, 1528, 2342, 2574
WILLIAMS, J. M. (1827)   738
WILLIAMS, John (N.D.)   201, 546, 721, 929, 2232
WILLIAMS, John (1671-1683)   313, 384, 689 (2)
WILLIAMS, John (1786-1798)   370, 549, 1481, 1715, 1914, 1946, 1954, 1980, 2643
WILLIAMS, John, Bishop of London (1637)   1172
WILLIAMS, John, D.D. (1579, 1586)   336, 1210
WILLIAMS, John, D.D. (1681-1695)   119, 153, 585, 643, 1852, 1853, 2364, 2676, 2741, 2749, 2750, 2756
WILLIAMS, John, D.D., Bishop of Chichester (1686-1694)   108, 263, 630, 1155, 1753, 1852, 2044, 2056, 2338, 2569

WILLIAMS, John, LL.D. (1767, 1771)   536, 961
WILLIAMS, John, M.A. (1801)   1704
WILLIAMS, Mary (1861)   1496
WILLIAMS, Mitchell (1826)   913
WILLIAMS, Morgan (1791)   2630
WILLIAMS, Philip, D.D. (1733, 1734)   2173, 2427
WILLIAMS, R. (1718)   1352
WILLIAMS, Robert Folkestone (1835-1851)   526 (2), 835, 1536, 1581, 1585, 1598, 2313, 2348, 2391, 2502, 2851
WILLIAMS, Roger (1644)   242
WILLIAMS, Rowland, D.D. (1846-1857)   622, 1332, 1825
WILLIAMS, Sir Charles Hanbury (1713)   2685
WILLIAMS, T. H. (1856)   744
WILLIAMS, Thomas (1795, 1796)   56, 57, 1105
WILLIAMS, W. (1761)   798
WILLIAMS, William (1660)   1798, Errata, vol. iv.
WILLIAMS, Zachariah (1755)   14
WILLIAMSON, J. (1703)   1826
WILLIAMSON, James, M.A. (1774)   1821
WILLIAMSON, John (1722-1793)   53, 503, 1749, 1815, 2088, 2153, 2272, 2306, 2470, 2544, 2642
WILLIS, Browne, LL.D. (1717, 1733)   2106, 2535, 2601, 2811
WILLIS, Duke (1827)   2062
WILLIS, Francis (1683)   80
WILLIS, H. Norton (1795)   237
WILLIS, John (1700)   1287
WILLIS, John, D.D. (1690)   1286
WILLIS, Katherine (N.D.)   1350
WILLIS, Richard (1700)   44
WILLIS, Richard, D.D., Bishop of Winchester (1696-1698)   1794 (3), 1795 (6), 2116
WILLIS, Robert (1821)   195
WILLISON, John (1714-1719)   151, 583, 1353, 2631
WILLOUGHBY, Sir Henry, Bart. (1827)   155
WILLS, —— (1813)   2142
WILLS, John (1714)   1999
WILLS, Rev. James (1821)   2712
WILLS, Rev. William, A.M. (1795)   218
WILLS, William German (1859)   1485
WILLSON, Samuel (1753)   197

WILLUGHBY, Lord, Peregrine Bertie (1589)   2359
WILMOT, George (1751, 1752)   1384, 2331
WILMOT, James, D.D. (1813, 1817)   1287, 1438
WILMOT, John (1802)   1589
WILMOT, John, Earl of Rochester (1679-1701) 764, 1756, 1951, 2260, 2716
WILMOT, R. (1832)   169
WILMOT, Sir John Eardley (1778-1822)   5, 1589, 2364
WILSHERE, W. (1817)   486
WILSON, —— (1667)   548
WILSON, —— (N.D.)   2067
WILSON, Alexander (1821, 1826)   1944, 2794
WILSON, Andrew, M.D. (1750-1788)   215, 532, 862, 1186, 2113, 2372
WILSON, Charles Henry (1792-1804)   219, 286, 1969, 2530, 2787
WILSON, Daniel, D.D. (1824)   1426
WILSON, Daniel, D.D., Bishop of Calcutta (1818)   586
WILSON, Daniel, LL.D. (1853)   2064
WILSON, Daniel, M.A. (1816)   2186
WILSON, David (1773)   1645
WILSON, Dr C. (1761)   1829
WILSON, Edmund (1675)   2460
WILSON, Edward (1675)   2460
WILSON, Henry Bristow, D.D. (1807, 1861)   265, 717
WILSON, James (1775)   180
WILSON, James (N.D.)   552
WILSON, James (1759-1766) 1631, 1951, 1952
WILSON, James, Advocate (1823-1824)   924, 2614
WILSON, James H. (1853)   2550
WILSON, John (1696-1712)   565, 802
WILSON, John (1684-1760)   367, 715
WILSON, John (1608-1668)   759, 1709, 2774
WILSON, John (1692, 1703)   2105, 2768
WILSON, John (1825-1832)   942, 1149, 1682
WILSON, John, D.D. (1828, 1832) 1476, 1929
WILSON, John   Errata, vol. iv.
WILSON, John, M.A. (1709)   2759
WILSON, John, *or* Willson   Errata, vol. iv. (2)
WILSON, Matthew (1630-1684)   365, 1223, 1603

WILSON, Mrs (1830)   1492
WILSON, Professor John (1811-1842) 1487, 1489, 1892, 2102, 2425, 2652
WILSON, Rev. David (1768)   1415
WILSON, Rev. John (1814)   1975
WILSON, Robert (1856-1877)   228, 496, 824, 2243
WILSON, Sir Robert Thomas (1817) 2400
WILSON, T. (1836)   609
WILSON, T. (1757)   2202
WILSON, Thomas (1828)   334
WILSON, Thomas (1667)   1286
WILSON, Thomas (1648)   1305
WILSON, Thomas (1761)   1829
WILSON, Thomas (N.D.)   1917
WILSON, Thomas, D.D. (1736)   681
WILSON, William (1731)   643, 700
WILSON, William, M.A. (1864)   1093
WILSON, William Rae (1837)   1751
WILSON, Right Hon. Countess (1841)   183
WILTS, Archdeacon of, Henry Stebbing, D.D. (1718-1757) 103, 589, 595, 657, 692, 768, 848, 953, 1769, 1842
WILTS, Archdeacon of, Rev. William Coxe (1823)   2404
WIMBLEDON, Richard (1575)   2333
WINCH, N. J. (1805)   250
WINCHELSEA, Countess of, Anne Finch (1713)   1631
WINCHESTER, Archdeacon of, J. Philpot (1554)   2650
WINCHESTER, Bishop of, B. Duppa (1673)   558
WINCHESTER, Bishop of, C. Trimnell (1708)   1865
WINCHESTER, Bishop of, Dr J. Poynet (1556)   2380
WINCHESTER, Bishop of, George Morley (1641-1660)   360, 1644
WINCHESTER, Bishop of, Richard Willis, D.D. (1696-1698) 1794 (3), 1795 (6), 2116
WINCHESTER, Bishop of, T. Cooper (1589)   46
WINCHESTER, Charles (1802-1869   1247, 1631
WINCHESTER, Thomas (1773)   678
WINCOP, Nicholas (1731)   2141
WINDHAM, Sir William (1739)   1355
WINDHAM, William (1759)   1930
WING, Rev. J. (1820)   2794
WINGATE, Edmund (1644-1677)   842, 1295, 2491

WINGATE, Edmund (1754)   1525
WINGATE, John (1635)   2272
WINNARD, Jane M. (1854)   1182
WINSCOM, Jane Anne (1857)   1939
WINSLOW, Dr Forbes (1839)   1906
WINSLOW, Edw. (1653)   1932
WINSTANLEY, William (1687, 1702)   1176, 1723
WINSTON, Charles (1847)   1228
WINSTON, James (1805)   2560
WINTER, Mary (1830)   72
WINTLE, Thomas, B.D. (1796)   1399
WINTRINGHAM, Clifton (1726)   1772
WIRGMAN, George (1839)   1688
WIRT, William (1812)   1443
WISE, Francis (1758)   2423
WISE, Francis, B.D., F.S.A. (1764)   1129
WISE, Rev. Thomas (1732)   6
WISE, Thomas, B.D. (1714)   378
WISE, Thomas Turner (1795)   2200
WISEMAN, Nicholas, D.D. (1839)   1501
WISEMAN, Nicholas P., Cardinal (1855)   871
WISHART, George (1660)   455
WISHART, George, Bishop of Edinburgh (1648)   1158
WISHART, William, D.D. (1702-1729)   652, 2357
WISZNIEWSKI, Michael Prus de (1853)   2400
WITHER, George (1623-1660)   79, 878, 987, 1045, 1196, 1432, 2039, 2081, 2186, 2513, 2805
WITHERS, John (1713, 1714)   345, 710
WITHERS, Philip (1789-1790)   65 (3), 176, 1898
WITHERSPOON, John, D.D. (1753-1791)   485, 722, 1130, 1346, 2274, 2328
WITT, John de (1703)   873
WOGAN, William (1753)   811
WOLCOTT, John, M.D. (1785-1817)   53, 143, 225, 252, 287, 346, 440, 460, 506, 865, 884, 895, 902, 1012, 1061, 1237, 1254, 1316, 1460, 1517, 1529 (2), 1661 (2), 1741, 1803 (2), 1804 (3), 1818, 1835, 1845, 1871, 1893 (3), 1915 (2), 1955, 1956, 1958, 2165, 2213, 2218 (6), 2234, 2235, 2236, 2255, 2277, 2390, 2510, 2543, 2549, 2657, 2798, 2830, 2840
WOLFE, Rev. J. (1828-9)   624
WOLFENSBERGER, Hannah D. (1844, 1845)   942, 2789
WOLLASTON, Francis (1774)   2067
WOLLASTON, G. H. (1827)   409

WOLLASTON, William (1691, 1724)   610, 2130
WOLLEY, —— (1684)   573
WOLSELEY, Sir Charles, Bart. (1668-1673)   313, 883, 1460 (2), 2715
WOLSEY, —— (1675)   689
WOMOCH, Dr Laurence, Archdeacon of Suffolk (1682)   2696
WOMOCH, Laurence, D.D. (1643-1683)   136, 167, 189, 475, 852, 1665, 2056, 2187, 2379, 2412, 2702
WOMOCH, Laurence, D.D., Bishop of St David's (1681)   2725
WOOD, Alexander, M.D. (1867)   1121
WOOD, Benjamin (1828-9)   1085
WOOD, Captain George (1826)   2076
WOOD, Dr Thomas (1693)   2756
WOOD, E. (1838)   2281
WOOD, Hans (1787)   2191
WOOD, James (1659)   2194
WOOD, James, D.D. (1815)   1779
WOOD, John (1819)   2121
WOOD, John George, M.A. (1837-1864)   194, 2231, 2436
WOOD, Lady (1866)   2229
WOOD, Mrs Henry (1825-1864)   1430, 1471, 2650
WOOD, Professor James (1632)   2754
WOOD, Rev. James (1881)   2500
WOOD, Rev. John George (1858)   1065
WOOD, Robert (1753)   2237
WOOD, Thomas (1682-1697)   80, 164, 618, 671, 1296
WOOD, Thomas, D.C.L. (1708, N.D.)   2444, 2762
WOOD, Thomas, LL.D. (1704, 1705)   1724, 2637
WOOD, William (1718)   2528
WOOD, William, B.D. (1826)   569
WOODBRIDGE, Robert (1793)   1844
WOODBURN, Samuel (1811)   724
WOODD, Basil (1852)   1812
WOODDESON, Richard, D.C.L. (1783)   738
WOODFALL, William (1777)   2392
WOODFIN, Mrs (1756, 1757)   1142, 1750
WOODFORD, S. (1658)   1693
WOODFORD, T. (1756)   2633
WOODFORDE, —— (1795)   2323
WOODHEAD, Abraham (1669-1689)   257, 340, 396, 448, 462, 483, 644, 655, 689, 1051, 1057, 1481, 1669, 1912, 2045, 2079, 2222, 2306, 2691 (2)
WOODHOUSE, J. (1763)   1187

WOODHOUSE, John Chappell, D.D., Dean of Lichfield (1802, 1818)　839, 2353
WOODHOUSELEE, —— (1771)　1916
WOODHOUSLEE, Lord, A. F. Tytler (1771-1835)　538, 807, 811, 1110, 1904, 1949, 2219
WOODLEY, George (1804)　1670
WOODMAN, William (1861)　2703
WOODMASS, —— (1797)　1966
WOODROFFE, Benjamin, D.D. (1690)　884
WOODROOFFE, Anne (1819, 1827)　1142, 1611
WOODS, Joseph (1784)　2582
WOODWARD, Dr (1799)　2162
WOODWARD, G. M. (1796)　889
WOODWARD, H. (1644-1656)　388, 470, 617
WOODWARD, Hezekiah (1656)　853, 1222
WOODWARD, John, D.D. (N.D.)　41
WOODWARD, John, M.D. (1696, 1723)　267, 2161
WOODWARD, Josiah, D.D. (1699-1718)　28, 381, 680 (2), 718, 1301, 1705, 1869 (2), 2097, 2159, 2360, 2444
WOODWARD, Mrs (1873)　1673
WOOLCOMBE, Dr (1811)　374
WOOLEY, Richard (1692)　455
WOOLLCOMBE, Henry (1812)　1909
WOOLLS, C. (1839)　214
WOOLMER, Joseph Benson (1851)　1659
WOOLSEY, R. (1803)　736
WOOLSTON, Thomas (1720, 1721)　1403, 2300
WOOLSTONECRAFT, Mary (1788, 1790)　1829, 2764
WORBOISE, Emma Jane (1866)　2815
WORCESTER, Bishop of, G. Morley (1670)　1376
WORCESTER, Bishop of, John Gauden (1644-1663)　351, 649 (2)
WORCESTER, Bishop, John Hough, D.D. (1688)　1212
WORCESTER, Earl of, J. Tipcroft (1530)　2685
WORCESTER, Bishop of, Richard Hurd, D.D. (1746-1794)　152, 599, 624 (2), 640, 676, 1385, 1407, 1444, 1656, 1820, 2136, 2140
WORCESTER, Bishop of, William Lloyd, D.D. (1667-1692)　630, 1320, 2006, 2086, 2288

WORDE, Wynken de (1820)　2650
WORDSWORTH, —— (1823, 1825)　935, 2531
WORDSWORTH, Charles, D.C.L., Bishop of St Andrews (1848)　431
WORDSWORTH, Mrs Dora Quillinan née (1847)　1274
WORDSWORTH, Christopher, Bishop of Lincoln (1862)　1172
WORDSWORTH, Rev. Christopher, D.D. (1802, 1842)　516, 2395
WORDSWORTH, Rev. John (1842)　516
WORDSWORTH, William (1798)　1529
WORLIDGE, John (1669-1677)　141, 2534 (2), 2769
WORNUM, Richard N. (1877)　2260
WORSLEY, Edward (1665, 1674)　642, 1222, 2040, 2084, 2681
WORTHINGTON, Thomas (1615)　2813
WORTHINGTON, William, D.D. (1773)　2283
WORTLEY, Charles Stuart (1833)　1277
WORTLEY, Sir Francis (N.D.)　1522
WOTTON, Anthony (1626)　562
WOTTON, T. (1851)　755
WOTTON, W. (1693)　1723
WOTTON, William, D.D. (1704, 1711)　322, 1380
WORTY, William (1760-1770)　303, 909, 2381
WRANGHAM, Francis (1792-1828)　917, 1573, 1877, 2053, 2117
WRAXALL, N. W. (1787)　2374
WRAY, Daniel (1741-1743)　192
WRAY, Daniel (1830)　1438
WRAY, Mary (1714)　1311
WREAKS, Barbara Hofland née (1813-1854)　1297, 1559, 1600, 1872
WRECKHAM, H. L. (1820)　676
WREN, Matthew, M.A., Bishop of Ely (1657)　481
WRIFFORD, A. (1835)　262
WRIGHT, —— (1827)　69
WRIGHT, A. (1668)　83
WRIGHT, Charles (1851)　328
WRIGHT, Frances (1821)　2738
WRIGHT, G. (N.D.)　2563
WRIGHT, James (1685, 1709)　449, 522, 1104, 1905, 2590
WRIGHT, J. H. (1846, 1847)　1179, 1256
WRIGHT, John (1831)　236
WRIGHT, John (1693)　1651
WRIGHT, Rev. James (1865)　307
WRIGHT, Rev. S. (1715)　889

WRIGHT, Rev. Thomas (1838)   1544
WRIGHT, Richard (1807)   1444
WRIGHT, Robert (1728)   1187
WRIGHT, Robert, D.D. (1625)   2098
WRIGHT, Samuel, D.D.(1716-1741) 118,
        365, 397, 428, 1796, 2320, 2646
WRIGHT, Th. le (1658)   1660
WRIGHT, Thomas (1742)   892
WRIGHT, Thomas (1822-1868) 691, 895,
    1050, 1271, 1320, 1663, 1686, 2425, 2673
WRIGHT, Thomas (1601)   1868
WRIGHT, William (1697-1714)   435,
                          1260, 1372
WRIGHT, William (1616, 1619) 2637 (2)
WRIGHT, William, S.J. (1619)   277
WRIGHT, W. W. (1777)   1695
WROE, Caleb (1725)   948
WROTHE, Sir Thomas (1620)   4
WYAT, Matthew (N.D.)   445
WYAT, T. (N.D.)   445
WYBARD, J. (1650)   2537
WYBORNE, P. (1581)   368
WYCHE, Joseph, M.O.S.B. (1735) 532
WYCHE, Sir Peter (1669)   2373
WYCHERLEY, William (1682)   786
WYETH, Joseph (1692)   193
WYLD, R. S. (1863)   2505
WYLIE, James Aitken, D.D. (1848) 2343
WYLIE, Robert (N.D.)   2359, 2471
WYLIE, Rev. Robert (1703) 1349, 2359
WYNDHAM, Henry P. (1775-1794) 1007,
                               1909
WYNDHAM, Miss (N.D., 1842) 716, 2682
WYNG, John (1715)   2092
WYNNE, Edward (1765-1790) 834, 1786,
                               2506
WYNNE, Jane, Countess of Rosen-
    berg (1785)   1656
WYNNE, John H. (1772-1794) 373, 2539
WYNNE, Dr Robert (1689)   315, 321
WYNTER, Andrew, M.D. (1855) 1800,
                               1911
WYSE, B. (1828)   499
WYSE, George (1822)   2244
WYSE, Thomas (1828)   499
WYVILL, Christopher (1647)   351
WYVILL, Christopher (1771)   2578

                 Y.

YALDER, Thomas (N.D.)   2481
YARDLEY, Edward, B.D., Arch-
    deacon of Cardigan (1762) 1904

YATES, —— (1700)   2356
YATES, J. (1826)   2578
YATES, John (1849)   1201
YATES, W. (1816)   1315
YEARDLEY, John (1829)   378
YEARDLEY, Martha (1829)   378
YEATES, Thomas (1833)   674
YEATS, G. D., M.D., F.R.S. (1818) 236
YELVERTON, Sir Henry, Bart. (1641-
    1662)   656, 1334, 2215, 2746
YETSWEIRT. Charles (1594)   179
YONGE. Charlotte M. (1847-1874) 2, 166,
    224, 247, 249, 327, 357, 388, 416, 507,
    520, 559, 563, 702, 714, 968, 1078, 1081,
    1083, 1085, 1133, 1148, 1177, 1298, 1306,
    1316, 1317 (3), 1318, 1341, 1496, 1548,
    1723, 1912, 2012, 2263, 2393, 2494, 2650,
                     2694, 2793, 2850
YONGE, Sir Wiiliam (1731)   2315
YORK, Archbishop of, S. Harsnet (1599,
    1605)   574, 664
YORK, Archbishop of, Sir W. Dawes,
    D.D. (1731)   85
YORK, Archbishop of, W. Thomson,
    D.D. (1842)   1837
YORKE, Charles, Lord Morden (1746)
                             2422
YORKE, Hon Charles (1741-3) 192 (2)
YORKE, Hon. P., Earl of Hardwicke
    (1727-1783) 192, 654, 1629, 2701, 2786
YORKE, John (1783)   1249
YOSY A. (1822)   2539
YOUATT, Elizabeth (1848)   1297
YOUATT, William (1840)   1180
YOUNG, Arthur (1770-1811)   47, 858,
    896 (2), 897, 1002, 1194, 1202, 1700,
        1783, 2037, 2241, 2396, 2733
YOUNG, Arthur, LL.D. (1734)   1116
YOUNG, Dr J., or Younge (1703) 2343
YOUNG, Edward (1753, 1755) 287, 348
YOUNG, Edward (1728)   1519
YOUNG, Edward, LL.D. (1727-1762)
    451, 477, 493, 556, 1214, 1740, 1799,
                 1868, 2184, 2693
YOUNG, Hannah (1818)   735
YOUNG, H. H. (1827)   732
YOUNG, John (1791, 1808)   541, 1228,
                               1423
YOUNG, Major Gavin (1822, 1827) 899,
                          988, 1228
YOUNG, Marianne (1853)   1888
YOUNG, Portia (1863)   135
YOUNG, R. (1855)   354, 460
YOUNG, Richard (1652)   1177

YOUNG, Richard, *or* Younge (N.D., 1658) 1849, 1995
YOUNGE, Richard (N.D.) 1030
YOUNG, Samuel (1696-1700) 147, 296, 473, 953, 972 (2), 2182, 2409, 2817
YOUNG, Sir Charles George (1829) 330, Errata, vol. i.
YOUNG, Sir William (1793) 2213
YOUNG, Thomas (1641) 106, 2741
YOUNG, Thomas (1672) 1514
YOUNG, Thomas (1849) 949
YOUNG, Thomas, M.D., F.R.S. (1821) 737, 1571
YOUNG, William (1762, 1774) 1275, 2641
YOUNGE, Dr J. Young *or* (1703) 2343
YOUNGE, Richard (1663) 2320

YOUNGE, Richard Young *or* (1658, N.D.) 1849, 1995
YOUNGER, —— (1665) 1159
YOUNGER, William Errata, vol. iv.
YUILLE, Major-General (1856) 2617

Z.

ZIEGENHERT, Sophia F. (1811) 2284
ZINCKE, F. B. (1847) 2337
ZINZANO, —— (1725) 2341
ZORAWSKI, V. S. (1844) 918
ZORNLIN, —— (1819) 2489
ZOUCH, Dr (1808) 1573
ZOUCH, Richard, LL.D. (1639) 2455

CORRIGENDA ET ADDENDA.

Col. 2, line 19, *after* " 1980," *read* " *sic.*"

Col. 28, line 46, *for* " William Gordon," *read* " James Gordon." Leave out on line 50, " Second edition," and insert in line 50, " The second edition was published in 1723, having the author's name."

Col. 48, line 56, *for* " W. H.," *read* " E. J."

Col. 53, line 48, *for* " John Williamson," *read* " Francis Grose."

Col. 53, line 53, *for* " J. Maidment," *read* " Taylor's Records of my Life, vol. i., pp. 318, 319."

Col. 55, line 33, *for* " Mrs S. J. Penny," *read* " Mrs A. J. Penny."

Col. 66, line 44, *for* " Noel Radcliffe," *read* " Noell Radecliffe."

Col. 73, line 28, *for* " Elias Taylor," *read* " J. Lukin."

Col. 104, line 56, *for* " Nunnery," *read* " Nunnez."

Col. 130, line 2, *for* "Fisher," *read* "Piercy, *alias* Fisher."

Col. 133, line 28, *for* " —— Boston," *read* " Michael Boston."

Col. 150, line 55, *for* " —— Constable," *read* " John Constable ; " line 58, *for* " Charles Dodd," *read* " Hugh Tootle." *See* col. 397, lines 15 and 20.

Col. 168, last line, *add* " *See* View of Antiquity."

Col. 188, line 47, *for* " Charles " *read* " Cecil."

Col. 206, line 47, *for* " Elkanah Settle," *read* " Samuel Pordage," and omit line 50.

Col. 220, line 6, *for* " Bedukal," *read* " Bedukah."

Col. 256, line 34, *for* " bride," *read* " bridle."

Col. 306, line 34, *for* " Rev. Andrew Bonar," *read* " Rev. Andrew R. Bonar."

Col. 311, line 45, *for* " Rev. Samuel Marsters," *read* "Rev. Samuel Masters."

Col. 335, line 17, *for* " Christopher S. J. Anderdon," *read* " Christopher Anderdon, S.J."

Col. 336, line 15, *for* " Doulevy," *read* " Donlevy."

Col. 339, line 59, *for* " —— M'Vicar," *read* " John Gibson M'Vicar, D.D."

Col. 343, line 30, *for* " Thomas Roscoe, jun.," *read* " William Bennett."

Col. 370, line 4, *for* " Bennett," *read* " Bennet."

Col. 370, line 14, *for* " —— Bickersteth," *read* " Edward Henry Bickersteth."

Col. 383, line 16, *for* " Drape," *read* " Augusta Theodosia Drane."

Col. 389, line 43, *for* " —— Bickersteth," *read* " Edward Henry Bickersteth."

Col. 390, line 36, *for* " Ethelfled," *read* " Ethelfield."

Col. 434, lines 43 and 48, *for* " P. Lee," *read* " Percival Leigh."

Col. 525, line 41, *for* " Henry Brougham, Lord Brougham," *read* " Probably by Lord Belfast."

Col. 528, line 54, *for* " James Hogg," *read* " Rev. James Hog of Carnock."

Col. 548, line 4, *for* " —— Wilson," *read* " John Wilson *or* Willson, minister at Backford, Cheshire."

Col. 556, line 17, *for* " Houston," *read* " Houstoun."

Col. 559, line 26, *for* " Houston," *read* " Houstoun."

Col. 572, line 16, *for* " Beborah," *read* " Deborah."

Col. 573, line 13, *for* "Grey," *read* "Gray."

Col. 608, line 2, *for* " Rev. R. Traill," *read* " Rev. James Traill."

Col. 615, line 15, *for* " French," *read* " Trench."

Col. 666, line 49, *after* " Gwillim," *read* [Dr John BARKHAM].

Col. 748, line 17, *for* " Leveson," *read* " Leverson."

Col. 755, line 45, *for* " J.," *read* " Joseph."

Col. 758, line 9, *for* " T. H. Ottley," *read* " William Brown Hockley."

Col. 771, line 23, *for* "—— Gordon," *read* "Thomas Gordon, minister at Speymouth."

Col. 791, line 37, *for* "founded," *read* "found."

Col. 798, line 50, *for* "M.," *read* "Frances Mary."

Col. 818, line 53, *for* "—— Ballantyne," *read* "Rev. James Ballantyne."

Col. 895, line 50, *for* "Ross Hickey," *read* "Rev. William Hickey."

Col. 903, line 49, *for* "Murray," *read* "Murphy."

Col. 1048, line 39, *after* "*appendix*," *read* ["by Thomas Wagstaffe."]

Col. 1075, line 37, *for* "Elizabeth Missing," *read* "Rev. William."

Col. 1090, omit line 23.

Col. 1159, line 10, *for* "—— Younger," *read* "William Younger."

Col. 1160, line 29, *for* "205," *read* "255."

Col. 1207, line 24, *for* "Maish," *read* "Marsh."

Col. 1209, line 47, *for* "Dr Hay," *read* "John Hay, D.D."

Col. 1215, line 41, *for* "John Dove, D.D.," *read* "John Dove, usually called 'the learned tailor.'"

Col. 1219, line 9, *for* "Wedderburn," *read* "Weddell."

Col. 1224, line 20, *for* "—— Shiels," *read* "Alexander Shiels *or* Shields."

Col. 1231, line 22, *for* "—— Adam," *read* "John Adams."

Col. 1231, line 23, *for* "—— Maclaurin," *read* "John Maclaurin."

Col. 1249, line 16, *for* "David Hamilton," *read* "Sir David Hamilton, M.D."

Col. 1249, line 24, *for* "—— Johnston," *read* "William Johnson, author of 'Iophon,' who has also written a History of England under the name of Cory."

Col. 1286, line 35, *for* "Thomas Wilson," *read* "John Wilson *or* Willson, minister at Backford, Cheshire."

Col. 1291, line 43, *for* "—— Hodge," *read* "James Hodges."

Col. 1295, *omit the entry*, "Justina, a play, etc." This translation is not by D. F. M'Carthy.

Col. 1304, line 16, *for* "Thomas Roscoe, jun.," *read* "William Bennett."

Col. 1310, line 8, *for* "——," *read* "J. K."

Col. 1438, line 19, *for* "Snett," *read* "Suett."

Col. 1449, line 19, *for* "Sidney," *read* "Sydney."

Col. 1470, line 40, *for* "John Francis Campbell," *read* "Walter F. Campbell of Islay, edited by his son, John Francis Campbell."

Col. 1487, line 26, *after* "Barbour," *read* "farmer, Bogue, Dalry, Kirkcudbrightshire."

Col. 1543, line 51, *for* "Manslauhter," *read* "Manslaughter."

Col. 1552, line 39, *for* "Toutroud," *read* "Toutrond."

Col. 1638, line 53, *for* "Crookwige," *read* "Crookridge."

Col. 1639, line 57, *for* "—— Williams," *read* "William Williams."

Col. 1663, line 32, *for* "Mrs S. J. Penny," *read* "Mrs A. J. Penny."

Col. 1683, line 51, *for* "Ascribed to Major Bunbury," *read* "By Colonel George Bruce Malleson."

Col. 1717, line 5, *for* "Melmonth," *read* "Melmoth."

Col. 1816, line 11, *for* "—— Dunlop," *read* "John Dunlop, Greenock."

Col. 1952, line 15, *for* "1858," *read* "1811."

Col. 1960, line 51, *for* "George Jabet," *read* "George S. Jabet."

Col. 2051, line 4, *for* "——Pike," *read* "Samuel Pike."

Col. 2070, line 37, *for* "Rev. James Morrison," *read* "Rev. James Morison, D.D."

Col. 2155, line 1, *for* "George P. Robertson," *read* "George Home Robertson."

Col. 2161, line 56, *for* "Lawrence," *read* "Laurence."

Col. 2164, two last lines, *for* "Sir Thomas Powell Buxton," *read* "Sir Thomas Fowell Buxton."

Col. 2183, line 9, *for* "—— Gordon," *read* "James Gordon, minister of Banchory."

Col. 2198, line 46, *for* "—— Jefferies," *read* "Thomas Jefferies *or* Jeffery."

Col. 2257, line 26, *for* "V. Llanos," *read* "Valentine Llanos."

Col. 2277, line 11, *for* "William Carstairs," *read* "William Carstares, Principal of Edinburgh University."

Col. 2307, line 4, *for* "Bishop John Jackson," *read* "John Jackson, rector of Rossington, Yorkshire."

Col. 2346, line 53, "The Shady Side" is *not* by Elizabeth S. Phelps. Authorship unknown.

Col. 2435, line 28, *for* "William Carstaires, D.D.," *read* "William Carstares, Principal of Edinburgh University."

Col. 2464, line 16, *for* "—— Constable," *read* "John Constable, Jesuit."

Col. 2553, line 51, *for* "—— Bennett," *read* "Thomas Bennett, minister at Ceres, Fife."

Col. 2564, line 10, *for* "Levesque de POUILLY," *read* "LEVESQUE DE POUILLY."

" English (the) Martyrologe" is by John WILSON.

For " ENQUIRY into religion," and " ENQUIRY into the powers of ecclesiastics," *see* " INQUIRY."

In several entries, *for* " Louise de La Ramée," *read* " Louise de La Ramé."

In numerous entries by Hesba Stretton, *for* " *Hannah* Smith," *read* " *Sarah* Smith." Stretton is her birth-place, and Hesba is composed of the initials of five sisters, of whom the authoress is the third.

In several entries by George Eliot, *for* " Marian Evans," *read* " Mary Ann Evans."

In numerous entries by Ann of Swansea, *for* "Ann Kemble," *read* " Frances Ann Kemble."

In numerous entries by Martin Doyle, *for* " Ross Hickey," *read* " Rev. William Hickey."

In several entries under " William Henry Logan," *read* " William Hugh Logan."

In the first volume, omit the asterisk in the titles taken from Mendham Collection Cat.

" Priviledge (concerning the) " should have been entered under " Concerning."

ABBREVIATIONS AND AUTHORITIES.

Aberdeen Lib.—University Library, Aberdeen.

Adv. Lib.—Library of the Faculty of Advocates, Edinburgh.

Allen, Bib. Heref.—Bibliotheca Herefordiensis. By John Allen.

Allibone.—A critical dictionary of English literature, and British and American authors. By S. Austin Allibone.

Almon's Biog. Anec.—Biographical, literary, and political anecdotes. By John Almon.

Athen. Cat.— Catalogue of the Library of the Athenæum, London.

Bib. Anglo-Poet. — Bibliotheca Anglo-Poetica; or a descriptive catalogue of a rare and rich collection of Early English poetry, in the possession of Longman, Hurst, Rees, Orme, and Brown.

Bib. Parriana.—Bibliotheca Parriana: a Catalogue of the Library of the late Rev. and learned Samuel Parr, LL.D.

Biog. Brit.—Biographia Britannica.

Biog. Dict., 1816.—A Biographical Dictionary of the living authors of Great Britain and Ireland. [By John Watkins and Frederic Shoberl.]

Biog. Dram.—Biographia Dramatica; or a companion to the playhouse. By David Erskine Baker. Continued by Isaac Reed and Stephen Jones.

Blakey's Lit. of Angling. — Historical sketches of the angling literature of all nations, to which is added, a bibliography of English writers on angling. By Robert Blakey.

Bliss' Cat. — Auction Catalogue of the . . . library of Dr Philip Bliss.

Boase, G. C.—George Clement Boase, one of the authors of the "Bibliotheca Cornubiensis."

Boase and Courtney, Bib. Corn.—Bibliotheca Cornubiensis. By G. C. Boase and W. P. Courtney.

Bodl.—Bodleian Library.

Boyne's Yorkshire Lib.—The Yorkshire Library, a bibliographical account of books on topography, &c., relating to the county of York.

Brit. Crit.—British Critic.

Brit. Mus.—British Museum.

Brook's Puritans.—The lives of the Puritans. By Benjamin Brook.

Brydges, Cens. Lit.—Censura Literaria. By Sir Egerton Brydges, Bart.

Burton, J. Hill.—John Hill Burton, historiographer-royal, author of " History of Scotland."

Cat. Lib. Trin. Coll. Dub.— Catalogus librorum impressorum qui in Bibliotheca Collegii Sacrosanctæ et Individuæ Trinitatis, Reginæ Elizabethæ, juxta Dublin, adservantur.

Cat. Lond. Inst.—A Catalogue of the Library of the London Institution.

Cat. Phil. Inst., Edin.—Catalogue of the Library of the Philosophical Institution of Edinburgh.

Chalmers, Biog. Dict.—The General Bibliographical Dictionary. . . . A new edition, revised and enlarged by Alexander Chalmers.

Chalmers' Notes.—Probably the Notes in Chalmers' Biographical Dictionary.

Chambers' Worcester. — Bibliographical illustrations of Worcestershire. . . . By John Chambers.

Chetham Lib.—Bibliotheca Chethamensis.

Coleridge's Worthies of Yorkshire. — Lives of Northern Worthies. By Hartley Coleridge.

Cradock's Mem.—Literary and Miscellaneous Memoirs. By J. Cradock.

Crit. Rev.—Critical Review.

Darling, Cyclop. Bibl.—Cyclopædia Bibliographica. By James Darling.

Davidson, Bib. Devon. — Bibliotheca Devoniensis. By James Davidson.

Dodds, Ch. Hist.—The Church History of England, 1500-1688, chiefly with regard to Catholicks.

Douce Cat.—Catalogue of the printed books and manuscripts bequeathed by Francis Douce, Esq., to the Bodleian Library.

Dyce Cat.—A Catalogue of the printed books and manuscripts bequeathed by the Rev. Alex. Dyce, Science and Art Department of the Committee of Council on Education.

Ecl. Rev.—Eclectic Review.

Edin. Select Subscription Lib. Cat.—Catalogue of the Edinburgh Select Subscription Library.

Edin. Univ. Lib.—Edinburgh University Library.

European Mag.—European Magazine.

Fishwick's Lancashire Lib.—The Lancashire Library. By Lieut.-Col. Henry Fishwick, F.S.A.

Gent. Mag.—Gentleman's Magazine.

Gough's Brit. Topogr. — British Topography. By Richard Gough.

Horne's Introduction.—An Introduction to the critical knowledge and study of the Holy Scriptures. By Thomas Hartwell Horne, D.D., ed. 1846.

Inglis. Dramatic writers.—The Dramatic writers of Scotland. By Ralston Inglis.

Inglis, R. — Ralston Inglis, author of "Dramatic writers of Scotland."

Jervise, A.—Andrew Jervise, author of "Memorials of Angus and Mearns."

Jones' Peck. — A Catalogue of the collection of tracts for and against Popery, in which is incorporated the whole of Peck's list of the tracts in that controversy, with his references. Edited by Thomas Jones, B.A., librarian of the Chetham Library.

Kennett's Wisdom.—The wisdom of looking backward, to judge the better of one side and t'other. . . By White Kennet, D.D., Bishop of Peterborough.

Laing, D.—David Laing, LL.D., late librarian of the Signet Library, Edinburgh.

Lathbury's Nonjurors.—A History of the Nonjurors ; their controversies and writings. By Thomas Lathbury.

Lavington's Moravians.—The Moravians compared and detected. . . . By George Lavington, LL.D., Bishop of Exeter.

Lit. Gazette.—Literary Gazette.

London Cat.—The London Catalogue of books published in Great Britain.

Lowndes, Bibliog. Man.—The Bibliographer's Manual. By W. T. Lowndes. Edited by H. G. Bohn.

Lowndes, Brit. Lib.—The British Librarian. By W. T. Lowndes.

M'Cull. Lit. Pol. Econ.—The Literature of political economy. . . . By J. R. M'Culloch.

Madan, F.—F. Madan, sub-librarian of the Bodleian Library.

Maidment, J.—James Maidment, Advocate, Edinburgh.

Martin's Cat.—Bibliographical Catalogue of privately printed books. By John Martin.

Masters' Corp. Ch. Coll., ed. Lamb.—The history of the College of Corpus Christi. . . . Cambridge. By Robert Masters. With additional matter . . . by John Lamb, D.D.

Mendham Collection Cat.—Catalogue of the Mendham Collection : being a selection . . . from the library of the late Rev. Joseph Mendham, M.A.

Mon. Rev.—Monthly Review.

Moule, Bib. Herald.—Bibliotheca Heraldica Magnæ Britanniæ. By Thomas Moule.

Murch's Dissenters.—History of the Presbyterian and general Baptist Churches in the west of England ; with some memoirs of their pastors. By Jerom Murch.

N. and Q.—Notes and Queries.

New Coll. Cat.—Catalogue of the printed books and MSS. in the Library of the New College, Edinburgh.

Nichols' Leicestershire. — History and antiquities of the county of Leicester. By John Nichols.

Nichols, Lit. Anec.—Literary Anecdotes of the 18th century. By John Nichols, F.S.A.

Nichols, Lit. Illust. — Illustrations of the literary history of the eighteenth century. . . . By John Nichols, F.S.A.

Oliver's Jesuits. — Collections towards illustrating the biography of the Scotch, English, and Irish members of the Society of Jesus. By George Oliver, D.D.

Olphar Hamst.—Handbook of fictitious names. By Olphar Hamst.

Orme Bib. Bib.—Bibliotheca Biblica. By William Orme.

Park's Walpole.—Catalogue of the royal and noble authors of England. . . . By Horatio Walpole, 4th Earl of Orford. Enlarged and continued to the present time. By Thomas Park.

Queen's Coll. Cat. — Catalogue of the Library of the College of St Margaret and Saint Bernard, commonly called Queen's College in the University of Cambridge, methodically arranged by Thomas Hartwell Horne.

Rich, Bib. Amer.—Bibliotheca Americana Nova. By O. Rich, Member of the Massachusett's Historical Society, &c., &c.

Rogers, Mod. Scot. Minst.—The Modern Scottish Minstrel. By Charles Rogers, LL.D.

Rose, Biog. Dict.—A new general biographical dictionary, projected and partly arranged by the late Rev. Hugh James Rose, B.D.

Scott, Fasti Eccl. Scot.—Fasti Ecclesiæ Scoticanæ. By Hew Scott, D.D.

Sig. Lib.—Library of Writers to the Signet, Edinburgh.

Smith, Bib. Ang.—A bibliographical catalogue of English writers on angling and ichthyology. By John Russell Smith.

Smith, Bib. Anti-Quaker. — Bibliotheca Anti-Quakeriana. By Joseph Smith.

Smith, Bib. Cant.—Bibliotheca Cantiana. By John Russell Smith.

Strype's Annals. — Annals of the Reformation and establishment of religion. By John Strype, M.A.

Taylor's Records.—Records of my life. . . . By John Taylor.

Tedder, H. R.—Henry R. Tedder, librarian of the Athenæum Library, London.

Turner's Unitarians.—Lives of eminent Unitarians, with a notice of dissenting academies. By William Turner, Unitarian minister.

U. P. Lib.—Library of the United Presbyterian College, Edinburgh.

Upcott.—Bibliographical account of the principal works relating to English topography. By William Upcott.

W. signifies that the title to which this initial is affixed was contributed by Mr H. B. Wheatley.

Watt, Bib. Brit.—Bibliotheca Britannica. By Robert Watt, M.D.

Westwood, Bib. Pisc.—New Bibliotheca Piscatoria. By T. Westwood.

Williams' Lib. Cat.—Catalogue of the Library in Red Cross Street, founded pursuant to the will of Rev. Daniel Williams, D.D.

Wilson, Hist. of Diss. Ch.—The history and antiquities of dissenting churches in London. By Walter Wilson, of the Inner Temple.

Wood.—Anthony à Wood.

Wood, Athen. Oxon. — Athenæ Oxonienses. . . . To which are added The Fasti. . . . By Anthony à Wood.

Wood, Fasti Oxon.—*See* Wood, Athen. Oxon.

Wrangham's Cat.—The English portion of the Library of the Rev. Francis Wrangham.

Turnbull & Spears, Printers, Edinburgh.